FUTURE / PRESENT

Printed in China through Porter Print Group, Bethesda, Maryland on acid-free paper ∞
Project Editor: Ihsan Taylor | Designed by Aimee C. Harrison
Typeset in Portrait Text and Univers LT Std by Aimee C.
Harrison and Copperline Book Services

Library of Congress Cataloging-in-Publication Data
Names: Alvarez, Daniela, [date] editor. | Uno, Roberta, [date]
editor. | Webb, Elizabeth M., [date] editor.
Title: FUTURE/PRESENT : arts in a changing America /
Daniela Alvarez, Roberta Uno, and Elizabeth M. Webb, editors.
Description: Durham : Duke University Press, 2024. | Includes
bibliographical references.
Identifiers: LCCN 2023001615 (print)
LCCN 2023001616 (ebook)
ISBN 9781478025160 (paperback)
ISBN 9781478020271 (hardcover)
ISBN 9781478027256 (ebook)
ISBN 9781478093718 (ebook other)
Subjects: LCSH: Racism and the arts—United States—History—
21st century. | Arts—Political aspects—United States—History—
21st century. | Arts and society—United States—History—21st
century. | Racial justice—United States—History—21st century. |
Anti-racism—United States—History—21st century. | United
States—Race relations—History—21st century. | BISAC: ART /
American / General | ART / American / Asian American &
Pacific Islander
Classification: LCC NX180.R3 F88 2024 (print) |
LCC NX180.R3 (ebook) | DDC 700.1/03—dc23/eng/20230727
LC record available at https://lccn.loc.gov/2023001615
LC ebook record available at https://lccn.loc.gov/2023001616

Cover art: Dyani White Hawk, *Stealing Horses Back*, 2016.
Oil, vintage glass beads, thread on linen, 18 × 48 in. Photograph
by Rik Sferra. Courtesy of the artist.

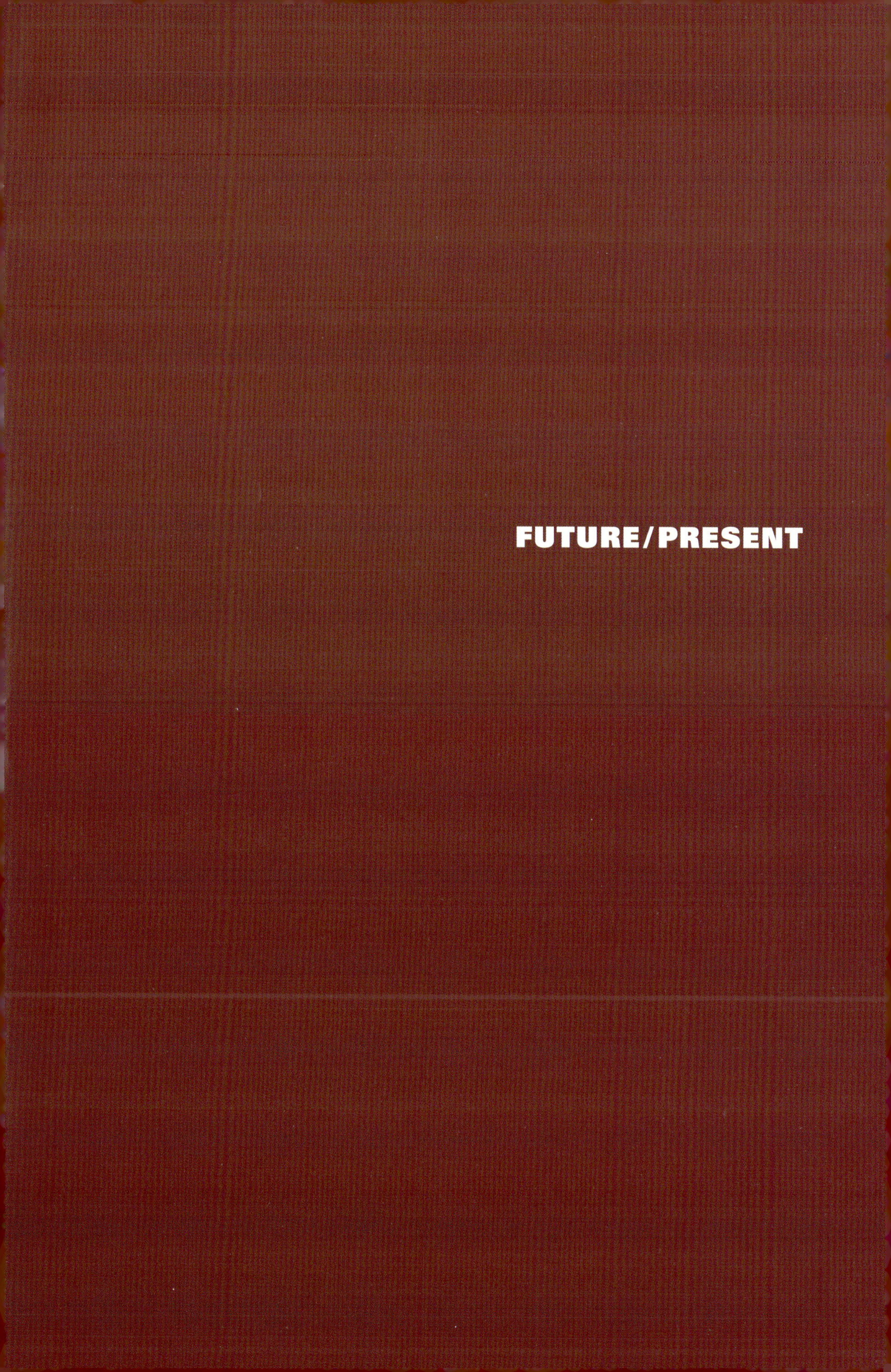

FUTURE/PRESENT

Daniela Alvarez

Roberta Uno

Elizabeth M. Webb

EDITORS

ARTS IN A CHANGING AMERICA

Duke University Press

Durham & London

2024

This book honors our cultural wellsprings, including:

Julia Bogany
Grace Lee Boggs
Elinor Bowles
Claudine Brown
Judy Heumann
C. Bernard Jackson
Yuri Kochiyama
Michelle Materre
Sam Miller
José Esteban Muñoz
John O'Neal
Diane Rodriguez
Randy Ross
Fred Tillis
Urvashi Vaid
Keith Wade
Keo Woolford

And is dedicated to the water carriers of our future.

CONTENTS

PART 2 / DISMANTLING BORDERS, BUILDING BRIDGES: MIGRATION AND DIASPORAS

PART 3 / CREATING A WORLD WITHOUT PRISONS: CULTURE AND THE CARCERAL STATE

PART 4 / EMBODIED CARTOGRAPHIES: RENEGOTIATING RELATIONSHIPS WITH LAND

PART 5 / LIVING OUR LEGACY: ANCESTRAL KNOWLEDGE AS RADICAL FUTURITY

PART 6 / CURRENTS BEYOND: ARTISTS SHIFTING PARADIGMS OF INEQUITY

INTRODUCTION

Roberta Uno

Roberta Uno is a theater director and the founder of Arts in a Changing America. She was formerly senior program officer for arts and culture at the Ford Foundation, the founder and artistic director of the New WORLD Theater, and professor of directing and dramaturgy at the University of Massachusetts at Amherst.

Think about how much blood has been shed for America to exist in our heads.

—**Lyla June**, Indigenous musician and community organizer of Diné (Navajo) and Tsétsêhéstâhese (Cheyenne) lineages, Taos, New Mexico

What are you saying with your body that you can't say with your words?

What do we say together as a group that you can't say as an individual?

—**Nobuko Miyamoto**, singer and choreographer, Los Angeles, California

Creativity provides meaning when all else fails. The work is alive.

—**Spel**, artist, State Correctional Institution at Dallas, Luzerne County, Pennsylvania

This book is the resonance of a five-year cultural organizing journey across America.[1] Through words, images, sound, movement, and actions, its contributors speak a collective text that is an echo from within, directions home, instructions from the future, and the whispered wayfinding of ancestors. This text is the weaving forward of deep listening and revelation. It is the joy, fury, and balm of unceded lives, land that remembers, bodies refusing to be mapped. It is the assertion that our future is in our presence now.

The seeds for this book were planted in 2014 when I gathered twelve artists, academics, and cultural organizers, working across geography, disciplines, races, and generations to imagine how we could lift up cultural leadership in communities on the ground, connect our networks, and embody cultural equity in practice.[2] My work as the artistic director of the New WORLD Theater (1979–2002) and later programming the US arts portfolio for the Ford Foundation (2002–15), had a through line of calling us to the watershed moment of the US demographic shift. Demographers project that by the year 2042, Black, Latine, Asian, and Native American people in aggregate will eclipse the historic majority Caucasian population. This flip is rolling up from the next generation; it has already happened for the nation's children under eighteen, the majority of metropolitan centers, and in the states of California, Hawai'i, New Mexico, and New York.[3]

Our gathering was not of sociologists, funders, or policy makers, but of culture makers, most of us peoples of color—Global Majority, artists. We were not looking at demography as a science, but as a window exposing inequities in funding, and structural racism, as well as bringing into sharper focus legacies of ongoing resistance and social movement building. In 2014, nativist opposition to the browning of the country promoted racism and xenophobia, peddling nostalgia for a "real America"—a delusional construct denying the history of genocidal wars against Native Americans, the enslavement of Africans, racist laws and institutionalized practices, and discriminatory immigration policies. An unmasked, violent reality conflated past and present in ways that writers like Octavia Butler and Leslie Marmon Silko had forewarned. But at the time, many were in denial that the extreme right would become the center of American governmental power: rolling back hard-earned civil rights, environmental, and gender advancements; isolating the United States globally, promoting lies, insurrection, and civil discord through the elevation and normalization of white supremacy, and grossly warping American character. In retrospect, the 2014 rhetoric seems almost quaint compared to the ensuing escalation of racism and terrorism promulgated by the forty-fifth presidency.

When we came together, we saw the ascending majority of peoples of color, not as threat, but as the possibility of narrative and power change; not as a monolith, but as the potential for a shared future. Our communities, long excluded from the bounty of our labor, had always been sources of generational wisdom and courage, self-sustainability, creativity and genius work-arounds, and the anchoring of spirit and humanity. Aware of our abundance, we began with two simple questions:

How can we be resources to each other?
What can we do together that we cannot do individually?

The result, Arts in a Changing America or ArtChangeUS, was originally a five-year, time-bound project launched to lift up demographic change as a cultural asset, validating artists and organizers on the forefront of cultural equity and racial justice, in communities on the ground. ArtChangeUS was envisioned as a national platform, a collaborative, and a connector. This radical notion of a horizontal table of equity nurtured the possibility that arts organizing could move across disciplines, geographies, and organizational budget size. ArtChangeUS was prescient in its call as an artist-led, Global Majority–driven, antiracist model of partnership, intergenerational leadership development, and network organizing.[4] We planned to sunset in 2020.

And then the world changed.

The Compass

Our ancestors laid the foundation for this work and this moment. So many movements are running parallel that ripples are becoming waves. Decolonizing work, Movement for Black Lives, visionary organizing continue.
—**Halima Cassells,** artist and community advocate, Detroit, Michigan

Through the arts people are able to hear truths that they're never able to unhear. . . . We are in a period of regaining our languages, but the bigger picture is helping other people remember.
—**Brenda Toineeta Pipestem,** associate justice of the Eastern Band of Cherokee Indians, in conversation with Lori Lea Pourier and Roberta Uno, December 19, 2021

Over the course of five years, ArtChangeUS collaborated with our Core Partners to produce intersectional gatherings called REMAP. Modeled after the Intersections program I had produced at New WORLD Theater, REMAPs started with participatory arts workshops where participants could connect interpersonally and through their senses by art making, moving, singing, writing, cooking, beat making, and putting their bodies into the work.[5] Workshop leaders were encouraged to also be participants, especially outside their disciplines, and gain exposure to their peers' methodology.[6] Once grounded in art processes, REMAP expanded to art-centered convenings and Future Conversations, the seeds of cultural strategy. REMAPs took place in the San Francisco Bay Area; Detroit; Los Angeles; Pine Ridge Lakota Territory and Rapid City, South Dakota; Richmond, Virginia; and the Twin Cities of Minneapolis and St. Paul, Minnesota. We followed the compass of our relationships, only going where invited, by partners who were working on the ground long before and after our presence. Our planning methods were organic and responsive, usually a year long, but Los Angeles, due to its extensive geography, was a protracted process of nearly four years.

We avoided the convention of summoning stakeholders around a table to discuss our project. Instead we went to individual people, learning context and practice in workplaces, in studios, in neighborhoods, in homes, and over meals. Those visits led to introductions to others. We practiced exchange instead of extractive listening. As artists, we could bring a workshop and mutually share methodologies or offer an event to grow participants. Conversations were moored by exploring how we, as an outside national entity, could bring greater visibility, amplify voices, and expose wider publics to the challenges of cultural communities of color, as well as focus on their robust artistic leadership. We listened for issues, priorities, methodologies, resources, while strengthening relationships.

As we traversed the country, we documented the work in real time by commissioning thought pieces, essays, and interviews and publishing them on REFRAME, our e-journal, conceptualized by folklorist and cultural producer Maribel Alvarez, with Daniela Alvarez serving as editor. Our target audience was practitioners, but also policy makers and the academy. We sought accessible language, images, and audio/visual links from artists, scholars, and organizers. These notes from the field serve as the spine of this collection; the content was expanded to a widened array of voices from thirty-three states and Washington, DC. Coeditors Daniela Alvarez and Elizabeth Webb conceptualized the book's parts, drawing from the topics that surfaced in the REMAPs: "Cultural Presence: Placekeeping and Belonging"; "Dismantling Borders, Building Bridges: Migration and Diasporas"; "Creating a World without Prisons: Culture and the Carceral State"; "Embodied Cartographies: Renegotiating Relationships with Land"; "Living Our Legacy: Ancestral Knowledge as Radical Futurity"; and "Currents Beyond: Artists Shifting Paradigms of Inequity." In every location we worked, we saw the overarching failure of public and private funding structures to equitably invest in communities of color.

Faces of Power

> What we think of as neutral is often just a mask of normality over the horrific inequalities and injustices that the most privileged few want us to buy into, for their benefit.
> —**adrienne maree brown,** Afrofuturist writer, Detroit, Michigan

> Racism is a national emergency.
> —**Eleanor Savage,** artist and program director, Jerome Foundation, Minneapolis, Minnesota

In 2016, in the wake of #OscarsSoWhite, the *New York Times* published "Faces of Power," a stunning full-page graphic representation of the most powerful people in US business, government, education, the arts, and sports.[7] Of five hundred faces, there were only forty-four people of color. As ArtChangeUS organized in different locations, we adapted the graphic to give a snapshot of arts leadership in the different cities of our work. For example, in 2018 in Minneapolis, we looked at organizations with budgets over $10 million and found one leader of color out of twelve. In Los Angeles in 2020, zero out of eight, in a city and a state that had shifted to a Latine majority in 2018.

Of course, facile representation is not a solution; a rainbow of gatekeepers can uphold the status quo. But the "Faces of Power" graphic underscored inequity in arts funding and our absence at decision-making tables. Funding inequity was significantly quantified in Holly Sidford's 2011 landmark study for the National Committee for Responsive Philanthropy.[8] The report validated what was obvious empirically. The biggest organizations, those with budgets larger than $5 million, make up just 2 percent of the sector, but they receive the majority—more than half—of all arts funding. And only 10 percent of arts grant dollars go to supporting arts that explicitly benefit communities of color.

Self-assessments by concerned public arts agencies have disaggregated and given local detail to this national data. Cultural strategist Debra Padilla, a member of the 2017 Los Angeles County Arts Commission Cultural Equity and Inclusion report, pointed out that $88 million in public funding went to four organizations, while $4 million went to two hundred-plus organizations in competitive application processes.[9] These self-studies, in Los Angeles, New York, Seattle, and other cities, have given a baseline for public officials to pilot strategies to achieve equity. For example, the New

York Department of Cultural Affairs collaborated with the Metropolitan Museum of Art to introduce an admission ticket for out-of-town visitors with one-third of the revenue added to support for organizations of color and lower-income areas. The City of Seattle's Office of Arts and Culture provided antiracism training to grant reviewers prior to their panel service; they assert that this tactic has transformed award results.[10]

As more Global Majority, queer, and disabled grant makers and their allies have come into philanthropic spaces, pressure to effect change from within has grown. In 2008, arts and social justice trailblazer Claudine Brown started the Grantmakers in the Arts (GIA) Social Justice Funders Group.[11] In 2015, under the leadership of Eddie Torres, GIA adapted a Racial Equity Statement of Purpose built on ongoing racial equity self-audits, publications, and conversations with the field.[12] Significant presidential leadership shifts, including Darren Walker at the Ford Foundation, Elizabeth Alexander at Mellon, Don Chen at Surdna, and Angelique Power at Skillman, have elevated foundation presidents who, from their bully pulpits, have advanced and deepened commitments to social justice.

This book replaces the *New York Times* "Faces of Power" with the perspectives of individuals whose work revolutionizes the center, redefining culture, power, and agency. They include choreographer Antoine Hunter, founder of the Bay Area International Deaf Dance Festival; Samara Gaev, founder and artistic director of Truthworker Theatre Company, a hip-hop company for youth impacted by mass incarceration; Dareen Hussein, creator of the digital space *A Partial Restoration of the Palestine Archaeological Museum*; Patricia Berne and Nomy Lamm, directors of Sins Invalid, a disability justice–based performance project; Scott Oshima, artist and former director of community arts at the Japanese American Cultural & Community Center; Aaron McIntosh, creator of *Invasive Queer Kudzu*, an ongoing community storytelling and archive project across the LGBTQ+ South; and Faith Bartley, Courtney Bowles, and Mark Strandquist of People's Paper Co-op, an arts advocacy project led by incarcerated women in reentry.

The Arts Understory

> People like to refer to these communities as food deserts, but ... deserts are thriving complete ecosystems. What we are experiencing in our community ... is food apartheid, where some communities have and others don't, mostly based on race and class.
> —**Carlton Turner,** performing artist and founder of the Mississippi Center for Cultural Production (Sipp Culture), Utica, Mississippi

Arts policy discussions for years have referred to an arts ecology, a term that implies a symbiosis between the diversity of organizations that make up the arts sector. However, the enduring funding paradigm more accurately resembles 1980s trickle-down Reaganomics, presuming benefit to those at the grassroots level by philanthropic and individual donor support to large-budget, historically white-led and -serving organizations. As the arts sector has become increasingly corporatized, community-based organizations have been treated like research and development nodes, where artists and ideas are incubated, and the best products rise to the attention of elite spaces that then exacerbate inequities by hiring talent away from communities of color and co-opting their work. At worst, concentrating resources in white flagships has upheld values and practices of white supremacy and settler colonialism, where communities of color, far from the wealth of the anointed cultural metropole, are places of extraction or token charity. These critiques are long-standing. In 1996, playwright August Wilson created a firestorm when he railed against the white regional theater system, where he had found a career without finding home. In "The Ground on Which I Stand," he also objected to grant incentives to white theaters for ancillary diversity programming, instead of supporting theaters of color, particularly Black theaters, themselves.[13]

A true arts ecology might better be equated with the layers of a forest, where the health of the understory, the place where the teeming diversity of flora and fauna is found, is critical to a flourishing woodland. The practice of replacing forests with monocultural planting not only prevents other vegetation from growing back, it creates vulnerability for all.[14] In her Mother Tree Project, ecologist Suzanne Simard describes mother trees in the forest that act as hubs, supporting a "large, interconnected community creating a vast below ground network with their own and other species."[15] The cultural mother tree organizations of communities of color, most born out of Civil Rights–era activism, represent so many others that have fallen by the wayside due to underinvestment. In 1981, Elinor Bowles produced a milestone report for the National Endowment for the Arts, *Cultural Centers of Color: Report on a National Survey*, that documented 551 vibrant cultural organizations of color.[16] Prepandemic, only 287 in the report were still active. Director and playwright Dominic Taylor posed a parallel question: "What if more organizations that started as a result of the Black Arts Movement survived?"[17] Queen Quet Marquetta L. Goodwine, elected chieftess of the Gullah/Geechee Nation on St. Helena Island, South Carolina, provides an answer in her question, "How do you live in such a way that creates the future you want when you must survive today?"

This collection includes mother tree–voices of iconic artists, fearless cultural organizers, and tireless policy advocates like Carol Bebelle, Ofelia Esparza, Hinaleimoana Kwai Kong Wong-Kalu (Kumu Hina), Guillermo Gómez-Peña, Nobuko Miyamoto, Cleo Parker Robinson, Vicky Holt Takamine, Carrie Mae Weems, and Ofelia Zepeda. Intergenerational dialogues with younger artists mine the interconnectedness of generations, including conversations between Aloha ʻĀina educator and spoken-word poet Jamaica Heolimeleikalani Osorio and her father, musician and educator Jon Kamakawiwoʻole Osorio; singer and choreographer Nobuko Miyamoto, her son Kamau Ayubbi, and granddaughter Sufi musician Asiyah Ayubbi; gender-nonconforming writer and performance artist Alok Vaid-Menon and their aunt, LGBT activist Urvashi Vaid; and Sadie Barnette, whose installation project is in artistic dialogue with her father, the proprietor of San Francisco's first Black-owned gay bar.

Trust US

This is a calling-in to institutions and entities with power and privilege to relinquish it. . . . This is a calling-in to the philanthropic, nonprofit, and education sectors to expand their circles of trust beyond white or white-adjacent executive leadership, to loosen their grip on time and space, in order to water the roots. This is how to support and elevate Black and Brown leadership, and (finally!) take a nonstop journey toward an anti-racist future. It's time.
—**Quanice Floyd,** founder, Arts Administrators of Color, Washington, DC, "The Failure of Arts Organizations to Move toward Racial Equity"

The best part about bad policy is that it can be changed.
—**Linda Campbell,** Detroit activist and director, Detroit People's Platform, quoted in Halima Afi Cassells, "Collectively Directing the Current"

Conventional cultural maps of cities focus on real estate: museums, theaters, galleries—places that exist through brick and mortar. But how does one map the ephemeral, the longitudinal, the actual ways that culture lives in communities? City Lore and the Alliance for California Traditional Arts have done extraordinary work to make visible places that matter—spaces like El Maestro, a Bronx boxing gym that is an informal cultural center, with a boxing ring that transforms into a stage for music and poetry events.[18] Large-budget white organizations have been equated with the mainstream and the canonical center of critical discourse. So often, Global Majority artists and organizations are characterized as new, emerging, next generation, and lacking in capacity. But in parallel universes, culture exists at scale, particularly in Indigenous and immigrant communities. Festivals and parades like the Brooklyn West Indian Day parade, which draws an estimated two million people annually, half of which are participants; the Tribal Canoe Journeys of the Pacific Northwest, associations of Native American basketweavers, and hālau hula are examples of widespread cultural activity, often nestled within language revitalization, traditional knowledge, and land steward-ship. In this volume, the rhythm of language also courses from the cultural movements of hip-hop rap artists and beat makers, poets, and spoken-word artists like Dahlak Brathwaite, Tani Ikeda, Douglas Kearney, Devin Kenny, Talon Bazille Ducheneaux (Cheyenne River Lakota/Crow Creek Dakota), Tanaya Winder (Duckwater Shoshone), Kondwani Fidel, Alison Akootchook Warden (Iñupiaq), and Yosimar Reyes. These voices represent influential cultures at scale, often unhoused, but fearlessly defying, repurposing, and expanding far beyond the limits of institutionalized spaces.

So what would it mean for large-budget white institutions, recognizing a transformed majority population, to assume the role of learners, not lead-ers, on issues of cultural equity? How would their positionality realign and their practices transcend performative solidarity? And what if public and private funding radically shifted to recognize leadership on the ground—if the forests were truly tended at the roots? In 2021, MacKenzie Scott made a breathtaking set of grants totaling $2.74 billion to 286 arts organizations, the majority of which are Global Majority–led and grassroots.[19] This book includes numerous contributors whose leadership organizations were rec-ognized by the Scott grants: Jeanette Lee, Allied Media Projects; Carol Bebelle, Ashé Cultural Arts Center; Favianna Rodriguez, Center for Cul-tural Power; Lori Lea Pourier, First Peoples Fund; Vicky Holt Takamine, PAʻI Foundation; Jeff Chang, formerly with Race Forward; Patricia Berne and Nomy Lamm, Sins Invalid; Carlton Turner, Sipp Culture; Maribel Alva-rez, Southwest Folklife Alliance; Faith Bartley, Courtney Bowles, and Mark Strandquist, the People's Paper Co-op at the Village of Arts and Humanities; and Yanina Chicas and Belise Nishimwe, poets from the Youth Speaks Brave New Voices Network. The Scott investment sent a simple, brilliant message to philanthropy and the art world: trust and invest in those doing the work.

But it doesn't take being the third wealthiest woman in the world to rad-ically reverse the long-standing egregious practice of rewarding those with the most dollars by giving them even more money as incentive to engage with diversity. Redressing the chronic underfunding of Native America, the Northwest Area Foundation committed to invest 40 percent of their annual grant dollars in support of Native-led organizations. From 2012 to 2020, they invested nearly $63.4 million in Native-led organizations—45.6

percent of their $139 million in awarded grants during that period.[20] This collection trusts in those who move beyond research and case making, beyond unmaking, to the bold work of iterating the future.

A Multiverse of Change

Given that the universe is infinite, everyone is in the center of it.
—**Talon Bazille Ducheneaux** (Cheyenne River Lakota/Crow Creek Dakota), rap artist and poet, Fort Thompson, South Dakota, in conversation with Genevieve Fowler, January 2021

How did I find my own home, from which I endeavored to build other homes?
—**Marlène Ramírez-Cancio**, cultural producer, Brooklyn, New York

In 2020, when the world was newly in pandemic lockdown, millions of people became virtual bystanders to the Minneapolis police murder of George Floyd. For nine minutes and twenty-nine seconds, a curtain was parted to the unabated lynching and violence against Black people, stretching far back in history and reaching widely into the present. In all of the communities where we worked, the issue of police profiling and brutality, and the impact of the carceral state, was named. A few weeks after we started our planning work for our REMAP in Minneapolis, Philando Castile was murdered by police in front of his girlfriend and child. The week we produced the REMAP there, his killer was acquitted, and the city arose in rebellion.

Activist-philosopher Grace Lee Boggs, who passed away at one hundred the year we began, said, "Change takes place in living systems, not from above, but from within, from many local actions occurring simultaneously."[21] The contributors to this book are enacting reverberating change from the centers of multiple locations; collectively they speak to a groundswell of connecting movements for justice. Artist Aydinaneth Ortiz's epicenter is the collision of mental illness and the police state; architect Teddy Cruz and theorist Fonna Forman imagine a cross-border citizenship spanning the militarized San Diego/Tijuana border; bassoonist Garrett McQueen confronts being the sole Black body in white orchestras as impetus to build a community of instrumentalists of color; fashion designer Sky Cubacub celebrates Radical Visibility for Queer and Disabled people in their accessible clothing designs; artist Favianna Rodriguez turns to her Oakland neighborhood and migrant roots to awaken a relationship to the environment; and Arshia Fatima Haq's project invokes the concept of azadi (freedom), writing in Urdu script across the sky above detention centers.

ArtChangeUS exists at the intersection between these different centers—personal, communitarian, geographic, and disciplinary. Jeff Chang opens this book with a catalytic Call and series of questions, urging the responses that follow. Similarly, in March 2020, as the early pandemic lockdown set in, Chang called to ArtChangeUS partners to join together on a cultural front line to challenge a postpandemic recovery of the status quo. In an email to artist Favianna Rodriguez and me, he imagined "a national call at this time when many of our organizations and artists of color are suffering from the closure of our doors, the loss of work and jobs, and the potential flagging of momentum around field-wide equity efforts. Funding and jobs may be the main issues of the art sector when quarantines end, but what about cultural equity? Can artists of color and arts organizations of color drive the agenda this time around?" We reached out to ArtChangeUS Core Partners: María López De León, National Association of Arts and Culture; Lori Lea Pourier, First Peoples Fund; and Carlton Turner, Sipp Culture. From our vantage points in Oakland, New York, San Antonio, Lakota Territory, and Utica, Mississippi, we invited other colleagues and collaboratively crafted the Cultural New Deal for Cultural and Racial Justice (CND).[22]

Part call to action, part arts manifesto, and part road map, the CND urges a transformation of our personal, institutional, and global thinking and actions to address racism and inequality from within the cultural sector. Prioritizing communities of color, it forwards artists and culture bearers as the first responders to the soul of our communities as stewards of the imagination and as healers of society.[23] It is a living and evolving collaborative body of work that ultimately seeks accountability and transformation in the arts and culture field, and connection to justice movements beyond. Contributors like choreographer Ananya Chatterjea embody this change on the ground. Her company is aesthetically "flexing hope," making dynamic choreographic work adapting to the ongoing uprisings in the Twin Cities. Mel D. Cole's powerful *Ballers* image shows the reclamation of a Confederate monument as communal space, expunging the statue through the presence of free Black bodies. Jeanette Lee, writing about Allied Media Projects and capturing the relationship of cultural and political change writ large, states, "These are human evolutionary changes, which unfold in the realm of culture through practices of creativity. They may materialize as policy change eventually, but that will be the evidence of change that has already occurred."[24]

A Future That Is Already Here

> You are the living representative of your ancestral lines. You are the ancestor from the future, peering back through time and forward through time with your intent gaze and wisdom. As an artist, cultivate these ancestral spaces and make work for not only your great-great-grandchildren, but also for your great-great-grandparents. You are the connective portal in the now. Cultivate a space for your song to come through.
> —**Allison Akootchook Warden,** New Genre artist, Kaktovik, Alaska

In the shadow of the COVID-19 pandemic, a monumental Supreme Court decision was made July 9, 2021. Writing the majority opinion for *McGirt v. Oklahoma*, Associate Justice Neil M. Gorsuch, an avowed conservative textualist, affirmed tribal sovereignty and territorial boundaries by recognizing the integrity of a US government–to-government document signed 154 years ago with the Muscogee (Creek) Nation. The decision begins, "On the far end of the Trail of Tears was a promise. . . . We hold the government to its word."[25] This recognition that about half of Oklahoma is Native land, based on treaties which established the Muscogee (Creek) reservation before the founding of the state of Oklahoma, has far-reaching implications. *McGirt*, a landmark decision resting on the tireless efforts of Native American legal champions, came at a moment of national reckoning about racism and accountability.

Throughout the country, individuals and communities are grappling with righting historical and structural wrongs. Evanston, Illinois, became the first US city to pay reparations to its Black residents; white supremacist statues have been removed from the heart of the former Confederacy and in public squares around the world; and in the arts field, leadership is being held accountable. In 2021, Americans for the Arts, a national arts advocacy organization, finally heeded field protests and retired its founder, a steadfast arts advocate who nonetheless had failed to build inclusive leadership and racial equity within the organization. But in this time of unveiled assault, meaningful change in the arts sector is tied with urgency to larger battles as legislators double down on voter suppression, the Supreme Court reversal of *Roe v. Wade* strips women of our most basic rights, white supremacists promulgate replacement theory, and critical race theory becomes the latest lightning rod in the culture wars. Organizing—beyond ally statements; diversity, equity, and inclusion plans; and land acknowledgments—must move reckoning from rhetoric to accountability and resistance.

Thus, the many contributions to this book are creative actions, subversions, and reframing propositions that exist in resistance to the present moment but ultimately draw a connection to long lineages of embodied and ancestral knowledge. All constitute a radical shift in values, power, and perspective. Hawaiian navigator and filmmaker Nāʻālehu Anthony expresses a relationship to the stars, winds, and currents that is both cosmological and scientific, predating Western contact: "These waʻa were moving throughout the Pacific a full one thousand years before Westerners would figure out how to use the compass and sextant to leave the sight of land. By the time Westerners got here, the millions of square miles of ocean and islands in Polynesia were already fully cultivated by Pacific Islanders." Artist Wendy Red Star proposes an "Apsáalooke feminism" grounded in the matrilineality of the Crow Nation. Artist Silvi Naçi centers healing as a decolonizing act: drinking tea together, and making the tea bags into bricks—a form that dates back to 7000 BCE as one of the oldest building materials. Ruben Ulises Rodriguez Montoya's sculptures reach simultaneously to a primordial past and to a mythic future, conjured from detritus found along the US-Mexico border. He writes, "*Sopa de Ostión* is a being of a future that is already here, as well as a creature of a time when desert used to be ocean and our hands were not hands but a thick foot of a muscle leaving behind glutinous slime over an already ancient rock." Similarly manifesting a Sankofa vision, Kenyatta A. C. Hinkle's project, *The Evanesced Series* (2016–), is an expression of the #SayHerName movement, asking, "What would it look like to emerge from erasure?"

It is our hope that, just as we began our journey with two questions, the readers of this book will hear and respond to the call of the many explicit and implicit questions embedded here, and that they come away with new questions that draw us closer to a thriving future that is not beyond our imaginations. Most people stand at the shore and see the ocean as a barrier that separates us. But these cultural navigators see the waters' pathways and possibilities, connecting the guidance of the stars above and the currents ahead.

Notes

1. Epigraphs come from the contributions in this book, unless otherwise noted.

2. The twelve original Core Partners were Maribel Alvarez, founder of the Southwest Folklore Alliance at the University of Arizona; artist Marc Bamuthi Joseph, then director of performing arts at the Yerba Buena Center for the Arts; James Kass, cofounder of Youth Speaks; writer Jeff Chang, then executive director of the Institute for Diversity in the Arts at Stanford University; Teddy Cruz, codirector of the Cross-Border Initiative at UC San Diego; Vicky Holt Takamine, kumu hula and executive director of the PAʻI Foundation; María López De León, executive director of the National Association of Latino Arts and Cultures; Lori

Lea Pourier (Oglala/Mnicoujou Lakota), president of First Peoples Fund; artist Favianna Rodriguez, then executive director of CultureStr/ke; Diana Taylor, founding director of the Hemispheric Institute of Performance and Politics, New York University; artist Carlton Turner, then executive director of Alternate ROOTS; and Clyde Valentín, director of Ignite/ArtsDallas at SMU Meadows School of the Arts.

3. Hawai'i has never had a white majority; it is the only officially bilingual state, with English and 'Ōlelo Hawai'i.

4. In 2015 when ArtChangeUS launched, I was questioning my sanity to do another start-up at sixty, having founded New WORLD Theater in my twenties. I worked the first three months alone, unpaid, before raising funds to hire actor and playwright Kristen Calhoun as program director. Steven Lavine, president of the California Institute of the Arts (CalArts), persuaded me to bring the project to CalArts. He posited that if artists and aesthetics were central to the project, it should be located at an arts school in a city like Los Angeles, with a majority Latine and people of color population. The student population was demographically shifting, but administration and faculty were predominantly white. CalArts provided half of my salary, office space, and freedom to work across schools by developing an ArtChangeUS Fellows program for graduate students from different métiers, who entered a leadership pipeline. Three became ArtChangeUS staff; others are ongoing collaborators of mine in the theater; and several made significant contributions to this collection, including as coeditors. With CalArts as an institutional base and with a fiscal agent, eventually NEO Philanthropy, as the infrastructural home providing back office, we were able to start a five-year heavy slog of fundraising, which enabled us to evolve into a national team of seven, all working up to 80 percent time, with medical and retirement benefits, while also pursuing our arts practices. Kristen left ArtChangeUS to become the first program manager for the Intercultural Leadership Institute, and I stepped down as director in 2022. Kapena Alapa'i and Kassandra L. Khalil became codirectors, joined by Daniela Alvarez, REFRAME and research manager; Michele Kumi Baer, CND manager; Genevieve Fowler, program associate; and Elizabeth M. Webb, senior creative producer. I tell this part of the story because programming is public facing, but infrastructure and process are often where the real equity issues lie. One needs only look at diversity reporting from predominantly white institutions to see that racial diversity is typically concentrated in support staff, adjunct, contracted and part-time workers, interns, and fellows, and, cutting across many of these categories, the undercompensated and unbenefited.

5. The legacy of the New WORLD Theater is examined in Chinua Thelwell, ed., *Theater and Cultural Politics for a New World* (London: Routledge, 2017).

6. REMAP workshops included "Hula as Resistance," Vicky Holt Takamine; "Social Justice Comedy," Negin Farsad; "FLEXn Your Story: The Art of Social Justice," Reggie "Regg Roc" Gray; "Listening to Our Landscape: Voice, Movement, Story," Sayda Trujillo; "The Aadizookaan: Beat Work, Beading with Beats," Sacramento Knoxx and Christy B.; "The Push and Pull: Screen Printing," Ron Watters and Elijah Ford; "The Freedom Chamber," Ron Ragin and Rebecca Mwase; "Lakota Game Making," Mike Marshall; "Loomworking and Beadwork-

ing," Molina Parker and Tasha Abourezk; "Counting Coup," Cannupa Hanska Luger; "Heart and Hearth: Bread Making for Community Strength," Seitu Jones; "Decolonizing Our Culture with Collective Songwriting and Dance Making," Nobuko Miyamoto and Quetzal Flores; and "Embodying Justice," Gabrielle Civil and Tamica Washington-Miller.

7. Haeyoun Park, Josh Keller, and Josh Williams, "The Faces of American Power, Nearly as White as the Oscar Nominees," *New York Times*, February 26, 2016.

8. Holly Sidford, *Fusing Arts, Culture and Social Change* (Washington, DC: National Committee for Responsive Philanthropy, 2011), http://www.ncrp.org/paib /arts-culture-philanthropy.

9. T. Dang, H. Hernandez, and M. R. Jackson, *LA County Arts Report: Cultural Equity and Inclusion Initiative* (Los Angeles: Los Angeles County Arts Commission, April 2017), https://www.lacountyarts.org/sites/default/files/pdfs/lacac17 _ceiireport_final.pdf; Debra J. T. Padilla, "Our LA," Arts in a Changing America: LA Cultural Equity Summit Remarks, April 17, 2019.

10. ArtChangeUS remap: LA Cultural Equity Summit Recap, April 17, 2019, https://artsinachangingamerica.org/remap-la-recap-2/.

11. A debt of gratitude to Claudine Brown, Tomas Ybarra Frausto, and arts philanthropy change makers, especially Maurine Knighton, Joan Shigekawa, Sam Miller, Emiko Ono, Denise Brown, Eddie Torres, F. Javier Torres-Campos, Margaret Morton, Taryn Higashi, Vickie Benson, Eleanor Savage, Arleta Little, and Regina Smith.

12. "Outline of gia's Work in Equity, 2008–Present," Grantmakers in the Arts, July 17, 2021, https://www.giarts.org/outline-gia-work-equity-2008-present.

13. August Wilson, "The Ground on Which I Stand," transcript of speech delivered at the Eleventh Biennial Theatre Communications Group national conference, Princeton University, Princeton, New Jersey, June 1996.

14. Forest fires rage on the US West Coast and in Australia, regions where fire season is now year round. But fire has also been an invaluable tool in the hands of peoples who steward a diverse ecosystem. According to abc Adelaide Facebook, May 13, 2021, Aboriginal elders say history was made May 2021 in Tartanya (Adelaide), which held the first Aboriginal cultural burn in two centuries. "The Kaurna people used fire to manage the Adelaide plains for millennia. It has shaped our ecosystems and it is a very important cultural practice for the Kaurna people," according to Adelaide Lord Mayor Sandy Verschoor. In a Zoom conversation on July 14, 2021, with Lori Lea Pourier and Menominee musician Wade Fernandez, he described his nation's forests, a vast area so green nasa astronauts have observed them from space. He notes that Menominee forest keepers' practices ensure a cycle of replenishing: "It goes on forever."

15. "About Mother Trees in the Forest," Mother Tree Project, accessed November 23, 2022, https://mothertreeproject.org/about-mother-trees-in-the-forest/.

16. Elinor Bowles, *Cultural Centers of Color: Report on a National Survey* (Washington, DC: National Endowment for the Arts, December 1989), 129, https:// www.americansforthearts.org/by-program/reports-and-data/legislation-policy /naappd/cultural-centers-of-color-report-on-a-national-survey.

17. Dominic Taylor, "What If . . . More Theatres from the Black Arts Movement Survived?," *TCG Circle*. Published as part of the 2011 TCG National Conference, TCG at 50: What if . . . ?(Los Angeles, CA, June 16–18).

18. City Lore's Community Anchor report, *Community Anchors: Sustaining Religious Institutions, Social Clubs, and Small Businesses That Serve as Cultural Centers for Their Communities*, 2016, https://citylore.org/place-matters/community-anchors/; Place Matters, "The Census Map," accessed November 23, 2022, https://placematters.net/; Alliance for California Traditional Arts, *Building Healthy Communities: Approaching Community Health through Heritage and Culture in Boyle Heights*, https://actaonline.org/wp-content/uploads/2019/06/BH-Cultural-Report-2017.pdf.

19. Laurel Wamsley, "MacKenzie Scott Is Giving Another 2.67 Billion to 286 Organizations," NPR, June 15, 2021.

20. "Northwest Area Foundation: Native-Led Work," Northwest Area Foundation, 2021, https://www.nwaf.org/approach/native-led-work/.

21. Grace Lee Boggs, "Seeds of Change," *Bill Moyers Journal*, August 31, 2007, http://www.pbs.org/moyers/journal/blog/2007/08/seeds_of_change.html.

22. See part 6 of this book for greater detail.

23. In 2022, ArtChangeUS was tapped by the CND partners to manage its next phase. They pivoted from the original calling-out of a white-led/serving arts sector to a calling-in of the Global Majority–led field. The Cultural New Deal elevates the learning, challenges, and culture of collaboration between our communities, while still pressing for accountability and equity. It has infused and expanded ArtChangeUS's work in cultural community benefits, a methodology grounded in the work of our Detroit partners, adapted from the powerful organizing history and ongoing efforts to legislate community benefits, ordinances, and agreements to ensure that for-profit real estate developers, using public monies, provide benefit to the people and neighborhoods of Detroit. For more information, see Detroit People's Platform, https://www.detroitpeoplesplatform.org/.

24. Jeanette Lee, idea lab speech, Grantmakers in the Arts Conference, Detroit, MI, October 29, 2017.

25. Neil M. Gorsuch, McGirt v. Oklahoma, 591 US (2020).

The Call

Jeff Chang

Jeff Chang is an author, cultural strategist, and organizer. He is the author of award-winning books, including *Can't Stop Won't Stop, Who We Be*, and *We Gon' Be Alright*. He is based in Berkeley, California, and Honolulu, Hawai'i.

Early in 2016, when the Black Lives Matter movement was in the streets, Black filmmaker Arthur Jafa took a file of videos he had been collecting on his desktop computer—including minstrelsy cartoons and the murder of Walter Scott, Biggie Smalls freestyling on a Bed-Stuy corner, and President Obama singing "Amazing Grace" from the pulpit of Charleston's Emanuel AME—and, in a two-hour creative burst, pieced together a seven-minute video. He set it to Kanye West's then-new song "Ultralight Beam" and titled it *Love Is the Message, the Message Is Death*.

Drawing from a century of moving images of Blackness in American visual culture, Jafa's video moved breath-to-breath juxtaposing images of Ferguson with images of Selma, Angela Davis and Amandla Stenberg, twerkers and line dancers, ordinary people experiencing joy and pain, children torn from their parents and beaten by police and lectured by parents using the language of police. This haunting visual meditation on the agita of the times, he later said, meant to speak to "the space of the abject sublime."[1]

Jafa had not intended it to be seen by many. He sent it to select friends, including the Los Angeles–based filmmaker Kahlil Joseph, who, unbeknownst to Jafa, began screening it at the Black art hub, the Underground Museum. He then took it to Art Basel Miami Beach and played it before an early screening of a film he had directed for Beyoncé's new album, *Lemonade*. It was soon being celebrated as a masterpiece of American art.

Its title, both compelling and disturbing, seemed to reference both the Black raise-your-hands disco classic and Frank Wilderson's philosophy of Afropessimism. The work captured all of the complexities of Black life that lay in between. "There's a certain feel of abjection that seems to swirl around us [Black people]," he explained. "And at the same time we are the emblem of life force and power and potentiality."[2]

Joseph himself had already been working on a project he called *blknws*, a two-screen installation that included viral internet memes of music videos, photos and screencaps of Black life, and clips of Black artists like Herbie Hancock or the painter Noah Davis, Joseph's late brother, in acts of creation, footage from documentaries and news coverage, and conversations between *blknws* "anchors" like Amandla Stenberg and Helen Molesworth. The images, fed live via satellite, scrolled and tugged and poked at each other across the split screens, evoking something between a Black-centered culture-friendly newscast and Jafa's more impressionistic work.

Joseph had been watching ESPN one night and noticed that the subjects whom the white sportscasters were talking about were all Black. He wondered what it might look like to have a Black news channel, a kind of twenty-four-hour CNN just for Black people. He seemed to be returning to the idea that Public Enemy's Chuck D and Harry Allen had voiced a generation before, when they argued that rap music was Black America's news network. Joseph had initially played with the notion of installing *blknws* in neighborhood spots—laundromats, barber shops, or bodegas around the way—and although he scaled back the plan and took it to the Venice Biennale, he did eventually also install it in destinations across the United States where Black creative communities gathered, such as the Eaton Hotel in Washington, DC, and Stanford University's Harmony House.[3]

blknws, too, was of its time. On August 9, 2014, when Officer Darren Wilson executed Michael Brown, the birth of the movement in a Black suburb of St. Louis called Ferguson had been documented in real time on Twitter, reigniting the hashtag #BlackLivesMatter and powering the longest, largest demonstrations in national history. Racial justice now fed the culture's riverflow, represented not just in the scroll of names of Black people killed by police and white vigilantes, but in the real-time assemblage of a justice movement and a new attention on artists and culture bearers of color, their works, and their presence—or absence—across an arts and culture sector blinded by whiteness.

Love Is the Message, the Message Is Death and *blknws* remind us of the role of the artist and the culture bearer in their community—to signal that our humanity cannot be denied, to remind us and prepare us for our practices and processes of resilience, to stir in us through delight, challenge, and inspiration our empathy and an urge to act, to point us toward complexity as the world is being flattened into binaries, to sound our traumas and dreams as burdens and aspirations to be collectively shouldered.

When, led by Roberta Uno, a group of us artists and culture bearers met in 2014 to launch what would become Arts in a Changing America (ArtChangeUS), it indeed seemed as if the world had finally cracked open, like the very surface of the earth at the beginning of Yuri Herrera's *Signs Preceding the End of the World*. The revolution had come, and it was being represented in the flow of images and sounds pouring up from the chasm.

For years we had been voicing warnings of this moment, usually to powerful but circumspect leaders. But the election of Donald Trump confirmed that our national culture had cleaved into two opposed visions: what Vincent Harding had called "a possible America" hopeful and yearning, per Langston Hughes, to "be America again," and, on the opposing side, a fearful America inflamed by the toxic mirage of whiteness, gripped by apocalyptic terror and raging in red hats to "be great again."[4]

In this moment after Trayvon Martin's and Michael Brown's murders and before the protests at Standing Rock against the Dakota Access Pipeline, Trump's election and the Muslim ban and #MeToo and Charlottesville and Parkland and El Paso and Mauna Kea and the biological and man-made violence of the coronavirus, we knew what we knew. Confusion and fear were miasmic. Politics had broken down. We needed artists and culture bearers to help us see through the fog. We thought that arts and culture might be the only place for us to start to make change.

The #BlackLivesMatter meme was the spark. Created by community organizer Alicia Garza, artist/activist Patrisse Cullors, and media organizer Opal Tometi in response to the 2013 acquittal of vigilante George Zimmerman in the murder of Trayvon Martin, the hashtag would catalyze the largest uprising for racial justice in national history.

#BlackLivesMatter made sense of different movement vectors—including efforts to end state violence, abolish police and prisons, end sexual assault, transform immigration, and win cultural justice. It centered Black leadership in the making of a new political insurgency and a new cultural front. In turn, these twin efforts reaffirmed the truth that Black-led movements produce and connect generative spaces for all. #BlackLivesMatter lent language, method, and moral force to the #MeToo movement to end sexual assault and abuse, the Parkland movement for gun control, and the Women's March. It connected to the movement for immigrant and undocumented migrant rights and the Standing Rock movement to deepen and strengthen intersectional critiques of systemic racism.

This new consciousness highlighted how much mainstream politics had abandoned "the art of the possible." But the possibilities of art and culture multiplied on digital and physical platforms. The latter half of the 2010s were astonishingly creative, as the culture thickened with new visions, new voices, and new ideas. Emergent strategy, codified by adrienne maree brown in Detroit, brought Grace Lee Boggs's ecosystem-building notions into cultural organizing and helped to describe and advance the ferment of consciousness, creativity, and community and cultural organizing.

Reimaginings spread across everyday life, positing joy and rest as forms of resistance (such as the Black Women Dreaming and the Nap Ministry projects). Artists and organizers came together to transform the narrative and therefore the culture (including Color of Change, US Department of Arts and Culture, the Center for Cultural Power, Pop Culture Collaborative, Harness, Define American, the Butterfly Lab for Immigrant Narrative Strategy). Community-centered collectives (such as those in the Intercultural Leadership Institute) matched their convening powers by building new independent centers, farms, and venues in long-neglected towns, neighborhoods, and reservations. By the end of the decade, facing a global pandemic, economic apocalypse, and environmental collapse, artists were actively developing futurist visions, whether in policy (the Black Futures Lab) or community building (Wakanda Dream Lab) or both (IllumiNative's Indigenous Futures).

These movements gave us pictures of people rising up—even while masked against the COVID-19 pandemic—fighting the Trump administration's attempts to defend a murderous imperial whiteness that could leave even white women attacked, suburban white high school students cut down by mass murderers, and white death rates soaring. The images multiplied, with new faces in the frame: millions at the Women's Marches, sexual assault survivors and activists in Hollywood awards ceremonies, and pop cultural storytelling that turned the spotlight on transgender people of color. #BlackLivesMatter had generated the existential current that gave these movements their momentum: here we are in all of our humanity, and that should be enough.

Artists and culture bearers of color had inherited the struggles of the multiculturalists to undo the invisibility that Ralph Ellison spoke of when he wrote in 1952, "I am an invisible man. . . . I am invisible, understand, simply because people refuse to see me. . . . When they approach me they see only my surroundings, themselves, or figments of their imagination—indeed, everything and anything except me."[5]

Following the Combahee River Collective's naming of intersectionality, radical people of color and feminist of color collectives began to call themselves multiculturalists.[6] In the 1970s, multiculturalism was not the toothless, corporate tokenism it would become, but a recognition that those who lived under multiple and cross-cutting oppressions might best articulate the paths toward collective liberation. They believed that by making and circulating their images, songs, and stories, they might be able to end erasure and invisibility and, in doing so, enable bonds of empathy to be built.

But empathy was not about artists of color begging whites to recognize their humanity. It was about imagining equity and the action required to restore cultural justice. As Toni Morrison had once told a white interviewer, "I would like to write novels that were unmistakably mine but nevertheless fit first into African-American traditions and, second of all, this whole thing called literature." She added, "It's very important to me that my work be African-American. If it assimilates into a different or larger pool, so much the better. But I shouldn't be *asked* to do that. Joyce is not asked to do that. Tolstoy is not."[7]

By the end of the 2010s, Arthur Jafa explained his work in a similar way. Artists of color were not merely seeking white recognition, whether through empathy or awards or jobs, but something much more—the end of whiteness altogether, a leveling of cultural power. He said, "My secret weapon is I am addressing Black people. Everybody else gets to listen in. I'm very happy that people want to listen in. I think maybe there's something to be gained from listening in, but I'm not speaking to white people." He said: "Black people, People of Color, women—they have developed that muscle. It's an empathy muscle. It's the capacity to be able to sit in front of something that's not coming from your subject position and to process it, have an opinion about it, feel something, be in that person's skin, see the world from their perspective. So, in effect, I would say the most caring thing I can do for white people is to not address them, to not speak to them."[8]

The radical multiculturalist uprising of the 1970s—a direct cultural outgrowth of the Black Arts, Chicano, American Indian, Native Hawaiian, and Asian American arts movements, with overlapping links to the North American Third World student movements—coincided with an expansion in funding for the arts and government cultural policy that had fostered the growth of organizations serving artists and communities of color. During this period, creative ecosystems expanded, sustaining artists and culture bearers like Morrison, Audre Lorde, Carrie Mae Weems, Amalia Mesa-Bains, Ruth Asawa, and so many more. By the early 1990s, some white leaders in the art world, in acts of self-examination that recalled a similar turn in the 1960s and prefigured yet another in the late 2010s, established initiatives and programs meant to increase diversity and inclusion.

But at the same time, protectors of whiteness—Republican and Democrat alike—slashed government budgets for arts and culture. They did so by first scapegoating artists of color, women artists, queer artists, and—yes, intersectionality—queer femmes and queer artists of color and queer femme artists of color. Their cuts eviscerated long-standing institutions that supported many artists and communities of color, and entire creative ecosystems vanished.[9]

Yet artists of color and communities of color never stopped making art or advancing culture. For those who came of age after the culture wars of the early 1990s and who didn't grow up to know the difference between the NEA and the CIA—as the visionary hip-hop gen arts advocate Clyde Valentín once playfully put it, to the groans of some elders—the impulse to make work, build venues, and develop creative ecosystems continued largely outside of the realm of government and cultural policy.

Hip-hop generation organizations did mature, and many turned to the nonprofit arts sector to harvest the expansion of arts funders. Here is where Roberta Uno was building a national program at the Ford Foundation she called Future Aesthetics. Established in 2002, about a decade from the peak of the culture wars, the program helped to popularize hip-hop aesthetics in the performing arts and eventually expanded to looking at underfunded but socially significant arts organizations in geographic areas and communities largely ignored by funders primarily in sustaining long-standing, well-resourced mainstream organizations such as symphonies, operas, and ballet companies.

Because the appetite for racial and cultural equity was not very strong during this period, Future Aesthetics described its mission as funding arts and culture at the convergence of the leading edges of aesthetic, cultural, and demographic change.[10] During its twelve-year run, the program managed to redirect and generate renewed attention and resources not just for young people, but for Black communities, Indigenous communities, Latinx, and Asian American and Pacific Islander communities all across the country, but notably in the South, Indian Country, and Alaska and the Pacific.

It may help to contextualize how radical Future Aesthetics actually was in that moment. After the culture wars of the 1990s, the field had moved so far away from communities of color that there were no studies of note that did a basic accounting of their underrepresentation. It was just a given, until 2016, when a study by the New York Department of Cultural Affairs revealed that although the city was two-thirds people of color, its arts and cultural sector staff was two-thirds white.[11] Studies by the Helicon Collaborative found that less than half a cent of each philanthropic dollar funded arts and culture organizations serving communities of color.[12]

So when we came together in October 2015 to launch Arts in a Changing America at the Ford Foundation, we were profoundly aware of the history that had brought us to that point. We recognized that the US arts and culture sector had begun in the late nineteenth century, during another gilded age, when wealthy industrialists had funded the creation of institutions that would elevate North American standards of culture to compete with European standards. We knew that the periods in which government funding and cultural policy lifted up artists and culture bearers of color had been brief and accompanied by vicious periods of whitelash. We knew that it was the millions in the streets who had made it possible for us to be taken seriously in halls of privilege. We knew that, no matter what lay ahead, we would continue to do what we needed to do. And we knew that this was a moment to push forward, so that even if another backlash lay ahead—which we were certain was the case—at least those who followed us would start at a position further along than we had been given by previous generations.

And so we asked ourselves:

- What does art and culture concerned with the question of freedom look like now? What kind of freedom movement do we want for the twenty-first century?
- How can we together dream of new futures that are sustainable and that center radical diversity again?
- And how can we make this dream delightful and, as Toni Cade Bambara once put it, irresistible to all?

And as 2016 accelerated toward the turn of the decade on the vast expansion of racial justice movements, those questions became very real very quickly. We moved beyond questions of diversity. We realized that we needed to define where we wanted to go.

We returned to the notion of cultural equity, advanced by musicologist Alan Lomax in the early 1970s and revisited amid the culture wars in the late 1980s by arts advocates like Marta Vega, Dudley Cocke, Arlene Goldbard, and many others. We needed to articulate the ongoing lack of representation—in terms of both aesthetic content and structural power. We defined *cultural equity* as the condition that all people are fairly resourced in artistic and cultural expression and fairly represented in systems of exhibition, performance, and decision making. We were clear, because we had learned from the cultural activists and organizers of the late 1980s, that cultural equity demanded a redistribution of cultural power.

Cultural power, we knew, was the ability to lift up—and also to marginalize, suppress, or erase—people's artistic, aesthetic, and cultural practices, processes, and products. In naming cultural power—and calling out its gaping imbalance in the arts and culture sector—we reminded arts and culture sector leaders that the history of the philanthropic sector was rooted in the preservation of whiteness. During the late nineteenth century, museums and cultural institutions were established and funded by a white American elite who had not only hoped to define American highbrow culture against European standards, but to maintain the imperialist impulse of looting, debasing, and appropriating non-European cultures.[13]

Racism and exclusion were built into the system and therefore required leaders directly to dismantle them. Cultural equity, in this regard, could be that process of change, but also a measure of the progress made. But where were we progressing toward? Here is where we felt compelled to define cultural justice as well.

Cultural justice needed to include two parts—the first, as we learned from Indigenous peoples and culture bearers, was about restoration; the second needed to speak to the ways in which we innovate our artistic practices to articulate and manifest our evolving identities. We defined *cultural justice* as the healing of the erasure, suppression, and marginalization of people's artistic and cultural practices. Cultural justice would restore and build for communities of color ways of living, being, and sense making, and it would also allow all of us to express ourselves and be recognized in our full, complex humanity.

A set of values marked a throughline in all of our work from Future Aesthetics through Arts in a Changing America—excellence, mutuality, and generosity.[14] We set out to theorize and then practice building sustainable creative ecosystems. In our praxis we did not see these ecosystems as ends in themselves. We wanted to build them because we wanted for our communities to be, or to continue to be, cauldrons of sustainable and protean creativity, and spaces that recognized the diverse encounters key to growth, security, and transformation. If we could strengthen our communities in these ways, we would then be changing society from the bottom upward.

In the spring of 2020, the global pandemic spread. Subsequent quarantine orders across the country shut down the arts and culture sector. An Americans for the Arts study in April found 62 percent of workers in the sector out of work.[15] Virtually every arts organization experienced massive drops in revenue. And yet, again, the impacts were not felt equally but fell harder on already underresourced artists of color, arts workers and cultural workers of color, and communities of color. In museums, galleries, theaters, and performing arts venues, those who were laid off and furloughed were in positions already disproportionately filled by people of color—security, frontline workers, visitor services, and so on.

Groups around the country, such as BLD PWR, Black Artists for Freedom, and We See You, White American Theater, began to organize to discuss these questions. Nationally, organizations like the US Department of Arts and Culture organized a People's WPA, and the Creative Justice Initiative organized discussions on cultural equity. Six of our own organizations—Arts in a Changing America, Race Forward, Center for Cultural Power, First Peoples Fund, National Association of Latino Arts and Cultures, and Sipp Culture—came together to discuss how we should address the crisis.

We now faced four interlocking crises—the pandemic, state and vigilante violence against Black people, the climate crisis, and the economic crisis. After the shocking May 25, 2020, murder of George Floyd and the uprisings in its wake, the Black Lives Matter movement swelled to new heights. Polls reported a massive cultural shift had occurred. For the first time in over a half century, majorities of white Americans now felt racial discrimination, particularly anti-Black racism, needed to be addressed.[16]

Rushing to get on the right side of history, corporations and institutions signaled their support for Black Lives Matter. In the arts and culture sector, arts workers and culture bearers of color made even stronger demands against leaders and institutions. On social media, they advanced critiques of institutions' performative solidarity, and as ad hoc groups formed all across the country, some of them moved to call for the abolition of museums.

As artists and culture bearers seeking to address our own complicity with a deeply inequitable and unjust arts and culture sector, with its funding and governance structures born of white supremacy, we had difficult, stop-start discussions about the way forward. This shift in discourse helped us to be real about our values and pushed us to deeply consider our roles as artists and culture bearers in our communities and in society.

During the 2007–9 Great Recession, some of us had joined calls for the Obama administration to establish an expansive cultural policy that would act as an economic stimulus, including programs that would put artists to work, along the lines of Franklin Delano Roosevelt's Works Progress Administration, a key jobs program in his New Deal.[17] In 2009, these proposals were dead on arrival. In 2020, we concluded that appealing to the federal and state governments for jobs alone actually missed the point. Even in the New Deal jobs programs for artists in the 1930s, and then again in Comprehensive Employment and Training Act (CETA) programs of the 1970s, artists had largely been instrumentalized. For liberals, they were a constituency to service and placate. Ironically, only cultural conservatives actually cared about what artists did in communities, and their sense was that artists were largely doing radical, anti-American organizing.

So we chose to write a document that we called the Cultural New Deal (see part 6). We did not come to the name easily. We passionately debated the value of the New Deal frame. We knew that the concept of the New Deal retained an enduring appeal for a certain kind of nostalgic political liberalism associated with big-D democratic ideals, especially during times of recession. Many of us knew the racial impact of Franklin Delano Roosevelt's New Deal policies had suppressed home ownership for Blacks and other people of color and reinforced urban and suburban racial segregation, as one example.[18] We knew that the cultural implications of many of those policies still resonated in the content and structure of North American arts. We also knew that many of the cultural programs of the New Deal had begun as a way to blunt the much more radical small-d democratic visions of the Cultural Front and the Black Cultural Front.[19] But we also understood that the notion of a New Deal tapped into a broadly held feeling in our communities around the urgent need to rebuild, and that the converging crises pushed all of us to think about how to do so on stronger, more sustainable foundations.

For this reason, the process and the resulting document of the Cultural New Deal intentionally centered the roles and perspectives of artists and culture bearers, especially those from Black communities, Indigenous communities, and communities of color. We wrote: "We ask ourselves the question: arts and culture for what? We work in culture and the arts because we believe that stories weave together the moral fabric of our societies. We aim to build and sustain our communities, those most impacted by racial and cultural inequity. We believe that art and culture are never separate from the undoing of inequities in health, employment, wealth, detention, incarceration, deportation, housing, and the environment."

Even now, our nation is still caught in a stalemate between two opposed visions—one that takes us toward the realization of a vital, inclusive, democratic America that has not yet been and the other that keeps us bound to an unjust, sclerotic, authoritarian America. We still believe in the power of arts and culture. And we still yearn to be free, together. Justice is the horizon we still look toward, even if after years of fire and chaos and brutality, the ways forward are as obscured from us as they have ever been.

This book responds to an urgent call. Here we ask:

How might we turn arts and culture to call out the lie that force, greed, and domination are the only way to organize and realize progress?

What are the possibilities that we might be able to imagine into that still foggy space between where we stand and where we want to go?

And again, how might we realize a shared, sustainable future that will be irresistible to all?

INTRODUCTION

Notes

1. Arthur Jafa, "Scholl Lecture Series: Arthur Jafa," Pérez Art Museum Miami (video), YouTube, posted January 23, 2020, https://www.youtube.com/watch?v=YnXCHVy6CGU.

2. Jafa, "Scholl Lecture Series."

3. The installation has also been included in Black-centered museum exhibitions as well, such as *Mothership: Voyage into Afrofuturism* at the Oakland Museum of California, October 2021 to February 2022.

4. Vincent Harding, *Is America Possible?* (Kalamazoo, MI: Fetzer Institute, 2007), https://fetzer.org/sites/default/files/images/resources/attachment/2018-03-16/FI_DAD_Harding_E-Version-Rev_0.pdf; Langston Hughes, "Let America Be America Again," in *The Collected Poems of Langston Hughes*, edited by Arnold Rampersad (New York: Alfred A. Knopf, 1994), https://poets.org/poem/let-america-be-america-again.

5. Ralph Ellison, *Invisible Man* (New York: Vintage, 1972), 3.

6. For more on the foundational thinking of the Combahee River Collective, see Keeanga Yamahtta-Taylor, ed., *How We Get Free: Black Feminism and the Combahee River Collective* (Chicago: Haymarket, 2017). For the radical roots of multiculturalism in the arts, see Jeff Chang, *Who We Be: A Cultural History of Race in Post–Civil Rights America* (New York: St. Martin's Press, 2014).

7. Elissa Schappell and Claudia Brodsky Lacour, "Toni Morrison, the Art of Fiction No. 134," *Paris Review*, no. 128 (fall 1993), https://www.theparisreview.org/interviews/1888/the-art-of-fiction-no-134-toni-morrison.

8. Jafa, "Scholl Lecture Series."

9. The complete story here has not yet been told, as it is one of absence rather than presence, and history is usually written by the winners. But for one perspective on the impact of these structural shifts on Black theater specifically, see Henry Louis Gates, "The Chitlin Circuit," in *African American Performance and Theater History: A Critical Reader*, edited by Harry Elam Jr. and David Krasner (New York: Oxford University Press, 2001).

10. Jeff Chang, Jakeya Caruthers, Kai Kanē Aoki Izu, with Jonathan Leal, Stewart Grrey, Yeji Jung, Colin Kimzey, Cody Leigh Laux, Lan Anh Le, Taylor Litchfield, Malcolm Lizzappi, Yinshi Lerman-Tan, Maia Paroginog, and Mia Ritter-Whittle, *Up from the Underground: Documentation of the Ford Foundation's Future Aesthetics Program, 2002–2014* (Stanford, CA: Stanford Institute for Diversity in the Arts, 2016), https://artsinachangingamerica.org/future-aesthetics-report/.

11. New York City Department of Cultural Affairs, "NYC Department of Cultural Affairs Releases Overview of Survey Results Measuring Staff and Board Diversity of NYC Cultural Organizations," press release, January 28, 2016, https://www1.nyc.gov/site/dcla/about/pressrelease/PR_2016-01-28_DiversitySurvey.page. "Cultural Workforce Demographics" describes the report (https://www1.nyc.gov/site/dcla/programs/diversity.page). The original report has been taken down and replaced by an updated report by SMU DataArts, released in July 2019. The numbers are equally disheartening. SMU DataArts, *New York City Department of*

Cultural Affairs Workforce Demographics Pilot Study Results (Dallas: National Center for Arts Research, July 2019), https://www1.nyc.gov/assets/dcla/downloads/pdf/NYC%20DCLA%20Full%202018%20WfD%20Report%207-24-19.pdf.

12. Helicon Collaborative, *Not Just Money: Equity Issues in Cultural Philanthropy* (New York: Surdna Foundation, July 2017), https://heliconcollab.net/our_work/not-just-money/.

13. For more, see the radical multiculturalist manifesto-as-rollickingly-good-novel that many of us took as bible and blueprint, Ishmael Reed, *Mumbo Jumbo* (New York: Doubleday, 1972)!

14. Another program in that group was called Artography, which was a place-based arts project that incubated and lifted up cultural hubs across the United States, such as PA'I Foundation in Honolulu, Hawai'i; La Mujer Obrera in El Paso, Texas; and Los Cenzontles Cultural Arts Academy in San Carlos, California. Amid the early 2000s craze for "creative placemaking," Artography focused on culture bearers and their hubs of arts, food, music, and other cultural practices in communities of color.

15. See Americans for the Arts, "The Economic Impact of Coronavirus on the Arts and Culture Sector," https://www.americansforthearts.org/by-topic/disaster-preparedness/the-economic-impact-of-coronavirus-on-the-arts-and-culture-sector.

16. Kim Parker, Juliana Menasce Hernandez, and Monica Anderson, "Amid Protests, Majorities across Racial and Ethnic Groups Express Support for the Black Lives Matter Movement" (Pew Research Center, June 12, 2020), https://www.pewresearch.org/social-trends/2020/06/12/amid-protests-majorities-across-racial-and-ethnic-groups-express-support-for-the-black-lives-matter-movement/.

17. Jeff Chang, "The Creativity Stimulus," *Nation*, April 15, 2009, https://www.thenation.com/article/archive/creativity-stimulus/.

18. Two books that discuss the racial impacts of the New Deal are Ira Katnelson, *When Affirmative Action Was White* (New York: Norton, 2005); and Richard Rothstein, *The Color of Law* (New York: Norton, 2017).

19. Two books worth reading on the praxis of radical US artists in the Great Depression are Michael Denning, *The Cultural Front: The Laboring of American Culture in the 20th Century* (New York: Verso, 1997); and Brian Dolinar, *The Black Cultural Front: Black Writers and Artists of the Depression Generation* (Jackson: University Press of Mississippi, 2012).

vestibular mantra
(or radical virtuosities
for a brave new dance)*

taisha paggett

taisha paggett makes things and is interested in what bodies do. They/she believes language is tricky, thoughts are powerful, and that people are most beautiful when looking up. paggett received the Foundation for Contemporary Arts' Merce Cunningham Award in 2019 and is an associate professor in dance at UC Riverside.

(Lights up)

> stay wild. stay feral, stay mystified. stay throwing
> fits, stay having no answers. stay
> heart-centered, stay permeable.

(Enter stage left)

> stay high-low brow, stay curious, stay rioting,
> stay asking tough questions, stay unclassifiable,
> stay getting crazy looks.

(Group two go)

---

* The vestibular system is a system of the body essential for spatial orientation and balance. In psychology, it explains the abilities to stand, move without falling, and focus the eyes on a single object even when the head is in motion. "Vestibular System," Chegg.com, accessed November 23, 2022, https://www.chegg.com/homework-help/definitions/vestibular-system-13.

stay crying in public, stay out of sorts,
stay forgetting the combo, stay with the
ripped pantyhose and the pit-stained tees.

(Music go)

because in this new dance we
play gravity like a pick primping its last 'do.

(Slow rise the volume)

stay visible, stay wanting more, stay addressing
what's not there and what the
audience isn't willing to see.

because as fish swim and birds fly, we stand against
the pressure—up, out, off, in, for and against
the ceaseless, creaseless pressure.

(Enter chorus)

stay fearless and momentous. stay
unwieldy and excretory. stay oceanic. keep
letting this piece drag on. stay humble.

because we were born with resistance in our spines.

stay chained to that fence, that tree, that railway
track, one another. stay over the rainbow, kaleidoscopic.

(Canon go)

because we don't collapse so much as
fold over, like prostrate
origami tumbling through dense sky.

(Sidelights at half)

in this duet you're looking at me—the real me—and
the air is a substance, like cherry hair gel; it disturbs
your body enough to send it writhing toward the
upstage diagonal and into the wings. it should elicit laughs.

stay with the senses.

stay in the nectar, the marrow. stay deep
listening. stay daydreaming. stay being
the last person clapping, but stay honest.

i'm up to my knees and inverted. there's a
little room to my side to insert about four
measures. we beat, we slide, but the ground
could never hook us.

stay staying and stay letting go.

because we don't collapse so much as bellow
in and out, collectivity lunging into one another like
an accordion before its next breath, and
in these folds lies the fervor.

stay loving everyone. stay eating the veggies
and the fruits. stay worshipping the sun. stay
knowing the street as the open museum of
our collective unfixable be-ings and
the art of living as the last reliable medium. stay
reading that heavy-weight theory shit but stay
knowing when to put it the fuck down. stay believing in
the classroom of your grandma, bus driver,
neighborhood tagger, pharmacist, dog, and the song
you can't ever stop listening to.

because we don't collapse so much as bend like light.
because we don't collapse so much as stand on the brink.
because we don't collapse so much as collapse together—
big bang bodies born into spontaneity.
because, anatomically antonymical,
resistance is what we are. because this dance did not
happen by accident. because we are the
we we've been bating our breath for.

(Spotlight go)

stay metaphysical. stay knowing vision is a process
and seeing is not always believing.
stay questioning the frame—including this one here.
stay victorious in those psychic acro-antics,
standing yet again and again because the ground
is a process and our homes are mobile(s). ever, forever.

because we don't collapse so much as swim
into the thick with-ness of pain and pleasure,
history and memory.

stay panoramic.

a woman. a man. a refusal to be either. a child. an
elder. an oracle. this theater. that house. age without decay.

this time i'll reach for your neck—your real neck—and i won't
let go until the plate is clean and the music climbs to silence.

stay knowing that if they *get* this dance, there might be something wrong.
stay knowing that if something is only to be *gotten*, we
might all be doing something wrong.

(Music fading . . .)

in technicolor canon we rise and fall. rock. roll.

(Blackout)

Note

vestibular mantra (or radical virtuosities for a brave new dance) was first printed in 2012 in theoffcenter's "Blog Salon #3: On Collectivity and Collapse" as a companion piece to the author's *Fila Buster* performance. It also appeared in the exhibition catalog for *that I am reading backwards and into for a purpose, to go on:*, at The Kitchen, New York, in 2017.

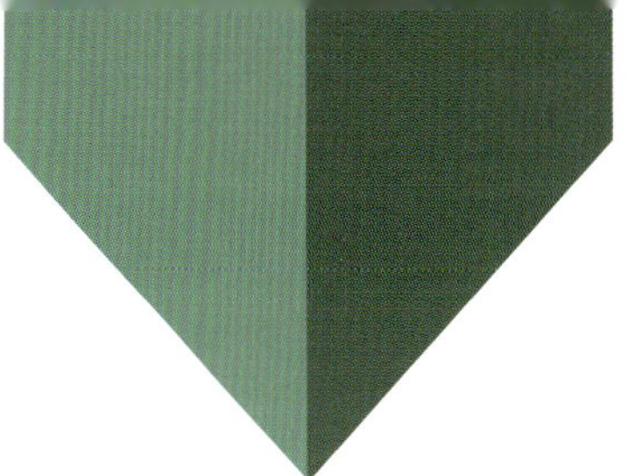

PART 1

CULTURAL PRESENCE

PLACEKEEPING AND BELONGING

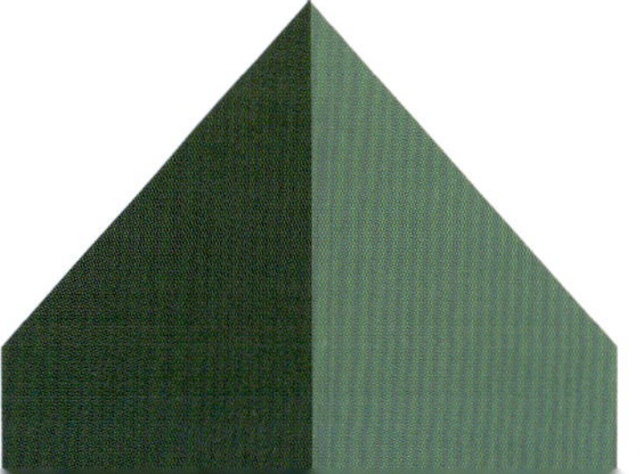

Introduction

Daniela Alvarez

Daniela Alvarez is the REFRAME and research manager for Arts in a Changing America and the public programs coordinator at the Getty Museum in Los Angeles. Her work as a cultural organizer and programmer centers on promoting community benefits and in creating spaces of belonging.

In May 2017, Harlem residents were incensed with real estate agencies and developers over their latest attempts to rename a portion of their historic neighborhood. This time the streets between 110th and 125th streets were targeted with the proposed moniker SoHa (South Harlem) as part of a re-branding campaign to attract new tenants to the area.[1] The reaction by the community was swift and unforgiving. As New York Senator Brian Benjamin stated, "How dare someone try to rob our culture, and try to act as if we were not here, and create a new name, a new reality as if the clock started when other people showed up?"[2] Protests organized by community leaders garnered considerable media coverage and generated a social media firestorm that pressured the real estate agencies to quietly drop the name SoHa from public advertising.

And while the act of renaming a neighborhood may seem innocuous, it insidiously echoes the historic and systemic practice of forced removal, segregation, relocation, racist exclusionary zoning practices, and redlining that violently erases people from their lands, neighborhoods, home—from history. Moreover, today many locations across the country face an un-precedented acceleration in gentrification and displacement that primarily threatens historically marginalized neighborhoods and communities of color.[3] What happened in Harlem has parallels in Boyle Heights, Oakland, Detroit, Atlanta, Baltimore, Chicago—you name it. And significantly, in many of these places, the arts have been viewed as either a vital cultural anchor providing resources to the community or as harbingers of displacement that exchange culture for capital.

For many, gentrification is not a question of when but a bitter reality. Illustrating a gentrified landscape through a political tirade, performance artist, writer, activist, and director of the international performance troupe La Pocha Nostra **Guillermo Gómez-Peña** guides the reader through a dystopian San Francisco neighborhood. As a result of Big Tech moving in and driving out locals through rent hikes, Gómez-Peña reminisces on the culture and people that once made the Mission vibrant but, now gone, leave him stranded. He sharply observes, "As the community continues to shrink, so does your sense of belonging to a city that no longer seems to like you." Similarly, multimedia and visual artists **Kiyan Williams** and **Jazmín Urrea** respectively capture the magnitudes of gentrification in their neighborhoods. In Williams's piece, *An Accumulation of Things That Refuse to Be Discarded*, the artist suspends 150 pounds of bricks collected from a demolished residential building cleared to expand Columbia University's campus. The precarious exhibition of material serves as evidence of the removal of families, adding to the artist's growing archive of gentrification in their community. The history and impact of displacement from systemic racism are also present in Jazmín Urrea's *Red 40*. The viewer is seduced by a dazzling pool of three hundred pounds of Flamin' Hot Cheetos in the center of the room, surrounded by images of red candy plastered on every available wall space. The inability to escape the irresistible lure of junk food is what Urrea's economically underinvested neighborhood in South LA experiences, as the lack of available and affordable fresh produce makes it one of the many urban food deserts that disproportionately affect people of color.[4]

But where does one begin to change the gentrified landscape? Efforts to dismantle entrenched narratives of white supremacy look to strategies that reflect and amplify the voices of the people. For Detroit-based artist and activist **Halima Afi Cassells**, bringing the community into the fold of policy making and organization is imperative to the work. After witnessing the lack of accountability and benefit to communities where private real estate development profited, artists and activists focused on building collective empowerment by creating a memorandum of understanding: "The document begins by uplifting our value, then lists points of constructive collaboration, and an agreement for benefit to the neighborhood in very specific ways." Visually, questioning and challenging the economic practices in a community through an aesthetic lens is also the inspiration behind **Daniel Andres Alcazar**'s photographs titled *Local Fruit Still Life: Ralphs $6.02, Sprouts $4.30, Super A $4.09, El Super $3.49*. Staging the same fruit bought from four different groceries at different prices, Alcazar allows the viewer to appreciate the elements of still life paintings in a modern context that simultaneously probes the relationship between community and corporations. And as artists, activists, and organizers pursue different approaches to creating and supporting community placekeeping, urban ethnographer **Alesia Montgomery** reminds us of the importance of working beyond good intentions as "cultural work is in danger of becoming the *performance of movement*—a catharsis from oppressive realities rather than a catalyst to battle them."

For others, the bonds to place and community are manifested through cultural work. For Sins Invalid cofounder **Patricia Berne** and creative director **Nomy Lamm**, lack of access to space is a physical and political concern that informs their mission and art. As Berne recounts, "One of the reasons I started Sins Invalid was because I needed to see us. I needed a place where we existed." And in creating a platform for hot, queer, disabled people of color to tell their stories, Sins Invalid also creates networks that further build community beyond its site. The idea of networks is further explored by interdisciplinary artist **Devin Kenny**, who looks at Black underground networks created through different junctions of sound. Through his performative script that mines the memory of American domination, Kenny highlights the instances where need and ingenuity help grow a culture. Through anecdotes of disruption, Kenny posits to the reader, in the large mechanism of marginalization, how can we act as resistors? Shifting from creating music in marginalized spaces to taking up space in white-dominated culture, acclaimed orchestral musician **Garrett McQueen** brings together musicians of color across the country to address racial inequality in classical music. Writing in the wake of the murder of George Floyd, McQueen cites that for many classical musicians of color, "Being the 'only one' in a room can be so much more than just an isolating experience, and without a support system, many have found themselves in situations that are not musically fulfilling, but violent and exclusive." Creating a community that shares experiences, doubts, and success in a safe space helps redefine what classical music can be and for whom. Likewise, music as a medium can also validate oneself as belonging. For rap artist and poet **Talon Bazille Ducheneaux** (Dakota, Lakota), the categorization of music as being "Native or not" is part of a larger conversation on Indigenous identity and expectations. But through his own experience, Ducheneaux "showcases rap music as a tool for Indigenous resiliency, just as it serves for all oppressed peoples," further strengthening his bond to his music and community.

Challenging the history of oppression and racism to create a sense of belonging is a daunting task, but one that is also accompanied by a long history of resilience and joy. Ashé Cultural Arts Center, New Orleans, cofounder **Carol Bebelle** and the US Department of Arts and Culture's (USDAC) Chief Ray of Sunshine, **Carol Zou**, converse about the power of art and artists during times of unrest and instability brought about by natural and systemic disasters. In the wake of Hurricane Katrina, Bebelle states, "culture provides the arms that make it possible to reach out to people and connect when they need comfort most." And much like the site-specific history and strategies recounted by Bebelle of New Orleans, the cross-disciplinary artist **Aaron McIntosh** digs deep into Appalachian culture and its relationship to Southern queer narratives. Inspired by the invasive plant kudzu, McIntosh's *Invasive Queer Kudzu* creates a monument of fabricated vines with glimpses of flesh and queer text that speaks to the undesired and persistent nature of the plant and queer community. Similarly, the artwork by **Sadie Barnette** also reclaims symbols from overlooked archives to preserve the past and present. *The New Eagle Creek Saloon* is a welcoming glowing neon, deliciously pink and glittering installation that reimagines the first Black-owned gay bar in San Francisco sourced from personal history and "a collective history of repression and resistance." The intergenerational dialogue that comes from celebrating the archive expands when the histories of a place and its many intersections are further acknowledged. The former director of community arts at the Japanese American Cultural & Community Center and lead for the Sustainable Little Tokyo initiative, **Scott Oshima**, centers their work on "a holistic conception of community sustainability—one that is culturally specific, historical, economic, and environmental, and is realized through organizing, art, culture, equitable development, and, above all, joy." Oshima unveils the layers of history and communities that built the Little Tokyo neighborhood, diving deep into what Oakland cultural affairs manager and cultural policy researcher Roberto Bedoya notes as the "politics of belonging or dis-belonging," making it clear that communities learn, grow, and thrive best together.[5] And so, we begin part 1 with the beautiful painting *Aqui Estoy* by artist and educator **Jose Ramirez**, who, in a myriad of colors, forefronts everyday people against the skyline of Los Angeles. Influenced by "the struggles of Mexican and Latino populations in the US," Ramirez makes visible the marginalized and recenters them as the heart and soul of every community.

Notes

1. Past attempts to rebrand New York neighborhoods include *SoBro* for South Bronx in 2005 and *SpaHa* for Spanish Harlem in 2014, to name a few. Amanda

Luz Henning Santiago, "The New York City Neighborhood Names That Failed or Prevailed," *City and State New York*, May 31, 2019, https://www.cityandstateny .com/politics/2019/05/the-new-york-city-neighborhood-names-that-failed-or -prevailed/177294/.

2. Taryn Finley, "Gentrifiers Want to Rename Harlem Area 'SoHa' and Residents Are Pissed," *HuffPost*, May 26, 2017, https://www.huffpost.com/entry /gentrifiers-want-to-rename-harlem-area-soha_n_592830a5e4b0df34c35b7e0c.

3. For a more in-depth read on gentrification and displacement, see Ananya Roy and Chris Carlsson, *Counterpoints: A San Francisco Bay Area Atlas of Displacement and Resistance* (Oakland, CA: PM Press, 2021).

4. In California, Latine people make up two-thirds of the state's food-insecure households. Dominic Borrelli, Ryan Gunn, and Andrew Lang, "Food Deserts in South L.A.," ArcGIS StoryMaps, Esri, November 19, 2020, https://storymaps .arcgis.com/stories/4ef7d78c52ec4b29a6073ffdc6809e83.

5. Roberto Bedoya, "Placemaking and the Politics of Belonging and Disbelonging," *GIA Reader* 24, no. 1 (2013): 20–21.

Aqui Estoy

Jose Ramirez

Jose Ramirez is an artist. In the past twenty-six years, he has illustrated children's books, painted murals, and completed numerous commissions. He has taught in the Los Angeles Unified School District for over twenty-six years and is currently teaching third grade at Esperanza Elementary in the Pico-Union neighborhood of Los Angeles. He received a BFA (1990) and an MFA (1993) in art from UC Berkeley.

As an artist and educator, my paintings are influenced by Mexican and Chicano art history. My work is inspired by the struggles of Mexican and Latino populations in the United States. My work is informed by our role in shaping and imagining the future of Los Angeles and other urban centers. As a Chicano/Latinx artist, it is important for me to recognize the importance that Mexican culture has played in shaping US culture, but it is equally important for me to push past nationalist rhetoric and promote the inclusion of all cultures.

Aqui Estoy is about recognizing and celebrating the daily lives of people of color, the undocumented and the poor, who are scapegoated and blamed by the dominant society. It shows the crucial role we play in bringing life to our cities.

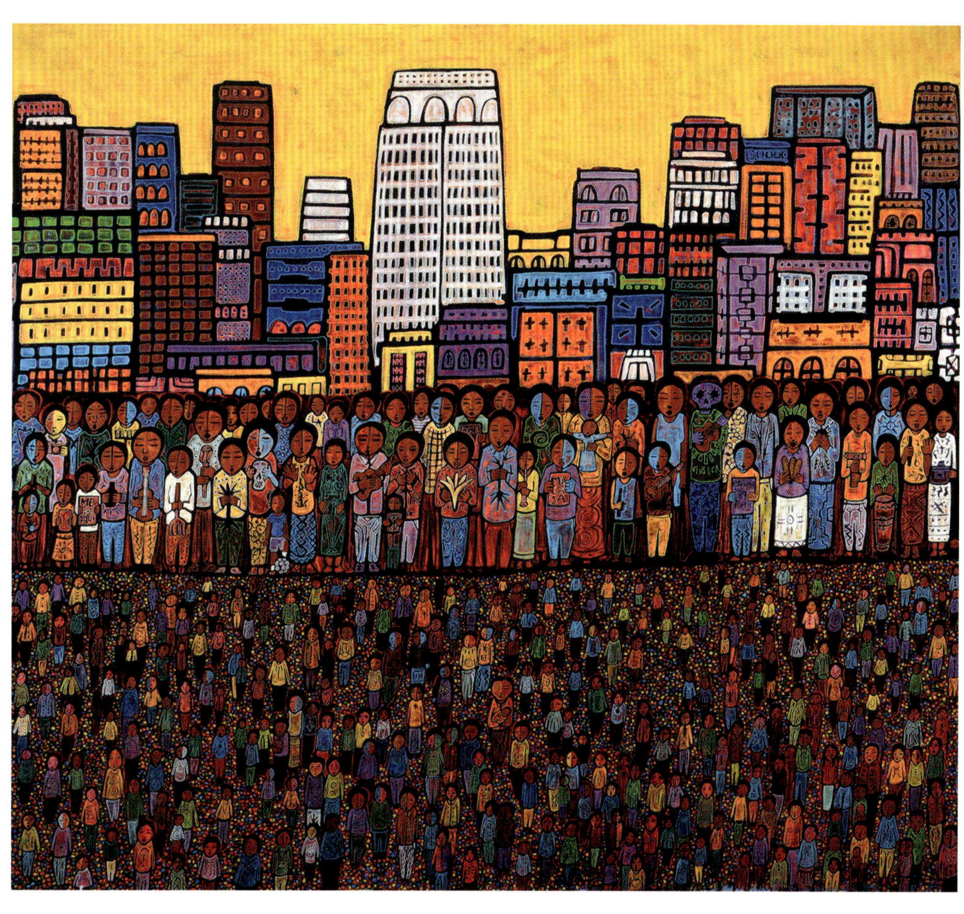

Jose Ramirez, *Aqui Estoy*, 2018.
Mixed media on canvas, 92 × 80 in.

Beauty, Justice, and the Ritual of Performance

Patricia Berne and Nomy Lamm

Patricia Berne is the cofounder and executive and artistic director of Sins Invalid. Their experiences as a Japanese Haitian queer disabled woman provide grounding for their work creating "liberated zones" for marginalized voices. Patty was awarded the Disability Futures Fellowship in 2020 and is widely recognized as a leader in establishing the framework and practice of Disability Justice.

Nomy Lamm is the creative director of Sins Invalid. Nomy is a multimedia artist, a singer, a writer, a riot grrrl, a Kohenet/Hebrew priestess, and a nonbinary femme who spends their time tending their fat disabled body and loving their partner Lisa in their home on Squaxin/Nisqually/Chehalis lands.

Sins Invalid is a disability justice–based performance project founded in 2005 by Patricia Berne and Leroy F. Moore Jr. in the San Francisco Bay Area. Led by disabled people of color, Sins Invalid incubates and celebrates artists with disabilities, centralizing artists of color and LGBTQ/gender-variant artists as communities who have been historically marginalized.

PATRICIA BERNE: We were talking about place and space in one of our meetings the other day. The idea of how much space we take up as individuals is so intimately tied to the political space that we are granted. Or that we take. The more political space somebody has, the more cultural space they have. It's interesting how that can be reflected in how much space people

Editor's Note: This contribution was edited from a virtual conversation between Patricia Berne and Nomy Lamm on June 30, 2020.

are comfortable taking up in public—like speaking your mother tongue, or taking up physical space on a BART train. For people with disabilities, we've long been shamed about how much space we take up if we have mobility aids. And all this is in the context of the reality that we're all on colonized land. This is Ohlone territory, and we need to call in the first peoples and the ancestors of this land. It's important to lift Indigenous voices in our work, to use our work to expand their taking of space, so to speak, and to assert Indigenous political space.

When we're calling in ancestors, for me that includes my Haitian ancestors and my Japanese ancestors, and all the best of the best of resistance to colonization that I can invite in.

NOMY LAMM: Yes, amen.

PB: Within that, how do we create a sense of belonging? We don't see ourselves reflected in many places. Sins Invalid has often been treated as a form of home or intimate community. We create this sense of belonging by accepting that everybody has strengths and everybody has needs. Like rolling on crip time, letting someone speak and waiting if they need more time, or listening at a different, nonnormative pace.[1] A lot of it is just engaging with other humans as human.

NL: In a lot of ways Sins Invalid is such a creation of the Bay Area and its history of the Black Panthers and movement work on Disability Rights and queer liberation. Before living in the Bay Area, I hadn't really had the experience of having a community of disabled people who are really politicized, so I would find myself in other kinds of politicized work, being one of the only disabled people and feeling like I had to speak for a whole community that I felt isolated from. Going to a Sins Invalid show for the first time— and this is an experience that I see so many people have repeatedly—I got to experience a place where all the parts come together, where disability is centered. It's not a side issue; it's about wholeness, and sexuality and racial justice, and telling more complicated stories about our bodies.

It's been interesting to move away from the Bay Area, back to Olympia, Washington (Squaxin, Nisqually, Chehalis land), where I grew up. I've stayed really involved with Sins Invalid virtually. But in terms of the local Disability Justice community, it's been a different process. There isn't the kind of grounded holding to create from, so I've been focusing on building relationships one by one and slowly watching them grow.

In terms of space, I feel like my experience as a white, Jewish, queer, fat person disabled from birth, I've been taught and given permission to use my voice in certain ways that take up space. Physically, I take up a lot of space—both in my literal body, and once I take off my leg and get myself comfortable, there's a radius of like five feet around me. It's definitely been a process of coming to accept "this is how much space I actually take up." Growing up as a fat person, I always felt a need to shrink; being both fat and disabled, there's a feeling of always being in the way. Being in the Disability Justice community, there's a certain amount of finding ease in the specificities of my body and also becoming more mindful of the space that I take up with my voice and my energy.

PB: I really appreciate you saying the piece about how coming into our bodies also means coming into this space that we take up in public and private settings, and the radius that you have around you. I also, as a chair user, have had many experiences as a kid, being told that I'm taking up a lot of space or that I need to not move because I will take up too much space. . . . Like in a restaurant, the easiest way for me to get assistance from servers is just to move. Before the pandemic, when I could go to restaurants, all I had to do was move my chair and suddenly everybody is flipping out that I moved and trying to contain me again. And that's kind of funny, and also really fucking insulting. I can be strategic with that as an adult. As a kid I just felt embarrassed.

One thing I love with chair users is going down the sidewalk together taking up space. I remember me and Stacey, a dear friend, would hold hands and walk down the sidewalk, and just take up space. Before the pandemic, I remember seeing people flatten themselves against the wall of a building, like I need the entire sidewalk. Which is quite an exaggeration. And it more describes their fear and focus on their safety around the disabled, as opposed to the reality.

NL: I relate to that as a fat person and as a slow walker, and also as a scooter user now. Sometimes people I'm in relationships with get stressed out by it, like, "We're taking up the whole sidewalk!"

PB: Right? And now I'm like, "Uh huh?" Ableism is funny.

NL: When you talk about just shifting your chair a little bit and everyone jumps at you, I relate to that. Every day of my life for my entire life, I put my leg on and take my leg off, and the performance of that in public can be so anxiety producing, people get so nervous and think that I need help. I look up and away from everyone and just pretend I'm in my own space. 'Cause it takes a while, and people very often want to help me.

PB: One of my pet peeves is people telling me how to drive. Like . . . this is how I walk. I've been walking like this since I was three years old. I'll ask if

I need to know where something is. But I'm sorry, I got into this physical space. I think I can get myself out of this.

NL: I'm thinking about the disability narratives that Sins Invalid challenges in our art. The most obvious disability narratives are those of overcoming and inspiration. And Sins Invalid complicates that. The idea that all that an artist has to share about their experience is "This thing was hard, and then I felt confident and I got over it!" is such a boring story. As artists, there's just so much more about us, including all our life experiences—all of who we are, politically, in terms of our identities, our location, the things we think about. My work throughout my life has focused on beauty. I'm kind of obsessed. And I think it did come from feeling like it was denied to me, so I wanted to access it and reinterpret what beauty is or means. I think that's something that really impacts people, to have a fat person and a fat disabled person say, "I'm beautiful!"

PB: Exactly. And be beautiful, which you are.

NL: Thank you. That in itself can be jarring for people and shake up their own assumptions about themselves. But that only goes so far, if you're not looking at deeper layers around access to space, systematic oppression, constant medicalization of our bodies—if it stays at the level of, "I can be fat and fabulous. I look good!" I've always been really interested in the dynamics of capitalism as it relates to our bodies, the ways that we're supposed to market our bodies, and the difference between a commodified idea of beauty versus a more liberation-based *experience* of beauty.

PB: Experience of beauty, yes. I think you and I are similar in having an aesthetic that is kind of everywhere and represents us everywhere. The subtitle of Sins Invalid is "An Unshamed Claim to Beauty" for a reason. Because we are, and I mean we *are*, beautiful. And that disrupts people. I remember being a little kid, this cute little girl in a wheelchair, and people would be like, "Oh, should I respond to her like a cripple, or should I respond to her as a cute little girl?" First of all, fuck you and your patriarchy and ableism. But as an adult I see, again, the same kind of disruption but in a different way. As I'm getting older I see the way that older women are treated differently. And I'm seeing some of the currency that was tentatively given to me and snatched back; the social or sexual currency, I just have less of it now. Which is interesting. And insulting. For me to live, I have to disregard so much shit and have a pretty thick skin because the broader narratives around disability are that we can't be seen. If we're allowed to exist, we shouldn't be seen, we should try to conform.

And that's the disability narrative that Sins was set up to challenge, the fact that we were not seen as sexual or beautiful. The whole reason that we originally thought of using this as the point on the arrow, so to speak, was to pierce through this erroneous image of people with disabilities. That is one of the strongest stereotypes around disability, that we've been neutered by our disability. There's so many nuances to that around eugenics and politics of desirability, and people's guilt. Able-bodied guilt if they're attracted to us, and then on the other end devotees who fetishize certain types of—not even people with disabilities—but just fetishize the disability itself.

NL: I have tried to monetize that. It didn't go well.

PB: It's not as attractive, right? When it's consensual. And all of that is, at the end of the day, still an able-bodied and power-over narrative around our bodies. I have been so in awe of some of what has been shared through the Sins Invalid performances about our desires. And about the way they get expressed or the way we've had to desire ourselves. I think it's true of everybody. But it's so important for us to center our own beauty because in a broader social-political context, we're just not there. I think every marginalized community has to do that. One of the reasons I started Sins Invalid was because I needed to see us. I needed a place where we existed, as hot, queer, disabled people—as hot, queer, and disabled people of color. I needed that in the world. I need to see myself reflected in that. That narrative was critical.

NL: Before I ever went to a Sins show, what I had access to was so limited, in terms of complex, embodied, hot performance or information that centered disabled people. . . . There's that *Ultimate Guide to Sex and Disability* book. There was E. T. Russian's *Ring of Fire* zine. I was fortunate to grow up in queer community with E. T., and they modeled so much about being a hot, sexy, kinky, queer, poly, crip person. So I did have that experience of embodied crip sexuality in my immediate queer community, but I was always looking for more and having a hard time finding it. In the performance work I did before coming to Sins, there was sometimes a little bit of a "freak show" feeling about it, because of being viewed by mostly able-bodied people, because disability isn't completely woven into all the politics.

In those early days I did find some reflection and relationality with trans, intersex, and nonbinary narratives that related to my experience of my disabled life. I am nonbinary, and also my experiences of medical trauma related to choices made about my body have resonance with choices that get made for intersex people. So there have been spaces where I've been able to get some of that kind of reflection, but before Sins Invalid, I just hadn't really experienced so much possibility for all of the pieces coming together. And there was a visceral lightning in my body from experiencing it.

PB: That's awesome. I think that's why in our mission and our vision statement, we mentioned other communities that have been medicalized. We're not the only ones that are nonconforming, and we're not the only ones that have been labeled as other and labeled as dangerous. But simultaneously, I think also there's a specificity to disability. And I heard you say that you had community in these places, but not necessarily with other disabled people. For myself, I was very lucky to have had some modeling and experience, not just of my own hotness, which I appreciate, but also in a local disability scene, as a teenager, coming up and working at a local CIL [Center for Independent Living] and going to their parties. I was working there half-time and going to their parties, and they were making out and like, just getting it, and I was like, "Oh my god, I'm not the only one!"

NL: Patty, I'm so jealous. That's so awesome.

PB: Yeah, it was great and so important for me because before that I really felt like I was the only one. And then, having a dear friend with a disability as an adult that I found so fucking hot. And I would see the way that he was just negated. I was like, "How can you do this to him? He's just the hottest ever. How can there not be a line of people around the block? This needs to be resisted. This is bullshit." That's in some ways part of the historical context that led to Sins, was just me wanting to create a space for us to exist. Because where we exist is incredibly valuable.

In 2005 when we founded Sins, there was certainly no framing of Disability Justice, other than how to incarcerate people with disabilities. When you Googled it, that's what came up. So it's great that we have created a framework of Disability Justice, where we can look at the interactions between the ways in which we're racialized and othered, as well as experiencing processes of disablement and how they interact with each other, or the ways in which our bodies need to be decolonized, just like the land needs to be decolonized. I do have imaginings of what reparations could look like. And what truth and reconciliation committees could look like in the United States. Wouldn't it be amazing if we think about how we can have reparations around disability?

What harm has happened to people with disabilities? And how can we speak the truth to that and have reparations as disabled people of color and as disabled queers? I don't know where this moment of liberatory potential is going to lead. But my hope is that it's going to lead to more and more political openings, and open up more and more political space.

NL: One thing I really love about Sins Invalid is that we are able to create a container for complex experiences within the ritual of performance. With what's going on in the world, the increasing difficulty of travel, the impact of air quality and COVID and whatever is going on in our bodies, minute to minute, it makes performance more and more difficult. There's something really special about Sins Invalid being a performance project. It's not the exact same thing as practical movement building. Performance transforms people's consciousness—I can create this vision and this world and transmit it to others so they can experience it too. And even though we do all this other stuff, I think there's a reason that people have been so transformed by Sins Invalid's work that is connected to the ritual of performance.

Thinking about the trajectory of performances that Sins has done over the years, it started specifically to explore disability and sexuality, and every piece was related to those themes. Then we did Disability Liberated, which was about incarceration and disability, all the different ways disabled people are incarcerated. And then Birthing, Dying, Becoming Crip Wisdom, looking at different developmental stages of being a crip. And really wrapping our arms around each other and ourselves and embracing the way people come into cripness at all different ages. Both of us were born disabled. Many people become disabled at different points in their life. Many, many people consider themselves able-bodied until they get old, and then they become disabled. So holding all of that along with the becoming process, and then the dying process, letting it be all the different ways it is and not just a story of tragedy.

And now, the piece that we're working on, moving forward in a slow crip rumble, is about disability and climate chaos. Patty, I remember you saying years ago that in twenty years, people will look back at us and say, "Why wasn't every single thing you did about climate change?" We're seeing more and more how we're being impacted. And we're going to see it more and more, the ways crips are both the canary in the coal mine, some of the first to really show the impacts of the degradation of the world that we live in and how it's harming us because of colonization and capitalism.

And seeing that in crisis, crip bodies and crip lives are the ones that are least tended to. It breaks my heart, stories of disabled people who were just straight up not treated for COVID, just allowed to die. We've been warning about this, saying, "Hey, these guidelines, these care rationing plans are really scary and dangerous." Disabled people, people with preexisting conditions, fat people, older people are not going to receive care, are going to be systematically denied care for COVID. There's lots of examples about how this played out with Hurricane Katrina, Hurricane Harvey, and the fires. Who's worth "saving," who's worth tending to, checking on, making sure they're okay? During the power outages, crips were barely given any notice, and we were just told to fend for ourselves. People who need power to live. The organizing that came out of it is so powerful: mutual aid projects, the Disability Justice Culture Club, Fat Rose and #NoBodyIsDisposable, and other organizing that's continuing to develop. On one hand, the fact that we as crips have to make these plans, build these strategies, do this work . . . that's beautiful. And also, it's just so fucked up because there's so much money out there in the world and crips are not the people that have it.

PB: That's why it's so critical that we build community and connect with each other as crips. I remember reading Essex Hemphill, and him speaking about the fact that in early days of queer visibility, Black queer men in the Castro didn't acknowledge each other, because of internalized white supremacy and all the internalized homophobia. That lack of acknowledgment of each other as crips, I've seen it a million times. I'm thinking of a support group we offered not that long ago, called Holding Our Own.

The Holding Our Own group was about how we hold ourselves, because at the end of the day, we need us. We always needed community. It is a frickin' shame that we can't always count on our able-bodied allies as coconspirators. They are just oftentimes lip service. So in order for other people to value my life, I need also to value my life, and to have my community valued. One of the biggest organizing tools that we use in Sins is love. Developing relationships that are really steeped in love. Any movement that operates as though our mental capacities are all that we're worth, or our physical capacities to labor are all that we're worth, is going to experience a lot of shortcomings and . . .

NL: . . . a lot of burnout.

PB: Yeah, because love is who we are as humans. Reflecting that in everything that we do is critical for us as an organization, and for the creative work that we produce, and for the movement that we are trying to build.

Note

1. In *Feminist, Queer, Crip* (Bloomington: Indiana University Press, 2013), 27, author Alison Kafer writes, "Crip time is flex time not just expanded but exploded; it requires re-imagining our notions of what can and should happen in time, or recognizing how expectations of 'how long things take' are based on very particular minds and bodies. Rather than bend disabled bodies and minds to meet the clock, crip time bends the clock to meet disabled bodies and minds."

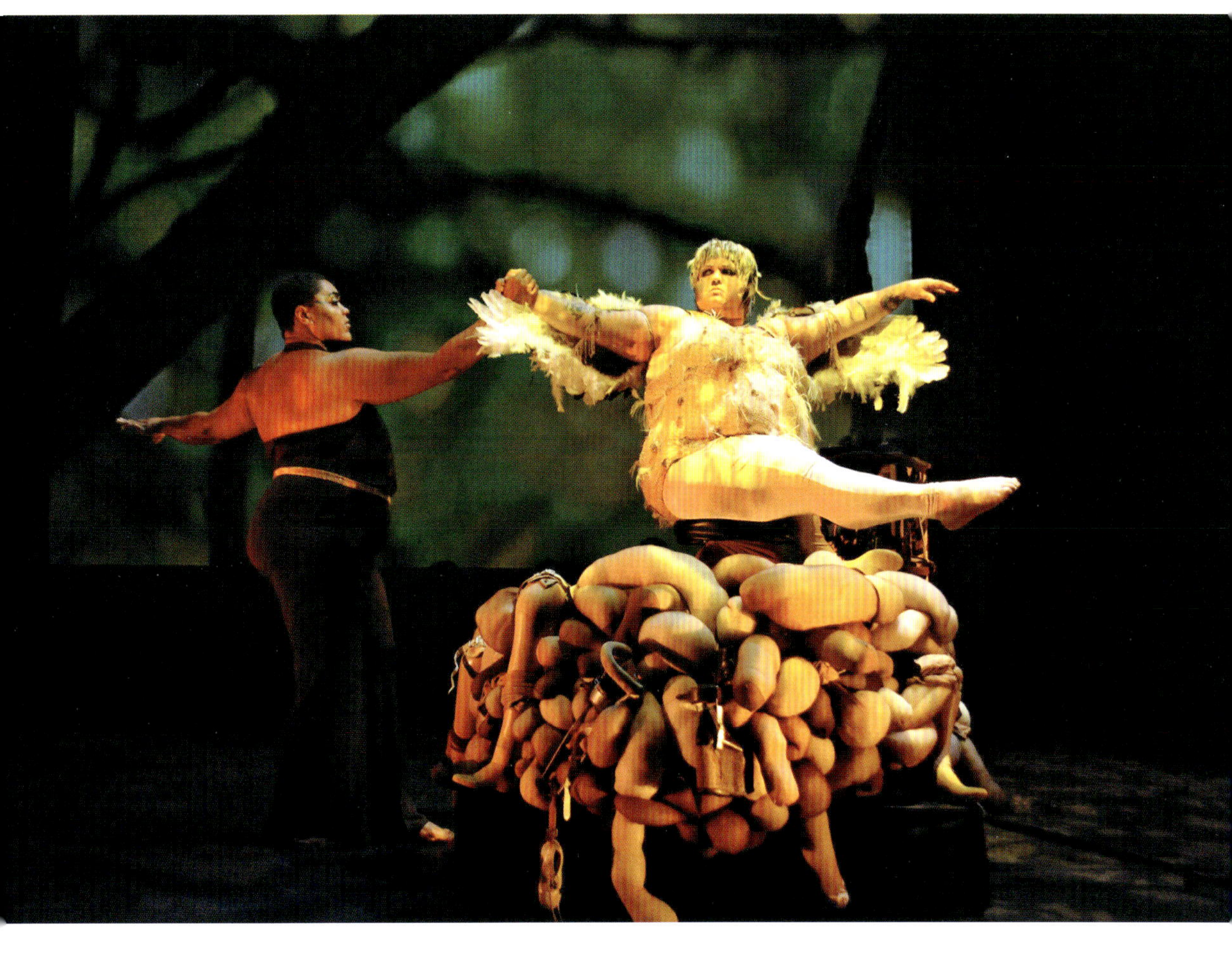

Nomy Lamm and Cara Paige in *Bird Song*, 2009. Copyright Richard Downing. Courtesy of Sins Invalid.

An Accumulation
of Things That Refuse
to Be Discarded

Kiyan Williams

Kiyan Williams is a multidisciplinary artist from Newark, New Jersey, who works fluidly across sculpture, performance, video, and 2D realms. Rooted in a process-driven practice, they are attracted to quotidian, unconventional materials and methods that evoke the historical, political, and ecological forces that shape individual and collective bodies.

An Accumulation of Things That Refuse to Be Discarded consists of 150 pounds of bricks from a residential building in West Harlem demolished by Columbia University in order to build its Manhattanville campus. The bricks, gathered while I was in graduate school in Columbia's MFA Program, suspend precariously from an entanglement of braids. I first began to collect bricks from bulldozed buildings in 2014 after my former high school—Science High in Newark, New Jersey—was demolished in order to build luxury condominiums. Collecting became an act of care in the wake of historical and ongoing annihilation. In my recent body of work I excavate soil and debris from sites of loss within the African Diaspora. I am attracted to materials that are silent witnesses to the historical and ongoing dispossession of Black people in America. I am driven by an impulse to recover the residue of Black loss and transform it into objects that contend with collective amnesia, systemic erasure, and social neglect.

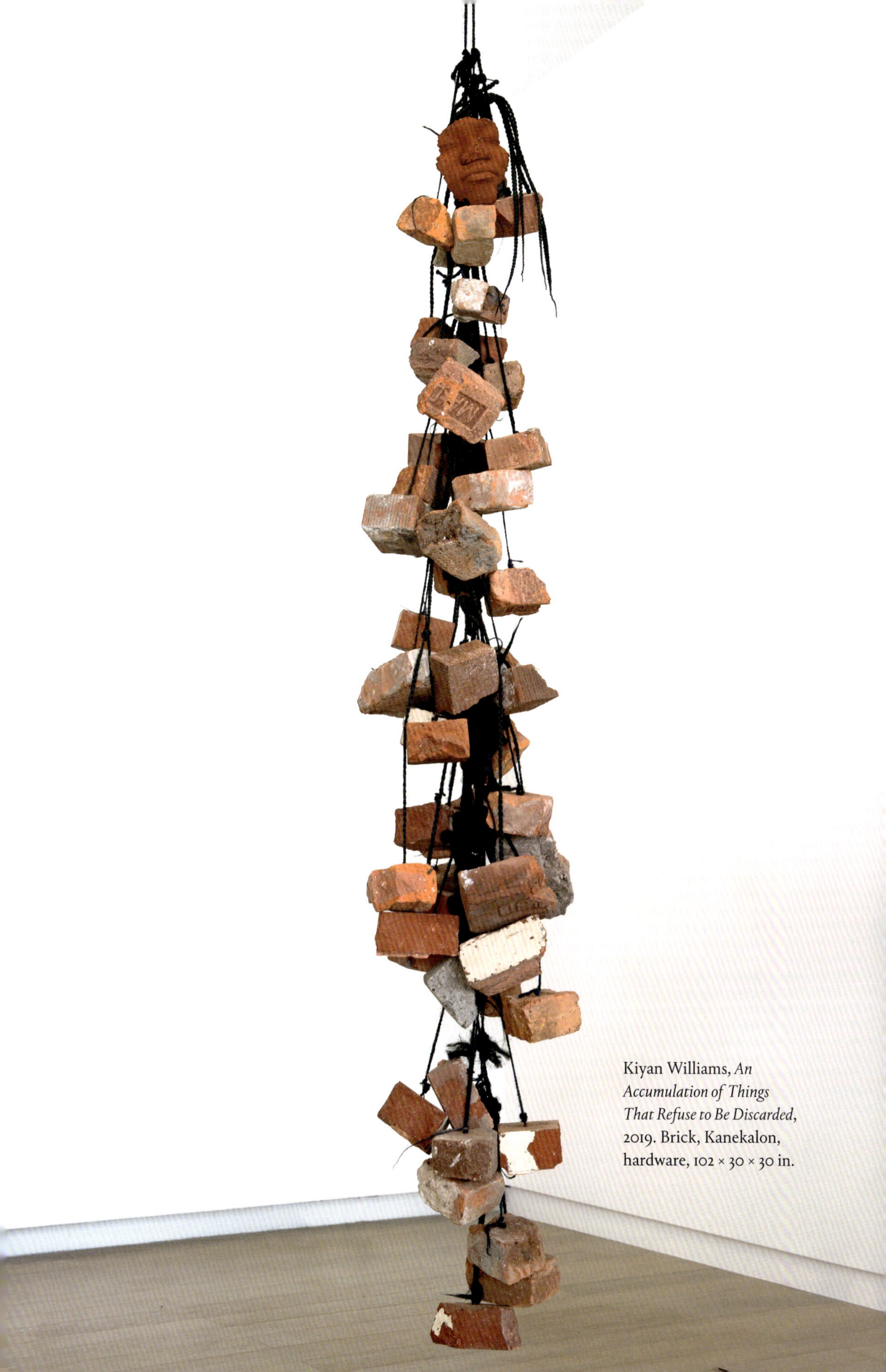

Kiyan Williams, *An Accumulation of Things That Refuse to Be Discarded*, 2019. Brick, Kanekalon, hardware, 102 × 30 × 30 in.

Counting Coup on the Compartmentalization of Indigenous-Made Rap Music

Talon Bazille Ducheneaux

Talon Bazille Ducheneaux is a rap artist and poet from the Oceti Sakowin (Dakota, Lakota) whose work has gone from rez to city to rez. An alumnus of the University of Pennsylvania, Bazille is also the head of Wonahun Was'te' Studios/Records—a studio that provides free access to community members and allies.

> Drop the beat and I'll spit that Black Hills gold.
> —"Souled Out," 2018

When it comes to hip-hop, some make the argument that its culture doesn't have a valid place within Indigenous culture (and/or vice versa), especially since most reservations are rural. Others would go as far as to state that it is a harmful fusion altogether, with some pressuring for more "culturally based" rap music "if such a thing must exist." And even as time moves forward and the overall acceptance of these sounds is rising, we can still see dominant pop culture attempt to categorize this music on the spectrum of "Native or not."

> Walk with pride, through the life I lead.
> Jammin' out to Pete [Rock], reading *Black Elk Speaks*
> —"Every Direction," 2015

Analyzing my own experiences and the music that was created in reflection, I hope to showcase rap music as a tool for Indigenous resiliency, just as it serves for all oppressed peoples. It is my aspiration as an artist to demonstrate the universality within this example of interculturalism.

I felt a small cue, my vision is fixed in a hue,
not because of some lean, but because of a new
view. It came with purple lights. She said, "Oh word, you like?
What does it mean ancestrally? Can you put meaning to light?
Oh you ain't 'tradish,' right? I guess you're a 'modern leader.'"
I said, "No, no, this purple has a meaning."
Even if I don't see it . . .
—"Smells the Earth," 2018

I never did go to powwows to dance or to sing. In those days, it was hard to walk around without feeling judged about anything. There were still things to feel welcomed/comforted in, though. The sound of the drum mixing with the carnival and laughter. The smell of truck foods and show-worthy rez-cooks. And on each side of the arbor, one could walk directly into horseshoe tournaments, softball games, rodeos, novelty vendors, and more. What spoke that energy to me the most were the rappers walking around with backpacks of CDs to sell.

In those years I got to meet the main artists that I had looked up to on my rez. Maniac the Siouxpernatural, Franc Castle (then Genocide), and Rezonate sold me a copy of almost everything. They gave me encouragement after I had expressed dreams of doing what they did. It fueled me more than anything to hear, "Yup, keep writing, man. One day you could be like us!" Maniac would later give me my first microphone.

Messages to my younger-self, like, "You're gonna get through it—
through the rain and the meth pipes." Whole lot of pain, and it's
still there, but we're gonna get through it, because we still care.
—"Still Care," 2022

Rap would nestle my first experiences of kola—a term given to a friend that represents real loyal friendship in the Lakota/Dakota/Nakoda way. At age thirteen, I would join my uncles in a group called R3zolve, and being around ten years younger than them gave me a group of mentors early on. By the time that I got into high school, the group disbanded, and I had learned enough studio basics to start getting by on my own.

I walk with cutthroats, and none of us know how to follow.
You follow?
—"Message to Your Chairman," 2018

In school, I'd finish work early and write verses for the rest of the period. But career goals had to "make sense" or be brushed under the rug, especially in a place of scarcity. I quit just before my senior year, having made around ten mixtapes up to that point. During this time, I focused on college admission, but deep down I couldn't let go of the one thing I could always turn to.

> One time. No eyes, just faith.
> I jump. I've lost my taste.
> Swear to God I won't slam brakes.
> See how many skid marks I make.
> I'm a fast rez car steady rollin on an ocean
> of blacktop pavement slidin
> swear, my life has seen some ice and
> I'm gonna tire up, and drive it
> —"Faith," 2019

I asked every recruiter, "Do you have a psychology program and radio station?" and one week after getting my driver's license I was navigating my rez-bomb to the University of Pennsylvania. Back home I was used to seeing my destination thirty miles out. Now I couldn't even see beyond the street I was on. Disoriented and claustrophobic, I took a breath and started my four-year commitment.

> So he pushes on the pavement with the spirit of his moccasins.
> He don't got a pair, but he wears them til he's off again.
> To home, he's a dope, but is he dope to those off the rez?
> No. He's alone, but he knows that he'll be on again.
> —"Reservation Pavement," 2014

Getting to curate and host my own college radio show every weekend helped my mental health and willpower to stay in one of the nation's top-ranked stressful schools. It felt good to run a show that could expose a major city to the rap that came from the rez. As a rez-rapper, you never imagine that the music you make will even get played in your community, let alone somewhere like Philly. Through the platform I was able to showcase, interview, and even premiere artists' songs every weekend.

Being a work-study student at the Greenfield Intercultural Center and an active member in the Natives at Penn student group, I was privileged to coordinate Native hip-hop events. It taught me the business and advocacy side of things, how to take care of performers. In doing so, I struggled to stay successful in school, but I remembered that my Ate' (father) taught me that as a Lakota I always had to "go all the way or don't go at all," and to always remember that "sometimes you won't even get a thank you, let alone money. That's not what it's about."

> Shout out to my cante [heart], it don't crack under pressure.
> Damn those French, made me an iyeska [mutt/mixed breed].
> —"No Bizz," 2017

Graduating in 2015 felt like a dream. The family I had gained along my collegiate journey attended some of the ceremonies since my family couldn't afford to. I had their support, but still I recall looking around and feeling lonely as gowns dispersed into the crowds of families after one of the evening's ceremonies. The beats and unfinished mixes in my headphones kept my spirit strong through these things.

> I swear it was a dream come true,
> to tell my Ina [mother] I'd be seeing her soon.
> —"I'm Coming Home," 2015

"You shouldn't have come back here, you know." A grandma I rarely met gave me a hug as I returned to South Dakota. "So-and-so might have told you this was the right path, but he isn't from here, he don't know. You came home too soon. You and your dad, are you behaving?"

> I swear they treat me like I'm slangin cocaine,
> just because I saw the images and said "No way."
> I ain't a role model, I'm just this real individu-owl—leave a feather,
> grant a wake
> watch the beat get funeral'd
> —"Not Even," 2018

Native education is a trip. The elders and ones with authority preach it all throughout high school, but in a way that makes it seem like you won't actually finish. Then when you're finally in college, it's a mixture of high praises and heavy expectations. Reminiscent of toxic celebrity stardom, it feels like everyone is watching what you do, what you post, what you consume, what you decide to do with your life, for better or for worse. And finally, after you graduate, the eyes slowly depart, checking in to see if your four years were worth it. In a twisted irony, the very sacrifice you made for your people can be the very aspect of your journey that ostracizes and discredits you. I had no choice but to put this into my lyrics. There was no other way to feel like I had power over uncontrollable situations.

I got optimists at my side that I don't see.
I got doctors, they try to tear inside of me,
but I got nothing of value to them, they just don't see
why they gotta bother me?
—"Bluha Sni," 2018

I spent six months in South Dakota where I took on performance contracts, as permanent jobs seemed impossible to find. I moved into a trailer outside of Eagle Butte with my dad and little brother after saving up enough. We'd find out that it was used to cook meth before we had moved in, but like anything on the rez, we made it work. I really wanted to ensure that my little brother had things every adolescent should have, like his own room. I felt that if anything, my degree should at least be able to help with that, because nearly every choice in my life was based on being an older brother. As a Dakota/Lakota, I could never let go of that responsibility to my relatives.

Bet you'll never see a lightbulb the same again,
I done lost a few family, lost a few friends.
But who is really lost when the pipe-dream begins?
Who really loses when usin' syringe?
—"See It," 2015

Deep-seeded struggles I had once traveled to college to defeat began overwhelming me, and after a suicide attempt on January 1, 2016, I was welcomed back into Philadelphia by extremely supportive hunka (adopted) family at my alma mater. I regretfully said goodbye to home again, feeling so defeated and lost. I took that plane back to save myself, but in doing so it became hard to find myself worthy of peace.

Free time spent in the city at punk rock and activist-run open mics gave me fuel. I loved exchanging music, culture, and ideas with communities that cared about justice and equality. Though as I began to settle in Philly, back in South Dakota pipeline companies were kickstarting what would become the next major historical event in Indigenous-US relations.

You can't mess with Unci Maka [Grandmother Earth], you must be gone.
Gone from the way you were.
You can't mess with Mother Earth.
So who are you, and who will you run to
when your mother repays you? Punishes you?
You can't turn to greed no more,
or kill green with your green no more.
—"Unci Maka," 2016

Just like in college, I found myself struck with survivor's guilt. It killed me to not be home to support my little brother, to not be on a front line somewhere. On *Democracy Now!* I'd see a picture with the blood of my cousin on a security dog's mouth, and later video of other cousins chasing out buffalo and evading cops through the hills. Everything I saw on a broadcast or livestream would be sampled into music I made. It was the only way I could fight and show my solidarity.

> There's blood on the dogs.
> Still singing our songs.
> 'Cause you can't stop our fight.
> No. Oh, you can't stop our fight.
> —"Tribute to #NODAPL Warriors," 2016

Eventually, dreams led me home again. After another failed attempt at my enrolled tribe's rez, I ended up at my aunt's home in Bad Nation, South Dakota. I tried doing what I could to help with menial tasks for the horses and cattle, mostly outside with nature and my music.

> I see Ikto [spider] in these salesmen, their corporate sheening eyes,
> but grew up watching hustlers still give their nephews rides.
> So I walk sharp and face this. They only look at crime,
> while I get eight eyes scribed with the pain from every life
> I try to save with music. Still, I see creepy creatures
> that only focusin' on frames, never my paintings features.
> —"Spider Bite," 2021

I probably could have sought employment or contracts like before, but I lost that ambition when communications became sour. Staff from outreaching tribal programs would question my abilities and argue whether or not I could be a good role model. On top of that, it seemed people only came to me at the last minute for a cheap get. Questioning my worth, I stuck to tending cattle and modestly released music.

> I don't care about what they're telling me,
> because when I grow up, I know what I'm gonna be——
> Same as I always was, black suit and all.
> My life's a downward spiral, I'm bound to fall.
> —"Rezified," 2006

Through prayer and nature, I learned to embrace the struggle and love my life. On my own private terms, I stopped using alcohol and worrying about money. Coincidentally, a council member would ask me what it'd take to run a free studio for our reservation around the same time. Choosing to live my life differently, I took advantage of the home that I had once missed out on and began pushing myself into ceremonies and focused on community work.

> Crazy, any one of us at any time could do a bid,
> sometimes even when we're not committing any sin.
> Got me wonderin' the lessons that I'd teach my kid,
> dealing with a system we weren't meant to thrive in.
> Opened up my eyes and all I seen were the lies,
> but within me lies a passion to make this right.
> Not for everyone, just workin' for me and mine.
> I could never convert a person or make them try … I just try to pray.
> —"Try to Pray," 2019

I fell back in love with singing prayer songs. Listening intently and learning, it dawned on me that traditional music had often come from an unsika (pitiful) and ikce (common, humbled) place, just like the rap music that I had been making my whole life! I sang harder and put that prayer into my everyday walk and creativity. My fusions of Lakota/Dakota sounds and lyrics increased as I discovered what felt natural and honest to my experience.

> I call upon a death … a death to all of this hopeless-
>   ness … and every piece of meth.
> A death to increases of these young-old deaths.
> A death to not prayin' anymore,
> not sayin' to my main people "love you" anymore
> A death to me fearing consequences to the real,
> a death to the thought that I've ever been that ill.
> A death to hesitation just to love, just to pray,
> hesitating to be something greater than I am today.
> —"Hoot," 2020

Wonahun Was'te' Studios—which my ciye' (older brother, mentor) explained as meaning, "Bringing good things through the music … in a whole different way. For the people"—kept me thriving. Hearing this encouraged me to apply for a fellowship with First Peoples Fund and from there I have been more empowered as an artist than ever before.

Break a heart with the tales of a sav[age] from the land.
Women to the Males, feeling like we're all damned.
"What's the plan?" I don't know, son. Take it as it comes.
If you see the cavalry, best to not run.
Our spirits are way stronger than a finger, trigger, gun.
Fast-forward, now we're fighting with the law, with the plug.
Now there's meth, so the love so shunned in a slum.
Same Custer, different day: death, alcohol, drugs.
Hechetu [so be it], so be it. We are stronger than the negative.
Gotta laugh at tricks gettin' played. On my s#*^ again.
We all gotta suffer just to get on up and live again.
So live again! Really couldn't tell you any different.
—"Oven Heater," 2020

I continue to create works like "Mastincala" (Rabbit) with Sicangu Lakota artist Tani Gordon, or "Taku Sni" (Nobody) with Oglala Lakota artist Ray Janis. I find my validation and come to terms with my living identity through the music I create and support. As a youth, I was indoctrinated into an ancient society outcast by colonial modernism, full of artistic truth-expressers. I walked among warriors who fearlessly battled the system (and, sometimes, each other) with their pens in a world focused on fighting wars with illusionary power. I participated and witnessed a culture of demonized members of an already oppressed people grow and develop what we call Native rap. While some may consider it a modern art form with some of its artists being more contemporary than others, I'd argue for letting go of these concepts entirely.

I'm from the death camps, you can't impress that.
I grew up drinking fluoride water, tasting food stamps.
F*%@ what they say about me. They don't know nothin' about me.
They question how I'm sounding, these enemies around me.
I had these organizers stressing on my 4G,
I was just "too rez" for 'em, they don't adore me.
That's why these tokenizers just cannot afford me.
I come from something greater, something that they don't see.
—"Cutthroat," 2018

Throughout the history of colonization, art has found ways to grow under any circumstance, sometimes deriving from seemingly nothing. When I rapped in my life, I really was praying and crying out to the Creator. When I made my beats, I was still in rhythm with the cancega (drum) of the people.

I grew up thinking and being told that I wasn't "acting Indigenous," not realizing that everything I did was Indigenous all along.

> I cried a lot for Zane, didn't make it to his wake
> so saying this doesn't really feel like a mistake.
> The sacrifices and success have both taken a toll.
> Counted many coup, but I never ever stole.
> And I don't think that I could ever let go of my soul.
> I tried so many times, and I know Creator knows,
> so I'm just here just trying to live and do it for my folk.
> Fill a hole in my home. For the rez, I will grow.
> —"Howl," 2020

Cultural Resiliency in the Face of Crisis

LEARNING FROM NEW ORLEANS

Carol Bebelle and Carol Zou

Carol Bebelle is a New Orleans native, a cofounder and executive director of Ashé Cultural Arts Center, and a constant voice and advocate for the primal role of culture in establishing equity, justice, and compassion in American society. Her new platform is AKUA Productions NOLA where her artist self is more present in her efforts.

Carol Zou is an artist, writer, educator, and cultural organizer who has worked for over a decade on the relationship between arts, culture, community, and activism. Her work has spanned various collaborative modes with Yarn Bombing Los Angeles, Michelada Think Tank, Trans.lation Vickery Meadow, Asian Arts Initiative, and the US Department of Arts and Culture, among others.

This conversation revisits the original conversation between the US Department of Arts and Culture (USDAC) and Carol Bebelle in Art Became the Oxygen, *a 2017 publication by USDAC on the roles of artists in emergency response. The original interview addressed the ways in which Ashé Cultural Arts Center and New Orleans artists responded to the 2005 devastation of New Orleans by Hurricane Katrina. Current USDAC team member Carol Zou and Carol Bebelle reprised the conversation in June 2020 on artists as emergency responders in the context of the 2020 COVID-19 pandemic in the United States, drawing out lessons learned from 2005 and beyond.*

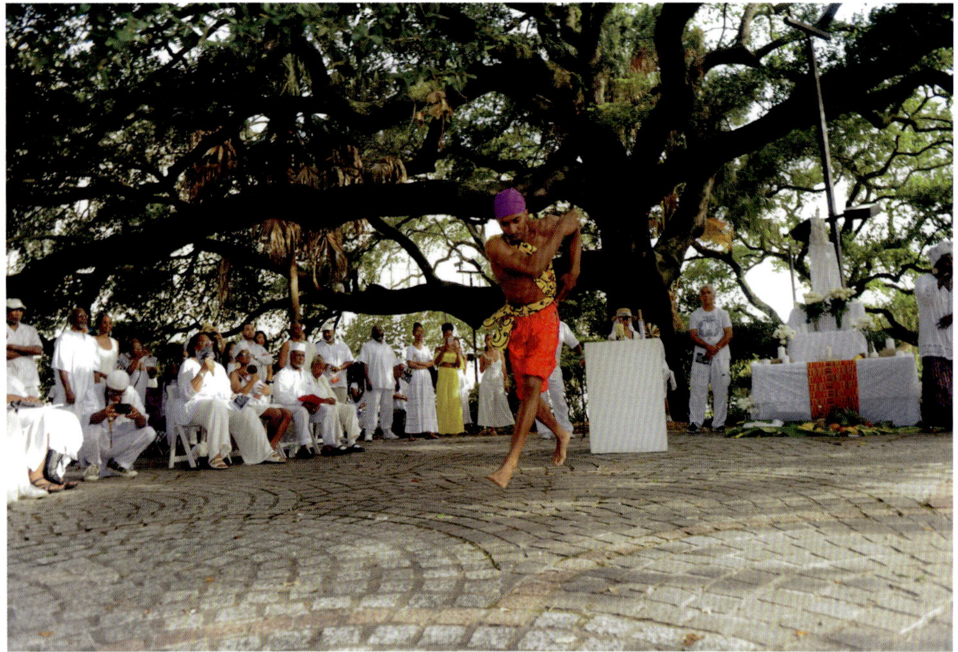

MAAFA commemoration, 2017. Annual sunrise gathering of hundreds of New Orleanians, including community, culture bearers, artists, and visitors to commemorate the ancestors, known and unknown, from the transatlantic slave trade. Courtesy of Ashé Cultural Arts Center.

CAROL ZOU: How has COVID-19 affected New Orleans and how has it affected New Orleans arts and culture?

CAROL BEBELLE: The arrival of a pandemic threat just after hosting Mardi Gras, our annual high-profile community event, created a real sense of crisis and vulnerability in our city. Mardi Gras combines festivity, libations, proximity, and lowered inhibition mixed with millions of people from around the world. Add a virulent pandemic and you have the making of a nightmare. All day every day for a couple of months, we were hearing about deaths of family members, friends, and widespread hot spots.

Tourism is one of the top three economic drivers for the city. In New Orleans's tourism industry, artists and culture bearers make a living from the gig economy. Tourism was severely hit by the mandated shutdown. The remaining workforce in the hospitality industry was devastated. For a city that's usually alive with festivals and cultural activity, it's been rather calm and very trying.

This shutdown is very reminiscent of the post-Katrina period. We have food lines at the food bank. The food bank has been struggling to meet this demand. Our hospitals were straining to meet the demand for beds. Being ventilated was certain death. Even our convention center opened a COVID-19 unit. Now we have rebounded, with fewer patients going on ventilators and treatment regimens having greater success.

We are also dealing with the uprising. Our young people have been protesting in the streets around many social justice issues. A protest group showed up recently at the mayor's house demanding that some of the potential defunding from the police department be made available to compensate hospitality workers for lost wages. These efforts have joined an ongoing challenge to reform the criminal justice system in Louisiana. We find ourselves in a cultural shift.

An additional complexity is the real possibility that this is going to be an active hurricane season, which is bad news for us. Our sewage and water board is currently unable to prevent street flooding after torrential rains—god forbid a hurricane! Suffice to say, New Orleans has a daunting immediate future.

In times like these it's important to keep people nurtured culturally and spiritually. This shifting and vulnerability is causing us to dramatically experience our interdependence, our "we-ness," more than before. This "we consciousness" is becoming stronger and driving our alignment with our "others." As a result, we are working together more. The New Orleans cultural community has a dogged determination to meet this demand with innovation.

A handy metaphor for me is the New Orleans second line. Second line is this cultural tradition that's related to funeral rituals. Mourners and friends follow the casket as it travels to the grave site, and then there is a jovial, dancing parade that returns from the grave afterwards. This signifies a celebration of the deceased's life. The uprising frontliners are the first line. The second lines are supporters, investors, donors, promoters. The third liners are the arm's distance folks, there when you need them. Too many of us have retreated to the third line and offline position. We've got to find our place in the first, second, or third line to be able to be active in getting this done.

CZ: What is the role of culture when it comes to making policy, and when it comes to recovery from a national crisis like this? What are the learnings that all of us can take away from what happened post-Katrina?

CB: Place really matters. Place can be a land mine with so many triggers of memories and feelings of belonging that we are hardly aware of. In a time of a pandemic, you can deeply feel the loss of place. When a place is lost, you lose a certain balance in your life. Your sacred memories are in jeopardy. It depresses your ego. So, we recognize the role culture plays in the human experience of place. Belonging is a core element of culture and must be a core element of any cultural/social healing strategies we employ.

There's a reason people come to New Orleans to write, to take their art residencies and their retreats to prepare and to think about creative projects, because this place, steeped with cultural and creative influence, is seductively welcoming and stimulates their sense of belonging. After the storm, everybody left, but everybody hasn't returned. There are still people trying to get back home sixteen years later. The loss of culture bearers and artists who served as familiar teachers and models was cause for great anxiety and sadness. The intimate belonging in the city was disturbed. Absent was the inspiration and usual support that had once been a regular part of life.

The ultimate value of New Orleans culture is its healing and restorative qualities, the "it's gonna be alright" spirit that helps to generate courage, to assuage loss, grief, anger, and sadness. The culture provides the arms that make it possible to reach out to people and connect when they need comfort most. So people are still concerned about the soul and spirit of New Orleans.

Gentrification has become a real threat here. Some of the people who came to Central City were folks looking for the opportunity to be a part of creating a more equitable existence. Some folks who came just had profits in mind and were looking to make big bucks. A physical disaster can create a crisis, bringing both danger and opportunity. I think it's also going to be a part of what's going to happen with the COVID pandemic and the uprising.

CZ: As we are having so many policy conversations about what recovery from COVID-19 looks like, how do we make sure that the efforts of our grassroots cultural workers and culture bearers trickle up to the policy level? And how do we also make sure that policy supports them, as well?

CB: I'm reminded of a young man who grew up in a cultural organization here, and who went off to Howard University, got his degree, then went on to law school, came back, and said to me, "Ms. Bebelle. I've got ten years that I'm gonna give to my community. Then, I got to take care of my family." He went on to run for the city council, and he served the council for eight years. Because he was there, there were instances when he could inform and bear witness to other viewpoints and realities that just wouldn't have gotten considered without him.

As artists and culture bearers, we could be more present at the tables of decision making and planning. Artists and culture bearers bring powerful insight, imagination, and creativity to these tables. Some tables are handling mundane matters. But it's in the mundane that we get a chance to make sure that the things that we need, those basic needs, are being served. As artists and culture bearers, we need to accept greater responsibility for sitting at more tables.

But folks that are tasked with deciding and planning ought to be looking to include us. The ideal is to have artists and culture bearers be seen as thought partners, ideators, communicators, etc., like we think about the data wonks, and the content specialists and practitioners. This is what I'd like to see. The growing presence of citizen artists and culture bearers in the civic world.

There are many artists whose practice is or includes community involvement. Artists have transformed neighborhoods for decades, only to be pushed out by developers. We are models and teachers of how to turn trash into treasure, how to make a way out of no way. So having artists in the community is a valuable thing. It is strategic to make sure that they have places to live in communities, particularly communities that have challenges. Making certain that they've got places to live means that they get to be stabilized. When they're fine, then they influence youth who may want to become artists, or who may understand science differently or better because of the artist that was their neighbor, their teacher, their friend. Artists can become literal heroes of the community. The years 2020 and 2021 have been successful in clarifying and dramatizing the need for America to create a culture that values equity and justice. This is not the current reality, and the shifting of culture is the work of artists, cultural bearers, healers, and spiritual guides. If there ever was a time that artists and cultural bearers were needed, it is now. They are bridge builders, motivators, innovators, and the visionaries and guides to the better society we all want and all deserve. Laws, policies, resources, infrastructure, and networks will be needed to support that world once we get to it. But seeing it and getting to it is the work of imagination, creation, and inspiration.

Collectively Directing the Current

Halima Afi Cassells

Detroit-based artist/community advocate **Halima Afi Cassells** occupies a myriad of roles that are unified by a deep and unwavering devotion to foster community interconnectivity. In practice, she designs spaces for authentic engagement and collaborative artistic expression, as well as projects that engender new economy practices.

Salt mine canaries—
Soaring, dive bombing, finding
Future's curved edge—still.

Morphed into starlings
Holding space, in formation,
We are those brave birds.[1]

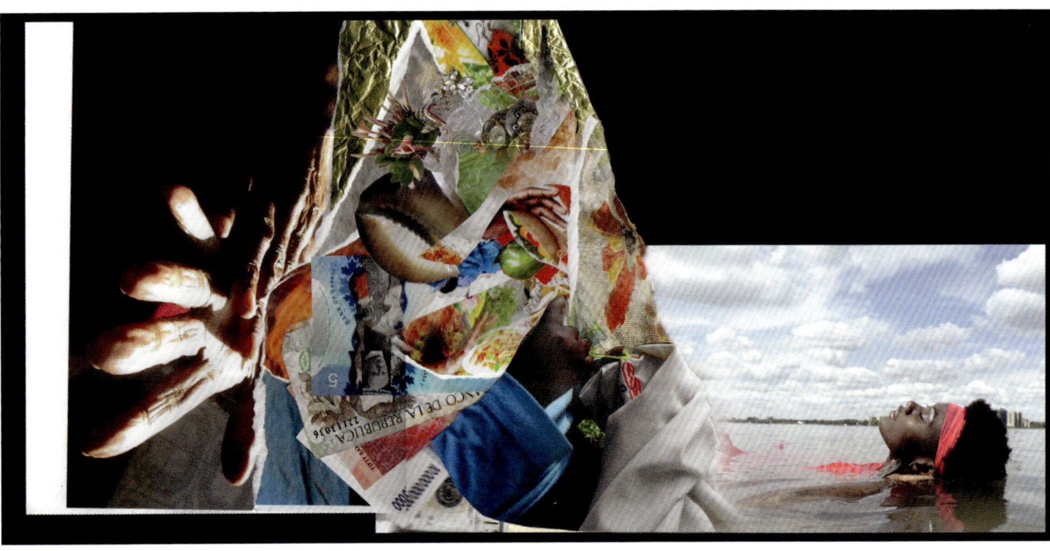

Detroit has been an epicenter for creativity, innovation, and social justice organizing that continues to change the world. Detroit is often a synonym for resilience and strength; I am proud to be from such a place. Everywhere that I've gone, Detroit is on my chest. Walking with a cloak of untouchability, "I'm from Detroit," I would say slowly, maybe giving a sideways glance or an affirmative chin-down nod if anyone ever tried anything stupid. My parents and grandparents worked hard, made a home, and struggled in revolutionary movements here. Their histories in this place have shaped me.

As an interdisciplinary artist, my practice is intertwined with my life in community as a mother, gardener, facilitator, and cultural organizer. I was embarrassed one day when I realized I did not know the original name of this land. I was thirty-five before the name Waawiiyaataanong passed my lips. The original Anishinaabe name describes "where the water goes around [the land]," an all-important marker of this landscape. The name that has existed for millennia was new to me. I had to sit in that discomfort. It offered me questions like, How did I not know this? Why was I uncomfortable speaking the name, even after I learned it? It was a moment for me to confront how internalized colonization informed my identity. As I continue to grow and learn from comrades, fellow artists, and friends, my own understanding of place in community deepens. I realize that decolonizing and transformational work happen differently, but that they must start with an upheaval of everything we "know," and a willingness to be open.

Art and culture hold the power to profoundly shift our perceptions. Although often thought of as being pent up in an ivory tower or behind the marble walls of museums, art and culture are actually everything. The songs, symbols, stories, architecture, news media, ways we gather, dance . . . all of it documents our humanity and how we collectively agree on reality. Most of us can remember song lyrics for a lifetime. Art and culture equal manifested imagination. And as the visionary author adrienne maree brown teaches, "we must always ask the question—whose imagination are you living in?"[2]

We are fortunate to be in a moment of monumental shift. The icons, structures, and mythologies that uphold terra nullius and white supremacy are crumbling. Artists and cultural workers are taking up the charge to boldly reimagine and lead visionary organizing in our communities to

(opposite) Halima Afi Cassells, cover image for *Fashioning the Free Market*, 2019. Mixed-media digital collage. A chronicle of seven years of the Free Market of Detroit's community participatory multimedia installations.

shape the future. We know the power of narrative. We know narrative drives policy.

So when a group of well-financed folks arrived in Detroit in 2015 proposing to create a week-long conference in an abandoned power station, with ruin-porn promotional material and plans to invite artists, architects, and designers from around the world, we called an intervention.[3]

I recall someone saying it felt as if Detroit was a trendy backdrop, and we (local cultural workers) were the props, set within a narrative of white saviorism. It took a collective process for us to come together, express our anger and grievances, and then find a way to uplift what we know to be true and figure out how we wanted to engage them, if at all. Dozens of Detroit luminaries, including ill Weaver, dream hampton, Piper Carter, Jenny Lee, Ingrid LaFleur, Marsha Philpot/Music, Taylor Renee Aldridge, Sacramento Knoxx, Devita Davison, Bryce Detroit, Wes Taylor, Ryan Meyers-Johnson, Gabrielle Knox, and many more got to organizing. We communed over dinners at Allied Media Projects, and pored over a Google doc. We naturally deepened the trust and bonds among ourselves as we articulated our shared values, decided on our process, and then developed possible strategies for engagement.

We decided on creating an MOU (Memorandum of Understanding) document that would address our collective concerns, agreeing that any of our participation was contingent on agreement to these terms. The document begins by uplifting our value, then lists points of constructive collaboration and an agreement for benefit to the neighborhood in very specific ways. Some of these include fair compensation for local artist participants, documentation of all sessions with attribution to the authors, dedicating the majority of the budget to hyperlocal woman- and BIPOC-owned prioritized procurement, and inviting neighbors to be at the table with city leaders, among many others. The museum director negotiated with us, and we agreed on some terms. In the end, many of us participated and used the opportunity to practice and champion a community benefits process. They took the model and principles and applied them forward to the next iteration of their gatherings in other cities across the world. Most importantly, it was a moment for our community to cocreate a working framework that could be used as a model for future engagements.

We patterned our course of action from the Community Benefits Agreement (CBA) process laid out by Rise Together Detroit Coalition (now Equitable Detroit Citywide CBA Coalition).[4] Stemming from many conversations within the Storehouse of Hope Food Pantry in the North End neighborhood of Detroit, people raised the question of respect and equity with regards to tax incentives being given to developers with no accountability to the community. Their rallying cries to Detroiters were "Nothing about us, without us" and "If we got to pay, then we should have a say." Over a period of several months, those who would be most impacted created the frame for a proposal to institute a process so that all voices would be considered when development happens: Proposal A.

A network of thirty-plus grassroots volunteer groups, including West Grand Boulevard Collaborative, Detroit People's Platform supporters, and the People's Action (an arm of New Era Detroit), gathered thousands of signatures to petition the city for an ordinance that required private development projects of $15 million or more receiving $300,000 in public subsidies to engage residents in a CBA process and create legally binding agreements. Almost immediately, a well-funded countermeasure (Proposal B), which watered down the original intent, was introduced and placed on the ballot to confuse voters. Proposal B raised the threshold to $75 million in tax incentives and took out the "legally binding" language. The Rise Together Detroit Coalition managed to garner over 98,000 votes from Detroiters for Proposal A, yet Proposal B managed to win by a slim margin. Although the CBA ordinance on the books is an extremely watered-down version of the community-led one, it's still another first for the nation. And as Linda Campbell, one of many Detroit women of color movement leaders, says, "The best part about bad policy is that it can be changed."

Once cultural organizers had practiced this process and model, we had a set of principles and a framework ready for conference organizers and cultural institutions coming into Detroit. In 2016, organizers from Art-ChangeUS entered the scene, working on their "ArtChangeUS REMAP: Detroit" conference, in partnership with the Arab American Museum, the Charles H. Wright Museum of African American History, and Complex Movements. They enthusiastically began working on how to incorporate the principles into their conference design and organizational practices. After the conference, which modeled what we sought in the first and much more, they went deeper with us, looking at how they could iterate and improve their impact for their next convening. Then director Roberta Uno asked the question, "How can we create ripples in the field?" ArtChangeUS extended their resources to continue consulting organizers in Detroit, as well as conducting national interviews and collecting stories, data, and best practices from cultural organizations nationally working to create equity. All of this is compiled in the *Cultural Community Benefits Principles Toolkit*, edited by Cézanne Charles and advised by ill Weaver and myself. This open-access document continues to be built upon and has been adopted by a growing number of national institutions and individual practitioners.

Our ancestors laid the foundation for this work and this moment. So many movements are running parallel that ripples are becoming waves. Decolonizing work, Movement for Black Lives, and visionary organizing continue. Back in 2015 in Detroit, artists bloodied and "cleaved" the statue of Christopher Columbus in the head with the addition of a hatchet. Through the creation of open mics, concerts, potlucks, and other community events, these organizers were explicit about building Black and Indigenous solidarity. Because of continued efforts, in 2018, cultural organizers successfully moved the city to abolish Columbus Day and officially recognize Indigenous Peoples' Day. The Aadizookan, Raiz Up, Frontline Detroit, Detroit Will Breathe, BYP100, and We the People of Detroit have been at the forefront of creating collaborative spaces for publicly demanding justice and integrating cultural organizing within social and environmental justice frameworks. Symbols have power. The way we pass down narratives has power. The way we create new traditions, rituals, and language has the power to bring the future we all deserve. As noted storyteller/music producer Bryce Detroit proclaims, "So many folks are concerned with being on the *right side of history.* My focus is being on the 'right side of the Future.'"[5]

As I write this, two museums in Detroit, the DIA (Detroit Institute of Arts) and MOCAD (Museum of Contemporary Art Detroit), are undergoing a radical shift to look into their practices and find ways to embrace transparency and a lens of equity—not inclusion. They are thinking about what decolonization looks like. Of course it is paradoxical, as museums are monuments to white supremacy. So what is causing this shift? Groups of artists, curators, educators, cultural workers, and community members demanding change as collectives. MOCAD Resistance and the DIA Staff Action came together in a moment of crisis in leadership at these institutions, and what is being birthed is much larger. The Waawiiyaataanong Arts Council—a nascent autonomous body—will work to inform decolonization practices and guide cultural institutions on actionable steps to operationalize land acknowledgments. We are continuing to connect movements and struggles as well as grow our understanding through solidarity.

I recognize you.
Put some respect on my name,
We breathe the same air.

Sitting on silt atop salt, fresh water runs into the backyard gardens our grandparents nurtured. We hold each other, stare into the future, and direct the current.

1. This poem references adrienne maree brown's work and her frequent referencing of the murmurations of starlings, citing their intelligence of the whole; thousands of these birds move as one body, creating intricate patterns in midair—each taking turns to lead.

2. "ArtChangeUS REMAP: Detroit" conference, "Writing the Future," workshop with adrienne maree brown, Detroit, MI, October 6, 2016, https://artsinachangingamerica.org/remap-detroit-recap/.

3. The New Museum hosted a conference called "IDEAS City: Detroit" in the spring of 2016 at the Herman Kiefer Complex and the Jam Handy Building.

4. The Equitable Detroit Coalition now consists of member organizations from all City Council districts in Detroit and represents 100,000 constituents.

5. Bryce Detroit (@BryceDetroit), Twitter, August 12, 2020.

The New Eagle
Creek Saloon

Sadie Barnette

Sadie Barnette is from Oakland, California, and holds a BFA from CalArts and an MFA from the University of California, San Diego. Her work is in permanent collections of museums such as LACMA, the Studio Museum in Harlem, and the Guggenheim. She is represented by Jessica Silverman.

My multimedia practice illuminates my own family history as it mirrors a collective history of repression and resistance in the United States. The last born of the last born, and hence the youngest of my generation, I have long held a deep fascination with the personal and political value of kin. My materializing of the archive rises above a static reverence for the past; by inserting myself into the retelling, I offer a history that is alive. My drawings, photographs, and installations collapse time and expand possibilities. Political and social structures are a jumping-off point for the work, but they are not the final destination. My use of abstraction, glitter, and the fantastical summons another dimension of human experience and imagination. Recent projects include the reclamation of a five-hundred-page FBI surveillance file amassed on my father, Rodney Barnette, during his time with the Black Panther Party and my interactive reimagining of his bar—San Francisco's first Black-owned gay bar. *The New Eagle Creek Saloon* (2019) installation is an invitation, a place to be, an invocation. I built the glittering bar structure to glow somewhere between a monument and an altar, reanimating the bones of the Eagle Creek in an intergenerational revival.

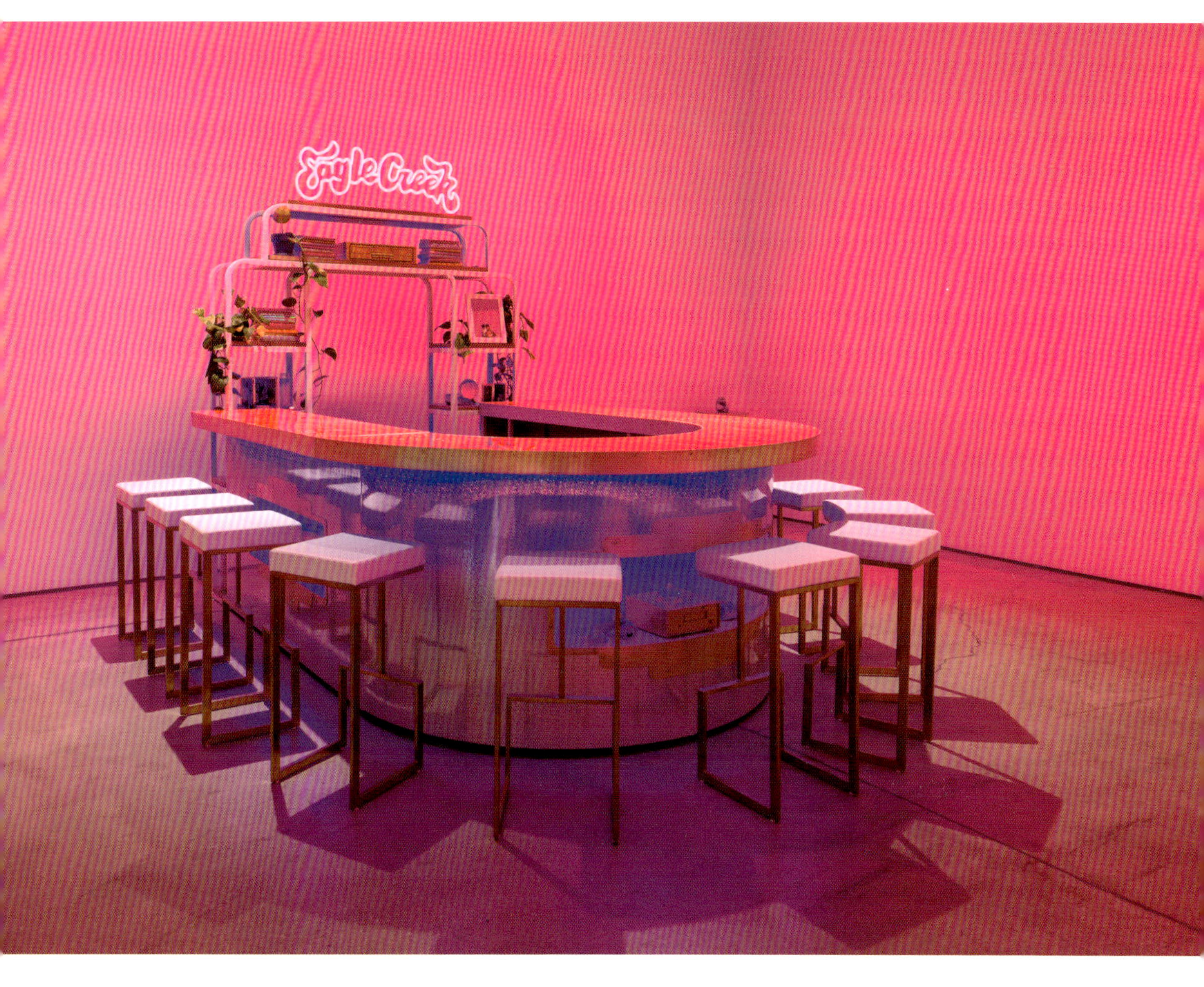

Sadie Barnette, installation view of *Sadie Barnette:
The New Eagle Creek Saloon*, Institute of Contemporary
Art, Los Angeles, 2019. Steel, plywood, plexi, holographic
vinyl, metal flaked objects, photographs, walnut
wood, LED lights, barstools, houseplants, matchbooks,
coasters, artist book, altar objects, dimensions variable.
Photo: Jeff McLane.

Notes from Technotopia 3.0

ON THE "CREATIVE CITY" GONE WRONG—
AN ANTIGENTRIFICATION PHILOSOPHICAL
TANTRUM, 2012–2016

Guillermo Gómez-Peña

(WITH CONTRIBUTIONS BY EMMA TRAMPOSCH,
BALITRÓNICA GÓMEZ, ANASTASIA HEROLD, AND ELAINE PEÑA)

Guillermo Gómez-Peña is a performance artist, writer, activist, radical pedagogue, and artistic director of the performance troupe La Pocha Nostra. Born in Mexico City, he moved to the United States in 1978, and since 1995, his three homes have been San Francisco, Mexico City, and the road. His performance work and twenty-one books have contributed to the debates on cultural, generational, and gender diversity, border culture, and North-South relations.

From 2012 to 2015, I wrote obsessively on the dangers of the ultimate creative city, the much-touted postgentrification era and what it meant to be a foreigner in my own neighborhood waiting for a surely inevitable eviction notice. During this time, my own troupe was evicted from our infamous studio in the Mission District of San Francisco. My obsessions were also driven by what some may describe as philosophical or material anxieties. In both cases, I ask a similar question: how do I wait … or should I even continue to wait?

This updated 2016 manuscript remix has been expanded and restructured as a series of literary postcards. They are meant to be published, performed live, on radio or for video, without a particular chronological order.

2020 Disclaimer: Since lockdown began in March 2020, the creative city has experienced dramatic shifts. The multiple pandemics at play (COVID-19, systemic racism, police brutality, wildfires, and the Trump Effect) have pushed out of the city a huge percentage of the tech workforce from companies responsible for gentrifica-

*tion in the first place. Or rather, many techies have decided to leave now that they can work remotely. In the meantime, many of the populations of San Francisco who were evicted during the last fifteen years are slowly coming back. Think of this text as a pre-*COVID *snapshot of the creative city. Who can predict what will happen in the next few years? Stay tuned for the Technotopia sequel.*

1. Dear ex-local artist, writer, activist, bohemian, street eccentric, and/or protector of difference...

Imagine a city, your city and your former "hip" neighborhood, being handed over by greedy politicians and re/developers to the crème de la crème of the tech industry. This includes the seven most powerful tech companies in the world. I don't need to list them: their names have become verbs in lingua franca; their sandbox is the city you used to call your own. Case in point, San Francisco.

Their Faustian iDeal involves radically transforming the city of your dreams in a few years into an unprecedented "creative city"; a bohemian theme park for the young techies who constitute their Darwinian workforce. It comes with dormitories, food courts with catchy theme bars, and entertainment centers. In the worst-case scenario, the entire police force is their private security.

Imagine that during the reconstruction process, the rent—your rent—increases by 300 percent overnight. The average city rent is now $3,500 a month for a small one-bedroom apartment, the highest in the country. The artists and the working class at large can no longer pay it. Your community is being forced to leave, at best to a nearby city (also in the process of gentrification), at worst, back to their original hometown. The more of an intimate history you have with the old city, the more painful it is to accept this displacement. You have no choice.

2. While you hang on by a thread, friends and colleagues receive eviction notices. This is death. Perhaps this whole process is a form of dying? You might never see them again—on that street, waiting for that bus, sharing a bite on that corner, hanging out in your local bar.

You spend a large part of your civic time attending antigentrification demonstrations and collaborating with other artists and activists in anti-eviction and techno-artivist projects. But it only seems to get worse. The number of dramatic eviction cases increases constantly, leaving you heartbroken and exhausted. Meanwhile, the diminished politicized citizenry and the progressive media begin to experience compassion fatigue.

As the community continues to shrink, so does your sense of belonging to a city that no longer seems to like you. You begin to feel like a foreigner and internal exile: freaky Alice in techno-Wonderland; remember the Alien Caterpillar who inhaled? Unless you own your home and studio, your hours "here" are numbered. You carry this feeling of imminent orphanhood like a very tight and stylish noose around your neck—a dandy walking through a cemetery of inevitable memories.

3. Dear ex-local artist, writer, activist, bohemian, street eccentric, and/ or protector of difference . . .

Imagine that all the classic and familiar places in your hood—the emotional spaces which have been your main source of inspiration, creativity, and community—are forced to close because the pinche greedy landlord tripled the rent overnight. Imagine those funky, decades-old Latino restaurants and immigrant bars full of memories and ghosts, barber and specialty shops, bohemian sex clubs, experimental art galleries, indie theaters and bookstores—yes, shops where bound books are still sold— disappear because some offshore millionaire bought the building or the entire block to rent out microunits to Airbnb. And all the new laws and acts protect him.

Coño! Your imagination is a painful companion—one that forces you to entertain tolerance and providential acceptance.

In a few months, these wonderful places that for decades provided the city with a strong cultural identity are destroyed and reopened as (get ready) homogeneous "live/work/play" spaces, "micro-condominium" buildings, and tech plazas in the works. The original tenants and workers of those buildings are now wandering around homeless, burning with rage. You can hear their heart-wrenching howls at night from the window of your apartment. *(I howl.)*

The new city begins to look like a generic global metropolis imagined by Italo Calvino. To make the lives of the transient workforce somewhat pleasant, hundreds of similar "smart cafés," trendy restaurants, overpriced "eateries," and "celebrity bars" open up in each neighborhood. These words are meaningless. Even the last standing old-school dive bars are being "discovered" (a euphemism for taken over) by the transplants via their Yelp or Foursquare mobile apps. But you, no matter how long you lived "here" or how much you have paid in rent throughout the years—even if it is enough to own your hipster remodeled Victorian upper unit—you are not welcome. Let's face it, in Technotopia, even hipsterism is a thing of the past.

You hit the streets looking for a place to eat and drink: What you used to call an average-priced dinner is way above your price range now. Your sacred $4 night cocktail, now served by an aloof "celebrity mixologist," costs $15, and your daily jugos and licuados, now called "cold pressed vegan organic cleansing juices," go for $12 in a "recyclable, sustainable" bottle. It's hard to be a dandy here. For the first time in history, they have chic taquerias that are run exclusively by Anglo hipsters whose job is to teach you the history of tacology and how to eat them properly, chilango (Mexico City) or Oaxacan style, $7 each.

> We (the artists), used to eat delicious inexpensive foods from around the world. Now we can only afford cups of noodles, shwarmas, burritos or burgers.
> —Anonymous tweet

But don't worry: Remember that this is just a sci-fi nightmare, a perverse exercise of radical imagination, or rather, a psychomagic challenge to deliver your daily dose of survival humor . . . with a side of "organic" guacamole or "tofu curry."

4. Imagine that your own building, a legendary (ex) artist building, is now just another revolving Airbnb miniunit for frat boy–cum–zombie techies who make well over two hundred grand a year. If you are the only one of three Mexican tenants left, when you open the front door for a new neighbor, they either perceive you as the building's janitor or report you to the manager as a "suspicious character." And yes, in Technotopia: your new identity is that of "suspicious character."

The nightmare unfolds: full of Maseratis, Ferraris, Porsches, and Mercedes Benzes, the private parking lot is now protected with barbed wire fences and a digital display keypad encoded by microchips. The "vintage bike" racks and trash containers also have contraseñas (passwords).

Video surveillance cameras are omnipresent. New management techniques keep the homeless, the day laborers, and the "scary" young people of color at a distance. They are unpleasant memories of the old city of sin and compassion. Pariahs and freaks—they recall distasteful and economically disadvantaged, at-risk neighborhoods. Who wants them roaming around their picture-perfect babies, fancy bikes, and groomed dogs?

The newly empowered cops drive around looking for criminal "difference" to make the hood safe for the new dot-com cadre. The homeless, the day laborers, and the "gang bangers" aren't the only ones being removed from the streets; with them go the poets, the performance artists, the experimental musicians, the frail transvestites, the politicized sex workers, the gallant mariachis, the cool lowriders, the urban primitives, the angry punks, the defiant radical feminists, and the very activists who used to protect us all from the greedy landlords and politicians who conceived of this macabre project.

The latest American version of ethnic and cultural cleansing is invisible to the newcomers, and highly visible to those of us who knew the old city. The press labels it "the post-gentrification era."

Prehistory is only 7 years old and nostalgia is pure style, a bad selfie of a fictional memory.
—Anonymous tweet

5. There are suspicious fires happening constantly, in apartment buildings and homes inhabited by mostly Latino and black working-class families. And you cannot help but wonder if landlords and redevelopers are setting these fires.

Is there a secret garden of violence in the heart of techno-bohemian paradise?
—Anonymous tweet

On June 18, 2016, Balitronica and I posted on Facebook:

It's a very sad day for San Francisco in the final chapter of the "post-gentrification era": The entire historical block of Mission St, between 29th & 30th streets, just a block from our home, was leveled by another seemingly "mysterious" fire. . . . From the legendary 3300 club, our daily bar and refuge for social outcasts, rebel artists and many working class folks, to El Paisa as well as other taquerias that feed economically frail locals. Playa Azul, one of the oldest iconic Mexican restaurants in town, Coronita's nightclub which is also a night sanctuary for newly arrived immigrants, and the historical Cole Hardware store, all burnt down.

This happened within a span of 4 hours! 60 people lost their homes, mostly working class, and hundreds, their jobs and small businesses. These establishments were beacons for bohemians and for cultural difference and the apartments above them were homes to many long time Latino, black and white working class residents.

City officials were prompt to say, while the fire was still going on, "it is not related to the other (equally suspicious) fires in the Mission" and that they "won't investigate arson." Of course, have they ever really investigated any of the fires of the last 5 years? Has any landlord or developer been prosecuted or even implicated?

Two blocks away from the madness in a parallel San Francisco, while locals watched in tears, a techie frat party unfolded as the city crumbled in flames around them.

Do we want to live here anymore? Will our "artist building" be next on the list of uninvestigated arsons? This city of greed is literally becoming a living hell (to the point of actual fire and brimstone) to anyone who is not an engineer in the tech industry, an upper class hipster, a venture capitalist or a redeveloper. Is there a way to recapture the city of our original dreams?

We are crying.

6. Looking for metaphors that explain this incommensurable crisis, I come across the Millennium Tower in San Francisco, touted as one of the "Top 10 residential towers in the country" and a symbol of the city's new techno-wealth.

Paradoxically, the tower is slowly sinking. As of mid-2016, seven years after construction began, it has already sunk 16 inches. And the problem continues to get worse. (The sleazy owners are trying to avoid paying for the digging of a new Transbay Terminal, which basically means that tax-payers would be screwed into paying the physical reinforcement costs to fix their building.) In the meantime, hundreds of upper-class tenants and CEOs are being forced out of the Tower.

Is this the ultimate symbol of Technotopia? Can Technotopia be so cruel and stupid—reverse eviction caused by shoddy, accelerated-for-profit work-manship and bad planning?

7. One begins to wonder, who are these people taking over my neigh-borhood?

> Techno-haiku:
> San Francisco sans differance,
> a nostalgic fiasco
> The Gold Rush Era Part 12
> 4 people who can't spell "nostalgia"
> & 2 loonies down the street
> who don't know their real names
> —El Aztec High Tech, 2018

Metaphysically speaking, where did the techno-zombies really come from? And how long will they stay? Are they merely taking a quaint stroll through the backyard of Technotopia? Will they return to the suburbs of the Red States when the Chicano intifada begins? Or when the new homeless popu-lation begins to attack them physically?

Day after day, enticed by the new digital bonanza, hundreds of new people arrive. They seem unfamiliar. They lack manners or style, social or historical consciousness; mostly middle- and upper-class white people from the suburbs and small cities from throughout the country, along with some wealthy foreign entrepreneurs and programmers from similarly upwardly mobile techno cultures.

They walk with yoga mats and wear gear bearing the logo of the company they work for. They push designer strollers and lead their designer-wearing pups down the street. So many of them are glued to their smartphones to the point where they can't even acknowledge your presence as you pass them.

> Of course, you, lucky YOU, queer, tattooed, eco-minded, Salvador-
> an or Peruvian teckie, you are an exception to all rules.
> —Anonymous tweet

> . . . But dear reader/audience member, don't take it personally, you
> are an exception to the rule. You are somewhat different.
> —Anonymous tweet

8. What these cyber-adventurers have in common is that they are in a hurry, determined to make lots of money . . . ayer! Their neocolonial dreams must be attained instantly. It's the latest San Francisco Gold Rush, the second digital bonanza, a true new Wild West; definitely the latest chapter in savage capitalism.

Upon their arrival they are willing to take any job on their way to a better one, displacing the working class, which made the city function for decades. They are even willing to be waiters, gardeners (as long as they are referred to as "landscape designers"), house cleaners (or rather "facilities personnel"), taxi drivers (for Uber or Lyft), and even nannies and dog walk-ers to the rich and famous. The difference between then and now is they charge three times as much and have no sense of labor ethics or a culture of service. After all, it's just a temporary gig on their way to Utopia 5.0.

I fear they are a virtual mob, not an informed citizenry. Their limited spatial awareness, for example, is troubling. Their navigation and com-munication devices are installed in their iPhone or iPad. And so are their identities, hollow dreams, "real" experiences; their nouveau families, and all of their fictional memories.

> In this imaginary city, we no longer have citizens: we have self-involved
> "consumers" with the latest gadgets in hand.
> —Anonymous tweet

9. In the new tech culture there's never a full presence; there's only auto-voyeurism . . . and the selfie. The selfie entails a profound anxiety: "I must tell the world I was 'here,' even if only for a few minutes, even if 'here' is nowhere. It might be my last day on earth."

For the poetic record: the strangers I speak of are mostly "white" (meaning gender or race illiterate). Eighty percent are male and seem blithely unaware of the history of the streets they are claiming with their daily rounds. Their behavior makes you wonder if they know, geographically and culturally speaking, where they are. Are they aware of the profound impact of their presence in the lives of the older inhabitants? Last night at a bar one of them felt compelled to confess to me he was angered by a "racist poster" he saw outside: the photo of a handsome mariachi pointing a gun to the viewer with a text underneath that reads: "Gringas si; gringos no." His lack of humor and imagination made me feel sad.

> In the way these vatos behave you begin to wonder if they exist in the same city you are or in a parallel quantum reality you are making up?
> —Anonymous tweet

In fact, they are easily annoyed by "difference" and have no problem letting you know or confessing it online. *Verbi gratia*: "Don't believe the hype: This neighborhood is not a safe place! There's still way too many Mexicans, hookers, lesbians & street freaks. Don't come to live here! The Dogpatch is where it's at." In the "creative city," the words *racism*, *sexism*, *homophobia*, and *classism* are passé. . . .

But the problem of unbearable difference has a deadline. The cops are working around the clock to solve it. In the past five years, Bay Area law enforcement has killed twelve Latinos and African Americans, including a pregnant woman. There are updated versions of old manuals circulating in the Real State milieus: "Don't rent to Latino or black families, artists or single moms. Preferably rent to young white males with a salary over $150,000 a year." There are also new laws proposing the relocation of the entire homeless population outside of the city. The techies, pobrecitos, are truly irritated by them. This makes me think of a novel that could be inspired by Ernest Hogan.

10. **I continue citing my poetic field notes:** "These techno-vatos have no sense of philanthropy. They spend their savings on gourmet food, gadgets, clubbing, fancy apartments and very expensive puppies, like French bulldogs, Italian Greyhounds, and Pomeranians. It's a solipsistic frontier economy. And if you are mildly politicized it is hard not to wonder: what if each one of those prosperous locos would contribute five percent of their income to improve housing, social services, schools for the poor, and the yearly art budget for the arts commission. But this is me, *my* plan—too sensitive, too logical, perhaps too Mexican?"

"Here," the future will come in a few days and the money they make must be spent in the immediate process of getting there. But "there" is actually nowhere.

—Anonymous tweet

The running mandate is to create, by any means necessary, a city for the rich. Our ex-mayor Willie Brown, paradoxically a Black "progressive Democrat," purportedly said: "We want to create the Monaco of the US, and if you can't afford it, you can leave!" Thanks, Brother Willie!

Well, it already happened . . . and yes, we, the authors and vehicles of cultural difference, "can't afford it." But here's the thing: We are doing everything possible to stay. Even if it feels so lonely here. As a colleague recently stated, returning to San Francisco from being on the road is like arriving at a party that's nearing its end. There are only a few wounded people left at the bar, which is just a sticky mess.

II. By now, as I reread my diary, I realize I am clearly experiencing acute philosophical vertigo and political despair.

The symptoms reveal themselves through devastating questions in my notebook:

- Whatever happened to San Francisco's original bohemia?
- Are we, the artists and activists left, merely stubborn?
- Are we delusional and engaged in a losing battle? Will I become the last standing Mexican performance artist in my neighborhood?
- Are we waiting for the bubble to burst, the San Andreas Fault to open up, or for the Mission shamans to conjure up the collapse of the new economy? But what if all the Mission shamans have already been evicted?
- Will the city get so unbearably expensive and will the "outsiders" and the evicted come back armed with a sense of relentless revenge to stage the next instalment of the "Purge" series? Will the leaders of the tech industry themselves decide to relocate to another place? Portland, Austin, Charlottesville or Seattle perhaps? If only we stick around a little longer . . .
- Is it too late to talk about this? Hello? Auxilio!!!

. . .

Three pages later my obsessive questions continue:

- Should I attend tomorrow's antigentrification march or is it time to finally pack up and go back to Mexico City?

- I wonder what is worse, overt organized crime or the covert forms of organized crime and ethnic cleansing in Technotopia?
- What is more violent: the menacing gaze of a sicario (hitman) or the absolute indifference of a techie? Dangerous difference or dangerous sameness?

12. During the revision of the final draft, I become fully aware of my poetic subjectivity. I know that my words are somewhat careless, partially unfair and devastating. But I can't help it. I am struggling to hold on to my sense of humor. I am not a journalist. I am a performance artist and a poet. It hurts to walk the streets of my refurbished ex-bohemian "city of tolerance, compassion and radicalism." It hurts to be an internal exile, a permanent foreigner in my hometown.

13. Strange prophetic dream: Last night I dreamt "the bubble bursted," the tech industry collapsed, and the evicted "criminals" and the homeless pushed out of the Golden Circle of Chili-con Valley had returned to the city enraged and armed with a vengeance.

The creative city was in ruins (remember Italo Calvino's *Invisible Cities* or the film *The Purge*?); hundreds of thousands of dot-com square feet empty; gang-controlled territory; robo-squatters everywhere; the obnoxious electric sound of white noise, techies getting kidnapped. The few start-up kids, the CEOs with designer families, and the techno-hipsters who were lucky enough to survive panicked and ran for their lives.

There were fires all over the city. But this time, they had been started by angry citizens of the old city and the homeless in cahoots with Antifa. "Outsiders" (proletarian zombies) were all returning to the city en masse. The Mexicans and the Central Americans were also back, and so were the evicted artists, and the X-treme bohemia. They all came back from the outer "neverland."

Shit! We were all dancing around bonfires made out of dated computers and techno-gadgets, where unemployed techies and retro-hipsters were roasting their designer dogs and drinking their piss. It felt like a more serious "7th Day" at the end of Burning Man. A very impressive sound system was broadcasting activist poetry and performance texts.

It was a beautiful day for mankind. But it was only a dream.

Was it?

14. I'm delusional! I want to move forward with my life, stop complaining and embrace the inevitable changes of the "postgentrification era." Hey! Starting a dictionary will help me get my thoughts on track or at least make them more cohesive for my audiences and readers. So here I go:

bohemian theme park: A multicultural entertainment and heritage park for monocultural adults working in the tech industry located in the "global metropolis."

creative: A euphemism for financial success in the tech world PR departments. It also includes graphic designers working in the tech, fashion, and entertainment industries. Critical performance artists and digital artivists don't qualify . . . luckily!

creative city: A desperate city without a working class.

here: Nowhere; nothingness; nada de nada. Caput.

hipster: No one really knows. You just think you know. If you think you know, you most definitely are not one.

local: Someone who used to live "here" when here was a place.

eviction: A euphemism for ethnic cleansing and the eradication of difference.

Facebook: My virtual landlord looking for ways to evict me.

Google bus: A traveling gas-guzzling half-full office with chairs and no cubicles, where people actually work on the way to work.

networking: A safe "alternative" to making actual conversation and flirting.

Neverland: That mythical place west of your imagination, where you never grow old or mature.

radical: An adjective for a franchise. Branding terms generated by a think tank about "content."

Technotopia: San Francisco sans differance—A/critical techno-utopia.

organic: Another franchise.

underground: Yet another franchise.

vintage: Secondhand object or a previously worn item of clothing, or used furniture or jewelry, sold for over $100.

white: A bizarre state of mind that makes you attribute "race" to "others" with darker skin.

white supremacist: An undercover techie or programmer in the Trump era.

TO BE CONTINUED IN MY NEXT BOOK

....

I wish to thank Balitrónica Gómez, Emma Tramposch, Anastasia Herold, and Elaine Peña for helping me to prepare this version of the manuscript.

"Building Temples for Tomorrow"

CULTURAL WORKERS AS CONSTRUCTION CREWS

Alesia Montgomery

Alesia Montgomery, an assistant professor at UCLA's Institute of the Environment and Sustainability, is the author of *Greening the Black Urban Regime: The Culture and Commerce of Sustainability in Detroit.* Her publications also include articles in the *International Journal of Urban and Regional Research, City and Community, Ethnography, Antipode,* and *Global Networks.*

I moved back to Oakland in 2018, two years before protests filled downtown streets that had been emptied by COVID-19. As crowds chanted, artists made murals of George Floyd and Breonna Taylor on the plywood barricades of stores and offices. A headline proclaimed, "Oakland Artists Unite in Historic City Takeover."[1] It was not a takeover, but the guerrilla art showed what a revolution might look like. Artists joined with dockworkers on Juneteenth 2020 at a rally of the International Longshore and Warehouse Union (ILWU). The ILWU had shut down West Coast ports, including the Port of Oakland, in solidarity with marchers. Generations of activists were there. Angela Davis raised her fist from a car; rapper and filmmaker Boots Riley shouted to the crowd, "Our power comes from the fact that we create the wealth. Wealth is power. We have the ability to withhold that power. We have the ability to withhold our labor, and shut shit down."[2]

Back in 2018, market-driven redevelopment had seemed unstoppable. I saw new luxury apartments—block-long fortresses—surrounded by (mostly

Black) people living in tents, RVs, and makeshift shacks. I had seen poverty in Oakland during the late 1980s and 1990s, but nothing like this. The *climate gap*—race-class inequities in climate change impacts—makes social disparities more deadly.[3] As I write these words, I breathe the thick smoke of wildfires burning out of control in Northern California as I gaze up at an orange sky. Droughts, floods, and heat waves will increasingly endanger households already struggling to pay for shelter, food, and water. If the past is any guide (New Orleans after Hurricane Katrina comes to mind), intensive policing will be used to suppress panic, anger, and disorder as these disasters multiply.

COVID-19 and other unnatural disasters have erased the illusion that building fortresses within cities can protect anyone from the multiplying threats. Seeing the misery on the streets, a new generation asks, "Is another world possible?" To answer this question, we must analyze the *interior architecture* of a city—what people feel and dream about it.

Cultural workers (artists, scholars, clergy) have the power to transform what people feel and dream. Planners and developers harness cultural work to lure young professionals of all races to *Black urban regimes*—heavily Black cities such as Oakland and Detroit. Murals, concerts, and gardens—defanged of their radical context—draw shoppers and tourists who generate wealth for financial and business interests. These artful spaces appeal to longings for the good community. However, low-income Black residents are *minoritized* in these spaces, by which I mean that they are treated as minors—children to be controlled and "helped" by gentrifiers who supposedly know what's best for them.[4]

An uprising amid a global pandemic has disrupted the ways in which the market uses the labor power of cultural workers. Will we cultural workers, in the words of Boots Riley, "withhold our labor" from corporate projects and "shut shit down"? Beyond disruption, can we help to build spaces that preserve human dignity and save lives?

> **demolisher:** "Demolition workers tear down and remove unsound structures . . . and make jobsites safe and ready for new construction work. . . . [They] perform their duties within a collaborative work environment that can be dangerous, even life-threatening, as jobsites may feature unsound structures and explosives."[5] (see also PILE DRIVER)

In the late 1980s, my girlfriend managed an apartment building on Telegraph Avenue; I was the maintenance crew. She collected rents and complaints; I polished the staircase, mopped the floors, cleaned the laundry room, kept the front sidewalk sparkling, and ran down to throw pails of water on dumpster fires set by bored teenagers who got a laugh out of seeing me run. I had the easy job: the old man who lived upstairs patted me on the back and called me a "hard worker"; the middle-aged mother who lived with two kids downstairs offered me chocolate cake and told me how much she appreciated me. My girlfriend, on the other hand, had the impossible job: the tenants yelled at her when their ancient plumbing broke, and some of them hid when she knocked on their doors for rent. The property management company took forever to respond to her calls about clogged toilets and broken laundry machines, but they expected her to be quick in squeezing rent from poor people. We felt for the tenants. And many tenants felt for us too, perhaps because our Black faces resembled their own, maybe because they saw the wooden boxes that we used for tables and chairs in our tiny studio. "Okay, I understand," the tenants would sigh. "I'm mad at *them*, not you."

When my girlfriend's supervisor—a white butch with a mullet (let's call her Jai)—would stop by for a chat and the rent checks, she'd tell us of her dream to turn the building into a queer space that was artsy and profitable. I asked my girlfriend to interpret: Was Jai talking about kicking out our tenants? (I was just a baby dyke and not yet schooled.) My girlfriend, who was older than me and thus wise to the world, shrugged; she had her own vision—without telling Jai, she had placed a homeless family in a vacant apartment and told them how to apply for government assistance.

In the late 1980s and early 1990s, there was an explosion of art and activism among young "out" Black dykes in Oakland—poets, dancers, musicians, scholars, painters, photographers, comedians, novelists. You won't find out about this efflorescence in any history book (yet), but it was a kind of Harlem Renaissance. This early cultural work paved the way for Oakland to become an epicenter of the Black Lives Matter movement today—a movement whose cofounders include a young Black queer woman, Alicia Garza, based in Oakland. Back before Twitter, we read *Aché*—a local Black lesbian journal founded in 1989. *Aché* swiftly drew readers across the United States and then throughout the African diaspora in far-flung places such as Canada, Germany, and the Virgin Islands. *Aché* focused on Black lesbians yet extended its concern to Black people in general, discussing topics such as police brutality that have resonance today.

This sense of community, reinforced by cultural work, inspired my girlfriend to bring in that Black family from the street. But then she and I broke up, and we moved away. The units got new paint and appliances, the rents shot up, and the building gentrified. I do not know if Jai caused the shift. Perhaps her talk was only talk, a dream-wish to create a space where she did not have to fear getting beat up or ridiculed. Some white lesbians in those days had a vision of autonomous women's communities. Jai's talk of a queer haven had the flavor of those times, but she dreamed of a capitalist venture. She was onto something: market logic served up with radical ideals now sells like hotcakes.

One afternoon, some months after my return to Oakland, I drove to Telegraph Avenue to meet with a friend of a friend—a young Black artist on a spiritual quest to build the Good Community. My friend had told the young man that I study utopian communities, so he wanted to talk to me. (Years after my job as a maintenance crew, in my unending and contradictory quest to be fed and free, I had gotten a PhD in sociology.) I found the bohemian coffeehouse that the young man suggested; I went inside. He stood up to greet me with outstretched arms and the glowing eyes of a mystic. He told me about himself: he was a musician and a seeker. He planned to go to India and live in a commune where he would give up everything and free his mind. He had a vision of building a network of collectives around the world where people would grow their own food and get in touch with each other, with Spirit, and with the earth. They wouldn't fight the existing order—they would peacefully replace it.

I told him that visionaries had attempted something similar for centuries. He asked me what happened to their communities. I said that some of them failed because their leaders were incompetent or nuts; others failed because of government persecution, market competition, or inadequate resources; still others survived but did not expand because they did not have broad appeal. He asked me if his vision appealed to me. I told him I was unsure—would it help people get homes who were now living in tents under freeways? He smiled: "They already have homes . . . the tents . . . " I looked him up and down. I almost said, "Child, why don't you pitch a tent under the freeway?" But I held my tongue because the stinging words used by Black folks to read uncaring rich folks—*bougee, hincty, seddity*—did not fit him. He responded to my raised eyebrow, "I don't mean it like that. I mean, I saw vacant land next to some tents, and I thought that the people who lived there could grow food next to their homes and become part of the network." I asked him where they would get the money for seeds and tools, and how would they stop the landowner from calling the police? He did not have an answer. I left soon after, but I did not dismiss his dream. There is a brilliance in the idea of building a new world from where people stand. Troubling the category *home* might deepen discussion of the settler colonial roots of land ownership in the Bay Area.

But I feared that the musician would inevitably feel the need to go, cap in hand, to ask for help from landowners and foundations. Their support would tether his vision to their requirements, limiting the ability of un-housed people to have a say. If he created a space of beauty, it would raise property values, which would entice the landowner to sell the land. The exploitation of cultural work would be complete. How can we move from vision (on the one hand) and critique (on the other) to dialogues about strategy? Is there a way to discuss the challenges of demolishing racial capitalism without demolishing each other?

> **pile driver:** "A pile driver is a device used to drive piles into soil to provide foundation support for buildings or other structures. The term is also used in reference to members of the construction crew that work with pile-driving rigs."[6] (see also DEMOLISHER)

Africans entered the public space of the Americas on the auction block, but from the abolition movement of the nineteenth century to the Civil Rights and Black Power movements of the twentieth century to the Black Lives Matter struggles of today, our resistance—our "simple and daily and nightly self-determination" (to quote June Jordan)—has shaken the walls of racial capitalism.[7] Our music, our stories, our ways of seeing have mobilized movements that have changed the public as a space and a people. Thus, we have helped to build a foundation for real freedom. As Langston Hughes declared, "America never was America to me, / And yet I swear this oath—America will be!"[8]

To build an enduring foundation, we must combat the tendency for radical cultural interventions to turn into their opposite. Francks Deceus, reflecting on his struggles and the battles of other Black artists, notes how the market dominates cultural production: "We have to take blame for a lot of the things that happened because we subscribe to a lot of commercialism. . . . Artists have to be careful in terms of their work. Is it really their work? Is it really what they want to say?"[9]

Even when artists express what they want to say on city streets, they must attend to what their work is made to mean by its setting. One of my favorite griots, Storme Webber (whose poems I read long ago in *Aché*), speaks about the concept of negative space in art—how the space around a thing defines that thing.[10] Foreground and background/center and periphery shift in our perceptions. Given that the *space* of public art is not contained by the *work* of art—it does not end at the mural on the wall, it extends beyond the limbs of the street performer—in whose design is it centered?

In the financial cores of US cities, cultural work is in danger of becoming the *performance of movement*—a catharsis from oppressive realities rather than a catalyst to battle them. The solution is not the creation of better and truer art. There is a crass sameness in much of popular culture, but finely tailored truths are also on the market. I do not share the concerns of critical theorists who bemoan the *aesthetics* of the culture industry.[11] Propaganda is not so much in the brushstroke as in the relations that frame the work of art. Muralists are paid to paint visions of a green commons as business interests privatize parks and hire private security forces to guard them. Thus, visionary art becomes pacification. Before the rents rise and evictions proceed, one may imagine that one lives in the beloved community.

Meanwhile, critics of the social order are quarantined in the academy. Today's high theory, distant from the street, is ineffectual against racial capitalism and its placemaking. Indeed, complicit with it, high theory does not let everyday people get a word in edgewise. Speaking truth to power has evolved into (*just us*) justice-speak conferences, at which critical theorists dine on buffets dished by silent Black and brown service workers. Thus, the critique of the race-class order becomes its affirmation, and speaking truth to power becomes duplicity. I do not doubt the good intentions of scholars who labor for a better world. I simply ask that we look unflinchingly at what our work is made to mean as it is structured by the policies, norms, and funding structures of the academy.

To mean what it says, if it means to save lives, cultural work must not simply protest market-driven placemaking—it must displace it. Business interests should not dictate urban life. The same street talent that lures gentrifiers could be deployed to draw together longtime residents and their allies on an everyday basis, deepen reflection, and build bridges to other places in the fight for social and environmental justice. The threat of co-optation would remain—racial capitalism will not fund its demise. There is a need for collective strategizing about alternative economies (in the short run) and structural changes (in the long run) to support cultural work that advances societal transformation.

To build on the interior architecture of cities and provide a foundation for future generations, we must liberate the space and time surrounding the work of art. The performance matters. But to control our work, it is not enough to represent the world that we see—we must see and transform *that which we represent.* In so doing, we will keep faith with the construction work of ancestors such as Langston Hughes, who said of his generation of Black artists:

> We build our temples for tomorrow, strong as we know how,
> and we stand on top of the mountain, free within ourselves.[12]

Notes

1. Alan Chazaro, "Oakland Artists Unite in Historic City Takeover," *SFGate*, June 9, 2020, https://www.sfgate.com/sf-culture/article/oakland-george-floyd-protests-street-art-15328278.php.

2. Daniel Kreps, "See Boots Riley, Angela Davis Deliver Speeches at Juneteenth March in Oakland," *Rolling Stone*, June 20, 2020, https://www.rollingstone.com/culture/culture-news/boots-riley-angela-davis-juneteenth-march-oakland-1018203/.

3. Rachel Morello-Frosch, Manuel Pastor, James Sadd, and Seth Shonkoff, *The Climate Gap: Inequalities in How Climate Change Hurts Americans and How to Close the Gap* (Los Angeles: Program for Environmental and Regional Equity, University of Southern California, 2009).

4. Michel S. Laguerre, *Minoritized Space: An Inquiry into the Spatial Order of Things* (Berkeley, CA: Institute of Governmental Studies Press, 1999).

5. "Demolition Worker Job Description," JobHero, accessed August 20, 2020, https://www.jobhero.com/job-description/examples/mining/demolition-worker.

6. "Pile Driver," *Wikipedia*, July 26, 2020, https://en.wikipedia.org/w/index.php?title=Pile_driver&oldid=969710030.

7. June Jordan, "Poem about My Rights," in *Passion: New Poems, 1977–1980* (Boston: Beacon, 1980).

8. Langston Hughes, "Let America Be America Again," in *The Collected Poems of Langston Hughes*, edited by Arnold Rampersad (New York: Knopf Doubleday, 2020).

9. Francks Deceus speaks about the struggles of black artists in the 2007 documentary *Colored Frames*, directed by Lerone Wilson (Boondoggle Films).

10. Storme Webber reflects on negative space in *Venus Boyz*—a 2002 documentary, directed by Gabriele Baur, that explores gender performances (Clockwise Productions).

11. Max Horkheimer and Theodor W. Adorno, *Dialectic of Enlightenment* (Stanford, CA: Stanford University Press, 2002).

12. Langston Hughes, "The Negro Artist and the Racial Mountain," *Nation*, June 23, 1926, 692–94.

Invasive Species

Aaron McIntosh

Aaron McIntosh is a cross-disciplinary artist, fourth-generation quilt maker and fiber educator. His work has been exhibited widely in the United States and internationally. His honors include fellowships from United States Artists and the Center for Craft. Since 2015, McIntosh has managed *Invasive Queer Kudzu*, a community storytelling and archive project across the LGBTQ+ South.

My work mines the intersections of material culture, family tradition, sexual desire, and identity politics in a range of works including quilts, sculpture, collage, drawing, and writing. I have long used quilt making as a language, form, and tool, and my inherited traditions of working with scraps are the primary platform from which I explore the patchworked natures of identity and community.

Sadly, domination versus cultivation are primary ways I know my Appalachian homeland. Earliest memories include picking weeds in our family garden, and I draw an overt line of connection between these unwanted plants and my own anxious efflorescence as a queer person from a culture steeped in heteronormative tradition. Ruminating further on weeds led me to thornier relations Southerners have with kudzu, an invasive species that engulfs hills, trees, and old buildings when left untended. Using kudzu as a slippery metaphor, the *Invasive Queer Kudzu* project invades dominant Southern narratives and monuments, reclaiming the "monstrous" vine as a symbol for Southern queer tenacity in the face of homophobic institutions that legislate our livelihoods and obscure our rich histories. Engaging with queer communities and archives, the project has created an *undeniably queer mass* of quilted kudzu vines and leaves adorned with 7,200+ LGBTQ+ stories that celebrate Southern queer culture.

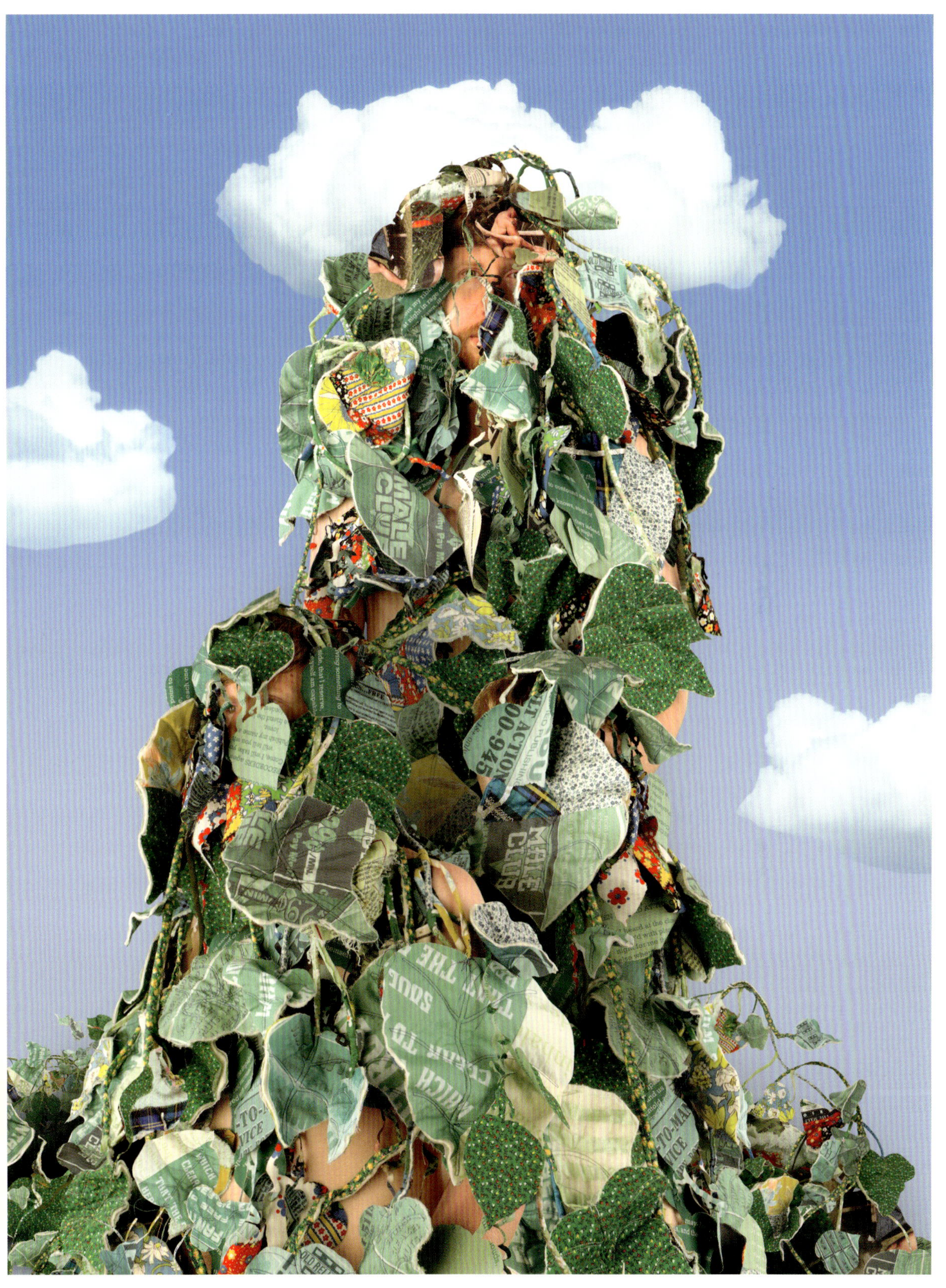

Aaron McIntosh in collaboration with Nick Clifford Simko, *Invasive Species*, 2014. Digital collage printed on archival paper, 31 × 40 in.

Sunny and 150 Years of Placekeeping in Little Tokyo

Scott Oshima

Scott Oshima is the former director of community arts at the Japanese American Cultural & Community Center and lead for the Sustainable Little Tokyo creative placekeeping initiative. They are a Chinese Japanese American artist and organizer, born and raised in Los Angeles on Tongva and Chumash land. Scott received their BFA in photography and media from the California Institute of the Arts.

Sunny the Grapefruit Tree is growing in the corner of the Japanese American Cultural & Community Center (JACCC) in Little Tokyo, Los Angeles. Over 150 years old, Sunny has witnessed the transformation and continued fight for this place with many names: Yaangna, Wolfskill citrus groves, Azusa Street, Nihon-machi, Sho Tokyo, Bronzeville, Japantown, J-town, Little Tokyo. Today, as one of three remaining historic Japantowns left in the nation, Little Tokyo stands as a cultural and spiritual center for Japanese Americans across Southern California and the many communities of color that have always called this place home.

For Sustainable Little Tokyo, we call this place ibasho: a place to be, to sit, to be oneself, and to belong.[1] We are a group of people and organizations who came together to imagine and bring to life a future that sustains our historic Japantown and community of color. We follow the saying mottainai, which roughly translates to "do not waste" and connotes respect for oneself, one's community, and one's environment. Ibasho and mottainai represent a holistic conception of community sustainability—one that is culturally specific, historical, economic, and environmental, and realized through organizing, art, culture, equitable development, and, above all, joy.

Sunny is one of over 150 treasures in Takachizu, Sustainable Little Tokyo and Little Tokyo Service Center +LAB's growing community archive and cultural asset-mapping project.[2] A made-up Japanese word combining takara (treasure) with chizu (map), the project collects Little Tokyo objects, photographs, memories, places, and other ephemera through show-and-tell gatherings. Through these treasures, we learn the story of Little Tokyo and what our community values.

Sunny the Grapefruit Tree is rooted in land cared for by the Tongva, who have inhabited present-day Los Angeles and its surrounding region for nearly ten thousand years.[3] Beginning in 1769, Spanish missionaries enslaved and displaced the Tongva, forcibly erased their culture and communities, and decimated their population. Mexico achieved independence from Spain in 1822 and sold the mission lands to private landowners, further displacing the Tongva. What was left of Yaangna, one of the largest Tongva communities, was forcibly relocated to what later became Little Tokyo before being again displaced.

When the United States took over California in 1848, the remaining Tongva and other Native Americans in Los Angeles were systematically enslaved through a notorious 1850 antivagrancy ordinance.[4] The city arrested Native Americans and auctioned them off for one week of forced labor. Sunny the Grapefruit Tree is a remnant of the Wolfskill citrus orchard, which, like many of the city's vineyards and farms, was worked by Tongva and Native Americans enslaved by this very ordinance.

Despite colonization, the Tongva remain in Los Angeles. Today, there is a resurgence of Tongva culture and community, and a reclaiming and celebration of their history, language, art, basketry, dances, rituals, and sacred lands.[5]

A city grew around Sunny as segregation, redlining, and racial covenants made the surrounding neighborhood one of the few places where people of color could live and own businesses. Sunny witnessed Biddy Mason purchase property along Azusa Street—a road named after a Tongva healer. Biddy was a former slave who was forced to walk 1,700 miles from Mississippi to Utah in 1848, before freeing herself in California in 1856 and settling in Los Angeles. She amassed a fortune as a skilled midwife and became one of the first Black landowners and philanthropists in Los Angeles and one of our city's cultural mothers. With Azusa Street, she created the first Black street in the city, and founded the First African Methodist Episcopal Church, the oldest Black church in Los Angeles. After her death, the church passed to William Seymour, a Black preacher who founded the multiracial Azusa Street Mission in 1906—considered the birthplace and a holy site for Pentecostalism.[6]

While Azusa Street continued to grow, Hamanosuke Shigeta's small American-style diner opened in 1884 and planted the seed for Sho Tokyo, Little Tokyo. Japanese American temples, churches, shops, food, and culture blossomed around it. Both Rafu Shimpo Japanese Daily News and Fugetsu-Do Confectionary opened in 1903 and are now the neighborhood's oldest operating businesses. Koyasan Beikoku Betsuin Temple opened in 1920, followed by Japanese Union Church and Hompa Hongwanji Buddhist Temple. These churches and temples were the primary cultural centers and are active to this day.

In 1941, Japan bombed Pearl Harbor and the United States entered World War II. Sunny watched posters "To All Persons of Japanese Ancestry . . ." go up when President Roosevelt's Executive Order 9066 sanctioned the forced incarceration of over 120,000 Japanese Americans. Little Tokyo's Japanese American community, estimated around 30,000 people, disappeared in buses and were taken to "camps."

During World War II, Black migrants from the rural South moved to Los Angeles and other urban cities searching for work in wartime factories, but faced racist, anti-Black residential restrictions in 95 percent of the city. They found a place to call home in the empty shell of Little Tokyo and named it Bronzeville. Black entrepreneur Leonard Christmas helped form the Bronzeville Chamber of Commerce and promote the neighborhood as a center of Black business, culture, and community. Bronzeville became the premier jazz scene in Los Angeles and was home to remarkable clubs: Cobra Club, Creole Palace, Shep's Playhouse, Club Rendezvous, and the Finale Club—which the city recognized as a historic site in 2019 through efforts by the Little Tokyo Historical Society. Then Sunny watched Japanese Americans return in 1945.

Only about half of Los Angeles's Japanese Americans were able to return after the World War II incarceration camps closed. They sought out their temples and churches to find temporary shelter and their former storefronts and apartments to find a home again in Little Tokyo. Bronzeville's Black community faced sudden unemployment, dwindling business, and eviction as wartime industries shuttered and racist, largely White property owners preferred Japanese American tenants over Black ones. While Japanese Americans benefited from this new postwar racial hierarchy, there were moments of solidarity and compassion: Kiichi Uyeda hired Black employees for his dime store; Samuel Evans hired Japanese American servers at his Bamboo Room restaurant; and some Black business owners sold their leases so the former Japanese American owners could return. Pilgrim House, a Black social services organization that was housed in the Japanese Union Church, created an outreach committee to improve relationships between Blacks and Japanese Americans—despite being displaced by the returning church congregation.[7]

Just as postwar resettlement offered a glimpse of a "Little Bronze Tokyo," the city used eminent domain to seize and demolish three blocks for the LA Police Department (LAPD) headquarters. Both the Japanese Union Church and Hompa Hongwanji fled their buildings, fearing further seizures and destruction. And most devastatingly, over 90 percent of the three thousand displaced residents were Black, and what remained of Bronzeville slowly disappeared.

More was taken in the name of revitalization in the 1970s and '80s, and Little Tokyo shrank to a quarter of the size that it had been. But Sunny continued to grow behind Amerasia, an activist-run bookstore, art gallery, and gathering space. Sunny heard shouts to "Save Little Tokyo" by Little Tokyo People's Rights Organization; protests to stop the eviction of Sun Building residents; and organizing to create affordable homes for our elders, the JACCC, Little Tokyo Service Center, and over thirty-five new public artworks to anchor our community.

The Japanese American National Museum opened in the former Hompa Hongwanji temple during the first days of the 1992 LA Uprising: protests against anti-Black police brutality and the National Guard collided at the LAPD headquarters on Little Tokyo, Bronzeville, and Tongva land. The Japanese Union Church was red tagged for demolition after the 1994 Northridge earthquake, but activists and the Nikkei Student Unions saved it. The building is now Union Center for the Arts and home to landmark Asian American Pacific Islander arts organizations: East West Players, Visual Communications, Tuesday Night Cafe, and LA Artcore. Sunny quietly witnessed over a century and a quarter of the growth, transformation, loss, joy, and activism that sustain Little Tokyo, this land and its many layers, to this day.[8]

For me, Sunny is Sustainable Little Tokyo's unofficial mascot. A symbol for the generations of people who built, nurtured, fought for, and loved this place; for the history of racism that we have yet to reckon with; for our responsibility to carry on this work; and for the future generations we fight for, even if we may never meet. In the long term, our community initiative is a fight for equitable development and for more permanent spaces for our culture, small businesses, and land to thrive. But the true spirit of this work is in stories like Sunny's—in continuing to care for this place, the people who call it home, and the memories and hopes it holds: ibasho.

In 2018, artists Beth Peterson, Nancy Uyemura, and Jennifer Racusin transformed Sunny into a puppet with the face of Aric Nakamoto, our longtime JACCC staff member who cares for Sunny and our campus. Sunny

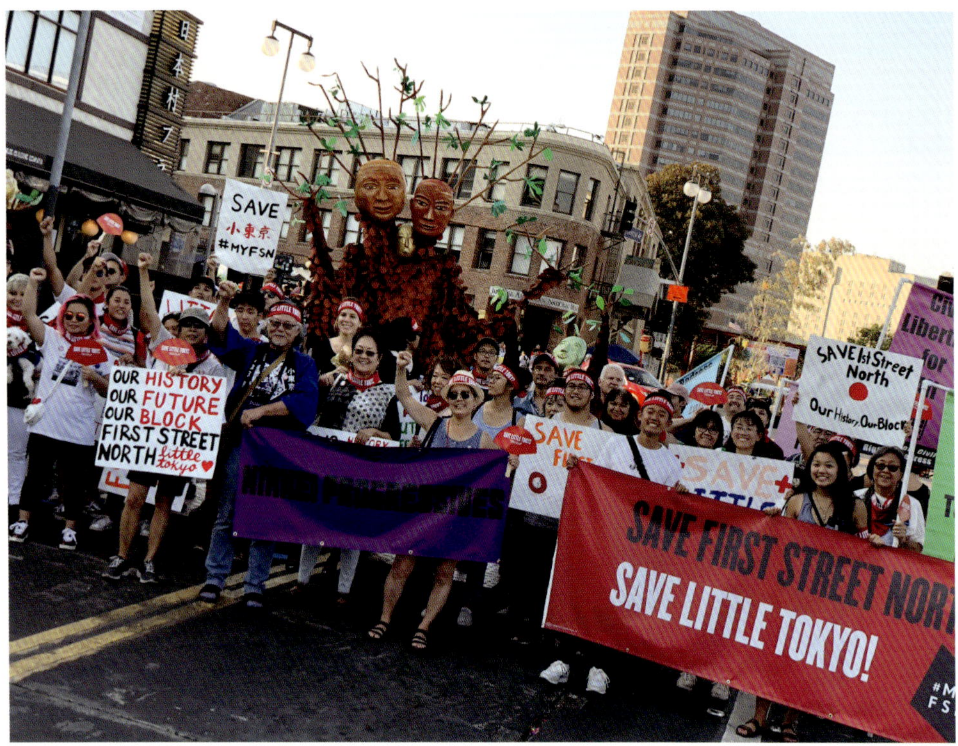

Nisei Week Parade, 2018. Photo: Scott Oshima.

took their first steps in the Nisei Week Parade, drawing attention to our campaign for community control of the First Street North block. Sunny then danced in FandangObon, an annual festival founded by legendary activists and musicians Nobuko Miyamoto and Quetzal Flores. The festival connects Japanese, Mexican, African, and Sufi Muslim American communities around traditions of circle dance, music, and caring for the land.

As I write this, Sunny is seeing a devastating pandemic and a national uprising against systemic anti-Black racism and police brutality. Our Buddhist Obon festivals, a tradition of honoring our ancestors, are canceled. The Nisei Week Festival, which would have celebrated its eightieth anniversary, is canceled for the first time since World War II. FandangObon, which planned to expand with the inclusion of Tongva artists, is on pause. The future of Little Tokyo, the city, and the country is uncertain. Yet Sunny provided us with an extra harvest of grapefruit this year: an early batch before the pandemic and a surprise harvest a month before I wrote this article.

Sunny may be offering us a reminder of our shared history, our hope for a future out of this crisis, and the work, love, and people needed to do it.

We will recover, we will heal. I look forward to dancing and celebrating our communal, cultural, spatial, and political connections—all beneath and with Sunny the Grapefruit Tree.

Notes

1. The word *ibasho* was brought to our attention by Yuji Sakuma and Jonathan Ja-en Crisman, who organized the exhibition *Ibasho: Arts Activism in Little Tokyo* as a part of the SLT Arts Action committee's ART@341FSN project, 2018.

2. "Asset mapping was developed as an alternative to needs based assessments of communities that defined places by their deficiencies. Asset mapping supports community based development strategies built from community identified strengths." Kofi Boone, "Disembodied Voices, Embodied Places: Mobile Technology, Enabling Discourse, and Interpreting Place," *Landscape and Urban Planning* 142 (2015): 235–42.

3. William McCawley, *The First Angelinos: The Gabrielino Indians of Los Angeles* (Banning, CA: Malki Museum Press and Ballena Press, 1996), provides a detailed record of Tongva history and culture, though only through the nineteenth century. Thanks to Julia Bogany for this recommendation.

4. McCawley, *The First Angelinos*. The deceptively titled 1850 Protection of Indians Act also arrested and sold Native American women and children, many into sex trafficking.

5. For more on the Tongva's efforts to reclaim stolen sacred lands and contemporary cultural practices, see Claudia Jurmain, William McCawley, and Colleen Delaney-Rivera, "O, My Ancestor: Recognition and Renewal for the Gabrielino-Tongva People of the Los Angeles Area," *California Archaeology* 2, no. 2 (2010): 290–92.

6. Dolores Hayden, *The Power of Place: Urban Landscapes as Public History* (Cambridge, MA: MIT Press, 1997), 138–65.

7. There is a need for deeper research into Bronzeville and the postwar transition back to Little Tokyo. I am indebted to the work of Hillary Jenks for laying the groundwork with "Bronzeville, Little Tokyo, and the Unstable Geography of Race in Post–World War II Los Angeles," *Southern California Quarterly* 93, no. 2 (2011): 201–35.

8. See Kelly Simpson, "Three Waves of Little Tokyo Redevelopment," KCET Departures, July 31, 2012, https://www.kcet.org/shows/departures/three-waves -of-little-tokyo-redevelopment.

Local Fruit Still Life

Daniel Andres Alcazar

Daniel Andres Alcazar (b. 1988, Los Angeles) holds a BA in art history from the University of California, Los Angeles, and an MFA in photography and media from the California Institute of the Arts. Alcazar works with photography, sound, video, and installation.

I am the son of countless generations of working-class people, and my allegiance lies there. In my work, I want to illuminate issues that affect the working class—issues that are not often considered in contemporary art, given the nature of the art market. My goal is not only to create an aesthetic experience but to nudge the viewer to a more critical view of the inequalities around us and, ultimately, to take action.

Each photograph in *Local Fruit Still Life* depicts the same fruits purchased on the same day at each of the four grocery stores near my home in Glassell Park. The project is influenced by secular still life paintings of the sixteenth and seventeenth centuries—specifically, the bodegones of Baroque Spain that depicted pantry objects from everyday life. I'm interested in the Spanish tradition of still life, as opposed to those of Northern Europe, because of its austere tone and its de-emphasis of pleasure and luxury.

Each photograph is titled based on the store and price of the fruit, which raises questions: Why are prices different for the same food? How do corporations cater to specific communities? How do we reconcile mundane, everyday actions and the systems behind them? How can we find beauty in a consumerist and commodified society?

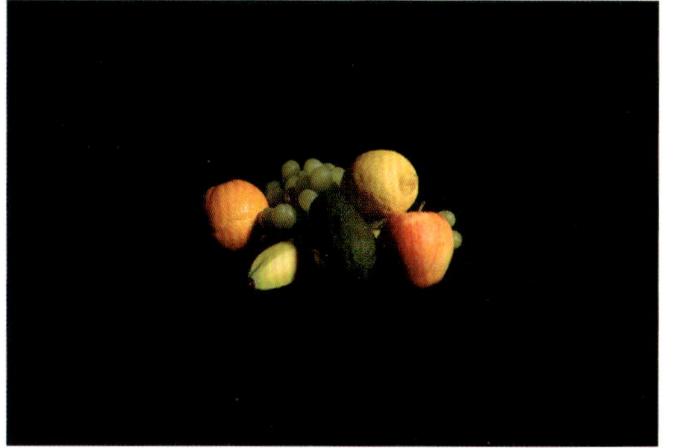

Ralphs, $6.02

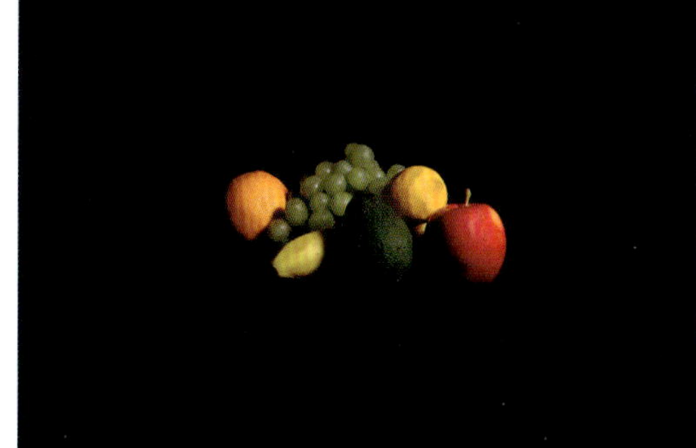

Sprouts, $4.30

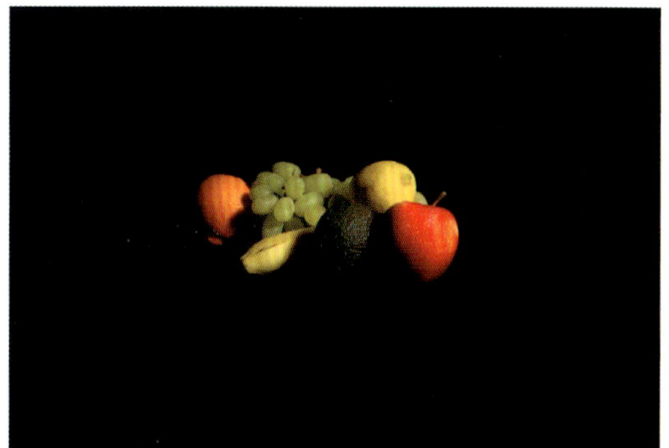

Super A, $4.09

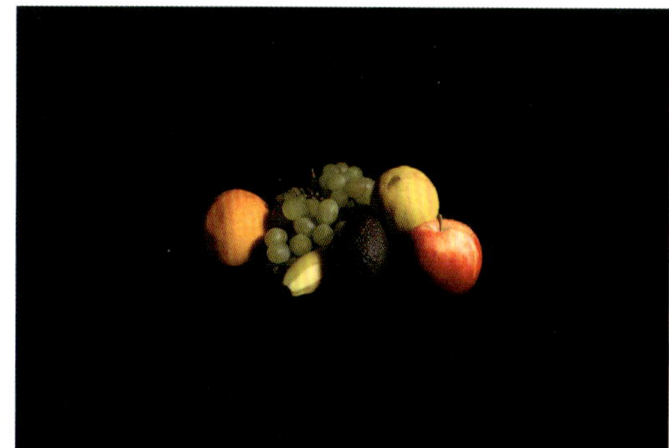

El Super, $3.49

Daniel Andres Alcazar, *Local Fruit Still Life: Ralphs, $6.02; Sprouts, $4.30; Super A, $4.09; El Super, $3.49*, 2019. Digital photograph, 15 × 10 in.

Stage One

ESTABLISHING COMMUNITY

Garrett McQueen

A proud native of Memphis, Tennessee, **Garrett McQueen** has performed as a member of the South Arkansas Symphony, Jackson Symphony, American Youth Symphony, Memphis Repertory Orchestra, the Eroica Ensemble, and, most recently, the Knoxville Symphony Orchestra. Today, Garrett works on radio broadcast and digital stages with nationally syndicated programs.

It was a night that no one would forget—least of all those who were in the Twin Cities, Minnesota. The smoke from businesses set ablaze could be smelled for miles. So-called looting had reached almost every part of the cities. The police had retreated and were nowhere to be found. This is just a glimpse of what the response to the killing of George Floyd looked like, and it would only be the beginning. Since those nights of unrest, the protests (mostly peaceful) have continued, and not just in the streets; local institutions have taken a second look at their relationships with law enforcement, and some have even cut ties altogether! What most would consider the biggest impact is the heightened attention to conversations of race and racial equity. Who facilitated these dialogues? How was such a large, impactful response to a monumental tragedy possible? The answer to those and many other peripheral questions is simple: community. The power of community has been an integral part in moving toward systemic change, and this is something that's already been proven in the world of "classical" music.

For far too long, the unfortunate reality for countless musicians, specifically Black musicians and other musicians of color, has been a lack of community. Being the "only one" in a room can be so much more than just an isolating experience, and without a support system, many have found themselves in situations that are not musically fulfilling but violent and exclusive. This was my reality, until my work led me toward a community.

Once I understood the lived reality of being Black in classical music as a professional bassoonist, I knew there were stories that needed to be told. This inspired my first radio series on the relationship between race and classical music, which featured three Black musicians with whom I would begin cultivating a community. The first of those people was Kelly Hall-Tompkins, a New York City violinist and entrepreneur who has blazed a trail for many other musicians of color by proving that musical excellence and virtuosity sees no color. In addition to founding an organization that brings classical music into underserved spaces, Kelly was Broadway's first Black "fiddler" and has participated in initiatives which trace the history of Black involvement in classical music all the way back to Europe.[1] The two other participants in that series were Alex Laing, principal clarinetist of the Phoenix Symphony and winner of several awards given to those who work at the intersection of music and social justice, and Lecolion Washington, my first bassoon teacher, and a musician who's now dedicated himself to the power of community as the executive director of Boston's Community Music Center. We didn't know it then, but those conversations would evolve into many other conversations that would impact the music field and further cultivate a community of musicians fighting for change.

Part two of the series moved beyond changing the general discourse of classical music and looked at how the actual music could sound. Jeffrey Mc-Neill and Andrea Coln (known professionally as "Thee Phantom" and "The Phoenix," respectively) used social media to build a community of musicians who perform together as the Illharmonic Orchestra. For Jeffrey, the formation of this ensemble has been almost a lifetime in the making. When he was about eight years old, he decided to mix the Beastie Boys' "Paul Revere" with Beethoven's Fifth Symphony. "I had been taking piano and flute lessons at the time," he explained, "so when my father introduced me to hip-hop it sounded like it all fit. At the time I had no idea what I had created or even if I had created something. I just knew that those [were] the sounds that I heard in my head, so I got the idea to mix them. I was excited. I took the tape to my friend's house. Fast forward and now that's what we do."[2]

It wasn't just about creating a community of musicians who loved hip-hop and classical but about engaging a community of audience members who hadn't always been at the center of concert hall programming. This is something that drives Andrea's approach to this work. From the start, she knew that orchestral music could engage more diverse communities of people, but she didn't foresee the pushback that this new approach to the art form would elicit.

"We actually started out working with members of the Philadelphia Orchestra," Andrea recounted in the conversation.

> As you can imagine, the concept of meshing the two genres was really frowned upon. We had a few people who were willing to do it with us because they thought that Jeff was a nice guy. But for the most part we were met with a lot of, you know, side eye, if you will. And really, we were told that we were bastardizing the form of classical music. We had someone who actually kind of threw his sheet music back at us after we did a big performance at the Kimmel Center in Philadelphia. It was not something that classically trained musicians were really open to.

At least, not the community of musicians whom the two initially worked with. With a light shed on this fresh take on the meshing of two seemingly opposing genres, Thee Phantom and The Phoenix have convinced countless audiences that a person *can* be a B-boy who loves Beethoven, and that communities can be enriched by this approach. The Illharmonic Orchestra's Carnegie Hall debut was historic, as it was only the third hip-hop act to headline a show there (after Jay-Z in 2012 and Wyclef Jean in 2001).[3] It enriched not only the hip-hop lovers in the crowd but Carnegie Hall regulars who were curious as to what this type of music could be. The idea of enriching a vaster community through unique performance manifested in an ever bigger way when the Illharmonic Orchestra headlined the New Year's Eve celebrations at the Kennedy Center in 2017. There were obviously people in the audience, dressed in their concert hall best, who didn't know what they were in for when they bought tickets for a show that included the word *orchestra*. After the initial shock of being met with an unapologetically Black art form mixed with symphonic sounds, audience members who were more familiar with the tradition of orchestral music had the opportunity to engage an experience that they otherwise would not have.

The perspective of musicians and performers is vital, but so are the often-overlooked perspectives of those working in the arts behind the scenes. Ariel Elizabeth Shelton (now Ariel Elizabeth Davis) was one of the Kennedy Center's program managers who participated in my three-part feature on race and classical music. When it comes to using music to engage and empower communities, she said, "I just started to produce things on my own.... We all have a lot of responsibility. Institutions have a responsibility to really listen closely to the community wherever possible. If community members are saying that they feel uncomfortable in an orchestral hall, we can't ignore that and then think that we're going to work toward diverse audiences. It's impossible to ignore someone and then cultivate a stronger relationship with them."

The fires in the Twin Cities born from community frustration and distrust of local police may be out, but thanks to vigilant community members, the impact is still burning brightly. Protests have continued, and while they are mostly peaceful, the levels of awareness that they foster continue to spread. Local institutions, including the University of Minnesota, have pledged to no longer contract the Minneapolis Police Department. There has even been a push for more neighborhood collaboration for basic needs, like food and childcare. The same work is happening across communities who are defined not by proximity to one another but by their individual proximity and love for the arts. The musicians who have been inspired by the stories of people like Kelly, Alex, and Lecolion, the audiences who have been entertained by the vision of Thee Phantom and The Phoenix, and the citizens who have been engaged through programs managed by cultural organizers like Ariel don't just represent the fruits of this labor. They represent a community of their own—one that amplifies the work started by an amateur radio host who could have never known where a journey like this could take him.

Establishing, teaching, and empowering communities is only the start—step one, if you will, but a necessary step. The late Coretta Scott King once said, "The greatness of a community is most accurately measured by the compassionate actions of its members." Thanks to arts conversations and content rooted in a desire for change, communities of change makers in the arts have been formed. The compassionate actions of those community members are underway, and the change that will be born from those actions undoubtedly lies ahead.

Notes

1. For media, see Kelly Hall-Tompkins, "The Fiddler Expanding Tradition," Kelly Hall-Tompkins, accessed November 29, 2022, http://www.kellyhall-tompkins.com/fiddler_expanding.html.

2. Garrett McQueen, "Race and Classical Music—Part 2," interview with Jeffrey McNeill and Andrea Coln, Afternoon Concert, WUOT, February 1, 2018, https://www.WUOT.org/arts/2018-02-01/race-and-classical-music-part-2?_amp=true.

3. For media, see "Illharmonic Orchestra Media," Thee Phantom Hip-Hop, accessed November 29, 2022, http://www.theephantomhiphop.com/media.

Red 40

Jazmín Urrea

Jazmín Urrea is a visual artist working in installation, photography, video, sculpture, and performance. Urrea's works have been exhibited at the Studio Museum in Harlem, Getty Museum, and galleries across the United States. She recently received the Rema Hort Mann Foundation Emerging Artist Grant and is based in South Los Angeles, California.

I grew up and currently live in an area formerly known as South Central LA. Most consider South LA to be a disadvantaged area, a food desert, and the "hood." But in reality, South LA is a cluster of communities, and it is the place that I call home. My home influences me. It forms my identity and practice, and it serves as subject matter and inspiration.

In *Red 40*, I explore the lack of access to fresh food faced by underserved communities and the health risks posed by artificial dyes and additives. Without healthier edible alternatives, neighborhoods are polluted daily by additives such as FD&C Red No. 40, FD&C Yellow No. 6, and many others. Growing up, I witnessed the effects of obesity, hypertension, and other illnesses in my family, friends, and myself. I created this project because the junk foods I was consuming led to my hospitalization, appendectomy, and poor health.

Red 40 was vital for me to make because it allowed me to address food insecurity on a larger scale. Through this project, I expanded my practice, started a dialogue, and began a platform for awareness and change with members of my community.

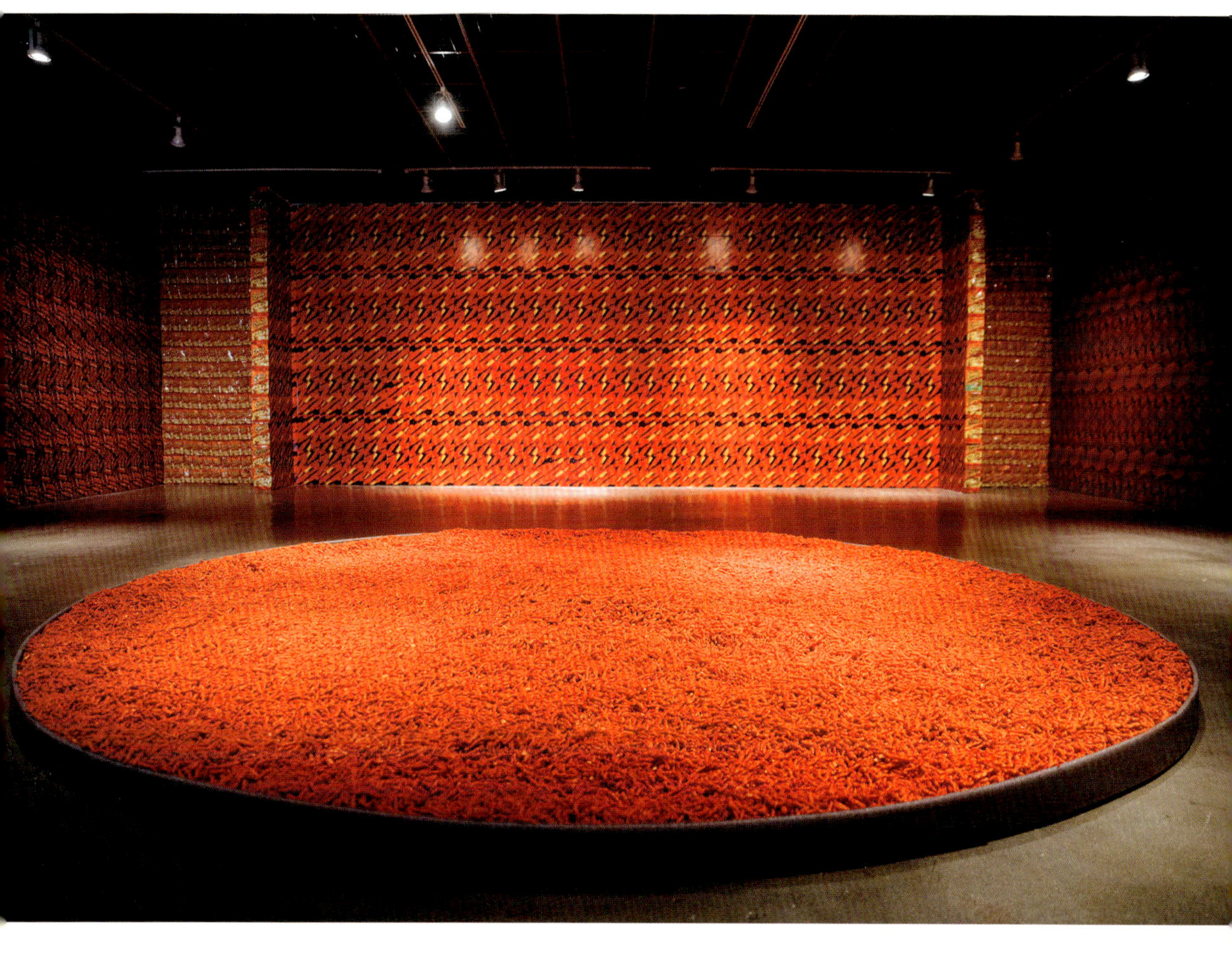

Jazmín Urrea, *Red 40*, 2017. Installation view, Flamin' Hot Cheetos, Flamin' Hot Cheetos bags, Xerox prints of Rellerindos, Jabalina, and Dedos. Gallery D301, California Institute of the Arts, Valencia, California.

More Nodes from the Performance Essay
Los Giros De La Siguiente/ the turns of the Next

Devin Kenny

Devin Kenny is an artist, writer, musician, and independent curator. Their work centers around products and processes of the African Diaspora in the Americas with a particular focus on the aesthetics of network culture before and after the advent of the internet. Kenny is a graduate of Cooper Union and received a Master of Fine Arts degree in 2013 from UCLA.

They can't take away your house if it's your *house*.
They can't take away the neighborhood if it's *yours*.

I asked "What about gentrification?" he said "They rented."

I moved to Houston. 3rd Ward. I turned down an apartment that would
choose me over the various refugees created by Hurricane Harvey.

I turned down an apartment that had a clause saying wearing baggy pants
or no shirt, even if in your home, was possible grounds for eviction.
I had the privilege to wait it out.

In "the Tre," Black homeowners are being pushed out monthly and annually as property taxes soar.
They can take away your house even if it's your house.
They can take away the neighborhood even if it's yours.

An oversimplification of the timeline: Indigenous peoples steward the land;[1]
white settlers attempt eradication and erasure of these peoples through

violent removal, the introduction of disease, and cultural "integration"; the settlers and their offspring claim ownership and redevelop the land; and finally the Tre becomes the home of one or more marginalized peoples, but largely Black Americans because of the city of Houston's segregationist policies. One jewel of the neighborhood was Emancipation Park, the oldest park in Houston, and the oldest in Texas. From 1922 to 1940 it was the only park available to Black Houstonians. I lived down the street.

A bustling capitalist economy would grow in this area; that would not be forever, though, and eventually the area would be deemed "in need of urban renewal" and nearly never receive it from outside, only from the ones that lived there and raised families, held businesses. The mythic American self-reliance in action: community interdependence.

Looking back, I could reinterpret what I was told in a "home is where the heart is" kind of way, but I think he was insinuating that without owner-ship, nothing in this country is truly held. I think even with ownership, for significant swaths of the population, nothing in this place is truly held—whether we are referring to racial covenants that would restrict Black citi-zens, or hateful white mobs that would create sundown towns, or destroy prosperous Black communities in Tulsa, Oklahoma; Rosewood, Florida; and elsewhere. To extend it further, how can one own land or lay claim to it, when the machinations that allowed the philosophical and governmen-tal shifts are tied to broken promises and stolen lives?

> *Confusion is bitter—Have a nice day—*
> *When using the shitter—Please use the spray—*
> *Or light a match(rimony)—Paying the debt to a bachelorette—*
> *Plastered with sweat—Hop on a pony with Ike and Tina—*
> *My cough is phony—My emphysema—*
> *Little old ladies and African surfers from Pasadena—*
> *Pass through Medina—*
> *After the cheetah has captured a zebra, and laughing hyenas are happy and*
> *   mean it—*
> *They're clapping their hands—They're stomping their feet—*
> *Me and myself and the family meet—*
> *They like my roommates—*
> *And my new place—And my garage—Pick my padlock—*
> *In my flip-flops—*
> *Don't even knock—*
> *Open the door—She used to snore—Now she does not.*
> —Radioinactive and Antimc, "Movin' Truck"
> (*Free Kamal*, Mush Records, 2004)

OOOOOOOOHHH! PWN'D!

What does it mean for the rhetoric of "America as a nation of immigrants" to be pushed forward, when there are significant portions of the population for whom that is not the case? These include people whose lineages have been altered permanently by the Maafa and the many peoples whose heritages are intimately connected to those indigenous to the continent. Given, many members of these populations also have some recent ancestors of European descent, too—by force, or not—which should push us even further from binary thinking. Still, to forefront that aforementioned aspect over others is white supremacist and deleterious to growth.

What does it mean for the histories of immigrants, some of whom came fleeing religious persecution, some who came seeking personal wealth which they were perhaps barred from in their prior countries of origin, some who came punitively, and still others who came seeking a place in a country that economically or politically repressed their homeland, coming home to roost so to speak . . . for all these various impeti to be flattened? Who gets to be an expat? Whose patriotism gets read as un-American? *Immigration* and *migration* as terms are about movement, but they are far too open to provide effective cover.

bracing yourself

dancing

kicking

rubbing

walking

sleeping

grinding

cartwheeling

breathing

grappling

stretching

blinking

punching

stepping up

and smizing

are all movement too.

"We are a nation of immigrants" is an update to the "melting pot" metaphor, which referred to new aspiring Americans of European descent in the United States who were encouraged to assimilate to the frame of whiteness and whose power was wielded by Anglo-Saxon Protestants primarily for the material benefit of the landowning men among them, but with psychic ramifications rippling through every tier.[2] The melting pot categorically excluded those who would later be called People of Color. "A nation of immigrants" as a summation does not function in the same way, but it still doesn't do the due diligence or the right thing.

> cumbe
> cambio
> combien ça coûte?
> kombination
> cumbia, (cambio) change, how much:
> what truths come from a false cognate?
> *Cumbia is a latinization of cumbe, a word of Bantu origin referring to dance.*

I began thinking of cumbia as the music of the Americas, one which is founded on an encounter of West and Central African–derived music cultures, infused with Indigenous instruments, along with a splash of European poetics and scales in there also, though not privileging a white gaze. In the current climate, with the continued rampant violence against Black people of all ages, genders, religions, sexual orientations, and neurological statuses, where Black, Indigenous, and Latine people are being incarcerated and brought to harm with US tax dollars, the emblem and history of this music struck me, though not because it's the only form of resistance.

Still, there are the things made in the crevices, in the in-between times, the births, deaths, rites of passage et cetera, and living well is the best revenge. West African rhythms and structures, Indigenous melodies and woodwinds, a West African courtship dance combined with Spanish formalities and affect, Indigenous melodies and organizing principles of two continents forced into Western notation, plus accordions thanks to the legendary Andrés Landero, as well as electric guitars, keyboards and drum machines, and vocal processing and data; new audiences were introduced to the sounds by Selena, still more by Shakira a generation later, and so many more. Not a smelting process, but an uneven admixture: a combination, syncretism, creolizing, coexisting if possible, and resisting and creating alternatives when the latter is a . . .

And I feel some kind of kinship with and hope to honor those who continue on in the work of others. I had a world studies and US history teacher who posited this country as a stew instead of a melting pot. That seems like a utopia, but we can experience it in spoonfuls. So long as we don't accept tastes as the full thing, we should be good.

[cue Mortal Kombat Kotal Kahn vs Jax Fatalities video montage]

[sung]

Parody will sting all the more because the heart was in the right place.
And yet there are still common struggles and ones slow to go away.

Like *cumbia*, hip-hop too is syncretic, but with a history arguably further away from the slave trade (though there were instances of Black people sharecropping in the United States even into the 1960s, segregation, and peonage that were based largely on the anti-Black policies of the slavery period). US descendants of enslaved Africans and Afro-Caribbeans of Jamaica and Puerto Rico drew influence from the sound system tradition, postwar music culture, and the dominance of vinyl; drew electricity, plugging into lampposts to power the party, using city money, flattening packaging for material goods into a dance floor, making a temporary home into a dance floor, making a temporary autonomous zone of a dance floor, making a discursive space of a dance floor wherever it may be; trying to curve skirmishes, hip-hop as the work song for a city in decline, that ran out of jobs for people like you, a music made by people seeking a better life and being rewarded with a ghetto, a music for a generation that just-missed the optimism of their parents, first out the gate, and this vehicle mutated and adapted to every place it touched, leaving the NY metro area and traveling all across the country and eventually the globe.

"While blues obsesses over the theme of mobility, hip-hop is as local as a zip code."[3] He [William Jelani Cobb] continued: "In hip-hop . . . railroads have been replaced by another central reference: the city. Or, more specifically, the fractured territories known collectively as the Ghetto. Innumerable hip-hop songs reference the term [and] all allude to a socioeconomic blind alley, a terrain defined by the lack of mobility of its residents. Scarface—formerly of the Geto Boys—underscores this point on the single 'On My Block,' where he rhymes, 'It's like the rest of the world don't exist/We stay confined to the same spot we been livin' in.'"[4]

(illegible header)

1. Back tha Ass Up (Juvy)
2. Rosa Parks (Outkast)
3. Range Rover (Pokey)
4. Throw Yo Hands Up (8 Ball & MJG)
5. Geto Stars (C-Note)
6. Thats tha Nigga (Mystikal)
7. Break Ups 2 Make Ups (Method)
8. Ballin' Parlay (Pokey)
9. Belly (8 Ball & MJG)
10. Too Hot (Hot Boys)
11. Spottie Ottie Dopaliscious (Outkast)
12. EPGH (Cool Breeze)
13. Like Some Hoe's (Geto Boys)
14. Stuntin' (Big Tymers)
15. Murda 4 Life (Ja Rule)
16. Street Talkin (Slick Rick)
17. Go Deep (Janet Jackson)
18. ~~Favor 4 a Favor~~ (Nas) Game Is Strange (Southcide)
19. Playas Holliday (T.W.D.Y.)
20. Playas Get Chose (Lil O')

Steve

In Houston, I delved into the legend of Robert Earl Davis Jr., better known as DJ Screw, a producer and turntablist, responsible for popularizing an audio manipulation technique whose influence is still heard today across various genres.[5] For his sprawling, psychedelic live sessions, slate-gray Maxell cassette tape was the recording medium of choice. I was fascinated by lists like the above, and stories of people coming up to Screw's house at all hours seeking mixes, with cars wrapped around the block. Coming with requests and returning fulfilled, expectations far exceeded, as it wouldn't just be the songs they wanted, but also other songs to contextualize, paths they may not have thought to draw. This is what algorithms try to do today, but there was accountability there, not just metrics. Before the first Screwed Up Records and Tapes, people would get music hand-to-hand, from car trunks at functions, and at DJ Screw's own home. At some point there was a police raid because law enforcement presumed he must have been selling drugs to have cars lined up around the block at all times of the day. I saw this event as a node, a singular instance in the history of Black networks, again resulting in a disrupted connection.

Hip-hop dance crews and Black American street gangs in the 1960s and 1970s were two approaches to a shared set of problems. The year 2019 marked the one hundredth anniversary of what James Weldon Johnson called the Red Summer. That year also marked the fiftieth anniversary of the Stonewall Rebellion, initiated in large part by Marsha P. Johnson and further supported by S.T.A.R. and others. Finally, it also marked the twentieth anniversary of the WTO battle in Seattle. The throughline of connections here is the role police played in repressing members of the community whose ideologies, identities, or combination of the two were seen as a threat to the way things were, their very survival throwing into question the way things are.

There is another node: understanding that cumbia has become a vehicle for many diasporas, that it is built off of a foundational encounter of the Americas as we know it today. Perhaps one can find in it a model to be built out in ways it had not been before. The legacies of redlining paralleled drawn borders, displacement, forced or coerced migration, the barrio, the ghetto, colonia, economic corridors, neighborhoods, genres, parties, parties. If the music has stories in Spanish, in lyrical poetics, it also builds on the African call-and-response forms, the social conditions that push the music, indeed all culture, to create a call to action. How do we respond?

Law is malleable to some extent, expansive in how it can contract the life possibilities of those punished by it. We cannot forget that apartheid was legal, as were slavery, segregation, antimiscegenation laws, laws preventing Black people from owning property or even merely congregating (see: the bombing of Black Wall Street, the MOVE bombing in Philadelphia, early twentieth-century "race riots" in Chicago and across the country, the uphill legal battle manifesting in the Loving generation). The restrictions unduly set have been influential on Black culture in myriad ways, not only from the development of distinctive religious, intellectual, and artistic networks (bell hooks speaks in depth about this in terms of education, James Baldwin in terms of religion, and the legacies of the Harlem Renaissance, Art Ensemble of Chicago, Native Tongues clique, Teklife, Hieroglyphics Imperium, the Soulquarians, Quannum, and others speak to artistic, literary, and musical sides of this equation), but also we cannot forget that a major influence in urban gang culture is the marauding mobs of white people disrupting Black businesses and livelihood, a state of being virtually ignored by the white police officers who legally are sworn to serve and protect the citizenry. What was once on the books later became de facto. The coda of Steve McQueen's *12 Years a Slave* includes an anecdote about Solomon Northup attempting to get legal recompense (as he was a freeman, illegally forced into servitude and immense physical, psychological, and emotional distress for over a decade). He could not legally testify against a white man.

In thinking about the notion of "the law of the land" and the irony of certain laws falling harder on particular peoples of "the land" than others, laws of protection that can only be called upon by some peoples and not others have been a recurrent phenomenon.

The American Dream is not allowed to be pursued by all people.

[Cue video of Patricia Okoumou on the Statue of Liberty from newscast]
[Cue song: dkyk, "Eres Mi Todo"]

Throw the past like milk splashes poured in air over eyelashes
Throw the past like orange straps tossed overhead of their bronze assets
Tarda un Swipe en conocerte
y solo un dia en enamorarme
Pero me × 3 llevará toda una vida poder olvidarte
estado pensando en ti
Pienso en ti todo el tiempo y
Solo puedo pensar en ti
Eres mi todo.—You are my everything. You are my everything.

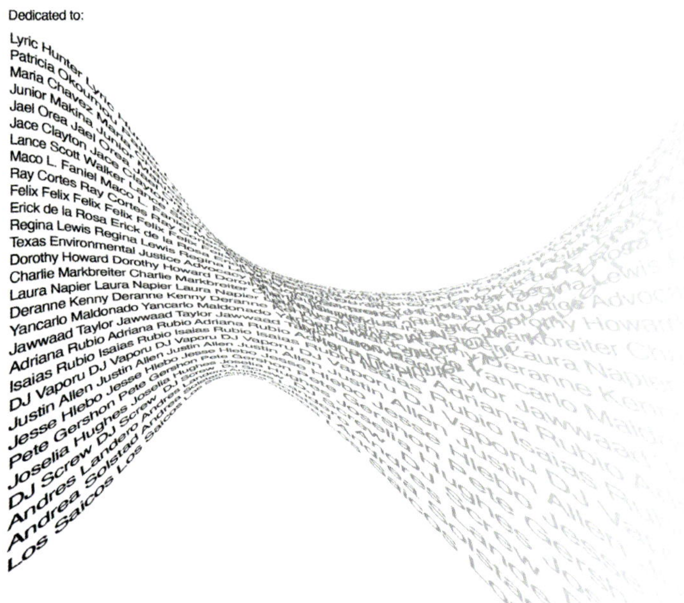

[Cue song: DJ Screw, "My Mind Went Blank"]

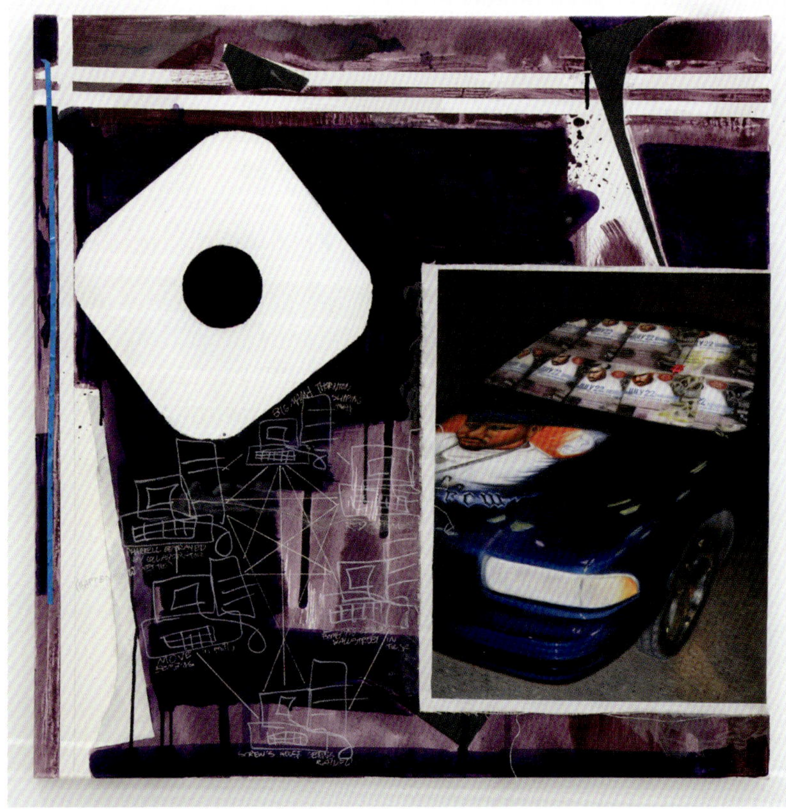

PART 1

Notes

1. Including Ishak, Karankawa, Esto'K Gna (Carrizo/Comecrudo), Sana, and Coahuiltecan peoples.

2. Barack Obama, "Remarks by the President in Address to the Nation on Immigration," White House Office of the Press Secretary, November 20, 2014, https://obamawhitehouse.archives.gov/the-press-office/2014/11/20/remarks -President-address-nation-immigration.

3. Maco L. Faniel, "Introduction," in *Hip-Hop in Houston: The Origin and the Legacy* (Charleston, SC: History Press, 2013), 6–7.

4. Faniel, "Introduction."

5. DJ Screw received the nickname because, while working on mixes, he would be found dragging a screw across the grooves of vinyl records he couldn't use, destroying the record's ability to be played normally again.

(opposite) Devin Kenny, *Black Networks*, 2018.
Acrylic, oil, and mixed media on canvas, 36 × 36 in.

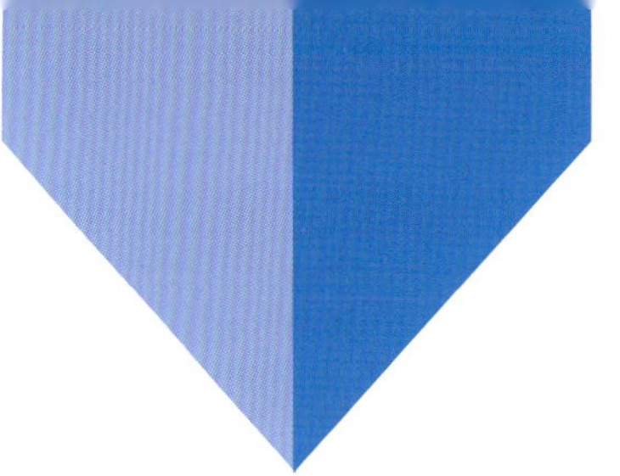

PART 2

DISMANTLING BORDERS, BUILDING BRIDGES

MIGRATION AND DIASPORAS

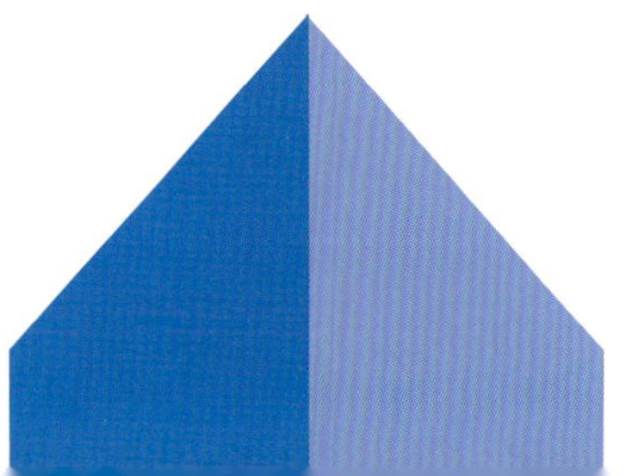

Introduction

Sarah Sophia Yanni

....

Sarah Sophia Yanni is a Mexican Egyptian writer, educator, and editor. She is the author of the chapbook *ternura / tenderness* (Bottlecap Press) and was a finalist for *bomb Magazine*'s 2020 Poetry Contest, Poetry Online's 2021 Launch Prize, and the *Hayden's Ferry Review* Inaugural Poetry Contest. She is managing editor of *TQR* and lives in Los Angeles.

....

> I am among the millions of people who are forced to
> reckon with what it means to reconnect to a motherland.
> Am I a sun or a planet? The moon that pulls the tide
> or a buoy that drifts between landmasses?
>
> —**Vinhay Keo,** interdisciplinary artist and researcher,
> Los Angeles, California

The vibrant diasporic communities peppered across the United States speak to the persistence of migration and to the strength of cultural ties, insistent on continuing even amid challenges. These challenges, too, persist in various iterations, encouraged by a rhetoric of fear. All too quickly, and with great fervor, we have witnessed how those in positions of privilege and power, or even those who have historically struggled at the bottom of the economic ladder, grasp desperately onto a self-destructive dichotomy: *us versus them.* It is a dichotomy so strongly embedded in their minds that steps toward racial justice and economic equality are translated as a threat, some sort of impending doom to rupture the postcolonial status quo.

How does a diasporic community respond to this? Artistry, perhaps, is one pathway to sense making; it is a vessel for geographic and identitarian reflection. It's also an entry point to remembering countries abroad—those mother/father lands whose echoes reside in the displaced body.

In this remembering, strength and resilience are conjured. So, too, are grief and loss. Migration does not end with a settling down, and once "settled," American imperialism continually wields its force, repurposing the same dynamics of power and capital that are often used abroad to "improve" the third world. In the United States, these imperial systems work to create stark divisions between winners and losers, belonging and nonbelonging. For migrant communities operating in this context, movement, negotiation, and sacrifice are constant—the push and pull of here and there, self and ancestry, holding on to memory in order to survive.

The writing in this section calls upon those memories, the sometimes nonoptional journey of leaving one's homeland, and the way contemporary language shapes the systems we land in. It also disrupts existing categorization, relying on data to propose a new understanding of what it means to be *other*. Journalist **Jose Antonio Vargas** presents us with a critical question: *Who is the emerging US?* Using demographic information, he reorients our understanding of minority and majority in America, reminding us that "the emerging US is more multiethnic, more immigrant, more colorful, than ever before." An imagined future in which bodies of color are dominant is no longer a fantasy; it is a societal shift that will be realized. Vargas also urges that, at this moment, the "survival of this emerging America requires that we see each other more fully and more humanely." This mode of recognition can spring from a concept as simple as increased empathy— through a mutual understanding that every individual carries a past. Painter and Iraqi refugee **Hayv Kahraman** begins her essay recounting moments when such treatment was not the case: "I've always felt 'dirtier' than my Swedish schoolmates, both in image (as in the way I look) and in experience (as in the way I feel). Foreign, dirty, filthy and impure. Contaminated." Through personal recollection and epidemiological research, Kahraman's essay investigates the intersections of military, medical, and bodily language, calling for an ongoing examination of how we situate difference. Also considering the intergenerational traumas of war is **Christine Her**, who offers readers a text that is both critical and personal, grounded in the ripples of her father's experience as a teenage soldier in Laos. She recalls the rifts between herself and her immigrant parents growing up, and how challenging but ultimately necessary pursuing artistry was in such a context: "To me, art was liberating. It was a way to overcome the pain I felt internally without hurting myself physically. Art was a language I understood."

Continuing this interrogation of language and inheritance, **Yosimar Reyes** and **Vinhay Keo** expand the lens of cultural diaspora toward a queer intersectionality. Reyes, informed by his status as an undocumented artist, pushes back against narratives of arrival, challenging societal expectations surrounding the "good immigrant." He insists on embracing an undocumented rhetoric that makes room for variance and thriving. Keo's writing is largely located postarrival and unpacks the lingering of intergenerational trauma, as well as how it manifests itself through art. Stemming from his own experience as a Cambodian American immigrant, he traces his body of work and proposes new methods of queer futurity. Furthering our understanding of violence against queer bodies, Dreamer and photographer **J Molina-Garcia** considers collective grief through his hybrid text, largely inspired by José Esteban Muñoz and his notion of "brown feelings." Molina-Garcia looks at the contemporary recurrence of violence against brown bodies, including events like the Pulse nightclub shooting in Orlando, and prompts readers to reflect on communal mourning, mimicry in artwork, and our affective responses to ongoing pain.

But what does it mean to look beyond violence? Is that even possible? What do we do with these diasporic histories, and how do we rupture them in order to create something new? Speaking to these inquiries, **Evelyn Hang Yin, Pamela J. Peters,** and **Rebecca Mwase** bridge past and present in their respective texts. Writing from the point of view of both an artist and an international Chinese student in America, Hang Yin looks at histories of colonialism to address both anti-Blackness and anti-Chinese sentiment against the current global backdrop of COVID-19. Recognizing that the past is never truly past, she searches for the "wandering spirits" of early Chinese immigrants to the US West Coast, and these encounters are what create the impetus for art making. Similarly, Navajo photographer Pamela J. Peters thinks about the overlap of healing, art, and heritage. Walking readers through Los Angeles's Indian Alley, she delves into the history of United American Indian Involvement, the largest provider of human and health services for American Indians/Alaska Natives living in the county of Los Angeles. It is a story of pervasive struggle, but it is also one of joy—an ethos similarly reflected in *Vessels*, a "seven-woman harmonic meditation on the transcendental possibilities of song during the Middle Passage." Producer and creator Rebecca Mwase, in conversation with performers from *Vessels*, addresses diasporic modes of belonging, asking, "What does it mean to communicate across distance?" They arrive at an answer that contains multiplicities—while diaspora makes room for the intrinsic and ancestral knowledge that is stored within our bodies to arise, it also unleashes "the grief that comes with constant change." Operating beyond constraints, it is art that ultimately serves as a tangible vehicle for community building, within and across national divides.

Poetry from **Belise Nishimwe** as well as art from **Silvi Naçi**, **Njideka Akunyili Crosby**, and **Rosalie López** shine as testaments to this statement and remind readers of the complex and remarkable thinking that immigrants enact. Nishimwe's poem "Fence," which won the ArtChangeUS Youth Speaks Poetry Contest, is grounded in her early childhood in a Tanzanian refugee camp. Now a US citizen and attending Washington University in St. Louis, Nishimwe aims to "create a platform that gives a voice to immigrants and refugees and the representation they need." Representing her own journey from Nigeria to the United States, Crosby's *Harmattan Haze* combines the domesticity of a Nigerian immigrant home with references to classical Western art history. Crosby sees this layering as a way to "invent a new visual language that represents my experience—which at times feels paradoxically fractured and whole—as a cosmopolitan Nigerian." She aims to expand the audience's generalizations about the African or diasporic experience, creating kinship with many others in this section who aim to interrogate cultural assumptions and preset understandings of the role that migrant communities play. Naçi's *building bricks for communal healing* began during the 2016 presidential election, springing from moments in Naçi's studio, drinking tea with friends, attempting to process the political realities of our time. As a nod to their family's army backpacks found in archived photos, Naçi began to fold these used tea bags into a similar shape, creating monuments not only to the Albanian immigrant community but to historical forms of gathering and healing. López's artwork blends traditional Mexican and contemporary experimental methods of art making. Responding to iconic religious imagery, López's work is a perfect example of an intergenerational object—art that reinterprets the past without losing it, paying homage to what came before and reinscribing it into the present's changing conditions. Immigrant art, specifically through the experience of cross-border citizenry, is deeply interrogated through **Teddy Cruz** and **Fonna Forman**'s text as well, which recounts their research-based architectural and political practice along the Tijuana–San Diego border region. They remind us that by looking at the unique microcosms of border cities, we can be immersed in community-based knowledge, radical survival strategies, and counternarratives, pushing our understanding of cultures and the vitality of the stories we tell.

Confronting both rhetorical and bodily violence, migrant communities reimagine maps and borders; they show us the ways in which traditions and language are porous. The writing in this section lives in that in-between arena and both celebrates and grieves culture. It investigates the ways in which the othered body takes up space and sits with the reality of the often oppressive pushback. It recalls cultural and family traditions, and ultimately looks at the way that artists bring these to the forefront, in ways that perhaps only artists can.

Mano Poderosa

Rosalie López

Rosalie López is from the Harbor area of Los Angeles, California. She creates artwork that blends influences from her family and Chicanx history with kitsch memorabilia, papel picado, and representations of Day of the Dead offerings. López has an MFA in printmaking from Indiana University and a BFA in graphic design and printmaking from CSU Long Beach.

Mano Poderosa mixes traditional and contemporary art-making methods and references the iconic religious kitsch imagery of *La Mano Mas Poderosa* (The most powerful hand). The artwork is a progressive response to an earlier artwork I created called *Her Hands Remind Us*, which used an aged and weathered hand and referenced the milagro charm of the Heart in Hand. To show the resulting impact on the younger generations, I depict a sprouting plant coming from the center finger.

The artwork was created in two phases. First, the hand, a replica of my own hand, was printed at La Ceiba Gráfica (Coatepec, Veracruz, Mexico) by hand using a traditional Mexican marble lithography process. The cutout portions and three-dimensional components were then created at TEG (El Taller de Experimentación Gráfica), which is an experimental print lab in Mexico City.

The combination of old lithographic printing and new laser cutting happening in the artwork echoes the conversation happening between this reimagined interpretation of the traditional and familiar and the impact of elder generations on the younger generations.

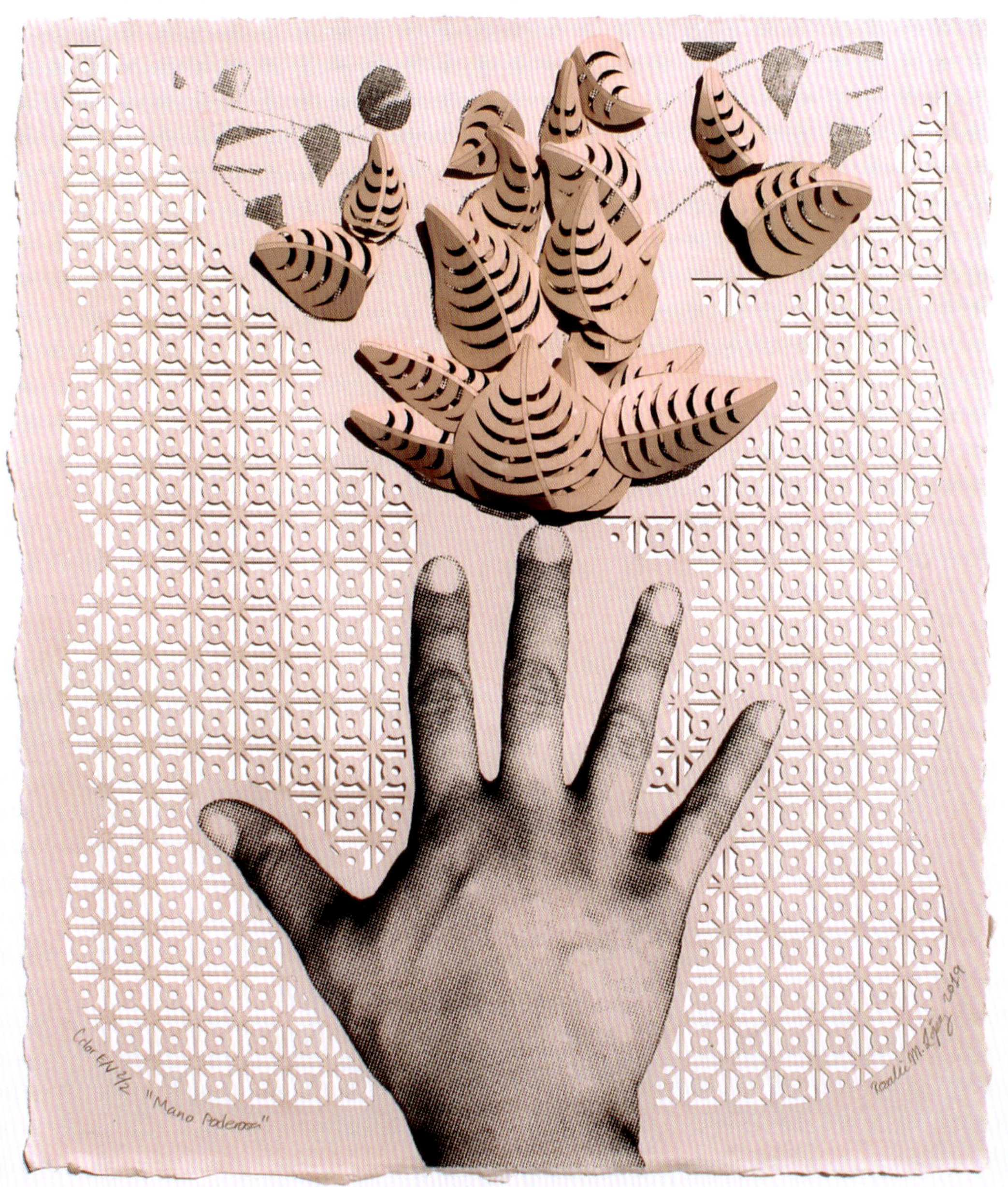

Rosalie López, *Mano Poderosa (Pink)*, 2019. Lithograph with laser cutouts on handmade kozo paper, 19 × 24 in.

A Cosmos of Dis/Joints

Vinhay Keo

Vinhay Keo is an interdisciplinary artist and researcher who operates within various media including photography, video, installation, performance, sculpture, and writing. His work interrogates the hauntological framework of historical residue— the effects of intergenerational trauma—from the Vietnam War, Khmer Rouge genocide, French colonialism in Indochina, and queer temporality.

After the 1979 fall of the Khmer Rouge regime, a radical communist party that enacted a harrowing genocide claiming 1.7 million lives—21 percent of the population in Cambodia at the time[1]—the surviving members of my family were flung apart; some remained in the country, while others fled to refugee camps in Thailand. My great-aunt and uncle are among those who fled. In the early 1980s, aided by the International Center of Kentucky's church sponsorship program, they resettled in Bowling Green, Kentucky, as refugees. Despite the presence of distinct diasporic Cambodian communities in the United States today (Long Beach, California; Lowell, Massachusetts; Minneapolis, Minnesota; etc.), the initial policy of the US government aimed to disperse the first wave of the Cambodian refugee population.[2] This policy played a crucial role in how my family landed in the South, far from other established Cambodian communities in the United States. My great-aunt and uncle were forced to assimilate into their new way of life. A continent and an ocean apart from their homeland, they built their lives in Kentucky and became a community lifeline for other Cambodian refugees who wanted to relocate. They were the thread that tugged my mother to later immigrate with her two children in 2004, a re-threading of our torn family connection. My existence, like others who traversed before me, is a byproduct of a violent history, birthed into a viciously imperialistic framework, born outside, raised inside. The United

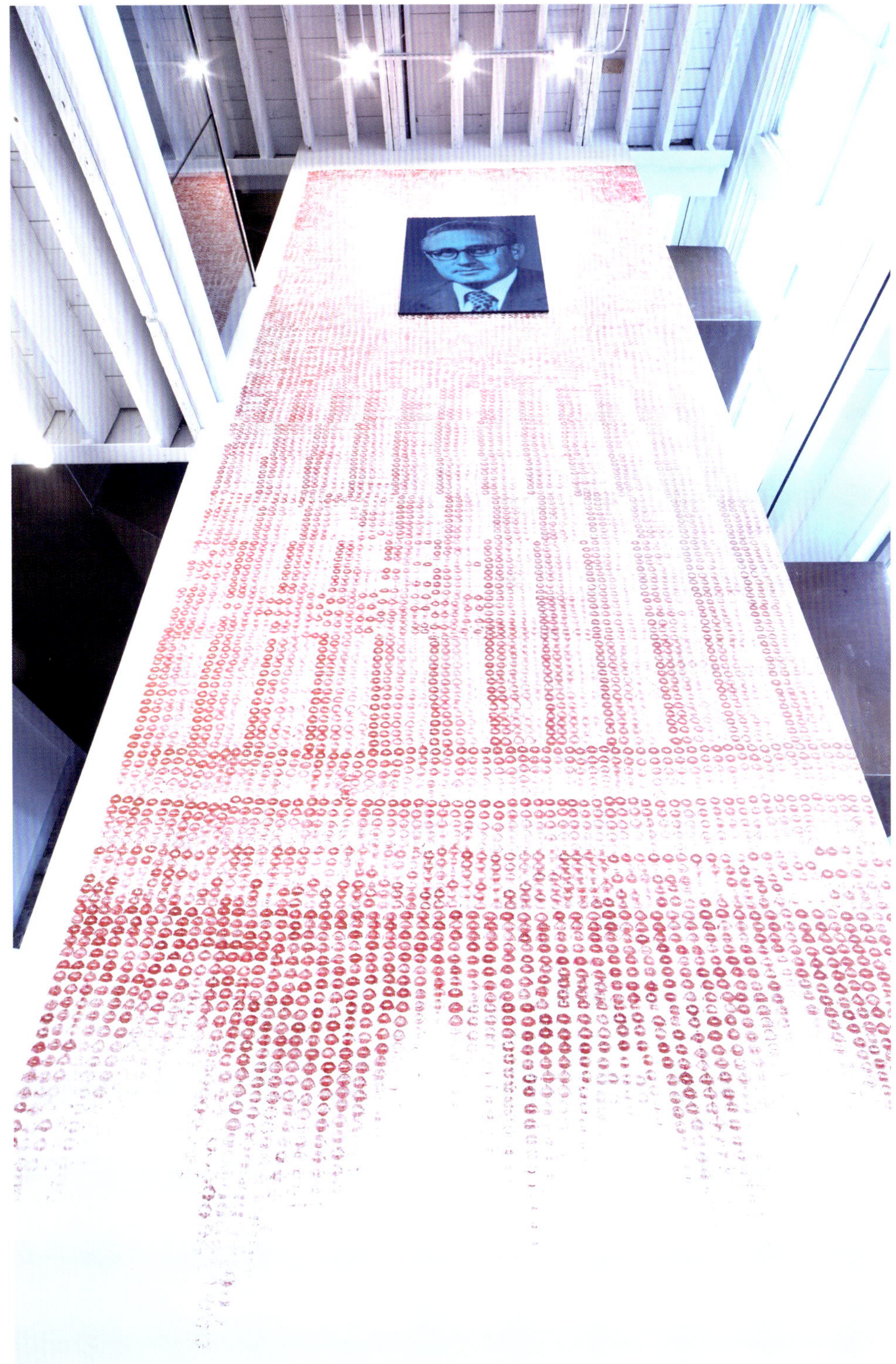

Vinhay Keo, *Kissing Kissinger (Portrait of a Nobel Peace Prize Winner)*, 2019. Performance installation of kiss marks applied to a wall, installation view, KMAC Museum, Louisville. Acrylic paint, inkjet print, 10 × 27 ft. Photo: Ted Wathen.

States is an empire that is built from historical residues—the entangled effects of generational trauma.

Inundated by the specter of violence, my interdisciplinary studio art practice harnesses historical materiality and situates sites of encounter within a perceived dis/joint/ness. Through a liminal identity as an immigrant, a Cambodian American, and a queer person, I examine the legacy of the Khmer Rouge genocide, Vietnam War, French colonialism in Indochina, and queer temporality. These histories are forces that dictate my world—ruptures that become gravitational pulls, a tethering for the displaced. This is how lives are trans/form/port/ed, how satellite communities arise, how Cambodia Town exists in Long Beach, California, and how a Cambodian kid came to grow up in the southern United States.

I am an interdisciplinary visual artist, performer, and researcher, and my work is a constellation that inquires into the state of hauntology, a concept coined by Jacques Derrida in *Spectres de Marx*.[3] Unlike its near-homophone *ontology*, hauntology replaces "the priority of being and presence with the figure of the ghost as that which is neither present nor absent, neither dead nor alive."[4] My artistic practice employs a Samsarian approach, a cyclical strategy that harnesses residual forces, in order to create a channel to/from/within marginality.

> When they ask you
>   where you're from,
> tell them your name
>   was fleshed from the toothless mouth
>   of a war-woman.
> That you were not born
>   but crawled, headfirst—
> into the hunger of dogs. My son, tell them
>   the body is a blade that sharpens
>   by cutting.[5]

The body as a container, an intra-vessel that harbors intergenerational knowledge, is a source of the materiality found within my performance work. In 2019 I began ចិត្តធ្ងន់ *(heavy feelings)*, an ongoing collaborative performance piece where I carry my mother on my back while she recounts anecdotes of her life during the Khmer Rouge genocide. Our backdrop is the sprawling bluegrass landscape of Kentucky. Her body stacked on mine, an entangled intimacy, induced by a childlike gesture to reconnect the generational loss, from genocide and from assimilation. Our bodies are dis/placed into a strangely un/familiar setting, and we are forced to confront a history that un/binds us. The work lives in the format of a video

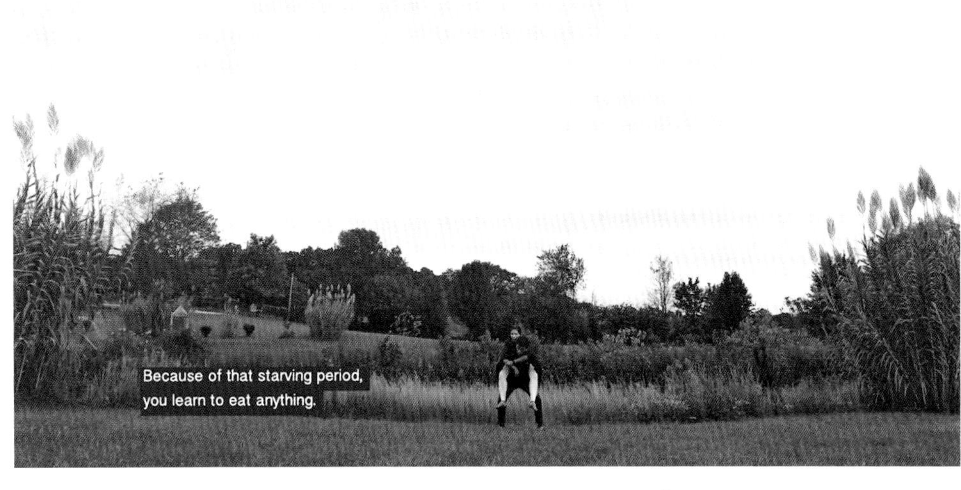

Vinhay Keo, still from ចិត្តធ្ងន់ *(heavy feelings)*, 2019. High-definition video, with sound, 11:25 min. Subtitle: "Because of that starving period, you learn to eat anything."

installation, a familial archive as anecdotal evidence to fill in the gaps caused by erasure. The wide shot frames the viewers within a fixed distance to the subjects and creates space for the audience to address the em/a/pathy upon encountering horror in mundanity. The task of confronting historical trauma demands a dissipation of individual burden and transfers it into a notion of carriance—a connection between caring and carrying, a responsibility of wit(h)nessing.[6]

Time and labor in relation to the body is another crucial element to engaging with history. In the 2019 piece *Kissing Kissinger (Portrait of a Nobel Peace Prize Winner)*, I created an installation of kiss marks applied to a multistory wall with a portrait of Henry Kissinger looming over. Henry Kissinger, President Nixon's national security advisor and recipient of the Nobel Peace Prize in 1973, led a series of bombing raids (1970–73) blanketing Cambodia, where Vietcong troops were hiding, in an all-out effort to end the Vietnam War.[7] Historians Ben Kiernan and Taylor Owen estimate that the bombings killed between 50,000 and 150,000 innocent people in Cambodia.[8] The seemingly endless kiss marks are incorporated into a visually monolithic motif that illustrates both the atrocity of war and the absurdity of awarding a war criminal. A kiss mark, a gendered construct, also serves as a femme gesture that pierces through patriarchal structure and pulls back the veil on a violent history. The work interrogates the power imbalance between those who are remembered and those who are erased from society.

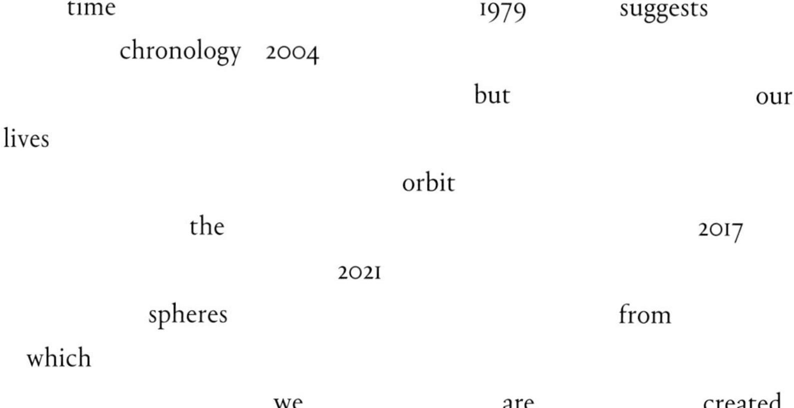

My great-aunt and uncle, along with my immediate family, are establishing the first, second, and so on generations of Cambodian Americans in Kentucky, while my extended family remains in Cambodia. My mom, brother, and I returned to Cambodia for the first time in 2017, nearly fourteen years after our uprooting. I am among the millions of people who are forced to reckon with what it means to reconnect to a motherland. Am I a sun or a planet? The moon that pulls the tide or a buoy that drifts between landmasses?

I am born into a/an un/binding, a life of un/doing and un/learning, a stage of genocidal history that nearly eradicated the practitioners, artists, musicians, dancers, and so on of the Cambodian cultural canon. I am a queer Cambodian American artist and researcher looking beyond the imperialistic system, a tangled structure that serves few and disposes of many. We are byproducts of violent histories, secreted lives cast into the margins. Yet, as bell hooks invokes, marginality is more than a state of deprivation: it is also a site of radical possibility, a space of resistance.[9] It is in this condition, moving between outside and inside, a Du Boisian consciousness, that we can come into our own double agency, an oscillation between il/legibility and in/visibility, a tethering to a whole universe.[10]

Notes

1. "Cambodian Genocide Program," Yale University, Genocide Studies Program, accessed September 18, 2020, https://gsp.yale.edu/case-studies /cambodian-genocide-program.

2. Khatharya Um, "The Cambodian Diaspora," Asia Society, accessed September 18, 2020, https://asiasociety.org/cambodian-diaspora.

3. Colin Davis, "Hauntology, Spectres and Phantoms," *French Studies* 59, no. 3 (2005): 373–79, https://doi.org/10.1093/fs/kni143.

4. Davis, "Hauntology, Spectres and Phantoms."

5. Ocean Vuong, "Headfirst," in *Night Sky with Exit Wounds* (Port Townsend, WA: Copper Canyon, 2016), 20–21.

6. Bracha L. Ettinger, "Carriance, Copoiesis and the Subreal," in *And My Heart Wound-space* (Leeds, UK: Wild Pansy Press, 2015), 343–51.

7. Ben Kiernan and Taylor Owen, "Bombs over Cambodia," *The Walrus*, October 2006, 62–69, https://gsp.yale.edu/sites/default/files/walrus_cambodia bombing_oct06.pdf.

8. Taylor Owen and Ben Kiernan, "Making More Enemies Than We Kill? Calculating U.S. Bomb Tonnages Dropped on Laos and Cambodia, and Weighing Their Implications," *Asia-Pacific Journal: Japan Focus*, April 27, 2015, https://apjjf .org/Ben-Kiernan/4313.html.

9. bell hooks, "Marginality as Site of Resistance," in *Out There: Marginalization and Contemporary Cultures*, ed. R. Ferguson, M. Gever, T. T. Minh-ha, and C. West, 341–43 (Cambridge, MA: MIT Press, 1989).

10. John P. Pittman, "Double Consciousness," in *Stanford Encyclopedia of Philosophy* (Stanford, CA: Stanford University, March 21, 2016), https://plato.stanford .edu/entries/double-consciousness/.

Cross-Border Citizens

Teddy Cruz and Fonna Forman

Teddy Cruz and **Fonna Forman** are principals in Estudio Teddy Cruz + Fonna Forman, a research-based political and architectural practice in San Diego that transgresses conventional boundaries between theory and practice and merges the fields of architecture and urbanism, political theory and urban policy. The practice investigates issues of informal urbanization, civic infrastructure, and public culture, with a special emphasis on Latin American cities. Cruz + Forman lead a variety of urban research agendas and civic/public interventions in the San Diego–Tijuana border region and beyond. They are also professors at the University of California, San Diego (UCSD), and together lead the UCSD Community Stations, a platform for community-engaged research and teaching on poverty and social equity in the border region.

Our embedded research-based political and architectural practice has always forwarded the Tijuana–San Diego border region as a global laboratory for engaging the central challenges of urbanization today: deepening social and economic inequality, dramatic migratory shifts, urban informality, climate change, the thickening of border walls, and the decline of public thinking. Now that this zone has become the main site of arrival for people seeking asylum from Central American violence, poverty, and the accelerating impacts of climate change, geopolitics has once more turned intensely local.

We are compelled to localize the global, to move from *critical distance* to *critical proximity*, from the abstraction of globalization, the "out there" somewhere in the world to the specificity of the political inscribed in the physical territory, the "here and now" of our immediate political context. Obviously, the local can easily devolve into selfish protectionism and identitarian myopia. The local is not an end in and of itself; instead, we propose moving simultaneously across scales, from the global border, to the border region, to the border neighborhood, to understand the implications of global conflicts in shaping the contested power relations inscribed in the everyday lives of people impacted by those conflicts on the political ground itself. Tackling the urban crisis demands visualizing it and naming what produced it. We construct methods to visualize political and civic processes and their spatialization across the border territory. We seek to expose the urban conflicts and controversies caused by collisions between exclusionary top-down urban policies and bottom-up social and ecological networks.

The San Diego–Tijuana border is our protagonistic conflict zone. This is where our practice has deepened its strategies of research and intervention, exploring hidden correspondences between global, regional, and metropolitan crises, and tracing critically the cross-border conflicts inscribed across the divided US-Mexico territory, one of the most contested continental borders in the world. This "geography of conflict" is the site from which we challenge all walled worlds, whose protectionist political economies are organized around surveillance, criminalizing immigrants and erasing Indigenous peoples, the polarizing of top-down and bottom-up systems of urbanization, and expanding the gap between wealth and poverty everywhere. Here, the millennial presence and knowledges of the Kumeyaay, the Tohono O'odham, the Yaqui, and other enduring sovereignties contest the geopolitical imposition of border.

In this piece, we will share the contextual and theoretical scaffold of our environmental, social, and architectural work, moving across geographic scales—from the global border to the border neighborhoods—and arriving at the scale of migrant communities, with whom we are codeveloping the UCSD Community Stations, a cross-border infrastructure of sanctuary spaces for citizenship culture.

Global

The Political Equator

Taking the Tijuana–San Diego border as a point of departure, *The Political Equator* traces an imaginary line along the US-Mexico continental border and extends it directly across a world atlas, forming a corridor of global conflict between 30 and 38 degrees North Parallel. Along this imaginary border lie some of the world's most contested thresholds, forming a continuous necklace of geographies of conflict, including the US-Mexico border at San Diego/Tijuana, the most-trafficked international border checkpoint in the world and the main migration route from Latin America into the United States; Fortress Europe along the Mediterranean, the main funnel of migration from North Africa into Europe; the Israeli-Palestinian border that divides the Middle East, emblematized by Israel's fifty-year military occupation of the West Bank and Gaza; the India-Pakistan border at Kashmir, a site of intense and ongoing territorial-religious conflict since the British partition of India in 1947; and the border between North and South Korea, which represents decades of intractable conflict, carrying Cold War tensions forward to the present day.

When this political equator is visualized alongside the climatic equator, the convergence of environmental and social injustices across the world becomes evident, as communities most affected by political marginalization likewise often bear the brunt of the accelerating impact of climate change. The collision of geopolitical borders, environmental calamity, political marginalization, and human displacement is the great crisis of our age.

The Nation against Nature

When the forces of division and control produced by these global zones of conflict "hit the ground," they are amplified and manifest in border regions like ours. Here, the global border is physicalized into a solid wall, bisecting the eight main watershed systems shared by the United States, Mexico, and Indigenous nations within and across the border region—a deliberate collision between nature and politics that damages social, economic, and environmental assets on both sides.

The Nation against Nature is a visualization project that documents how, through the hardening of an antagonistic political line against the "other," the United States will inflict a violent blow to its own natural resources and to those of Mexico.

As the border continues to thicken with massive militarized, surveillance infrastructure, it performs more as a partition than a border, because its purpose is more to separate than to demarcate, willfully obstructing the flows that have always defined life in this region. As such, we challenge the legitimacy and wisdom of a rationalist nineteenth-century line imposed on complex systems and want to provoke a more ecological way of thinking about border spaces and, again, a more inclusive idea of regional interdependence.

MEXUS: Geographies of Interdependence

The border is not simply a place where things end, and this reality challenges us to consider a more porous border region, rather than a flat line imposed on territory, truncating the social and environmental systems that ecologically bridge divided nations. In contrast to *The Nation against Nature*, MEXUS is a visualization of the continental border region without the jurisdictional line, presented instead as a transnational bioregion composed of eight watershed systems.

By focusing on this continental swath of land as a region rather than as a border, unwalling this "thick" system of interdependencies, MEXUS confronts the validity of an undifferentiated line between nations. It argues that even though the wall is regularly presented as an object of national security, it may prove to be a self-inflicted wound and the cause of great international environmental and economic insecurity as it undermines vital regional ecosystems that are essential to the coexistence and survival of the communities on both sides. As MEXUS visualizes the conditions that a physical barrier wall along the political border cannot contain—watersheds, Indigenous lands, ecological corridors, and migratory patterns—it provokes a more inclusive idea of citizenship based on coexistence, shared assets, and cooperative opportunities between divided communities.

Regional

The Cross-Border Commons

As we zoom deeper into the westernmost part of *MEXUS*, we arrive at the Tijuana River watershed, which is shared between the border cities of San Diego and Tijuana, but truncated by the border wall (25 percent of this watershed is located in the United States, 75 percent in Mexico). New invasive border wall infrastructure continues to interrupt the many canyons that travel tangentially to it, exerting a devastating impact on sensitive environmental and hydrological systems that flow from Tijuana into San Diego as they descend into the Pacific Ocean.

The collision between natural and administrative systems, and between ecological and political forces, is most profound at a specific juncture, the Laureles Canyon in Tijuana. It is an important finger of the binational watershed, crossing the border line and draining into the Tijuana River estuary in San Diego, an environmentally protected zone that is now layered with militarization. An informal settlement in Laureles Canyon, home to ninety thousand people, sits at an elevation higher than that of the estuary. Wastewater from Tijuana flows northbound, carrying tons of trash and sediment with each rainy season, contaminating the estuary, considered the "lungs" of the bioregion. Here the wall becomes an infrastructure of environmental insecurity, exacerbating conflicts between the informal settlement, the border wall, and a protected natural estuary.

The Cross-Border Commons begins in this site of environmental insecurity, a problem belonging to Mexico only, but proposes it as a common problem for Tijuana and San Diego—a condition that must be tackled collaboratively between the two cities. We are now curating a transnational coalition of state and municipal governments, grassroots organizations, communities, and universities to steward a *cross-border environmental conservancy*, linking the Tijuana River estuary in San Diego with the Los Laureles informal settlement in Tijuana to form a continuous political, social, and ecological zone, protecting the water and environmental resources shared by these cross-border cities.

The need to reimagine the border through the logics of natural and social ecologies is the foremost challenge for the future of this binational region and of many other border regions across the globe. A community is always in dialogue with its immediate social and environmental context; this is what defines its political nature. But when this relationship is disrupted and its productive capacity is splintered by jurisdictional power, it is necessary to find a means of recuperating its agency. This is the space where art and architecture practices need to intervene today.

Local

Decolonializing Knowledges

Michael Connolly-Miskwish, an elder of the Kumeyaay Nation and a frequent collaborator of ours, proposed that we could learn a lot about climate adaptation from his tribe's approaches to water management. He explained that water was the spatial organizing system for Kumeyaay clans (Sh'mulq), who used watershed boundaries to define their territories and situate communal life. Oral histories narrate the traditional practice of "rock drop" to confront drought conditions. Piling rocks and brush in drainage zones helps to recharge streams, raise water tables, and fortify the boundaries of the wetlands. Wetland restoration is also the key to maintaining supplies of food, medicine, and building materials, including reinvigorating the juncus, a root used in basket weaving, a source of local economy.

Confronting climate change requires top-down planetary coordination of policy, finance, and clean energy technologies deployed equitably at grand scales to replace our dependence on fossil fuels. It also demands that we cultivate a new value system from the bottom up, along with new ways of thinking and doing. Learning from cross-border practices has transformed our design practice and illustrates a kind of paradigm shift that we believe can decolonize power relations, integrate what our technocratic and bureaucratic ways of thinking and doing have divided, and inspire new approaches to community and economic development. Our engagement with Kumeyaay elders taught us that oral history is generative; that water is social; that science is embedded in the everyday; that civic participation can yield bottom-up technologies for habitat restoration, cultural sustainability, and economy; and that recognition of bottom-up strategies can help to stimulate a new urban-ecological public imagination.

Cross-Border Citizens

We have always resisted the criminalization of the US-Mexico border and have advanced it instead as a site of urban and political creativity. For us, the San Diego–Tijuana border is the site from which a new cross-border public policy can emerge, based on empathy and collaboration, mobilizing the hidden shared social and environmental flows, and disrupting our very understanding of belonging, identity, and citizenship.

We believe that the most compelling ideas about the futures of cities are emerging from peripheral communities in sites of conflict, such as the San Diego–Tijuana border region, where community agency, human resilience, and adaptation manifest in the ingenious reinvention of everyday life. In these zones, survival strategies shape new social, cultural, environmental, economic, and political dynamics that become models and, ideally, catalysts for alternative urban practices and policies that enable more inclusive, sustainable patterns of urban growth. In fact, a major area of our work has focused on making Indigenous practices like "rock drop" more visible, as resources for broader regional resilience and collective well-being. Additionally, we elevate the positive impact of immigration on the transformation of the American city, generating more socially inclusive and environmentally sustainable urbanization.

The border neighborhoods that flank the wall have been our sites of investigation and engagement, to visualize and expose both the top-down institutional mechanisms that have accelerated structural racism, exclusion, and inequality everywhere, as well as the many bottom-up communities of practice that counter and transgress the imposition of exclusionary political and economic policies. Immigrant neighborhoods are the epicenters of urban activism from below, and it is from these marginalized communities that we envision new paradigms of civic infrastructure, affordable housing, and a more solidaristic transjurisdictional imagination.

In conditions of scarcity and displacement, the communities adjacent to the wall have always produced alternative modes of encounter, dialogue, and circulation, sharing resources and infrastructure, recycling at the most outlandish levels the fragments and situations of these two cities, and constructing bottom-up social practices of adaptation, overlap, and encroachment that resist and challenge top-down forces of economic privatization, social marginalization, and cultural exclusion. The discarded postwar bungalows of San Diego are transported to Tijuana; their garage doors become the new skins of emergency housing. Discarded tires are unpeeled and stitched into retaining walls that stabilize informal dwellings on precarious canyon hillsides.

Immigrants bring with them diverse social-cultural attitudes and sensibilities regarding the use of domestic and public space as well as the natural landscape. In these border neighborhoods, multigenerational households of extended families shape their own programs of use, taking charge of their own microeconomies in order to maintain a standard for the household, generating nonconforming uses and social densities that reshape the fabric of the residential neighborhoods where they settle. An informal economy is plugged into a garage and becomes a taco stand, a small carpentry business, a day care; housing additions in the shape of illegal companion units are plugged into existing suburban dwellings to provide affordable living, while next-door neighbors negotiate their property line to generate shared spaces. Alternative social programs begin to spring up in large parking lots; informal economies such as flea markets and street vendors appear in vacant properties; and underutilized alleys might become alternative zones for cultural exchanges and pedestrian circulation, blurring private and public boundaries.

This is how the survivalist urban strategies of immigrant communities generate new spatial configurations that thrive through solidarity and resilience, anticipating new paradigms for shared urban infrastructure. We have archived many stories of urban adaptation in San Diego, for example, to visualize these creative acts of citizenship. These are socio-spatial anecdotes that narrativize moments in the city when immigrants have retrofitted the mono-use and homogeneous spaces of San Diego's mid-city, transforming them into more complex social and economic environments, exemplary of more inclusive and dynamic land uses.

The "nonconforming Buddha" is one of the stories we documented, about a group of Vietnamese monks who acquired two adjacent parcels, each containing a small postwar bungalow, located in the City Heights neighborhood of San Diego—one of the most demographically diverse communities in this city. Throughout the last twenty years, these tiny homes have been transformed from single-family detached dwellings into a Buddhist temple. The monks incrementally altered the small parcels, adapting them into a micro social-economic infrastructure for the neighborhood. The small decorative lawn that filled the front yard has been hardened into a shiny marble plinth that serves as an altar for a huge, white statue of the Buddha that encroaches illegally into the front setback. The driveway has become a dining room, leading into the main interior altar, meditation space, and community room. The old setbacks that define the separation of these houses have now been filled with small sheds to accommodate other shared programs related to the temple. From far away, though, and framed by the small street it occupies, this small bungalow resembles just another typical house.

While the spatial alterations of these parcels are a compelling evidence of the incremental and extraofficial adaptation of spaces in these neighborhoods, to accommodate a more diverse set of bottom-up land uses and everyday practices, this story also revealed to us that it is not only the urban process of physical retrofit that is important to notice here, but the fact that these houses have now transformed into a social agency inside the neighborhood, facilitating social relations, pedagogical programs, cultural support, and economic exchanges. Community-based agencies, such as the Buddhist temple, become urban facilitators that compensate for the lack of municipal support for social, economic, and educational services for these immigrant communities.

Ultimately, migrant neighborhoods have taught us that urban density should not be measured as an abstract number of objects or people per area. Density must be understood instead as the intensity of social and economic exchanges per area. For us, these exchanges mobilized by bottom-up urbanization are the DNA for democratizing the city into more inclusive and plural environments.

The UCSD Community Stations: Spatializing Justice

But while many of these off-the-radar environmental and social flows across the US-Mexico border must be the armature toward more inclusive and collaborative policies, the invisibility of this information prevents new, more deliberate transborder publics from emerging. An investment in an urban pedagogy—the transfer of knowledge across institutions and communities—is essential to construct a knowledgeable and engaged civic culture that demands inclusive urbanization beyond walls. In our practice, designing inclusive cities is not only, or primarily, about spatial intervention, but about designing the programmatic frameworks to reorganize institutional protocols, knowledges, and resources. Visualizing and mobilizing cross-border knowledge lies at the heart of our urban pedagogical work. In this context, we see our primary role as researchers in horizontal terms—as mediators, facilitators who translate both bottom-up and top-down urban knowledges and curate their meeting. We have been particularly interested in the role that universities can play, stewarding knowledge exchange between marginalized border communities and institutions to address urgent city and region-wide deprivations.

We founded the UCSD Community Stations as a platform for the coproduction of knowledge, linking the specialized knowledge of the research university with the community-based knowledges embedded in immigrant neighborhoods on both sides of the border wall. Through this initiative, we have been advocating for a more rooted, embedded, and long-term infrastructure of partnerships, spatialized through a network of "public spaces that educate," as we think of them, taking a longer view of resistance, strategic thinking, and anticipatory planning. The Community Stations are a cross-border network of sanctuary spaces where research and urban pedagogy are curated collaboratively between university researchers and community-based activists. They perform as a programmatic and spatial infrastructure of inclusion, to increase community capacity for political and climate action.

Programmatically, the UCSD Community Stations advance cross-border citizenship through cultural action, but as physical, spatial projects, they also present a new model of shared urban development. We have mobilized the economic power of our public research university as leverage for our community partners to be developers of their own social housing and public spaces. We codeveloped four Community Stations with our community partners, two in Tijuana and two in San Diego. They include the EarthLab, a four-acre climate action park in partnership with Groundwork San Diego, an environmental justice NGO; Living Rooms at the Border, a prototype for affordable housing connected to a community theater, outdoor classroom, and social service pavilions, in partnership with Casa Familiar, both in San Diego; and in Tijuana, Border Sanctuary, which connects migrant housing to fabrication and kitchen economic incubators, led by our community partner, Embajadores de Jesús.

Unwalling Citizenship

The Community Stations become a cross-border observatory for generating different stories, counternarratives about life in this border region, grounded in the experiences of those who inhabit it. We are a region of flows and circulations, shared practices and aspirations, alliances of hearts and minds, regardless of the wall that restricts the movement of our bodies. Ultimately, they are a platform for constructing what we call an *elastic civic imagination* from the bottom up, a cross-border res publica.

Here at the border, the idea of the bioregion—the binational watershed system that traverses politically inscribed boundaries—has been a powerful imaginary for activating more elastic civic thinking. With our cross-border partners we curate "unwalling experiments" that dissolve the wall—using visual tools like diagrams and radical cartographies to situate border neighborhoods within broader spatial ecologies of circulation and interdependence—from local to regional, to continental, and ultimately to global scales. We see elasticity as a civic skill, the ability to stretch and return, between local and more expansive ways of thinking, over and again, to understand one's challenges within broader dynamics and processes, and to envision opportunities for solidarity and collective action across walls.

Indian Alley, Where Art Is Healing

Pamela J. Peters

Pamela J. Peters is a Diné multimedia documentarian from the Navajo Reservation currently living in Los Angeles. Her multimedia work explores the vision that she calls Indigenous Realism, which examines the lives and complexities of contemporary American Indians today. Her creative outlet pushes viewers to critically analyze the psychological and historical structures of Native Americans in film, storytelling, and visual images.

Los Angeles is a city with an exceptionally diverse cultural landscape. There are vibrant neighborhoods with rich cultural identities, including Chinatown, Koreatown, Armenian neighborhoods, and a large Persian community in Westwood, to name a few. However, one culture that many are not aware of is that of the original people of North America. The city is situated on the homeland of the Tongva people; the entire Los Angeles basin is known as Tovaangar. Most people don't know about the Indigenous landscape or about the many tribal people who live, work, and create in this place—Los Angeles has one of the highest concentrations of American Indians in the country.

In the spring of 2019, I was invited to give a tour of the gritty downtown landscape of Skid Row known as Indian Alley. As a Navajo woman who migrated from the Navajo Reservation in the late 1980s, I became familiar with the Native community by searching out Indian centers. While living in the San Fernando Valley, I contacted the Southern California Indian Center, which referred me to United American Indian Involvement (UAII), then located in a decaying downtown location at 118 Winston Street, next to Indian Alley.

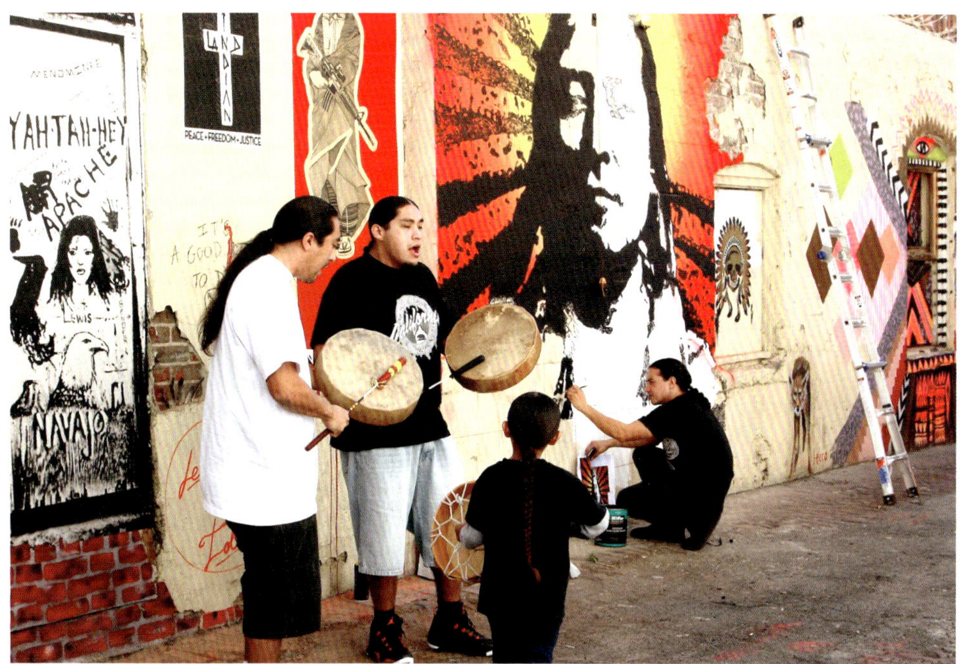

Indian Alley: Phoenix brothers drumming (Julian, Julius, and Adrian) while artist Votan is painting Crow Chief Plenty Coups during the open exhibition of *Legacy of Exiled NDNZ*. Jan 2013. Photo: Pamela J. Peters.

Downtown Los Angeles in the 1980s was nothing like it is today. During the tour of the Alley, I gave a brief history of urban Indians living and moving through downtown LA. In the early 1970s, the Red Power movement was one of many cultural groups that organized and fought for equality. This history started most spectacularly with the occupation of Alcatraz Island near San Francisco by mostly college students, which drew national and international attention to Indian rights and concerns. The American Indian Movement (AIM) occupation of Wounded Knee in South Dakota likewise also garnered national and international attention.[1] During these acts of resistance, a federal program that was initiated in 1953 as part of the Termination Act continued to encourage and subsidize the relocation of Indians from reservations to designated urban cities. Much of the American Indian migration to Los Angeles occurred due to the Indian Relocation Act of 1956. By this act, the federal government offered American Indians the opportunity to work and live in major cities with the promise of job opportunities, yet many were not aware they would be competing with others for blue-collar jobs. For some this meant assimilation, for others, a better life than on their tribal reservations.

Many Natives who came to Los Angeles in the 1950s lived in the decaying neighborhood of Bunker Hill, as seen in Kent Mackenzie's 1961 film *The Exiles*. The Native population grew from roughly 12,000 in the 1960s to more than 25,000 in the 1970s. Today, more than 175,000 tribal members live in Los Angeles (the highest population of urban Indians in the United States), many of whom migrated from Montana, South Dakota, New Mexico, and Oklahoma, among other communities. Many came in hopes of finding a better life, yet failed to realize those hopes and unfortunately wound up addicted to drugs or alcohol, and homeless. This is not uncommon when people who are distant from their home communities struggle with poverty and depression in unfamiliar urban environments.

United American Indian Involvement was created at 118 Winston Street and established in 1974 by Baba Cooper, who is described as a Sioux Indian woman in old newspaper clippings. A recovering alcoholic, Baba wanted to help the impoverished and displaced Natives she knew and encountered in downtown Los Angeles. Initially, UAII served primarily as a recovery home for those addicted to drugs and alcohol. Today, UAII provides health and support services to Los Angeles's Native American population, ranging from culture workshops to job placement and elderly services, with many more programs too numerous to list. Additionally, the center continues to assist addicts through their Robert Sundance program. Robert Sundance, a former alcoholic who had been arrested over one hundred times for public intoxication, initiated a landmark class-action lawsuit against the Los Angeles Police Department for the mistreatment of addicts on Skid Row. His case helped reform how the LAPD treated alcoholics, which led to a nationwide change in law enforcement and increased public health programs in LA County. His activism created a sea change in public health and generated many rehabilitation programs along with the one started by Baba at UAII, which continues to run today.

United American Indian Involvement became the first stop for many Indians coming to Los Angeles for the first time. It was a place where they were able to reconnect with friends, loved ones, and family members, just like me in the late 1980s when I too was searching for relatives. By the 1970s and 1980s, 118 Winston Street ultimately became the center for the Skid Row community, until UAII moved to its new location at 1125 West Sixth Street in the early 1990s, where it still resides.

Today, Indian Alley, which was named by many Indians who have visited UAII over the years, has been reconstructed with murals and public art installations commemorating the relocation history of American Indians in Los Angeles, designed to acknowledge the ongoing existence of urban Indians despite the vast neighborhood changes. Stephen Zeigler, the resident caretaker at 118 Winston Street, has been instrumental in inviting well-known street artists to depict Native American icons, Indian leaders, and social activists within the walls of Indian Alley. Since 2011, Mr. Zeigler has recruited local street artists to install murals in the Alley for the purpose of showcasing the American Indian heritage of the place. Some portraits include depictions of local American Indian activist Robert Sundance and eighteenth-century California anticolonialist Tongva leader Toypurina.

In 2013, I launched my first photography and multimedia project, *Legacy of Exiled NDNZ*, which addresses the historical and contemporary legacy of the US Indian relocation from the 1950s through today. Shot in a neo-realist visual style reminiscent of Kent Mackenzie's 1961 film *The Exiles*, it shares the stories of those who relocated from their reservations. During the opening of the photo exhibition, I asked my artist friend Votan if he could do a live piece, and we agreed on a visual he created of Chief Plenty Coups, a Crow leader. Thereafter, I collaborated with Zeigler to bring some well-established American Indian artists into the Alley's mural space.

The site today is commemorated by artwork created by noted Native American and non–Native American local artists, including Wild Life, Bandit, Sketchy, Free Humanity, Random Act Teacher, and Shepard Fairey. All of the murals, regardless of the artist's ethnicity, comment on the history of American Indians. The showcasing of Native artists has brought new lifeblood to the Alley, which has become a tourist attraction as well as a local point of interest, especially in Indian Country. Many art fans from different tribal nations come to the Alley to see work from Native American artists such as Jaque Fragua (Jemez Pueblo), who created two collaborative art pieces titled *Decolonize and Keep Calm* and *Indian Country*. There is also Votan (Mayan), who expanded his first artwork with another piece titled *Indian Roll-Call*. Steven Judd (Kiowa/Choctaw) stamped his work with a piece called *War Paint*. Christian Armstrong (Akimel O'odham) created a piece that invokes his tribal creation stories. Carrie Curley (Apache), the first Native female muralist to showcase her work in the Alley, created a piece called *Strength of Native Women*. Most recently, River Garza, an artist from the Tongva tribe, created a mural of the traditional mapping of his Tongva landscape that is both educational and a depiction of the perseverance of the original caretakers of the land base known today as Los Angeles.

While other ethnic groups have towns named after them, Native people get an alley, despite having the largest urban population of any city in the United States. I want the city of Los Angeles to recognize the Alley as a historical landmark, and by sharing the contributions of these young Native trailblazers from the 1970s I want to remind this city that there is a vibrant contemporary community of Native Americans who express their creativity visually to share a history that has long been silenced in Los Angeles.

Located on the homeland of the Tongva people in the Los Angeles basin known as Tovaangar, it's time that this landscape memorializes the many Native Americans who have contributed so much and recognizes that we too are part of this diverse cultural landscape. The Alley with its artwork is providing the capacity to heal and recover while contributing to the culture of Los Angeles in significant ways.

Note

1. For more on the Red Power Movement, see Paul Chaat Smith and Robert Allen Warrior, *Like a Hurricane: The Indian Movement from Alcatraz to Wounded Knee* (New York: New Press, 1997); and Kent Blansett, *Journey to Freedom: Richard Oakes, Alcatraz, and the Red Power Movement* (New Haven, CT: Yale University Press, 2020).

Vessels

A CONVERSATION

Chanice Holmes, Mykia Jovan,
Rebecca Mwase, and Mahalia Abéo Tibbs

Vessels is a seven-woman harmonic meditation on the transcendental possibilities of song during the Middle Passage. Experienced within an interactive and acoustically rich sculptural environment that invokes those infamous ships, this interdisciplinary ritual performance explores singing as a survival tool and asks, "What does freedom sound like in a space of confinement?"

REBECCA MWASE: Since coming out to Baltimore, I've been thinking a lot about what it means to build community in diaspora and how so much of the work of *Vessels* has been doing that. We've had twenty-seven different Black women participate in the creation process over the last five years from all over the Americas and Ghana, and we're still in communication in some way with everybody. And so, I've been thinking a lot about what it means to be [part of] a diaspora. What does that mean? What does it mean to communicate across distance?

I think about *Vessels* as a metaphorical womb. That womb, or cauldron, was a space in which blackness was created; in the Middle Passage, all these boats, different tribes, nations, people, and languages got massaged into this thing we now call blackness. Beaten, brutalized, transformed, joy [finding], all of it was grieved into this thing that we now call blackness. What does that mean for us now? And given that experience, how do we imagine beyond the idea of borders? I'm curious from y'all when you think

Editor's Note: This contribution was edited from a virtual conversation between Vessels performers Rebecca Mwase, Mahalia Abéo Tibbs, Chanice Holmes, and Mykia Jovan on August 14, 2020.

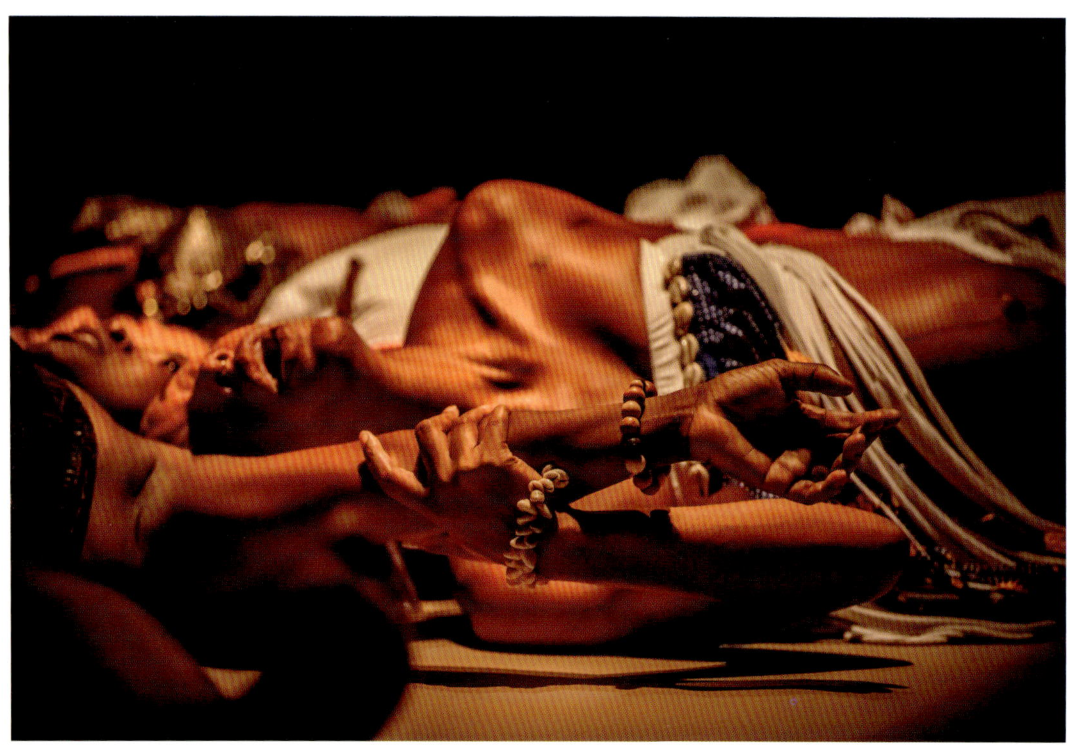

Vessels, 2019. Photo: Melisa Cardona.

about diaspora movement, when you think about *Vessels*, what comes up for you? What have you learned? What have you witnessed? What have you embodied?

MAHALIA ABÉO TIBBS: As far as diaspora and the work of *Vessels*, I really think of a cellular and astral reprogramming. I feel like *Vessels* helped me connect back to some portal where all the information that I knew intrinsically and ancestrally was stored. And I kind of like avatar[ed] myself, and it really has been a forum—a held, supported forum—to sift and to discard, and to grow the things that are useful to me and to us.

RM: That makes me think of epigenetic memory and activation. I think about this all the time now that I'm pregnant—if, when I was born, or when my mom had me in utero, I held the mitochondrial DNA of her mother's mother's mother's mother's mother. What does it mean to be of the Black diaspora because all that shit's right here, at least in these lineages, right?

CHANICE HOLMES: And I think a lot about circles. I think about feeling really rooted, really grounded, really centered. I feel the fullest I could be, the most aware I can be. It feels like a transfer of energy when I connect to that place, and really sit in that place. That's why I'm always dancing and expressing myself. I'm trying to get it off of my body. I'm trying to let you know, this is what it is. So, I feel like it's always kind of circling. I have a lot of the knowledge already in my body because of the diaspora. I have the tools I need. So just trying to hone in to that place. It feels like a transfer of energy and an investment into self and to the other people around me who are connected in this diaspora with me. We're investing in ourselves when we connect back to that place.

MYKIA JOVAN: I think with *Vessels* in particular, with this work that we've done and are continuing to do together, something about tapping into what's already inside of us opens up portals. Like making ourselves literal vessels. We have three kids on the way since this work. So, it's kind of like a measuring stick to see even after we're done with this work, how far it'll go just based on our offspring.

MAT: Something about the *Vessels* work has allowed for us to work with an innumerable amount of suffering that most people find terrifying. When I began organizing after COVID and was talking to people about freedom farms, I encountered so much terror from Black people about living in the South or living off the land. We've gotten so, I won't even say comfortable, but we've gotten really skilled at honing our anger and our fear and recognizing how useful it actually is. And then being able to create some sort of memorial and visit it. Now we have very healthy relationships, I think, to the suffering in our lineage. But I don't think any of us did—I know I didn't—in the beginning. So, I feel like it's also offered us a way to deal with our own communal pain, which then taps into our personal pain, and allows us to use it and not let it inhibit us from moving forward, which is a huge collective problem in the Black community that I'm still running up against. I just wish that other people had processes to confront this amount of pain because it's real. And also, how can we use it?

MJ: Through this work, I know it's been less terrifying to deal with grief, and the loss of loved ones, and recognizing what we always say—that death is a myth. And I don't think I could have gotten through the things that I've been through since this process, without this process. Going back to what Chanice said about grounding, being a grounded force in my family now, that I was not before. When tragedy happens, when things happen, I know all the tools to get us through this.

RM: Yeah, the grief though. The motherfucking grief. I thought a lot about multiple displacements. My parents were displaced from Zimbabwe. And then I went to New Orleans, which is a place of continuous displacement. I even remember being so intentional, [in] conversations, at the beginning. I said, we have to have a majority from New Orleans cast. And that took us two and a half, three years to get there. But we're learning things about what it means to work with the Black diaspora in that process, and the grief that comes with constant change. I know for me now, being in Maryland, and not being in New Orleans anymore, I've just been navigating so much grief around [losing] place and space. There's so much in *Vessels* that made it easier for me to not feel like I lost y'all in the move. There was never an instance where I felt loss of y'all ever. And that to me, I think, is a testament to the work that we did in the process of being connected, being together, knowing that people can tap in and out, but the container is strong enough. I have never not felt y'all with me. And there's something to that. When you talk about process, Abéo, when I imagine what *Vessels'* future looks like, we need to be teaching the process. We need to be inviting people into the process, to learn new skills and tools, to dig into ancestry, to look at the lineage that's held in this body.

There's something that one of y'all said, or maybe it was in my brain, about home—how do we think about what home is? For me, *Vessels* is also a reiteration of home. If home is in this body, if home expands and is held between the tips of my fingers, the top of my head, and the bottom of my feet, then what does it mean for me to protect that, love that, hold that, and also extend that place of belonging to yours? Let's talk about that. What and how has your vision or understanding or concept of home shifted in the process of *Vessels*?

MJ: I think what you just said makes me feel like one of the key elements to maintaining a sense of home all around us is to first start within. In *Vessels*, you cannot really connect with others without connecting with yourself first. And I'm really well versed at connecting with other people and just keeping parts of myself closed off from myself and from others. With this work, you feel more like yourself the more you relate to the ensemble, which I've never experienced in any other work that I've done. It's wild because, especially as a person that likes to keep to herself, my growth and this process has been letting go of that, and allowing you guys to look in. And that helped me expand more. And the whole concept of knowing that you're held, wherever you are, is because I am really everywhere now, because you all are everywhere now.

MAT: The funny thing is, if we sat here and made a list outside of *Vessels* of the main five issues, let's pretend, that affect our community as a whole, I feel like *Vessels* somehow addresses those things without us ever really having to discuss them. We figure that out in process. But I think boundary setting is very hard for Black women in general. And it's something that we had to learn in real time with one another, whether that was physical, because of the work we're doing, reminding everyone in the room that they are allowed their own boundaries. And having to navigate that amongst the natural sisterhoods that emerge. I know for me and Jalisa, that's something I've had to do outside, offstage. So, I just feel like it really helps us access all of these obvious points of fissure in the blackness block. Because we come as our whole selves so obviously, we bring our shit with us. And I feel like it actively kind of laser beams everything. I think that there are some people who probably wouldn't even want the process, or would start it and be like, "Oh, that's too much for me." But it really calls in your own willingness, and it forces you to see where you're at and how you're willing to grow within your own container, or if that's even important to you.

Vessels also taught me that I can change my pronouns, whenever I feel like it. Like from this morning to this afternoon, I can. And I can also dream up my own pronoun, which is something in this trend, in the whole larger trans conversation. I wish we could talk about that more—the agency of being able to name yourself and not feel like you have to exist within this structure. Because there were a lot of days when I was like, "Oh, I don't have to be a she, or a him, or a they? I can be the loam of the sea?" *The agency in that*. I think it requires everyone to be much more intentional. It requires a certain amount of focus. It changed my world. As I literally move and change, I have the agency to say how you interact with me. Whether that be my body, my name, my soul, anything. And that, I think, is revolutionary, and I wish that was something that we could include in more building practices. You don't have to choose within these binaries if we say this binary doesn't exist; you could be whatever the hell you like.

RM: I want to shout out my LOUD babies because I cultivated that shit with them.[1] Working with young transgender people, I was like, "Y'all can do whatever you want." It allows for [an] expansiveness that I feel like blackness requires. And queerness, and all the other juicy fluid things that we aspire to over here.

MAT: I think I would be remiss if I didn't also mention the deep and profound and very intentional level of care that we both give and receive to one another, but also that the process offers. *Vessels* fortified me to be able to keep my boundaries [within] all this, so that after that, shows became very different for me. My contract process became different. What I was willing to do for the money became very different because of the immense care that was put into our own process. And I was like, "Oh, actually, I never have to work for shit I don't believe in anymore." This level of care fortifies us to then go out into the world and create the ways in which [we] allow all the things, what we want to be called, how we want to work, and what that looks like. That, I think, stems [from] bell hooks and that love ethic.[2] This deep level of love and care that actually comes out in this very fierce and protective thing that imbues us as soldier people on the way out into the world.

CH: Yeah, being intentional with not overworking and asking: What does freedom look like? Reclaiming my time? Okay, I need all my time back. I think a big part of it is easing that sustainability, those practices that were put in place in *Vessels* that is like, oh . . . this is what rest feels like when you just sit down and don't do nothing. This is fueling my body throughout my day. So just thinking about all the ways that I can be more intentional.

RM: I have to have autonomy and choose to be in a place. Yes. I love y'all.

Notes

1. For more on LOUD, visit "Our Mission," LOUD Nola, https://www.loudnola .org/our-mission.
2. See bell hooks, *All about Love: New Visions* (New York: William Morrow, 2000).

Fence

Belise Nishimwe

Belise Nishimwe is a student at Washington University in St. Louis, attending on a full ride. Extremely passionate about social justice, international relations, and law—especially pertaining to immigrants and their rights—Nishimwe was born and lived in a refugee camp in Tanzania until the age of five, when she and her family moved to America.

There is a field and beyond it is a gate
That beckons me to it like a siren
Tempting me with its green fields
And flowers unstained by the blood
Of mothers
Dying by their ten-year old's hand

Rero, nirutse
So I ran

Towards it
But I succumb to the chains
wrapped around my throat

To the faces of brothers and sisters
Fallen in the streets
Holding my legs to the land
My ancestors were dragged
To boats to take them beyond that fence

The fence I now crave
I recall the
Words heeded by my grandmother,
Abazungu biba ibintu vyose bafise
White people steal everything they have
Biba Ibiyiko biri muminwa yabana bacu
They steal the spoons from our children's mouths
Bakabaha inkoho zokwicana
Giving them guns to kill each other
So I stay
Within the chaos
Lying in between
Tribes rested
Dreaming of the girl
 beyond the fence

A Touch of Otherness

Hayv Kahraman

Hayv Kahraman was born in Baghdad, Iraq, in 1981 and now lives and works in Los Angeles. A vocabulary of narrative, memory, and dynamics of nonfixity found in diasporic cultures is the essence of her visual language and the product of her experience as an Iraqi refugee-cum-émigré.

I've always felt "dirtier" than my Swedish schoolmates, both in image (as in the way I look) and in experience (as in the way I feel). Foreign, dirty, filthy, and impure. Contaminated. Never belonging to the tight-knit group of those who are "immunized." Instead, I'm a migrant Other who could threaten the imaginary of a pristine border wall around these purified, immunized bodies. I'm hypervisible through my skin, yet utterly invisible in being. Like a virus, my pathology renders me nonhuman in their eyes. Men fetishize me, women find me threatening, and both see me as subhuman. The colonial wound is so deep that I question my validity.

I fled Iraq after the first Gulf War, and when I settled in Sweden, I remember enrolling in ballet classes. I had studied ballet in Baghdad and had aspirations of becoming a ballerina. My teacher, however, made it clear that Black Swans were not welcome in Tchaikovsky's lake. I could do my Arabian saut de chameau, but le saut de biche was not made for the likes of me.

What I can hold on to, however, is what Walter D. Mignolo has coined an "awareness of the coloniality of being."[1] This is a migrant consciousness of sorts; it's the moment you realize that your body, your voice, and your life are worth less than those of your Swedish schoolmates. And so you learn to survive, being well aware of this fictional state imposed upon you, in which your existence is classified as dispensable. And in this awareness, there are possibilities to create interventions which question that very paradigm.

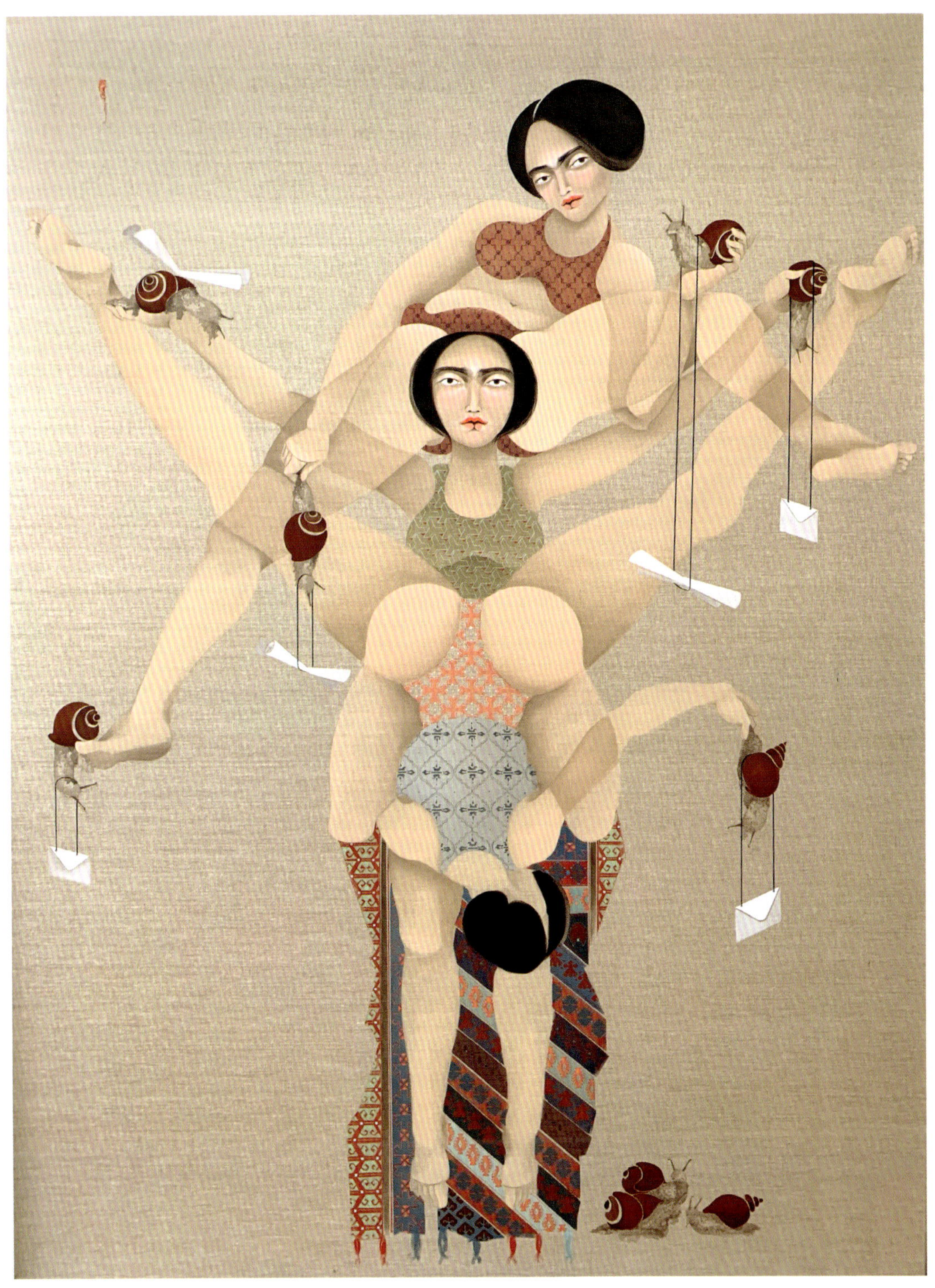

Hayv Kahraman, *Snails*, 2020. Oil on linen, 60 × 80 in. Image
courtesy the artist and Susanne Vielmetter Projects LA,
Jack Shainman Gallery, Pilar Corrias, and The Third Line.

I had never really thought critically about the language of contagion or immunity. And why would I have? This was an established language; how could a little immigrant girl question that? When my mother got diagnosed with cancer, I started noticing the innumerous phrases in medicine and popular culture that fed a militaristic view of our bodies, such as the "body as defense," "pathogens invading or attacking," "the patient is winning or losing the fight," "the physician as general," and most recently with the onset of SARS-CoV-2, Donald Trump announcing himself as a wartime president fighting against the "invisible enemy." My mother had survived multiple wars in her lifetime (the oppression of the Kurds by the Ba'athist regime, the Iran/Iraq War, the first Gulf War) and she was now clearly at war again, this time with her own body.

The militaristic metaphors we read in the news about the virus and our bodies are endless. They justify ideas of conquest and war, and they also have immense implications for how we relate to difference in our everyday lives.

In my most recent work, I have been examining different ways in which I can question political notions of individuality that are embedded in the rhetoric of immunology, especially where concepts of self and nonself play a central role. This self/nonself relationship is rigid and absolute. There are clear delineations of where the self ends and where the nonself or the Other begins. As a refugee, this discipline that studies foreign pathogens resonates with me. I was a virus before the virus. My denigration from the category of being "human" is a construct put forth by masculine, Euro-American-centric and heteronormative thought processes. The field of epidemiology breeds the imaginary of an Other as defined by imperial modernity (a dirty immigrant) who then becomes the carrier of the disease into the confines of the State and, in so doing, into the body—the body-state. An example of this is the 2018 migrant caravan in which thousands of migrants from Central America arrived at the US-Mexico border, fleeing persecution, violence, and poverty. Charles Payne, a Fox News personality, and former immigration agent David Ward openly spoke on the network, proclaiming, "these migrants will infect *our* people."[2] The idea of the "immune" turns into a charade through which specific bodies come to personify a legitimized, hermetically sealed entity or fortress, and aberrations from this fabricated normativity belong to the pathological and need to be eradicated. It's the "fear of the alien Other pillaging the white body."[3]

I've chosen to depict this in my paintings by both erasing the borders around my figures and contrarily, using thick, black charcoal to emphasize them so severely that they evoke a sense of mockery. The black borders around the flesh define the body as it repeats on and in itself, alluding to a structure or a language. The image becomes a collision of lines that, if chased, ultimately emerge as mutant bodies. Concepts of visibility and invisibility are at the forefront of how I approach my work. I think of invisibility both as a state of dehumanization but also as a proximity to dying. As a nearing to an end. The figures in some of the works dissolve so naturally into the chaotic background, it seems as if the process of assimilation has been successful. This makes me think again of Mignolo's "coloniality of being." The erasure of who you are in your entirety. Some figures, however, demand to be valid. The charcoal around their flesh is a statement of visibility. Their gaze, looking directly at you, the audience, is an act of confrontation. Part of this action to reclaim visibility is unearthed by inventing a new species of women in my paintings. I'm creating a collective of superwomen contorting their multiple limbs in extraterrestrial ways. These superhumans are not part of normative conceptions of a woman—some have six legs, some don't have feet, and some bend precipitously backward without breaking. They resemble extraterrestrial beings or organisms that clearly do not belong on this planet and attempt to implicate the viewer in thoughts of fetishization and eroticization in a rather explicit way. They are looking right at the viewer, enacting a sort of "double consciousness" in the Du Boisean sense, so as to confirm their awareness of what they are and how they are seen.

When researching immunity, I inevitably came across antibodies. We develop these Y-shaped protein molecules called antibodies after we are subjected to something "foreign." Our immune system scans our body for nonself substances called antigens that, once detected, cause a series of events in which antibodies bind to antigens and either signal to white blood cells that a pathogen is nearby or neutralize the pathogen on the spot, debilitating it and paving the way for the white blood cells to "clean up" the mess. The antibodies act as a bridge between the foreign and the self. They are translators that tirelessly negotiate how, when, and if our body will respond. I find this role of mediation interesting, as it reminds me of dwelling in the border; of being in between one, two, or multiple spaces. Antibody or Antikörper is a term coined in 1890 by the German physician Paul Ehrlich as a description of something that recognizes a body. The etymology of the word *anti* goes back to the Greek meaning of going against, opposed to, or opposite. Despite the problematic language that exposes the divisive constructs now present in popular culture, what if we think of this antibody as a trickster figure that exposes "us" to "them"? The symbol of an antibody in my work becomes a source of intervention and perhaps a cry for peace. This antibody is, in loose terms, a result of an "invading" body that goes against *our* body. It is something essential to the survival of our species, yet it's a consequential development stemming from the nonself.

These precarious mediators have a very stoic molecular form of the Y shape, which I've introduced in the paintings. The Y is placed in the background and foreground in such a way that the figure is absorbed by it, yet completely extruded from it. There's a mutual reciprocity happening between the antibody and the figure in the paintings. The figure seems to bathe in washes of broad translucent paint that take the form of a Y. Perhaps these Ys resemble protective waves of color in which collaborative processes of healing or cleansing the vulnerable are enacted. In another group of paintings the focus lies on the role of mediation where figures are acrobatically assembled, creating the shape of a large Y, one on top of the other. Carrier pigeons are flying around them carrying secret messages. A baby with an envelope taped to her stomach hangs on the leg of one of the women. This is a reference to the late 1960s when my mom, at age ten, served as an undercover messenger for the Shia party and the first women's liberation party in Kurdistan. Covert messages were taped to her stomach as she delivered the information. Another painting replaces the pigeons with snails carrying rolled paper messages on their backs, hinting to ask the inevitable question of what consequence a delayed message can have. For me, the body is a site where trauma resides, and subsequently a site in which a sort of mending is enacted by reimagining different worlds where multiple heterogeneous ideas and ways of living are played out.

Immunology is slowly changing as new discoveries about the human body are being made. We now know, for example, that human cells make up only 43 percent of the body's total cell count. The rest are microscopic colonists: bacteria, viruses, and other microorganisms, which populate our human body ubiquitously. So when you look in the mirror, you're seeing more microbe than human, according to Lita Proctor of the National Institutes of Health, who is leading the Human Microbiome Project.[4]

I believe that the apparatus and semantics of immunity and the immune system need a reinvention in which we acknowledge the porosity and permeability of our skin, and our dependency on other organisms for survival. As Donna Haraway says, "The immune system is everywhere and nowhere."[5]

And so, can we shed the hegemonic discourse against difference by surrendering all troops and starting instead to think *from* the border or *inside* the border? Can we lean toward a new body language that does not see self and Other as enemies but rather speaks from the border between them? While this pandemic has unearthed vulnerabilities across the board, we have to remember that we are actually not in this together. My experience differs from yours and from others', and what matters at this point is that we are heard. My invisibility, as well as that of anyone touched by coloniality, needs to be rendered visible and valid. Let us heal our wounds, shatter the imagined barricade we've built around our bodies, and lean toward a symbiotic relationship to difference.

Notes

1. Nelson Maldonado-Torres, "On the Coloniality of Being: Contributions to the Development of a Concept," *Cultural Studies* 21, no. 2–3 (2007): 240–70, https://doi.org/10.1080/09502380601162548.

2. Jason Le Miere, "Fox News Guest Claims Migrant Caravan Carries 'Leprosy,' Will 'Infect Our People,' Offers No Evidence," *Newsweek*, October 30, 2018, https://www.newsweek.com/fox-news-migrant-caravan-leprosy-1192605.

3. Laura Diehl, "American Germ Culture: Richard Matheson, Octavia Butler, and the (Political) Science of Individuality," *Cultural Critique* 85 (2013): 84–121, https://doi.org/10.5749/culturalcritique.85.2013.0084.

4. Audie Cornish, Rob Stein, and Lita Proctor, "Finally, a Map of All the Microbes on Your Body," *The Human Microbiome: Guts and Glory*, NPR, June 13, 2012, https://www.npr.org/transcripts/154913334?storyId=154913334.

5. Donna Jeanne Haraway, "The Biopolitics of Postmodern Bodies: Constitutions of Self in Immune System Discourse," in *Simians, Cyborgs, and Women: The Reinvention of Nature* (New York: Routledge, 1991), 203–52.

Harmattan Haze

Njideka Akunyili Crosby

Njideka Akunyili Crosby was born in Enugu, Nigeria, and currently lives and works in Los Angeles. She has exhibited at venues around the world, including the Fifty-Eighth Venice Biennale. She received a MacArthur Fellowship and is the recipient of honorary doctorates from University of the Arts and Swarthmore College.

I was born in Nigeria, where I lived until the age of sixteen, and in 1999 I moved to the United States, where I have remained since that time. My cultural identity combines strong attachments to the country of my birth and to my adopted home, a hybrid identity that is reflected in my work.

Many of my works feature figures in scenarios derived from familiar domestic experiences: eating, drinking, watching TV. These gestures are underscored by a second layer of imagery, only truly discernible close-up. Photo-collage areas are created from images derived from Nigerian pop culture and politics. Some of these images are from my archive of personal snapshots, magazines, and advertisements, while others are sourced from the internet.

Western art historical references are also included in the work as a means to counter generalizations about African or diasporic experience. In much the same way that inhabitants of formerly colonized countries select and invent from cultural features transmitted to them by the dominant or metropolitan colonizers, I extrapolate from my training in Western painting to invent a new visual language that represents my experience—which at times feels paradoxically fractured and whole—as a cosmopolitan Nigerian.

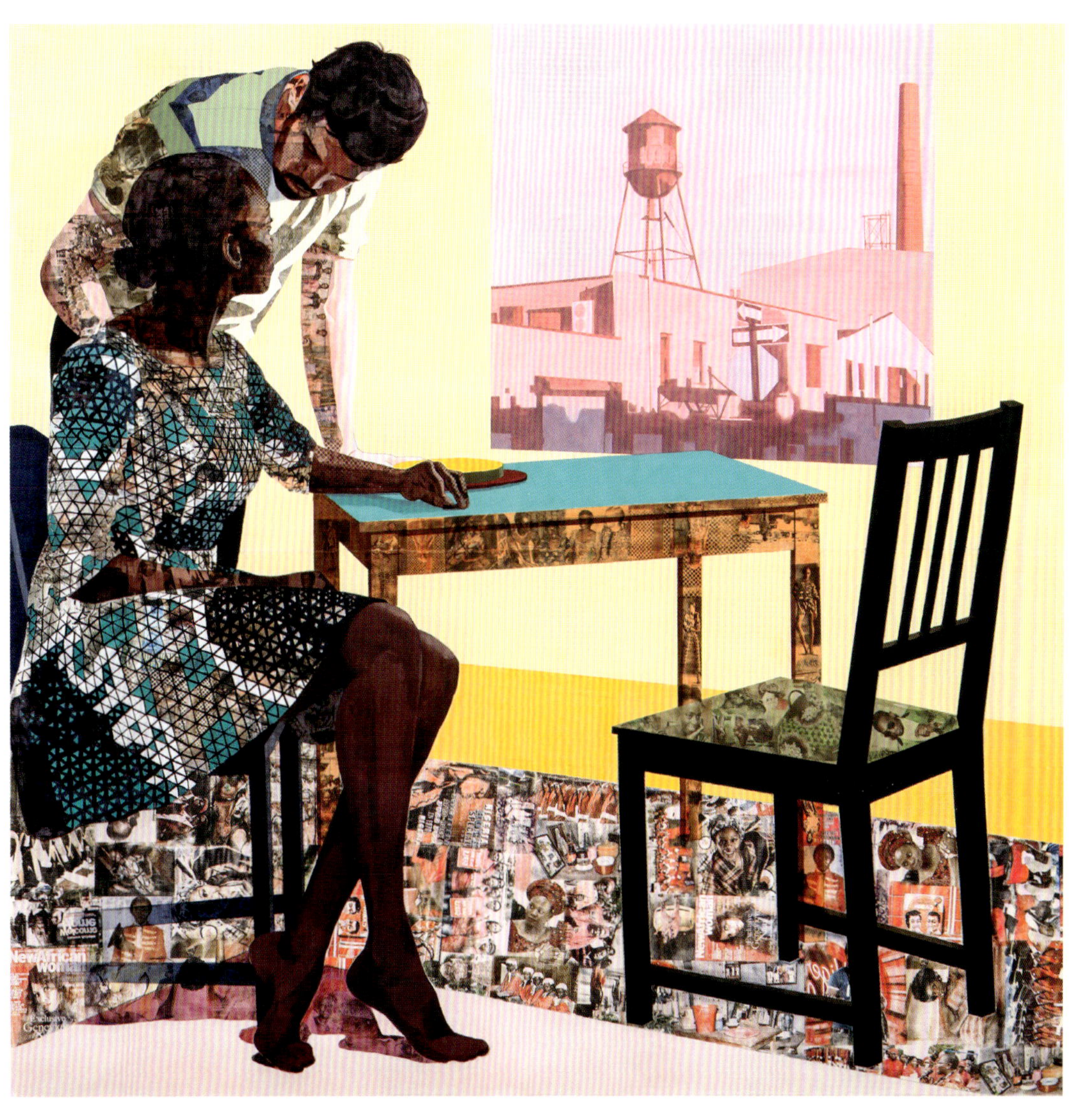

Njideka Akunyili Crosby, *Harmattan Haze*, 2014. Acrylic, color pencil, charcoal, and transfers on paper, 84 × 84 in. Photo: Mario Todeschini. Courtesy the artist, Victoria Miro, and David Zwirner © Njideka Akunyili Crosby.

Who Is the #EmergingUS?

Jose Antonio Vargas

Jose Antonio Vargas is a Pulitzer Prize–winning journalist, Emmy-nominated filmmaker, and Tony-nominated producer. A leading voice for the human rights of immigrants, he founded Define American, a nonprofit that uses stories to shift the narrative on immigrants. His memoir, *Dear America: Notes of an Undocumented Citizen*, was published in 2018.

Along with many others, I share a mission to document America's demographic earthquake, and it is an earthquake that we are all living through. All of us use the same tools of storytelling, and we share a vision of a changing and emerging America that is truly inclusive. We are the stories we tell. Yet when it comes to the stories that the media tells about us, when it comes to the art that should reflect the reality of our daily lives, there is a tremendous and unacceptable imbalance. The emerging US is more multiethnic, more immigrant, more colorful, than ever before. Although East Coast media people seem to think that America is mostly Black and white, the emerging US is also Latino, it's Asian, it's Native American, it's Middle Eastern, it's mixed race. *In the next fifty years, Latinos and Asians will make up 88 percent of total US population growth*. This emerging US is more intertwined than ever. Our lives and the issues that we live with—immigrant rights, LGBTQ rights, women's rights, #BlackLivesMatter, income inequality among all races—they all intersect with one another, resisting being categorized and simplified into one box.

We can't talk about immigration and not talk about race. We can't talk about race and not talk about what's happening in our own communities—the anti-Blackness that is pervasive in the Asian and the Latino communities in this country. So how do we have all of these conversations at once?

"

The reality is that this country is only going to get gayer, Blacker, browner, more Asian. Women of all ethnic and racial backgrounds will continue to break every possible barrier there is to break. So what's left? Straight white men.

Prior to the 2020 election, somebody asked me what I thought was at stake. I argued that what was at stake was the soul of white heterosexual men. How much change could they handle? Were they willing to give up space? Were they willing to actually realize that the very people that created the laws and founded the institutions now have to make room for a truly inclusive emerging America that is not going to go backward? That is the question that still faces the arts; it's a question that absolutely faces journalism; it is a question that faces all forms of media. The reality is that the emerging US is here, and we are the ones who make this country great. Not only that, the emerging US are the ones who will insist that this country lives up to its promise of a more perfect union.

We are living at a time (James Baldwin is probably smiling up there) in this country in which the Other, the Other in America, is now all of us. Because white people feel that they are Othered. They feel under attack; not all white people (younger ones seem more willing than previous generations to address racial issues and colonization in both the past and present), but many white people. And what's fascinating is, white people, for the first time, are an emerging racial minority across the country. In 2014, for the first time in American K–12 public schools, white students were in the minority.

When we talk about diversity, how do we include white people in the conversation? People of color talk about white people behind their backs. How do we do that now in front of them? How do we now insist on more uncomfortable conversations about race and privilege and class in this country?

Moreover, we can't talk about America being a nation of immigrants without acknowledging the struggle of Black Americans and Native Americans in this country. We cannot emphasize our commonality without first confronting what makes our experiences different. What laws were created that made them different? (There is a whole branch of federal law, for example, about inventing papers that subjugate American Indians.)[1] The survival of this emerging America requires that we see each other more fully and more humanely.

Some years ago, I made a film called *Documented*. We had a screening at the University of Minnesota, and this African American law student got up and said, "Jose, I'm really conflicted about this. Of course I want you to be a US citizen. You've been working really hard to get citizenship. I feel conflicted because I'm born here. My ancestors are from here. We helped build this country, but sometimes I don't feel like I'm treated as a citizen because I'm Black." Then, a month later at a screening in South Carolina, this elderly Black woman came to me (she saw me on Rachel Maddow's show) and she said, "I just thought it was really interesting that you say that your life is subjected and limited by pieces of papers, because my great-great-great-grandmother got here, and when she landed in South Carolina, she was given a piece of paper, it's called the Bill of Sales, saying that she's a slave. So can you connect the papers that you can't seem to get to the papers that she was given?"

And here we are stuck talking about walls. And talking about Mexico as if Mexico didn't used to own parts of the United States. Talking about all these very simplistic issues that the media just runs with. At such a political and partisan and divided time, we need more than ever artists, writers, journalists, poets. We need all of the artists, all of our artists, to do something that has never been done in this country: to tell the fuller story of America. Politicians are not going to do that. They're too busy trying to get elected, to divide us. The only people who will do that are artists. Artists always lead the way to where we are going, transcending politics and speaking to people.

Note

1. Many thanks to Emmy (Lorna) Her Many Horses (Sicangu and Oglala Lakota) for directing us to learn about Certificate Degree of Indian Blood (CDIB), which led us to readings including Paul Spruhan, "CDIB: The Role of the Certificate of Indian Blood in Defining Native American Legal Identity," *American Indian Law Journal* 6, no. 2 (2018): article 4, https://digitalcommons.law.seattleu.edu/ailj/vol6/iss2/4.

Justice and Equity

WE'RE COMING FOR IT ALL

Christine Her

Christine Her is the daughter of Hmong refugee parents from Laos. She graduated from East High School in Des Moines, Iowa, and pursued her BA at Drake University, majoring in creative writing, philosophy, and political science. She is highly motivated to interrupt social and systemic injustices with hope and opportunity while helping others rise in their own power and lean into their purpose.

My dad was a teenage soldier.

Between the ages of fourteen and sixteen, his responsibilities were to protect the thousands of Hmongs who sought refuge in the jungles of Laos to escape genocide. The Hmong were recruited and trained by the United States to fight against communism in Southeast Asia during the Vietnam War.[1] My grandfather, Cher Kao Her, was a US army recruiter. When the war ended, Hmong people were persecuted and murdered. My grandfather, fearing for his life because of the role he played in the war, fled to the jungles with my dad.

My dad's uncle who made the journey to Thailand learned his son was left behind in the jungles with my dad. Because of this, my dad's uncle came back to Laos to find his son. Luckily, they were reunited, and my dad's uncle told my dad and grandfather to join them on the trip back to Thailand so they could start over again in America. Then something changed, and my dad's uncle left without saying a word. In the Hmong culture, family is everything. My grandfather was heartbroken and believed starting over again in America without family wasn't worth the dangerous journey. Even though he felt this way, he wanted more for his son. He encouraged my dad to leave the jungles because he was too young to die. He needed to fall in love. Become a father. Grow old. Cher Kao wanted his son to live.

In the middle of the night while protecting the community with other young men, my dad kept thinking about his dad's words. He knew his dad was right. He wanted to live. My dad, at the age of sixteen, encouraged twenty other young men between the ages of fourteen and twenty to join him in finding a way to Thailand.

They all left without the opportunity to tell their families, "Goodbye. I love you. I will come back for you." The young men made promises to each other to return and take their families with them to Thailand after finding a safe passage. The journey wasn't easy, but they eventually made it to Thailand. Through word of mouth, my dad's mother, who had made it earlier to the camps, heard he was in jail. When she arrived in Thailand, she filed documents in his name in hopes that if he did make it, he would be able to start a new life in a new place away from the war. When he finally arrived, together, they made the long journey to their new home: Des Moines, Iowa.[2]

Some of my earliest childhood memories are my parents explicitly introducing me as their "fat daughter." Other memories involve my parents telling me to quiet down, not cause trouble, or to put my guitar away because I needed to study. It felt like I could do no right even though I was a straight-A student. When they vocalized their disappointment in my job choice after graduating, it hurt. After years of feeling like I wasn't enough and the relentless criticism by my parents, I started to believe I was the problem. Life wasn't going to get better, because I was never going to get better. I spent almost a year not talking to my parents. When I did, it was to be spiteful and cause harm. I couldn't regulate what I was feeling. I didn't have the words to explain what was going on because we didn't talk about it. Suicide. Mental health. Depression. Beyond the stigma and shame, I faced barriers with translation and access.

In February 2013, I called my older brother, who was living in Texas, and said, "I want to die." He listened. He asked, "What can I do? What do you need?" It was the first conversation I had where I felt like I could breathe again. That same month, my aunt passed away from cancer. My brother came to Iowa for the funeral. After we said our goodbyes to her, I said goodbye to Iowa. Two months after I moved, my great-aunt passed away. She was one of the few people who loved me for me. She's the reason why I love runny scrambled eggs over freshly cooked rice. She was the first person I ever made a meaningful promise to and the first person in my life whose promise I will never be able to keep.

After living in Texas for six months, I moved back to Iowa for a job. None of them worked out. Then in July 2016, I accepted a position with ArtForce Iowa to manage their arts program for refugee and immigrant youth, called the DSM Heroes program, now called the Heroes program.[3]

After a year, I was asked by the board to serve as executive director. Each leadership transition came with highs and lows. What was consistent was the trauma of starting over again with unstable financials, issues surrounding trust between staff and the board of directors, the trauma our youth faced in their schools and homes, the racial disparities leading our youth to be fed into the school-to-prison pipeline. As a team, we were struggling with our own trauma from the transitions at ArtForce Iowa. As humans, we were dealing with our own personal and historical traumas. Serving young people who face traumas and disclose them to us meant we were also struggling with secondary trauma.

At the end of 2017, as an organization we chose to pivot. We wanted to change the oppressive systems, knowing our youth didn't always feel safe or welcomed, and learned about the Adverse Childhood Experiences Study (ACES).[4] Those with significant trauma are more likely to have heart disease or diabetes, be depressed or suicidal, have substance addiction problems, and have financial problems. Recognizing that our youth artists were living through their adverse childhood experiences, we made it our priority to educate those who worked with young people. ArtForce Iowa is the only arts organization to provide trauma-informed care arts-based workshops utilizing the healing-centered engagement approach for young people in the state of Iowa.[5] We are also the only arts organization doing this work in Iowa's juvenile detention center.

As I learned more about historical and intergenerational trauma along with ACES, I began to understand young Christine. I grew up believing my parents didn't love me, and it was the story I told myself until a few years ago. Doing trauma work meant facing my own trauma in the process of healing. It led me to reflect on my childhood with empathy for my parents, who experienced significant trauma as young people fleeing genocide. My parents were still healing too. I had the comfort of playing guitar, singing, and writing poetry and short stories, whereas my parents had the stress of learning a new language and supporting their families by being adult teenagers.

To me, art was liberating. It was a way to overcome the pain I felt internally without hurting myself physically. Art was a language I understood. Through my songs and stories, I could be authentically myself. Now as an adult on my healing journey, I'm learning my parents didn't have the same opportunity.

My dad never made it back to the jungles of Laos. None of the young men kept their promise to each other. Each was forced to "move on" and start over again without the ones left behind. My grandfather died alone with no family around him, in the jungles with no proper burial because he fought for a country that never fought for his liberation.

It's taken my dad over forty years to share his complete story, holding onto survivor's guilt and the shame of not going back to save his dad. In 2019, I sat down with him to talk. I never imagined I would have this experience with my dad where we could talk about hard things, cry together, and hold each other. He shared what sixteen-year-old Meng Her felt when deciding if he should leave his dad. He shared that he silently cried every night on the journey to Thailand. He shared that he had two sisters who died by suicide and how sad he was to be the only living son carrying his father's name. He shared with me how a handful of the young men who fled the jungles with him died from strokes or heart attacks. My dad survived a heart attack in 2008. He ran every day, had a healthy diet, and still does to this day.

In 2021, ArtForce Iowa moved into Mainframe Studios, one of the nation's largest nonprofit creative workspaces. We built a video production studio to continue collecting stories of community members, recording workshops for our youth to have our content on demand with the purpose of preserving and sharing our communities' stories through curricula and various art mediums. Through every traumatic event, our youth artists have shown and taught us how to adapt, how to remain true to ourselves, and how to stay humble. Our youth artists continue to remind us how art changes us for the better and how art connects us when we feel alone and isolated. We've witnessed how it takes a community to build resiliency and how it requires community for our collective healing.

We each hold the power to make the change needed to have a more kind and equitable society by humanizing and empathizing our individual experiences that make up the collective. We cannot demand one without it impacting the other. We want justice and equity in schools, in the workplace, in the arts, in social services and in the doctor's office, in politics and policies, in housing, in the disbursement of wealth. We want true liberation where everyone has the opportunity and access to thrive and embrace their purpose without systemic oppression. And that's why we are coming for it all.

Notes

1. "The Split Horn: The Journey," Public Broadcasting Service, accessed November 30, 2022, https://www.pbs.org/splithorn/story1.html.

2. In July 1975, President Gerald Ford wrote to every governor asking them to help find new homes for the Southeast Asian refugees. Iowa Governor Robert D. Ray was the first governor to respond to his call. Clare McCarthy, "Resources for Refugees Change over Decades," *Des Moines Register*, August 9, 2015, https://www.desmoinesregister.com/story/news/2015/08/09/burmese-refugee-history-iowa/31388507/.

3. ArtForce Iowa was conceived by a man convicted of attempted murder in a drive-by shooting in the summer of 1999 in Des Moines. After his release from jail, he met Yvette Hermann, and through their mentor-mentee relationship, he shared with her how he wanted to be the last Black kid to recognize he was an artist while serving time.

4. Adverse childhood experiences are traumatic events that can dramatically upset a child's sense of safety and well-being. These events create a toxic level of stress for a child and can lead to lifelong problems with school, work, health, and mental health. For more information, see Iowa ACES 360, accessed August 20, 2021, https://www.iowaaces360.org/.

5. To learn more, see Shawn Ginwright, *Hope and Healing in Urban Education: How Urban Activists and Teachers Are Reclaiming Matters of the Heart* (New York: Routledge, 2015).

building bricks
for communal healing

Silvi Naçi

Silvi Naçi is an artist and writer working between Albania and Los Angeles. Their interest lies in the subtle and violent ways decolonization and migration affect and reshape a people, language, and gender identity as well as social and cultural dynamics.

building bricks for communal healing began in 2016 during the US presidential election. I sat with friends in the studio drinking tea, trying to make sense of the nonsense happening around us and understanding the effects this election would have on us, on queer, immigrant, Black, people of color, and all marginalized bodies. During this time, I was going through archived family photographs and noticed my parents' army backpacks. In a trance in the studio, I began folding the used tea bags into similar forms—small army backpacks. The work continues in collaboration with the Albanian and immigrant community in Boston, and currently in Los Angeles, where I reside. This work offers space to think collectively about immigration, belonging, and queer-femme national identity while reading and dissecting important feminist texts together, drinking tea, and making the tea bags into bricks—a form that dates back to 7000 BC as one of the oldest building materials. As the work grows, I will continue to host reading–making–drinking tea gatherings as creative interventions in various spaces to bridge the gaps that this nation has built to separate us, and make our own healing space.

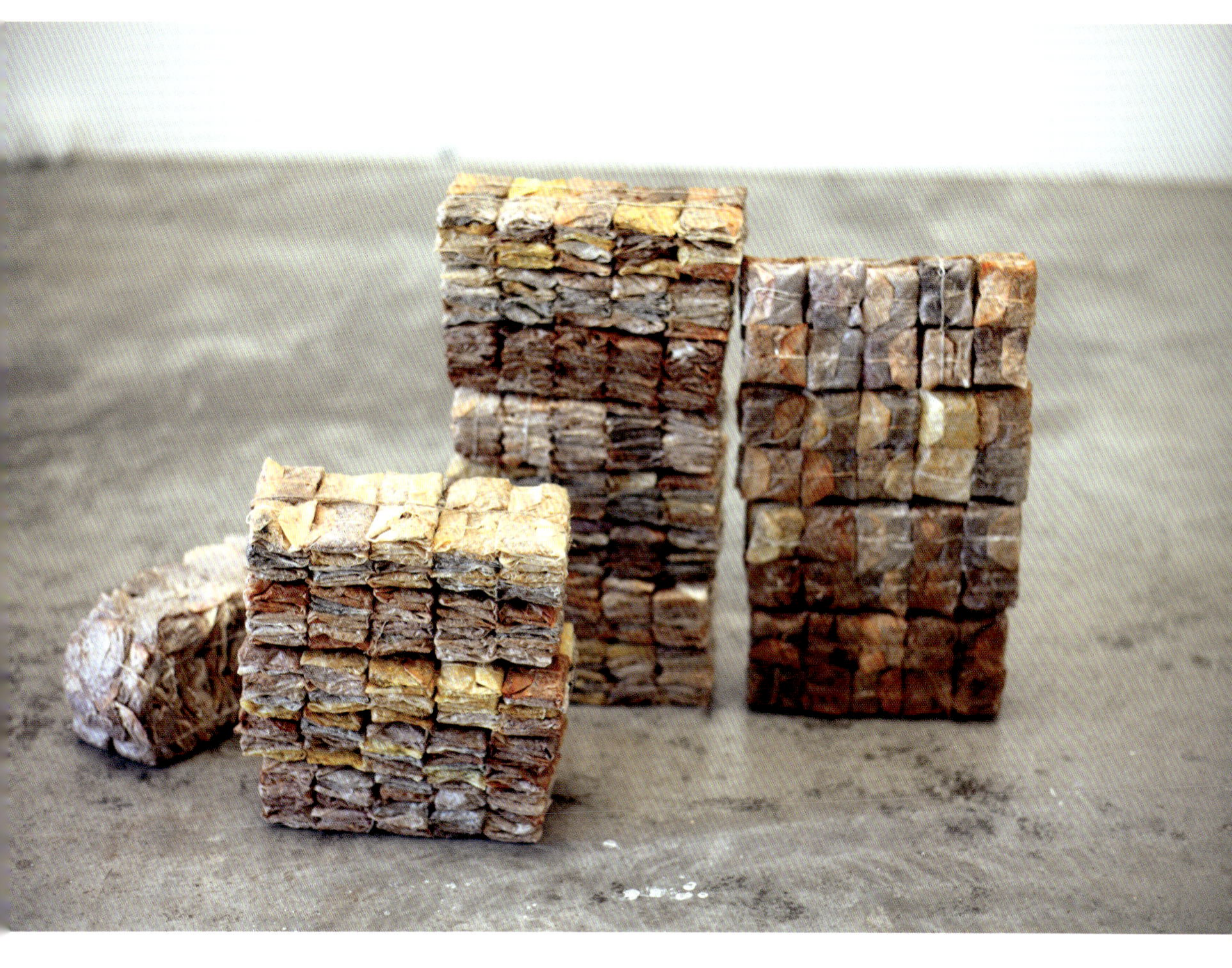

Silvi Naçi, *building bricks for communal healing*, 2016–
ongoing. Tea drunk cross-continentally, thread, hair,
each brick approx. 3.75 × 2.25 × 7.75 in.

We Never Needed Documents to Thrive

Yosimar Reyes

....

Yosimar Reyes is a nationally acclaimed poet and public speaker. Born in Guerrero, Mexico, and raised in Eastside San Jose, Reyes explores the themes of migration and sexuality in his work. The *Advocate* named Reyes one of "13 LGBT Latinos Changing the World" and Remezcla included Reyes on their list of "10 Up and Coming Latinx Poets You Need to Know."

....

I am powerful—and I've always known that.

When I was ten, my Abuela told me I was undocumented. She did this not to scare me but to convey that I would have to work twice as hard to make something of myself in this country. At an early age, I was forced to make peace with the fact that my life as an undocumented queer was going to be one filled with challenges. The biggest one being not allowing the limitations set for me by the government to stop me from living a life filled with joy.

Coming out of the Shadows™ was not a phenomenon for me. I grew up in Eastside San Jose, California, in a community with strong, established mechanisms for survival. We created our own rules to keep afloat and an underground railroad of resources. You'd know which coyote was reliable to cross your loved ones over and what jobs hired undocumented people.

I never saw my life as an undocumented person as anything worth discussing. I never imagined that there would be scholars forensically analyzing how we survive in the future. "Undocumented" has never been my identity. I have always known that just like growing up poor, it's a social condition that influences my identity. When you sit down to think about it, nothing in my physique is undocumented; my status is not tangible.

Immigration became a topic of national conversation in 2006 with the Great American Boycott on May 1. Despite the fact that undocumented immigrants lived in the United States long before 2006, our little boycott gained us national visibility. Reporters and filmmakers became interested in our narratives. The media went wild looking for all the undocumented people they could showcase. Due to social media trends, the most immediately accessible were young people brought to the United States as kids wanting to pursue higher education. The stage became ready for us to become "Dreamers," a term born out of failed federal legislation called the DREAM Act.

That same year, we saw a rise of undocumented people in news specials and documentaries. It was particularly interesting that we were repeatedly asked to relive our trauma. "How did you find out you were ille—I mean, undocumented?" However, instead of being asked to recount our pains to understand ourselves as undocumented people better, our narratives were weaponized to create a moral crisis for citizens—a bloc of people with actual voting power.

As a result, the very same autonomous, independent, undocumented people I grew up with were chopped and edited to become victims with no agency—none of this made sense. I never wanted to be showcased crying on camera. Being undocumented was an experience only to be shared with folks in my same predicament. We did not and do not need saving. We needed people to understand how this country reaps and exploits the (often literal) fruits of our labor so that we could move forward with creating practical immigration laws that made sense.

We needed them to see that immigration was not a people problem but one set forth by racialized policies. The immigration conversation has been framed as a social problem, but we need citizens to understand that immigration is a racial justice issue: certain immigrants are targeted as being problematic based on their race. Beyond being undocumented within the US border, we represent migrants globally forced to leave their homes because of the economic imperialist power countries like the US have over our homelands.

Since 2006, undocumented people have been positioned as subjects that constantly need to prove their loyalty to this country while simultaneously living up to the expectations of being a "good" immigrant. The good immigrant is law-abiding, taxpaying, and contributing. The good immigrants aren't like the myths nativists promote, that undocumented people are lazy criminals who rip off the system. The good immigrant can win over the hearts and minds of every American! This would later be the framework from which nonprofits and progressive politicians would operate, using the same tired talking points. Our narratives are funneled into three main frameworks:

1. Our academic accolades: stories of undocumented students with 4.0 grade point averages being accepted into prestigious universities.
2. Our economic contributions: stories about how much undocumented immigrants contribute to local, state, and federal taxes.
3. Our labor: stories of the jobs that would not get done without undocumented immigrants. Emphasis is placed on jobs that make the lives of citizens easier.

Our lived experiences' nuances and complexities are overshadowed by the sentiments of having to showcase us as "useful" people.

In 2008, then-Senator Barack Obama swayed the Latinx vote with promises to pass comprehensive immigration reform by the end of his first year. After completing two terms, Obama left with the legacy of being the "deporter-in-chief"; as the forty-fourth president, he deported more than three million people—a new record for any administration. Deferred Action for Childhood Arrivals (DACA), a form of administrative change in 2012 granting work permits and relief from deportation, is undeniably one of the biggest wins to come out of the immigrant justice movement in recent history. Many attribute it to Obama's goodwill, but immigrant youth remember otherwise.

Since 2008 and the death of DREAM, many young activists have shifted away from respectability politics and opted to demand action from the president. Although Democrats wanted undocumented people to have pride for this country by giving them American flags and calling them "Dreamers," many simply got tired. The expectation to continually prove ourselves and fit into the narratives set out for us was unrealistic, exhausting, and dehumanizing. So undocumented immigrants started disrupting Democrats and Republicans alike. They shut down campaign offices. They went rogue.

They were warned. They were given an explanation; nevertheless, they persisted. The reality is that undocumented people are not monolithic. There are eleven million undocumented people and eleven million complex narratives from different parts of the world. Now, more than ever, undocumented storytelling needs to disrupt the "good immigrant" and "criminal alien" dichotomy. It must consist of a spectrum of stories that allows undocumented people to be human.

Frameworks around the stories of undocumented people should take into account an undocumented audience. Our voices as undocumented people need to be the focal point instead of being edited for a citizen audience. War was declared on undocumented communities when America handed Trump the presidency. What we needed then and still need now is to let undocumented people lead. We should edit the framework of our stories *for us*. From the undocumented Salvadoran nanny in upstate New York to the undocumented Kenyan doctoral candidate at UC Berkeley, it is time to build a bridge between our narratives and tell the true story of migration.

Let it be known that undocumented people have never needed saving. Let it be known that we are simply people who are caught in a game of political football. Undocumented people are powerful because waking up every morning to a country that vilifies you and choosing to actively participate in it is an act of resilience. Our energy is often spent trying to convince xenophobes of our humanity, but I argue that we have already given enough as undocumented people. Instead of repeating the same stories we have been telling for the last two decades, it is time that we tell stories of our strength. It takes a level of genius and ingenuity to survive as an undocumented immigrant in America.

In the future, I imagine an abundance of narratives that capture our joy, our magic. We are powerful—and it's time that the world knows that too. Stop co-opting our message. Let undocumented people create, let us dissent, let us lead.

prop·er

Kassandra L. Khalil

Kassandra L. Khalil is a visual artist and former codirector of Arts in a Changing America. Kassandra's drawings and sculptures explore how movement and gestures evoke personal and cultural memory. Kassandra channels her interest in Caribbean communities and the culture of resistance into organizing arts programming for her Haitian diaspora in New York.

prop·er

/ˈpräpər/

adjective

1. truly what something is said or regarded to be; genuine
2. of the required type; suitable or appropriate.[1]

My mother used to make me copy down sections of the dictionary when I told a lie. She said that writing down each line exactly, taking down honestly what the page said, would teach me what it meant to be straight with people. To be a proper young lady. To sit up right. To keep your feet on the floor. To not make obvious one's discontent. My mother, Esther, learned this version of womanhood from her mother, Marie, a serious but kind woman who raised her nine children as a seamstress in Port-au-Prince.

My mother brought herself to the United States in her twenties and learned what it meant to be a proper American woman. To still sit up straight, but to make it sexy, to make yourself *for* yourself. I believe both of these women were being honest when they taught me these versions of propriety. What they did not know is that I skipped whole sections of the dictionary.

Only two weeks after I finished painting this series, my grandmother, Marie Lorvanette Laborde, transitioned to the Glory after ninety-six years

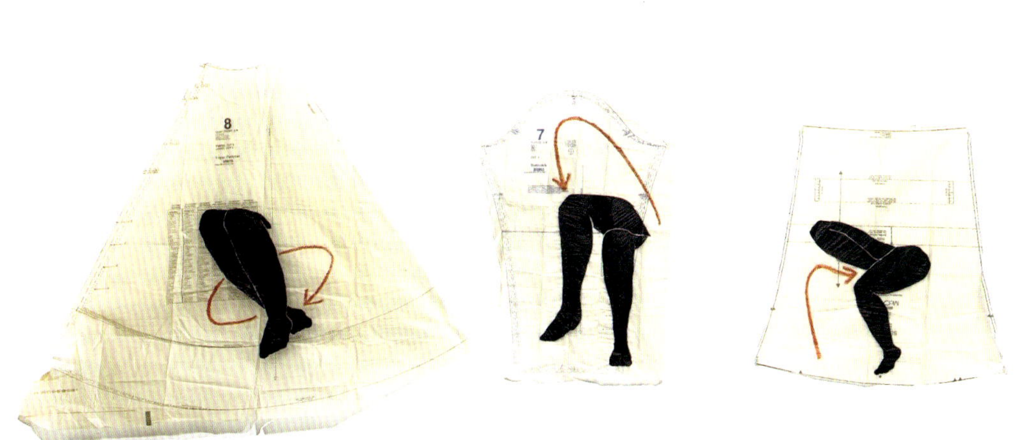

Kassandra L. Khalil, *prop·er*, 2020. Vintage sewing patterns, wax marker, ink, acrylic medium, 10 × 4 ft.

of love in action. This piece is about finding myself through the lessons of the women who raised me. It's about the marks laid for me as a guide and about my matriarchs' respect and love for me, however I cut the cloth.

Note

1. *Oxford Pocket Dictionary of Current English* (Encyclopedia.com), s.v. "proper," https://www.encyclopedia.com/humanities/dictionaries-thesauruses-pictures -and-press-releases/proper-0.

Alongside

ON CHINESE STUDENTS IN THE UNITED STATES AND THE FIGHT FOR BLACK LIVES

Evelyn Hang Yin

Evelyn Hang Yin is an interdisciplinary artist and filmmaker based in Los Angeles. Yin investigates how her experience moving between China and the United States informs her cultural identity and is invested in issues of race, history, place/displacement, and collective memory.

I was hiking deep in the Cascade Range two years ago when I discovered a hand-stacked rock wall made of mining tailings that locals call the Chinese Wall. Since then, I have been tracing and documenting the footprints of early Chinese immigrants in rural parts of the West Coast in the United States. At an unmarked burial ground full of body-sized indentations, in narrow alleyways filled with temples, herb stores, and gambling houses, and in the reclaimed swampland of the Sacramento–San Joaquin Delta, I search for their wandering spirits.

More than 150 years after Chinese laborers first came to the United States, I arrived in San Francisco. I am one of the over 300,000 Chinese students in the United States who make up a third of the total one million international student population.[1] International student enrollment dramatically increased after the 2008 recession, when US colleges started turning toward international students to fill the budgetary hole left by state funding cuts, and I am no different from many of my peers who benefited from China's recent economic boom.[2] Thanks to the one-child policy, the family culture that prizes its children's success, and China's psychologically damaging education system, both newly affluent parents and those who sacrifice to save decide to send their kids abroad.[3] While international students contribute over $30 billion to the US economy every year, we are gentrifying college towns and neighborhoods and taking resources away from those with less in the first place—with most institutions heavily relying on tuition revenue, our very presence strips away many domestic students' chance to receive higher education.[4] This is especially true at public universities, where in-state students pay a fraction of what out-of-state and international students do.

What is our role in the United States, especially when there are so many of us? Too often I see a disconnect between the lives we lead and the social issues that are happening around us.

Amid COVID-19, tightened China-US relations, and protests against police brutality (in Hong Kong and in the US), the large community of Chinese nationals living in the United States oscillates on a pendulum between hypervisibility and hyperinvisibility. We became hypervisible when Trump shouted "Chinese virus" and "kung flu" at his rallies and saw related, increased racially motivated attacks against Asians. However, when the killing of George Floyd sparked nationwide protests, we went back to hermit mode, and the aforementioned disconnect resurfaced. I observed a disappointing lack of interest in participating in conversations, let alone taking up the fight, as if it is a problem between Black and white people in the United States or, worse, a problem between Black people and the US government. Meanwhile, Chinese state media seized the opportunity to call out the United States' hypocrisy in condemning Hong Kong police brutality while mistreating Black Lives Matter protesters; the Trump administration planned to cancel visas of Chinese graduate students with ties to China's military; and US Immigration and Customs Enforcement (ICE), by presidential mandate, prohibited all international students from returning to or remaining in the States if their school planned to go fully online in fall 2020.[5] Although later retracted, this worsened the plight of many international students who had already waited for months to go home due to travel restrictions, and further deterred Chinese students who reconsidered US study plans even prior to the pandemic.[6]

I believe a few factors contribute to the political apathy of Chinese students despite our being constantly affected by policies in the United States. The sheer number of Chinese students in any academic institution makes it easy for us to socialize only with our fellow Mandarin speakers. With linguistic and cultural barriers, we don't feel the need to step out of our comfort zone to make non-Chinese friends and are thus not in tune with what others are talking about.[7] Schools also lack the staff and know-how to accommodate the needs of international students. The increasingly diverse student body is not reflected in largely white, majority-male faculty, who are oftentimes unwilling to adapt their teaching methods for students coming from a very different educational background.[8] Often unwelcomed by domestic students, who have joked that the University of California, Irvine (UCI), is the "University of Chinese Immigrants" and that California College of the Arts (CCA) is "Chinese College of the Arts," we are also branded and actively distanced by Chinese Americans as FOB (fresh off the boat).

Most significantly, we grew up in a comparatively homogeneous and politically censored environment where race issues seem absent (though not in reality). We are a generation showered in aggressive nationalist views yet are politically disengaged and taught to focus our energy on math and science, not politics or the arts. Only when I left China did I first see the photo of the Tank Man at Tiananmen Square. Only when I left China did I realize the omnipresence of colorism and xenophobic ideologies in my upbringing: the historic association of white skin with the elite class, the blatant racism in the 2016 detergent ad and the Africa skit from the 2018 CCTV Spring Festival Gala, and the evictions and mistreatment of African students in Guangzhou during the pandemic.[9]

A historical parallel might offer some perspectives on how the fate of Chinese students has always hinged on politics. After the failed attempt of the "Chinese Educational Mission" (1872–81) by the Qing dynasty to educate a group of Chinese students in the United States, the second wave of Chinese students arrived under the "Boxer Indemnity Scholarship Program" in 1909. They faced the same set of challenges and racial discriminations under the 1882 Chinese Exclusion Act, a law that wouldn't end until 1943. Not welcomed in the United States, many returned home, only to be politically alienated by both the Kuomintang (KMT) government and the Communist Party. When Mao took over China in 1949, having no tolerance for US influence, he completely cut off the flow of students to the States. Those who stayed, regardless of their political views, faced the new reality of the Red Scare. "In many American eyes, the day China became communist was the day that all of its students abroad did as well," writes Eric Fish.[10] They were monitored, interrogated, and denied job opportunities and housing simply because they were Chinese. Those who returned home received even crueler treatment, where they were accused as spies and traitors during the Anti-Rightist Movement and Cultural Revolution— also interrogated, humiliated, beaten, and even driven to suicide. Chinese students have been and always will be chess pieces in the geopolitical game, easily disposed of by both powers vying for greater global control.

Chinese students were, however, exempt from the Chinese Exclusion Act and allowed in the United States at that time. One should not forget the large-scale violence against Chinese laborers during the gold rush and the exclusion era, where entire Chinatowns were burned down, and Chinese people were lynched and massacred. Unlike students that were financially supported once by the government and now by their families, the earliest Chinese immigrants came to the United States as indentured laborers, substituting for the newly emancipated Black enslaved laborers. They mined gold, dug trenches, built the railroads, and were rendered hypervisible by ubiquitous racist cartoons and exclusionary laws, and yet historically invisible by a complete erasure of their contributions.

Chinese and other Asians have been, ever since the internment of Japanese Americans in the United States during World War II, described as the model minority who, despite discrimination, excel in academics and the workforce. As long as we keep our heads down and work hard, we will achieve "success." In response to the 2020 protests against police brutality, I've heard voices asking, "If we were also discriminated against, why did we make it and not Black people?" What these voices don't consider is the fact that the majority of Chinese immigrants in the United States today (and many other East and South Asians) came here *as* students and highly skilled laborers after the 1965 Immigration Act reversed quotas on Asian immigrants. The law wouldn't be possible without the civil rights movement and the activism of Black Americans, who, on the other hand, were forcibly brought to the United States as enslaved laborers (though also highly skilled) and endured over four hundred years of racial segregation, lynching, redlining, housing discrimination, and police brutality thereafter. How can we even begin to compare Asian "successes" to the struggles of Black people? The framework of white proximity is a tactic used by white supremacists to distance us from Black and Brown bodies, while masking our real struggles. It also discounts the huge socioeconomic disparities within Asian communities and the colorism that comes with it.

My goal in writing this is not to stand on high moral ground and exclude myself from my own complicity and the privilege of having financial support throughout my time in the United States. What I intend to do is to call attention to the importance of engaging in politics and our interconnectedness with the struggle of Black lives. Two years of researching and documenting rural Chinatowns led me to a gradual process of unlearning and relearning. In between paint-peeled walls and rusted artifacts, I found the wandering spirits of my Ancestors, who urged me to pick up this heavy piece of history. Greater privilege comes with greater responsibility, and it is on us to unlearn racist ideologies and relearn our own past so that we can reenvision a future, alongside our Black neighbors and other marginalized communities.

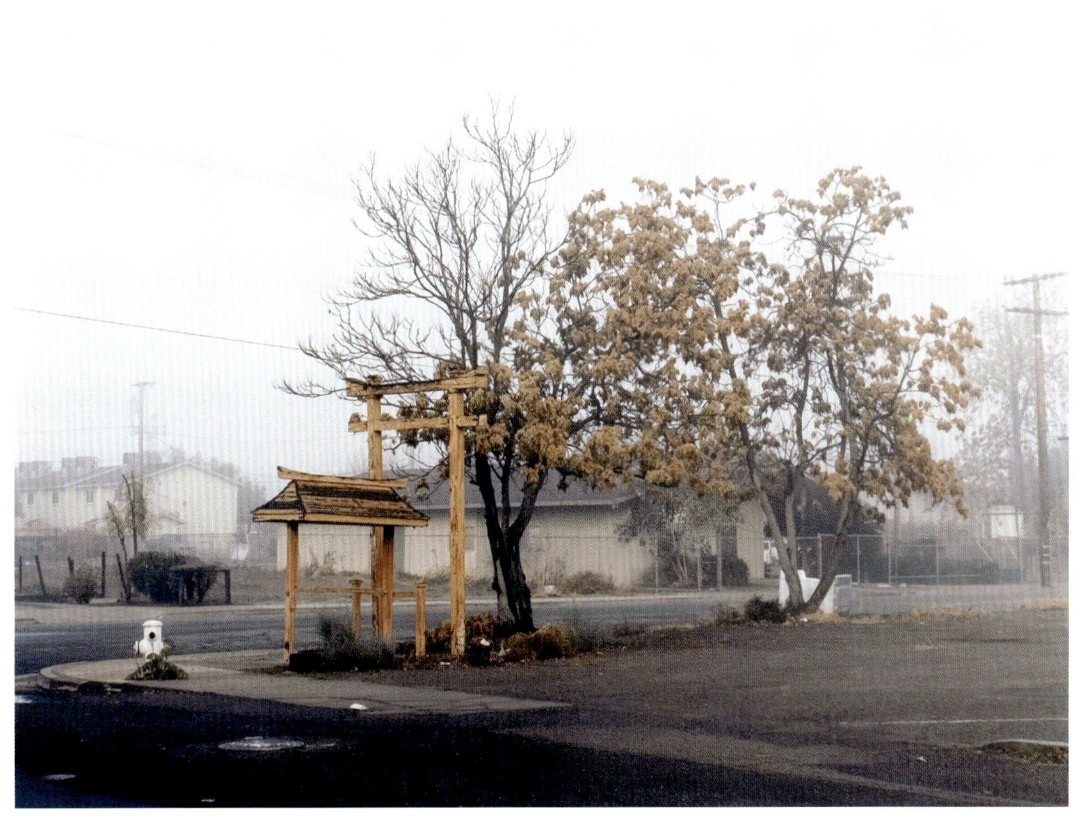

Evelyn Hang Yin, *Chinese Pagoda and Imperial Dynasty Parking I*, 2018. C-print, 40 × 50 in.

Notes

1. Institute of International Education, "Number of International Students in the United States Hits All-Time High," November 18, 2019, https://www.iie.org/Why-IIE/Announcements/2019/11/Number-of-International-Students-in-the-United-States-Hits-All-Time-High.

2. R. P. Deuel, "Not a Blank Check," *Inside Higher Ed*, June 16, 2020, https://www.insidehighered.com/views/2020/06/16/colleges-must-change-how-they-view-international-students-opinion.

3. Tom Bartlett and Karin Fischer, "The China Conundrum," *New York Times*, November 6, 2011, https://www.nytimes.com/2011/11/06/education/edlife/the-china-conundrum.html.

4. Institute of International Education, "Number of International Students in the United States"; Laura McKenna, "The Globalization of America's Colleges," *Atlantic*, November 18, 2015, https://www.theatlantic.com/education/archive/2015/11/globalization-american-higher-ed/416502/.

5. James Palmer, "How Is China Responding to the U.S. Protests?," *Foreign Policy*, June 3, 2020, https://foreignpolicy.com/2020/06/03/how-is-china-responding-to-the-u-s-protests/.

6. Xiaofang Wan, "Chinese Students Cautious about U.S. Study," *Inside Higher Ed: The World View*, October 27, 2019, https://www.insidehighered.com/blogs/world-view/chinese-students-cautious-about-us-study.

7. Bartlett and Fischer, "The China Conundrum."

8. Eric Fish, "End of an Era? A History of Chinese Students in America," China Project, May 12, 2020, https://thechinaproject.com/2020/05/12/end-of-an-era-a-history-of-chinese-students-in-america/.

9. Kristen Yee, "Skin Whitening, the Prejudice against Dark Skin and How Class in Asia Was Associated with Pale Skin Long before White Colonialism," *South China Morning Post*, April 20, 2020, https://www.scmp.com/lifestyle/arts-culture/article/3080423/skin-whitening-prejudice-against-dark-skin-and-how-class; Churan Zheng, "China Has No Problem with Racism, and That's a Problem," China Project, February 23, 2018, https://thechinaproject.com/2018/02/23/china-has-no-problem-with-racism-and-thats-a-problem/; Winslow Robertson, "A Brief History of Anti-Black Violence in China," *Africa Is a Country*, May 2020, https://africasacountry.com/2020/05/a-brief-history-of-anti-black-violence-in-china.

10. Fish, "End of an Era?"

Love Spirals

NOTES ON BROWN FEELINGS

J Molina-Garcia

J Molina-Garcia is a Salvadoran American media artist, professor, and writer. A graduate of the Photography and Media Program at CalArts, Molina-Garcia's visual and rhetorical output constructs assemblages of fiction, cultural criticism, and queer critical race theory to reanimate the dead (ancient knowledge and brown ghosts).

Family ruptures of the type characterizing contemporary mass death have created erratic unities between the body, self, and environment. Brown people are dying in high-def. Everywhere you look; it's panoramic and immersive.

Forty-nine people killed at Pulse, twenty-three at the Walmart shooting in El Paso, and an unknown number of child deaths at detention centers, under the oversight of a decentralized prison system run amuck, unregulated.

Something approaching the idea of national feelings has festered in my mind since the Pulse shootings occurred in the summer of 2016.[1] Living on the West Coast at the time, the distance between Orlando and me seemed entirely phantasmatic; the world had turned small, without borders. I turned to my friend and said, that could have been us.

Measurement foreclosed that day—a distance that grew small not only in spatial distance but in proximity to my body's politics. I saw only mirror copies in their wake. These names that sounded like mine: Almodovar, Torres, Martinez.

A news video appeared on my Facebook feed of Aurelia Martínez, the mother of one of the victims, speaking from Hidalgo, Mexico, in anguish on the first take: "Cuanto sufren las mamas para mantener sus hijos / How much do mothers suffer to tend/abide by/support/sustain/hold their children."[2] So many worlds were collapsing, and I thought, this must be what José Esteban Muñoz was talking about when he spoke of nationalized Brown feelings, Brown feelings felt on a mass scale. For if there is mass consumerism and viral action, there must also be mass feelings, operating on a mass scale, virulently. Other children and offspring of the Latin American diaspora would have understood these reactions—people for whom I wouldn't have to deliver the multiplicity of meaning that mantener holds. The word simply would have been felt, en masse.

Six years before his death in 2013, Muñoz had been writing on the outsized misery and politicized tears of the Brown subject in his quippy essay "Feeling Brown, Feeling Down," where the *feminized, racial* position of tears took central stage, boldly rejecting the generically or universally melancholic for the historically situated.[3] Reading now, I think he thought there was artfulness to *how* a Brown woman grieves (the methods *and recovery*).

If he were here now, I would ask him, *under the scale of violence* of Brown death (because it is truly a spectacle), what affective responses do I have in light of a nation intent on driving me to suicide? Muñoz hypothesized on how culturally bound vulnerabilities could battle conglomerates—dominant culture and the like—and how they might provide escape and liberation for minority identities or, as he might have said, the *minoritarian*; a word that remains foreign to my word editing application's spell checker because the idea of a minority identity holding a degree of control (-tarian) remains an unfulfilled syntactical promise.

The geographic shrinkage I felt at Pulse is but one very visible example of what I'm referring to, but it's not the exclusive domain of trauma, like some afterimage of violence that makes you feel as if you're next. There is a subtexture of closeness that keeps all disenfranchised populations affiliated. Had Muñoz lived, there is no timeline that would have prevented our inevitable kinship; one benefit of the subjection of a tyrannical sovereign is that it creates predestined pathways of overlap for the impoverished.

Is this not the same experience of relating to the dead, queer mentors of the AIDS epidemic? All that mythical gay life of creation and creative accomplishment banished. Black life in America must understand this as well. We go throughout our day communing with ghosts more than living ancestors because of systematic wipeouts of inherited knowledge and legacy. Does the minoritarian subject simply grieve like no other? Is this why the death of a known stranger feels like a deprivation, regardless of the distance that separates us across time and space? Hurt for the other remains.

In his works and case studies, Muñoz exhibited an effervescent thinking around belonging, companionship, and resistance, with a palette and taste for the particular radicality of cultural artifacts to intervene in the everyday. These are the seeds that inform my own research as an artist—how suffering stretches us closer across space and dissimilar temporalities—and why something like the misspelling of the word *minoritarian* appears like a margin of opportunity to blast open the rhetoric of violence deployed through official language.

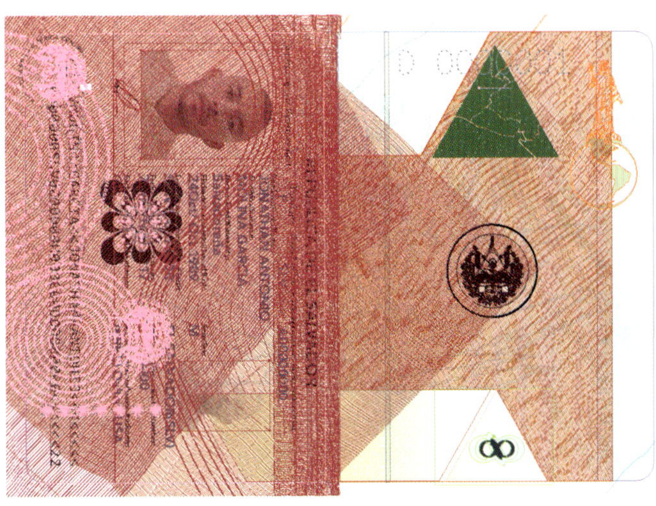

J Molina-Garcia, *Superpasaporte (digital reconstruction of anti-theft patterns)*, 2017. Adobe Illustrator file, 4.75 × 3.5 in, 7.5 × 5.25 in.

Most of the processes I employ are shelled within their own respective box of depressive labor, directly outputted from a melancholic need to repair.

I spent hours illustrating digital copies of the antitheft patterns that appear on passports, so that I could print infinite copies of my Salvadoran passport, whose internal language I amended to translate a phrase in Spanish that is left curiously untranslated in English: "Este registro tiene por objeto facilitar la protección legal debida a los Salvadoreños en el extranjero / The purpose of this document is to facilitate the legal protection *owed* to Salvadorans in the foreign land" (my italics). I grew up to become a forgery artist, making counterfeits to catalog the range of Brown feelings reacting against state control. In an unfair game, the local pickpockets, petty thieves, and criminals will have the best methods of analysis. Looking to artifice and reassembly, you find: the doctored deceptions, the pickpocket's nimbleness, the border-crosser's survival tactics. People cheating to survive.

Muñoz writes that tragedy begets a rip, a breakdown in the revolutionary imaginary, making us feel helpless or out of ideas. These outsized events get so big that they can't be contained or managed. Our hearts stop, we are speechless; we are made senseless. Rationality (common sense) fatigues.

Muñoz's theory is no longer speculative; anyone surviving the COVID era will know the immobilizing mannerisms of national feelings; they have become embodied; we are paralyzed. Why are we so fatigued in the days following the mass spectacle of Black death in America? Do you remember your tired body the summer George Floyd died? You can barely stand it because collective anguish must work like an incantatory contagion, like internal screams amplifying a Wi-Fi signal, so that we're all in misery, en masse.

(Brownness, Muñoz notes, in its use and deployment of depressive positions, is a mode of attentiveness *to the* self *for* others. *To* the self *for* others. This idea/concept never made sense to me until after I understood the pain of self-love.)

Here's the short of it. Depression suspends thought. Ethics emerges out of it, providing greater insight into psychic reality. The depressive condition interjects obsessive attachment that can clog the emotional sores left by Capital. Obsession (which can take the form of an attachment behaving like a spiral; fractal and exponential) can become self-destructive because it is a deluge: however unpredictable, it holds its own quiet, efficient agency. Love does this as well. You want to do its bidding, but it might kill you in the process.

Optimistically, Muñoz thought the deluge could be leveraged to drive our civic interactions with the state, creating pools of nationalized Brown feelings held together through membership in near disintegration ("Brownness is a kind of uncanny persistence in the face of *distressed* conditions of possibility").[4]

Of the ashes, we take the anger and the hurt and metabolize it as an external spectacle that cauterizes the wound. Aesthetics are crucial here. Jordan Peele does something Muñoz would have heralded—a truly disidentificatory response to the genre of horror; Peele constructs cinematic representations of the nightmares of the Black mind, demonstrating the merit of publishing the terrors of the subaltern and their origin, *for they are shared* among more than one.

Brown feelings are not destiny—not a dogma or ideology that would bind Latinx subjects to any predetermined course of action or a space of belonging (like a cookie cutter mold), although maybe you'll cry harder, *together*, when you finally see yourself represented in culture or suffer the death of your worshipped idol. Selena's death was Brown feelings maximized.

Muñoz said it like this: "Communal mourning by its very nature, is an immensely complicated text to read, for we do not mourn just one lost object or other, but we also mourn as a 'whole.'"[5]

Affective attachment made possible through racial conditioning doesn't create mechanical (unfeeling) clones, but it certainly provides a matrix of induction whereby racialized subjects understand each other at the level of the material, which can make way for a stronger, coalition-based politics. It's about weaponizing our shared *affinities*.

Brown feelings make possible the physical vibration of matter, making things appear as if in a circuit, where one injury inevitably reverberates along the net. It's not about knowing; it's about quaking and turbulence—the feeling, unspoken, that you and I are vibrating on a genealogical wavelength.[6]

Love Spirals, Act II

It's 2016—I'm watching that VICE documentary interviewing a white supremacist at the Charlottesville rally who tells the correspondent he's readying for a war, and immediately, I go to my pull-up bar and do ten pull-ups.

It's 2020—video of unmarked vehicles driven by federal agents kidnapping protesters in broad daylight, cleaving them from indignant and helpless friends and bystanders, and later in the news, a seventeen-year-old shoots two protesters in Wisconsin. I keep my mouth closed, but mournfully, I think we've already entered a new stage of civil war in America.

Inside, you start miming warfare, playing out fears and gothic spectacles of capture in your head. All that I see on social media, whether real or artificial, tells me something about something I already knew: I Hate America and America Hates Me.[7]

An ongoing project begun in 2016 involved making mechanical camouflage and invisibility uniforms for border crossers. I started miming warfare, calling my mother about ICE stopping points for her to avoid. I sank into despair, and out of it, I brainstormed artful deceptions: mechanical camouflage suits changing their spots in response to their environment. What criminal methods are these? Mimicry is one of the most curious artifacts of fiction and fantasy: a product of decorative forgery and yet fully operational, particularly in realms of zoology, it functions to hide the threatened or *threatening* organism from death and danger.

Imitation, however, can come too close to the real thing, like when an insect mistakes its own kin, killing it: "with the imitation of the leaf serving as an incitement to cannibalism in this particular kind of totemic feast." Caillois called it a collective masochism[8]—groups deciding to trend toward their collective death, toward an abyss. What the surrealist French philosopher hoped to uncover were these pathologies of perception: those moments of sick sight (ill perception) that could express certain truths about our social topos and metaphysics.

Visual mimicry can only happen in light. It requires vision to be functional, and the patterns of nature in which it is observable, particularly those moments when anthropomorphic projection takes flight—like when humans look at butterflies and see eyes—demonstrate a fundamental seduction of lighted space. Mimicry emerges out of the organism's enchanted desire to disappear in light—a photo frenzy.

The utility of mimicry or its instrumentalization by the artist, the writer, the philosopher-engineer is truly apotropaic magic, the "oculus indiviosus, the evil eye that not only harms but can also protect once it has been turned against the evil powers to which it naturally belongs, as an organ of fascination par excellence."[9]

Idealistically, or naively, I thought COVID-19 would make the digital more personable, a better conduit and interface for feeling, and media artists would helm the movement toward a new leviathan: a novel, networked reality of human and nonhuman compact.

Do you know what I mean? The accelerated union of flesh and metal holds the promise of cyborg transcendence; we camouflage in the mystique of the lighted screen to disappear and become anew. Napster would let you curate the everyday with songs for free, turning a generation into pirates. The digital represented an outsized field of potential precisely because there was nothing behind it; it was all light show, phantasmagoria, and empty masquerade.

When Byung-Chul Han talks about the fickle social organizing of online forums, he says, "the digital inhabitants of the Net do not assemble. They lack the interiority of assembly that would bring forth a *we*. They form a gathering without assembly—a crowd without interiority, without a soul or spirit" (my italics).[10] One feels the need to interject from the sides of Generation Z and their free-form anarcho-primitivistic approaches to technology. Hellfire will be raised by their kind, and this is a source of both great

(*opposite*) J Molina-Garcia, *Girl's Tactical Camosuit (a prototype)*, 2019. Wearable custom inkjet-printed canvas and silk, dimensions variable. Photo: May Makki.

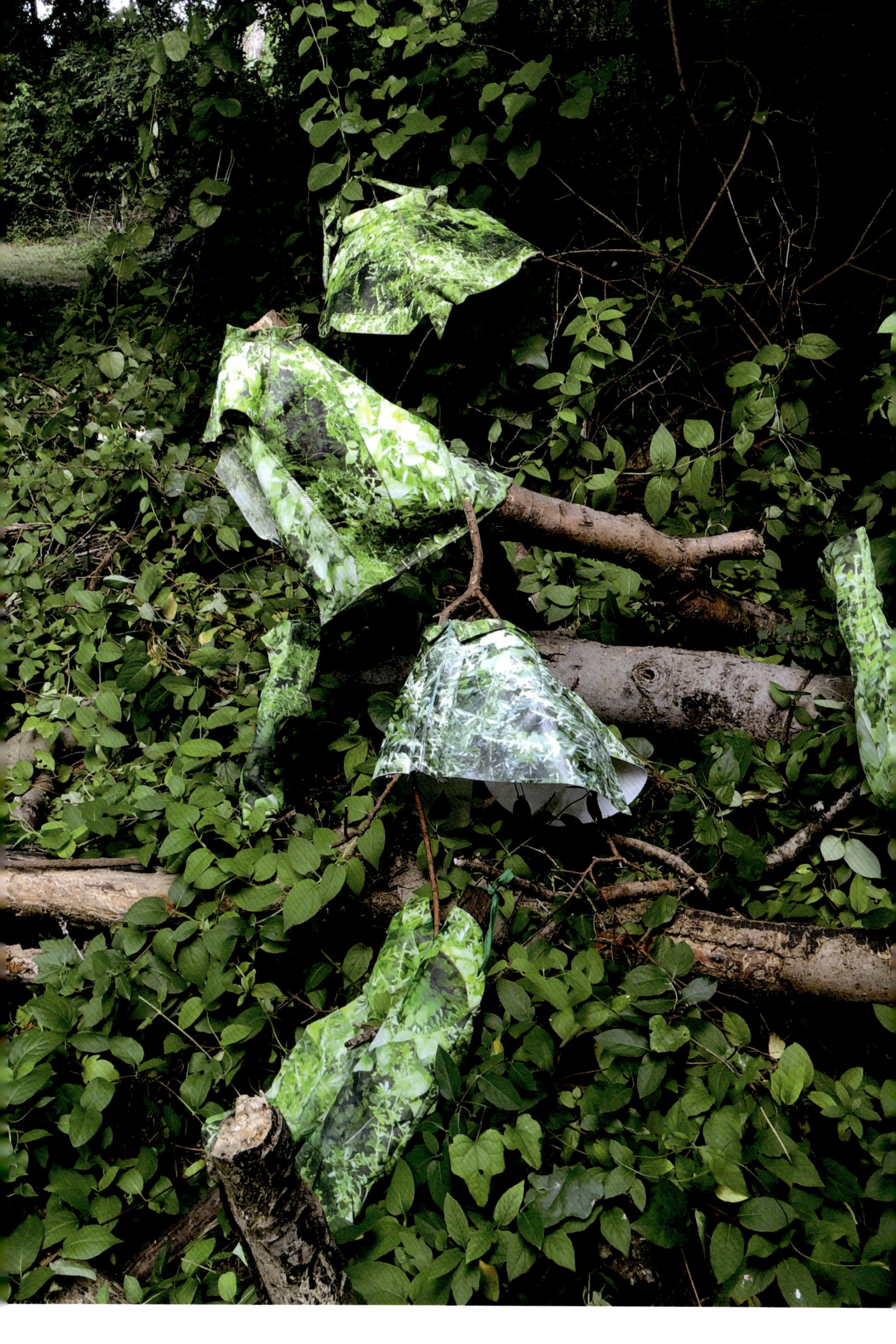

fear and awe. What affliction of sick sight will possess the lost children of detention centers? How evil will their eyes be?

When the child concentration camps worsened and family separation policies were introduced into law, it seemed obvious that my suits should be worn by children, so I employed two of my nieces to model the first set of prototypes. After a live, outdoor performance at a sculpture park in Dallas, the words of a friend echoed from months earlier: "the children are already invisible," he said, in response to my project, while admiring its speculative, world-building angle.

A live performance of hidden Brown girls intimated one level of invisibility, but represented like this, they were virtual to the point that they might already not exist. Muñoz was clear that there was a necessary distinction: a difference between engaging in clinical depression (its paranoid-schizophrenic representations that continue the numb repetition of the negative) and a war of provisional positions that deliberate on the sacred boundaries that keep us connected. The second is a habitual and daily praxis of love: a *spiral of doing love* that sharpens hope, instead of dulling it.

"Representation is an anthropocentric demand," Jasbir Puar writes—a way of saying that the merit of having an identity in the first place is a political privilege of the capable, adult, speaking population.[11] No condition of visibility improves what regulated national feelings do, that is, what they deem capable of being retrieved, represented.

I sought to stage a new set of disappearances of the child inside machines, turning them into digital-point clouds, and thus into crude avatars (poor imitators). Massive is a Hollywood FX software built to generate virtual crowds, conceived for the epic battle scenes that awed audiences in the *Lord of the Rings* film trilogy. The program uses an intricate node system of if/then statements to control the "brains of computer-generated crowds," variegating responses to the environment without the human worker having to rig the skeletal framework of individual figures.

The dark winter of AI research—a period spanning the 1970s and '80s in which AI funding and research halted—was in large part resolved by the mathematics underpinning the "fuzzy" logic at the heart of the Massive software, which outputs values outside of the confining true/false dichotomy provided by Boolean logic. The nonlinear functions behind modern-day algorithms, moreover, perform in such a way as to imitate imprecision and human randomness, nurturing an intelligence by introducing decimals, where before there were only totalizing integers.

The circuitry of artificial life is therefore built on the introduction of difference and multitude. The more diversified data you feed the artificial neurons of generative algorithms, the more perfected the digital copy becomes; the imitation is granular, down to its defects. The imperfections are in fact greater proof of its efficacy. The artificial neurons evolve because they cannot know the other, and this difference (the incommensurability of the other) is constitutive of their own wholeness in the world. "To touch something is to make contact with it even while remaining separate from it because entities that touch do not fuse together. To touch is to caress a surface . . . but to never master and consume it."[12] These are the spiral gifts of love, regenerating past, present, and futures: assembling respect, recognition, and a blueprint forward.

I've fantasized about a child army redrawing the Texas southern border, little soldiers chiseling the earth to liberate an Indigenous past, renaming and resettling land according to lines drawn by Native nations. Their maps are camouflaged too. Surveillance is a solar project, with no taste for the subdermal, subterranean, occluded/occult; a fear of it, perhaps. Indigeneity is its adversary.

Perhaps by methods of walking and dragging, the child schools (not an army, but schools, like those of fish) erode hills with tiny footsteps, this blind swarm simply feeling, erasing their way down, jumping into a void of trust. Or is it suicide? What's the difference? It's not collective masochism as Caillois would have called it, when the organ sees itself indistinctly from the organism; this is not a pathology of sight, it is mutual salvation—a *convergence*. Buddhists might call it devotional, abiding love.[13]

A photographic grid of victim portraits becomes hypercamouflaged within a sea of complacency when there aren't enough tears shed. The destitution of sight happens when we regard the dissolved mass without a beginning or end (a numb repetition): Almodovar, Ayala, Chevez, Carrillo, Fernandez, Ortiz, and the forty-two other names at Pulse that night keep repeating, making their hollow presence known each time another mass shooting occurs, but they appear as ghostly droplets without an aesthetic vessel to receive them, mediate their afterimage, much less purge the grief unto the world. This spectacle of consumption is only an ouroboros of paranoia-schizophrenia.

What affective responses do I have in light of the rot of Western civilization? Well, how many ways can one conceive to enlarge a given social reality, the onto-particularities that make up the ethics of Brown feeling, so that it occupies the entire screen of affect and sensation? We have far more depressives with imaginative truths than con-men delivering the same rote, scripted lies of corpo-neo-liberalism.

Nationalized Whiteness reproduces clinical depression in the world, and it is the true criminal of democracy, regulating body orientation, spinning you, craning your neck, establishing how you mourn with how many tears. The State is already looking the other way, enforcing you to do the same. They're dragging us away from the funeral by the neck.

The simulation—and the larger project of browning the world—is akin to the dark mirror of the screen or renegade maps redrawn by the crowded footsteps of a serpentine and virtual intelligence. Simulations don't own the Master's tools; they undo them.

Brown feelings suspend your breath, provide relief, and anticipate something better to come; performed and worked over, they become an "educated-desire" or a "critical hope"—"an active refusal and a salient demand for something else."[14] To touch, to quake, to reverberate, to vibrate, like a Wi-Fi signal in harmony: *to do love*. Is there a word for that?

Collectively, we must craft a war of positions (love) to command forfeitures, seizures, and wholesale desistance. A *we* that could be a *one* (because, it is, after all, an option to participate), or a *one* that is infinitely a *we*.

Notes

1. If you go on Wikipedia right now, take note of this: in the summer of 2016, just a few months shy of the Trump presidential victory, a twenty-nine-year-old American-born man demolished a total of 102 people at Pulse, a gay nightclub in Florida that was hosting its weekly Latino Night; he would claim the murder spree for ISIS amid speculation of his own repressed sexuality. He killed forty-nine people. Counting them is important. Fifty-three were wounded. One hundred and two families were ruptured (killed) that summer day.

2. Univision Noticias, "Historia de una de las víctimas mexicanas de la masacre de Orlando," June 13, 2016, YouTube video, 1:47, https://www.youtube.com /watch?v=VChgNNNx-sk.

3. José Esteban Muñoz, "Feeling Brown, Feeling Down: Latina Affect, the Performativity of Race, and the Depressive Position," *Signs* 31, no. 3 (2006): 675–88. He remains criminally underrepresented in collections of other white authors writing on the subject of what ultimately became a somewhat trendy philosophical discourse known as affect theory, germinations of which can be seen in Baruch Spinoza's *Ethics* or the oral traditions and metaphysics of Indigenous women of the Global South, if we are to be completely honest to the historical record. Affective chants, affective fire, vaporous body schema, and the vitality of touch for transference of spirit are all present in Mayan cosmology—hallmarks, too, of the studies undertaken by affect scholars. See Timothy W. Knowlton, "Flame, Icons, and Healing: A Colonial Maya Ontology," *Colonial Latin American Review* 27, no. 3 (2018): 392–412.

4. José Esteban Muñoz, "The Brown Commons," in *The Sense of Brown* (Durham, NC: Duke University Press, 2020), 4.

5. José Esteban Muñoz, "Photographies of Mourning: Melancholia and Ambivalence in Van Der Zee, Mapplethorpe, and *Looking for Langston*," in *Disiden-*

tifications: Queers of Color and the Performance of Politics (Minneapolis: University of Minnesota Press, 1999), 73.

6. "What has been derided for centuries as 'primitive superstition' has only recently been 'discovered' by Western scientists and academics as 'valid' knowledge. Nevertheless, knowledge alone has never ended imperialism." Nick Estes, "Prologue: Prophets," in *Our History Is the Future: Standing Rock versus the Dakota Access Pipeline, and the Long Tradition of Indigenous Resistance* (London: Verso, 2019), 9.

7. I borrow this elegant epithet with the permission of performance artist Vicente Ugartechea, who coined it for a 2017 processional flag-burning performance.

8. Roger Caillois, "Mimicry and Legendary Psychasthenia," in *The Edge of Surrealism*, ed. Claudine Frank (Durham, NC: Duke University Press, 2003), 97.

9. Caillois, "Mimicry," 93.

10. Byung-Chul Han, "In the Swarm," in *In the Swarm: Digital Prospects* (Cambridge, MA: MIT Press, 2017), 11.

11. Jasbir Puar, "Introduction: The Cost of Getting Better," in *The Right to Maim: Debility, Capacity, Disability* (Durham, NC: Duke University Press, 2017), 27.

12. Graham Harman, "On Interface; Nancy's Weights and Masses," in *Jean Luc Nancy and Plural Thinking*, ed. Peter Gratton and Marie-Eve Morin (Albany: State University of New York Press, 2012), 98, quoted from José Esteban Muñoz, *The Sense of Brown*, 7.

13. "When thus your mind is even with regard to all, / Then just as you would wish / That your own mother meet with happiness, / Think the same for all embodied beings. / All living beings thus become the object of your love, / The form of which consists / In wanting, in the immediate term, / That beings have the happiness of gods and humankind . . . / Beginning with a single being, / Train yourself to embrace all . . . "

Longchenpa, "7. The Four Unbounded Attitudes," in *Finding Rest in the Nature of the Mind: The Trilogy of Rest*, vol. 1, trans. Padmakara Translation Group (Boulder, CO: Shambala, 2017), 78.

14. Muñoz, "The Brown Commons," 6.

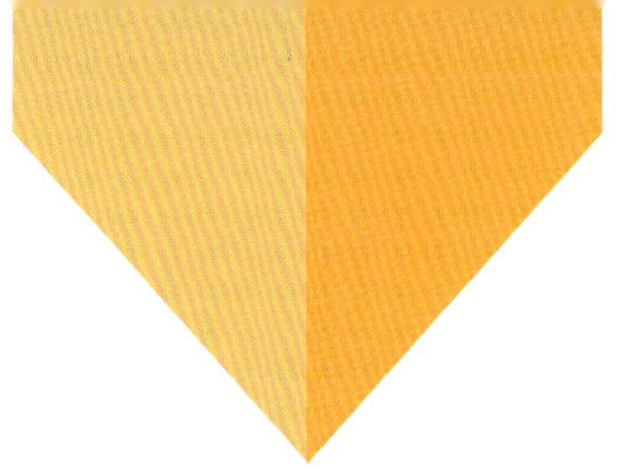

CREATING A WORLD WITHOUT PRISONS

CULTURE AND THE CARCERAL STATE

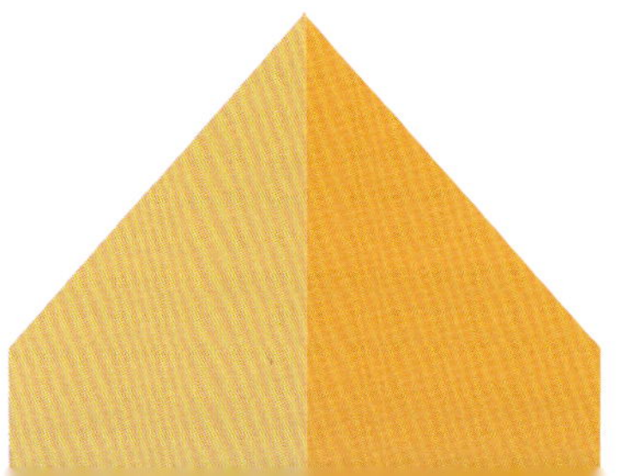

Introduction

Kassandra L. Khalil

Kassandra L. Khalil is a visual artist and former codirector of Arts in a Changing America. Kassandra's drawings and sculptures explore how movement and gestures evoke personal and cultural memory. Kassandra channels her interest in Caribbean communities and the culture of resistance into organizing arts programming for her Haitian diaspora in New York.

For the 2.3 million people incarcerated and detained in the United States and the millions more impacted by state-institutionalized violence, the 2020 uprisings for Black lives were a validation of what they already knew: the carceral system impacts us all.[1] Or as Critical Carceral Visualities' director Ruby Tapia puts it, the carceral state is wider than the formal mechanisms of the criminal justice system. It includes the social and ideological structures that perpetuate the "tangible and sometimes intangible ways in punitive orientations to difference, to poverty, to struggles to social justice and to the crossers of constructed borders of all kinds."[2]

As a country founded on controlled freedoms afforded only to a select few, the United States undeniably embodies the definition of a carceral state. Today we find ourselves pressed to understand its permeating impact on our freedom as well as on our relationships and responsibilities while we dream what other forms of corrective action might look like. We are gaining a more detailed popular understanding of the US prison-industrial complex as conversations on topics like surveillance, judicial prejudice, and discrimination take seats at our dinner tables and persist on our daily news feeds. But it's complicated. Sentence commuting for elderly and health-vulnerable inmates has become a politicized position rather than an active solution, even amid prisons' lethal inefficiency and lack of protocol oversight.[3] We see United States Immigration and Customs Enforcement

(ICE)–detained individuals experiencing family separations, coerced sterilizations, and coronavirus positivity rates thirteen times higher than those of the rest of the US population.[4] We nod our heads understandingly as young Black Instagramers share memories of getting the "cop talk" from their parents. Concurrently, we navigate mixed emotions when flicking through comments disbelieving or defending the victims of police violence as the media correlates morality and race with worthiness for life.[5] We seem to wrestle with recognizing the humanity of those who've had a brush with the law rather than understanding ways that the underresourced, disabled, and people of color have been targeted by our carceral system.

The work toward liberation is continually moving. We see it from the work to protect the disproportionate number of Native youth in the US federal prison system to the increasing practice of automatically expunging misdemeanors.[6] We are seeing communities take hold of leading reforms through landmark ballot box wins like civilian-proposed Measures R and J in Los Angeles by prioritizing care over a cell.[7] Many more recognize that a guilty verdict for Derek Chauvin is not justice for George Floyd; truthful accountability is only the beginning of saving lives from carceral violence. Change is happening. Key to this progress is that it has been led by those who have spent time inside, those whose daily existence is threatened by state violence, and the hard questions they ask. What do we imagine in a future where prison is abolished? What happens when we look to each other rather than our government to help us heal from violence? What part does artistic creativity play in this change?

Answering these questions between bars and across barriers, the organizers and artists included in this section are imagining a world without prisons. They center collective safety and healing through cultural knowledge, creative expression, and exchange.

A carceral state regularly attacks the fullness of our joy, inherited knowledge, and relationships to co-opt them within the state's operative power. So it is on us, the People, to activate and connect our forces in resistance and for reimagining. Organizer and former codirector of Southerners on New Ground (SONG) **Mary Hooks** reminds us that "our lives do not belong to the State." As such, an abolitionist future focused on healing and de-escalation must come from within our community. Hooks pushes us to recognize the tools used by our ancestors, elders, and neighbors by asking, "If you didn't have to call the police, who would you want to be able to call for help?" Disability Justice activist **Lydia X. Z. Brown** asks us a similar question as they critique the panoptical nature of the US carceral state, which does not differentiate between people in the criminal justice system and people seeking help but experiencing state control as a result of their ability status. They assert, "prisons and institutions do not keep us safe; they do not protect either the people outside them or the people in them." In this way, abolition becomes "a natural extension of and kin to the work of Disability Justice," as mutually aligned work challenges institutions that inhibit our ability to experience care, pleasure, and "justice without precondition." Change for a more just future requires us to re-evaluate our connection to one another. In **Aydinaneth Ortiz**'s *HOGAR*, mental illness and cultural differences are seen as punishable offenses. Even still, as Brown extends, the institutions charged with reforming are under-resourced and focus on whittling down who is acceptable and worthy of care. In San Antonio, artist **Mark Menjívar** places us in a secret sanctuary room and poetically traces a network of friends in migration from the Northern Triangle who are experiencing isolation, separation, solidarity, and repatriation. Looking through time and space, Menjívar shows us how personal memory becomes knowledge and, together with others, becomes part of the movement for immigrant rights. **Tani Ikeda** takes account of the othering in the name of nationalism through her poetic response. Following the intersections of xenophobia and US identity, she sets a tempo of solidarity that goes unbroken in her generation.

Researcher and curator Nicole Fleetwood tunes us to the significance of carceral aesthetics as art produced "under the conditions of unfreedom."[8] With this lens, the significance of incarcerated artists' approach to materials and content is imbued with dynamic social critique. **Spel**'s use of materials while serving life in prison weighs the use of contraband with expression, rather weighing the risk of further unfreedom with creative liberation. *I guess if you think about it we are all in it* provokes viewers to further contemplate the limits of unfree conditions while all people, inside and outside of carceral institutions, experience the consequence of the carceral state. In *Locked in a Dark Calm*, **Tameca Cole** refuses to reconcile the double consciousness of her self-portrait of metered calm and frustration, aiming to see herself as whole in her discontent but fragmented from truthful expression by systems of carceral control. The importance of looking within becomes more pointed when isolation is not a "new normal" reality. Truthworker Theatre Company's founder and artistic director **Samara Gaev** artistically shares correspondence with writer and death row inmate **Jarvis Jay Masters** about the impact of twenty-one years in solitary confinement and how to purposely focus on life and hope in the face of uncertainty.

One of the most violent components of life inside a carceral institution is the severing from one's community. For **Dustina Gill**, from the Wahpekute band of the Sisseton-Wahpeton Oyate of South Dakota, these connections to community and tradition are the singular path for healing Native incarcerated youth. Unpacking the legacy of the "3 As" (Annihilation, Assimilation, and Acculturation), Gill makes clear the deeply violent reality of incarceration on Native youth because of the ways it disrupts intergenerational relationships and systems of care. **Hinaleimoana Kwai Kong Wong-Kalu (Kumu Hina)** talks about the reckoning that hoʻoponopono or making "something correct . . . to bring to balance" offers Kanaka Maoli and non-Native people in the Hawaiʻi prison system. Reconciling past action with future choices is central to the wholeness of a person as well as the stewarding of Hawaiʻi's land and its sovereignty, a system grounded in mutual care and accountability. In Philadelphia, **Faith Bartley, Courtney Bowles,** and **Mark Strandquist** of the People's Paper Co-op know that life after incarceration necessitates rebuilding families and futures. They show us that an effective arts-based, people-centered strategy responds to real-life needs by supporting counternarratives, direct aid, and policy change. **Kenyetta A. C. Hinkle**'s *#107* from *The Evanesced Series* (2016–) offers a mere slice of the gendered ways in which the carceral experience endangers and erases bodies. Part painting, part performance, *The Evanesced* body of work expresses the power of the #SayHerName call to protect, mourn, and heal the Black female body by refusing the ways it has been made invisible and disposable.[9] In one moment during the performance, a woman's voice repeats a poem-chant in cycles. Hinkle stomps at each syllable: "Beauty walks beneath me, beauty be protecting me, for now and forevermore more more."[10]

Provoking the ways carceral institutions perceive some bodies as deserving incarceration, **Sherrill Roland**'s *Jumpsuit Project* uses his experience of fighting to clear his name and the visual disruption of the orange jumpsuit to engage in intimate, direct conversations about the complex impact of incarceration. Those who have not experienced firsthand the cost of incarceration don't fully understand how a person's life after imprisonment is dramatically altered. Shifting these perspectives and dismantling a carceral system ultimately require change from within. This change is not limited to those who are incarcerated. As musicians, Street Symphony's **Vijay Gupta** and **Duane Robert Garcia** reflect on the power of sound to generate dialogue and center the creative humanity of LA's unhoused and formerly incarcerated communities. The interconnectedness of our life experiences reveals the finite nature of a lifetime. This urgency is expressed through language and image: **Kondwani Fidel** with photographer

Devin Allen present the stark reality of the Black experience in Baltimore and how Baltimore's young people encounter the tilted mirror of the US criminal justice system. Together they ask back, "How many times did we tell you we were hungry for love? How many times did we tell you we were hungry for a way out? How many times did we tell you we were hungry for something as simple as a fair chance?" They stand waiting for the answer and knowing the reasons why.

These artists and cultural workers are revealing exploitation at the hands of the US carceral state and setting new precedents for community-led justice. They represent the undoing of centuries of race- and difference-based policies that since their establishment have been used to control the movement of communities of color. The efforts named above and endless more are moving us toward an ecology of care and restorative justice. Simply, they are all working to get more free.

Notes

1. Wendy Sawyer and Peter Wagner, "Mass Incarceration: The Whole Pie 2020," Prison Policy Initiative, March 24, 2020, https://www.prisonpolicy.org/reports/pie2020.html.

2. Gabrielle French, Allie Goodman, and Chloe Carlson, "What Is the Carceral State?," U-M Carceral State Project, Documenting Criminalization and Confinement, May 2020, https://storymaps.arcgis.com/stories/7ab5f5c3fbca46c38f0b2496bcaa5ab0.

3. "Reducing Jail and Prison Populations during the Covid-19 Pandemic," Brennan Center for Justice, August 2, 2021, https://www.brennancenter.org/our-work/research-reports/reducing-jail-and-prison-populations-during-covid-19-pandemic.

4. Maya Manian, "Immigration Detention and Coerced Sterilization: History Tragically Repeats Itself," American Civil Liberties Union, September 29, 2020, https://www.aclu.org/news/immigrants-rights/immigration-detention-and-coerced-sterilization-history-tragically-repeats-itself; Eamon N. Dreisbach, "COVID-19 Case Rates among ICE Detainees 13 Times Higher Than US Average," Infectious Disease News, Healio, November 4, 2020, https://www.healio.com/news/infectious-disease/20201104/covid19-case-rates-among-ice-detainees-13-times-higher-than-us-average.

5. Annie Waldman, "Michael Brown 'No Angel' Controversy," BBC News, August 25, 2014, https://www.bbc.com/news/blogs-echochambers-28929087.

6. "Native Lives Matter report," Lakota People's Law Project, February 2015, https://lakotalaw.org/resources/native-lives-matter; "50-State Comparison: Marijuana Legalization, Decriminalization, Expungement, and Clemency," Restoration of Rights Project, June 2021, https://ccresourcecenter.org/state-restoration-profiles/50-state-comparison-marijuana-legalization-expungement.

7. "Los Angeles County, California, Measure R, Civilian Police Oversight Commission and Jail Plan Initiative (March 2020)," Local Ballot Measures: The Basics of Direct Democracy, Ballotpedia, March 2020, https://ballotpedia .org/Los_Angeles_County,_California,_Measure_R,_Civilian_Police_Oversight _Commission_and_Jail_Plan_Initiative_(March_2020)#Measure_design; "Analysis: Measure J," County of Los Angeles, July 24, 2020, http://file.lacounty .gov/SDSInter/bos/supdocs/147585.pdf.

8. Nicole Fleetwood, *Marking Time: Art in the Age of Mass Incarceration* (Cambridge, MA: Harvard University Press, 2020), 25.

9. Kenyetta A. C. Hinkle, *The Evanesced Series*, KACH Studio, accessed December 2, 2022, https://www.kachstudio.com/the-evanesced.

10. Kenyetta A. C. Hinkle, *The Evanesced: Embodied Disappearance 2017*, KACH Studio, accessed December 2, 2022, https://www.kachstudio.com/performance.

To Create in Prison

Spel

Most individuals who observe my work at a glance are prone to say, "It's abstract, it's expressionistic, modern." It may be, but I believe that to categorize is to marginalize, and such labels I defy. My work includes personal elements conveying the unfettered spirit and soul. Creativity provides meaning when all else fails. The work is alive. It summons willing participants to hold dialogues, to be educated, to elevate their spirit and consciousness to the unknown. Through these paintings I am a vessel transmitting for the voiceless, rendering a symphony of balance and pure energy, reflections of the past, present, and future. Layers of dichotomous elements are symbolic to what exists in this life and thereafter.

Making art has always been instrumental in my journey through life. Being incarcerated forces you to have to acclimate and accept the conditions of life in a new world where rules and regulations are met from both the jailed and jailers. To survive is key. Creating becomes much more serious in such an environment, but with so many restrictions and rules about "what you can and cannot have," you again must adapt and become super resourceful; the adage "One man's trash is another man's treasure" becomes so real.

For a long time, I salvaged all sorts of discarded materials, foraging for what I viewed as being useful for the next masterpiece. Having created

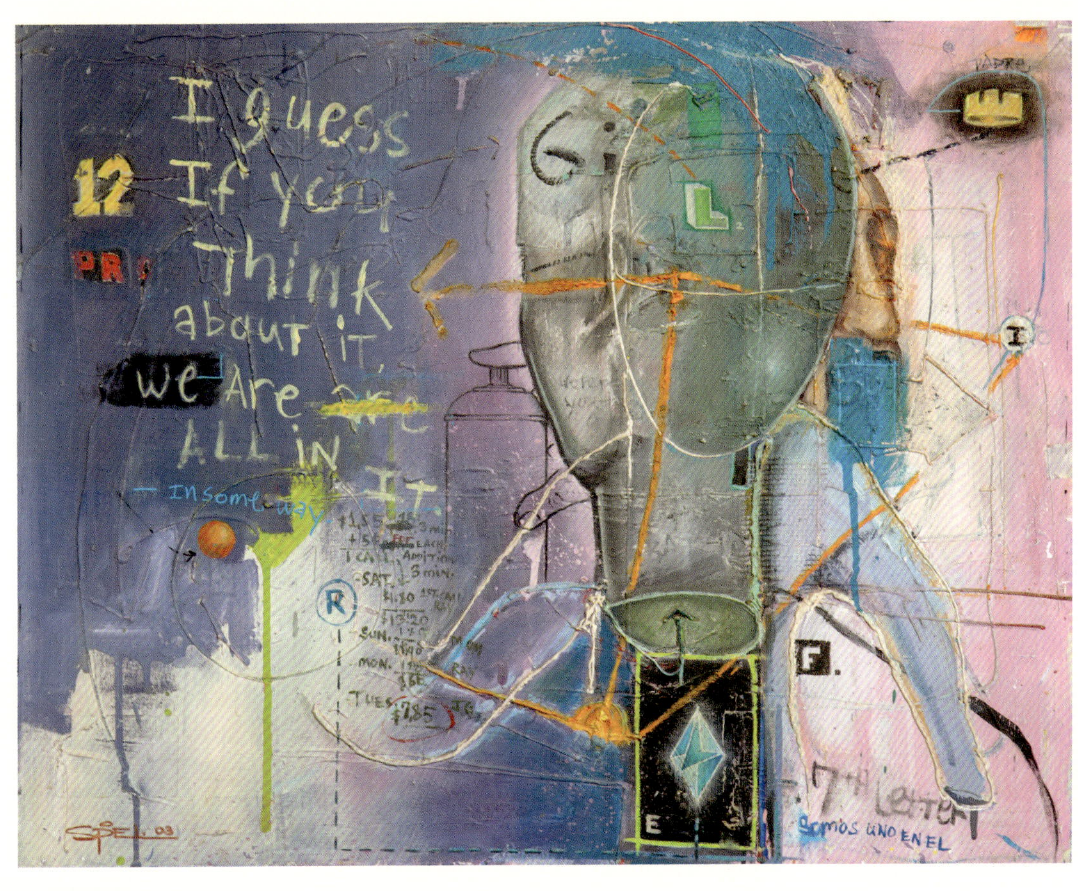

Spel, *I guess if you think about it we are all in it*, 2002–3.
Acrylic, oil, oil stick, spray paint, marker, drywall tape,
and sticker on paper mounted on panel, 24 × 19 in.

many works throughout my time in prison, I find that people (in the free community) are usually amazed to discover that I use such nontraditional materials. The works possess a raw grittiness that I think could not be achieved if not for the materials and manner in which they are used. The process of finding what I consider useful becomes in itself an act of mental gymnastics. "Okay, is this or that material considered contraband? Do I go for it?" you ask yourself. In the end, the risks far outweigh the repercussions. My work is my buoy. I guess I am most creative when my options are limited and I'm told I cannot.

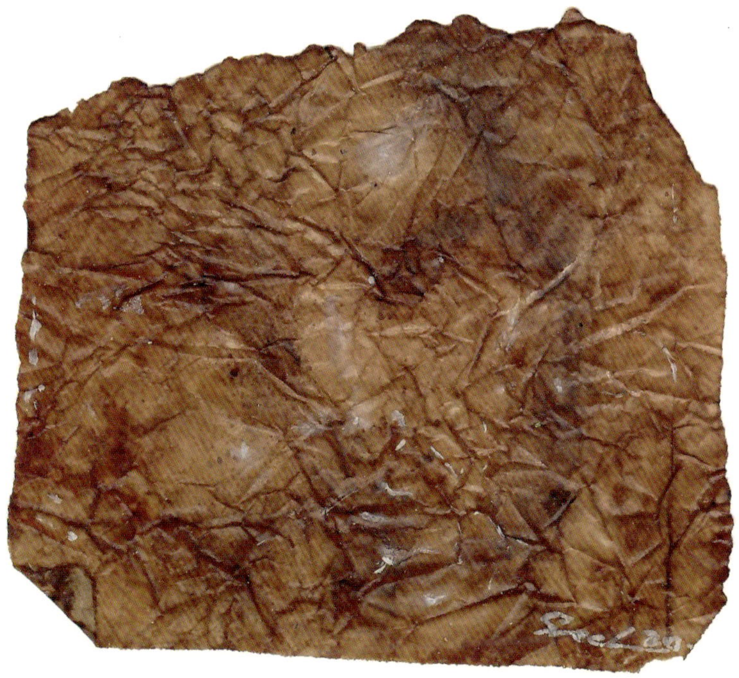

Spel, *with each day*, 2021. Hand-torn toilet tissue wrapper soaked in instant coffee, floor sealer, marker, 5.5 × 5 in.

A Measure of Joy

Samara Gaev and Jarvis Jay Masters

Samara Gaev, founder and artistic director of Truthworker Theatre Company, is a Brooklyn-based activist, educator, director, performer, doula, and single mama. Living and working at the intersections of social change, trauma-informed community engagement, and performance, she examines and challenges constructions of power, privilege, the prison industrial complex, and systems of oppression that enable cycles of violence.

Jarvis Jay Masters is a widely published writer and the author of *That Bird Has My Wings: The Autobiography of an Innocent Man on Death Row* and *Finding Freedom*. His poem "Recipe for Prison Pruno" won the PEN Award in 1992. In collaboration with Truthworker Theatre Company, Masters's work and life story have been adapted and performed in a variety of venues, including the National Cathedral and the Kennedy Center.

A Measure of Joy *excerpts and weaves together verbatim dialogue, transcribed and adapted from communications spanning over six months in the height of* COVID-19 *between Truthworker Theatre Company founder/director Samara Gaev, and Jarvis Jay Masters, an innocent man on death row. Jarvis, who has been incarcerated since the age of nineteen in San Quentin Prison, spent over twenty consecutive years in solitary confinement, and has been living on death row for over thirty. Through their decade-long collaboration, a powerful triangulation of healing has emerged between a dozen young visionaries directly impacted by mass incarceration, a survivor of a violent crime whose perpetrator is spending multiple lifetimes in prison, and a death row inmate whose capacity for liberation within the walls of confinement is astounding. Each continues to grow closer to themselves, their healing, their purpose, and compassion as they collectively strive to interrupt and transform the criminalizing and violent systems that permeate our communities.*

I open my palms to the sky,
surrendering to my human hopelessness,
that it doesn't despair me.
For life needs no more,
no more despair, I pray.
To turn a situation as bad as mine
into an opportunity
to be of some benefit.
To transcend my present circumstances
To transform everything around me into something almost radiant.
—Jarvis Jay Masters, *Finding Freedom*

JARVIS

I have COVID, Samara.
It's bad. Real bad.
There's no way around it.
Only choice I have is to let it move through me.
It's not trying to make you sick, it's trying to take you out.
This one, this is the killer one, Samara.
You need a respirator, a ventilator.
You need something to keep you alive cause you're gonna go.
It's been bad, real bad.

My neighbor died yesterday.
I had all these friends, man.
Everyone I know who got sick, they're in an outside hospital—in a coma,
    on ventilators—
It's bad, man.
There's a lot of mistrust going on around here and it displays itself with
    the noise.
And I don't even think people know how scared they are.
And I don't know how to say to them, you know,
"We all have a reason to worry about what's going on
Because we don't know what's going on."
But I do know, this is not the time to withhold us from our families.
We need to be in touch
And they're cutting the lines.
Phones hanging on the wall
For us to just look at—

Cut off from our loved ones
We need to check on our families.
People are dying.
I had no choice but to hunger strike.
I went 60 meals without eating.
And you know, when I did that, all the symptoms of COVID came back.
It was painful,
But it was necessary.

Samara, I was really really sick. I've never been so sick. I'm still sick.
This particular virus—it attacks your vital organs.
I thought we'd just get sick, and then it'd be over.
But this is the kind of sick where you can drown in your own lungs and
    die.
That shit ain't no joke. No joke at all. It's criminal. It's truly criminal.
It's a genocide in here.
San Quentin.
Death Row.

You know, most people in prison—
We have high blood pressure, we're diabetics, we were born with
    asthma . . .
Our medical histories are flawed from the beginning—from the first days
    of life—
It's systemic.

SAMARA

It's the architecture of this country.

JARVIS

It's racism.
Our parents were heroin addicts.
We grew up in poverty.
It's designed that way.
You'd have to look real hard to find somebody in here
Who's a completely healthy individual—

I went to the shower this morning and on my way I was looking at peo-
    ple's cells,

And I noticed they still had those red X's.
They used tape and those X's for the people who tested positive for COVID.
And it was like one cell, two cells, and then skip a cell,
Then three cells in a row . . .
Then skip one cell, then four cells in a row . . .
And, for some reason, I was thinking that it was the opposite, you know?
That all the cells that had red tape crossed out on the door,
Were the ones that didn't have it.
I didn't think it would be that many people who caught it, you know?
It was sort of biblical.

My neighbor died yesterday.
Right there in front of me, from the same virus I got.
I knew he wasn't gonna make it. I told him. I knew.
I think he would've been alive if they caught it two weeks ago.
Before they ran outta ventilators.
But he was on death row—and they let him die.
A diabetic on death row.
COVID knew exactly who he was.

All I know is that I have to find my center.
I have to know that all the possibilities are there
And that I'm going to settle with those possibilities.
You know, it's not about avoiding them, it's about looking at them for
    what they are.
Then doing the work to figure out what's going on inside.
Inside of me.
I meditate because I need to realign my space.
And, right now, it's keeping me safe.

I'm thinking of you and your daughter.
I hope you're holding her close.
Keeping *her* safe.
That baby girl I love.
She was born in the height of all this.
Masks. Quarantine. Social distancing. Sirens.
But she has you. That's all she needs, Samara. Her mama's love.
You know how lucky she is? To have her mama's love?

I'm the lucky one. This love is infinite. Potent. Just she and I from day
    one.
Never would've imagined it this way, but here we are.
Born at home under quarantine while COVID raged my city, this country,
    the globe.

I'm nursing her as I write this.
Sometimes she slows and deepens her tiny breath with such intention it
    seems—
She's teaching me, reminding me to ground.
Slow down. Breathe. Find my center. Be grateful.
Do the work of figuring out what's going on inside.
Inside of me.
Like it's you—checking me through her meditative breath—
When I have the audacity to wrestle with "isolation."
To cling to my attachments to what I thought it was supposed to look
    like.

I think of my grandmother's war stories from Auschwitz, younger than I
    am now.
She knew survival. Loss. Adaptation. Trauma. Genocide.
I remember tracing the numbers on her arm as a little girl, reckoning
    with violence. Hatred. Murder. Forgiveness.
Trying to grasp it all as I traced her tattoo with my fingers.
I think about the days she didn't die by the weight of a trembling finger on the trigger,
Pressed against her temple.

I labored in the wake of Breonna Taylor's murder.
Passed through the places in me where trauma still lives from the vio-
    lence I survived
To give birth to my daughter—her sacred brown body scriptured with
    prayer.
I think about the day I didn't die by the weight of a trembling finger on the trigger,
Pressed against my temple.
I wonder what she might have memorized as she moved through me.

She keeps shifting her attention between my breast and this photo of you
    and me.

The one the guard took through the bars, where our hands are clasped
    together
Around a string of prayer beads.
You led me through a meditation that day right there in the middle of
    visitation.
Mothers and sons, husbands and wives, children on laps, lawyers—
In a row of cages bound together by a system that still believes in
    execution.
I think about the days you didn't die by the weight of a trembling finger on the
    trigger,
Pressed against your temple.
We closed our eyes and meditated.
Disintegrated barbed wire with our breath.

You told me that was the first time you guided anyone but yourself
    through a sit.
Survived 23 years in solitary with your practice.
39 in prison.
My time on this earth.
With all the privileges in the world.
How dare I feel alone.
How dare I ever think I know anything about isolation.
Your phone lines have been cut since COVID came.
Visits halted.

I'm breathing with you, Jarvis.
Like you taught me.
Deep, slow breaths.
Breathing health into your lungs.
My daughter keeps reaching for your face.

JARVIS

You know, I reached my hand to the ceiling today.

I've been in here forty years and I've never tried this, I never understood it.
I just knew the ceiling was real short, real small.
But when I actually just reached my hand up and allowed myself to really
    lock that in,
That image of myself—a snapshot of me—a moment frozen in time in my
    mind—

It scared the hell out of me.
Because I realized that I'm nothing.
I'm not far from being in a coffin, you know.
Buried alive.
Something I've never felt before,
Something that I've never realized,
Something that I've never paid that much attention to—how low the
    ceiling is—
God, it scared the fuck out of me.

Am I living in a place like this?
How can I survive in a place like this?
Why did I do this? I'm asking myself why did I do this?
Reach my hand up, touch the ceiling.

You know me.
Imagine me, who I am, living with the ceiling this short.
40 years, Samara. 40 years.
How is this possible?
How is it possible that I can write a book, 2 books?
How is it possible that my sanity's been maintained?
My whole sanity's been maintained in something like this.
God, I wish I didn't touch that ceiling.
I won't ever reach my hand up like that again.
It's too scary.

An innocent man
A man who did nothing wrong.
On death row.
Almost buried alive.

And you know what?
I can sit down.
I can meditate.
I can write.
I can write books.
With this, with this over my head.
That's fucked up. It truly is.

And I'm sorry I had to tell you all this.
It doesn't sound like I'm a well prepared Buddhist.

I know I'm supposed to have all this experience, you know?
But tonight, when I stood up and put my hand on that ceiling,
It seemed like all the Buddhist in me
—All the time I spent in a cell—doubled, tripled.

I mean. I feel like I had to duck to get in the cell.
You know how you bend over so you don't hit your head on something?
I did that twice now 'cause I didn't know if I would bump my head on the
    damn ceiling. Now, of course not. That's not gonna happen.
But to realize that you're living in a cell this small . . .
It makes you wonder if you have to bend over to get in or to get out.

But times that by 40 years.
And then times that by an innocent man
In prison,
Times that by death row,
And then times that by the people who love me,
Who care about me,
Who know I'm innocent,
That they have lived this life with me on death row.

I can't say I hate being here, though.
Because I've learned so much, you know?
Oh, you can hate knowing that I'm here for no reason.
No reason.

My life.
The years in my life, in my thirties are all gone.
In my forties are all gone.
Now in my fifties, a few months away before they're all gone.
I can't get that back, Samara.
I know that. I really do.
And if I ever get out of here, I will not reach to bring them back.
They're gone. They're gone.
And for no reason. No reason at all.
This is my life.

Every year of your life, I've been in a cell.
But they felt like a hundred years when I touched that ceiling tonight.
I don't know how I can take my mind off that.
And I just hope that whoever reads this will understand my fear

And won't think of me as being flawed,
Without purpose of realizing who I am, where I am.
It hurts.

So, whatever I leave people,
I guess I'm leaving them with the understanding that I'm just—
I'm just like everyone else.
Confused. Hurt. Scared.
But not scared of no violence.
I'm scared because so many people anticipate me living without feeling
    these fears. Sometimes I'm just living the fear
So they can benefit from knowing that if I did it, they can do it.
I feel like I'm being trapped by that
While I'm holding so many people together.

And whatever I do, will become a part of my legacy.
You think about that on death row.
What am I gonna leave?
What am I gonna write that will stick?
That will make a difference
Whether I'm alive or dead?
It feels like everything I do
Will have a history to it, you know?

But you know what I realized?
I realized that, other than being here,
I'm happy being me.
I'm truly happy to be me.
And so many people don't feel that way about themselves.
I love being me,
Which allows me to wake up feeling blessed.
To have my heart, my spirit—
To have my fears, to have my joys,
And to understand that I can really look at myself with a measure of joy.
You know?
A measure of love.
It sustains me.
It holds me up and makes me feel so lucky.

So anyway, I just wanna say I love you
And I love that baby girl.

Hopefully, before she's three or four, I'll get a chance to meet her and
    hold her.
I can't wait to hold her.
Send me pictures.
And I hope your mom's doing alright.
I love talking to her.
More than you.
I'm kidding—
But I'm not.
She's special.
I love her too.
Kiss your baby girl for me.
Goodnight.

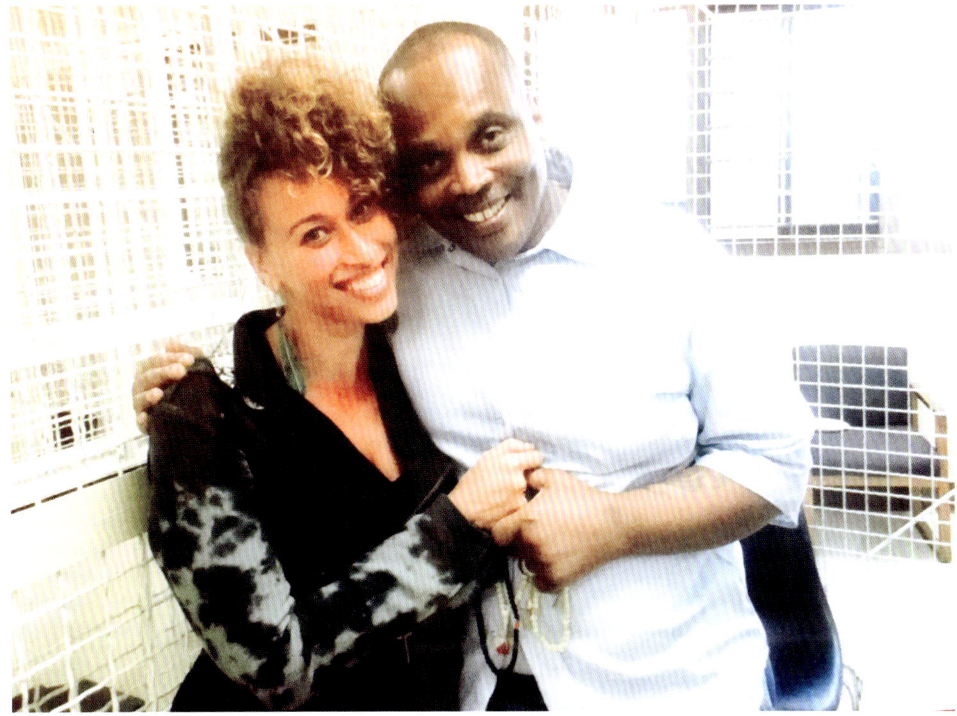

Samara and Jarvis at San Quentin Prison.

There Is No Abolition or Liberation without Disability Justice

Lydia X. Z. Brown

Lydia X. Z. Brown is a community builder and organizer, writer, advocate, educator, strategist, lawyer, and cultural worker dreaming of Disability Justice and collective liberation. Their work focuses on addressing and ending interpersonal, structural, systemic, and institutional violence targeting disabled people at the margins of the margins—especially surveillance, criminalization, and incarceration at the intersections of disability, queerness, race, gender, faith, language, and nation.

In Massachusetts, just south of Boston, there is an institution where so-called professionals subject disabled people to a form of "treatment" consisting of painful electric shock punishment from a patented device designed to be more powerful and painful than a police taser. This institution, the Judge Rotenberg Center (JRC), first opened in 1971 under a different name and, in the nearly half century since, has been responsible for at least six residents' deaths, received condemnation from the United Nations, and spurred grassroots activism by people with disabilities internationally to shut it down and stop the shocks.

What many do not realize is that the JRC's population is 90 percent people of color, and over 85 percent Black and Latinx—all of whom have intellectual, developmental, or psychosocial disabilities. The JRC accepts referrals from adult developmental disabilities services systems, local education agencies (as an out-of-district, and often out-of-state, alternative placement), and the juvenile criminal legal system—recently even from

Rikers Island in New York. That symbiosis is emblematic of the ways in which carceral spaces of all kinds operate in tandem. And the racial and disability dynamics of the place ought not go unnoticed and unnamed—as Talila Lewis has said, the intersection of disability and race is "the most dangerous that history has ever held."[1]

And yet, for all its horrors, the JRC is not a singular institution. While it is the only disability institution known to use painful electric shock punishments, millions of disabled people across the United States languish in other institutions—group homes, nursing homes, psychiatric wards and hospitals, large-scale public and private residential institutions, jails, and prisons. And some live in institutions as small as a single person, because in the end, institutional/carceral violence is defined not by a particular place or program but by power—who has power and control, who exercises power and control *over others*, and who is denied and deprived of power while subjected to control. Mel Baggs and Cal Montgomery often write of the phenomenon of an "institution of one" and institutions that mimic community life—when a disabled person's life and living space may appear to have all the trappings of freedom, but they are nonetheless institutionalized because of complete deprivation of control, autonomy, and the meaningful ability to exercise agency.[2]

Institutionalization and incarceration take many forms, and are constant, powerful forces in the lives of disabled people, especially those of us at the margins of the margins. I have a friend who lives in a large institution so far from where other people live that there is no reliable cell phone service. I have another friend who lives in their own place but for whom constant disruptions to their services—including outright denial of and refusal to provide care at all—keep threatening their ability to stay in control of their own life. I have another friend who has already survived decades in prison and may die there. I have another friend who chose to enter a disability institution at one point because the care they needed to survive outside an institution did not exist and was not available. I have another friend who has chosen intentionally to live houseless and in the streets.

We have conversations late into the night sometimes about what we will do if someone tries to file papers on us to have us committed or put under legal guardianship. Those of us who are disabled, sick, mad, neurodivergent, and self-advocates are all too familiar with the threats of incarceration and institutionalization in our lives. The possibility of institutionalization keeps people experiencing crisis suicidality from seeking support for very real fear that instead of receiving support and care, they will instead be carted (perhaps even in handcuffs, by police) to a hospital where they will be detained anywhere from hours to weeks or months. Sometimes years.

Disabled people fear that our relatives—including, in many cases, abusive, toxic, and manipulative family of origin—will seek guardianship orders to deprive us of the legal right to make any decisions about our own lives. By deeming a person legally incapacitated due to mental disability, a judge can strip that person of legal recognition as a person—a more overt form of juridical violence. No one should live with the fear that they can be judicially deemed a nonperson, and that everyone around them will believe and accept this determination.

It is impossible to meaningfully or authentically discuss the violence of mass criminalization and mass incarceration without understanding the necessity of ableism in upholding carceral violence.[3] Policing and prisons rely on the perpetuation of ableism as a force of racialized capitalism, white supremacy, settler colonialism, and gender oppression. Disability Justice requires full abolition—decarceration and deinstitutionalization. Disability Justice demands an end to carcerality, punishment culture, and white supremacist and settler logics. We fight until all our people can get free.

Incarceration is an ableist and eugenicist practice and system, borne of the desire to contain, control, and manage those whose bodyminds are deemed defective, disordered, and deviant—socially undesirable, undeserving, unworthy. Ableism is *violence*, as a form of systemic, structural, and institutional oppression, that embeds notions of whose bodyminds are valuable, worthy, desirable, and *human*, and whose bodyminds are instead expendable, disposable, tolerable collateral damage, *in*human.

Incarceration targets marginalized people because of impoverishment, which is itself deprivation and exploitation by design under capitalism. Incarceration targets marginalized people because of perceived or imputed sexual deviance, stemming from white Western notions of appropriate and acceptable gender, sexuality, intimacy, and kinship structures. Incarceration targets marginalized people because of disability, whether through psychiatrization, imputation of feeblemindedness, or incapacity. Incarceration targets marginalized people because of imputed criminality, which itself is always a fluid social construct defined by those who hold power, privilege, and resources. These categories elide clear boundaries and have always been deployed to infer one another's presence.

Disability Justice advocates, organizers, educators, community builders, and strategists have worked to catalog the enormity of ableist violence so pervasive in our society. Abolition is a natural extension of and kin to the work of Disability Justice. We recognize that prisons and institutions do not keep us safe; they do not protect either the people outside them or the people in them.

We affirm that no one deserves the violence of incarceration, that there is no justification for enacting this form of violence on a person. Prison is not a response to violence. Prisons are in fact a form of violence in themselves. The belief that some people belong in prison is the belief that some people do in fact deserve to be subjected to violence, that some people are expendable and disposable after all, that some people are so awful that they ought not be treated as persons.

This carceral logic pervades even many otherwise radical spaces dedicated to the work of antioppression. Abolition asks—requires—us to imagine responses to violence and harm, both interpersonal and systemic, that are not rooted in punitive, carceral logics. Why is it that the only response most of us can imagine to acts of sexual violence, mass political violence, or genocide is imprisonment? The same reason that the immediate response from those with privilege to accusations of harm is to rush to a person's defense as *a good person*—that is, a person who does not deserve to be punished, to lose their home, their access to health care, their mental and emotional stability, because of what they have done. A forgiveness and compassion only ever extended to those with power, privilege, and resources, but one that belies that those with access to privilege already know that noncarceral responses to harm are possible.

Assholes should be fired from their jobs, for instance, and we as community members should work to protect and keep safe the people at risk of abuse and harm from people with patterns of abusive actions who show no signs of wishing to take accountability to undo harm. And being fired from a job or asked to leave a particular place of residence should not result in loss of access to health care, homelessness, or destitution. The response to this harm should not be the infliction of structural violences (as happens in our current world), but the removal of the person causing harm from the immediate situations or people who have been harmed and are at risk of being harmed (as must become the norm in the next world).

Abolition does not mean freedom *to* harm, after all. Abolition means freedom *from* harm. Abolition means a world in which we are *all* safer and freer from all forms of violence—physical, emotional, psychological, sexual, financial, epistemic. In which we can and do respond to harm in ways that care for and support the people who have been harmed, that honor communities' needs following harm, that address the root causes of harm, and that provide support for people who have harmed in taking accountability and learning to live, do, and be better. Abolition makes us safer and brings us closer to justice. These are among the core principles of transformative justice praxis, which Mia Mingus and Leah Lakshmi Piepzna-Samarasinha outline forcefully and brilliantly.[4]

Disability Justice helps us imagine a world in which we may all experience care, support, rest, access, pleasure, and justice without precondition. One in which care is no longer synonymous with coercion as it so often is now for queer, trans, intersex, fat, disabled, poor, and negatively racialized people.[5] One in which it might become possible to witness, hold, and sustain multiple necessary truths about trauma, accountability, justice, and healing simultaneously.[6] One in which not only places like the JRC and all other sites of unspeakable violence are made history, but where we cultivate and sustain values and cultures that honor our wholeness, our worth, our magnificence, our *deservingness* of justice and love. Where we build networks, collectives, and systems to ensure that all of us receive the care and support we need, on our own terms. Where communities most directly impacted and targeted by violence define safety for ourselves. Where we constantly work on ourselves and with each other to reduce and minimize our capacities to harm, and maximize our capacities to do and live justly, in right relationship with one another, with our communities, and with the sacred earth around us. Where we leave nobody behind.

. . . .

With thanks and appreciation to many whose work and thought have shaped my own, including, among others, AJ Withers, Azza A. Altiraifi, Cal Montgomery, Dustin P. Gibson, Eli Clare, Johanna Hedva, Kai Cheng Thom, Leah Lakshmi Piepzna-Samarasinha, Leroy F. Moore Jr., Liat Ben-Moshe, Mariame Kaba, Mel Baggs, Mia Mingus, Mimi Khúc, Patricia Berne, Sara M. Acevedo Espinal, Shain Neumeier, Subini Ancy Annamma, Sunaura Taylor, and Talila (TL) Lewis.

Notes

1. Talila A. Lewis, "Emmett Till and the Pervasive Erasure of Disability in Conversations about White Supremacy and Police Violence," *Talila A. Lewis* (blog), January 28, 2017, https://www.talilalewis.com/blog/emmett-till-disability-erasure.

2. Mel Baggs, "The Problem Isn't That We Need Institutions Back. The Problem Is We Haven't Got as Far Away from Them as We Think We Have," *Cussin' and Discussin'* (blog), May 5, 2018, https://cussinanddiscussin.wordpress.com/2018/05/05/the-problem-isnt-that-we-need-institutions-back-the-problem-is-we-havent-got-as-far-away-from-them-as-we-think-we-have/amp/; Cal Montgomery, "Disabled People in the Mist," *Cal's Blog*, October 10, 2020, https://montgomerycal.wordpress.com/2020/10/10/disabled-people-in-the-mist/.

3. Talila A. Lewis, "Disability Justice Is an Essential Part of Abolishing Police and Prisons," *level*, October 7, 2020, https://level.medium.com/disability-justice-is-an-essential-part-of-abolishing-police-and-prisons-2b4a019b5730.

4. Mia Mingus, "Transformative Justice: A Brief Description," *Leaving Evidence* (blog), January 9, 2019, https://leavingevidence.wordpress.com/2019/01/09/transformative-justice-a-brief-description/; Ejeris Dixon and Leah Lakshmi Piepzna-Samarasinha, *Beyond Survival: Strategies and Stories from the Transformative Justice Movement* (Chico, CA: AK Press, 2020).

5. Shain Neumeier, "For Your Own Good: Coercive Care in the Lives of Marginalized People," Disability Intersectionality Summit at the NonProfit Center, Boston, Massachusetts, November 5, 2016, YouTube video, 27:49, https://www.youtube.com/watch?v=r2FOIqJkCAU.

6. Kai Cheng Thom, "What the Queer Community Should Have Told Us," *Marvellous Grounds: Special Issue #2—Bodies as Archives: QTBIPOC Art and Performance in Toronto*, 2018, http://marvellousgrounds.com/blog/original-poems-by-kai-cheng-thom/#poem3.

HOGAR

Aydinaneth Ortiz

Aydinaneth Ortiz received her BA in art at UCLA and MFA in photography at Cal-Arts. Her work focuses on intersections between familial relationships, mental illness, drug addiction, and immigration. Ortiz's work is in the permanent collections of the Pomona College Museum of Art and the Museum of Latin American Art.

Through photography and installation, I investigate personal relationships in order to open up larger conversations around vulnerability, mental illness, immigration, belonging, and drug addiction. Due to our current political climate and as a Chicana artist, my work is designed to reach a broader audience, break down communication barriers, and build new meanings.

HOGAR is an installation that includes three series of photographs: *Ingredients, California State Mental Hospitals,* and *Hija de tu madre.* A series of walls requires the audience to move through the space while encouraging them to make deeper connections with their own private lives. After a tragic event in my family, I spent a lot of time reflecting and questioning, leading to my ongoing study of the California mental health system. I concluded that the lack of mental health support for my brother was not an isolated incident but a part of a much broader systemic issue. Due to a lack of funding, state-run institutions cannot meet the needs of those who need assistance, and statistics show that there are more people with mental illness in prisons than in state-run psychiatric institutions. Through my work, I hope to draw attention to the devastating lack of mental health support and other common failures within the system.

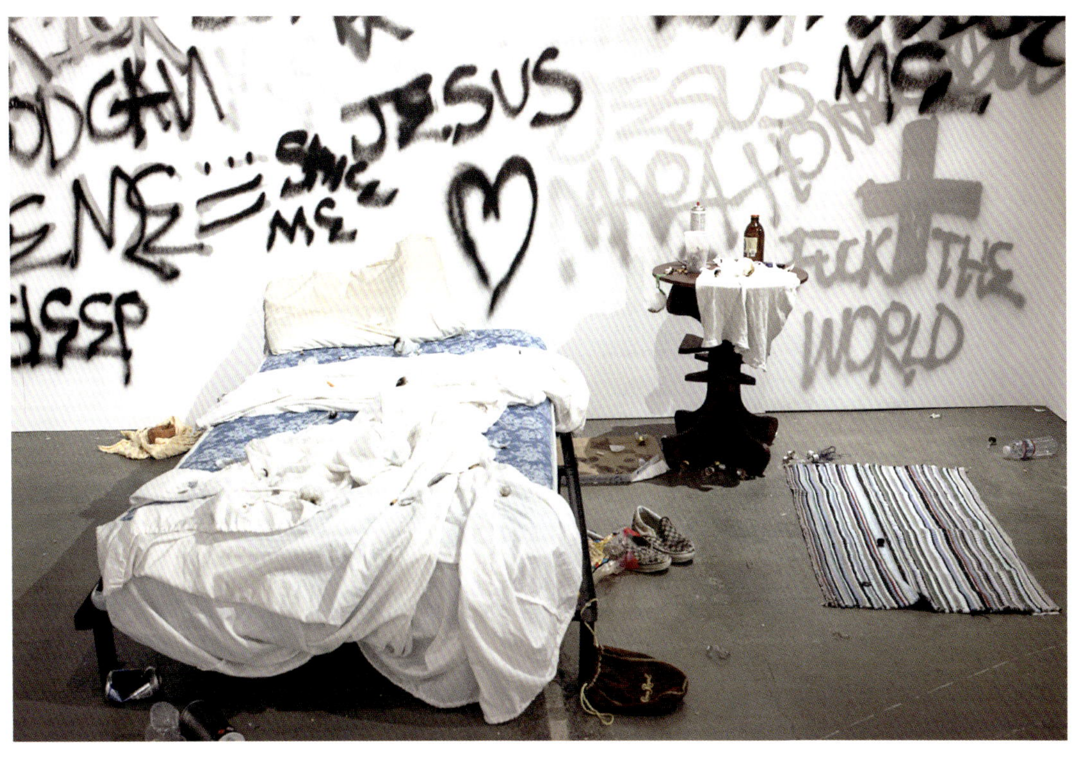

Aydinaneth Ortiz, detail from *HOGAR*, 2018.
Installation, dimensions variable.

I Remember

Mark Menjívar

Mark Menjívar is a San Antonio–based artist and associate professor in the School of Art and Design at Texas State University. His work explores diverse subjects through photography, archives, oral history, and participatory project structures. He holds a BA in social work from Baylor University and an MFA in social practice from Portland State University.

I was standing in the garden the first time I heard that there was a secret room behind the sanctuary. Most people stayed there after ICE released them in the middle of downtown with nowhere to go.[1] I didn't know any of their names yet or what their stories were, but the fact that the room existed was enough to make me remember.

I remember being nine years old and lying in my backyard in San Salvador watching the red streaks of the tracer bullets fly across the sky. It was November and the Offensive was the strongest attack on the capital yet.[2] United States–backed government forces were put back on their heels.

I remember hugging my Tio Julio and feeling the hard scars across his belly. He was kidnapped in the 1970s, and even though they paid the ransom, he was shot three times in the stomach.

I remember the first time I went to Santa Marta, in rural El Salvador, just over the mountain from Honduras.[3] The community elders invited me to sit and listen to the story of their community. Violence beyond my imagination. The recorder mysteriously stopped halfway through. At first I was devastated. Then I accepted it and was thankful.

I remember seeing a group of young men in a car whom I had not seen on any of my other visits. When I asked, I was told that the gangs were now coming out here. *Even out here*.

I remember deciding to not book a flight to go back for the sixth trip. My boys were getting older and the stakes seemed higher.

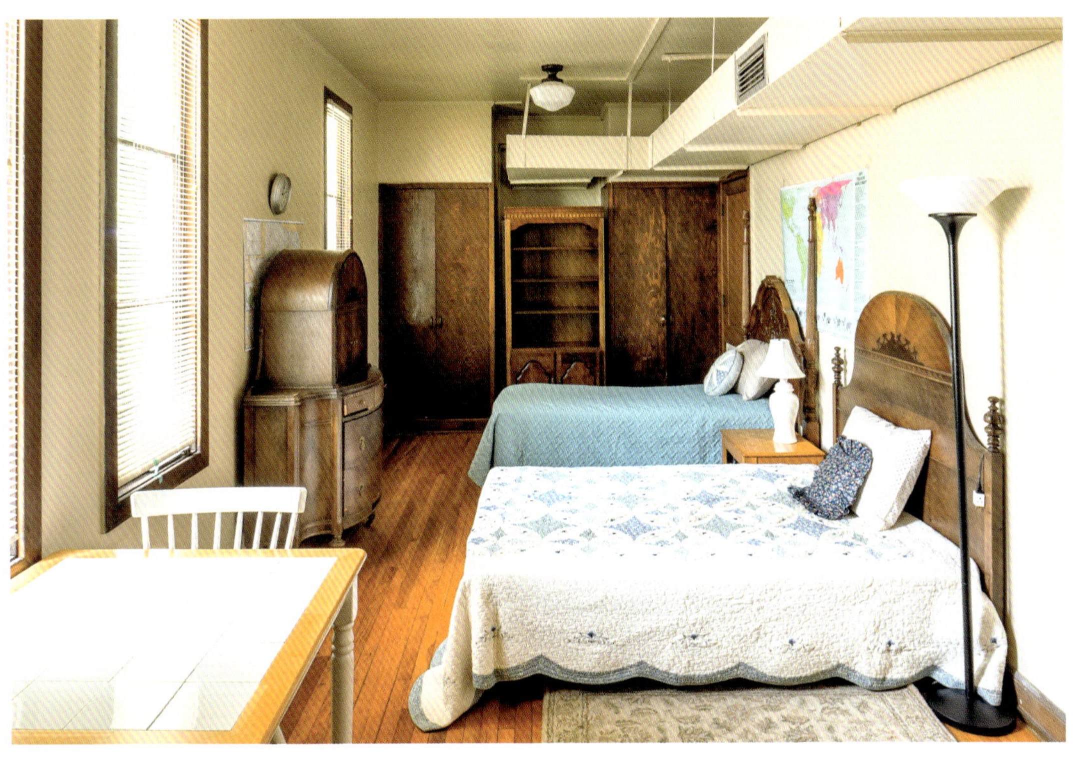

Mark Menjívar, *Secret Room*, 2020. Archival pigment print,
24 × 30 in.

I remember getting a phone call from the Karnes County Residential Center.[4] Carlos was there. I could barely remember his face, but his mother had made me pupusas one evening in Santa Marta and we talked for hours about crops and civil wars and babies. Carlos had to come north. He couldn't stay and do the things the gangs were going to make him do. His parents said he had to come north. The neighbors said he had to come north. His uncle was in Virginia. It was late 2013.

I remember the security guard telling me that I couldn't take my stack of papers in with me as I walked through the metal detector. He was barely eighteen and shrugged back when I told him I needed it. He paid no attention to me when I came back five minutes later with phone numbers, addresses, and questions written in black ink up and down my arms.

I remember finally finding an attorney who would take the case. She walked me through the documents we needed to gather. I remember writing checks. And making phone calls. And not knowing what to do. And friends and family helping. And I remember Carlos passing his credible threat hearing and heading north.[5]

I remember the news headlines that followed. Thousands of women and children were showing up at the border seeking asylum.[6] They were fleeing violence. Violence beyond my imagination.

I remember interviewing Stacey Merkt about her time spent in federal prison for helping families along the border in the 1980s.[7] She refused to take a "slap on the wrist" plea bargain. She was pregnant and sentenced to six months in federal prison. There is a photograph of her talking to the press on the courthouse steps next to a man holding a sign that said "God's Law, not Reagan's Law—Free Stacy Merkt." The Sanctuary Movement was strong during those years.[8]

I remember finally hearing someone on NPR say that what we were seeing was directly connected to US foreign policy that stretched back more than one hundred years. I was shaking with anger and gratitude because I thought if people could understand, then things would change.

I remember when ICE dumped more than twenty thousand women, children, and men on the streets of San Antonio. And the city set up a shelter. And the Interfaith Welcome Coalition started doing even more outreach and connecting people to family and friends in other parts of the country.

I remember getting a call from Jack Elder asking if I would like to see the posters he had found in his attic.[9] There were twenty-seven of them. About half spoke about El Salvador. One was for a 1984 US-Mexico border conference against US intervention in Central America.

I remember driving by a residential facility for youth on the south side of San Antonio that was surrounded by a tall chain link fence with barbed wire on top. It was being run by a private company to house and educate children who had been separated from their parents at the border by ICE.

I remember seeing the first picture of kids being held in cages, separated from their families.

I remember buying my first bouquet of flowers from a community of women who lived together on a farm. All of them seeking asylum from different parts of the world. All of them at different stages of waiting.

I remember when they couldn't find the parents of 545 children separated from their parents by the Trump administration.[10]

I remember making the bed and tucking in the corners of the sheet. He had been separated from his family by ICE. A child lost. He needed a place to stay while he learned the system.[11]

....

I'm grateful for Joe Brainard and his practice of remembering.

Notes

1. The US Immigration and Customs Enforcement (ICE) is a federal law enforcement agency under the US Department of Homeland Security. The stated mission of ICE is to protect the United States from the cross-border crime and illegal immigration that threaten national security and public safety.

2. Outraged by the results of the 1988 fixed elections and the military's use of terror tactics and voter intimidation, the FMLN launched a major offensive with the aim of unseating the government of President Alfredo Cristiani on November 11, 1989. This offensive brought the epicenter of fighting into the wealthy suburbs of San Salvador for essentially the first time in the history of the conflict, as the FMLN began a campaign of selective assassinations against political and military officials, civil officials, and upper-class private citizens.

3. The rural community is approximately twelve miles from the Honduran border, where many were forced to flee at the onset of the Salvadoran Civil War (1980–92). Indeed, thousands of families fled the scorched-earth policies carried out by the US-sponsored Salvadoran military. After years of living in refugee camps in Honduras and long negotiations with authorities, repatriation to their former communities began on October 10, 1987.

4. The Karnes County Residential Center is a detention center for immigrant women and their children in Karnes City, Texas. The facility is run by the GEO Group, a publicly traded real estate investment trust that invests in private prisons and mental health facilities in North America, Australia, South Africa, and the United Kingdom.

5. A portion of a legal asylum hearing. A "credible threat of violence" means intentionally saying something or acting in a way that would make a reasonable person afraid for his or her safety or the safety of his or her family.

6. The protection granted by a nation to someone who has left their native country as a political refugee.

7. Stacey Merkt is a longtime activist for illegal immigration from Central America, who was a prominent member of the Sanctuary Movement and co-founder of RAICES, the largest immigration legal services provider in Texas.

8. The Sanctuary Movement was a religious and political campaign in the United States that began in the early 1980s to provide safe haven for Central American refugees fleeing civil conflict. The movement was a response to federal immigration policies that made obtaining asylum difficult for Central Americans.

9. Jack Elder is a longtime activist for illegal immigration from Central America, who was a prominent member of the Sanctuary Movement and cofounder of RAICES, the largest immigration legal services provider in Texas.

10. These children were separated from their parents at the US border by border officials under President Trump's zero-tolerance policy from 2017 to 2018.

11. All of these endnotes were sourced from online outlets, including Wikipedia and KeyWiki, and edited to fit my own needs.

Coming Home

Dustina Gill

Dustina Gill, Sitomni Sa Yapi Win, Paints Red around Her, hails from the Wahpekute band of the Sisseton-Wahpeton Oyate of South Dakota. A lifelong advocate of native youth, Dustina established Nis'to Incorporated, a native youth nonprofit organization. *Nis'to* is a Dakota word that means concern for others outside of ourselves.

They said there was nothing good here for our children to return home to.

So they kept them.

When they returned, broken, bruised, and ashamed of their beautiful brownness, we wiped their faces with sage water and combed their hair with tea while we sang songs of ceremony, generations old.

We held cups of warm sage tea to their lips as their little brothers and sisters burned sage and smudged them, until their souls began to awaken.

Their grandpas stacked wood around the rocks and set them ablaze until the wood turned into ashes. The hot red rocks glowed brightly, waiting for the prayers to descend.

We sat outside the inipi by the fire and told stories of how our Kuns'ipi and Unkannapi ran back home in the darkness from the orphanages and boarding schools. Following the stars and their hearts.

We told them stories of how many did not make it back home and were forever lost.

We told them how we turn that pain into prayer

For the future generations to not know that fear.

And to not know that fear as parents for our own children, as they sleep innocently.

We took them into inipi, and poured water on the rocks and sang songs of prayer as the steam and smoke from the cedar and sweetgrass filled the air with the scent and feeling of the comfort of a mother's womb.

They emerged, strong. Resilient, knowing the creator had heard their prayers and knowing they were not alone.

That they would never feel alone again.

That the creator was always only a prayer away.

Because when the government said,

"The only good Indian is a dead Indian"

And then, when it became too expensive to kill us they said,

"Kill the Indian, Save the Man"

They took our ceremonies, they cut our hair and they broke our families when they stole our children.

But

Our children found their way home, back to their ceremonies, back to their relatives. Back to something that others fought to keep them from for centuries.

And

We only grow stronger

Epilogue

It's referred to as the three As in our history of Native Americans. Annihilation, "The only good Indian is a dead Indian"; Assimilation, "Kill the Indian, save the man," also known as the boarding school era; and Acculturation, when Congress passed the Indian Relocation Act, moving us off reservations in an attempt to not only assimilate us, but to terminate tribes from existence.

Each has a deep root of historical trauma that has become generational trauma. Each one taught the children that the worst thing to be was Indigenous.

The boarding school era did the most damage for our people. The children were taken on the spot and sent hundreds of miles away, and many were never seen again. Many that returned home had survived atrocities that were so traumatic.

Everything about us had been declared illegal: our ceremonies, our gatherings, and our way of life. Illegal up until 1978, when Congress passed the American Indian Religious Freedom Act. While we still practiced our ways, we had to in secret. Not many people practiced the traditional ways.

The Dakota people (formerly known as the Sioux) call the sweat lodge inipi. It is used for prayer and purification. It resembles the womb of the mother and brings a spiritual healing.

The grandparents were cherished, grandmother is Kuns'i and grandfather is Unkanna. Their roles were and still are crucial to spiritual upbringing of the children.

We are only a couple generations away from the eras of the three As. There has been much healing from them, but also still much healing needed.

Many of our children are on what is called the "school-to-prison pipeline."

The Indian Relocation Act is still ongoing, and foster care has become the new boarding school. A majority of Native Americans in the system were raised in foster care. Tribes and relatives struggle to bring them home because once in the system, our children become easily lost in a world they do not understand. When they do, there is much healing to be done because of the damage that has taken place.

Focusing on the strengths, using our Dakota culture in our work has brought many opportunities to our youth and has helped strengthen their families.

The eras our people have survived broke down the societal system that was a part of raising our children.

While we cannot bring back that entire system, we are applying parts of it to our work.

I am part of what is called a "trickle effect" of the boarding school era. I am a survivor of trauma. We are told time and again, historical trauma is in our DNA, but so is the resilience and strength of our ancestors. My Kuns'i taught me to focus on the strengths. It is this concept that I used in establishing Nis'to Inc. and that I use in my work. Happy memories are a form of resilience; this is one of the main goals of every single activity, to bring about the opportunity to make happy memories. Happy memories become foundations of a person's spirit. When they are having a difficult time, they hold them up.

Drawing on memories of having depression or loneliness, they have something positive to draw on as well, and that gives them strength. With those memories comes a smile of remembrance, a feeling of positivity, and the reminder of the good things in their lives.

For example, we take kids to dig our traditional medicines. Knowing that they have the knowledge of those plants, their uses, and have visited spaces their ancestors also harvested gives them such a strong sense of identity and pride; it makes them resilient when they come across something negative in life. Racism, for example. Living on a reservation has its challenges in a society where there are people who are not kind to native people. Having such knowledge makes them strong in those situations.

I am Sitomni Sa Yapi Win, Paints Red around Her. I am Wahpekute and am enrolled in the Sisseton-Wahpeton Oyate and reside on the Lake Traverse Reservation in northeastern South Dakota.

We are the walking prayers of our ancestors. They survived so that we may live.

Singing Our Way to Abolition

Mary Hooks

Mary Hooks is a Black, lesbian, queer, feminist, mother, organizer, and former codirector of Southerners on New Ground (SONG). Mary's commitment to Black and LGBTQ liberation is rooted in her experiences growing up under the impacts of the war on drugs. Her people encompass those of the Great Migration, factory workers, church folks, Black women, hustlers and addicts, dykes, studs, femmes, queens, and all people fighting for liberation of the oppressed.

For years, African descendants have worked to advance the freedom dreams of enslaved Africans, in the hopes of bringing about true liberation, both inside the US empire and across the diaspora. The demand for abolition—whether it be the demand to abolish chattel slavery, Jim Crow, redlining, apartheid, or mass incarceration—has always been rooted in the quest for self-determination as a people. As this iteration of the Black liberation movement continues to fight to change rules and laws and dismantle violent institutions like policing and the prison industrial complex, we know that the ultimate change must be that of hearts and minds. Our demands to defund the police are as much about our values and changing the ways in which we relate to each other as they are about taking power away from those that seek to kill and control us. It is a spiritual fight for who we want to be, and it is not just about having better material conditions. This is why art plays such an important role in the transformation of society. We must awaken the possibility and willingness to love ourselves and each other more than we hate the State.

Our work as organizers is to show the good news of abolition. Organizing is not just what we say and do but also *how we make people feel.*

I grew up singing. My sisters and I were a part of the trio called Mary's Angels. Our great-aunt, Ann H. Peel, who was raising us at the time, devoted much time and effort to ensuring that every Sunday, we stood in front of the small congregation and sang the latest Shirley Caesar hits. For a three-, four-, and five-year-old, we were very much out of our depths. Not one time do I remember us ever being able to finish a song without bursting into tears; the ushers in the church would have to come and escort us back to our seats. Decades later, I'm unsure if our tears were driven by our fear or by what singing did to our spirits. By the time I was a teenager and had found my way back into the church, I had also found my way back to singing. I learned that singing was medicine—throughout my life, it would be a place that remained sacred, and a place where I would connect to spirit.

When I came out as a lesbian, my traditional relationship with the church made it difficult for me to enter that sacred space. I was taught that to be a lesbian was to be against God, so I made a decision to be honest with myself and be exactly who I was, which also meant I let go of the singing that brought me much joy and comfort. When I moved to Atlanta, I discovered a community of radical Black lesbians and queer folks who were all in their twenties and discovering their purpose. Eventually, a few of us took refuge together and became roommates. We'd bring folks together to party, talk, watch TV, paint, and debate. Our time together reminded me of the ways I was taught to build community through the church. We always broke bread and welcomed a new stranger. For years, I would not bear to listen to any gospel music, a boundary that kept my voice harnessed and my spirit grappling with how I was to tap into a new voice, as a community organizer. However, one day, our rowdy household, which had become known as the Juicebox, was overtaken by the gospel music that I'd enjoyed as a young person; what had become a stony place in my memories became running wells of joy again. The sounds of Kirk Franklin's 1990s hit "The Storm Is Over Now" compelled the roommates and myself to grab our best faux microphones and sing like it was the Last Supper. By the end of the day, we'd sung all the songs our hearts could muster and our minds could remember. It was the start of a tradition that we still carry to this day.

This revival of singing was also happening at a time when I was being deeply politicized through the work of Southerners on New Ground (SONG) and Southern movement-building spaces. I began to learn words to freedom songs that likened to the gospel songs I'd learned in my church days. It was freedom songs that reminded me of the long history of struggle and resistance in the South. It was freedom songs that were sung as a way to unite a room and center us on our purpose. It was freedom songs that kept us steady and unrelenting when I engaged in my first direct action.

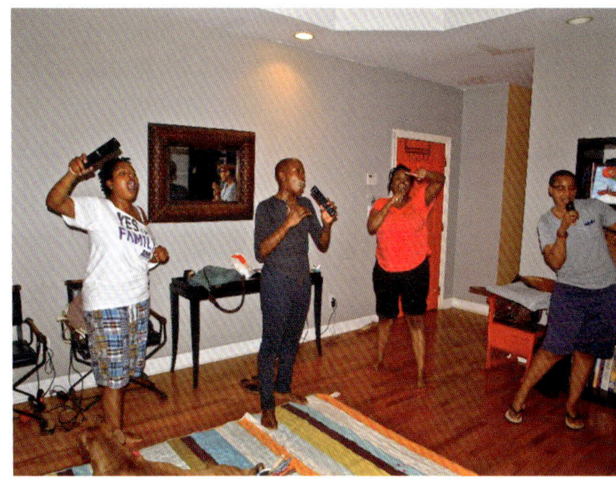

The day that singing arrived at the Juicebox, circa 2011.

Freedom singing has remained a sacred practice inside of SONG and other Southern freedom movements that were passed down by divine cultural workers like Bernice Johnson Reagon, Brother Hollis Watkins, Sister Tufara Muhammad, and Wendi Moore-O'Neal, to name a few. The more songs I learned, the more I understood the power of collective singing to declare our demands, fortify one another, teach history, and invite spirit into the work of getting ourselves free. For literally two years, the song "I'm On My Way" rang in my spirit and stayed on my tongue. It grounded me in work that has always been bigger than myself. If ever there was a time when we needed congregational singing in our movements, it would be now. The depth of isolation and mediocrity that plagues our lives and movements must be met with the salve of singing that frees everyone, in that moment, who is willing to lift their voice. Singing has been medicine and a balm in some of my hardest moments of fighting for freedom. I've sung to mothers locked in cages that we couldn't get them out of, but in that moment, we'd elevate their hearts to a place outside of the cage. We sang when we shut down highways and disrupted meetings of politicians. We've used singing to encourage each other to carry our water and put our hands on the freedom plow when we were tired and weary. One of my greatest joys is hearing my kid sing the old freedom songs that have kept Black people standing when all else has failed us. Passing on this freedom tradition has been essential to those who have come before us and those whose voices are yet to be heard. Freedom singing tells our histories, but it can also speak of our possibilities. Singing is a tool we have to paint the vision of the world we are striving to create.

We must be able to have a vision and articulate it to the world. Even the good book says that without a vision the people perish. Do you think our ancestors knew the path north before they forged it? Nah, they took the risk because to not try, to not be willing to get lost, to not run, would kill them and any possibility of the taste of freedom. One of my elder comrades, Mariame Kaba, says, "We must be willing to try a thousand experiments and fail until we bring about something new." The truth of the matter is, we are not starting from scratch. Our ancestors and elders have much to teach us, especially in how we create a world that doesn't rely on our enemy to come to our rescue when we harm each other or are going through crisis. What have your people done to care for each other? What have you learned from them about dealing with conflict and anger? How do you and your family deal with a crisis? What freedom traditions and familial traditions can be harnessed in those moments of disrupted peace? If you didn't have to call the police, who would you want to be able to call for help? What types of people? Would having a bunch of kids show up to your house while a domestic dispute is happening stop you from abusing your partner? Would a squad of grandmothers who are also trained in mental health support be what you need? Are you willing to learn how to de-escalate heated arguments on the block? Do you know how to disarm someone? Are you a good solid hugger? Are artists willing to draw murals showing what a community without police can look like? What other things in our community do we need that promote life, love, and wellness? More gardens? A drive-in? A community grill? A conflict clinic? Affordable nice housing for people to own and rent? Dignified work that makes neighbors clap for each other when we get off the bus from work? A twenty-four-hour drop-in center for village members to build with each other? A community school that teaches us how to transition from trapping to being storytellers, teachers, and mediators for the young people? We all we got, y'all, and we got to believe in each other more than we believe in the state. Our lives do not belong to the state. We can govern ourselves. As one of the freedom songs we sing reminds us, "We've got all our medicine right here, right here."

Standing in the Gap

MUSIC AS FIRST RESPONDER

Duane Robert Garcia and Vijay Gupta

Duane Robert Garcia was born in 1948 and is a veteran who was deployed to Vietnam and beyond from 1965 to 1968. Duane's trajectory as a professional radio broadcast engineer was interrupted by thirty years and forty-four days of incarceration in the California state prison system. During his period of incarceration, Duane continued to pursue his passion for music.

Vijay Gupta is an esteemed violinist and a leading advocate for the power of music to foster social connection. A 2018 John D. and Catherine T. MacArthur Fellow, Gupta is the founder and artistic director of Street Symphony, a nonprofit organization providing musical engagement and dialogue and teaching artistry for homeless and incarcerated communities in Los Angeles.

EXCERPT FROM "LA VIA DOLOROSA" BY SANDI PATTY

Por la Vía Dolorosa, triste día en Jerusalén
Los soldados le abrían paso a Jesús.
Más la gente se acercaba,
Para ver al que llevaba aquella cruz.
Down the Vía Dolorosa in Jerusalem that day
The soldiers tried to clear the narrow street.
But the crowd pressed in to see,
The Man condemned to die on Calvary.
Por la Vía Dolorosa, que es la via del dolor
Como oveja vino Cristo, Rey y Señor,
Y fue Él quien quiso ir por su amor por ti y por mí.

Por la Vía Dolorosa al Calvario y a morir.
Down the Vía Dolorosa called the way of suffering
Like a lamb came the Messiah, Christ the King,
But He chose to walk that road out of
His love for you and me.
Down the Vía Dolorosa, all the way to Calvary.

Tonight, in Los Angeles, 66,000 people will walk the way of suffering. The epicenter of the crisis of homelessness in America today, Los Angeles County is only 8 percent African American, but Black people make up a whopping third of the homeless population. As early as the 1960s, Skid Row—the fifty-square-block neighborhood of downtown LA—was the terminus of "Greyhound therapy," when an institution would buy a patient with severe mental illness a one-way bus ticket to the City of Angels. Skid Row is often the end of the line for many who are consumed by intergenerational trauma, manifested through chronic addiction and mental illnesses.

Defining a neighborhood by its afflictions is a convenient excuse to erase it. Skid Row is precious land to developers and gentrifiers but could also be considered a recovery zone—one of the largest in the nation—a precious, vital place of new beginnings.

In 2009, Americans for the Arts conducted a case study on the role of arts and culture in Skid Row. Part of the Animating Democracy program, the seminal study, which gathered testimony from community members and leaders of neighborhood organizations, was coauthored by Maria Rosario Jackson—then of the Urban Institute—and my mentor and friend John Malpede, the founding director of Los Angeles Poverty Department, the first theater company to be made up primarily of unhoused people and the first arts program of any kind for the homeless community of Los Angeles.

Respondents of the study saw the power of art as being core to reclaiming their neighborhood, their cultural lineages, and their very lives, while also challenging a stigmatizing narrative. A community member stated, "We are creating the recovery process. . . . A part of the wisdom that has been discovered and is operational in the neighborhood is that once you are given a safe space, positive things happen."

Since 1985, Los Angeles Poverty Department has celebrated the art and cultures of Skid Row with projects like Walk the Talk—the parade commemorating neighborhood initiatives and the people behind them; an annual two-day Festival of Skid Row Artists, which has created a registry of over eight hundred artists working and living in Skid Row; and the Skid Row History Museum and Archive, a gallery space for Skid Row artists, and a center for challenging, generative conversations with community activists and policy makers across the city to create a vision for a healthy, vibrant Skid Row. Skid Row is an artistic ecosystem, composed of the painters of Studio 526, the tile mosaic makers of Piece by Piece, the singers of Urban Voices Project, and the musicians of Street Symphony—to name a few.

The work of Street Symphony is to create a relational laboratory through music. The music we offer is just the beginning of a dialogue, of a relationship—whether we're playing jazz or Schumann at a county jail, singing the "Hallelujah" of Handel or Leonard Cohen at the Midnight Mission, or playing the music of mariachi, reggae, and West African traditions on the very streets of Skid Row—the music we play is a conduit of relationship, a way to listen to the voices and experiences of a community. In Skid Row we were taught that listening is one sure act of love.

Street Symphony serves to hold up a mirror to communities in reentry and recovery—to offer a pathway to wholeness: for those with histories of pain to orient themselves toward hope, and for us with questions about our role as artists and citizens to find a role as stewards of change. In that liminal space that only art can create, we might find the tiniest window—in the form of a glance, a smile, a pause in conversation—to peer beneath the veneer of armor, to transform.

Today, Skid Row serves as a point of reentry for thousands of Californians emerging from incarceration in the state's thirty-five prisons, and from the billion-dollar LA County Jail—which is effectively the planet's largest psychiatric facility. In 2018, Street Symphony started a program called Music for Change, supported by the California Arts Council's Reentry through the Arts Program, which empowers our musicians to engage individuals paroled from life sentences in prison.

In 2018, I met a man named Duane Robert Garcia. He sat in the audience of a program called the Messiah Project, an annual culminating event of my organization Street Symphony. It was Duane's first public outing after an incarceration lasting three decades. Nearly one hundred musicians performed for an audience of hundreds more in the gym of the Midnight Mission in downtown Los Angeles's Skid Row. There were songs from the community of Skid Row, nestled in the frame of George Frideric Handel's beloved oratorio *Messiah*.

Throughout the next two years, my team and I got to know Duane more informally as De—a humble, devout man with the soul of a poet. At the next Messiah Project, De was one of our opening acts, sharing his voice and his story with the people he came to call his new family. Each week now, even through COVID, De speaks and sings to us through his phone or Chromebook like some grand priest of music, a constant human reminder of the power of love.

In June 2020, I was honored to give the thirty-third annual Nancy Hanks Lecture for Americans for the Arts. Of course, I had to ask De to be my guest. From his tiny cell of a room at the Weingart Center, garlanded by art he had created during his incarceration, honey flowed from De's heart:

> Words the spirit longs to express are many times best quickened to life in melodic forms we cordially and lovingly call music. Single notes, triplets, arpeggios strung together like a precious pearl necklace adorn the listeners' heart and soul. Music stands in the gap when even the human embrace does not suffice, a first responder, if you will, to the longing of the spirit at the very core of who we are. Our divinity drinks from the fountains of sound. Ever refreshing the drought that at times can be a desert of space and time. Music, second to none, stands alone—the go-to place accessible to all—knocking at the doors of our being, crying out from the rooftops and on the highways and byways of all of our life experiences.
>
> Always eager to please, ever pleasant, kind and loving, soothing the troubled waters of our sojourn—onward and upward lilting and lifting us to crescendo—resolving in the rapture of auditory bliss. It's not about the gift, it's about the giver, ever giving glory to the Creator. Loving in its expression, music solely gives to all asking only that we share the unveiling of itself with each other.
>
> *Music lends grace to the hearers.*
> *Music is purity.*
> *Music is perfect love.*

....

In 2008, I encountered the monumental heart and work of the artist J Michael Walker, who created a geographical and historical testimony to the saints of Los Angeles in a project called *All the Saints of the City of the Angels: Seeking the Soul of L.A. on Its Streets*. As J Michael became a beloved friend and mentor, I learned about San Julian Street—one of the main thoroughfares of Skid Row—miraculously named for the patron saint of wanderers, of those who make shelters and hospitals, and of violinists. I wonder if Duane would say that San Julian is the patron saint of those who "stand in the gap."

What does it mean to stand in the gap? What does it mean to stand where few are willing to stand—to serve as the bridge, a conveyance—between seemingly irreconcilable worlds?

Recently, I have been enraptured by the image of the Hindu world tree—the Asvattha—which is upside down, its roots in the sky and branches in the earth. This tree, the sacred fig, or peepul, is also known as the Bodhi—the very same tree under which the prince Siddhartha Gautama became the Buddha. I am struck by the image of this metaphor, particularly because of the inversion of the image—the fruits of the tree are invisible. They reside within us, hidden from plain view. We must manifest and grow fruits within the darkness of our being, nourished by the transcendent. We must stand in the dark gaps of ourselves, if we are to stand in the gaps of the world. What gifts, within us—within all people—beckon to emerge from the darkness, in order to nourish the world?

That conveyance—between the transcendent universal of our roots and the slow cultivation of inner fruit—is the specific work of the artist. Like pearl divers, we constantly search for gems in the muck of ourselves, manifesting our deepest intuitions into some soul-nourishing form. In that movement from cultivating deep inner fruits to manifesting gifts for the nourishment of all—we may enact a profound loving grace.

When I visit with individuals emerging from life sentences in California prisons, I encounter an alchemical force embodied in people who have been told to wait, people we have locked away in the darkness of our carceral state. Little do we know, many of them have taken the calcified container of the cell and turned it into a cocoon. In the complicated nuance of people waiting for their SSI, waiting for an ID and a job and a Greyhound bus out of Skid Row to hopefully reconnect with their families, I meet my teachers—those who have weathered the drought of care, who have walked the Vía Dolorosa.

Locked in a Dark Calm

Tameca Cole

Tameca Cole is a visual artist and writer from Birmingham, Alabama. She also performs with the abolitionist arts organization Die Jim Crow. Cole's art has been featured in *Art in America*, *Artforum*, *ArtNews*, *Momus*, the *Nation*, and the *New York Times*.

My name is Tameca Cole. I'm forty-nine years old. I'm a lifelong resident of Birmingham, Alabama. Currently, I'm serving life on parole after serving approximately twenty-six years in the Alabama Department of Corrections.

I went into the prison system at a young age but always with a hopeful attitude that a better future awaited. Most of my time was spent going to trade school to upgrade my job skills and reading. I signed up for a creative writing class sponsored by Auburn University and that's when I found my purpose in life. Once I reconnected with my creative side I never looked back.

Art and writing allow me to address my personal demons in a way that doesn't hurt others. They give me an outlet to express how the cruelty of my incarceration, injustice, and experience with racism has affected me. They give me the power to show other human beings how degrading it feels to be Black in America and still live under systemic racism.

I consider my art to be an educator, a weapon, and a thought-provoking conversation about change. I would be grateful for any support that allows me to continue to elevate as an artist as well as a civil rights soldier.

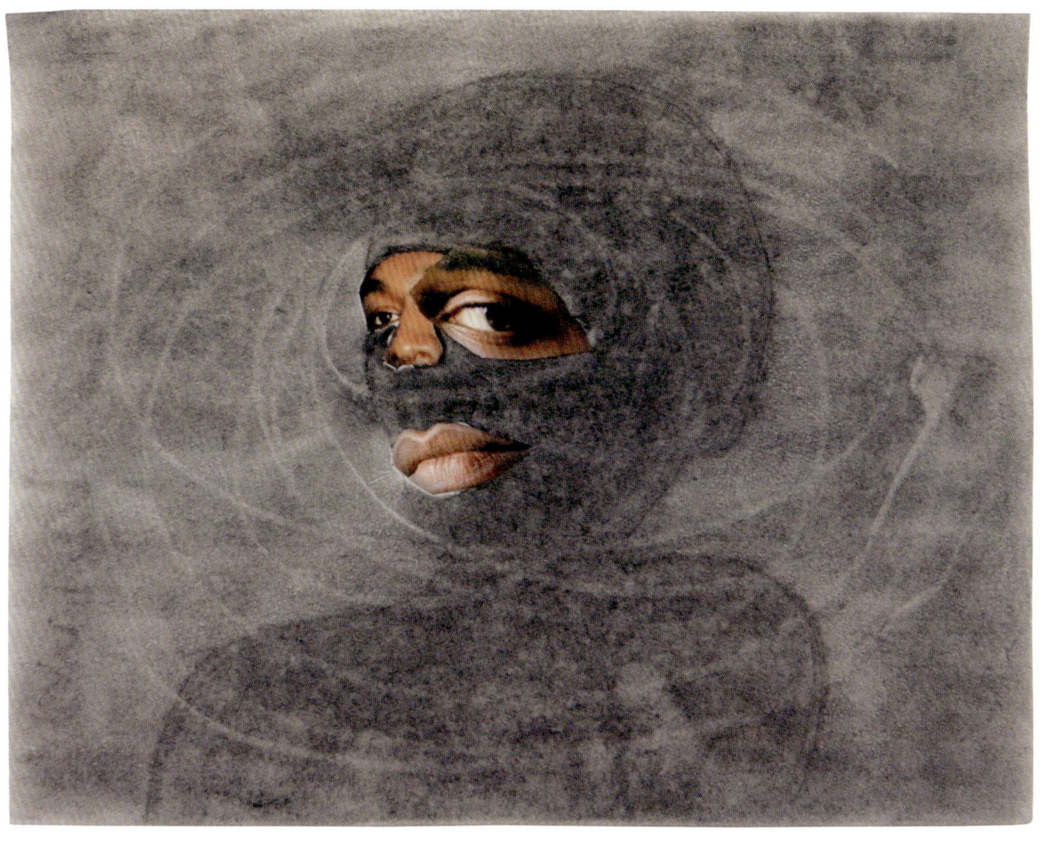

Tameca Cole, *Locked in a Dark Calm*, 2016. Collage and graphite on paper, 8.5 × 11 in. Collection Ellen Driscoll.

As Crazy as the World Is, I Do Believe

Kondwani Fidel

with images by Devin Allen

Kondwani Fidel is a poet and essayist from Baltimore who has used the power of storytelling to confront education reform and civil rights all over the world. Fidel is the author of *The Antiracist: How to Start the Conversation about Race and Take Action, Hummingbirds in the Trenches,* and *Raw Wounds.*

Devin Allen is a self-taught artist from West Baltimore. He gained national attention when his photograph of the Baltimore Uprising was published on the cover of *Time* in May 2015. Allen is the winner of the 2017 Gordon Parks Foundation Fellowship and was nominated for an NAACP Image Award for his book *A Beautiful Ghetto.*

As youngins, me and my friends weren't knowledgeable when it came to politicians and their job descriptions; however, it didn't take rocket science to see that there wasn't a political party to represent our interests, and the police in our neighborhoods who were supposed to "protect and serve" did the complete opposite. Still, my friends and I were repeatedly told by adults that our living situations would not improve unless young Black people like ourselves voted when we became of age. The men and women that I saw running for office on television were not blasting Boosie or Lil' Kim or Jay-Z or Lil Wayne during their campaign trails. None of these politicians and candidates spoke in the same vernacular as me and my friends. I didn't see any guys with suits and ties ordering from the same carryouts we ate from. If they did come to our neighborhoods, it was for photo ops and to gain

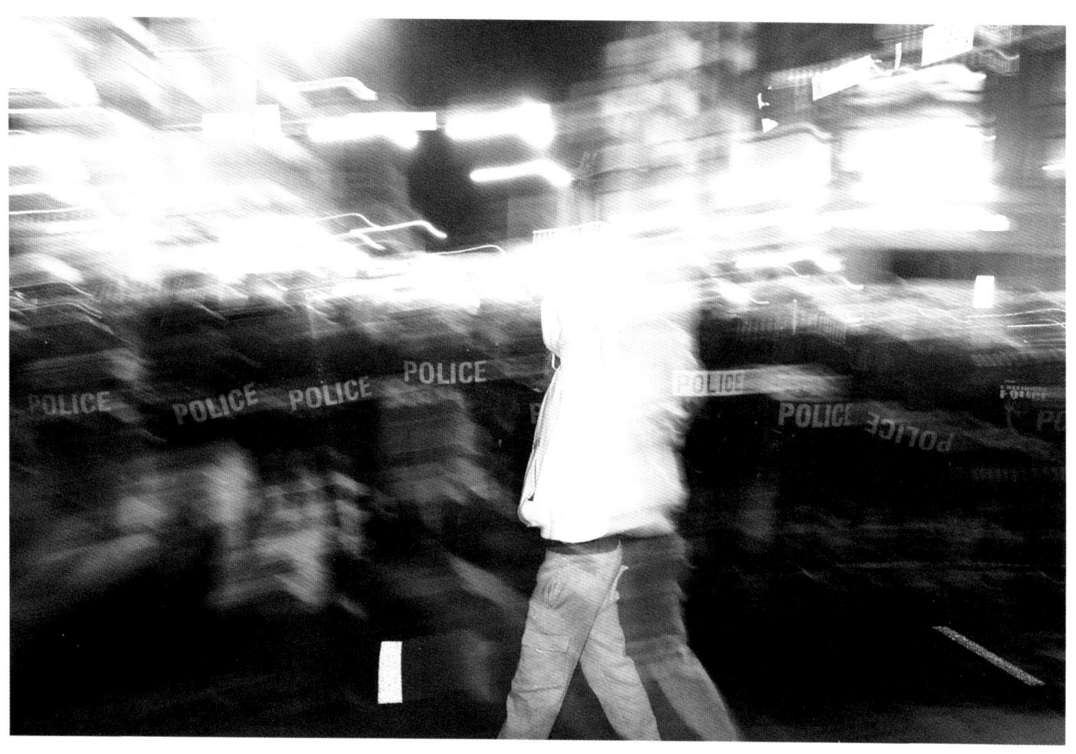

Devin Allen, *Untitled*, 2015. Digital photograph.

media attention to create a false perception that they cared about us. None of these people in positions of power were reflections of my friends and me. So we didn't rally behind officials, but, instead, behind one another. We roamed the streets that conceived us and took ownership of public spaces, stole valuable items from those who had plenty. We created our own laws and delegated representatives in our neighborhood who we saw fit. There wasn't any love for kids like us on the big screen, in newspapers, or in books, so we found love and loyalty in one another. Growing up, everyone wanted to speak for us. Not to us. Not with us. But about us. We were always the topic of discussion when it was about violence, welfare, criminality, or low test scores. This was our experience growing up, and it is still commonplace for the younger generation of Black children growing up in Baltimore City.

How many times did we tell you, America, that we were hungry? How many times did we tell you we were hungry for love? How many times did we tell you we were hungry for a way out? How many times did we tell you we were hungry for something as simple as a fair chance? How many times did we show you we were hungry for the truth?

In a 1994 interview, 2Pac tells a story about some folks inside of a hotel room with an abundance of food, who deny entry to a hungry and poor group of friends. Every day, this group tries to sing their way into the hotel room: "We are hungry, please let us in." A week later, the song becomes more demanding: "We hungry, we need some food!" After three weeks, the voice grows thick and angry: "Get me some food or we breaking down the door!" The group of friends goes back to the drawing board and realizes they have to adopt a new language if they want to eat. Out of the many languages they could've chosen from, they choose the one that's closest to them, an American manifesto—gun talk. That group of friends traded in their "Kumbaya, My Lord" for Biggie's "Gimme the Loot."

"We asked 10 years ago. We was asking with the Panthers. We was asking with them . . . with the Civil Rights Movement. We was asking. You know, now those people that were asking—they're all dead or in jail. So now what do you think we're gonna do. Ask?"—2Pac.[1]

"Fuck the police" has been a popular phrase in my community since I was a kid, and long before I was born. My favorite rappers rapped it over instrumentals and my father said "Fuck the police" as if it were his second language. "Man, the police will lock you up for nothing," was another frequent saying of his. Young and ignorant, I remember asking my father why did police routinely harass the people in our neighborhood without "reasoning." "It's because we're Black," he said. My father has several stories about his run-ins with Baltimore City police, and crazy racist White boys in our city. Everything from being called "ain't shit little niggers," to "monkeys," to being chased out of Patterson Park in East Baltimore.

There was nothing more poetic than me being a youngin, and having troubles with the law, in this same exact park that my father once did. One night, my friends and I were sitting on Luzerne Avenue, the block where most of us lived, four blocks away from the park. For us, the park was a hub for pickup basketball games and swimming, and it hosted Virginia S. Baker, a recreation center where kids from the neighborhood attended after-school programs and summer camp. But on this particular day, we had different plans for how we would deal with the park. My homie Mark had just gotten released from a juvenile detention center a few days prior and was venting to us about his difficulties in finding work, and about his family disowning him because of his recurring run-ins with the police, on top of dropping out of school. He pulled three black metal BB guns out of his backpack and sat them on the marble steps.

"Yo, you see these? They look real, don't they?"

"Hell yeah."

"Exactly, so if we catch somebody slippin' down the park, ain't nobody gonna crack slick. It's like ten of us."

We agreed. I took one of the guns, Mark had one, and our homie Ryheem had the other. The rest of the gang marched with us just in case we had to get physical with someone resisting the stickup. We touched all bases of the park and ran into absolutely no one. We realized we were on a dead mission and decided to walk back home. As we made our way back to Luzerne, lights and police sirens lit up the park, and we made the smart decision to toss the BB guns and run. Some of the homies had lightning for feet and got away—if you were behind them, all you saw was ass and elbows. Cop cars sliced through the grass, and before I knew it, five of us had police boots on our throats. The cops stomped our stomachs and ribs and called us pieces of shit as they handcuffed us. They tossed us in the paddy wagon and ignored us as we asked them why we were being arrested. Once we arrived at the police station, they told us that we were being charged for assaulting a Hispanic male and robbing him of $500 and his moped. Later that next day, my grandmother picked me up from the station, cursed me out, and lectured me about making better decisions in life. She didn't believe me when I told her that we didn't do what the police said we did. She didn't believe me but was glad that I was safe at home, nonetheless. Fast-forward to our court date regarding this alleged assault and robbery. Neither the arresting officers nor the alleged Hispanic male that was involved showed up to court, so the judge dropped the charges and allowed us to walk. To this day, I think about the outcome and my future, and wonder: If they had showed up to court, what would that have looked like for us? Would we still be incarcerated? If convicted, in what ways would it have threatened our future employment? School? Our lives? This wasn't the first or last time that me and my friends had guns pulled out on us by the Gun Trace Task Force (a so-called elite squad of highly trained officers tasked with seizing illegal guns) or were harassed, threatened, and periodically jailed, for just existing. Back then, my friends and I didn't know what "constitutional rights" were, let alone that they were being violated.[2]

Sister Souljah once said, "The sincerity of all of the programs and all of the education has to be questioned, indicted, convicted, because the bottom line is that America is not and has never tried to produce African adults who are functional, self-sufficient, who understand their politics, their economics, and their relationship to the world politics and world economics."[3]

I didn't know what systemic oppression was, and that the pain I suffered from was a product of my era of racism, until I was an adult. I didn't believe that mass incarceration was a real thing. Although I knew people, including myself, who were arrested and jailed for crimes we didn't commit, it was difficult for me to understand that millions of Blacks got arrested because

Devin Allen, *Untitled*, 2020. Digital photograph.

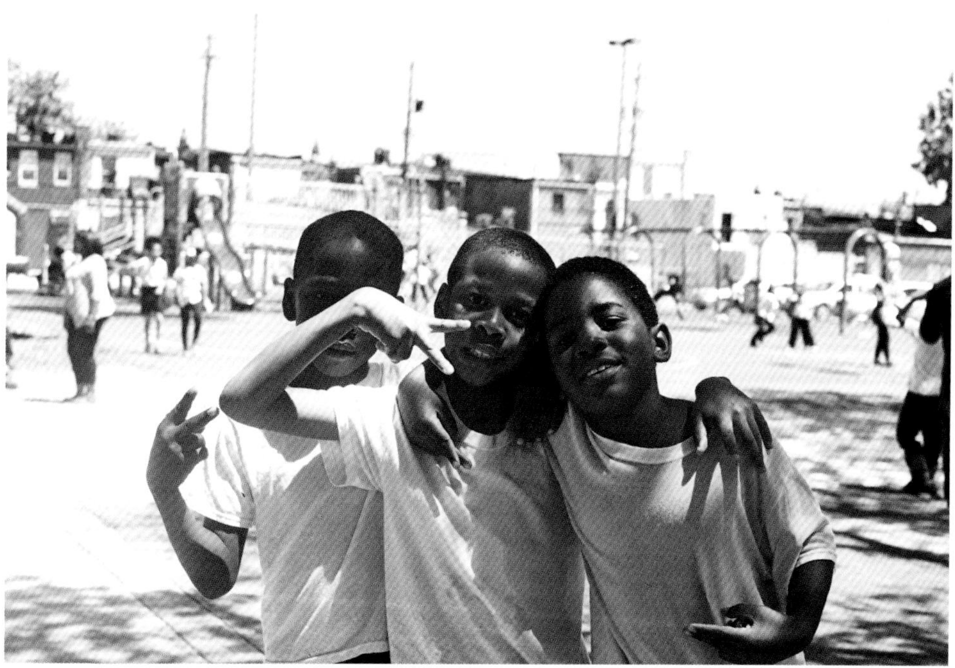

of an "agenda." I just always thought that there was something wrong with Black people.

The pain that I endured, without any truthful context as to why that pain exists, is what forms and nourishes racist ideas. If I see someone get shot, then see someone else get shot, the smart thing for me to do is to get a gun. Now I'm staying dangerous—staying on the alert. Then, say I get arrested with that gun—people from all sides will call me a thug, and a no-good knucklehead, when in all actuality, I'm trying to protect myself and my grandmother because the dudes across the street and around the corner from me got shot. I might step foot on the campus of an HBCU and not know what the acronym stands for, because I've never seen anybody go to one before, so an elite Black person might say I'm an idiot, when in actuality, I haven't been exposed to it, or never seen it on television. Or add to the fact that some of our parents, including both of mine, didn't even graduate high school, so how could they ever teach us what Historically Black Colleges and Universities are?

Baltimore operates the way it does because people made conscious decisions to fund highways for White people in the suburbs, instead of jobs and education in the city for Black students. People made conscious decisions to pay out millions of dollars in lawsuits because police can't stop terrorizing the people they are supposed to protect and serve. A conscious decision was made to fund the police department and prisons, and not to build up underserved Black communities. There are both White and Black Americans who support the construction of more prisons, and they champion the strategy to add more police on the streets because there's a fixed image in their minds of poor Black people—that they are inherently criminal—and the eradication of crime will protect their lives and valuables in their suburban homes. Studies show that more police and more prisons do not lower the crime rate, but jobs and opportunities do. The decisions that benefit White suburbia are the same decisions that make the lives of Black residents in Baltimore City difficult, and played a part in creating the conditions of my life story that I speak about. I've had several White people tell me that they can count how many times they've seen police in their neighborhoods, which is a luxury, being that people in my community see the police 24/7. In White suburbia, their schools and youth programs are funded, instead of policed. The adults in these suburban communities have the luxury to swoop in and support their kids who misbehave, instead of them being punished by the legal system. Their kids' futures are protected, rather than encumbered with criminal records, even if they are arrested.

Ethan Couch, a White sixteen-year-old, was sentenced to ten years of probation in 2013 for a drunk driving crash that killed four people and injured two. The prosecutor urged that Couch should receive twenty years; however, he did no jail time because a psychologist testified that Couch was a victim of "affluenza." He blamed this for Couch's dangerously violent lifestyle, citing his affluent upbringing and irresponsible parenting.

In 1990, Jonathan Fleming was convicted and arrested for the murder of his friend Daryl Rush in New York. In 2013, the case reopened, and in 2014, after spending over two decades in prison, Fleming was released and exonerated: new evidence showed that he was in Florida at Disney World hours before the murder took place. Fleming's black skin robbed him of over twenty years of his life.

For us, criminality is considered the rule, and for them, it's the exception. Since racist laws aren't as cut and dry as they were decades ago, racists who crave the need to dominate and control who lives in their neighborhoods and who occupies their spaces take it upon themselves to do the controlling.

On May 25, 2020, Melody Cooper posted a video on YouTube, which her brother, Christian Cooper, recorded. Christian asked a woman to "put her dog on the leash," in an area in Central Park where it was required of dog owners. The White woman, Amy Cooper, who was asked to follow the laws of the park, got violent, pulled out her cell phone, and said, "I'm going to tell them that there is an African American man threatening my life," before calling the police. The internet called this woman "Karen," which has become a label for problematic White women initiating and pursuing racist and violent behavior in public places toward Black people. I personally believe that we should leave the term "Karen" on the playground and call them what they are—White women exercising racist, violent, and deadly behavior.

Having the luxury to be able to use the State as a resource to eliminate something that is uncomfortable for you is an example of White privilege and White power—and it's available to some by the simple act of picking up the phone. You want Black children out of your pool? You don't want people barbecuing in a public park? You don't want Black people entering an apartment building in which they live? You call the police.

My experiences of being Black and from Baltimore have been buried under politics, polls, and mainstream media. Not only have I survived violent murders, police brutality, and poverty, I've been diving deep and examining my experiences, analyzing my suffering, and developing liberatory ideas to help me grow, and share truth through my poetry and storytelling which I hope can be useful to others. I'm not here to police or gain authority over Black liberation, but I am here to make people aware of the injustices that are rarely covered or encountered in depth by mainstream media, whose spokespeople have little direct knowledge of the real issues, providing only quick statistics and surface analysis, and hardly ever giving a platform to people who truly know the issues—from their root causes to workable solutions. It's past time to work together to give insight on how we all can do better.

One of the most important things that I learned on my journey is that there is nothing wrong with Black people, and there is nothing extraordinary about White people. Black people are not inferior, but their opportunities in this country are. White people are not superior, but their opportunities in this country are. As crazy as the world is, I do believe that we can live in a humane society one day. I believe that there will come a time when mothers and fathers won't have to bury their kids because they are victims of poverty. Through my own experiences and research, I came to an understanding that growth and becoming antiracist are not one-stop shops, or a fixed state to be satisfied with, but a lifelong commitment to reexamining the way one thinks and the way one acts. Being on the journey to become antiracist is a freedom that I never knew existed. A freedom that is available to us all. A freedom that belongs to us all.

Notes

1. Lauren Lazin, dir., *Tupac: Resurrection* (Paramount Pictures, 2003).

2. In 2018, eight of those "elite" and "highly trained" Baltimore police were convicted on charges of racketeering, conspiracy, multiple violent robberies, and overtime fraud. In 2017, Mayor Catherine Pugh ordered a forensic audit of police overtime, and during that time it was discovered to be $1.6 million every two weeks. Back in 2014, the *Baltimore Sun* reported that since 2011, city police officers have faced 317 lawsuits for civil rights and constitutional violations, such as false imprisonment, assault, and false arrest. The *Sun* investigation also showed that even though the city had paid out $5.7 million over that period in lawsuits, police leaders, city attorneys, and other top officials weren't keeping track of the officers who repeatedly faced lawsuits with allegations of brutality. The entire state needs to be held accountable for its participation and aiding in the terrorizing of Baltimore citizens that was carried out by police. One of the many repeat criminals was former Baltimore Police detective Daniel Hersl, who was convicted and sentenced to eighteen years in prison in 2018 for his role in the task force's illegal and deadly series of schemes and his overtime fraud. In my neighborhood, if Hersl hadn't beat your ass before, then you knew someone who had gotten their ass beat by him. His reputation of being a thief, an abuser, and a certified cruddy individual is not just "he says she says." Before this GTTF investigation, Hersl had cost the city $200,000 in lawsuit settlements. He was accused of everything from breaking a guy's nose and jaw to beating up and arresting a woman who was selling church raffle tickets.

3. Citizen Stewart, "That One Time When Sister Souljah Schooled Cornel West," August 15, 2015, YouTube video, https://youtu.be/JokCToCAkE8.

Jumpsuit Project

Sherrill Roland

Sherrill Roland is an interdisciplinary artist who creates art that challenges ideas around controversial social and political constructs. Inspired by his experience in prison for a crime he did not commit, he founded the *Jumpsuit Project* to raise awareness around issues related to mass incarceration.

I create art that challenges ideas around controversial social and political constructs, and generates a safe space to process, question, and share. My work grows out of my personal history; in August 2012, as I first entered graduate school, I was issued a warrant in Washington, DC. In October 2013, I went to trial and subsequently lost, and ten months later, I was released from the county jail. Almost a year and a half after being released, I was exonerated of all charges and granted a bill of innocence.

Jumpsuit Project, a socially engaged art project, began at the University of North Carolina at Greensboro. During the 2016–17 academic year, I wore an orange jumpsuit every day until graduation. These performances engaged those who encountered the orange jumpsuit by igniting conversations around issues related to incarceration and encouraging them to address their own prejudices toward incarcerated people.

In 2019, I performed the *Jumpsuit Project* in Washington, DC, for the first time. It is the only time I've elected to walk freely in public wearing the orange jumpsuit. I walked 6.8 miles from the DCDC Jail, where I was incarcerated, to Georgetown University's Maria and Alberto de la Cruz Art Gallery, where I presented my project.

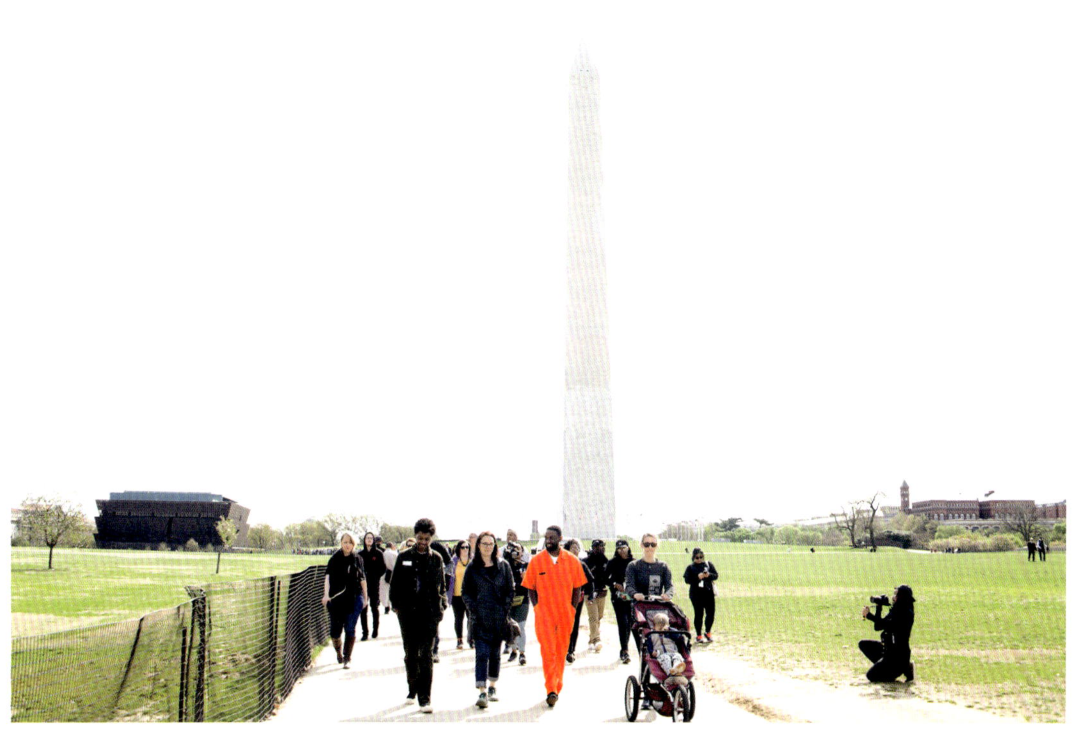

Sherrill Roland, *Jumpsuit Project D.C.*, 2019.
Photo: Christian Carter-Ross.

The Bonds of Aloha

CONNECTING TO CULTURE CAN FREE US

Hinaleimoana Kwai Kong Wong-Kalu (Kumu Hina)

Hinaleimoana Kwai Kong Wong-Kalu (Kumu Hina) is a Kanaka Maoli (Native Hawaiian) teacher, cultural practitioner, and community leader. In 2014, Hina announced her bid for a position on the board of the Office of Hawaiian Affairs. Although she lost, she was one of the first transgender candidates to run for statewide political office in the United States.

I was born and raised on my mainland, my homeland of Hawai'i, here on the island of O'ahu. This is my one hānau. I am a graduate of the Kamehameha Schools and the University of Hawai'i at Mānoa. I was formerly employed by the Office of Hawaiian Affairs (OHA) as a community advocate on issues that matter the most to us Hawaiians and to provide cultural support through education and community engagement. And I've been fortunate through OHA to be supported in my work within the incarceration system. I also served as the chair of the O'ahu Island Burial Council, a governor-appointed position to be a voice of advocacy for iwi kupuna, ancestral burials and the Kona Moku representative on O'ahu, aka Honolulu, aka Kou. Currently, I am the cultural ambassador for the Council for Native Hawaiian Advancement.

I am also engaged in filmmaking, most recently collaborating on the animated film *Kapaemāhū*.[1] It speaks to the arrival of four legendary māhū figures memorialized in history through four large stones in Waikīkī standing

Editor's Note: This essay was edited from a virtual conversation between Kapena Alapa'i and Kumu Hina, September 21, 2020.

between the Duke Kahanamoku statue and the police station on Kalākaua Avenue.[2] I also take care of my mother, and although she probably wishes she could fire me, she's got no choice [laughter].

I don't identify as an artist—engaging in filmmaking is just a part. My worldview and context are different from a lot of people: Hawai'i is my piko; my mainland; the center of my world.[3] And everything radiates out from that, including all that we do, the choices that we make, and how we interpret what comes back to us. That is said in the context of our current political status underneath the United States of America, bombarded with bipartisan politics.[4] Will I participate in the system? Yes, but not whole-heartedly. I'd have to side with who has more of a heart for me, as a māhū, and as a Hawaiian. I don't believe that Americans have any best interest at heart for us kānaka. People who are in positions of power—who aren't kānaka—keep us under foot in our own home.

My Hawaiian grandmother, Mona Kananiokalani Kealoha, who married my grandfather John Furtado Mathias, raised me. She emphasized the importance of Hawaiian language and culture; she pointed to all she could that would anchor and guide me. So even though she was not the kupuna who gave me the ability to speak our language, she planted the seed.[5]

Learning and teaching Hawaiian language and culture has become a life mission and journey. I was given the opportunity to work for Hālau Lōkahi Public Charter School teaching K–12. Working there for thirteen years, I saw the difference that could be made by teaching the next generation.[6] I also realized many of our Native youth came from broken homes where someone in their family, a sibling, an aunt or uncle, a mother, or a father, were incarcerated. So when I was given the opportunity to work with incarcerated Hawaiians, I took it.

In 2006 or 2007, a friend asked me to provide community support at the O'ahu Community Correctional Center (OCCC) and Hālawa Correctional Facility (Hālawa). My class is attended primarily by Native Hawaiian men and sometimes transgender women. I am allowed between twenty and twenty-five haumāna and in my class, behavior is everything.[7] My haumāna are to come in, greet the people who are already sitting, say "aloha" and "mahalo" on the way in and out. I don't emphasize being perfect, but if you can't conduct yourself in that manner, don't come. It helps to establish who's the boss in the class. Because in the Hawaiian school of thought, the classroom is a monarchy—I'm the reigning monarch, and none of them are allowed to be queen [laughter]. But it has been to my advantage, to be who I am, as a māhū, and to say to the menfolk: if I can do it, they can. If I can overcome my inhibitions and work and stand in front of the men, and not be ashamed, not be afraid, not have my doubts, then they can too.

This class is for what I call culturally based cognitive skills; it's a life skills equivalent. It's about decision making, analyzing, processing, assessing, and evaluating where we all are as Hawaiians today, and what we want for our tomorrow. And how we ground ourselves to our culture, language, and history to help determine that path. In an ideal world, the system would be set up where if I'm working with an inmate, I'm working with their family too. That way, the family would not feed their need for discord and conflict. But that's a different system altogether. The current system is a Western system, but if you returned our people to the land, they could do it. There's no reason why they couldn't.

In Hawaiian culture you are obligated to the bonds of aloha that require you to pay attention and be sensitive to know when you may have upset somebody and require you to admit when you are hurt. I don't always use the term ho'oponopono, because my 'ohana Ni'ihau doesn't use it.[8] Ho'oponopono is to make right, to make something correct, to fix, or to bring to balance. Ho'oponopono can be very useful when applied in context of our kānaka, but not when it is a seed for Western mysticism or hybridized with other shamanistic teachings. We should be conscious of ho'opa'apa'a before ho'o-ponopono.[9] In ho'opa'apa'a, it is up to the individual to be self-regulatory. When you know someone is upset, you say, "He aha ta'u mea i hana aku ai iā 'oe? He aha lā kāu e huhū nei? What did I do to you? Why are you upset?" And then it's up to the person hearing that to say, "Ka tumu au i huhū ai iā 'oe, 'o tāu 'ōlelo i 'ōlelo mai ai ia'u, no tou no'ono'o 'ole mai ia'u. I'm upset because you didn't think of me. I'm upset because of what you said." It means that you must speak up rather than be silent and allow something to happen passive aggressively. You have responsibly given some consideration to the impact of your words.

In incarceration, when you have Hawaiian or Polynesian policemen or guards, they look out for Hawaiian or Polynesian inmates. They'll cut each other slack in the system because they know what the system does to us. When they meet as kānaka, one who's on the side of power and authority, and the one who's not, there is still respect between the two as kānaka. It overcomes the Western system.

But at Mauna Kea in the aloha 'āina patriots, we saw something different: the collision of law enforcement and kānaka.[10] We saw Hawaiians in law enforcement who chose to do their jobs instead of walking out; there's no way they could leave because then they couldn't support their families. They chose the welfare and benefit of their family but also chose to stand against their people. The system makes us choose; it sits back, watches this happen, and lets Hawaiians do themselves in. Is there equity? Is there parity? Is there justice in our system? No. But it goes even more insidiously beyond.

We saw the collisions between law enforcement and community at Kalaeloa and Kahuku.[11] Police officers in a bike unit came to push back the community from blocking the road. They in turn blocked us. One of the wahine officers had a nephew in my school.[12] I know her well. She struggled. She looked at me and put her head down in shame, and she tapped out. She knew what we were standing for; she left, and another officer came in. I know there's a heart in all of our officers. They know what's going on. Any of us who are Hawaiian and were born and raised here are going to feel for the next person that was born and raised here.

But law enforcement training has gotten more and more rigorous. Why? Because our islands and our people have been colonized at every level. By taking on the colonizer's outlook, perspective, and worldview, we have been further embroiled into this American framework. Now I see Hawaiians driving around in caravans holding American flags high and Hawaiian flags just as high. If you are a proud American and you're ethnically Hawaiian, great. You want to hold up a Trump flag in the principle of being American? You have that right. But just don't hold the Hawaiian flag there with it. Because what the Hawaiian flag stands for does not equate to what the American flag stands for. We don't come from the same moral compass, the same values. The Hawaiian flag reminds me to have aloha in my heart. The American flag does not. And to see them flying together . . . never.

When things were ramping up in the States towards Black Lives Matter, I needed further research to take into account that I am not a Black person and that the system definitely oppresses Black people. I had to take myself out of the kānaka community model, the "all of us have a part to play, all of us matter equally," to really understand that the system in which Black Lives Matter exists is not our system. I had to make peace with that. It's definitely hard for me to explain that point of view to people on the continent. But we are all on the same side of equality, and that's what bands us together with Black and brown bodies in solidarity.

But I was very worried, because as someone who has led our community on numerous marches, you have to be aware of the fact that many of our people are going to be in a herd mentality. They're just going to move, and there's plenty of outliers who are ready, waiting, itching, hungry to do something. They are the ones who don't step in with Kapu Aloha.[13] Kapu is a law. It means forbidden or restricted, a law that governs what we do and why we do; what we don't, and why we don't. It's absolute. I interpret Kapu Aloha as a law requiring us to have aloha above and beyond. So when we're confronted with law enforcement, with a foreign culture, with things that hurt us to the very core—such as anticipating a development atop a mountain that our ancestors long ago said "No more" to—we have aloha in its highest form. Even when faced with prejudice, with discrimination, with tough situations that challenge who we are, we are required to have aloha, which is mutual care, kindness, and, at minimum, a respect for one another. If you're in Kapu Aloha, you don't have to ho'oponopono, at least not so formally.

If I stick to the understanding that Hawai'i is my piko, my mainland, my homeland—never will I call the United States the mainland. Because my mental, spiritual, emotional, and physical analysis of who I am, where I'm at in life, where I'm going, will always be grounded to and tied into the fact that Hawai'i is my piko. It is the community I serve, the culture I serve, and I would give my life for it.

> FOR THE LĀHUI
> *Composed by Hinaleimoana Kwai Kong Wong-Kalu and Josh Tatofi*
>
> E welo mau loa ku'u hae aloha
> My Hawaiian flag, may it wave evermore,
> I ka nu'u o ka lewa lani lā
> In the highest of heavens, above all else,
> E maluhia no nā kau a kau
> May there be peace and tranquility for all time,
> Eō Hawai'i ku'u 'āina aloha
> Answer, oh great and beloved Hawai'i, my beloved homeland
> E ku'u lāhui ē, wiwo'ole ē,
> (To my people) be fearless, be bold, be brave.
> Kū kānaka ē, 'onipa'a mau,
> Stand and be as Kanaka, hold fast to who you are
> Ua mau ke ea o ka 'āina i ka pono
> The life, the essence, the independence of who we are
> Ua mau ke ea o ka 'āina i ka pono
> Are supported by our culture and our language.

Notes

1. *Kapaemāhū* is a 2020 Oscar-nominated animated short produced and directed by Hinaleimoana Kwai Kong Wong-Kalu, Dean Hamer, and Joe Wilson with director of animation Daniel Sousa. It is based on the long-hidden history of four healing stones on Waikiki Beach placed as a tribute to four legendary māhū who first brought the healing arts to Hawaii. Puanani Fernandez-Akamine,

"Kapaemāhū: A Lost Story Found," *Ka Wai Ola*, March 30, 2020, https://kawaiola
.news/kiionioni/kapaemahu-a-lost-story-found/.

2. Māhū, n., homosexual, of either sex; hermaphrodite. Contemporary contexts include transsexual of either sex.

3. Piko, n., navel, umbilical cord. Figuratively, blood relative, genitals.

4. While Hawai'i is internationally recognized as a state of the United States, an underlying argument is that Hawai'i was overthrown and is an independent nation under military occupation. "Legal Status of Hawaii," Wikipedia, accessed December 2, 2022, https://en.m.wikipedia.org/wiki/Legal_status_of_Hawaii.

5. Kupuna, n., grandparent, ancestor, relative, or close friend of the grandparent's generation; grandaunt, granduncle.

6. *Kumu Hina* is a film by Dean Hamer and Joe Wilson about the struggle to maintain Pacific Islander culture and values told through the lens of a Native Hawaiian who is a proud, confident māhū and an honored and respected kumu, or teacher, cultural practitioner, and community leader (https://kumuhina.com /about).

7. Haumāna, n. (plural), student, pupil, apprentice, recruit, disciple.

8. Ho'oponopono, v., mental cleansing: family conferences in which relationships are set right (ho'oponopono) through prayer, discussion, confession, repentance, and mutual restitution and forgiveness.

9. Ho'opa'apa'a, n., dispute, argument, quarrel; ho'o.pa'a.pa'a, to argue, dispute; argument, quarrel.

10. From 2014 to the present protesters, both Indigenous and non-, have halted construction of the Thirty Meter Telescope and brought attention to over fifty years of mismanagement atop Mauna Kea, a mountaintop considered sacred to Kanaka Maoli. See Pu'uhonua o Pu'uhuluhulu, https://puuhuluhulu.com /learn.

11. On October 18, 2019, one hundred Honolulu police officers filled Malakole Street in Kalaeloa and prepared to arrest protesters who sat in the middle of Hanua Street to block the transportation of the turbine parts to the site of the planned Na Pua Makani wind farm in Kahuku. Blaze Lovell, "27 Arrested in Second Kalaeloa Standoff over Wind Farm," *Honolulu Civil Beat*, October 21, 2019, https://www.civilbeat.org/2019/10/27-arrested-in-second-kalaeloa-standoff-over -wind-farm/.

12. Wahine, n., woman, lady, wife.

13. Kapu Aloha is a multidimensional concept and practice inspired by our kūpuna. It is a discipline of compassion for all to express aloha for those involved, especially those who are perceived to be polar to our cause. Kapu Aloha helps us intentionalize our thoughts, words, and deeds without harm to others. It honors the energy and life found in aloha—compassion—and helps us focus on its ultimate purpose and meaning. Kapu Aloha arose from kānaka-led protests in Hawai'i at Mauna Kea as a law of nonviolence between protest groups, onlookers, opposition, and land. It is outlined in a set of protocols found at Protect Mauna Kea, https://www.protectmaunakea.net/.

The Nail That Sticks Out

Tani Ikeda

Tani Ikeda is an Emmy-winning director for the documentary television series *Wonder Women*. She is a published essayist in *Believe Me: How Trusting Women Can Change the World*, where she wrote about Survivor Love Letter, a love letter–writing campaign she founded for survivors of sexual assault. Ikeda was an executive producer and director for the Blackpills television series *Resist* with Black Lives Matter cofounder Patrisse Cullors.

I remember my grandfather,
who was a long-haired, radical, artist,
telling me when I was a girl,
"The nail that sticks out gets hammered."
At that time
I was getting taunted on the school bus rides home
"Chinese, Japanese, look at your dirty knees,"
I wanted to get so small I would disappear.
But my grandfather saw me.
He told me that everything I was experiencing
made me an artist.
He said I was born an artist.
Being Japanese American didn't make me ugly.
It allowed me to see the world
unlike anyone else.

As a little girl,
I remember Grandpa telling me stories
about being in McNeil Penitentiary for draft evasion
—how when prison riots raged,
inmates lit their mattresses on fire

and threw them between the bars.
Grandpa remembers banging his metal cup
against the cage.
"This was our way of crying,"
he said.

I memorized every expression—
every story he'd tell me.
At the end, Grandpa would shake his head and say,
"The nail that sticks out gets hammered."
Although Grandpa had tuberculosis and
could have avoided the draft
by naturally failing the army physical,
he believed refusing to enlist
was his way
of taking a stand
against a country that imprisoned
him, his family, and his community.
Now, when I think of my grandfather
looking down on his small, tender grandchild,
I know that he was afraid—
afraid that what this country had done to him
is what it could do to me.
Now I know he spent years and years
telling me stories about his life
so I would be ready
for the challenges
I faced in mine.

This past year
after the coronavirus spread
a stranger told me to go back to China,
swastika stickers showed up in our neighborhood mailboxes,
I was sprayed by a hose and forced to walk on the other side of the street.
I have been filming with the co-founders of Black Lives Matter.
I filmed the co-organizers of the Women's March on Washington
and documented them as they marched 18 miles from the NRA
    headquarters
to the Department of Justice
while hordes of white men
armed with assault rifles

intimidated and taunted them.
We were in Charlottesville
as Neo Nazis
beat Black and brown youth,
We witnessed children torn apart
from their undocumented mothers
by ICE,
We filmed as hundreds of protesters at LAX chanted,
"We welcome you!"
to those who were separated from their loved ones
after the Muslim Ban:
Executive Order 13769.
And what I see is this:
America is at war with itself.
Instead of defending democracy
from German Nazis,
Fascism has taken on the symbolism
of our own national anthem
and Star Spangled Banner,
and anyone who dares
take a knee
against racism
is deemed an enemy
of this country.

Now, as before,
our country is looking for an enemy within.
75 years ago,
Japanese Americans lived through a war
that rounded up our American families
and put us in concentration camps.
We were told we were not American.

Today's gray, Seattle weather
is like a day I would visit my grandfather.
Today I want nothing more
than to sit at the kitchen table
and ask him what I should do
in these times of fear and political terror.
Yet, all I have left are his stories.
I've been raised in a tradition of struggle

and the art of seeing what
does not yet exist.
As a filmmaker,
every day I am in the crossfire
of stories that echo
the injustices of the past.

Linda Sarsour walks on the opposite side of the street from her son for
    fear of being shot as a terrorist.[1]
11-year-old Leah fights for her mom with other children separated at the
    border as they chant "We Belong Together."
Patrisse Cullors chants Charleena Lyles' name.
She was a mother from Seattle shot in front of her babies by police.
"They win when we stop feeling," Patrisse says.
Many times I wake up shaking with anxiety.
But it is this pressing urgency,
that gets me out of bed.
Telling our stories will keep us alive.
They will open the heart
of this country
by breaking it.

Note

1. Linda Sarsour is co-organizer of the Women's March on Washington.

Art Is a Trojan Horse

RECLAIMING OUR NARRATIVES

Faith Bartley, Courtney Bowles, and Mark Strandquist

Faith Bartley has been lead fellow of the People's Paper Co-op since 2015. She is a tireless advocate and champion of those that society typically silos and discriminates against. Faith has spoken at local, regional, and national conferences, and in the spring of 2021 was the first in her family to graduate from college.

Courtney Bowles is an artist, educator, and community organizer. Her projects combine organizing strategies and urgently needed services, with collaborative, poetic, and performative actions that connect diverse and often antagonistic actors. She currently codirects the People's Paper Co-op and the Reentry Think Tank in Philadelphia, Pennsylvania.

Mark Strandquist has spent years using art to help amplify, celebrate, and power social justice movements. He is the creative director of the Performing Statistics project, codirects the People's Paper Co-op and the Reentry Think Tank, and founded the COVID-19 rapid response project Fill the Walls with Hope, Rage, Resources, and Dreams.

The People's Paper Co-op (PPC) is a women-led, women-focused, women-powered art and advocacy project at The Village of Arts and Humanities in North Philadelphia, Pennsylvania. It began in 2014 as part of The Village's Spaces Program, a five-month-long residency designed to bring artists

Editor's Note: This contribution was edited from a conversation between three leaders from the People's Paper Co-op, Faith Bartley, Courtney Bowles, and Mark Strandquist, on June 30, 2020.

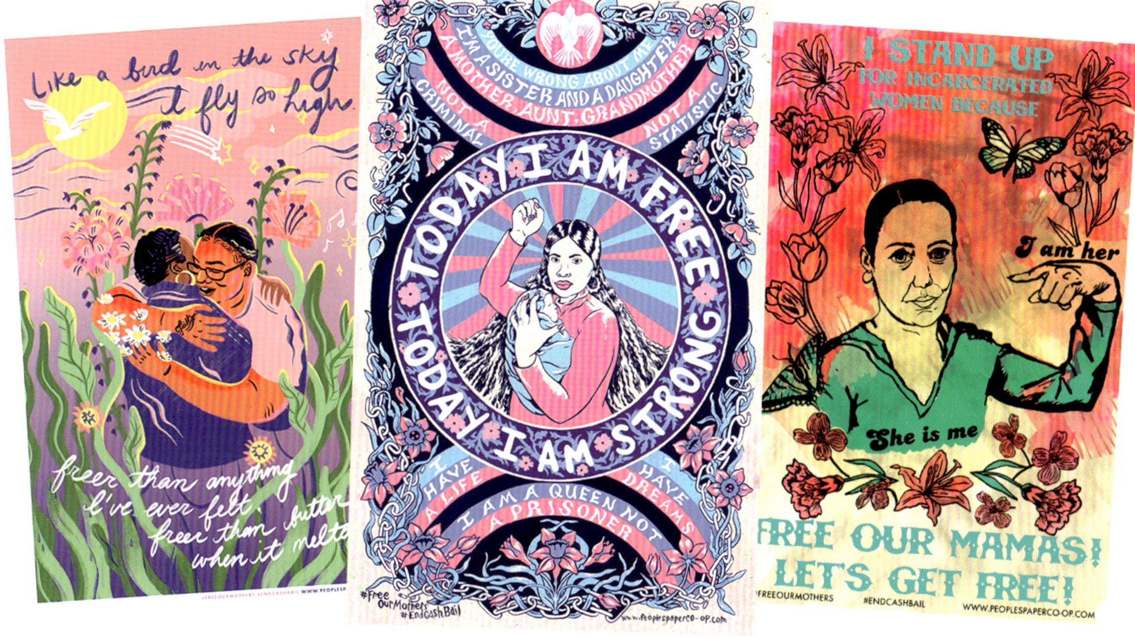

free our mamas! sisters! queens!, 2019–ongoing. Posters collaboratively designed by artists across North America and formerly incarcerated women in the People's Paper Co-op, created as a fundraiser for the Mama's Day Bail Out campaign. Photo courtesy of the People's Paper Co-op. Pictured posters created by Ashley Lukashevsky, Katie Kaplan, and Mary Tremonte. For a full list of contributing artists and PPC Fellows, visit http://peoplespaperco-op.com.

together with community and long-term residents around a variety of projects.

MARK STRANDQUIST: Throughout our work we've seen that starting with questions, not answers, is so important to building trust and a healthy foundation. Some of the project's initial framing questions were: If social services, legal services, and legal advocacy were led by community members with criminal records themselves, how would those social services change? How would that advocacy change? How could artists not impose art or ideas on a community but be in service of and in support of the visions and ideas and demands of local community members?

COURTNEY BOWLES: For context, there's a very high arrest rate where we're located. But also, Pennsylvania is a state where anything someone is charged with, regardless of conviction, stays on their criminal record. So a disproportionately large number of folks have criminal records in Pennsylvania and in North Philly where we're based. Also in Pennsylvania, anything that people are charged with but not convicted of can be expunged—cleaned or cleared. Typically, it's an expensive process, and people often don't know that it's an option.

FAITH BARTLEY: From my experience living in and growing up around The Village, having a criminal record is a discouraging thing. It creates barriers. Even if you just get the handcuffs on you, it's on your record. And for people like me that aspired and tried to do the right thing, knowing that I have a criminal history, I'm thinking, if I go for a job, they're not going to hire me. Or if I'm looking for an apartment, I have this criminal history. Once you get a record, it's like, well, hell, I might as well just keep messing up. Ain't nobody gonna hire me. Nobody's gonna help me do nothing.

MS: One of the main things we started doing was partnering with lawyers and community members to cofacilitate legal clinics where people could get free legal services to help clear or clean up their criminal records, but the actual events were designed by community members. After community members go through the process, they meet with a lawyer, and then, if they want, they can go to a paper-making station and take their criminal record, that's been holding them back, that's been telling their story for them, and turn it into something new.

FB: It is important that people like myself, who have been directly impacted by the criminal justice system, help design these social services. I can offer my lived experience with other members who are coming in getting their record cleaned up. Most social service spaces are drab and dehumanizing. We want to make these spaces inviting; we want to make them safe. So we have people, like myself, or another sister or another brother that was also formerly incarcerated, welcome you into a space. And when you come inside, you see art all over the walls created by formerly incarcerated men and women that speaks to what they need to survive and thrive, or some of the injustices that they might have gone through. Just going in front of a lawyer and pulling up the darkest moments of your life can be a retraumatizing experience. So when you're in a space where you're feeling welcome and invited, and it's a safe space for you to venture into those dark moments, and then after you get your printout and a person like myself invites you to transform that, or tear that paper up, get rid of that old past, get rid of the mistake you made, and transform it into a new sheet of paper—it was part of my healing process. To have not a mug shot but what we like to call a "reverse mug shot" of who people are today, and then include some forward-thinking writing, "Without my criminal record, I could be or I am . . ." is healing. Especially when our neighborhood is not set up like this. It's set up for us to fail.

MS: Everything we're talking about is about ownership of stories, ownership of services. It's about agency and about community power. If you can't control your story, you can't control your future. And telling a counternarrative, reclaiming your history is the starting point to speaking your dreams into existence. I think one of the things our project does right is that we're not asking you to apologize for what you've done. We're asking you to demand what you needed in the first place to stay free. What you needed to be the parent, the neighbor, the teacher, whatever it is that you wanted to be. While storytelling is part of everything we do, we're not trying to pull trauma out of people. We know these systems have failed people. What still excites me about art is that it's a rare place where we can both reclaim our stories, while illustrating a more just and beautiful future. It's the first step to building that world. It's like a blueprint.

FB: We use new stories to counteract those old stories. I have a piece of artwork that says, "Don't exploit me. Look at my résumé, not my record." Just because I have a criminal history, I still have all these things that I know that I can do to aspire to and be a better person. Don't hold that against me, don't exploit me because I've been in jail.

MS: Each person's transformed record then lives on and goes to the next clinic so that later, if a person comes in, they might see a neighbor or friend or just another person that's gone through a similar experience. And those have been exhibited in legal clinics all over the city, in the Philadelphia

Museum of Art, art galleries, City Hall, outside of the mayor's office, and in Philadelphia's federal detention center. It's important that our art is shown in all kinds of places. We know that every space has a self-selecting audience, so it's important that we are constantly fighting to get the work and these voices and stories into as many places as possible.

CB: When they're hung collectively in these spaces, people have to interact with each piece separately to understand what the individual who created it wants to share. But if you step back, you see hundreds of pieces that represent a larger group and a larger issue. It weaves the personal and the political together.

FB: It's encouraging. It feels like we're finally getting to be heard. It feels empowering to have our art outside the mayor's office where he has to take notice. We want to say we're here, we need help, we need support, and we need you to hear us. Since I started doing this advocacy work, I've learned that art is like a Trojan horse. We can use art to infiltrate places where formerly incarcerated people aren't even allowed. It's a way to get our message across. Because I always say, people always hear with their eyes.

Imagine an art exhibit of ours being in a university, where they don't even let ex-offenders go to school. I'm in college right now, and I got turned down from a few colleges that I really wanted to go to because of my criminal history. To have this art on those university campuses feels good in a way. It's a bittersweet moment for me because my prayer is to be on that campus *with* that art, *going* to that school and getting a degree. But because I'm an ex-offender, I can't. The question in the back of my mind is, is that the only way we can get on a campus? By using our art as our vehicle?

When policy is being made, people like myself are not sitting at the table helping draw this policy up. How can you have someone who has never been incarcerated, who has never been through half of the stuff that we've been through, making policy? We should be helping design things that help us, that make us feel human and not like animals. We're humans who have made mistakes and want to do better.

CB: Exactly, and it's not just about making mistakes; we all make them. Some people are more easily forgiven for them. It's also about systems setting people up for failure and a lack of being able to imagine a different world because of that. That's one reason our programs are about looking to people who've been through the process as experts that the city, the state, the country, and the world need to hear from. Because, as you were saying, how can anyone possibly presume to imagine what someone else needs when we haven't been in their shoes?

FB: And that speaks to our reentry program. At that time, there were not (and there still aren't) many programs in the city of Philadelphia for women, but there are tons of men's reentry programs. So we created a reentry program based on one I wish I could have come home to. When I came home, time and time again, I was getting discouraged, getting all kinds of doors slammed in my face because I built up such a heavy criminal history. We wanted to work with formerly incarcerated women or women coming home from prison who might not have access to resources or know what to do, and create a platform for them to survive, thrive, be out here, to get resources and access to nonjudgmental support. We keep passing the torch. Our program is different because it's led by women with lived experience who can speak to what it takes for others coming home to thrive and stay free.

We create a safe environment for the women to be vulnerable, for them to want to talk about their experiences. We get so guarded sometimes that we don't want to let people in for fear that they might judge us. And once a person feels safe, it opens them up a little bit, and that's where the creative energy comes in. The art comes from the heart, not from the mind, and it speaks to part of their story, some of the things that have been holding them back for so long, that they couldn't express before. But they express it through art, be it in photos, collective poems, in tears shed during our daily share and tear ceremony.

MS: One clear way that shows up in the work is when we're making art about what fellows dream of growing into and becoming. They visualize their dreams through art, which is powerful on its own, creates counternarratives, builds trust in the space as we learn about each other, and from a reentry support side, it helps our team understand what forms of support we could connect folks [with] to help them achieve that goal.

CB: I don't think that any of the work we do could be done without the relationships and trust that we build together. It opens a space for imagination, which we don't always have. It's hard to imagine a world without prisons; it's hard to imagine a world where everyone is treated justly, because we've been taught that that's not how it works. Art allows us space to dream and begin to create the world we hope to bring into fruition.

Let's go through some of the fundamentals about the Women in Reentry Arts and Advocacy program. Twice a year, we work with a cohort of women who have been nominated from reentry organizations across the city, know about the program from past participants, or heard about it from the halfway houses where they're staying. In addition to Faith, our lead fellow, and

Latyra Blake, our peer mentor, we typically work with an additional four to seven women. Fellows are paid a living wage for their participation, and each cohort of women meets between ten and twelve weeks, twice a week, at our storefront in North Philly. There are no rules per se, but we have principles we all design together.

Each spring, for the past three years, our big collaboration has been with the Philadelphia Community Bail Fund. In addition to organizing parades, press conferences, and pop-up exhibits, we've made artwork for the annual Mama's Day Bail Out, a national campaign to bring Black moms and caregivers home to be with their families and communities for Mother's Day. PPC Fellows make portraits and poetry that they share with artists across the United States to collaboratively create artwork. Both a digital version and limited pieces, hand printed on paper we made from criminal records, were produced. In 2019, the artwork raised $23,000 in two weeks to bail moms out. In 2020, we repeated the process with another group of fellows and artists—it, and everything, was complicated by COVID. Still, we raised $43,000 in just a few weeks! Typically, we close the store after Mother's Day, but we left it up to try to raise as much as possible to bring people back to their communities, where they belong, during the pandemic. And then the Uprising for Racial Justice happened. And in three days, we raised another $17,000 that went to bail out protesters from Philadelphia.

FB: Women, specifically Black women, Black mothers, are the women sitting in jail. Many have not even been convicted of a crime and are just sitting there because they can't make the bail. That's been my lived experience as well. To sit in a cell for three months on a $260 bail, not having the outside support to even bail me out. Finally, I got an opportunity to go before the judge, and I was found not guilty. And so, that's three, four months that I couldn't get back. During that time, my mom was dying of cancer, I lost my apartment, I lost a pretty good forklift job, all because I couldn't make bail. I believe it's important that we campaign for incarcerated women, we help lift their voices and make people aware that we're all human and that we're sitting in a cell rotting away. We haven't even been convicted. Almost all the women in our reentry program have had similar experiences.

MS: I feel like for many decades, if not centuries, people have been making art about the *idea* of freedom. And the women in the program, in collaboration with artists, we're making art that's *literally* freeing people. Our art has raised over $160,000 in three years. If we think about the work in concentric circles, or ripples, when a story is first told within the workshops it's hopefully helping to heal the person who's telling the story, but also the women around them. And then as it goes out and out, it's hopefully building empathy. It's hitting policy makers, it's raising money to free people, it's providing tools for advocates to do their work better. It reverberates. But if you can't create that space of trust within the workshops, that story isn't told, or it's told differently.

And we're not just talking about freeing people, we're talking about modeling a way of working with each other. You go into one of our workshops, and hopefully it doesn't feel at all like a typical reentry program. We want it to feel like a family. I think so much of the project is about transformation. It's literally about taking things that you want, that are sites of trauma, sites of incarceration, sites of policing, surveillance, and turning them into a site of liberation and community. I think that there's some symbolic and real ways in which a lot of the work we do together reinforces the idea that transforming society is part of the journey to true liberation, true freedom, and community. Our best moments are when we're trying to live up to that. When the system tries to divide us, when the world makes it hard for us to connect, artists and activists have powerful tools for building community and simultaneously dreaming of a better world. Art is a tool where you can literally imagine and visualize a different kind of world, imagine different forms of public safety, different forms of community.

CB: Cash bail removes people's presumption of innocence; it's designed to punish poor people. It's been amazing to see how much people across the country have donated to their local bail funds this year. We're keeping our fingers crossed since more attention has been made to the injustices of money bail that by next year it will have ended, and our focus can be on something else!

MS: To that point I think this year, in the wake of the Uprising, we're seeing changes, conversations, and coalitions being built that seemed unimaginable a year ago. It's of course a horrifying moment for so many reasons, but also one where it feels like society is ready to commit to (and hopefully build) something more just, more equitable, more creative, more whole.

FB: As we continue to grow, I'm excited to see what we've already been doing, done even better. I want to see the PPC completely led by formerly incarcerated women and helping other formerly incarcerated women; we're close. The idea of people like myself, people that had all these barriers in the past, now having a platform to speak to what we need to keep thriving, in a society where it sometimes feels like we're frowned upon because of our criminal records, is powerful. That it continues to live and that formerly incarcerated women lead. That the fight will continue.

CB: Yeah, we've been trying to work ourselves out of a job since this started! When we first began the program, we were hustling so hard because we thought we were only going to be around for the five-month residency. As a result, we didn't fully have space to create the blueprint of "how will this survive without us" because we didn't expect it to exist. Like you said, Faith, recently we've all been working on a sustainable business model, around the paper and book making, that is completely run by formerly incarcerated women. Employment is one of the main barriers people face when coming home; our hope is that the PPC will be able to provide jobs to women as they're being released. That's a beautiful legacy, and we're fortunate that we can create that together from the ground up and provide the blueprints to pass along.

MS: When I think back, I feel like one thing that has helped the project have the impact it has is that we constantly asked the question, "Who's missing from the conversation, who's missing from the collaboration?" We assumed that we didn't always know the answers. We assumed that we needed to reach out to other people to help make things more powerful. And it's brought in the invitation for more and more people to be part of the projects, to be more part of the campaigns, to find ways to connect across difference, and community.

And we've seen when that is done well, we're collaborating with incredibly brilliant neighbors, artists and activists, and lawyers, and city officials, rad parade designers, and filmmakers. The world is full of people, in this moment more than ever, that want to use whatever skills and privilege and networks and resources and dreams they have to be part of something that's building a better world.

CB: I think one of the takeaways is just how important it is not to do art *to* people but *with* people. I think the importance of trust building, communication, and listening, so much listening, and then building together is how we've been successful.

FB: My hope for what someone would take away from this is that for me, I can dream now. I can dream. I've been in and out of prison for the better part of my life, but I'm not who my records say I am. I'm a human being who's made mistakes and who's now trying to make the world a better place. And I'm doing everything I need to do. Just because a person has been locked up doesn't mean that they can't help change the world. Everybody deserves a chance and opportunity. And I feel like the PPC has given me the opportunity. I just keep dreaming, and that's the key, to follow my dreams.

Try/Step/Trip (Excerpt)

Dahlak Brathwaite

Dahlak Brathwaite is an award-winning playwright, composer, and performer. His work has been presented at the Smithsonian, Brooklyn Academy of Music, the Kennedy Center, Lincoln Center, REDCAT, the Public Theater, SXSW, and on HBO's last two seasons of *Russell Simmons Presents Def Poetry*.

Try/Step/Trip is a spoken-word, multicharacter, ensemble musical performed in the body through the choreographic language of step. The story is guided by a music man, the Conductor, as he reimagines his experience in a court-ordered drug rehabilitation program. Cocreated with director Roberta Uno and choreographer Toran X. Moore, the play was originally inspired by Brathwaite's own history. Try/Step/Trip *layers characters, poetic verse, and dialogue over the content of songs to create a theatrical piece that blurs the lines between hip-hop and dramatic performance.*

*THE CONDUCTOR begins a simple stomp-snap and sets the tempo quickly.
THE GROUP joins in after the first snap.*

ANONYMOUS (CONT'D)

The first time
A cop told me
I'd driven through the parking lot
Of a movie theater
Too many times

PASTOR

The second time
I made it inside the movie theater

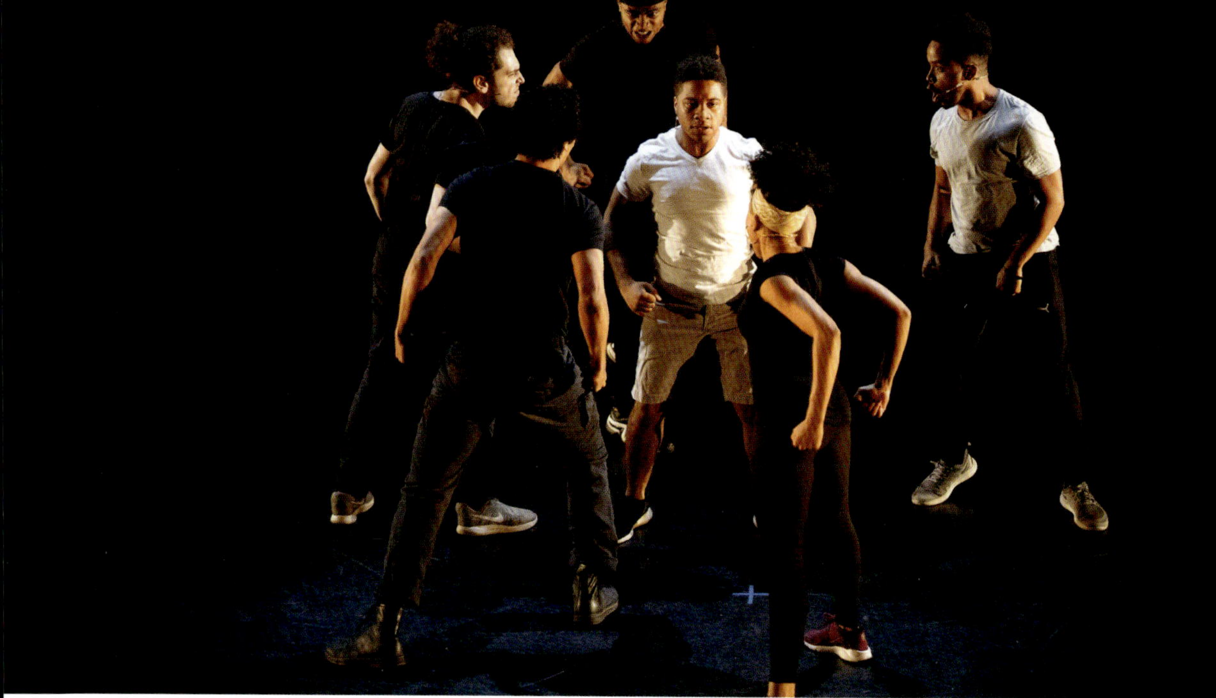

Dahlak Brathwaite, *Try/Step/Trip*, 2019. Directed by
Roberta Uno; choreography by Toran X. Moore.
Photo: Daniel Alcazar.

But the best fight scene
Happened before the movie
Even started
Two Chinese families
Literally punched each other
Out of the building
Leaving all the brothers just
Sitting there
Saying
Quote
"DAMNNNNNNNNNN . . ."
"It wasn't us."

MARY

The third time
A cop car followed
My car

Through a small town
For 15 minutes
Pulled me over
Checked my license
And when everything checked out
He said he couldn't see
If I had changed
My tags or not
Those tags are color coded
For that particular reason
You couldn't see?!
I don't think you should be walking around
With a GUN, playa
You can't see
I mean
Are you colorblind?
Clearly not.

SAMPLES

The fourth time
I'm walking across the street
When a parked cop car
Flashed his high beams
At me
It's awkward
So I'm inclined to wave
Hi
At least
I keep walking
And the car speeds at me
Then drives off
Like it was a bluff
Like I would run first
And wonder if I was guilty later
"Bitch, I might be"

ANONYMOUS

The fifth time
I'm parked at the park
When 5-0
Parks right behind me

Points a camcorder
So of course
I pose
Til the po's
Get all the info they need
I'm told to leave.
Notified that I've been registered
In a gang affiliated database
Great.
Thought I had to sign up for that.

MARY

The sixth time
I get a police escort
From closing club
To parked car
The officer got his arm out the window
Just staring at me
I mean I dressed up to get looked at
But this is not what I had in mind.

PASTOR

The seventh time
I'm around the corner
From my house
That's it.

SAMPLES

The 8th time
I spend the first hours
Of the year 2006
Outside my apartment complex
Face down
Oscar Grant style
Under an infrared police gun
Nervously pointed down

ANONYMOUS

The ninth time
I'm dragged by neck
Off steps

Of a Las Vegas hotel
And the 10th time

THE GROUP

The 10th time

ANONYMOUS

And the 10th time

THE GROUP

The 10th time

THE CONDUCTOR layers in the chords for "1 Time."

ANONYMOUS AND THE CONDUCTOR

(Raps)

And the 10th time
I was high
Cops stopped me driving in my ride
Marijuana got me all paranoid
All I want is to avoid a DUI
I'mma be cooperative officer
This car is marijuana free
I swear it you can search me

ANONYMOUS (CONT'D)

But forgot these mushrooms in my pocket
I was planning on
Tripping on a Thursday

THE GROUP

Ohhhhh

ANONYMOUS AND THE CONDUCTOR

Hands behind back

THE GROUP

Hands behind back

ANONYMOUS AND THE CONDUCTOR

Back up on the way

THE GROUP

Back up on the way

ANONYMOUS AND THE CONDUCTOR

Put me in the back

THE GROUP

Put me in the back

ANONYMOUS AND THE CONDUCTOR

Black man bad day

THE GROUP

Black man bad day

ANONYMOUS AND THE CONDUCTOR

Formally arrested me
Second cop questioned me
Telling me it's a felony
A felony?
A FELONY.
Tellin me the bail will be
Set at $10,000
And the judge and the bailiff
Won't see me till the end of week
Jumpsuit given now

THE GROUP

Jumpsuit given now

ANONYMOUS AND THE CONDUCTOR

Clothes taken off

THE GROUP

Clothes taken off

ANONYMOUS AND THE CONDUCTOR

I was driving down the street

THE GROUP

I was driving down the street

ANONYMOUS AND THE CONDUCTOR

How I get so lost?

THE GROUP

How I get so lost

THE CONDUCTOR

Heading to a cell
Can't call cell phones
Only landline number
I can find is mother's
But the sound on the other end
I couldn't stand that tone

GROUP MEMBER

But who need a number
When you are number?

THE CONDUCTOR

Another brother
That they drug in
For a drug offense
And judge him
Never had a gun on me
But they were gunning for me
It's custom for me to be
In custody
Always knew I's gonna be
A subject of the government
And of this narrative
Turned all our heroes to heroin
Heroines to single parent mothers

GROUP MEMBER

It's embarrassing

THE CONDUCTOR

Just "one of" in a system set up for me
It comforts
Can't resist it like a rhythm
I jump into it

Like fuck it!

Throughout the above section of the song, ANONYMOUS *begins to experience the content of his statement viscerally, until eventually* THE GROUP *morphs into the force of the system, deepening the experience of his story through their movement.* THE GROUP *calls out names of victims who have been slain by police violence and* THE CONDUCTOR *responds with "Say Their Name!"*

Another optional call from the group is: "Yeah it only takes one time" and/or "Yeah it only takes one!"

THE GROUP surrounds ANONYMOUS. *THE CONDUCTOR calls a step into motion. The scene transforms.*

THE CONDUCTOR'S SPACE

The percussion drops out and only THE CONDUCTOR's *chords for "1Time" remain.* THE GROUP *circle* ANONYMOUS *center stage as fraternity/sorority pledges in resting stance.*

THE CONDUCTOR

Context:
When I was in college
2% of the population was black
And 95% of that black population
Were either raised
By African immigrants
Or in the church
Or by both

MARY steps toward the center of the circle, looks ANONYMOUS *up and down, dismisses him, then walks back to her position.*

As though just being Black American alone
Was only right for a very different type of institution

When I was a freshman in college
I pledged for Sigma Gamma
A multicultural fraternity
I dropped out.

STEVE moves toward ANONYMOUS *to taunt him.*

As this white kid was hazing me
I just kept thinking slavery

My pro-blackness peaked during those years
And I wasn't letting no white folks talk crazy to me

I think now that I would have took
The hazing from the Black Sigmas

Because Black was always my higher power
Black power
Even if it made me
Powerless
Slave to rhythm

Never falling out of step
Or falling out of line
But that was always the problem
I had trouble fully following anything

Especially . . . "one time"

When I finished college
I'd been in a school system
For 16 years straight
I decided that I'd go my own way
Be as free as black boy hip-hop
Seemed to me

But I only got a 2 month break
And I was back
To a very different type of institution
With its own set of papers
And requirements for class
More important tests to pass
But essentially
The routine of things

The Evanesced Series (2016–)

Kenyatta A. C. Hinkle

Kenyatta A. C. Hinkle is an interdisciplinary visual artist and writer. Her artwork has been reviewed by the *LA Times*, *Artforum*, the *Huffington Post*, and the *New York Times*. She is the author of *Kentifrications: Convergent Truth(s) and Realities*, published by Occidental College and Sming Books, and *sir*, published by Litmus Press.

In *The Evanesced Series (2016–)*, over one hundred drawings, large-scale paintings, and a performance suite bring attention to a painful subject: missing Black women in America and the African diaspora, from history to the present day. I coined the term *un-portraits* to capture the rampant erasure of these elusive figures—channeled by drawing with handmade brushes, while I do improvised dancing to blues, hip-hop, and Baltimore club music. These un-portraits pivot between real and imagined narratives representing thousands of Black womxn who have disappeared due to colonialism, human trafficking, homicides, and other forms of erasure as well as within the prison industrial complex. *The Evanesced: Embodied Disappearance (2016–)* is a performance suite that evokes various types of womxn navigating historical and contemporary contexts. The performance—which includes a soundtrack of whispers, shuffles, and snippets of popular and underground music and prison work songs recorded by Alan Lomax—adds another dimension to this emotional examination of a fraught part of the Black femme experience. Although this work examines the acts of violence within erasure, it also asks the question, "What would it look like to emerge from erasure?" *The Evanesced* is an expression of the #SayHerName movement of mourning, awareness, and healing.

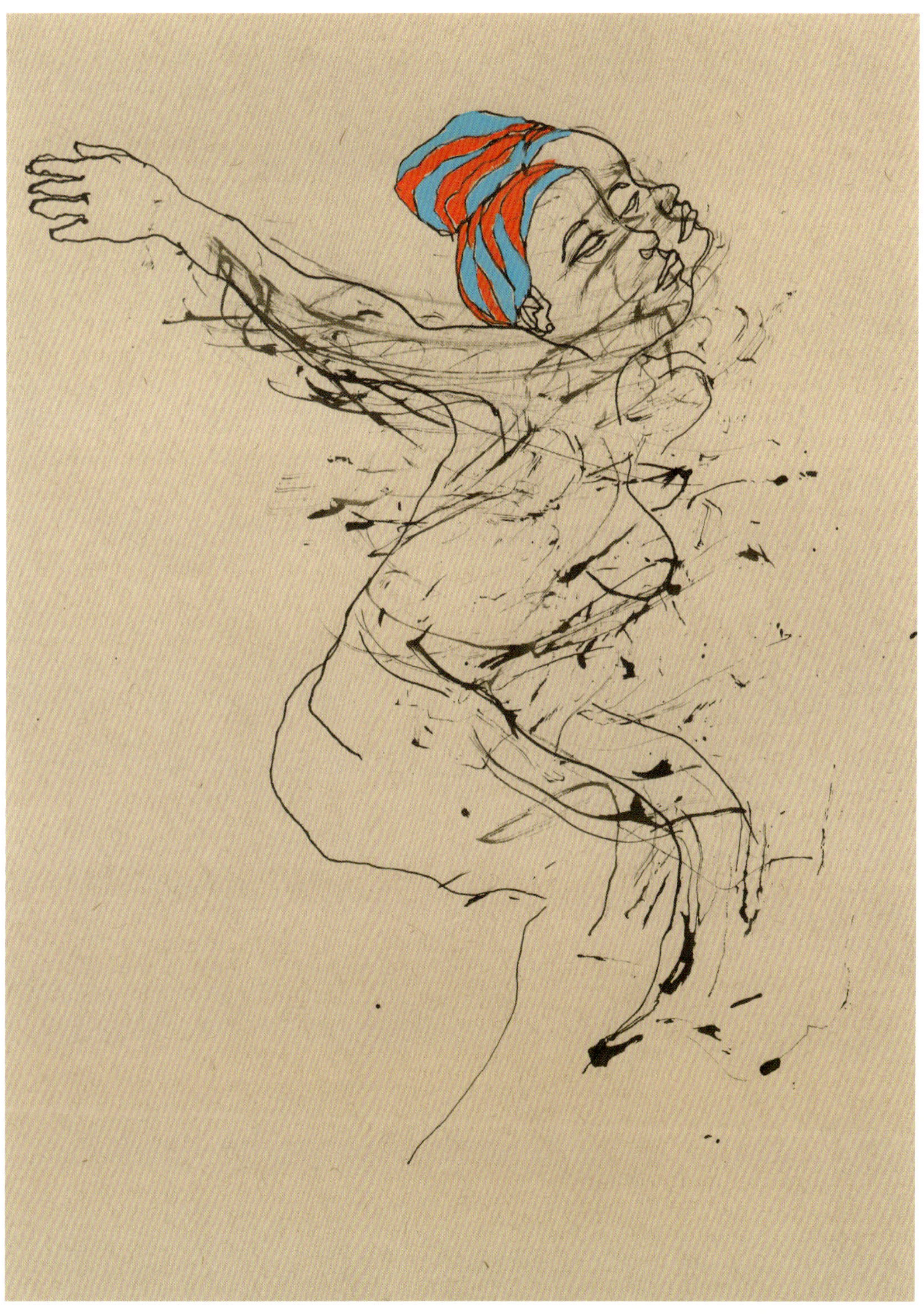

Kenyatta A. C. Hinkle, *The Evanesced #107*, 2016. India ink and watercolor on recycled, acid-free paper, chalk, and glitter, 12 × 9 in.

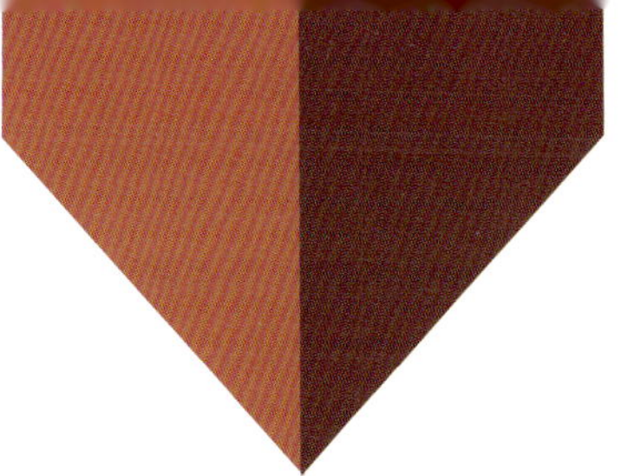

EMBODIED CARTO-GRAPHIES

RENEGOTIATING RELATIONSHIPS WITH LAND

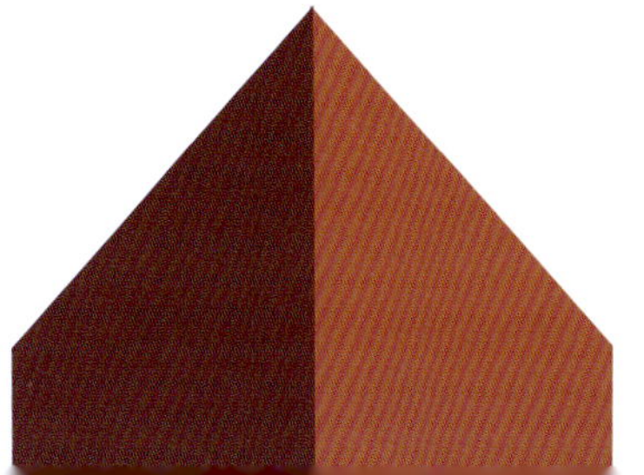

Introduction

Elizabeth M. Webb

Elizabeth M. Webb, an artist and filmmaker originally from Charlottesville, Virginia, is the senior creative producer for ArtChangeUS. Her work is invested in issues surrounding race and identity, often using the lens of her own family history of migration and racial passing to explore larger, systemic constructs.

> The story of our relationship to the earth is written more truthfully on the land than on the page. It lasts there. The land remembers what we said and what we did.
> —Robin Wall Kimmerer, *Braiding Sweetgrass: Indigenous Wisdom, Scientific Knowledge, and the Teachings of Plants*

Throughout the creation and development of the United States, legal frameworks and individual formations of citizen identities have been predicated on the idea of land ownership; that is, land as defined by property.[1] The Doctrine of Discovery, beginning with a 1452 papal bull and upheld in the US Supreme Court, notably in 1823 and again as recently as 2005, laid the groundwork for colonial expansion, the seizure of Indigenous lands by European settler colonists, and the attempted erasure of Indigenous peoples.[2] Maps were the representational tools that made both visible and tangible settler claims on land once stewarded by Indigenous populations, inscribing new social and political boundaries to support a burgeoning US (white) identity that came to rely on a plantation economy based on the slavery and subjugation of Black people. And now, four hundred years later, these extractive relationships continue to be inextricably linked to our society's extractive relationship with the earth. Scholar Mishuana Goeman, Tonawanda Band of Seneca, finds a way out of this destructive loop, calling on us to critically examine the common conflation of land and property (and the fixity upon which that definition relies), and instead to consider land as place—as an ever-evolving site for meaning making that holds and produces stories of our past, present, and future:

> Land [is] a storied site of human interaction; they are routed and rooted stories that provide meaning well beyond jurisdictional legal values.... Deconstructing the discourse of property and reformulating the political vitality of a storied land means reaching back across generations, critically examining our use of the word *land* in the present, and reaching forward to create a healthier relationship for future generations.[3]

What is at stake in this reformulation? What pathways, passages, and routes might be revealed in the process? For the artists in this section, questions like these are at the center of contemporary cultural discourse. Across the country, artists are resisting prescribed colonial concepts of space, creating in favor of fluidity over immutable boundaries, and exploring other kinds of cartographies—embodied cartographies based on relationships of equity, both between one another and with the environment.

For traditional Hawaiian navigators and voyagers **Nāʻālehu Anthony** and **Haunani Kane**, renegotiating our relationships with land extends to renegotiating our relationships with water and the stars. Interdisciplinary scholar Vincente M. Diaz articulates the need to resist the essentialization of islands as isolated land masses separated by water (as defined by a continent-centric, Western framework) and instead invoke "archipelagic identities" that emphasize water as a physical and narrative connector, blurring the distinction between land and sea.[4] Nāʻālehu Anthony urges us to apply the lessons of the voyaging vessel *Hōkūleʻa* to life beyond the canoe, reminding us, "A canoe is literally this floating island . . . and our honua or our planet is also in the sea of space, floating toward its next destination . . . and if we don't [take care of it], it cannot take care of us and we cannot persist into the next destination."

That borders and boundaries are social constructs with destructive effects (created largely in service of property ownership) underlies essays throughout this section. As Indigenous artist, scholar, and community organizer **Lyla June** powerfully asserts in her aptly titled poem "America Doesn't Exist," what we think of as America is only "an excuse we use to manifest a reality." June goes deeper in her conversation with performance poet and educator **Tanaya Winder**: "When I look at the land from satellite imagery, I see one contiguous landmass that is interconnected. I see rivers that don't stop at the border for customs.... They just go right through because those borders aren't real." Together, Winder and June offer insight into how Indigenous practices can work against colonial paradigms and move us toward healing. Working in the politicized border space between the United States and Mexico, artist **Ruben Ulises Rodriguez Montoya** uses both natural and human-made detritus found along the borderland as materials in his hybridized sculptures. A mariachi sombrero, a white polo, a toothpaste cap, a vaping cartridge, a Topo-Chico cap, hair, and black bean silicone molds converge to form *Sopa de Ostión* (2020), a mythological creature born of toxicity that calls out the ecological conditions that borders create as well as their effect on the health of those who live there.

Other contributors also radically insist on their own physical, cultural, and narrative presence, in spite of attempts to displace them. Photographer **Mel D. Cole** vividly depicts the community-led conversion of a former Confederate monument site in Richmond, Virginia, to a place of vibrant collectivity in *Ballers!* (2020). Multidisciplinary artist **Morel Doucet** affirms the rich cultural presence of his Haitian diasporic community in South Florida, despite continued forces of climate gentrification, migration, and displacement. In *Earth Mama II* (2019), artist **Favianna Rodriguez** also focuses on her ancestral connection to the life-giving powers of nature, emphasizing personal resilience and healing in the face of climate injustices. And in Los Angeles, artist **Jaklin Romine** uses her body to draw attention to LA's landscape of inaccessible art spaces and creates installations for care and possibility. In her powerful performance series *ACCESS DENIED* (2015–ongoing), Romine documents her body sitting outside an inaccessible art space for the duration of an art opening or closing. Here, the photograph (and video by extension) serves as a reminder of presence in place, even throughout institutional attempts at erasure.

In their essays, both **Dareen Hussein** and **Ashley Hunt** reframe the colonial history of arts institutions and their impact on political constructions of place. Artist, activist, and educator Ashley Hunt offers ways to move beyond land acknowledgment to tangible community benefit through his work with students in collaboration with the Tejon Indian Tribe, whose members reclaimed historical photographs and deployed them in their successful 2012 campaign for federal recognition. Palestinian American artist Dareen Hussein builds an online archive of photographs and artifacts from a home she had never before traveled to and discusses the politics of image making, diaspora, and how counterhistories can undermine colonial narratives.

Embodied connection to homeland underscores other pieces throughout this section. Public artist **Angela Two Stars** speaks of a return from exile to her ancestral homelands of Mní Sota and her efforts through public art to revitalize the Dakota language. Two Stars charts her own role in the

Bde Maka Ska lake name restoration (formerly Lake Calhoun) in Minnesota and offers insight into the deep cultural importance of place names, writing, "Our language is our identity. It grounds us within our place on this land." Artist and organizer **Kapena Alapaʻi** emphasizes the active labor required to untether land from Western notions of property. Describing his family's work to maintain stewardship of their ancestral land in North Kona, Alapaʻi writes: "Our collective process has necessitated unpacking historical trauma as well as joyful memories, and differentiating between the monetary value that Western society places on land and the value of Indigenous knowledge that originates from ancestral stewardship of this land." In his mixed-media work on paper *Kiksuya* (2018), **Michael Two Bulls** foregrounds the Lakota language as a way to hold layered histories of place. Alongside imagery of the Badlands and symbols that call forth the ongoing impact of the 1890 Wounded Knee Massacre on the Lakota people, Two Bulls prints "Kiksuya" in large, outlined text across the bottom of the work—Lakota for *remember*.

And in both urban and rural contexts, artists and organizers are turning to agricultural practices as models for sustainable futures, community growth, and liberation. In Utica, Mississippi, performing artist and founder of the Mississippi Center for Cultural Production (Sipp Culture) **Carlton Turner** honors his Black ancestors and works to build the future of Utica by harnessing the power of community storytelling and agricultural education: "If food is life, then land is liberation. What we do with it, who controls it, who benefits from it, are all questions deeply connected to our liberation." In Chicago, writer and chief operating officer at Sweet Water Foundation **Jia Lok Pratt** grounds her essay in her experience transforming vacant urban spaces into thriving sites for community gathering, knowledge-sharing, and agriculture. Lok Pratt argues against the high capitalist modes through which we have come to relate to each other and the land and instead proposes a return to an essential economy—one that is rooted in sustaining life.

Borrowing from Katherine McKittrick's seminal work on Blackness and geography, "Can these different knowledges and imaginations perhaps call into question the limits of existing spatial paradigms and put forth more humanly workable geographies?"[5] Throughout this section and beyond, artists are challenging the very terms by which we understand our relationships to land and place and moving towards these "more humanly workable geographies." Our society and the earth are at an existential tipping point. To return to Lyla June, *America doesn't exist. America doesn't exist*, but we—its artists, its educators, its organizers, its stewards, its navigators—

do. Whether by challenging the primacy of land over sea, questioning who
has access to a place, decolonizing place names and institutional practices,
or foregrounding ancestral knowledge to create a sustainable future, these
artists are modeling ways that our communities endure beyond maps, and
ultimately are creating geographies of freedom.

Notes

1. For more on the relationship between land conquest, property, and slavery,
see K-Sue Park, "Race and Property Law" (August 19, 2021), in *The Oxford Handbook of Race and Law in the United States*, edited by Devon Carbado, Khiara Bridges,
and Emily Houh (New York: Oxford University Press, in press).

2. City of Sherrill v. Oneida Indian Nation of New York (03-855) 544 US 197
(2005) (Supreme Court of the United States March 29, 2005), opinion delivered
by Justice Ruth Bader Ginsburg; Indigenous Values Initiative and American
Indian Law Alliance, Doctrine of Discovery, July 30, 2018, https://doctrineof
discovery.org/.

3. Mishuana Goeman, "Land as Life: Unsettling the Logics of Containment,"
in *Native Studies Keywords*, edited by Stephanie N. Teves, Andrea Smith, and Michelle H. Raheja, 71–89 (Tucson: University of Arizona Press, 2015).

4. Vicente M. Diaz, "No Island Is an Island," in *Native Studies Keywords*, edited
by Stephanie N. Teves, Andrea Smith, and Michelle H. Raheja, 90–108 (Tucson:
University of Arizona Press, 2015).

5. Katherine McKittrick, "Geographic Stories," in *Demonic Grounds: Black
Women and the Cartographies of Struggle* (Minneapolis: University of Minnesota
Press, 2006), xviii.

Kiksuya

Michael Two Bulls

Michael Two Bulls (Oglala Lakota) is a multidisciplinary artist and musician who has always believed that the true nature of art is not in the medium, but rather in the artist and their subject. He engages a vast array of art forms to deal with themes including identity, history, and place. These narrative works often draw from his family and experiences.

Kiksuya is a piece that activates memory of the 1890 Wounded Knee Massacre. The word *kiksuya* can be translated as "to remember." Not needed nor intended as American "never forget" sloganeering, this piece invokes some of the myriad ways that Lakota relatives remember and live the ongoing violence of the settler United States.

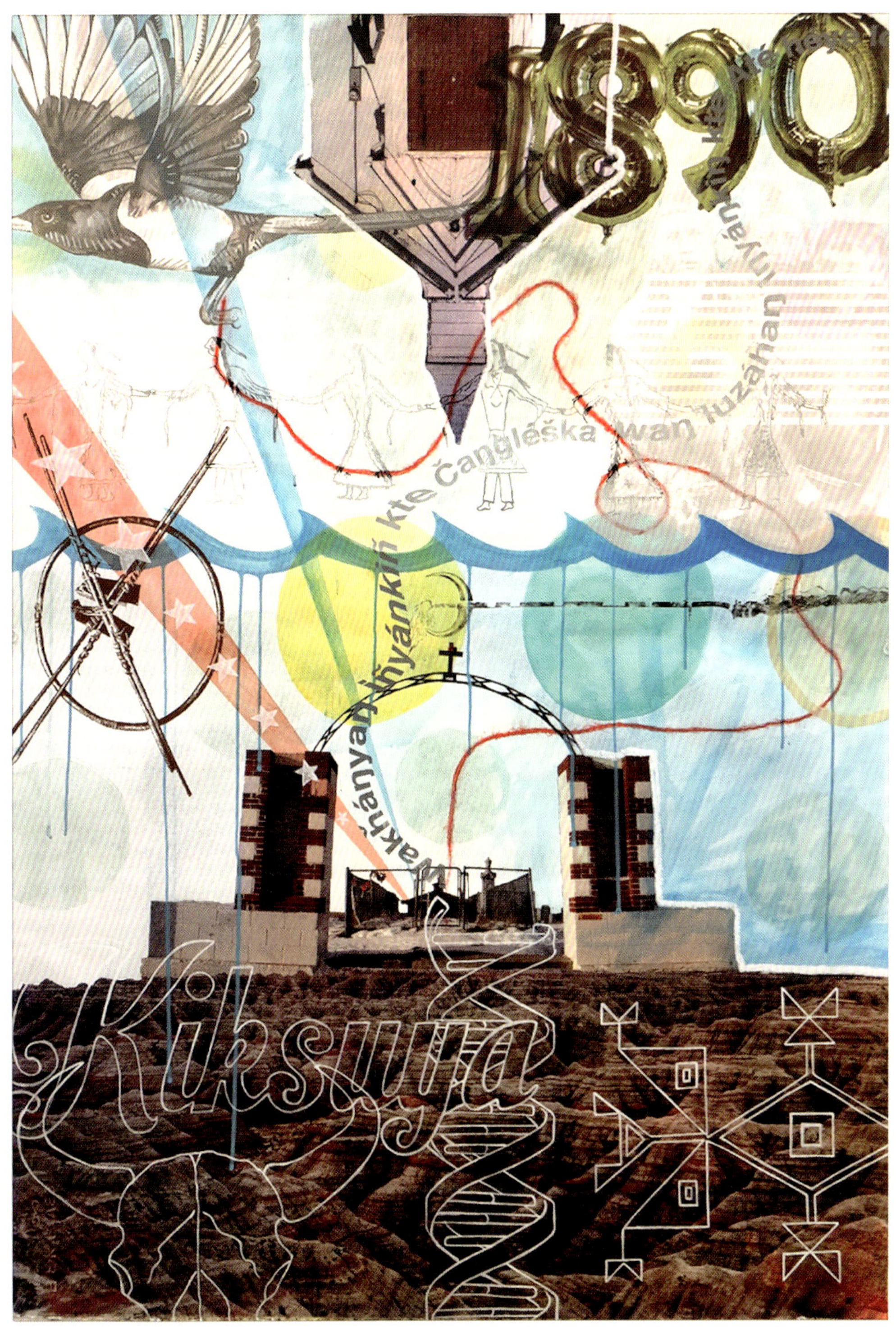

Michael Two Bulls, *Kiksuya*, 2018. CMYK acrylic serigraph, oil pastel and intaglio ink on BFK Rives, 30 × 44 in.

America Doesn't Exist

Lyla June

Lyla June is an Indigenous musician, scholar, and community organizer of Diné (Navajo), Tsétsêhéstâhese (Cheyenne), and European lineages. She blends studies in human ecology at Stanford, graduate work in Indigenous pedagogy, and the traditional worldview she grew up with to inform her music, perspectives, and solutions. She is currently pursuing her doctoral degree, focusing on Indigenous food systems revitalization.

America doesn't exist.
It's an idea men have obsessed over since 1776.
An excuse we use to manifest a reality
that destroys the destiny of all native peoples.
Native Americans once made one hundred percent of the population
and today they are less than one percent.
All because man forgot to separate fact from fabrication.
Once we believe America is real.
We believe we have a reason to kill, a reason to steal.
Do you remember what has happened ever since we dreamed up
this country,
this church,
and this state?
Trail of tears 1830—
Look on the twenty-dollar bill and you'll see Andrew Jackson, the man
    who ordered the forced expulsion of 15,000 Cherokee from their
    homeland.
Pregnant women, their children and the elderly
forced to walk from Georgia to Oklahoma.
Wounded Knee Massacre 1890–
US cavalry descends on a Lakota camp with 530 women and children.

America in their minds, red and white stripes blinding their sight.
They sunk bullets into the chests of children.
Trampled women with their horses and left two hundred Lakota
dead in the snow.
And this is how our beloved country was founded.
America doesn't exist.
It is a psychological sickness we catch with years of exposure to public schools
and baseball games.
Raising hands to our hearts for a fairytale
that America is anything more than a word.
We put labels on the land and draw imaginary lines in the sand
but it's a tragedy when the human mind forgets to separate fact from
    fabrication.
Projecting our imagination onto sacred mountains and ancient continents.
Ever since I was a child I was told I live in America.
But one day I realized that America lives in me.
In my mind
but today we drop our weapons.
Today we stop the cycle.
Today we unite with every plant and animal in this world.
To remember that humanity is real.
A beating heart is real.
The earth beneath us is real.
But America is but a thought that is used to turn brothers into contenders,
histories into myths,
entire cultures into forgotten languages,
and the free mind into a society, deceived.
So please do not call me American
Do not call me Native American.
Please call me human.
And do not call this land America.
Listen hard and she will tell you her true name as the nighthawks dive at
    twilight.
As the waterfalls rage cascading.
As the avalanches fracture, breaking.
She will tell you her true name with earthquakes that split states and
    break fences
to remind you that she does NOT belong to you.
But that we
belong
to her.

Between the Real and the Imagined

A CONVERSATION WITH LYLA JUNE AND TANAYA WINDER

Lyla June and Tanaya Winder

Lyla June is an Indigenous musician, scholar, and community organizer of Diné (Navajo), Tsétsêhéstâhese (Cheyenne), and European lineages. She blends studies in human ecology at Stanford, graduate work in Indigenous pedagogy, and the traditional worldview she grew up with to inform her music, perspectives, and solutions. She is currently pursuing her doctoral degree, focusing on Indigenous food systems revitalization.

Tanaya Winder is an author, singer/songwriter, poet, motivational speaker, and educator who comes from an intertribal lineage of Southern Ute, Pyramid Lake Paiute, and Duckwater Shoshone Nations, where she is an enrolled citizen. Her published books are *Words Like Love* and *Why Storms Are Named After People and Bullets Remain Nameless*.

LYLA JUNE: We grew up in a place where our history on the land and the destruction of that history is ignored everywhere we go. As Native students in middle school and high school, we were taught history that erases our imagination of this land. Everywhere we turn, there are monuments to those who destroyed our people and took our land. And it's not even really our land because you can't own land, but they took away our ability to feed ourselves and steward the land. So, I feel like we have an interesting positionality to reimagine space. For you, what does reimagining space look like? And how does that show up in your artistic practice as a poet, songwriter, and youth worker?

TANAYA WINDER: Your question makes me think of a time I went home. I visited my mom, and we watched a movie about the Utes in Colorado. It said that most of the roads we now travel on were trails that the Ute people used when they traveled through different seasons. Those routes were turned into the paved roads people use today. And so for me, reimagining space is like a reeducation, one that I wish could happen all across school systems. Growing up, we feel so displaced in school because we know those institutional spaces weren't built for us. But imagine if our education was Indigenized, if those spaces could be reclaimed so we'd learn our culture and history inside that place rather than constantly having to seek out that knowledge elsewhere. I would've learned long ago that the Indigenous people of this land made our travel possible today. The fact that you're able to drive from Ignacio to Denver is *because of* the Indigenous people who knew the land, the way it moved and flowed. Seeing yourself and your people's history in an educational curriculum means being able to see yourself in those institutional learning spaces. That sense of belonging is something we all need as human beings.

So, when it comes to my artistic practice as a poet and songwriter, I think of education because my art practice teaches. Reimagining the classroom space means reimagining what constitutes valued knowledge systems and what is deemed worthy of sharing in that space. Reimagining asks the question, what grounds you in who you are? Like when we perform, teach, or gather to connect, a lot of Indigenous people smudge. We begin with prayer. It cleanses the space. Starting with those kinds of grounding practices doesn't just reimagine the space, it transforms it into something safer, braver. As an artist and an educator, I strive to create spaces—whether physically, mentally, or emotionally—that allow people to stretch toward a bravery that allows them to connect with the vulnerable parts of themselves that they need to heal. And with my poetry and art, I try to write things that help heal people or help give people hope. For me, at the root, that is safety.

LJ: And what do you mean by that?

TW: I guess by safety, I mean, you feel protected, a sense of belonging, and trust for the people you're sharing space with. I feel that in ceremony, or when I'm out on the land. Imagine how to bring that safety that you feel in the natural world to these indoor spaces and the inner spaces that we carry within ourselves.

LJ: That's beautiful. Thank you so much for sharing that.

TW: I know you do a lot of work around education with empowerment. Teaching people about love, whether that's love for yourself or the environment. You're a person who's been in so many different kinds of spaces. What does reimagining space look like to you in your art practice and in your work?

LJ: I think for me, it's all about seeing the earth for what it is. I wrote a poem a long time ago called "America Doesn't Exist." In this poem, I talked about how America is not a place—it's an idea. And how we don't live in America, but America lives in us, in our minds. We're just projecting our imagination onto sacred mountains and ancient continents, and drawing all these imaginary lines in the sand. And that has consequences because once we believe America is real, we believe we have a reason to kill. Think about how much blood has been shed for America to exist in our heads. And so, when I look at the land from satellite imagery, I see one contiguous landmass that is interconnected. I see rivers that don't stop at the border for customs. They go right through because those borders aren't real. I see deserts that span across what we see as two different nation-states.

I see borders that are not defined by human arrogance but are defined by ecological conditions. Like the equator—the sun and the moisture that happen along that area create these discernible rain forest borders. I think about Native people and how we never named the land after ourselves. We're not like, "Oh, I'm gonna call this Lylaville or this is Tanayatown," you know; we named ourselves after the land. For example, the Paiute, the people of Pyramid Lake, their name refers to a specific fish they eat. So, we often name ourselves after how the land feeds us. Or the Winnemem Wintu, which literally means "middle river people." They're naming themselves after the river that they live on.

I try not to get too frustrated and disgusted with the world in its colonial paradigm. I try to have love for people who can't seem to see that these nation-states don't really exist, and that they're not worth fighting each other and killing each other for. And honestly, it makes me sad every time I hear the word *America* because it comes from Amerigo Vespucci, who was commissioned to look for slaves and gold. To name this beautiful part of the land after him and arbitrarily isolate it from the rest of the continent, it makes absolutely no sense to me. But of course, you have people who are very attached to it. Those who think that if you dare speak anything ill about America, you are the scum of the earth. I reimagine space by trying to remind people of what is real, and what is imagined.

PART 4

TW: Everything you said is so real, raw, and true. We don't think about that as a society enough—what is imagined and what is real. Listening to you speak made me think about my relationship with the land and how a lot of it is influenced by how the stories we were raised with were our source of education and knowledge. Like I can go visit Pyramid Lake in Nevada, and I know the stories my relatives have told me about how the lake got there. I know what the lake is for; I know I am in relationship with that lake. And I don't know that all tourists know or care to know just how sacred a place is and that the earth is a living being. When we go out looking for plant medicine, we never just take it. We offer a prayer and tobacco; you leave something because you're taking something. You offer something because everything is living, everything has a spirit. And that's what I know to be real. Walking in this world can be really frustrating because so many people are oblivious. They don't want to know the full history like how we got the name of America or attachments to objects. People get upset about statues being taken down or don't understand the importance of naming or rather renaming things. Why shouldn't we change the name of this street that's named after somebody who murdered many people? Why do we have this whole mountain named for somebody who destroyed the land and tried to destroy the people instead of listening to the people of the land? It's about renaming things to have a purpose.

LJ: Right. We've had our experiences of hardship, being Indigenous in this twenty-first-century culture; what kind of world do you want your children and grandchildren to grow up in? What kind of experience do you wish them to have?

TW: I want my children to be grounded in ceremony. I dream of having a piece of land where I can teach my children how to garden the way I was taught to garden and teach them about the different plants and medicines. For them to know that what we grow and make isn't ours, but we can share with elders or other people in the community. I want all of my relations to have a physical space where they can be who they are. It's going to be a lot of teaching and unteaching them what they learn in school if the education system doesn't change, because I want them to learn their languages, know ceremony, and be in relationship with their culture, their relatives, and the earth. I don't want them to struggle with attachment to things—to wealth, objects. Earlier, I saw the video you shared on social media about attachment to instant gratification and "likes" and how people are seen. I want them to know who they are and where they come from and be proud of that, because living can be really lonely with all these comparisons. Living can be really hard, and it's easy to get lost if you don't have something rooted to ground you.

LJ: How do you want them to relate to space? You know, given the struggles that we've been through relating to space.

TW: I want them to be aware of the land that they're on. I know I'm not always the best at doing it, but just stopping to pray and thank the land for allowing us to be on it, that we're just there visiting and mean to do no harm. I want them to have that "do no harm" mentality and be aware that they're in relationship with everything, every place they go.

I'd like to ask you the same question—how do you want your future children to be aware of space? Or what kind of world do you want them to exist in?

LJ: There's the part of me that is idealistic and the part of me that's realistic. Ideally, I would like them to be able to travel seasonally the way our ancestors did and steward the land in really sophisticated ways. We used to burn the understory of the forests across this country systematically before Columbus even got here. And we diversified our food systems in ways that America couldn't imagine doing because they aren't sophisticated enough. I would love for them to walk the land in a way that is in community. Because when you have to take care of a whole bioregion, you need a whole community. For instance, in Chile with the pehuen, that little nut that feeds them during a certain season—the whole community goes out and harvests them together. And while they do that, they tend the pehuen forests. Their name as a people is Pehuenche, the people of the pehuen. I would love for my children to be able to move seasonally and communally in a way that is both harvesting from the land and nourishing the land and reseeding the land and pruning the land and tending the land.

But then I butt up against reality, which is that this country has barbed wire fences every two miles. The ability to move freely is stifled by this false construct of property ownership, and I butt up against the reality that we don't have control of very much land anymore. And I butt up against the reality that a lot of the rivers are poisoned now, and they can't necessarily just walk from spring to spring and river to river anymore. What gives me hope, though, is that my elder told me that we control enough land to change the way the world thinks about food and water. So when I hybridize my realistic and idealistic dreams, it looks like having a community of people relearning how to tend the land together. And that's what I'm working on with my PhD, building a food and land university with my people.

TW: Holding all of that knowledge, what do you feel like your role is as an artist in all of this, in this world, knowing what you know and hoping what you hope for?

LJ: I always have to make music, no matter where I am or what's going on. There's always a song bubbling up or a rap or a melody. I want to create an album that has the four elements—earth, wind, water, fire. Four different albums that speak to these four different ways of making music that I do—hip-hop, poetry, electronic music, and guitar. I want to speak about these truths and educate people about the land through song. Not just about the landscape outside of them, but the landscape inside them, and how to navigate the trauma and pain of your inner world.

I wanted to ask: what gives you hope for the future as an Indigenous woman?

TW: Our youth. When we visited my hometown reservation last summer, the youth led us into prayer; they were wise beyond their years. I have a lot of experiences like that where the youth say or do something so profound, and in those moments I know we're all going to be okay. As long as we keep doing what we're supposed to do to prepare this earth in this world for them, they're going to continue to grow and help the world heal.

LJ: I share that hope with you. And I'm honored to call you my sister. I'm honored that we've gotten to work together over the past twelve years to try and help our people, and I hope we continue to do that for many more decades.

TW: Me too. I was thinking that as well. Our paths are intertwined, and I'm really grateful for you. I always try to pray for guidance—that Creator helps me find who I'm meant to help, and who's meant to help me. I definitely recognize the light and force that you are. You've been a blessing to me in ways I don't even know yet. I always enjoy sharing space in conversation with you and learning more about you.

LJ: Thank you, sister. I think one badass Indigenous woman is a force, and two together are just completely unstoppable. And when we have three and four and five and start bringing in our sisters from other cultures, we will continue to be unstoppable in our prayer to bring healing to the world.

Sopa de Ostión

Ruben Ulises Rodriguez Montoya

Ruben Ulises Rodriguez Montoya was born in Parral, Chihuahua. He emigrated with his family to an immigrant community in the US-Mexico border of El Paso, Juarez, and New Mexico. He received his MFA in sculpture and extended media from Virginia Commonwealth University.

Nahuales are mythological beings, witches/shamans that use ancient Aztec abilities of therianthropy to convert to animals; *Sopa de Ostión* is one of them. They exist and live alongside me and my family's cosmology. They too have inhaled the lethal landfill fumes that caused the premature death of my sister inside my mother's womb.

The insidious fumes of landfill waste distort the genetic composition of these nahualitic creatures. Their shapeshifting from human to animal becomes arrested and curdled, leaving them in between space of human and animal. A new transfiguration occurs, creating creatures made of a hypersensitivity that prevents and protects them from further environmental hazards. *Sopa de Ostión* takes that intrusion, licks the foul aberration over and over, forming a shielding layered lacquer of nacre around it, forming a pearl from a noxious agent.

Nahuales are a premonition of what a divergent body will look like as our world becomes more toxic, a rasquache mythological construction grounded in its new identification. *Sopa de Ostión* is a being of a future that is already here, as well as a creature of a time when desert used to be ocean and our hands were not hands but a thick foot of a muscle leaving behind glutinous slime over an already ancient rock.

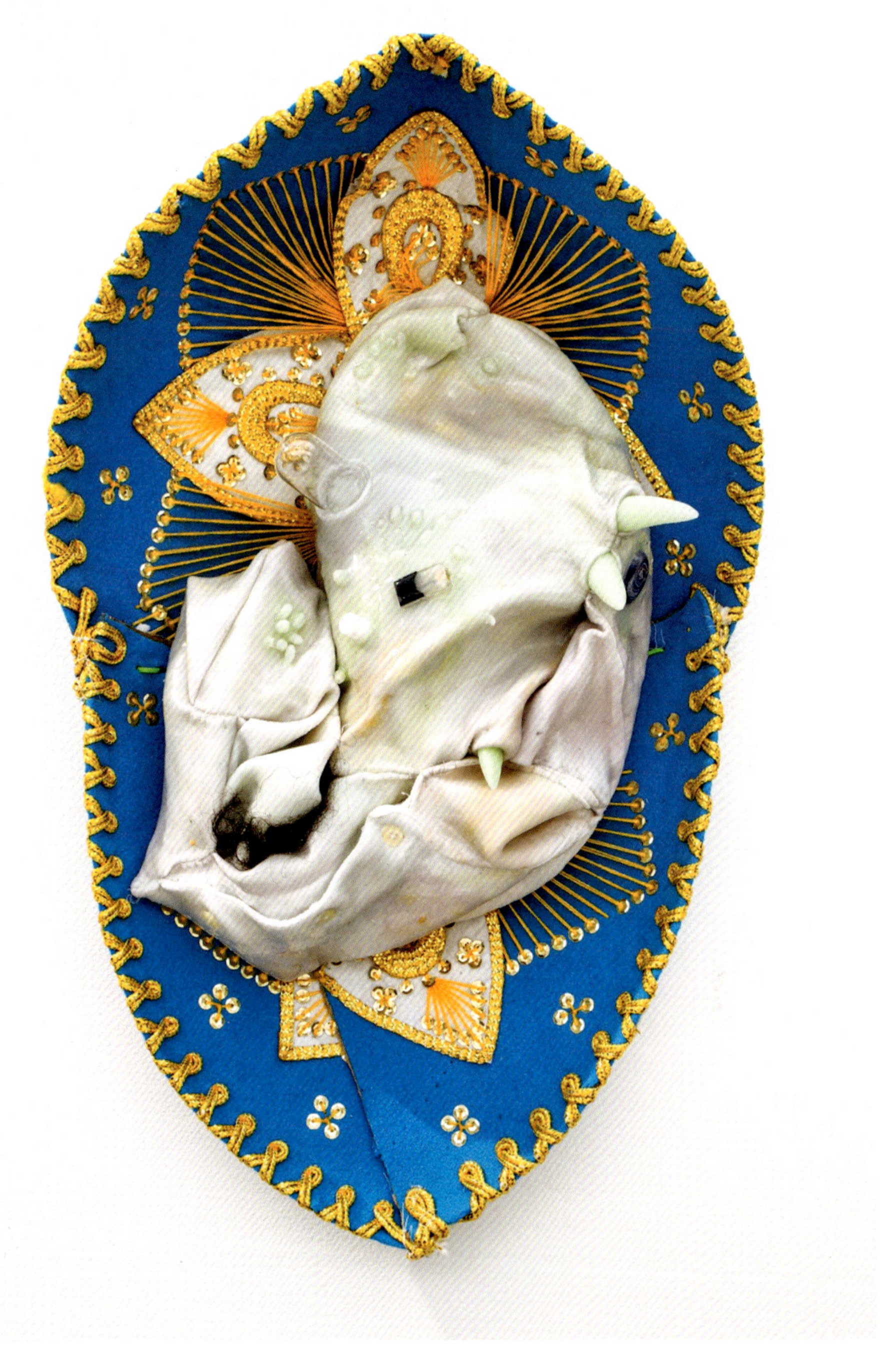

Ruben Ulises Rodriguez Montoya, *Sopa de Ostión*, 2020. Mariachi sombrero, white polo, toothpaste cap, vaping cartridge, Topo-Chico cap, hair, black bean silicone molds, silicone. 25 × 15 × 8 in.

Island Earth

WATER, WAYFINDING, AND
THE CURRENTS THAT CONNECT US

Nāʻālehu Anthony and Haunani Kane

- -

Nāʻālehu Anthony is the former CEO of ʻŌiwi TV and the principal of Paliku Documentary Films. He has produced and directed a number of films including the award-winning PBS documentary about Mau Piailug, *Papa Mau: The Wayfinder.* Nāʻālehu is a member of the Polynesian Voyaging Society and has documented many major voyages made by *Hōkūleʻa.*

- -

Haunani Kane is a scientist, surfer, and voyager from Kailua, Oʻahu. Currently an NSF postdoctoral fellow at the University of Hawaiʻi at Hilo, Haunani's life is guided by the values and storied history of her kūpuna (ancestors). Haunani uses the ocean as her classroom, the sky as her blackboard, and islands as models for sustainable living.

- -

Hōkūleʻa has voyaged traditionally since 1976, sailing over 150,000 nautical miles throughout the Pacific. The Mālama Honua Worldwide Voyage began in 2013 with a Mālama Hawaiʻi sail throughout the Hawaiian archipelago and continued on to circumnavigate the globe through 2014, 2015, 2016, and 2017. The Mālama Honua sail plan included more than 150 ports, eighteen nations, and eight of UNESCO's Marine World Heritage sites, engaging local communities and practicing how to live sustainably. June 2017 marked Hōkūleʻa's historic homecoming to Hawaiʻi, capping the global portion of the voyage.

Editor's Note: This contribution was edited from a conversation between Nāʻālehu Anthony and Haunani Kane conducted by Kapena Alapaʻi on November 6, 2020.

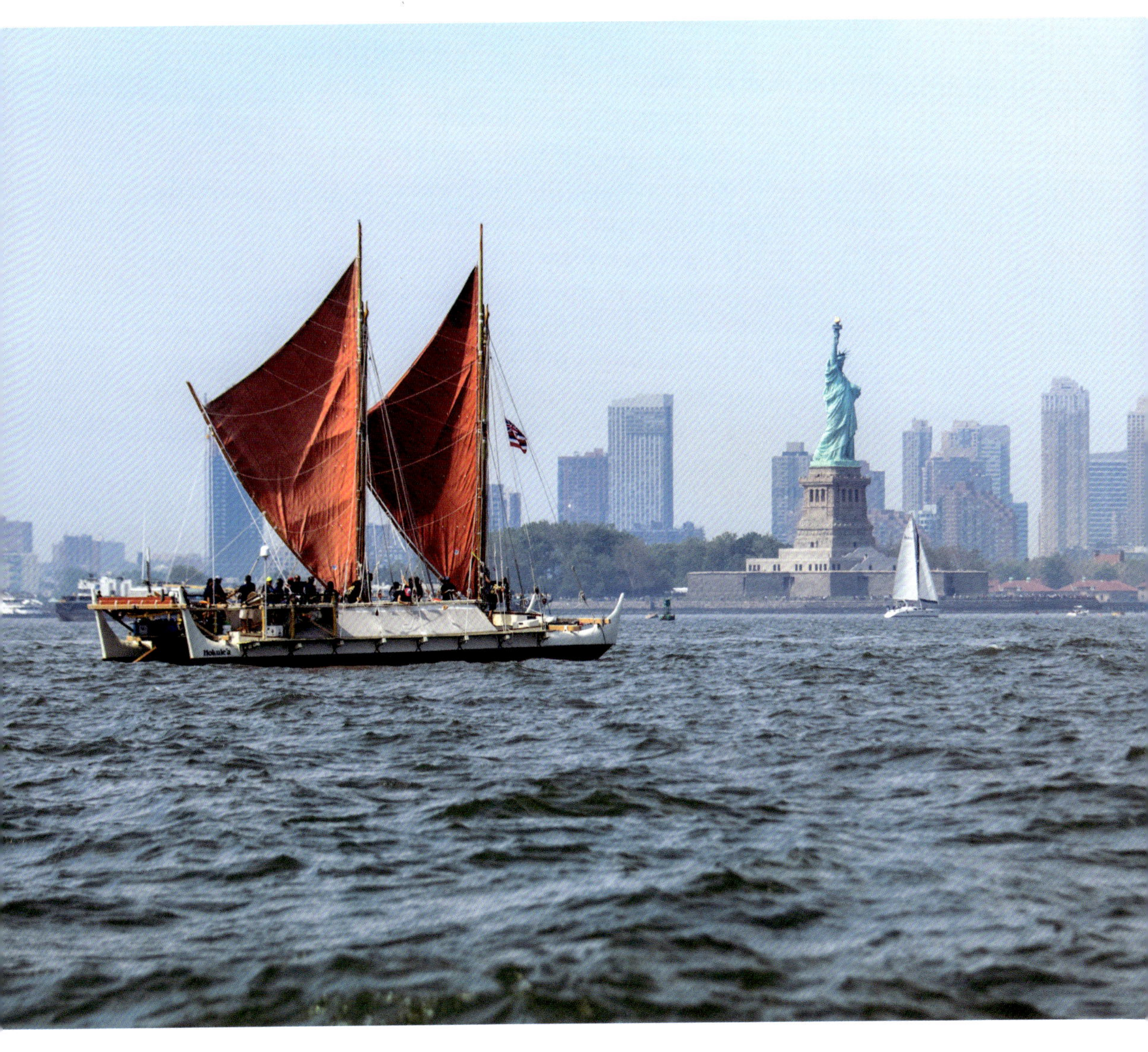

Hōkūleʻa arriving in New York City, 2016. Photo courtesy of Polynesian Voyaging Society and ʻŌiwi TV. Photo: Nāʻālehu Anthony.

NĀʻĀLEHU ANTHONY: Aloha nui kākou, ʻo wau ʻo Nāʻālehu Anthony. No Kaʻaʻawa mai au ma ka mokupuni o Oʻahu. My name is Nāʻālehu Anthony. I'm a filmmaker and storyteller from Oʻahu. If you go far enough back, my mother's family is from Hana, Maui, and right now I'm sitting in the house I grew up in, in Kaʻaʻawa.

Polynesian navigation and the canoe story is thousands of years old. We know that because of the stories that have been told throughout time, not only about how humans got to Hawaiʻi to become Hawaiians and the canoes that they came on, but also about how some of the gods that we still point to as being in Hawaiʻi got here. For instance, we know the canoe that brought Pele to Hawaiʻi was called Hōnuiākea. We also know that at the time, canoes were at the cutting edge of technology. These waʻa were moving throughout the Pacific a full one thousand years before Westerners would figure out how to use the compass and sextant to leave the sight of land. By the time Westerners got here, the millions of square miles of ocean and islands in Polynesia were already fully cultivated by Pacific Islanders.

Since then, Pacific Islanders have had the technology to build canoes that could go to sea for a month at a time. Navigating using the stars and other elements, they were able to sail for more than 2,500 miles. The crowning achievement would have been finding Hawaiʻi because it is the most isolated archipelago on the planet.

But over the years, the knowledge of Polynesian navigation was almost lost and only held in tiny corners of the Pacific.[1] The resurgence of voyaging came about as part of the cultural renaissance in Hawaiʻi in the 1970s. The following forty-plus years is really a story of resurgence, refining and relearning this art that is summed up by what Haunani does today. Using all of those tools, those values, and pieces of the puzzle helps us understand who we are as Hawaiians or Polynesians in a globalized society and unlock things we would have conceded to Western science. It forces us to rethink making sense of the world, and how we relate to what we call science and Western education. And for plenty of Native kids, Western science never made sense of their world. Now we're adding layers onto this idea of traditional knowledge: Why is it important today to have the story of *Hōkūleʻa*? How does it fit into the context of us now?

HAUNANI KANE: Aloha, ʻo wau ʻo Haunani Kane no Kailua ʻOʻahu mai au, akā noho au ma Pāpaʻikou, here in beautiful muggy warm Hilo. I started with *Hōkūleʻa* when I was in high school. I have a vivid memory of being on Molokaʻi, being on *Hōkūleʻa*—Uncle Snake, Uncle John Cruz, Uncle Kainoa, Uncle Bruce, Uncle Nainoa, I see all these people who were a part of this from the beginning. During that first voyage, they were under

immense stress. Knowing the old stories, knowing it's how we got here—
sailing to and from Tahiti—all of that kuleana rested upon their shoulders.
They had no choice other than to succeed, to learn, to carry their people,
and to bring pride back to their people. Flash forward forty years, and we're
still sailing in the old way.

I wouldn't say the burden is lighter now, but it has shifted in a way; we
want to make that first group of kānaka proud. The exciting part now is:
we can get creative in the ways that we sail, the ways we learn, the ways we
navigate, the places we visit—places we've never been to before—and we
can be creative in the ways that we document. This speaks to what *Hōkūleʻa*
has achieved and the ways we envision our future as our own.

NA: To understand what Haunani is referring to about the 1970s, you must
know that the last embers of navigational prowess were dwindling down,
because of the choices we were making as Native people. Did we value
spending time with elders and learning these old ways, or did we give in to
the ease of a compass, a sextant, and a GPS to get from point A to B?

Mau Piailug, who came to Hawaiʻi from Micronesia to teach Nainoa
Thompson, Shorty Bertelmann, Bruce Blankenfeld, ʻOnohi Paishon,
Kalepa Babayan, and others, was one of the youngest navigators of his generation. When I interviewed Mau in 2005, he could point to grandfathers,
and grandfathers before that, and grandfathers before that, who had passed
this knowledge down orally to him. There were star maps for places he had
never been, where he didn't know anyone who had ever been, but they existed as this body of knowledge of oral tradition that had been passed on
to him. It was not only very ancient, but it was also very detailed. We also
know now that he was looking at the edge of a cliff—who would take on
all this knowledge?

Over the course of thirty years of work of *Hōkūleʻa*, we saw not only a
resurgence in Hawaiʻi, where there had been zero navigators for several
hundred years, but we also saw resurgence in Micronesia within Mau's
ʻohana on the island of Satawal. The important part is that these contem-
poraries like Haunani have agreed to this contract of kuleana. Kuleana is
such an interesting word because you can define it as responsibility or jurisdiction, but it's also a physical weight of having to do something.

HK: My cohort and I had been learning primarily with Nainoa, navigating
as a team to each of the places we went, so we shared that kuleana or that
weight that Naʻalehu mentioned. One time, Nainoa wasn't able to come
with us as planned, so the navigation was up to four of us, his students. We
were tasked with finding Rapa Nui. It was a time when much was tested—
our trust for each other, all of the teachings we had received, and our faith

in the generations of knowledge either broken or unbroken. We were with Uncle Billy Richards, and toward the end of our trip we realized that if we were off by half of a degree, we'd be off about thirty miles. If we were off by measuring the stars to tell us when to turn west and start looking for Rapa Nui, we would miss the island. It was important to trust in our relationship with our kumu [teacher, tutor] and our relationship with *Hōkūleʻa* herself, trust we were where we needed to be. For some reason, at that point, it felt like we were just a little off course, so we turned the waʻa, just a little bit, and shortly after that adjustment we found the island. We found Rapa Nui.

Uncle Bruce wanted us to build a personal relationship with the stars. He said if you don't know the name of a star, or you can't vibe with its Greek name, name it after your grandkid or your partner, something that's really important to you, so every time you see it in the sky you connect it with something that means a lot and you start to build a relationship. You start to see that star is actually a little more blue, or it's a little more pink and when there's nothing else in the sky and it's just that star and a whole bunch of clouds, you're like, oh yeah, that's my daughter's star.

On our last voyage sailing *Hikianalia* home from San Diego, Uncle Bruce had us research one of the old navigators; we learned about fifteen navigators that trip. Growing up in Hawaiʻi, we weren't taught about our navigators. We were told that everything was lost, but it wasn't. Every night at dinner one of us shared about a different navigator, and it was super empowering. Because of Kaleo, Maya, Uncle Kihei, and Aunty Māpuana, I know where I come from in Kailua on Oʻahu and that our navigators were Kaʻulu and Paumakua; they were the first. So now whenever I talk to people from Kailua, the first thing I do is say the names of all those navigators, so we can breathe life back into them. I want to remind them that we know a lot more than maybe we think. It brings Indigenous knowledge to a whole new level.

And when we went to Tahiti for the first time, to Tautira, we stayed with the old families. Each crew member gets adopted by a family, and you live with that family for the time you're there. And then when you come back again, you stay with them again. So that becomes your mama and your papa; Mama Linda and Papa Sicky are my ʻohana. Those are the relationships that *Hōkūleʻa* has built since the 1970s. The last time *Hōkūleʻa* went to Tahiti, fifteen to twenty thousand Tahitians were in the water to greet them. *Hōkūleʻa* symbolizes more than just this reawakening of pride in our people here in Hawaiʻi but also all across the Pacific. And as we sailed through the Americas, up into the inland waterways and rivers, we met with a lot of the First Peoples of those places. We were able to bond over our similarities and our relationships with the canoe stories there as well.

As we sailed up to the Mohawk Nation in Canada, there was already a connection there through our shared efforts to build Native language school programs. They had help from the Hawaiians who started the Pūnana Leo program here in Hawai'i, so when we arrived it was a big reunion.[2] *Hōkūle'a* symbolizes not only voyaging, but those relationships with each other.

There was a whole group researching the First People of those places, so we could reach out and make sure that they were comfortable and accepting of us coming, and to make sure we were respectful coming to a place for the first time. It's funny to think of going somewhere without asking permission, in this modern world where you can just buy a ticket and jump on an airplane to go just about anywhere. Here at home, when you go and visit your friend you don't just walk up to the front door; you call out to announce you're coming: "Hūi, hūi!" It's not in the same traditional way that you would go to a place for the first time on a wa'a, but it's a similar idea.

NA: There are these embedded understandings of what people do when a canoe arrives in their community. And those are traditions that maybe haven't been practiced for hundreds of years. They are thousands of years old. And so, when a canoe approaches, the level of protocol and hospitality is immense. And when the canoe gets ready to leave, nobody has to say anything, but the bounty from those areas just shows up. They will bring whatever they have—bunches of rambutan, mango, and cacao. In Hawai'i, we have ho'okipa, a protocol that dictates how visitors seek permission to enter a space and how hosts welcome newcomers, including feeding, caring for each other, and sharing space. This mutual respect is something we see in many Indigenous cultures we encounter on voyages; the bounty our hosts share with us, whether food, prayers, or good wishes, supports the crew on their journey.

When we sailed 3,600 miles from Bali across the Indian Ocean to this island of Mauritius, which doesn't have a Polynesian canoe connection, it was dangerous sailing. The day we left, we had 'awa in Bali with the people who supported and embraced us there, and we closed the leg of the voyage with 'awa in Mauritius, with the staff that was hosting us. And they had never done 'awa. We brought a pōhaku [rock, stone] from Hakipu'u to give to them. This was not just any rock; it was part of the place where I was born. It wasn't a carved rock, but it had traveled several thousand miles on a canoe to get to this place. And you could tell that the people there, who did not have this long-standing history and understanding of what the voyage meant—they got it. They understood the weight of the kuleana. It is rooted in this understanding that we're now connected. The ceremony, whether big or small in scale, signifies a deep connection—to each other, to place, to our ancestors, and to our future. This floating island coming to connect to this other island, this other land, is universal. If we come with the right intention and values, we can connect to people anywhere. If we choose to.

HK: At the start of the voyage, there were two canoes, *Hōkūleʻa* and *Hikianalia*. *Hōkūleʻa* was going to be fully traditional, focused on traditional knowledge. *Hikianalia* had electric motors powered by the sun. She's wider; more of a technology platform and a communications platform, but navigated traditionally as well. When I think about that, I think about myself trying to live in those two worlds, being a Western scientist and also being trained in voyaging and hoʻokele [steersman, helmsman, navigator; to sail or navigate].

On our first trip down to Tahiti, we talked before about seeing the island for the first time. Growing up here in Hawaiʻi on a High Island, when you look for islands, you look for your mauna [mountain]. But when you go to Tahiti, there's a group of low-lying islands—first is the Tuamotus. You look for shifts and clues that tell you that you're approaching an island; the dominant open ocean swells start to get blocked. You see birds that live on land coming out to feed on fish or going home at the end of the day, and you might even see shifts in the color of the water or the types of fish you hook because you're entering shallower water.

And your kumu is trying to describe what you're going to see in the future, and for a lot of us it was really confusing because it was something that we hadn't seen before. He said you're looking for this hazy uneven surface, and that's the tips of coconut trees, because that's the highest part on these low-lying islands. You're looking when you're at the top of the swell. If you look when you're at the bottom, you're not gonna see it. When we saw the tips of the coconut trees and saw this swell that wasn't moving, it was everything Nainoa had described and told us to envision in our future. It was exactly spot on. But unless you had that experience out at sea, it was a really frustrating riddle you're trying to find. So when I think of Mālama Honua and the message of caring for our Earth, it reminds us of our connection and relationship to our place here on Earth to wherever we call home. It makes it so much easier to mālama, or to care for, because you're thinking about that future for the generations to come.

NA: For me Mālama Honua is also the reverberation of mana, of all of the hands that showed up at dry dock, all the people who lashed the canoe together. All of that collective effort sums into energy, that positive vibration that goes into the canoe. And when we share it around the world, we get more reverberations coming in, tying to the canoe. And when we're on the canoe in the bubble, working it every day, it's really hard to know how people are being affected by the message of the voyage, by the updates, by the images, by the video, or by the canoe coming to your port. But then you get to places like Florida, where this family showed up in Titusville after driving twelve hours just to see and to touch the canoe. They hadn't lived in Hawai'i for many years, but the canoe was a reminder of what Hawai'i was and what it felt like—if they could just touch the canoe, they would be reminded of it. On one hand, it's heartbreaking that there are so many people who are from Hawai'i but who don't live in Hawai'i. But on the other hand, it's a reminder that we need these data points, whether they're interacting with people, whether they're physical canoes, whether they are stories about people trying when it's hard, to help us to determine what we're supposed to be doing next and how we're supposed to be moving along as people.

And so, when the canoe came home, my question was, does this even matter? We just sailed 45,000 miles, we've been gone three years, we shot a thousand days in a row. People have been away from their families literally for months at a time. And when we got home, the answer was clearly yes, it matters: "The worldwide voyages inspired me to do these things"; "*Hōkūle'a* has inspired me to act this way." There were full-on murals! People did all these things to say, "We support the voyage. We support the idea of Mālama Honua."

HK: I think the voyage is about realizing our value, as Hawaiians and as Indigenous people, realizing our strength and our pride in all of those things that define us, and realizing that we as Hawaiians are more than enough. And in realizing that we, as people from that place, should have the ultimate authority over what happens to our home. If we decide to embrace that kuleana to care for our home because of our genealogical relationship with it, because of all of the work that we've put into becoming not only well versed in who we are as a people, but also in what it takes to be the best scientist or to be the best documenter or to be the best conservationist or artist. To be able to understand all those aspects of what it takes to be a modern Indigenous person. And when I think about the future, I think about the impact of not just *Hōkūle'a* but also all these other parallel movements happening worldwide.

NA: I think the worldwide voyage was in response, in one sense, to this fear—and in another sense, the hope of what might be possible in this time of tremendous upheaval and change. There has to be a recognition that our world is changing rapidly. And as our world is changing rapidly, we need to be reminded of how we could live in harmony with it, because if we don't then it is just going to spin out of control. A canoe is literally this floating island, and it sustains a handful of us, a family and ‘ohana, for everything we need for a set amount of time to get to a destination. The canoe needs to be rigged properly, she needs to be dried off, she needs to be seaworthy, so that she can be our floating island for this amount of time. And that is in direct parallel to how we treat our islands here in Hawai‘i; that we are also on this journey to a destination. And our honua, or our planet, is also in the sea of space, floating toward its next destination. And we need to take care of that island because it is the only one we have. And if we don’t, it cannot take care of us and we cannot persist into the next destination.

Hawaiians maintained Hawai‘i for thousands of years without one container ship, without outside resources. I’m sure it was not easy, and difficult decisions had to be made, but the values with which we made those decisions led us to this very day. And over time, Western thought and science have decoupled us from the values that sustained this place for all that time. If we don’t have ten million tourists a year or container ships every day, this place cannot sustain us. And that is increasingly apparent across the planet. The driving force to participate in the worldwide voyage was knowing that if we could make an impact with people understanding what life is like on a little canoe and how delicate that balance is and how important the values are that have carried us for thousands of years, then maybe we could replant those seeds in places and spaces that had forgotten. Places where they understood the reverberation of the mana of the canoe, but had forgotten the values that drive that canoe to continue. And so, as we planted the seeds as we went along, I think that maybe those things are starting to grow in terms of value and how we can interact so that we can make the right choices to find a new destination for Island Earth.

Notes

1. Most notably, Micronesians were using noninstrument navigation to go between islands even into the 1970s.
2. Hawaiian Medium Education schools started in 1984.

ACCESS DENIED

CREATING NEW SPATIAL UNDERSTANDINGS

Jaklin Romine

Jaklin Romine was born in Burbank, California, and currently lives in Pasadena. She studied studio arts at Cal State LA and completed her MFA at CalArts. She has lectured and exhibited extensively throughout Los Angeles and in 2019 received the Rema Hort Mann Foundation Emerging Artist Grant.

I'm a person with a disability. I've been disabled since 2006.

As a disabled person, I'm trying to (1) be an artist, and (2) participate in the art world. Both are very difficult things.

My visual art practice is ultimately about creating new understandings of space. Before I went to Cal State LA and before I went to CalArts, nobody took me seriously. People thought I was just that "poor little brown girl in a wheelchair" who worked for free at MOCA. They sympathized with me and would help me with different projects, but nobody thought that I had a true vision or believed I had a powerful voice. As soon as I got into CalArts, everybody started treating me differently. All of a sudden, I was treated like a person. I wanted to participate in the art world, meet other artists, and learn more about art. I thought a good way to do that would be to go to events and gallery openings to support other artists. But when? Only if I'm able to get in.

On the day I interviewed to attend the MFA program at CalArts, I went down to the photo lab in the sublevel (basement), and I couldn't open the

Editor's Note: This essay was edited from a conversation between Daniela Alvarez, Jaklin Romine, and Elizabeth M. Webb via Zoom on November 6, 2020.

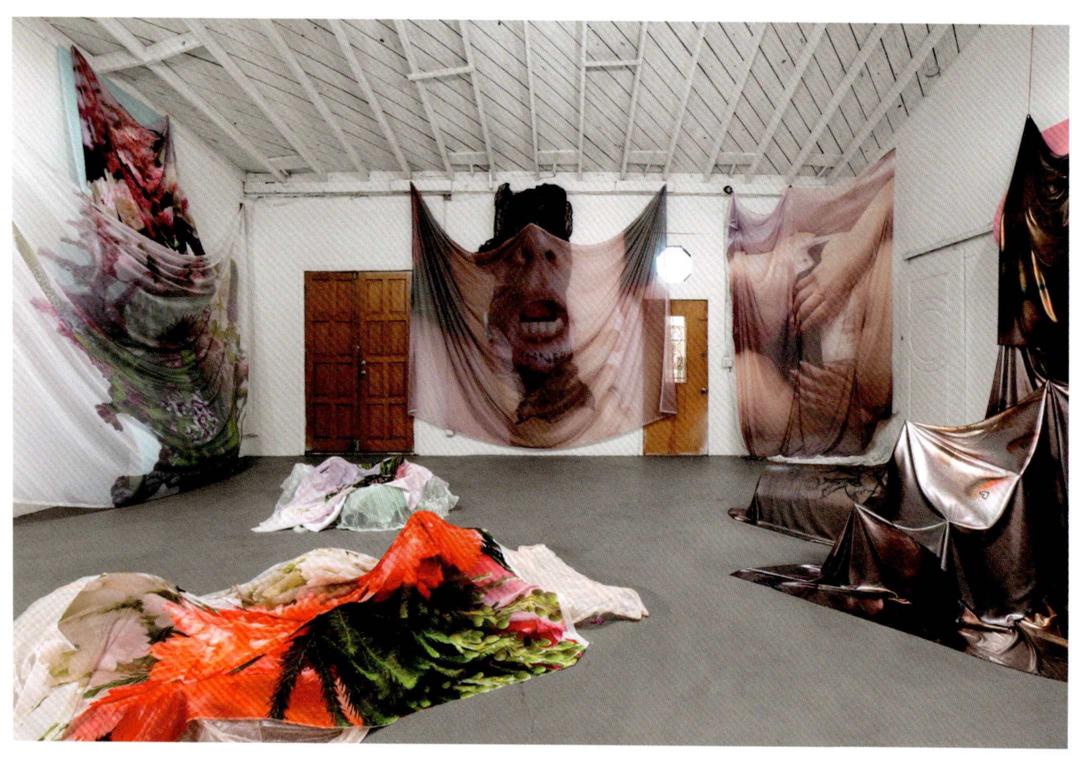

Jaklin Romine, *Living with SCI*, 2019. Installation at PSLA, dimensions variable.

photo lab door. The photo lab was inaccessible. And when I needed to use the bathroom on my tour, I couldn't; even though it was labeled accessible, it was not accessible for my body to fit within the stall. During my interview, I expressed my concerns about if I was going to go to school there. If I were to get in, they said, for sure, they'd address this. They'd give it to the right people. But when I came to school that fall, the facilities were still the same, still inaccessible. Nothing had changed. I don't think they realized the force they would create by allowing me to enter that institution. Because when I have to pay for something, and it doesn't work, and it's really hard, and I still have to pay the same price as everybody else, it really pisses me off. I paid the same amount of money as every other person that could get into that school, and I still couldn't go to the bathroom on every floor of the institution. (Technically now, I still can't.) I had meetings with the head of student access; I had meetings with the head of student affairs; I had meetings with the risk management officer, who was the most egregious of them all. I tried to help them make the necessary changes without having to sue them. All the while, I was being discriminated against and segregated.

At CalArts, I really wanted to make a point of not making work about my disability, partly because I knew everybody *wanted* me to make work about my disability. Classmates suggested, "You should make work about the assistive stuff that you use to open doors. Like the weird things that you have to use to adapt, you can make it bigger and it can be a sculpture." And I never wanted to do anything like that. I really wanted to make work about just being a woman, and I did. My first show was about online dating. Most people didn't even believe it was my show, even when I was sitting there, in the show. People would walk around, talking about the show, and they would never assume that it was my art. But I still kept going to school, kept asking for bathrooms to be accessible, kept asking for my studio bathroom to not be so dangerous—there was literally a water heater underneath the sink that was right in front of my shins—totally illegal and totally unsafe. I did make some changes, but I had to take legal action against them. I documented all the inaccessible stuff at school for the lawsuit and used that documentation, as well as different portraits of my wheelchair, and different portraits of my power wheelchair set on fire, in my thesis show.

While at CalArts, I wanted to start making work about inaccessible places in LA as well. I started making the project because there was a class outing to the galleries at Bergamot Station, and it was inaccessible. I had to stay outside while everybody else went into the galleries to look at the art. Literally, I got left outside. That's the first video that started my series *ACCESS DENIED* (2015–ongoing).

When I was twenty-five years old, before I had the fortitude that I currently have about my disability, I even allowed my art to be shown in an inaccessible gallery. It was one of the first art shows that I was in outside of community college, and I thought it was important. So I allowed my art to be shown in a gallery I could not physically get into. That was my first real experience with an inaccessible gallery. I didn't even know that it wasn't okay, because I just wanted my art to be shown in an art show. But then I started going to more and more art shows and not being able to get in, and I got frustrated.

When I finally graduated, I decided to make work about my disability because I needed to. I can't get away from it. When I would go to see art shows and not be able to get into some, I would document it and put it on Instagram. I would sit in front of an art gallery for an entire opening or closing, while somebody else took pictures and video of me. It was super lonely, super isolating. I thought I was speaking into a vacuum for a good year and a half. I would make the work because I was tired of this experience, and I wanted people to pay attention to it. I had no idea if it was going to take me anywhere or do anything because I was up against the art world. I never imagined that I would be let into the art world, because I was literally fighting them. But actually, it wasn't me fighting them, it was them excluding me. And it's not just me. And it's not just my body. It's any other physically disabled person who doesn't have the ability to walk up a flight of stairs.

My video, ACCESS DENIED, started at three minutes; it's fifteen now. And it's only because there's so many other spaces that have been documented.

During the COVID-19 pandemic and the mandatory quarantines of 2020, galleries closed, and everyone, including able-bodied people, temporarily experienced inaccessibility to art spaces that the disabled body experiences constantly. I was invited to participate in an outdoor exhibition where I showed one of my sculptural pieces and a fabric print at my studio. In addition, I made twelve or fifteen 3′ × 8′ vinyl banners to post at various inaccessible art spaces around LA that read:

ACCESS DENIED

is an ongoing project by JAKLIN ROMINE.

The project is based around her physical access being denied on a constant basis at different art, music, and performance spaces around Los Angeles: the segregation of the disabled body from the public space.

PUBLIC meaning accessible to or shared by all members of the community. SEGREGATION meaning the practice of restricting a person's rights and privileges in society/set apart from each other; isolated or divided.

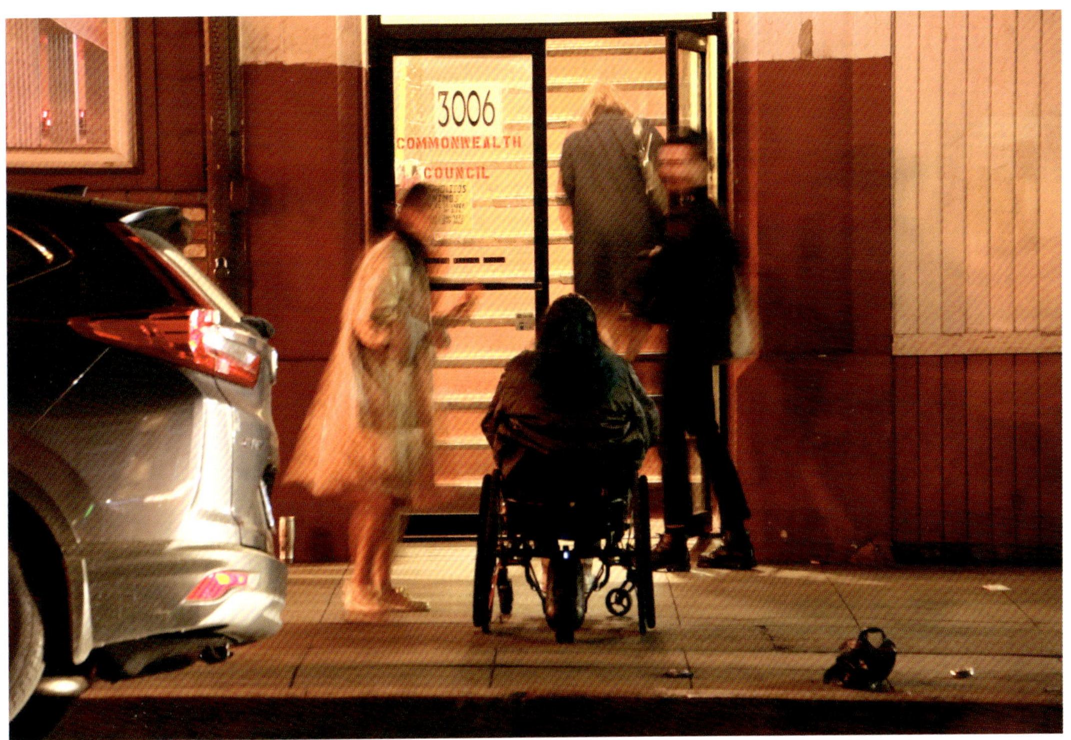

Jaklin Romine, *ACCESS DENIED*, 2015–ongoing. HD video
still.

The disabled body is segregated from the art community at [insert gallery].

Because of the physical distancing required by the state (COVID-19), You,
the VIEWER, are being temporarily denied access to this location, and
by extension temporarily performing the project.

Without the required modifications, the WHEELCHAIR USER'S BODY
will continue being DENIED ACCESS after these restrictions are lifted.
Romine's performance will continue as well.

I then put the inaccessible galleries on a virtual map so that anybody
could go to the location and perform that inaccessibility. The banners were
supposed to be up for a month, but they were all taken down within forty-
eight hours. Subsequently, I was blocked on social media by several of the
galleries. For those galleries that did and do reach out to me, they generally
don't deny that accessibility is an issue, but instead try to get me to understand a landlord's perspective. As if my disabled body is supposed to care
about the fact that they don't have enough money to make their public
events accessible to the public. If a space receives public funding, they will
often get money to make accessible changes. But they tend to give it back
because it's usually not enough for what they need and because the changes

would add no property value. They don't see access as an incentive, economically. Others have entered dialogue as if they had no understanding of the physical limitations of somebody with a disability or that somebody in a wheelchair would even want to participate. I think that's probably the biggest thing—the expectation throughout the art world that art is for everybody. But my body and the way my body manifests in social spaces is not seen as a priority. Our institutions have a very narrow view of who should be able to access art. A number of the more prominent inaccessible spaces get celebrated, highlighted, featured on lists of "What to do if you're coming to LA." But if you're disabled, you can't go. The *you* doesn't include me or bodies like mine.

My hope for this project is to be able to bring awareness to the exclusion of the disabled body, and that disability justice will be served by the art spaces actively choosing to no longer operate from inaccessible locations and instead move to physically accessible spaces. Some spaces have actually made change, have relocated, and made some of their talks and parts of their programming in courtyards in their bottom floors. One gallery contacted me after I did the quarantine callout because they have an upstairs area that has consistently been inaccessible. They told me they no longer show art on the second floor because of my project. They actually shared my project on their Instagram, and they've made the necessary changes, at least to the best of their ability so far. This is great. But we need to recognize the fact that the Americans with Disabilities Act (ADA) still isn't fully implemented. And it's been in accordance and in law for thirty years; 2020 was the thirtieth anniversary. And thirty years later, a physically and visibly disabled person is still trying to fight to get in the front door, still fighting to use the bathroom, still fighting to be able to use the counter, use the table—we're still trying to be able to get inside, sit down, and participate. And those are really basic things. I honestly never thought that I would still be making this project today. I thought I would have nothing to talk about, there would be no more inaccessible places, and people would just tell me to stop talking because, "it's not that many, it's not that serious." But these inaccessible galleries still exist. So, I'll keep talking.

Essential Economy

Jia Lok Pratt

Jia Lok Pratt is a mother, writer, educator, aspiring textile artist/printmaker, and chief operating officer of Sweet Water Foundation in Chicago. After ten years in corporate consulting and six years working with traditional nonprofits, she joined Sweet Water Foundation, where she works to build a more radical and imaginative future.

As I write this, humanity is facing a global pandemic, America is in the midst of an uprising sparked by police brutality and racial oppression, unemployment is at an all-time high, the global food supply chain is being tested as never before, and, once again, our planet is on track to reach the hottest year on record.[1] This complicated and interconnected layering of crises is forcing a values-based alignment of our way of living, calling into question what is truly essential versus what is not. And the greatest devastation that most of us will experience as a result of these crises will stem from the underlying fact that our economy is not structured to support that which is essential. It is not programmed to value and sustain life. Instead, its function is to drive conspicuous consumption of a consumer-driven culture to maximize profit. This is why a foreseeable, albeit unpredictable, event such as the COVID-19 pandemic unraveled the American economy, all while the pathology of profit justified a premature return to "normal," fueling deadly consequences.

We are witness to the dramatic effects of an irrational, single-bottom-line economy that has functioned for decades without regard to people or the planet and, thus, is wholly ill-equipped to function in a time of crisis. Our economy operates under a logic structure that is short-term, degenerative, and extractive. It is unable to preemptively acknowledge or proactively address crises because preventative measures do not make "economic" sense (i.e., profit). So, here we are.

In search of the cheapest labor and materials, we have devalued and outsourced the production of the most essential elements of life. We have neither the regional or national systems in place to support people impacted by the collapse of nonessential industries, nor the means to maintain essential industries capable of sustaining life locally. We do not grow the food we eat. We do not manufacture the appliances, equipment, medicine, and tools we rely upon.

The pathology of profit extends to the most fundamental and sacred element of our very existence, Mother Earth, from whom the essence of all life is derived. She, too, has been relegated to serve the single bottom line. Her land is parceled out to the highest bidder, with its value determined by the almighty market. Instead of serving as a common good, land use is subject to the whims of individual "owners" with little to no accountability to community or ecology beyond property taxes that fuel the very municipal systems that perpetuate the cycle of speculation, exploitation, hoarding, and extraction.

The fundamental flaws of a single-bottom-line economy that renders both humans and nature as expendable are now in plain sight, forcing a much-needed reassessment of our values. In what has been a time of worldwide political upheaval, rife with division and social disruption, we find ourselves intimately united in a fight to sustain life, both physically and economically. We have before us a rare moment—a once-in-a-lifetime opportunity as individuals and a never-before-experienced chance as a species—to change course. If we choose wisely, these crises will catalyze a new economic model, an *Essential Economy* rooted in that which matters most—sustaining life.

Toward an Essential Economy

The Essential Economy operates with a triple bottom line that recognizes *people*, *planet*, and *profit*. It employs regenerative and resourceful practices and is accountable not only to those among us today but to seven generations into the future. The Essential Economy shortens the supply chain of essential goods and services, decreasing the human and environmental impact of the current economy. It restores local manufacturing and production while carefully preserving and promoting technological advances that enhance the lives of workers. Most importantly, the Essential Economy restores our connection to that which is essential in our daily lives—caring for others, growing food, making art, and engaging in community and culture. It restructures and realigns our education systems to ensure the wisdom and know-how of essential practices are passed on and that academic resources (e.g., research, technology) are used to develop solutions, not products. And, most importantly, the Essential Economy requires us to renegotiate our relationship with nature and the land upon which we rely to nourish our bodies, make our homes, and sustain all life.

The Essential Economy grounds us by making visible and tangible the labor and environmental toll that our current system so masterfully has hidden from view. It has deep roots inspired and informed by the wisdom of elders, Indigenous peoples, and the writings of James and Grace Lee Boggs, Frederick Douglass, Paulo Freire, André Gorz, and E. F. Schumacher. The Essential Economy is emergent and flexible, able to prepare us for both impending crises and those unknown.

Sweet Water Foundation: The Essential Economy in Practice

In a community nestled at the nexus of the Englewood and Washington Park neighborhoods on Chicago's South Side, we are already demonstrating what the Essential Economy looks like in an urban setting. Here, the humans of Sweet Water Foundation have been cultivating a hyperlocal Essential Economy for more than five years. Our vision is simple—*Every community contains the seeds of its own regeneration, able to cultivate stable, healthy, and happy families*. Our work demonstrates how cities might begin to reconstruct urban life in a manner that sustains life. Our practice is rooted in the values of an Essential Economy: *Regeneration, Small Is Beautiful, Chaord* (harmonious coexistence of chaos and order), *Sankofa* (embracing history to rebuild the present), *Seventh Generation Principle* (a philosophy integral to Haudenosaunee life), and *Open Source*.[2]

Through a series of unique sequences of urban acupuncture interventions to the built environment, we have collectively begun to re-story and reconstruct a community situated on so-called blighted land that has been intentionally disinvested in and subjected to decades of systematic racism and municipal neglect. Through agriculture, art, carpentry, education, and outreach, we have built a dynamic site that contains the essential elements of life—art, culture, food, housing, and wellness. This place, known as the Commonwealth, spans four city blocks and includes more than three acres of urban farmland, open community gardens, a carpentry workshop, two formerly foreclosed homes transformed into live-work-learn spaces, and a hand-raised, timber-frame barn that serves as a visual and performing arts, reflection, and community gathering space. Here, we design and build furniture, craft home goods, and construct community structures from reclaimed wood destined for landfills. We reclaim vacant spaces, grow healthy food, and engage an intergenerational audience in programming that reconnects us to one another and our shared environment—from bee-keeping to yogurt making to canning to local historic preservation. Our work fills the void of food deserts, closed schools, and economic margin-alization through an approach that is ecological, accessible, and inclusive. The Commonwealth is a leverage point, a new model for land use and urban living that illuminates a paradigm shift capable of transforming the systems currently failing humanity.

Maybe most importantly, we nourish our humanity via a holistic practice that elevates and democratizes the arts through the integration of artistic practice as an essential element and integral part of our work. The notion of art as an isolated practice that elevates an individual is not aligned with the values of the Essential Economy because, far too often, even the most well-intentioned and thought-provoking social practice installations are hidden in abstract environments, great distances from the contexts which their objects portray and void of accountability or solutions. In an Essential Economy, investments in the arts would fuel communal practices and serve as a powerful catalyst for connection, healing, education, inspiration, and collective action. The Essential Economy insists that we move from art for the sake of art to art for the sake of change.

An Essential Economy approach to the arts is embodied by the fall 2020 exhibition *well·ness at The Commonwealth*, a collaborative project of Sweet Water Foundation, the Smart Museum of Art at University of Chicago, and artist Iñigo Manglano-Ovalle. *well·ness at The Commonwealth* is a catalytic assemblage of art, artifacts, and history that explores the many facets and dimensions of water as the source of all life. The "living" installation fea-tures an emergent and participatory research project that engages a diverse range of global citizens of all walks of life to critically examine the precarity of this precious life source and establish an accountability framework. Most importantly, *well·ness at The Commonwealth* is rooted in place and practice. It is embedded within a neighborhood grappling with the most dramatic effects of the content displayed and juxtaposed, with active practitioners engaged in solution seeking and new ways-making.

Today, amid COVID-19 and the myriad of other crises, Sweet Water Foundation's work continues with greater resolve each day. Founded on sustainable and regenerative practices, our community has been rehearsing for the future and is well positioned to thrive amid the events unfolding before us. Food shortages brought about by COVID-19 and the uprisings sparked by police brutality and racial oppression amplified the essential-ity and sacredness of growing food locally, exposing the delicate thread by which our global food system hangs. The seeds we sowed amid the fear and uncertainty reaped produce that has fed and will continue to feed thousands. To adjust to the new normal of social distancing, the Sweet Water Foundation team created virtual ways to engage our values-based partner network to continue sharing life-sustaining practices in the absence of in-person workshops and events. Doing work that is *rooted* in place, work that stewards the land, and work that cultivates our humanity is now more essential than ever before.

A Way Forward

As we look to the future and begin to reconstruct our global and local economies, may we carry with us a fresh perspective and profound understanding of that which is essential. In the days ahead, we have a choice. Do we continue to bolster existing economic structures that value profit over people and the planet? Or, do we chart a new way forward toward an Essential Economy that sustains life, nurtures land, and returns our capacity to provide for ourselves that which is essential?

The future is ours to create. Let us establish a new way of living in which every community contains the seeds of its own regeneration. There GROWS the neighborhood.

Notes

1. Zoya Teirsteing, "2020 Was the Hottest Year on Record. We'll Remember It as One of the Century's Coldest," *Grist*, January 16, 2021, https://grist.org /climate/2020-was-the-hottest-year-on-record-well-remember-it-as-one-of-the -centurys-coldest/.

2. "Values," Haudenosaunee Confederacy, accessed February 8, 2023, https:// www.haudenosauneeconfederacy.com/values/.

Earth Mama II

Favianna Rodriguez

Favianna Rodriguez is an interdisciplinary artist, cultural strategist, and social justice activist based in Oakland, California. Her art and praxis address migration, gender justice, climate change, racial equity, and sexual freedom. She is the founder and president of the Center for Cultural Power, a national organization igniting change at the intersection of art, culture, and social justice.

After a life crisis in late 2018, I put my focus into my relationship to plants, to surround myself with them so that I could wake up to their life-giving force. It was my way of healing my relationship to the natural world. I grew up in a cement city, with dead structures all around me, cement and buildings, hardly any green areas. Meanwhile, wealthy folks lived in the greenest and most beautiful mountains just a few minutes away. People of color and migrant families like mine were forced into hoods, next to freeways that spewed emissions and made us sick. I didn't do much camping as a kid because my parents were busy surviving, plus we didn't really know how to navigate that world. Therefore, my relationship to nature was dormant.

As I confronted headline after headline about climate catastrophes—from wildfires to floods—I had a vision in which I saw how colonizers ripped away my ancestors' traditional practices. They tried to bury our knowledge and our relationship to nature, so that they could exploit her.

But within me, the ancestral memory is alive, and my artistic practice is a vessel for that.

I created this work to represent the transformational power of tuning into nature's wisdom.

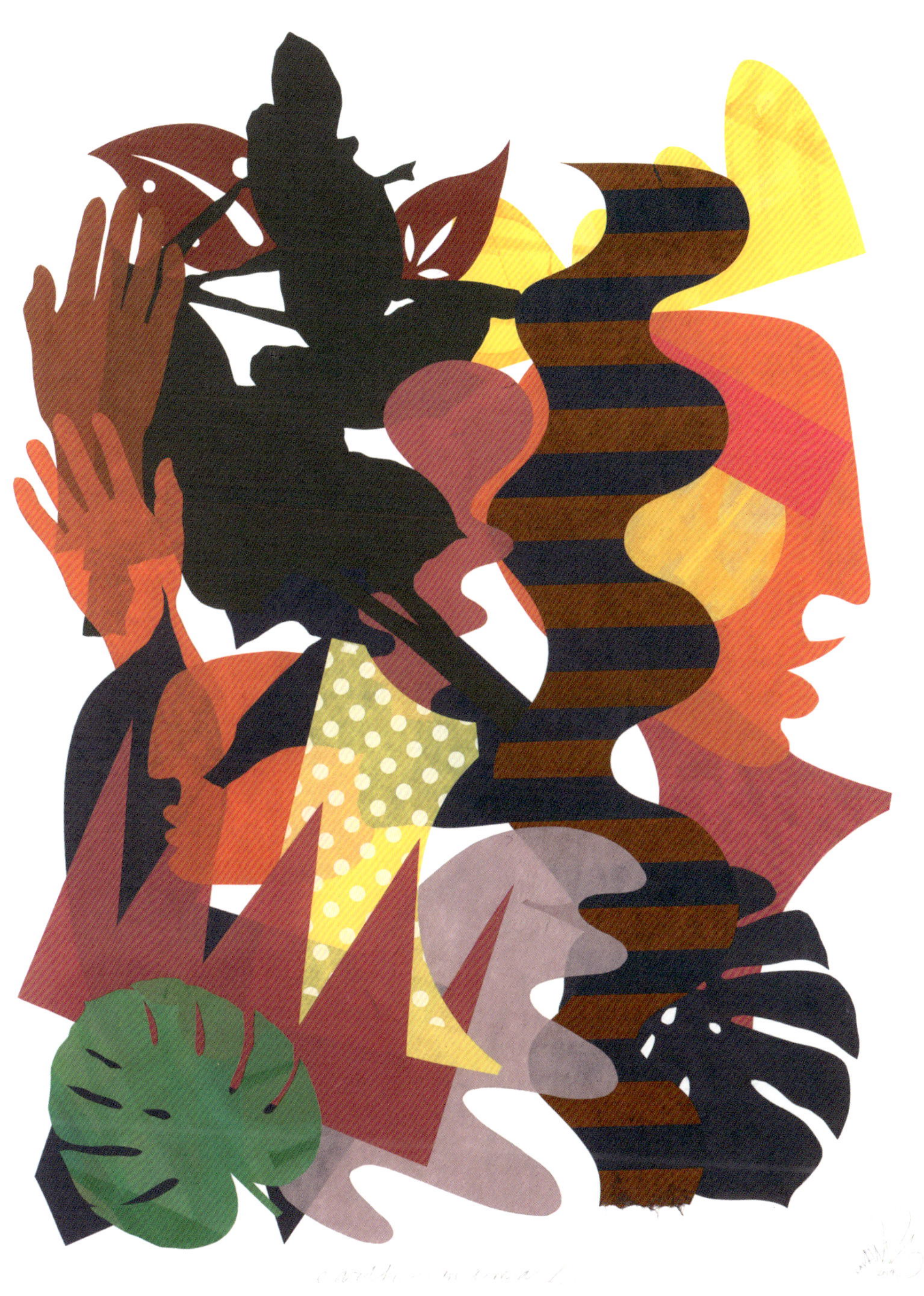

Favianna Rodriguez, *Earth Mama II*, 2019. Collage with monoprint and screen-print elements on cotton rag paper, 30 × 22 in.

We Are Part of This Land

Carlton Turner

Carlton Turner is a performing artist, agriculturalist, arts advocate, policy shaper, lecturer, consultant, and facilitator. Carlton is also founder of the Mississippi Center for Cultural Production. The MCCP uses arts and agriculture to support rural community, cultural, and economic development in his hometown of Utica, Mississippi, where he lives with his wife, Brandi, and three children.

I am the son of Emmett and Genevia Turner. Emmett, born in Harlem in 1935, was a product of the Great Migration. His parents came up from the Carolinas, his father Emmett from the North, his mother Armecer Brown from the South, near Charleston. Genevia is the daughter of Samuel and Epsie Roberts—Mississippi full blood on both sides; my mother was born on Choctaw and Chickasaw land in 1942. My roots are planted in a rich and fertile soil. Enriched with the sweat and blood of growers and builders, artisans and storytellers, preachers, teachers, cooks, and midwives. I live in Utica, Mississippi, a small town that sits at the foot of the Mississippi Delta, thirty minutes from the river. *Mississippi* is an Ojibwe word that means "Great River." This river ferried King Cotton and unnamed precious human cargo from weigh-ins and auction blocks into markets and plantation bondage up and down this country, providing a literal stream of income that would build white generational wealth across the nation and fuel the south block of Confederate political power up through Reconstruction and deep into the era of Jim Crow. Right down the road from us is Natchez, in its day a massive slave trading post, second only to New Orleans. There is direct correlation between states that mastered human trafficking pre–Civil War and those that have the highest incarceration rates today. South Carolina. Louisiana. Mississippi.

During the cotton boom, my community of Utica was perfectly situated in a small yet important location between the growers and the river.

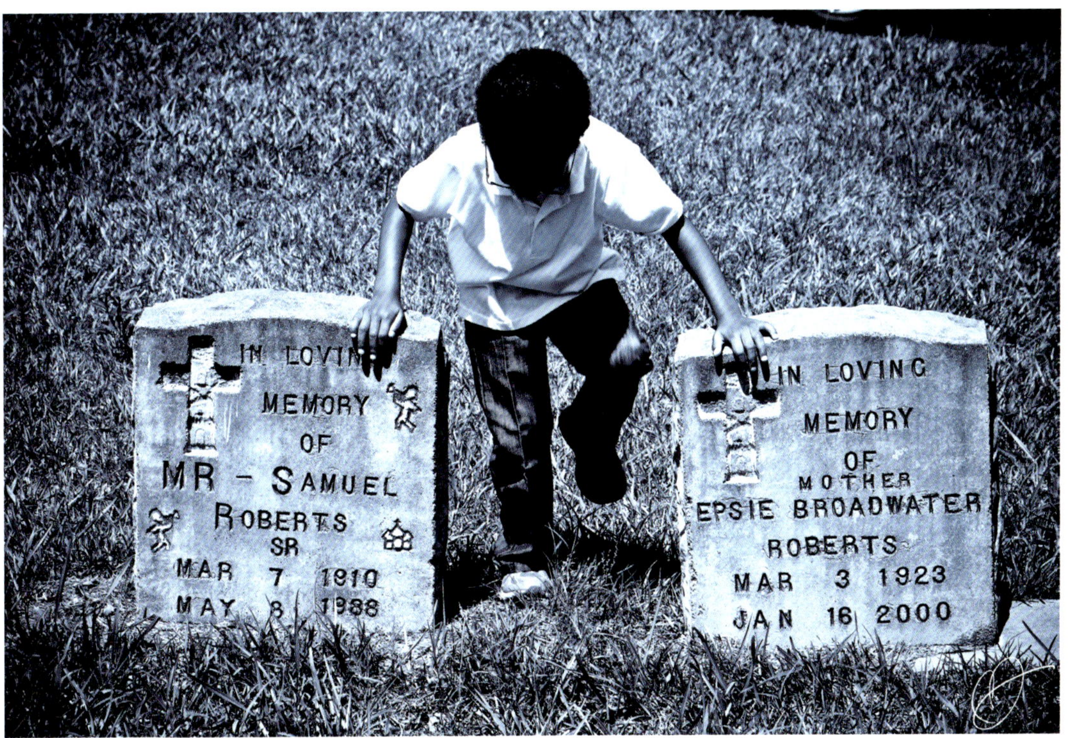

Warren Bailey playing on the gravestones of his great-grandparents Samuel and Epsie Roberts in Paige Grove cemetery in Utica, Mississippi, c. 2015. Photo: Carlton Turner.

A depot of sorts, where growers could bring their harvest to any of the three cotton gins to be weighed in and paid out. According to the stories, in its day, Utica had a top-of-the-line social scene that included jook joints, cafés, a hotel, a railroad depot, and even an opera house. Utica was the site of the first radio station and the first paved road in the state of Mississippi, a town built on the production of agricultural goods, lumber, and, most importantly, educators. At some point Utica held importance.

In 1903 the Utica Normal and Industrial Institute was founded by William Holtzclaw. Holtzclaw was one of many students of the Tuskegee Institute, a school founded by Lewis Adams and Booker T. Washington on July 4, 1881. Tuskegee's agricultural program was founded and directed by George Washington Carver. Alumni of this great institution were charged with duplicating the land- and food-based strategies throughout the South. George and Booker, and William and Fannie Lou Hamer after them, knew that land was the key to Black liberation.

Time moves on and industries inevitably change, and when they do, decisions about the future of communities like mine are made for us, rarely by us. These decisions are usually based on an analysis of the potential to exploit labor, land, and the means of production. The result is that our communities are adversely impacted by decisions they have little agency in. But Utica is still important to me and many other families that have been and continue to be here.

My third great-grandmother, Kea Bradbery—or maybe Barber; records of the enslaved are really difficult to find—was born in South Carolina in 1822. She was brought to Mississippi as the property of Samuel William Broadwater, also born in South Carolina in 1820. Kea was repeatedly raped by Samuel as part of her bondage. I am not sure how many children came of these crimes, but I do know Kea birthed my great-great-grandfather, Edmond Broadwater, in 1850. Born into enslavement, Edmond would later marry Alice Kidd from Georgia; to this union was born five children, the oldest of which was my great-grandfather, Willie "Soap" Broadwater, the first of my direct descendants on this line to be born free. They called him "Soap" because he stayed clean.

Please continue this walk with me: Soap married Eliza Terry, daughter of Gus and Sarah Terry, and they lived in Learned, Mississippi, in the same community as Willie's white grandfather Samuel. Willie and Eliza had seven children. Their oldest daughter is my grandmother Epsie Broadwater. Epsie married Samuel Roberts, and then came my mother Genevia and then me. Although I was born in Mount Vernon, New York, my family moved back to Mississippi when I was two years old. I have been here ever since. Today, I live here in Utica with my wife, Brandi Alexander, and three children in the same community that saw some portion of each of the aforementioned relationships. Relationships in this community are generational. My childhood best friend is David, and his mother, Ella, and my mother grew up together. His mother's mother and my mother's mother grew up together. Utica is built on these concentric circles of relationships in families that are connected to, and go back to, a relationship with the land and agriculture. Eight generations of my family have walked these same lands—Roberts, Broadwaters, Washingtons, and Terrys. I am no stranger here. I am a continuation of their intention to make a life with this land.

Utica is my home. It's where my children go to school, where my nephews, nieces, and little cousins are growing up, and it's a community vastly different from what it was just a generation ago. Like transformation, deterioration happens gradually over time. The Utica of my youth was a very different place. The future Utica will need to be radically different, if our community is to thrive. These shifts don't happen all at once—they occur over generations. It takes intention and time, and in these parts, you can't be afraid to put your hands in the soil. For many Black people across educational and socioeconomic statuses, working with hands in soil is seen as lesser than. Psychologically, we connect land labor to sharecropping and enslavement. I am working to shift that ideology to one of empowerment and liberation. If the land isn't liberated, if the land isn't bearing fruit, then our people, our community, cannot thrive.

For many, the enslavement of Africans is just a footnote in the history of White America. For me and others like me, it is a fundamental part of our story. It's an essential part of the American narrative of separate and unequal, of white supremacy and Black resistance and resilience.

The once-thriving town of Utica, with three cotton gins, two lumber mills, a textile factory, multiple grocery stores, a butcher shop, doctors' offices, two high schools, and a bustling retail and social district, has now been reduced to a bedroom community of less than one thousand people that line up at the Dollar General to shop for food or travel more than twenty miles to the nearest full-service grocery store. People like to refer to these communities as food deserts, but in reality, that moniker is off base. Deserts are thriving, complete ecosystems. What we are experiencing in our community and many like ours is food apartheid, where some communities have it and others don't, mostly based on race and class.

Food is the common denominator of humanity. There's not a street you can walk down in any major city, or any small town, that doesn't have food. There's food everywhere. It permeates every aspect of our lives. I grew up in a community where I had a deep and personal relationship with my food. Many people in my community share that experience. So, we use stories connected to food as a framework for accessibility, for people to enter and contribute their story to an ongoing conversation. They may not feel comfortable if the frame is the arts, but when you combine food and story, you get a backstage pass to the most prolific of venues for storytelling. Coming from a big family, collards, cornbread, fried chicken, and candied yams become the centerpiece of a visceral and ethereal experience, adorned by stories that bring layered emotions, tears, and some of the most gut-wrenching belly laughs you will ever experience. This is the place where arts and culture bloom and, at the same time, fade into the performance ritual of everyday life. It's not just "table talk"—it's theatrical and emotional, it's personal, it's comedy and drama, it's sometimes tragic, but always an art. My work as an artist is to acknowledge those stories and the legacy and future of our community that are encoded within them.

My mother was a seamstress and clothing designer. At one point, she led a team of women in Jackson, Mississippi, producing a line of underwear and lingerie for low-income women under her Genevia R. Turner label. My grandmother made beautiful functional quilts to keep her family warm through wet, cold Mississippi winters. She also embroidered flour sacks with intricate designs and figures of country life. My great-grandfather was a builder and a master basket weaver, a cultural practice that failed to transfer to the next generation. Our community has always been brimming with cultural producers and has always been a hotbed of creativity, ingenuity, and innovation.

Our ability to achieve health and wellness in our community is tied to our agency with the land. It is deeply connected to our ability to construct an analysis of the trajectory our community has taken to this current moment. It is grounded in our ability to tell our stories about food and our individual and collective histories to this land. And we believe that through the telling of those stories we can supplement parts of the social fabric lost over the past couple of generations and begin to construct a new community. One that centers the voice of the people that live here, fostering a place that provides health and wellness for all.

The central mission of the Mississippi Center for Cultural Production (MCCP), otherwise known as Sipp Culture, is to recalibrate the measurements by which economic prosperity is calculated and, in the process, redefine wealth for our rural community. We are taking an intergenerational approach to community cultural and economic development through the lens of cultural and agricultural production—shifting the community's dominant identity from consumer to producer.

The idea evolved from the creation of a school to the creation of a community cultural center to focus on collective community cultural transformation. That is the social and economic transformation of our community using arts and agriculture as intersecting points to engage the community in a conversation about past, present, and future. At the heart of our work is cultural production. It shows up in the production of stories in media, film, and photography, in audio stories, in the growing of food, and in creating an overall sense of growth as a community identity. In this process, Utica becomes the backdrop for a renewed community energy, embodied in the sense that anywhere you have land, we can grow something. The work began the moment we offered this idea as a seed to our community to nurture and grow. At that moment, when we asked permission to share our dreams with the community and have those dreams embraced, the people began to share and place their dreams on ours. Together, our ideas and aspirations became interlaced, and that process is the work—that is the community transformation. It can be difficult to see the incremental change, but remember—transformation takes time.

I have come to understand that we cannot depend on powerful people for our liberation; the only thing that can save us is our relationship to each other and the land. We have to adjust the way we consume, the way we create and produce. The very fabric of the way we live. If food is life, then land is liberation. What we do with it, who controls it, who benefits from it, are all questions deeply connected to our liberation.

I think of those as really important things that I've learned that I don't feel are about social justice. It's just about doing what's human, like taking care of everybody as if they're your children or as if they're your mother or your aunties or uncles. Treating the community as an extension of family. That may sound really naive, but to come from a community entrenched in these concentric circles of relationships that date back before any living memory, it's just a way of being. It ain't nothing special.

Mississippi offers hope because for us, the distance between connection and disconnection to the land is less than a couple of generations wide. There are still deeply seeded memories of a time when sustenance was part of a localized relationship between land and life. Through our work we will cultivate those seeds once again.

Freedom is an elusive and precarious concept. But as the great Fannie Lou Hamer said, "Nobody is free, until everybody is free!"

Mauka House

Kapena Alapaʻi

....

Kapena Alapaʻi (Kanaka Maoli) is the codirector of ArtChangeUS and a visual artist and organizer based in Kona, Hawaiʻi. He is a graduate of Ka Haka ʻUla ʻo Keʻelikōlani Hawaiian Language College and sits as board president of Kahilu Theatre in Waimea.

....

Mauka House is where my grandmother, my father, and most of my generation grew up.[1] It is thirty-six acres located in the kūāhewa, prime agricultural land in Hōlualoa, North Kona, Hawaiʻi. Before the barges came in, this is where the foods that sustained Kona's population were grown. This is family land.

This property, once alive with family gatherings, singing, dancing, playing, and imu, now lies overgrown and condemned, a heavy topic of conversation.[2] Since my childhood, my father's generation worked together to make sure land taxes were paid, never falling behind for fear of covetous colonizers making moves. With more than fifty people on title, subdivision was necessary to pay extended families and keep what land we could or risk losing all of it. Now ten acres, this land has been left to my siblings and cousins. As we renegotiate our relationship with this land and each other, our collective process has necessitated unpacking historical trauma as well as joyful memories and differentiating between the monetary value that Western society places on land and the value of Indigenous knowledge that originates from ancestral stewardship of this land.

Culture-bearing practices like mahiʻai, ulana lauhala, and imu are tied to a kanaka's relationship with land.[3] It is our responsibility to care for land, to steward it, to fight for it when necessary; caring for land is inextricable from our artistic or cultural practices. In *Mauka House*, I stand outside the gate, a Native Hawaiian among invasive species, looking back to see who is ready to enter with me, to do the work it takes to aloha ʻāina.

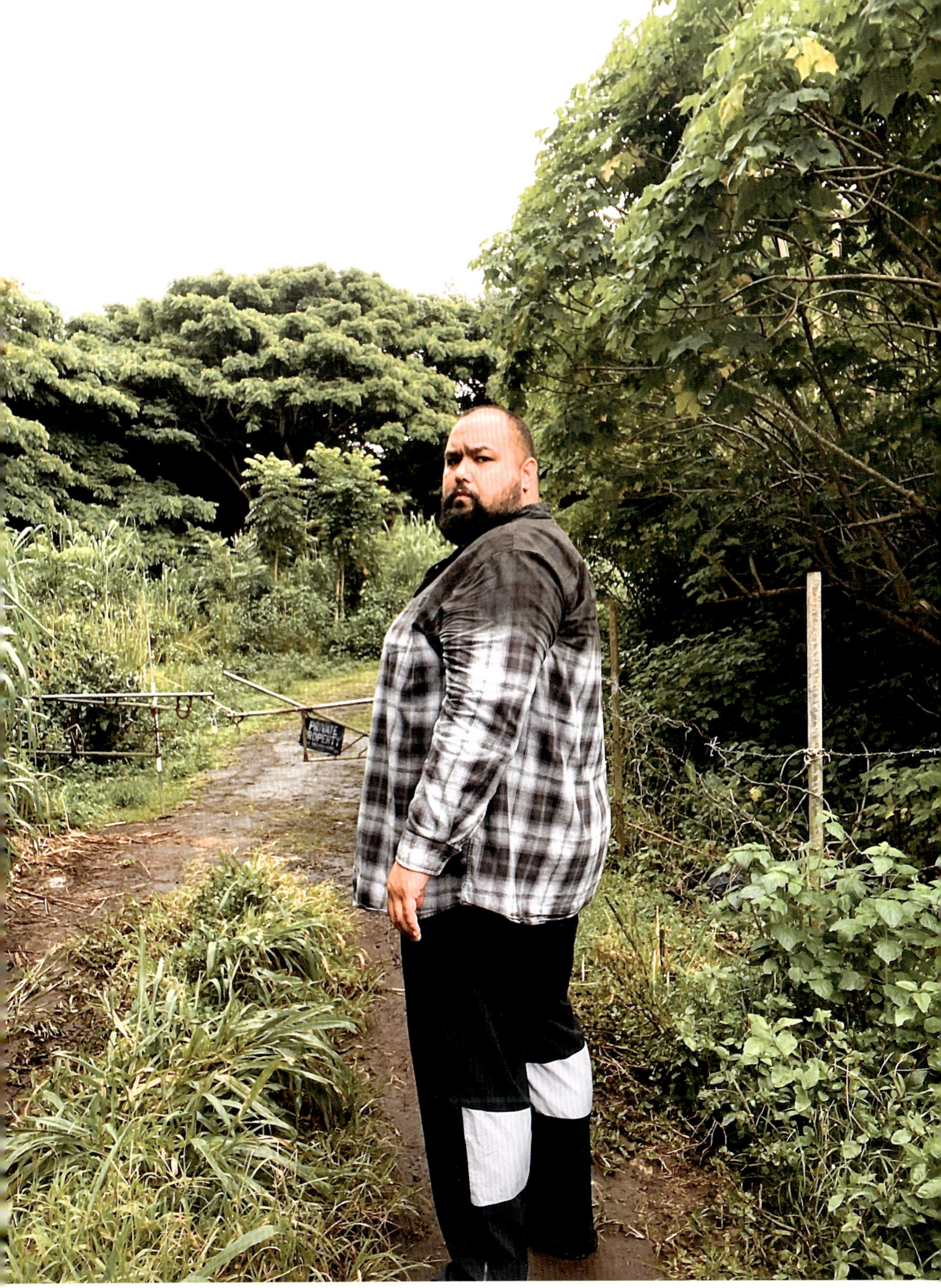

Kapena Alapaʻi, *Mauka House*, 2021. Digital photograph.

Notes

1. Mauka means inland, upland, toward the mountain.

2. An imu is an underground oven.

3. Mahiʻai: farming; ulana lauhala: weaving with pandanus leaves; kānaka: person, Hawaiian.

Withholding an Image

DISCIPLINARY DISOBEDIENCE
AND RECIPROCITY IN THE FIELD

Ashley Hunt

Ashley Hunt is faculty in the program in Photography and Media at California Institute of the Arts (CalArts). His work looks to structures that allow people to accumulate power and those which keep others from getting it, while learning from the ways people come to know, contribute to, or resist these structures.

1.

A picture shows a family on a rural piece of hillside land. An older woman, two younger women, and an older man in early twentieth-century, well-worn clothes, their likenesses, and that of the landscape are rendered in black-and-white film grain.

In conventional art and photo history, here are the questions that we might be expected to ask of this image: What other photographs are like this one? What does it tell us about photography? What does it tell us about the artist/photographer? What does it tell us about art as a field or discipline—about its discourses and conventions, about landscape and portraiture, documentary, or other classifications of genre, about representation or cultural questions of value and vision? Primarily, we would ask what it connects to among art history's other objects—its meaning shaped by the chains of meaning it links into ("syntagmatically," we would say) within art's canon(s).

These questions, we suspected, would be the wrong ones for us, a class of students learning on unceded Native land in what is now called Southern California, looking to challenge the status quo of our own curriculum.

No matter how these conventional questions would point our learning out into the larger world, they would boomerang, bending our learning back into that status quo, locked in a loop within Western art's disciplinary and institutional reproduction.

2.

We came to this photograph and others like it through a family friendship that had begun with Gloria Morgan and her mother, Kathryn Montes Morgan, who was at the time the tribal chairwoman of the Tejon Indian Tribe, a federally acknowledged tribe whose headquarters are based in what is currently known as Bakersfield, California. Chairwoman Morgan had presided over the reinvigoration of the Tribe and the 2012 reinstatement of their federal recognition as a "historical Indian tribe" by the US government. This image, one of a large body of images, played a role in that process, and we hatched an idea for a chance to work together. In it, we could redirect some part of the resources of the Photography and Media program at CalArts toward a more reciprocal model of education, opening our curriculum to parts of the world that our institutions historically disavow but profit from; to learn from but contribute to as well—in this case, toward an awareness of the Tejon Tribe as original inhabitants of Southern California "since before the sun first rose."[1]

Rather than utilize discipline-bound questions, the class would begin by asking an anticolonial question: Whose land are we on?

3.

While CalArts sits within a layering of unceded Indigenous territories, primarily those of diverse villages of Fernandeño Tataviam and Chumash peoples, their histories are intermingled with the Katenamuk people, the primary tribal group who would become known as the Tejon under Spanish colonial, Mexican, and then US imperial rule. Following the 1848 Treaty of Guadalupe Hidalgo, the United States broke its treaty obligation to honor the land bases that California tribes had been guaranteed under the Mexican Rancheria system, as the California legislature refused to ratify and then disappeared the eighteen treaties it had signed with California tribes.[2] This left the Tejon, among many others, exposed to rampant settler encroachment and land theft, backed by militaristic and legalistic methods, including the twentieth-century allotment system, the federal property scheme designed to undermine Native territorial and cultural integrity. But this didn't erase the memory that the Tejon's ancestral territory begins just north of CalArts, around the ruins of Fort Tejon in what is now called the Tejon Pass, extending up into the San Joaquin Valley.

There were twelve of us in the class from around the United States and the world, and we spent the semester moving throughout this geography, between our school and Tejon sites. This included their Tribal headquarters in Bakersfield, their annual Pow Wow on the Cal State Bakersfield campus, and a frustrated attempt to visit the Tribe's ancestral cemetery, which is enclosed within the privatized property of the Tejon Ranch real estate corporation—who, you will be told quickly, has nothing to do with the Tribe other than occupying their ancestral land, and who had once again changed the lock on the access road without notifying the Tribe.

This included Gloria, Chairwoman Morgan, and other family members visiting our campus, joining us in our classroom, meeting the institute's administrators, and seeing our galleries and the exhibition that our class held. This exhibition acted as a rough draft for our eventual task as a class to produce something for the Tribe in return for their generosity toward us, so that our learning would not be extractive but reciprocal.

4.

Our starting point was a return: in the early 2000s, the Tribe received a large body of photographs depicting their ancestors on their ancestral lands before their community's removal, given to them by the Smithsonian Institution in Washington, DC, as a "digital return." This "return" fit within a range of practices of repatriation that are expected of museums and archives today, to return collection holdings to the Indigenous communities from whom they'd been extracted or stolen, for whom it is their cultural patrimony and heritage, but are often credited to and owned by a Western anthropologist or institution.

Our task as a class was not to again peel these photos away from this diplomacy between nations and institutions and ask how they relate to art and photo history, but, given this context, to ask, what are the histories of these photographs, the histories in which they've come about and which they've played a role in shaping?

5.

The digital return of these photographs played a key role in the restoration of the Tejon's federal recognition, not only to help them retell their history but as documentary evidence proving familial lineage across generations.

Federal recognition is a status awarded to American Indian tribes, recognizing their existence as an independent nation and their inherent sovereignty before contact with European colonizers. It grants a limited form of sovereignty under US law, including a right to (partial) autonomy to self-govern, with forms of financial, social service, and economic development support and help with maintaining or building a tribal land base.[3] While recognition is refused by some as yet another colonial relationship, it is still valued, even if ambivalently, for what this autonomy and these resources can help to maintain and build.

The US government's criteria for recognition are onerous and contradictory though, including documented proof of lineage between current tribal members and their ancestors, and a continuous maintenance of tribal identity and political organization from 1900 to the present.

6.

The photographs that helped to prove the Tejon's descendancy were primarily attributed to the anthropologist, linguist, and ethnomusicologist J. P. Harrington (1884–1961), whose images, sound recordings, vocal notations, and field notes are, like the Federal acknowledgment process itself, ambivalently valued by many of the people whose descendants his materials describe. On one hand, Harrington is remembered as having played a disruptive and disrespectful role in their communities—extracting knowledge with manipulation and bribes; while on the other, the materials that have outlived him represent family and Tribal histories that would not be represented in the same way today. Because Harrington's own archives were notoriously a mess, however, institutions like the Smithsonian received them without much of his own ordering or archival metacommentary to define their meanings.

7.

As the history of art too easily becomes a field that defines everything in relation to itself—to its known actors, objects, conventions and tropes, its institutions, discourses, presumed purposes, and value systems—it often excludes what lies outside of those parameters. For all that it shows, it also erases the people, stories, political and economic realities, the meaningfulness and purposes to which a medium or practice is put, the relationships between images and daily life as they have commingled, shaped, and reshaped the world, if they do not appear relevant or legible to these received values, or if they contradict its reputation as always enlightening or democratizing.

Our class's history thinking would therefore be *through* photography rather than *of* it—watching these images in relation to the life of the Tribe, rather than assessing their relationship to canonical photographers and works—an Edward Curtis, Carleton Watkins, John K. Hillers, and so on. In other words, by practicing a kind of disciplinary disobedience, it would not be to assimilate these photographic objects into the discipline-bound stories of photography as a medium, but to consider the intersection of the medium's objects with social practices and forms of world making.[4]

An archive is more than a finding system or preservation scheme; it is also a story, a discourse, a structuring, a system of definitions, relationships, evidence, and arguments. Understanding this, what we thought we could offer would be archival assistance, helping to shape how the Harrington photographs sit within the Tribe's larger, growing archive, the site of its narrative building, and how that archive's ordering or metanarrative holds them in place.

8.

Where we thought we would encounter a raw photographic archive, in need of our specialized expertise to imbue it with an order and meaning, we found a meaningful archival system already in place. This system was in the form of an extended family tree, built up for and structured by tribal members themselves.

After the photographs' return, the Tribe had passed a set of copies around the community in family album form to notate one another's knowledge of who was who, and to whom each person is related. And it was this ordering of the photographs, this archival logic, that had allowed the images to play their role in the Tribe's historic federal recognition process. This had structured the images into chains of meaning built upon principles of kinship, community formation, a relationship to land, and the preservation of an identity that has survived its attempted erasure. This was already the photographs' interpretive framework, through a methodology that worried little for Western art or anthropology's valorized canons, enunciating instead—epistemologically and historically—the fabric of what, relationally, constitutes them as a tribe.

9.

When we shared this realization with Tribal members, they teased us with, "Okay, whatever with your artsy mumbo-jumbo," continuing, "what we could really use is for you to help us build a timeline of the Tribe's history."

This framed the rest of our curriculum. Beginning with the Tribe's own narrative, as they had formalized it for their recognition process, we looked at cultural and geologic histories of the region, Indigenous constructions of time, and questions of ecology, cosmology, and ontology, and we began to organize selections from their larger visual archive according to Tribal values and principles as they'd been shared with us.[5] The result became a two-part class exhibition at CalArts, followed by an installation at the new Tejon headquarters building, located outside of Bakersfield.

10.

For our class exhibition, we secured two identical, side-by-side galleries on campus. Coming to understand images of and by Indigenous peoples had also required us to understand the long history of Indigenous people's images and likenesses being manipulated and used against them for the cultural capital and colonizing ends of settler colonial states, institutions, and actors. So we considered how, here, an educational institution like CalArts might either repeat or challenge that history.

This meant a hard look at the exploitative roles that artists, ethnographers, and institutions, even the best intentioned, have played in disappearing, misrepresenting, and appropriating Native histories, objects, narratives, and cultural sovereignty. While CalArts was allowing the curricular freedom for this class to be developed and take place, its leadership wasn't moving to take up these questions, reflected most clearly in the lack of initiative around developing an institutional land acknowledgment or a relationship with surrounding Native communities.[6]

At the same time, photographs are continually taken on campus, including ones to document student exhibitions. These photographs become CalArts' intellectual property to use in documentary and promotional materials, while providing documentation to the students. Without any commitment from the institute to act politically or build relationships, we did not want to have our own "well-intentioned" work unwittingly become the institute's symbolic capital, used to help tick diversity boxes for funders and applicants, realizing that the Tejons' recovered images could inadvertently become a part of CalArts' own intellectual property, should they be pictured in exhibition documentation.

This dilemma challenged our ingrained assumption that what is liberatory about art lies always in its ability to *show* things. And we began to wonder what it might mean, on campus, to *not show* things.

11.

One of the visitors to our class, Maria Montenegro, a Chilean scholar based in Los Angeles who works closely with multiple Native communities throughout North and South America, and who was also an important connection to the Tejon Tribe in the first place, had shared with us a way that culturally sensitive objects are displayed/not displayed at the Museum of Anthropology of the University of British Columbia in Vancouver. Among other objects displayed throughout their galleries, objects that have been deemed "culturally sensitive" by collaborating Native communities are placed in illuminated displays behind opaque glass, through which only their silhouettes are visible. These silhouettes allow the objects to be present to the average museum goer while, at the same time, withholding from them full access to the object—the power or imaginary possession of an object that we expect to come through their visual apprehension or interpretation suspended.

Montenegro helped us to understand how this gesture questions the value of the right to know that is presumed within Western Enlightenment epistemology. While an important right of the public against the powerful in many cases, it has also been leveled uncritically as a demand against Indigenous and other historically subordinated or dispossessed communities: to reveal, to expose, to inform, to give up, to forfeit. This performs a kind of ethical violence that mirrors other dispossessions and appropriations by settler colonial and imperialist regimes, and it disregards the sophisticated protocols of stewardship, production, and sharing of knowledge within Indigenous communities.[7]

Inspired by this, we split the side-by-side galleries our class had reserved into two functions. In one, we exhibited what is the primary concern of the institute, artworks by the class's students, curated to reflect upon what they had been individually and collectively learning in the class, through the lens of their own practice and authorship. While one of these artworks related specifically to our engagement with the Tejon community—a watercolor by John Wu of a screen grab of the Native territories of Southern California as depicted on Native Land Digital (https://native-land.ca)—others dealt with questions of identity, land, extractive politics, citizenship, migration, and history, as they refracted through these students' own lives.

While this gallery was open to the public and the documentary practices of the institute, we kept the second gallery locked for the same duration, visitable by appointment only, and we used it as our dedicated workshop space for developing the timeline. In this, as in the class more generally, was a small gesture of redistribution: putting our institutionally and curricularly dedicated time, space, and resources toward the Tribe.

One of the functions of art that we arrived at here was not the power to show, but instead, the powers to withhold, to make space for and mark for the record without overexposing. Contrary to much of Western art value systems and pedagogy, this also taught the power that artists have to forge responsibility and relationship rather than individual autonomy, and to develop a collective and plural voice rather than only a singular, individuated one. Beyond the art school question of "who's your audience," it pointed us instead toward a social question, "who's your constituency, who are your allies or the communities of interpretation and meaning you're prioritizing," while inquiring into the forms of social organization toward which our resources, talent, privilege, and access as artists will be dedicated.

12.

A week after the exhibition and work process, we brought our final version of the timeline to install at the Tejon Tribe's new headquarters—a former elementary school outside of Bakersfield that their reacknowledgment had just allowed them to purchase and begin to renovate. We installed it as a wall display in a large room that would become the library, and we were invited to return the following weekend for their first Tribal gathering there, where we were able to offer this contribution, discuss it, and learn from Tribal members' reactions, while sharing in food and conversation, and share our gratitude for their engaging with us.

13.

In art education language, some would label this a social practice class, in that its methods involved social materials instead of art materials, a practice in social space rather than studio space, or which privileged a social world rather than an art world. But we would reject the terms of that question. Instead of asking "was it social practice," we prefer to ask, "with which social practice(s) of the world did the class engage and align its capacities and abilities?" Rather than center the capitalist-informed practices that Western and globalized art markets privilege, which recuperate the histories, economies, political formations, and epistemologies that fortify a colonial world and teach them back to us as mere questions of aesthetics and "free expression," we tried, however imperfectly, to situate our energies, time, know-how, and learning resources within the social practice of an anticolonial community-making.

As a class composed primarily of students of color with mixed class, linguistic, national, and ethnic backgrounds, looking for different paradigms of art and culture in which to situate their own practices, it offered an important counterpoint to a Eurocentric and institutionally centered history of photography. It recentered what an art history could mean and do, how artworks become meaningful, do things, and contribute to larger reconfiguring of curricula in ways that might be considered decolonial.

14.

A part of what we learned together that *decolonial* means, however, is that it is not a merely symbolic thing, based only on representation, inclusion, or the righting of just any wrong; and it is especially not about exonerating settler subjects or institutions from their own responsibility. Instead, decolonization starts with and comes down to questions of territory, land, and material life as they are affected by colonization—actively undoing that colonization and furthering anticolonial struggles and futures.

Our attempt to challenge what the study of art and photo history means within our art school is important, and it could be decolonial inasmuch as we were challenging the colonial erasures and violences that structure Western art's discourses and, by extension, the organization of cultural capital and other resources facilitated by it. But it could easily become what Eve Tuck and K. W. Yang describe as this kind of "move toward settler innocence": helping an institution to sanitize or (art)wash its hands of its role within or benefit from the persistence of colonial relationships, dispossession, and erasure.[8]

Perhaps this is where the idea of working in reciprocity and in the field became most important, situating and aligning our practice within an effort to support and dialogue with the Tejon Tribe's retelling of its past and the building of its future. This places the site of the decolonial not within our curriculum, program, the students' experience, or the larger institution, but in what the institution's resources do beyond its own reproduction.

Beyond, in the field, for example, we can look at the site and action of the Tribe building its new headquarters. After all, in one visit with the Morgan family, Chairwoman Morgan told us that this former elementary school was the very one in which she and others faced a tremendous amount of racism and discrimination as children, which told us that there was a tremendous amount of power in taking over that building. It was an overcoming of that past, symbolically, but also a recovery of space that had always been their historic territory; a reterritorialization that is a part of re-building a tribal land base. In my most recent contact with Gloria Morgan about this text, she wrote excitedly that the land of the new headquarters has finally been taken into trust by the federal government, meaning it is now "the first piece of 'fully' Tribal land our Tribe has had in 150ish years."[9]

15.

Another thing that came of our work with the Tejon Tribe was CalArts' first introduction to the leadership of the Fernandeño Tataviam Band of Mission Indians, facilitated by our colleague Roberta Uno, who had joined us on one of our visits to the Tejon headquarters and had been in dialogue with the class. From that introduction, and with the recent leadership of CalArts' inaugural fellow for Indigenous Arts and Expression, Chad Hamill/čnaq'ymi (Spokan), CalArts has begun to build a relationship with the Fernandeño Tataviam community, including a series of on-campus cultural education sessions facilitated by Fernandeño Tataviam culture-bearers and curriculum for Fernandeño Tataviam youth through the CalArts Community Arts Partnership (CAP). In November 2022, CalArts officially adopted a tribally endorsed land-acknowledgment statement that was written in direct consultation with Fernandeño Tataviam (Chaguayavitam) leadership. It reads as follows:

> The CalArts main campus sits on the unceded ancestral lands of the Chaguayavitam, the people of Chaguayanga, whose present-day descendants are citizens of the Fernandeño Tataviam Band of Mission Indians. They have been here for millennia and will forever call this place home. Through meaningful partnership and collaboration, CalArts is committed to lifting up their stories, culture, and community.

Notes

1. Arlinda F. Locklear, V. Heather Sibbison, Lawrence S. Roberts, and Suzanne R. Schaeffer, "The Tejon Indian Tribe Request for Confirmation of Status," June 30, 2006, https://tejon.libraries.wsu.edu/collection/tejon-indian-tribe-request-confirmation-status.

2. See Larisa K. Miller, "The Secret Treaties with California's Indians," *Prologue*, fall/winter 2013, https://www.archives.gov/files/publications/prologue/2013/fall-winter/treaties.pdf.

3. "Federal Recognition," National Congress of American Indians, accessed December 6, 2022, https://www.ncai.org/policy-issues/tribal-governance/federal-recognition.

4. While some would suggest this makes our task a different discipline, a social science rather than art, one could also argue that such a limitation of art has its own colonial and racial underpinnings, allowing some groups' histories and meaningfulness to be clear subject matter of the discipline, while others' are excluded and diminished, as one way that the value of "artistic ingenuity" is managed as a white, European-derived attribute or form of cultural capital.

5. Important texts included Mark Rifkin's *Beyond Settler Time: Temporal Sovereignty and Indigenous Self-Determination* (2017); the many authors in the volume edited by Simon J. Ortiz, *Beyond the Reach of Time and Change* (2004); and Roxanne Dunbar-Ortiz's *An Indigenous People's History of the United States*.

6. See Mishuana Goeman, "The Land Introduction: Beyond the Grammar of Settler Colonial Landscapes and Apologies," *Western Humanities Review* 74, no. 2 (fall 2020).

7. This privileging of Indigenous community-based protocols of access, information, and visibility through collaborative methods accompanies the movement to repatriate Native and Indigenous objects. It is what informs the Museum of Anthropology's display politics, and it is reflected in the Murkutu online platform (https://mukurtu.org) and the Local Contexts and Traditional Knowledge (TK) Labels project (https://localcontexts.org), both developed by Jane Anderson and Kimberly Christen as accessible digital tools that, respectively, allow Indigenous communities to archive their own cultural heritage behind their own customizable access protocols, and which allow them to create their own metadata labels for objects held in collections not their own, including at institutions who refuse to collaborate.

8. See Janet Mawhinney, "'Giving Up the Ghost': Disrupting the (Re)Production of White Privilege in Anti-racist Pedagogy and Organizational Change" (1998), as discussed in Eve Tuck and K. Wayne Yang, "Decolonization Is Not a Metaphor," *Decolonization: Indigeneity, Education and Society* 1, no. 1 (2012): 1–40.

9. Gloria Morgan, personal correspondence with author, March 2022.

Thinking through Fragments

SPECULATIVE ARCHIVES, CONTESTED HISTORIES, AND A TALE OF THE PALESTINE ARCHAEOLOGICAL MUSEUM

Dareen Hussein

Dareen Hussein is a writer, curator, and multimedia artist based in Ohio. She is a PhD student in the Department of History of Art at the Ohio State University. Her research interests meet at the intersection of documentary cinema, visual culture, and critical theory.

Abdullah Jaddallah was a native of Jerusalem. He was a devoted husband and father to seven children. Highly favored for his education, Jaddallah was employed by the British army during the years of British Mandate rule in Palestine. Following a successful career with the British military, in which he traveled across the Middle East on various assignments, Jaddallah permanently settled in Jordan. Jaddallah enjoyed drinking his black tea with milk, a ritual adopted during his tenure in the military; tea with milk would become a fond family tradition upheld by successive generations. Two generations later, and from a much farther distance, I was transfixed by the story of my grandfather, a man that I barely knew. Immersed in his memory, my practice as an artist evolved into one that traced lineage, familial histories, and, subsequently, the geopolitical forces which catalyzed our migration. I was left to wonder: What historical circumstances created these conditions? What constraints did he endure, and how did it impact his movement? How am I implicated within this meshwork of history, chance, and fate? Meditating on his story and the complexities of these intersections, a larger research project unfolded; while its major thrusts are historical, it still resides between the poles of fact and fiction.

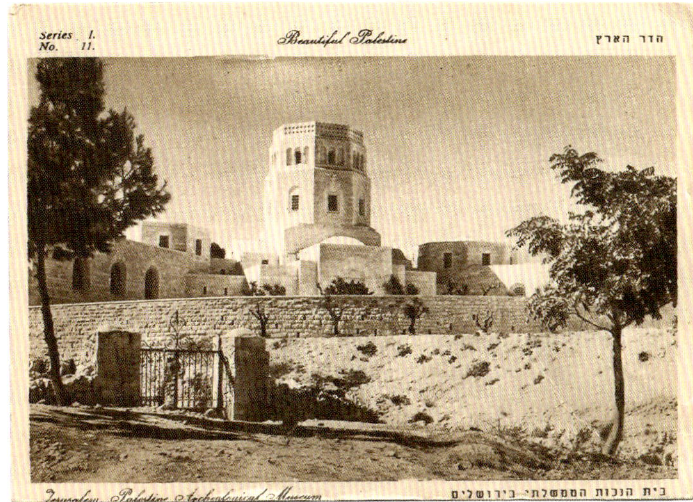

Dareen Hussein, *Beautiful Palestine*, 2019. Archival postcard of the Palestine Archaeological Museum, date and photographer unrecorded. Collection of the author.

In 2014, I stumbled upon the story of the Palestine Archaeological Museum; however, the brief history that I encountered felt wholly insufficient. While the Israel Antiquities Authority foregrounds central figures who oversaw the erection of the museum (like John D. Rockefeller and Henry Breasted, whom I introduce later in this essay), these historical accounts neglect to acknowledge the violent seizure of land that altered the fate of this institution.[1] It is through colonial theft that a more complex picture emerges of the Palestine Archaeological Museum; however, extant histories proffer a depoliticized image of the museum impacted by the occupation of Palestinian land. Meditating on the erasures in the museum's history, I could not help but feel that this story was an allegory for larger, more persistent efforts to suppress Palestinian history. This spurred the creation of *A Partial Restoration of the Palestine Archaeological Museum* (2014–19), a multimedia project that restores the memory of the former Palestine Archaeological Museum in Jerusalem, an institution entrenched in geopolitical turmoil and precarity. *A Partial Restoration of the Palestine Archaeological Museum* is presented as a museological installation, with an exhibition space formerly held online. Before embarking on this project, I had never been to Palestine, nor to the museum, and so my research and art making was carried out at a distance. Due to these constraints, imagination served as a vehicle that stitched together an otherwise fragmented history. Suddenly I stepped into the role of a collector, driven by an impulse to salvage any valuable material I could find. This collection became a bridge to a site that I could not physically access.

A Partial Restoration of the Palestine Archaeological Museum is composed of this makeshift archive; the collection also contains personal, familial heirlooms. By juxtaposing these intimate mementos with historical ephemera, I reclaim authority over personal experience, validating its role in the production of knowledge. Furthermore, it is through these personal histories and experiences that cultural memory is shaped and transmitted. Hours were spent mining and excavating hidden corners of internet marketplaces. I purchased photographs, stamps, and pamphlets from independent eBay and Etsy merchants. Some merchants sold aged books and press clippings as their official business line. Others sold more sporadically, auctioning off junk culled from drawers and cabinets. This collection does not, in fact, belong to the Palestine Archaeological Museum proper; however, it became a speculative archive for the "restored" iteration of the museum that I introduced to the public. Digitized portions of this collection were shared on an exhibition webpage.[2] This website played an integral role in the afterlife of the installation, connecting me to other Palestinian artists, researchers, and writers, all producing their own unique historical and archive-based research projects.[3] The story of the Palestine Archaeological Museum begins with its founding mission: preserving and recording the diverse cultures of the region. However, this vision was stymied in its infancy. By engaging the fraught trajectory of the museum, my project questions the ways that didactic institutions are implicated in the erasure of subjugated peoples and histories. Furthermore, the project confronts the colonial legacies of the institution as we know it. *A Partial Restoration of the Palestine Archaeological Museum* considers the rich possibilities in creating our own imaginative histories, institutions, and archives to bridge gaps in history and distance.

Ruminating on my grandfather's story and the course of his career, it became more pressing to consider how colonial entanglements played out across personal, political, and cultural registers. This led me to broader questions about archaeological practice, soft power, and Western cultural hegemony, and how this impacted Palestine in particular. These forces undoubtedly led to the erection of the Palestine Archaeological Museum. This museum was only one chapter within a larger history of extractive archaeological projects taking place in the Middle East at this time, initiated under the jurisdiction of colonial governments. James Henry Breasted, America's first formally trained Egyptologist and a professor at the University of Chicago, spearheaded the birth of the museum.[4] Breasted also founded the Oriental Institute at the University of Chicago, with generous philanthropic support from John D. Rockefeller. Breasted and Rockefeller formed a mutually beneficial relationship; between 1924 and 1927, Rockefeller supported Breasted's archaeological projects in the Middle East. Breasted insisted that archaeological artifacts had a home in the heart of Jerusalem. Following an unsuccessful attempt to open an Egyptian antiquities museum and research center in Cairo, Breasted proposed opening the Palestine Archaeological Museum in Jerusalem.[5] In January 1927, Rockefeller approved the museum's initial development plans, allotting two million dollars to subsidize construction costs and operating expenses. The British government provided necessary approvals for Breasted and fellow organizers to erect the museum. Austen St. Barbe Harrison, the architect at the helm of the project, combined contemporary European design with local architectural traditions, a style later defined as Mediterranean Modernism. The fusion of these aesthetics asserted British cultural prestige and further expressed its paternalistic role as a colonial occupier.[6] The Palestine Archaeological Museum was built on a hill overlooking the northeast corner of the Old City, officially opening to the public on January 13, 1938.

The museum endeavored to catalog and preserve the rich diversity within the region. But as political tensions heightened, the museum's mission was further out of reach. On April 1, 1948, the British government closed the museum to the public. The high commissioner assembled an international board of trustees to preside over the institution. The makeup of the board traced back to Britain and France, with members also recruited from various antiquities departments across Syria, Egypt, Jordan, and Lebanon, among others. The international board remained effective until November 1966, when King Hussein of Jordan nationalized the museum. During the Six-Day War of 1967, Israeli military forces seized control over the Old City of Jerusalem, and, as a result, the Palestine Archaeological Museum was captured and relinquished to the Israel Antiquities Authority. Bullet holes still line the library walls, serving as a memento from the battle.[7] Following the end of the war, the institution was officially renamed the Rockefeller Museum. It remains unclear who authorized changing the identity of the museum. However, the decision to rename the museum has remained a point of contention. The Rockefeller Museum continues to operate today, instilling a new collective memory throughout the region, one that undermines histories of Palestinian indigeneity.

In 2017, I left Ohio and journeyed to the Rockefeller Museum, which still stands on that hill overlooking the Old City. The edifice is officially deemed a historical landmark; old etchings, markings, and carvings on the museum's facade reveal its conflicted past. Exterior entrance halls direct visitors to the Government of Palestine Department of Antiquities offices. Upon entering through the front doors, patrons encounter the building's floor plan, guiding them to the exhibition halls. Above the map reads "Palestine Archaeological Museum," its maiden name hand-carved into the limestone wall. Wandering through these hallways, the museum felt virtually untouched—its interior halls unfixed and unchanged from the photographs I examined in the archives. While these appearances remained frozen on the surface, the wall text was quietly confrontational, promoting a narrative positioning Palestinians as "visitors" of their native land. The story of the Palestine Archaeological Museum is a painfully layered one, replete with the hauntings of colonial power and historical erasure. In many ways, its story is only a modicum of the more pervasive effacement of Palestinian historical and cultural memory that occurs ad infinitum. This institution was born out of a deep entanglement with colonialism and Western expansion, only to become the spoils of its new colonial occupier. *Palestine* was forcefully removed from its name, much like our names on villages, streets, and maps effectively erased by the violent workings of a settler-colonial regime. Reclaiming this institution's fraught history opened a pathway to creating *A Partial Restoration of the Palestine Archaeological Museum*, an imaginative space that reclaims and resuscitates the elisions of history.

Notes

1. Historical information about the Palestine Archaeological Museum, now named the Rockefeller Museum, is provided in Rachel Kudish-Vashdi and Yuval Baruch, "Historic Background," Israel Antiquities Authority, accessed December 6, 2022, https://www.antiquities.org.il/Article_eng.aspx?sec_id =39&subj_id=156&id=155.

2. As it stands, the exhibition webpage remains in personal archives and is no longer operating online; www.palestinearchaeologicalmuseum.org operated 2014–19.

3. In 2019, I received a note from Yazan Kopty, a writer, oral historian, and National Geographic Explorer. Kopty is currently the lead investigator on an archive-based research project titled *Imagining the Holy*, which examines images of historic Palestine from the National Geographic Society archive. Kopty makes space for the Palestinian community, providing opportunities to collaborate and restore Indigenous knowledge and narratives to the images in the archive. The photographic archive can be accessed on Instagram via @imaginingtheholy.

4. Jeffrey Abt, "Toward a Historian's Laboratory: The Breasted-Rockefeller Museum Projects in Egypt, Palestine, and America," *Journal of the American Research Center in Egypt* 33 (1996): 173–75, https://doi.org/10.2307/40000614.

5. Abt, "Toward a Historian's Laboratory," 104.

6. Yara Saqfalhait, "The Palestine Archaeological Museum (Rockefeller)," *56 Museums,* Palestinian Museum, March 13, 2014, https://www.palmuseum.org/news -1/newsletter/56-museums.

7. Michael Kimmelman, "In Jerusalem, a Museum's Treasures Go Unseen," *New York Times*, September 27, 1990.

Secrets That the Wind Carries Away

Morel Doucet

....

Morel Doucet (born in 1990 in Pilate, Haiti) is a Miami-based multidisciplinary artist and arts educator. His work portrays a contemporary depiction of the Black experience, cataloging a powerful record of environmental decay at the intersection of economic inequity and the commodification of industry, personal labor, and race.

....

I come from a legacy of oral historians and bush medicine magicians who danced in the face of adversity and memory. At dawn, the clouds greeted us with grace and a warm embrace at the base of the mountain. My experience growing up as a Haitian immigrant in South Florida is dedicated to my grandfather, a farmer who supported the education of all his eleven children. Over time, I've collected ephemera and developed a visual language rooted in magical realism to form the world around me. During my adolescence, I assimilated into American culture as a form of survival, while maintaining my Haitian traditions.

> It's midday afternoon. The sun is baking the soil like eggs over easy; the air is filled with the scent of jerk chicken and fried okra. Haitian kompa music beats the ground like caffeinated hammers. The men are gathered around the domino gambling table, making a fuss. The neighborhood boys are playing basketball with the broken milk crate for a hoop, and the girls are busy braiding one another's hair. The block is hot and vibrant—a tightly fitted community where everyone knows one another; some with three generations living in the same household.
>
> —Journal entry, April 12, 2008

Hurricane Katrina struck us hard in 2005, which was the beginning of a neighborhood climate exodus. The gentrifiers and developers followed, combing and canvassing the area like white on rice. Imagine two months without power and only cold showers—the darkness will do something to your soul. The silent chatter of the night stars will fortify your spirit.

My grandfather always said that "God was not the author of confusion and despair," but I wonder: Why he be putting us through all these obstacles so often? Aren't we creatures of free will and our own destiny?

The community I grew up in, La Petite Haïti (Little Haiti), sits on one of Miami's highest elevations. Most of the city's neighborhoods are, on average, seven feet above sea level, with other points going as high as fourteen feet above. Because of this, developers are aggressively gentrifying La Petite Haïti, lobbying for new zoning laws and higher property taxes on its residents. Miami is on the brink of experiencing a significant ecological disaster since the reconfiguration of the Everglades.

The Everglades is itself a natural wonder, a living ecosystem of biodiversity that is in danger of being consumed by the rising sea or decimated by development. Part of an interconnected system of waterways and channels to the Atlantic, coastal areas are steadily eroding, blanching coral reefs, while the Everglades struggles to sustain itself. Miami-Dade is undergoing continuous infrastructure development while preparing for conflict between land and sea. The Everglades seems to be caught in the middle between this earth's past and the idealism of American progress.

Miami's affluent residents can easily relocate, as they did during hurricanes Andrew (1992) and Irma (2017); they have the resources to escape such environmental instability. But what of those residents from low-income communities such as Overtown, Liberty City, and Little Haiti? How are these residents supposed to navigate a city destined to succumb to the sea? Are residents even aware of the impact climate change will have within our children's lifetime?

These questions, and a sense of wonder, have led me toward an archaeological study beneath the ocean's surface. I study motifs that reference a colonial past of my Haitian identity. I examine current events, the impact of environmental destruction across the globe, and the uncertainty of existence. My studies ultimately led to a phrase from my journal: "Water grieves in the six shades of death." This is an allegory for understanding those truths that may make us uncomfortable but are necessary for growth, change, and spiritual transformation.

Water has been a primary element since the formation of the universe. Water has been continuous within each earth cycle and during the six great extinctions. Water quenches the thirst, sustains life, and has displaced entire civilizations. Today, water *grieves*, as we've caused more harm than good. We pollute our drinking waters, dump trash and human detritus into streams, rivers, and waterways.

As an artist and educator, I started to envision ways of sharing insight with Miami's most vulnerable communities while navigating the changing landscape around me. I want residents to understand the reality of climate gentrification and potential displacement due to climate change and rising sea levels. This internal search led me to create a series of mixed-media illustrations exploring the phrase "water grieves in the six shades of death." This series examines the realities of climate gentrification, migration, and displacement within South Florida's Black diaspora. The title juxtaposes water as a body containing historical trauma, cultural dissonance, and memory—preserved in the flora and fauna of Miami's natural landscape.

Other works such as *Maroons over Green Mountains* examine ideas of migration, displacement, and movement between Miami Beach and the Caribbean. *Maroons . . .* features the profile of a Black man embellished with flora and fauna, which I gathered from public parks near South Beach. I then overlaid and silk-screened these pieces over the Black figure. The portrait is regal yet firm, standing behind Black fencing, a testimony to overcoming Miami Beach's segregated past—a time when Black residents were only allowed to be on the beach as domestic workers, not for leisure.

Butterflies float and scatter within the piece and foreground as metaphors for freedom, resilience, and the plight of Black and Brown people in Miami Beach. The titular Maroons give homage to the Indigenous people of Jamaica, Haiti, Dominican Republic, and Cuba, all communities establishing roots in South Florida.

Another work, *Every Horizon Line Is a Double Metaphor Waiting to Dispel the Truth*, is an active critique of the global institutions that make the vices of skin bleaching a viable option and a prevalent one throughout the Caribbean. The work is embellished with various layers of flora and fauna stripped of their natural color pigment through a chemical process, which removes the pulpy part of the leaf, leaving behind a clear fibrous skeletal structure. The method of distilling the leaf pigments parallels that of skin bleaching and cream application. The work is silk-screened with imagery of plants gathered from Allapattah, a Dominican American neighborhood located in Miami, Florida, that has deep-rooted issues of colorism, racism, and climate gentrification.

As I illustrate Miami's changing communities, my series of mixed-media drawings and collage portraits will reflect the resilience of residents from Little Haiti, Overtown, and Allapattah. As I explore each neighborhood,

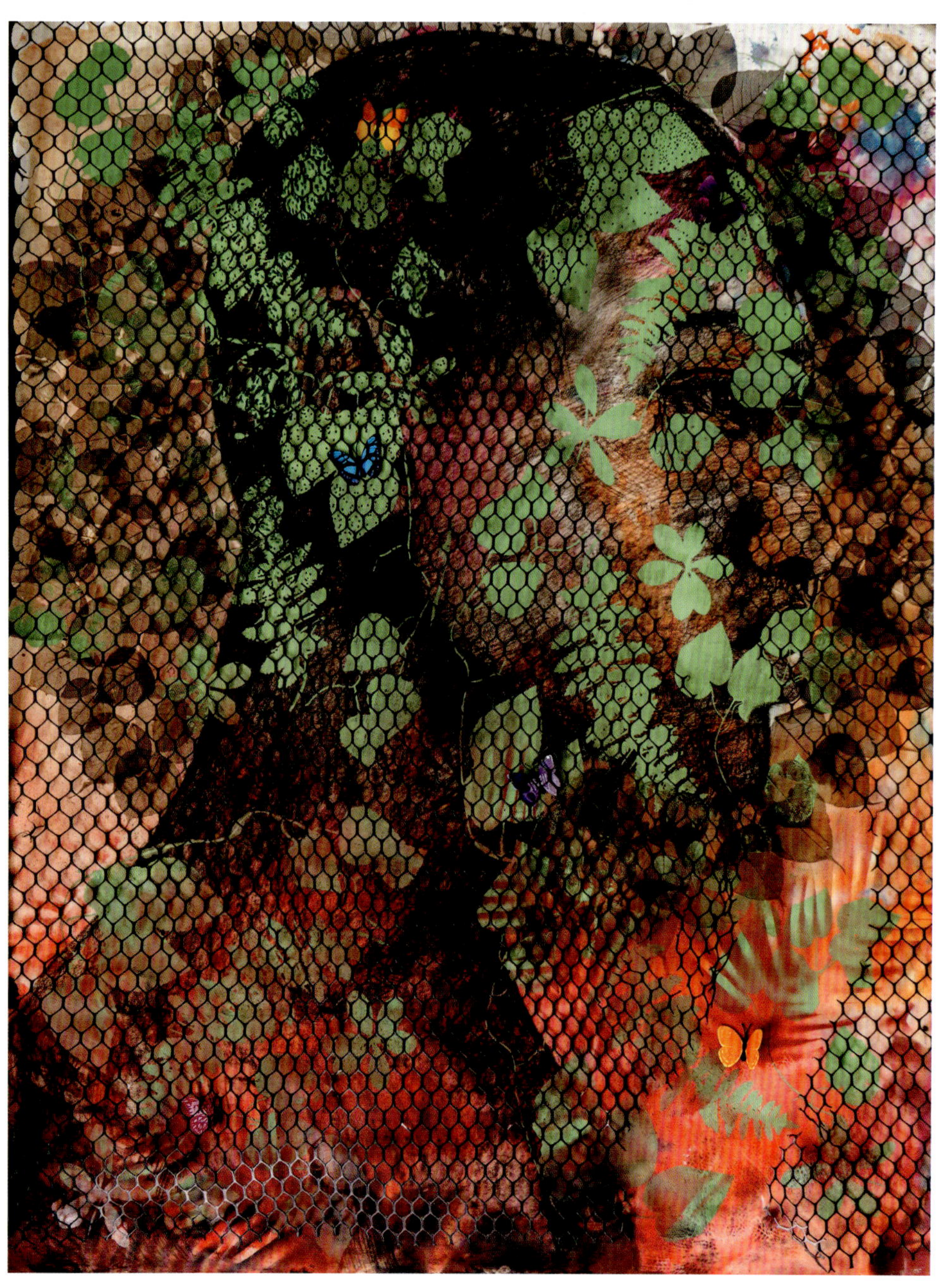

Morel Doucet, *Maroons over Green Mountains*, 2019.
Assorted charcoal densities, aerosol black, flora and fauna,
and found fencing, 44 × 55 in. Photo: Pedro Wazzan.

I see how sacred these areas are to those of us who live here. The land and sea, our shared history, legacies, and secrets connect one another.

Today these communities are changing; kompa and twoubadou music no longer flow through the small bungalow houses on Fifty-Fourth Street. The men have all disappeared from their domino tables, which have been replaced with new, modern architecture painted (ironically) white—the absence of color on the spectrum. The roosters no longer crow or roam the streets in the early morning. They've been replaced with pristine, manicured green grass. Teslas, Mercedes, and Range Rovers line the driveways of my old neighborhood, La Petite Haïti.

Historic Overtown, one of the first Black settlements in Miami, was a center for Black life and community. Now Overtown is overshadowed by fifty-story buildings overlooking downtown. The warm bowl of Dominican sancocho no longer lingers in the air; instead, all these communities have been stripped and robbed of their culture and voice. With time, only the wind will know the secrets of joy, laughter, and baby showers nestled in these coterie pockets. I write for these silent communities, I write midnight lullabies from memory, of songs and dreams to hold on to when their streets no longer welcome them. The humans of Black and Brown life navigating the unfamiliar and uncertain; a world within a world.

Ohiŋniyaŋ ded wati kte

THIS PLACE WILL ALWAYS BE HOME

Angela Two Stars

Angela Two Stars is a public artist and curator. She is the director of All My Relations Arts, in Minneapolis, Minnesota. Angela is an enrolled member of the Sisseton Wahpeton Oyate and lives in Saint Paul with her husband and three children.

Our language is our identity. It grounds us within our place on this land. I use my platform as an artist to highlight language revitalization. Most Indigenous languages are endangered; therefore, I focus on incorporating the Dakota language into my artwork. It is an oral language translated into a written language on the shores of Bde Maka Ska in the early 1800s.[1] Dakota language is the first language of the state of Minnesota, whose name comes from the Dakota word Mni Sota: the land where the water reflects the sky. Our identity as a state is rooted in Dakota language. That knowledge is what I bring into my work as a public artist.

Growing up, my dad told me the story of how we got our last name, Two Stars, from my great-great-grandfather Solomon Two Stars. He recounted how, when our people were being registered onto the reservation, a lot of Natives were given names by the white soldiers because the Natives could not speak English, and when asked what their name was, would give their Dakota name. Solomon Two Stars, when asked his name, said, Wicaŋhpi Nuŋpa. The white agent didn't understand and was about to make up a name when Solomon said, "Wait, I can speak English" (he had been taught by missionaries that had come through the reservation). "Wicaŋhpi Nuŋpa means Two Stars." Still, he was told he needed to pick a *Christian* name, a first name, so he chose Solomon from the Bible, because Solomon was wise. As a young girl who used to get teased for such a unique last name, learning this story gave me a sense of great pride, knowing that my ancestor was able to retain his identity in our language, and that I carried this proud name. "Who was Solomon Two Stars's dad?" I asked my father. "Maḣpiya Wicasta, Cloud Man," my dad would say.

It wasn't until early 2017, when I was traveling to Minneapolis to participate in an artist talk at All My Relations Gallery, that I once again saw the name Cloud Man. It was within a call for artists for public art that was to honor Maḣpiya Wicasta and the village Ḣeyata Otuŋwe on the shores of Bde Maka Ska.

This was a great opportunity to advance as a professional artist, while also connecting with my history through meeting extended tiospaye (family) and learning more about my ancestors. Being selected for this public art project was serendipitous—not only was I a Dakota artist, but I was also a descendant of the Dakota leader the public art was honoring.

After my selection, I traveled to Minneapolis for a site visit. The lake was then known as Lake Calhoun (1839), after former Vice President John C. Calhoun, who was widely known for strongly defending slavery. The lake was in the process of a legal dispute around restoring its original name, Bde Maka Ska (White Earth Lake).

The agricultural village at Ḣeyata Otuŋwe came about after Dakota chief Maḣpiya Wicasta endured a particularly hard snowstorm in which he and others in his hunting party were overtaken and forced to lie underneath their furs for three days and three nights.[2] During that time, Cloud Man was unaware if those in his party were alive or dead. He recalled the urging of the fort agent Teliferro to adopt farming. This pressure to adopt farming was another method of forcing the Dakota people into assimilation. Knowing that the traditional ways of survival were becoming more and more obsolete, especially with the decimation of the buffalo, Cloud Man decided to try something new. For ten years, the agricultural village at Ḣeyata Otuŋwe thrived, along with the neighboring villages, because although farming was not standard for Dakota, generosity was, and the village shared their abundance with those around them, ensuring the survival of many. This was at the disapproval of the agents, who admonished the Dakota for sharing their crops, but being Dakota was who they were, and that was not going to change even as their survival methods were adapting.

Using this newly gained knowledge of my ancestor, my assignment was to incorporate art into the new pedestrian sidewalk that would run alongside the gathering space at the location of Ḣeyata Otuŋwe. During my site visit, I walked along the lake and observed the relatives that shared the lake with us. This lake was home to birds, fish, and other animals; we, the humans, were visitors. I wanted to share the names of these relatives in my work. So I designed ten simple images of native plant medicines and animals in triptych patterns along the sidewalk with the Dakota name for each image, created to share the Dakota language with the five million visitors that come to Bde Maka Ska every year. I lived in Michigan at the time and frequently traveled to the Twin Cities for meetings related to the public art project. The more I came to Minneapolis, the more I wished I could stay.

I grew up on a small, rural reservation in northeast South Dakota. It wasn't until I was in college that I learned of the Dakota Uprising of 1862 that led to the exile of the Dakota people from Minnesota. I had an "aha" moment when I learned of that piece of my history. "So that's how we ended up here," I thought. This history was kept from me too. I did not grow up in a traditional way; I was kept from my language, the result of both my grandmothers being victims of boarding school. I moved away from the reservation in my early twenties and didn't return until 2013. It was then that I reconnected with my culture and language, and I decided I would share the Dakota language in the way that I could, through art. I have moved frequently, and of all the places I lived, none felt like home. It always felt temporary. I wouldn't hang pictures on the wall or even make friends because, "Why bother?" I would think. "I'm not going to be here that long to invest in my surroundings." That changed after my art was installed, I was offered a job in Minneapolis, and in December 2017, my family and I moved to the Twin Cities. There was an instant connection with the land. I felt settled, like, "Here is where I can invest in my future; here is where I can plant my roots." I had never felt that way about a place before. The reservation never felt like home; I had been desperate to leave for as long as I could remember, and now, I realize, the reservation was not our home, that was just where they had put us. This land—this was home. I could feel it. I felt so comfortable in my surroundings. I have a blood memory of this place, and knowing that this is where my ancestors lived, it makes sense that it felt so comfortable. I came home.

I enjoyed witnessing the public interact with my artwork. One day, a young man walking with two other friends looked down at the art, looked up, and said, "Hmm, Waŋbdi." What joy I felt that my artwork got this stranger to speak Dakota. How gratifying it was to hear the Dakota language spoken aloud. My goal was to create language pieces accessible to all, because if you want a language to survive, you have to share it.

The dispute over the name change finally ended, when the Minnesota Supreme Court ruled in May 2020 that the name of the lake would remain Bde Maka Ska. The name of the public artwork created by myself, Sandy Spieler, and Mona Smith is called *Zaniyaŋ Yutȟókča*, meaning Brave Change. I thought about the story of Maȟpiya Wicasta—how he considered the future survival of his people and how, with the change that was coming with colonization, he decided to do something different and adopt the colonizer's method of agriculture, which sustained his people and those in neighboring villages for years. It took courage for him to try something new. I thought of the people that presently had to deal with the name change of this lake; a familiar and, for some, beloved Lake Calhoun was now restored to Bde Maka Ska. It would take bravery to accept this change and acknowledge the full history of this place. There is a Dakota phrase in the public art that states, "Ohiŋniyaŋ ded wati kte," which translates to "This place will always be home." This phrase represents everyone who grew up loving this lake and affirmed for those Dakota who had been in exile, myself included, that yes indeed, this place will always be home.

Notes

1. Ella Deloria, Aŋpétu Wašté Wiŋ (1889–1971), was instrumental in the protection of the Dakota language, particularly through her 1941 book *Dakota Grammar*, written in collaboration with Franz Boas.

2. Gwen Westerman and Bruce White, *Mni Sota Makoce: The Land of the Dakota* (St. Paul: Minnesota Historical Society Press, 2012), 104–7.

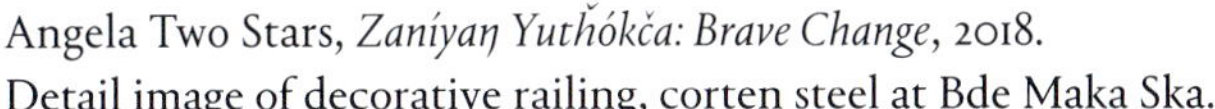

Angela Two Stars, *Zaníyaŋ Yutȟókča: Brave Change*, 2018.
Detail image of decorative railing, corten steel at Bde Maka Ska.

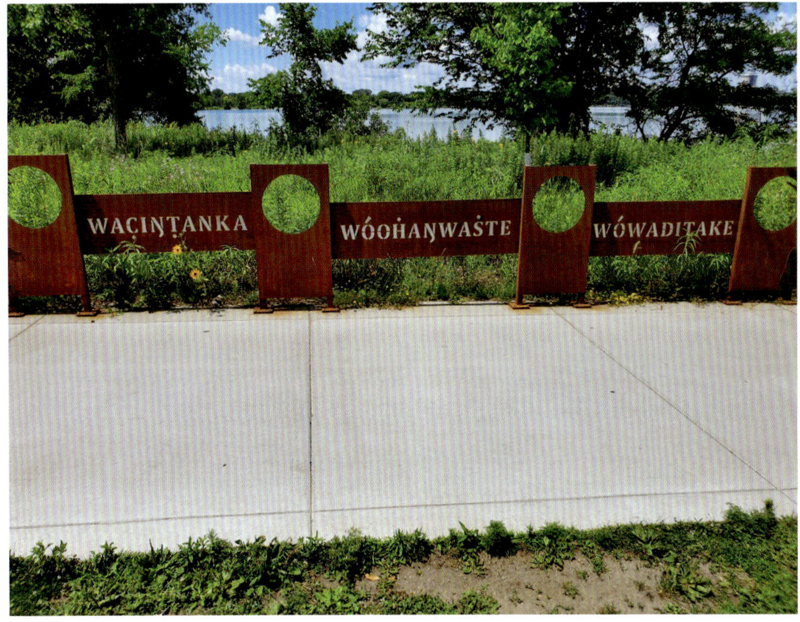

Ballers

Mel D. Cole

. . . .

NYC-based, Syracuse, New York–raised, self-taught photographer **Mel D. Cole** is one of hip-hop's most accomplished and celebrated photographers, with a career spanning almost twenty years. He released his first book, called *GREAT: Photographs of Hip Hop,* in February 2020. Mel is also known for his work in nightlife, travel, and street documentary.

. . . .

In early 2020, I focused my lens on documenting the pandemic. But when George Floyd was killed, I dedicated myself to documenting the Black Lives Matter uprising. I named this image *Ballers* because of the obvious, but also because of what ballers do! A lot of real ballers took over the Robert E. Lee monument soon after the murder of George Floyd. Ballers make shit happen! A baller is someone that started at the bottom and has now made it to the top! Ballers also know that the work is never done, and to continue to have status, they must keep at the hard work that got them there.

What's happening with the monument wasn't necessarily a renegotiating; it was more of a takeover, but still, it created a new map and a new name. The uprising created a different way to think about spaces and new ways to think about our pasts and our futures. Ballers ball!

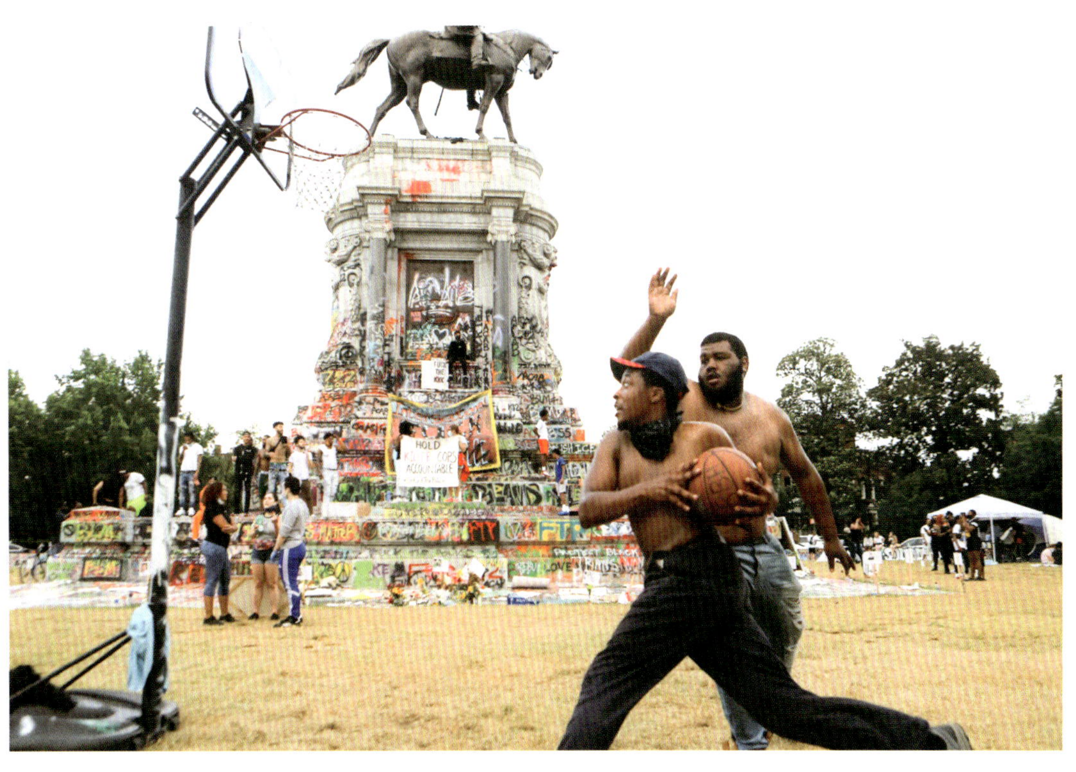

Mel D. Cole, *Ballers*, June 20, 2020, Richmond, Virginia.
Digital photograph.

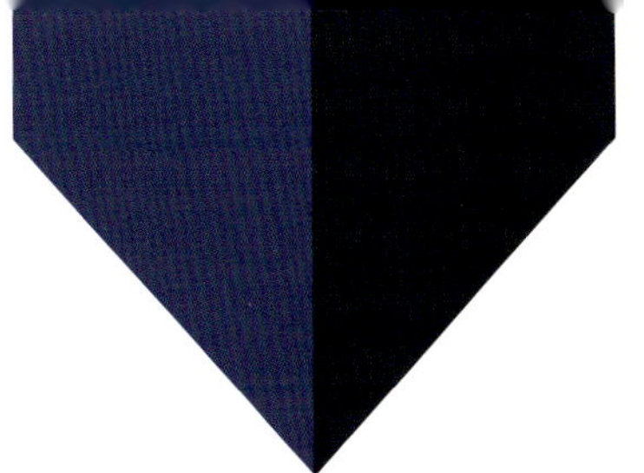

LIVING OUR LEGACY

ANCESTRAL KNOWLEDGE AS RADICAL FUTURITY

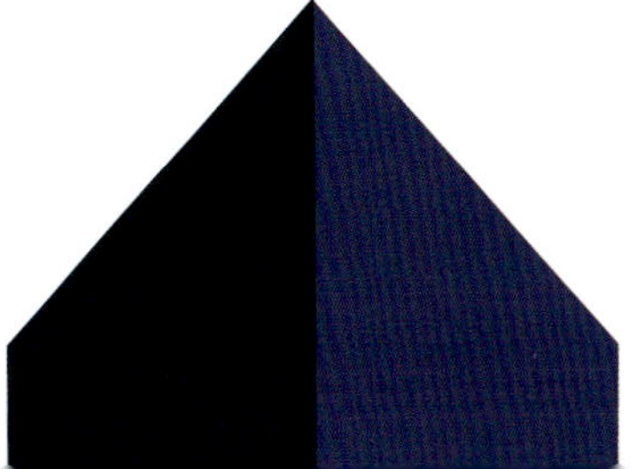

Introduction

Kapena Alapaʻi

Kapena Alapaʻi (Kanaka Maoli) is the codirector of ArtChangeUS and a visual artist and organizer based in Kona, Hawaiʻi. He is a graduate of Ka Haka ʻUla ʻo Keʻelikōlani Hawaiian Language College and sits as board president of Kahilu Theatre in Waimea.

> It's 2019, and I'm thinking
> of 1619 so I'm thinking past
> and thinking past them to
> think of us now and of
> then and now, then's
> next, what stay
> passing.
> —Douglas Kearney, "1619"

When you hear the words *ancestor* and *futurity*, where does your mind wander? Does it first recall the past or skip to the future? What would it mean to do both simultaneously, in a loop, calling backward for the lessons once again before us, for the morals once embodied, once natural, now buried deep within cell walls? If given a linear timeline to stand on, which direction would you face? Those with reconciled pasts and unencumbered access to its archives march forward, a path so clear its destination can be taken for granted. Others, whose pasts have been disrupted, severed, or stolen, encounter time differently—kinked, entwined, out of sequence, hands outstretched in search of connection. Our path and orientation on the timeline are influenced by our connection to ancestral history, self-determination, and legacy-mindedness, paving the way to reconciling our pasts and bridging our histories with our futures.

Douglas Kearney's "1619" exclaims, "Steal away, steal away, go. The song about going till gone. And I think about what comes after 1619. After what was stolen." For many people of color and Indigenous culture bearers, we can place a finger on a cultural disruptor, a point in time that altered the course of our people's past and their future. Our authors offer "that 1619 darkness," the 1893 Kingdom of Hawai'i Overthrow, the 1921 Tulsa Race Massacre, and the 1973 Occupation of Wounded Knee as examples. These, along with so many other traumatic events including the erasure of Indigenous languages, ripple through generations and into the future, manifesting in our family histories as shame, denial, guilt, rage, and abuse. With them, a severing occurs between the cultural past, present, and future, ripping ancestry from progeny. However, through that pain, there is strength and resiliency—a resolve that is maintained, located deep within our blood, a cellular memory, calling us back to heal the point of disconnect.

Jonathan Kay Kamakawiwo'ole Osorio and **Jamaica Heolimeleikalani Osorio** (Kanaka Maoli), noted scholars, activists, educators, and, most importantly, a father and daughter duo, share with us this dilemma of orientation, trusting that the keys (yes, multiple) to our liberation already exist in the lessons and stories of our ancestors, both contemporary and modern. They ask us to reject English-only histories in order to center an Indigenous retelling as a means to unlock ancestral knowledge embedded in our native languages and reconnect with the future our ancestors once held for us. Language erasure has been the universal tool of colonizers since . . . well, since forever, and it is an unfortunate connection many Indigenous peoples share. Poet **Yanina Chicas** openly shares her frustration at the "stripping" of her Indigenous language in intermixed lines of English and Spanish, calling both languages and their wielders out for their role in colonizer warfare. And yet the heart that beats for its tribe is strong and unyielding.

Also discussing temporal orientation is Art-ivist **Queen Quet Marquetta L. Goodwine**, elected chieftess of the Gullah/Geechee Nation in South Carolina. She brings us the image of a Sankofa bird, firmly rooted facing forward with a neck arched toward the past, symbolizing for her a rootedness to the place of her ancestors' enslavement and long-later emancipation. Embedded within this painful past, Queen Quet calls on us to listen closer for an ancestral drumbeat, a steady source of inspiration, connection, strength, and power in her community.

The AIM song, sung in times of joy, protest, and solidarity, exhibits just how resilient the message of Indigenous Pride is. Artist and composer **Elisa Harkins** (Cherokee/Muscogee) gives us a look into the history of the AIM song from Wounded Knee, South Dakota, to Tulsa, Oklahoma, and how when challenged at an Indigenous Peoples March in 2018 in Washington, DC, the song's message endured beyond ignorance, intolerance, and injustice. Black Fire, a collection of films by filmmakers **Kevin Jerome Everson** and **Claudrena N. Harold**, gives us insight into Black student life on the University of Virginia (UVA) campus in Charlottesville from the 1970s to the present. Intentionally steering clear of "summative statements on the Black experience" and "images of spectacular blackness," Everson and Harold locate stories of comradery through protest and the power of peer pressure for accountability and collective benefit.

And while oral and visual language and histories are the ancestral keys to some communities' radical futures, others unlock theirs through movement. **Cleo Parker Robinson** tells of an innate need to learn movement as a language to celebrate self, heal past pains, and connect internationally with others of similar vibrations. In conversation with her son, **Malik Robinson**, they share how innovations in movement contribute to a shared well of cultural assets "even as the new generation comes forward to inspire us all." **Nobuko Miyamoto**, **Kamau Ayubbi**, and **Asiyah Ayubbi** continue this notion of movement as language that connects, in a three-generation conversation on art, activism, and storytelling. Nobuko shares her story from the 1970s, '80s, '90s, and early 2000s leading to the work of FandangObon—not a fusion, but a "conversation" between cultures. "When we first put Fandango and Obon together, the community saw it. And when we invited African Americans in, they saw it too. They brought their element of drum from their practice; it was like synchronizing heartbeats."

In her work *These Roots Run Deep*, **Dyani White Hawk** (Sičáŋǧu Lakota) brings forward this idea of cultural continuity, pointing to the dynamic shifts a living culture takes in response to its environment and interactions with other cultures. With special care, living cultures still remain ancestrally rooted. An example of this is given to us by **Lori Lea Pourier** (Oglala Lakota), who shares how Lakota basket weaving and song traditions accompany both childbirth and death. Stewarded by Lakota culture bearers, basket weaving and singing songs were saved from the reach of Indian boarding schools. Pourier shines lights on the resiliency of her community and the strength of the next generations.

In a conversation between **Maribel Alvarez** and **Ofelia Zepeda** (Tohono O'odham), we further explore the pathways in which wisdom manifests through generations of living cultures through poetry and language. For Zepeda, the stories and sayings passed down by her mother are imbued with values and lessons derived from generational experiences. Especially in times of adversity, "the lesson they would have derived from it all was that you have to adapt and change to survive and go forward as a culture. And if my parents themselves had not lived through those catastrophes, they would have known the stories through their own parents and their grandparents, and so forth. They had that kind of memory."

These artists and culture bearers move forward without fear into the past, searching for the stolen faces of ancestors. **Elizabeth M. Webb** shares with us her journey to find her great-grandmother Paradise, unearthing stories and anecdotes from long-lost relatives. "She is, all at once, present and absent, the past and the future as imagined present." Webb shows us how timelines manifest physically on our streets, visible through a lens one can only inherit from family. "No longer looking for an image, I trace her edges in the landscape that witnessed her life." **Allison Akootchook Warden** (Iñupiaq) lives with the lens her ancestors gave her. Creating work from her cabin in the Arctic Circle, she asks, "How do we cultivate spaces and live practices that invite the ancestors in, allowing them to cocreate with us as artists?" Warden embodies the term *living our legacy*, composing songs and dances that are both new and traditional—yes, both, simultaneously. **Wendy Red Star** (Apsáalooke Crow) poses in a photograph with her daughter, bringing both an intergenerational element and a lesson on the matrilineal customs of the Apsáalooke Crow Nation. In using the term *feminism*, Wendy provokes a conversation not only around the imbalances of power between men and women generally, but also how, unlike Western cultures, many Indigenous cultures traditionally center women.

Ofelia Esparza, a sixth-generation altarista working out of East Los Angeles, shares the art and importance of the traditional Noche de Ofrenda ceremony, part of the annual Día de los Muertos celebration. In the wake of upheaval and loss, the altar and ofrendas (offerings) become an active site for personal and communal support. "We all need a time for reflection, for gratitude, for healing, and yes, a time for social awareness as a community. As we honor our loved ones, we remember our ancestors who are always with us."

In the wake of "progress," we peer through cultural remains, looking for knowledge, for understanding, for healing, for strength, for the point on the timeline at which we can restore the tether. The point at which we finally understand just how wildly nonlinear the timeline really is. Once we grasp the simultaneity of our orientation, we march alongside, in connection with, to, for, and as our ancestors, into a radically shifted future of our own imagination.

And, if we look to our periphery, we will surely see each other on our journeys, because we are not just one nation, we are many nations; we are made up of peoples, diasporas, layered histories, and entangled futures.

These Roots Run Deep

Dyani White Hawk

Dyani White Hawk (Sičáŋǧu Lakota) is a visual artist based in Minneapolis, Minnesota. White Hawk, a 2019 United States Artists Fellow, has work included in public collections such as the Museum of Modern Art, Whitney Museum of American Art, Walker Art Center, Crystal Bridges Museum of American Art, and Pennsylvania Academy of Fine Arts Museum, among others.

As a woman of Sičáŋǧu Lakota and European American ancestry, I was raised within Native and urban American communities. My work reflects these cross-cultural experiences through the combination of modern abstract painting and abstract Lakota art forms, weaving together conceptual influences, mediums, and aesthetics from each respective history.

By highlighting the strength and legacy of Indigenous art within a conceptual painting practice, the audience is invited to consider perceived parallel histories as truly intertwined. The complexity of visual and conceptual references encourages conversations that challenge the lack of representation of Native arts and people in the mainstream while highlighting the truth and necessity of equality and intersectionality.

The beaded lanes in *These Roots Run Deep* emerge in parallel rows from each side of the canvas, representing traditional porcupine quillwork and beadwork motifs. As they move across the canvas, they begin twisting and turning. This transition can be perceived as becoming unraveled and disheveled, or freer and more fluid. The shifting nature of the lanes represents cultural continuity. A living culture cannot be stagnant. Culture will inevitably shift to reflect the current environment, and while it may look different over time, with care, it can remain strongly rooted to ancestral origins.

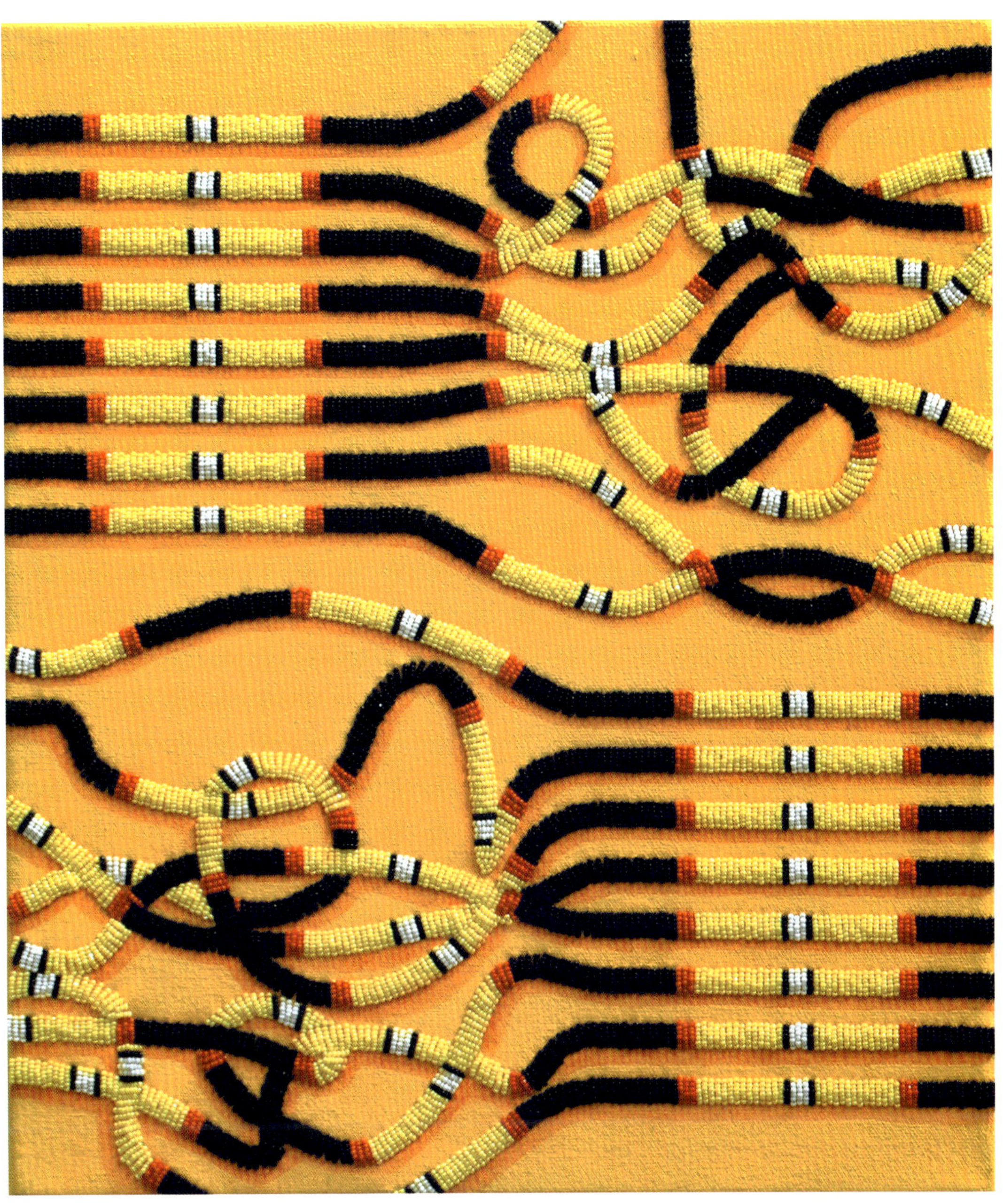

Dyani White Hawk, *These Roots Run Deep*, 2010.
Seed beads, thread on canvas, 11.5 × 10 in.

The Future Is Ancient

Allison Akootchook Warden

Allison Akootchook Warden is an Iñupiaq installation artist born in Fairbanks, Alaska, with close ties to Kaktovik, Alaska. Her work *siku/siku* debuted at the Arctic Arts Summit in Harstad, Norway, in 2017. In 2016, she debuted *Unipkaaġusiksuġuvik (the place of the future/ancient)* at the Anchorage Museum.

How do we cultivate spaces and live practices that invite the ancestors in, allowing them to cocreate with us as artists? How would you react if your great-great-great-grandparent materialized in front of you and needed attention and care? How would you care for them, feed them, introduce them to you and your modern world? What kind of space would they feel most comfortable in and how would your group dynamics change to allow for their wisdom and perspectives to shine through?

I have a photo of my great-great-grandparents that I keep affixed to the back of my laptop and my phone case. In the photo, it looks as if they are fully aware that this image will travel into the future, into the world of their great-great-granddaughters and grandsons. It is as if they are creating a portal through the photograph toward me; all of what they want to communicate is right there, in their eyes, their posture, the energy and love that they exude.

This photo has become the cornerstone of all of my artistic work and my approach to creating work not only for them but also for the now and future. I think of their lives, how they lived on the land, served their communities, and embedded stories within their children—stories that still live within me. Stories that were passed on for a reason.

It was in 2016 that I was given the space to create a ceremonial house in the Anchorage Museum. *Unipkaaġusiksuġuvik (the place of the future/ancient)* is an Iñupiaq ceremonial house that exists in the space between the hyperfuture and the superancient. I was physically present as part of the installation for the almost 380 hours that the museum was open while the exhibit was up. There were artifacts from the museum present, as well as objects from my own family that were passed down to me and objects 3D replicated by the museum under my direction.

Part of the ceremonial house included a modified traditional sleeping bench, which was used long ago to perform our bench dances, which are still popular today. I knew that I wanted to activate the space with a traditional Iñupiaq dance group. It made the most sense to start my own group in Anchorage; but I needed a coleader, someone who knew the songs and how to drum and dance.

I put the call out on social media and was introduced to my own cousin, Isaiah Patkutaq McKenzie, who was sixteen years old at the time and had a knowledge of over 250 traditional Iñupiaq songs, many of which he composed himself. We met and the Kisaġvigmiut Traditional Dancers was born. Our first practice was at the Anchorage Museum, and over the course of the two months of the installation, we rehearsed and performed in the modern ceremonial space, taking care for the women to dance the bench dances on the sleeping benches with the men drumming on the floor, in a way that we had never before seen or experienced.

We learned many songs together, and it was the new songs and dances that Isaiah had composed for ceremonial purposes that had us the most excited as a group. New ceremonies, new dances, new songs, yet all still traditional. Our relationship with the Anchorage Museum strengthened as Isaiah became the sole leader in 2019, and practices continue in Anchorage.

My time with the group deepened my curiosity about how traditional songs came to be, how songs were utilized in the everyday life of my great-great-grandparents' time. I had heard of personal songs—songs to change the weather, songs for hunting animals, songs for protection, songs for community dances, ceremonial songs, and many other types of songs. My research showed me that, not too long ago, every Iñupiaq seemed to have at least one personal song, and almost everyone in the community would participate in the community singing and dancing.

When I travel to my tribal home of Kaktovik in the Arctic Circle, I participate in the community dancing and singing with the Kaktoviġmiut Traditional Dancers, and it is so much fun to laugh and be laughed at as I sometimes struggle to remember all the motions in the right order.

I wanted a song to come through me—a traditional song, not my modern songwriting that I do and perform as a rap artist, but one that would be my personal song. A short song that I would sing that would be just mine, for my use. I created an expectation within myself that at some point the song would come, and my cousin Isaiah encouraged me, as he started to receive the songs and motions for the dances at a very young age. He was confident that my song would eventually arrive.

My personal song finally did come through, and many more songs continue to flow through me. When going back through my song memos to find the very first song that came, I was surprised to remember that my first Iñupiaq song arrived while I was on a plane leaving Atlanta after being part of my first session of the Art Equity 2019 cohort. Listening to the song, I remembered that at that moment, I needed the song for my spirit and what my spirit was going through after being part of the training. I recorded myself singing the song quietly while the person in the aisle seat slept soundly nearby. These songs have become my meditation, a way to connect to my ancestors one-on-one and as a community, and I am very thankful that the songs finally did arrive.

Today, I live in a one-room cabin where I haul water each day, in and out, and use an outhouse for a restroom. I have a huge Rubbermaid tub that leans in a corner when not in use, and I boil water to take a bath, then lovingly drag the tub outside to let out my bathwater onto the land. After waking, I meditate, and then I pick up my Mother's drum and start by singing my personal song, and then I wait to see what songs want to be present, as I imagine my ancestors sitting behind me, ready to join in and sing.

When I was a young girl, I remember an elder who lived in a cabin similar to mine. He had a radio, an oil lamp, and a drum, and he also hauled water that he would heat over a woodstove. I remember the quality of air that the elders around me cultivated. I remember exactly how their homes felt and how they impressed upon me their ways of life and being in the world. Today, I strive to re-create these spaces in my daily life. I talk to my great-grandparents and my great-great-grandparents when I need advice, and I tell them about parts of my day, about things that weigh on my heart.

Remember in the beginning, how I asked what you would do if your great-great ancestor arrived today, in your world, in physical form? You reflected on how you would care for them, how you would introduce them to the world, how you would nurture and feed their bodies, minds, and spirits. Now, like a Polaroid film that develops when you shake it just a bit, look in the mirror and imagine yourself as your ancestor, here in this modern world. Take care of yourself the way that you would if they were here; nurture yourself the way you would them; love yourself the way you would show love to them; be patient with yourself the way you would be patient with them.

You are the living representative of your ancestral lines. You are the ancestor from the future, peering back through time and forward through time with your intent gaze and wisdom. As an artist, cultivate these ancestral spaces and make work for not only your great-great-grandchildren, but also for your great-great-grandparents. You are the connective portal in the now. Cultivate a space for your song to come through.

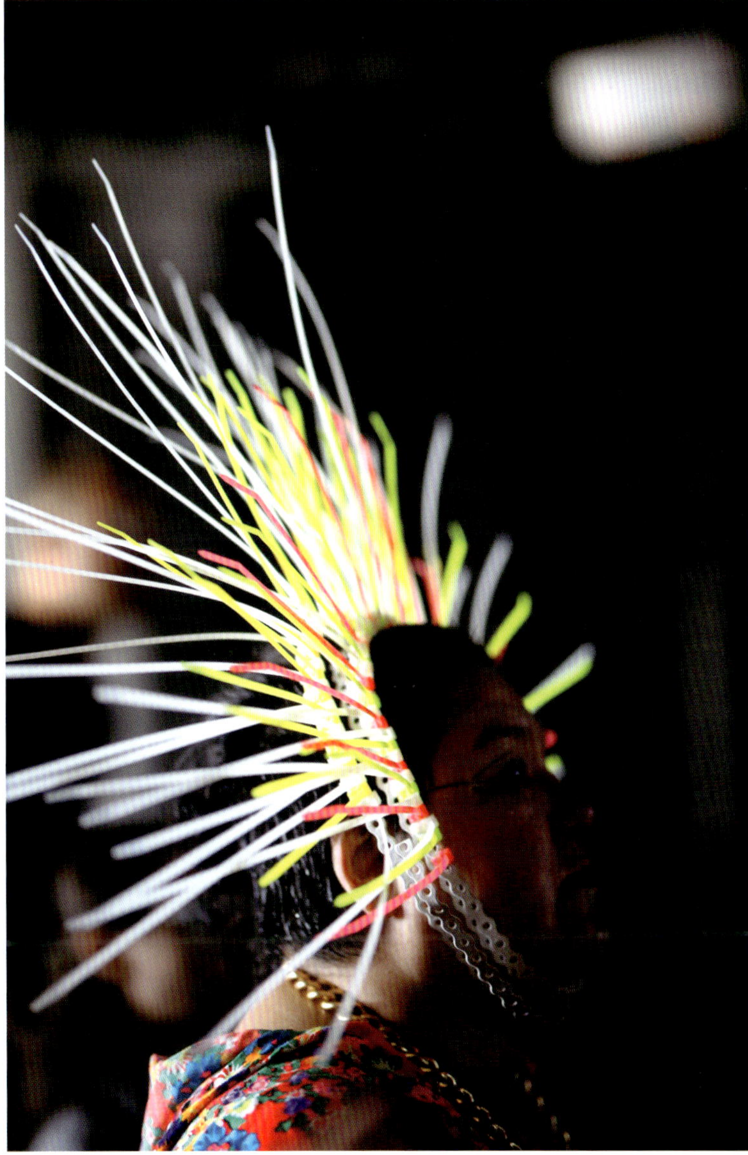

Allison Akootchook Warden in Ancestor from the Future headdress. Photo: Matthew Nuqingaq.

Being in Oneness

CONVERSATIONS WITH NOBUKO MIYAMOTO, KAMAU AYUBBI, AND ASIYAH AYUBBI

Nobuko Miyamoto, Kamau Ayubbi, and Asiyah Ayubbi

Nobuko Miyamoto, artistic director of Great Leap, has been using the power of music, dance, and theater for social change since the early 1970s. Her extraordinary life, spanning the World War II Japanese American concentration camp experience, a pioneering career as a dancer on Broadway and film in *Flower Drum Song, West Side Story*, and *The King and I*, and her social justice legacy as a singer, choreographer, theater artist, and movement activist, is chronicled in her memoir *Not Yo' Butterfly: My Long Song of Relocation, Race, Love, and Revolution* (University of California Press, 2021).

Kamau Ayubbi is a chaplain, visual artist, and meditation teacher. He received his bachelor's degree from San Francisco State University in visual art in 1998, his religious and spiritual education and training under the Islamic Supreme Council of America (ISCA), and was appointed as an Imam in 2002.

Asiyah Ayubbi is a Japanese African American Muslim musician and graphic designer currently based in the United States. She is a founding member of the Az-Zahra Ensemble, a Muslim women's qasida and nasheed group.

Editor's Note: This essay was edited from two interviews to focus on Nobuko's experience through an intergenerational lens and her intercultural journey, particularly with the African American cultural community. Its sources are two conversations: with Nobuko, Roberta Uno, and Evelyn Hang Yin on October 29, 2019, and a conversation with Nobuko, son Kamau Ayubbi, and granddaughter Asiyah Ayubbi with Roberta Uno on July 30, 2020.

Nobuko, 1968–Early 1970s

In 1968, I had gotten involved with the movement when I was helping to make a film about the Black Panthers.[1] I was totally green, but I felt the Panthers really saw Asian Americans as part of the oppressed people in the US and were very generous. Then I met Yuri Kochiyama in 1970. We were shooting at the Young Lords Church. They were Puerto Ricans in New York and, like the Black Panthers, had a free children's breakfast program in a church they had taken over in East Harlem.[2] This little Japanese woman there tapped me on the shoulder: "What are you doing here?" I replied, "Well, what are *you* doing here?!" Her name was Yuri Kochiyama. She started grilling me: "What camp were your folks in? Where are you from? . . . What are you?"[3]

It was winter, and it was *cold*. She invited me to a meeting of Asian Americans for Action. There were second- and third-generation Chinese, Japanese, and Koreans. It was a shock to me that there were people my parents' age who were politically engaged, as well as their children. That was my real wake-up. These were my brothers and sisters; so I just jumped in. My brother and I started organizing demonstrations against the Vietnam War. And they were doing things in Chinatown like the Chinatown Health Fair. Then Warren Furutani came out from LA to New York.[4] People were defensive because he was working at the time with the Japanese American Citizens League (JACL), which we thought were the middle-of-the-road betrayers, assimilationists, and apologists that helped put us in camps. We were suspicious, but he and Victor Shibata convinced us to come to Chicago for the summer 1970 convention.[5] They said, "Say what you believe, say what you want. We're going to bring Asian activists from the West Coast to be there."

It was a way of infiltrating the JACL. When we got there, there were activists from both coasts, and we went to visit the Panthers. Fred Hampton had just been killed.[6] And then Victor Shibata, Richard Taguchi, and others visited the Blackstone Rangers; Fred Hampton had been organizing Latino and Black gangs, getting them politicized before his murder. We were walking from the Panthers meeting and saw this Native American group who had this big teepee in front of Wrigley Field and they pulled us in! They were leafleting for better housing for Native urban people, but they just dropped everything and brought us in the circle and did ceremony with us. They told us the story about Warriors of the Rainbow: that there will be five thousand years of evil followed by five thousand years of good, and that change would come when warriors of all the colors of the rainbow

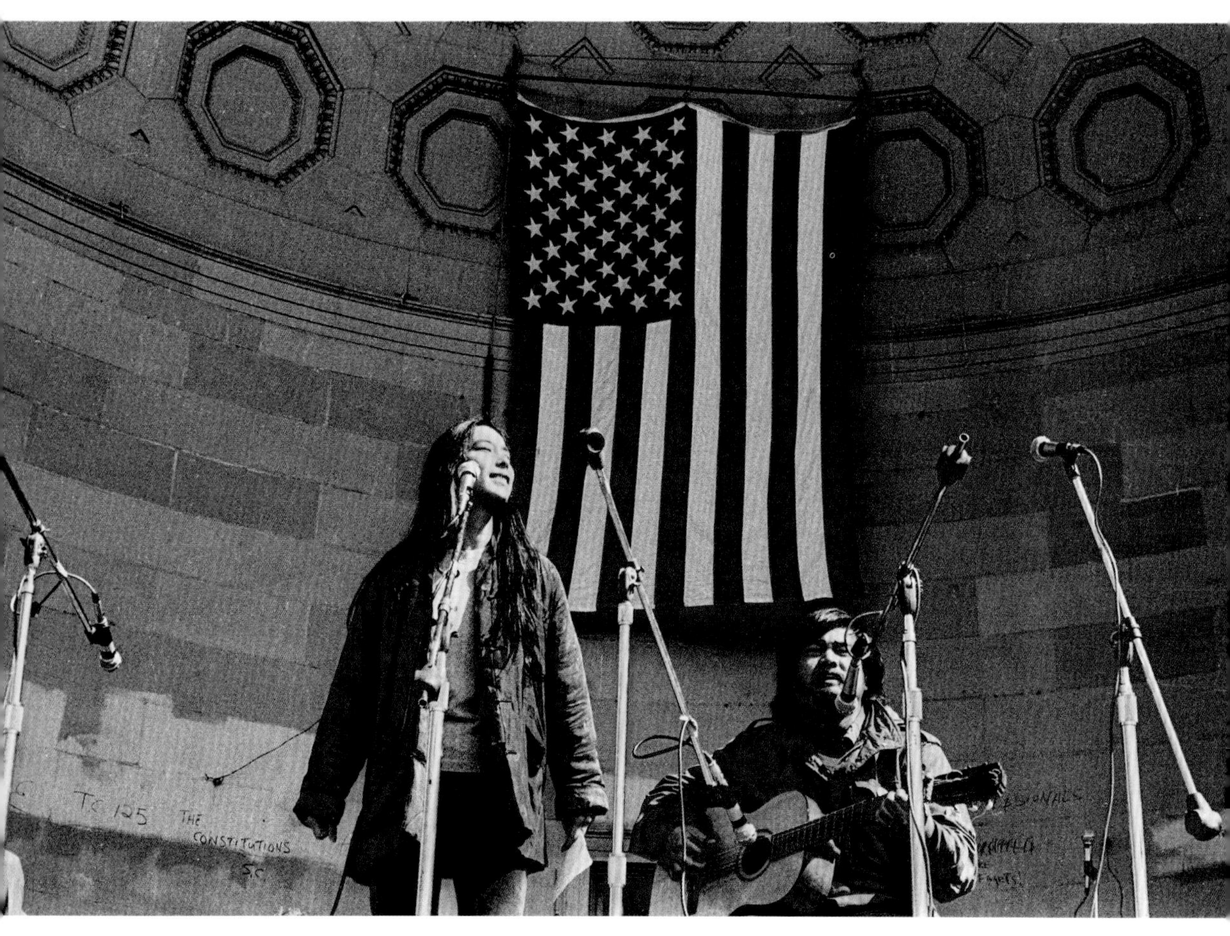

Nobuko Miyamoto and Chris Iijima performing in 1970 in New York's Central Park at a rally for Martin Luther King Day. Photo: Bob Hsiang.

would come together. They passed around the pipe, and it felt like time stopped—we were in eternal time.

When we went back—we were sleeping on the floor of the Japanese Christian church—Chris Iijima brought out his guitar. I didn't know he played music, and he didn't know I sang. He started noodling a chorus based on one of Fred Hampton's speeches called "The People's Beat." I started singing with him, and we quickly built this song. Warren Furatani said, "Let's sing that tomorrow at the big convention." We showed a film about Vietnam and about Hiroshima. We were trying to say, if you believe what happened in Hiroshima was wrong to our people, then you need to make a stand against the Vietnam War.

We sang "The People's Beat," and Warren spoke. Such a powerful speaker—it was a moment. People were into it; the young people sitting on the floor and people in suits in the back. The spirit in that room just woke up. The next day, Ranko Yamada, the roommate of Evelyn Okubo, was waiting downstairs for Evelyn, who wasn't coming down. She went up and found Evelyn with her throat slit. And then Ranko got her throat slit too. Evelyn died and Ranko lived. Nobody ever found out who murdered her. It was in Chicago, Cook County. Fred Hampton had just been murdered by the police. How did somebody come in the room and murder this girl? We took it as a threat. Taguchi told me we were leafleting the next day to say we support the Panthers. It was a turning moment where we knew: this is serious.

Chris and I went back to New York City and wrote the songs "Yellow Pearl," "We Are the Children," "Something about Me Today," and "I'm Alright Jack." We did a fundraiser at the New York Buddhist church on Riverside Drive and got enough money to go to the West Coast to connect with their movement. We toured to UCLA, Fresno, Sacramento, different communities, all by the end of 1970. It was fast! And everywhere we went, the Asian American movement was strong. We realized that that culture could speak about our values, dreams, and history in a way that speeches didn't. For three years, we performed around the country. I became a singer and a songwriter, a troubadour for the Asian American movement. And along with Chris Iijima and Charlie Chin, we made an album called *A Grain of Sand: Music for the Struggle by Asians in America*.[7]

In 1973 I left New York to live in LA—I wanted to dig into the community. I was a single mother, and I went to see Reverend Mas Kondani at Senshin Buddhist Temple, who said, "Here's a key to the temple, if you want to teach dance here." When I went into the hall, I saw a lot of taiko drums on the stage. That was the very temple where they started taiko drumming in America in 1968. There, then San Francisco almost simultaneously, and then San Jose. Reverend Mas believed that art is a way of learning about Buddhism. He saw the temple as a dojo—a place to learn about Buddhism, using martial arts or other practices. You do it here, you do it together; it's the idea of learning to harmonize together. My organization, Great Leap, was born at Senshin in 1978 based on those Buddhist principles.

People in the movement were asking me to teach dance. They wanted an expression. I said okay, but how? I was learning how to teach and how to work with people who weren't trained dancers, and to understand the principles of it. And when you start teaching, you want to create. C. Bernard "Jack" Jackson at Inner City Cultural Center was the first person who opened his doors to produce our own work. We learned by being in that space and seeing all the elements of production, and that was an inspiration for us.[8]

Nobuko, 1980–Early 1990s

I had a son, so the work was built around my life as well. Having a Black son, I said, how do I as a Japanese American raise a Black son? So I got involved in the Black community. I lived in a Black community in South LA, and Leimert Park was a burgeoning village with storefronts transformed into galleries and live-work spaces for artists. I got involved on the board of directors of Brockman Galleries. That exposed me to Ben Caldwell and Black visual artists and performers, including Kamau Daáood and the Pan Afrikan Peoples Arkestra led by Horace Tapscott, who I studied music with. I started working with the kids in Leimert Park with Kamau and others to create pieces where the kids could perform and we would present concerts. At that time, Alonzo and Dale Davis had many storefronts in Leimert Park and were part of the Comprehensive Employment and Training Act (CETA) program; they could hire artists, give them places to work out of, and present them in festivals.

When we had the '92 Uprising in Los Angeles, we were out in the front of the yard with our hoses because everything around us was burning. The next day, I said, "We need to shoot what's going on." So Magda Diaz and I went to South Central where it started. People were looking at us with hatred. I mean, Black people saying, "Fuck you, what are you doing in this neighborhood?" And I suddenly thought, "Oh my God, they don't know who I am. They don't know I have a Black son. They don't know anything about me." And that just woke me up again.

We had to do something to bring people across cultures together. And that's when we shifted to collaborate to bring out Black stories, Latino stories, *and* Asian stories. Shishir Kurup, Dan Kwong, and Chic Street Man worked with us. One of the most beautiful people in *A Slice of Rice* was Long Nguyen, a modern dancer from Vietnam, who told the story of a child seeing the monk burning in the street, protesting the war. You can imagine these stories—so powerful.

In the '80s we were hit with AIDS, and many people around us were falling. We lost some in our company, like Long Nguyen and Jose de Vega, a major force in Great Leap as a director. We were creating *Talk Story* when he got sick. And we wanted to keep going, even though he was in and out of the hospital. So we figured out how. He performed this piece called the *Pilipino Tango*; I have a beautiful recording of him singing this in the studio. And we created a dance piece around him while he told a story of a manong, an elder who dressed up on Saturday night to go out to a dance hall, to hold a woman and dance. Pilipino workers weren't allowed to bring a wife, and it was illegal to marry a white woman.[9] It was just a beautiful piece. AIDS showed us how fragile we were, but we kept going.

Nobuko, Early 2000s

Chris Iijima, Charlie Chin, and I did a reunion concert in the 1990s, in Michigan, and Grace Lee Boggs came.[10] She had actually been at that first JACL convention in Chicago in 1970! She came up and said, "You have to come to Detroit." So around 2000, I started the residency at the Boggs Center in Detroit. Grace introduced me to the concept of the urban place, how in Detroit they were starting to grow organic gardens in these abandoned lots. At that time, it still looked like a war zone; they were leading change through the urban farming movement. That was another turning point for me, to see the importance of the environment.

It was just right after 9/11 as well. Grace was taking me to these different conferences, and I realized political people separate the arts as entertainment. I wanted to show how we use the process of the arts to engage all people. So I did a workshop a few days after 9/11. Everybody told a story about where they were during 9/11, and I got the whole room moving in slow motion, prompting: "Why are you moving?" "What are you saying with your body that you can't say with your words?" "What do we say together as a group that you can't say as an individual?" It was about how we connected on an energetic level, not just an intellectual level. Grace gave me the place to do it.

She really was a spiritual being. And she loved young people and learning from them. She wanted to know: What are they thinking about? What are they doing? The last time I saw her, she said, "You need to write your book." I said, "What?!" "You need to write your book. It'll change your life. It changed mine." I said, "Yes, ma'am." She would give assignments to people, and she was giving me mine.

Then I met Quetzal Flores, because I was doing music videos to engage our communities of color about environmental issues. We did one about bicycling, and after, he invited me to a fandango class. Then he came to Obon, and his kid loved Obon. I said, fandango is in a circle around a wooden platform, and we dance Obon like that too. What if we put fandango and Obon together? And he said, "Yes. Let's try it." We went to Reverend Mas, who said, "It shouldn't be a fusion. *It should be a conversation.*" And that's what FandangObon is about. We each deal with our own cultural forms but also create a conversation between the two cultures. How do you make change easy and joyful? That's what FandangObon is really trying to do; it's saying, let's try to build traditional knowledge so that we have the knowledge to take care of our land. It's an elixir to bring us together and hold us together as communities who have been oppressed, to claim ourselves as who we are.

Asiyah and Kamau Ayubbi perform the Hadrah with members of FandangObon, including Nobuko Miyamoto and Martha Gonzalez, at the JACCC Plaza in 2018. Photo: Daren Mooko.

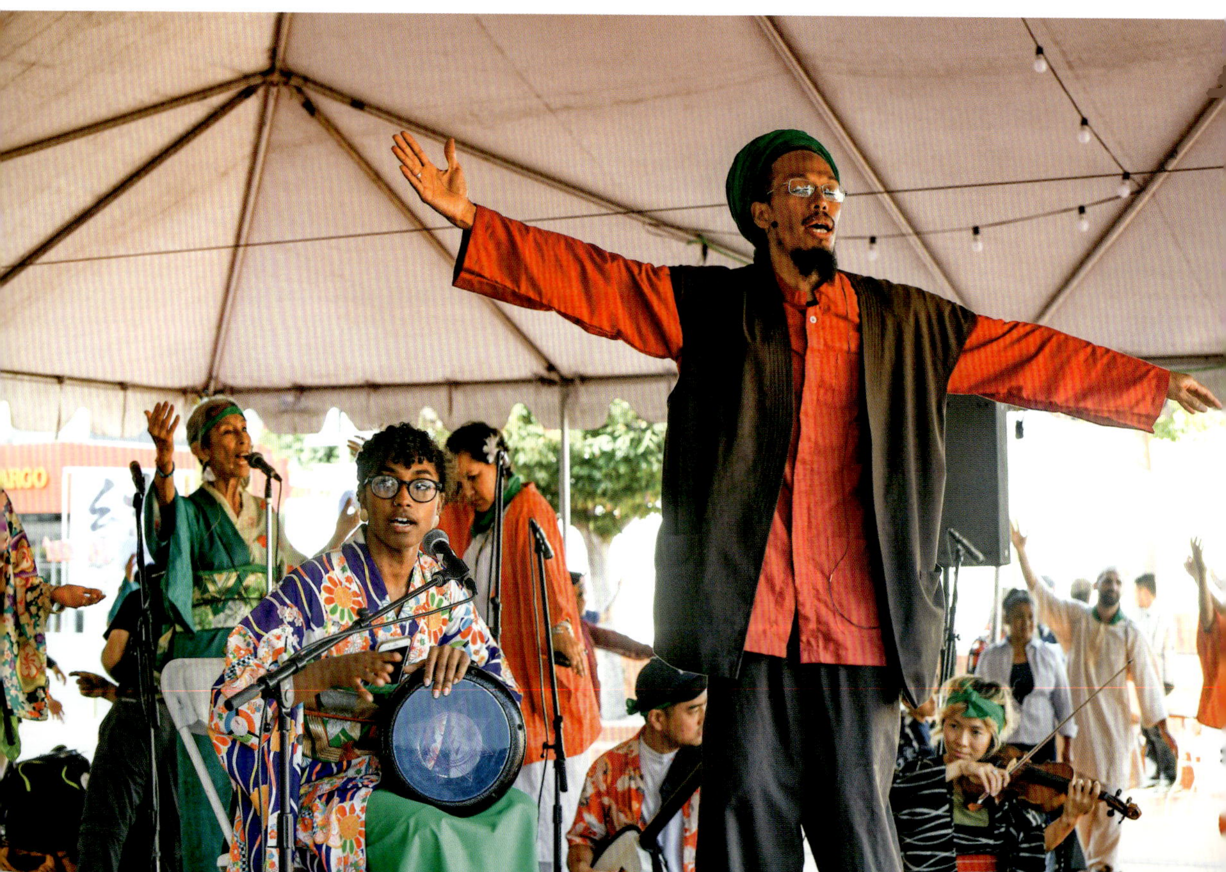

July 2020: Nobuko Miyamoto, Son Kamau Ayubbi, and Granddaughter Asiyah Ayubbi

ASIYAH AYUBBI: My name is Asiyah Ayubbi, granddaughter of Nobuko Miyamoto, daughter and child of Kamau Ayubbi. I've been a Sufi musician for almost ten years. I play the drums, percussion, and sing; I'm located in Ann Arbor, Michigan, right now.

KAMAU AYUBBI: And I'm Kamau Ayubbi, son of Nobuko Miyamoto. I live in Ypsilanti, Michigan, and as an Imam, I'm a hospital chaplain serving the spiritual needs of individuals and groups through teaching, facilitating, counseling, and listening across the University of Michigan health care system, especially with psychiatry and Muslim patients, but also people of all walks of life.

One of my early memories is my mother telling me the meaning of my name. And there are five names: Kamau Miyamoto Shigeki Ibn Attallah Ayubbi. And she told me the meanings of the names, like "quiet warrior," "to be concerned." There's Miyamoto Musashi, there's the tree Shigeki, and Ibn Attallah is from my biological father, Attallah Ayubbi. He wanted me to be part of a world community of Islam. I remember at a young age thinking, what does "quiet warrior" mean?

I remember touching the drums at a very early age and always going to events with my mother at Senshin Buddhist Temple: mochi pounding, rehearsals, meetings with activists. I was definitely a quiet observer of these people socializing about issues of importance and seeing processes of rehearsals that turned into cultural narratives.

My mother was pursuing things that were very meaningful to her. I've grown up in the same pattern. Whatever is meaningful to me at a given moment, I'll just go after it. Whether it's break dancing, skateboarding, I was finding and navigating an identity. Being multiethnic, it was a constant adjustment to navigate the containers—the confusion of culturalism, colorism, and bias that society has created—and find authenticity. Mom was very conscious of putting me in intentional spaces at an early age, where art, culture, and history were valued. Once I got into junior high, it was a culture shock of the generic race identities of mainstream American culture. And that turned into a spiritual quest at eighteen. That pretty much has shaped my life, reintegrating all these different aspects of my identity and my past, into my spiritual identity.

I embraced Sufism, an orientation toward spirituality and healing, when I was twenty years old. I consider healing an extension of self-awareness. It doesn't mean that you feel healthy all the time, but that you become aware of ailments and things that you may have collected through your lifetime and eventually will have to face and reconcile. It's a process of reconciliation and integration.

AA: Like my father, I absorbed a lot. We grew up in Oakland as kids; our parents exposed us to different environments and cultures and music. I was exposed to many different people of color. Growing up Muslim and homeschooling was also a big part of my upbringing. When we moved to Michigan is when I really started to be aware of dynamics that go on between races. We lived in a town that was mostly white and rural; we were one of the only Black families in the neighborhood. Very different from California's culture and the way I was brought up earlier.

At our mosque, a group of girls and I decided we were going to make a band. A friend of mine had gone to Indonesia, and she came back riled up: "We got to start a drumming band. We got to get together and do this thing!" So we did. And we started touring all over the Midwest, to Chicago, DC, New York, and to interfaith events. It felt like home to me, this sense of community, sharing stories, perspectives, and music; and people welcomed us wherever we went. We were just a group of seven girls growing up into women. And we had this tool to reach a crazy amount of people and really touch people and share light and love.

I was twelve or thirteen in 2010 when we started the Az-Zahra Ensemble. The type of music that I play is very spiritual. Some say it's religious, reciting Arabic poetry called qasida. The style that we would play and sing was our own, but it was definitely informed by the Indonesian salawat. There are many kinds of bands that sing this type of music and play drums and all types of percussion.

KA: There's a lot of qasida, worldwide, whether it be in West Africa, Indonesia, in Syria. And wherever Sufi masters or Sufi teachers are, sound is very important.

AA: My spiritual teacher, Sheikh Hisham, encouraged us as young adults to perform and go to all types of places. It was really a fight for women's power in communities where a lot of the time, people fall into patriarchal roles. It's only men in the front; only men can be seen. And we were in the front of the mosque, playing our music in front of everybody! I think we became very close as a community because of this music; people really supported us. It was a big part of me growing up and informs my practice today.

KA: It was interesting to watch her going to Indonesia to an international festival. There was . . .

AA: . . . a 200,000-person crowd—it was crazy! One of the spiritual leaders in Indonesia has this big Mawlid where you celebrate the birth of the Prophet Muhammad, and you sing "peace be upon him" and praise songs of his beauty and his kindness. The first night that we went to one of those big, mega Mawlids of over 200,000 people, we were not going to sing. Suddenly, somebody came to our hotel room saying, "Habib Sheikh wants you to sing." And we freak out: "How are we gonna do this? What are we gonna do?"

We sat on these raised platforms—the crowd was so big you couldn't see all of the people! But we sang, and everybody was singing with us at the same time. It was a warm and euphoric experience. And I've definitely had moments like that with FandangObon, doing this practice, singing these songs. And people, even if they don't know the lyrics, they're still moving, they're still doing the Hadrah, they're still in a circle around us. People have come up and said, "I've never experienced something like that. What was that feeling?" It's quite amazing, just what you can feel through art.

KA: From the middle tier, between generations, I've seen that Az-Zahra lives on in Asiyah as she develops. There's at least three girls' groups that developed out of the Az-Zahra group. There's one in Chicago; there's one in DC; there was another one in Michigan. Az-Zahra girls sparked an example for many other girls to express themselves and stay involved in their spiritual practice. That was the seed that was planted.

NOBUKO MIYAMOTO: It's so beautiful for me, as a grandmother and mother, to hear them articulate how art has affected their lives. My mother was Christian but also Buddhist, and art was her religion. She was born here, but she grew up in Japan. Japanese people take art very seriously. And it is a kind of a spiritual practice. I have been so lucky because I have been able to not only be Japanese, but to also raise a Black son, and to be in a circle with Sufis and be moved by that experience. I wanted to share this with the circle of FandangObon.

KA: Going into the FandangObon, you're doing Japanese Obon, you're doing West African dance, and Mexican dance that's meant to build culture and awareness. And then you bring Sufism, which comes in and tries to integrate all that experience in a very basic way. It's the breeze that runs through it.

NM: What Kamau said is true. It's a transformative experience to externalize what we have experienced in our bodies, in our lives. It's also transformative to be in a circle so there's no audience. We experience this together as a community. Where else are you going to get that opportunity?

When we first put Fandango and Obon together, the community saw it. And when we invited African Americans in, they saw it too. They brought their element of drum from their practice; it was like synchronizing heartbeats. It's going beyond allies. You're not saying words of solidarity, you are being in solidarity, in oneness with others. Once you come into that circle and you move together, no matter what color you are, you are changed by that experience.

AA: And across all generations, people are hungry for it. They want this participation. They want the euphoric feeling. I think it's important especially in activism for people to cross bridges and pull down walls across generations, because I feel like we're misunderstood.

People say about the younger generation, "Why are they changing so much?" It's a shock when somebody is expressing their queer self, or boldly being themselves. It's important that people from different generations understand young people and what we need. I think my grandmother did a very good job instilling that into my father, and my parents to us. I wasn't some kid in the corner hidden away, I was right in the center of it. I distinctly remember one of my grandmother's performances, *Sacred Moon Songs*, where stories were being told by people in their ethnic clothing. I remember thinking, "Wow, I want to do something like that when I'm older." Art transcends generations.

KA: I have that privilege of hearing culture being articulated consciously throughout my life. I grew up hearing about Malcolm X and Marcus Garvey, and all these righteous people. I thought that Black people were superheroes. But then you see the realities of disenfranchisement, and a way must be forged for dignity to walk in this land. I think that's why spirituality and art are so important—to build those connections that touch people in ways that can't be explained. Spirituality and art transform consciousness.

If you consider yourself part of the universe, then you'll know that everything in the universe is collaborating for your existence. And we struggle in this country of duality. Dualism is a very severe test on us, whether it be racial, whether it be political, or gender. But reality is a spectrum of human experience. Dualism is a convenient way of dividing people into categories so they can be marginalized. So the healing and reconciling of one's identity promotes that unified consciousness of recognizing these different stories and listening to them. This is the work that Mom's been doing. It's the work that is going to run through our family in some way, hopefully, for as long as the earth exists.

Notes

1. Antonello Branca, dir., *Seize the Time* (1973; Italy: Filmmakers Research Group, 2008), DVD.

2. See Michael Abramson and Iris Morales, *Palante: Young Lords Party* (Chicago: Haymarket, 1971).

3. For more on political activist Yuri Kochiyama, see her *Passing It On—a Memoir* (Los Angeles: UCLA Asian American Studies Center Press, 2004).

4. Warren Furutani is a pioneering Asian American Movement activist who helped many campuses establish ethnic studies programs, cofounded the Manzanar Committee to designate the former concentration camp a national historic site, was the first Asian Pacific American ever elected to the LA Unified School District in 1987, and served in the California State Assembly from 2008 to 2012. "Warren Furutani," Wikipedia, June 8, 2021, https://en.wikipedia.org/wiki /Warren_Furutani.

5. Editor's note: my uncle, Edison Uno, called a militant activist within the JACL, proposed at the 1970 JACL convention a controversial redress resolution calling for compensation for Japanese Americans confined in the wartime camps. He passed away in 1976 before it became a mass movement but is considered a founding father of Japanese American redress and reparations. Coincidentally, his cousin, Raymond Uno, was elected JACL president at the 1970 convention.

6. For more on Fred Hampton, see Mike Gray, dir., and Howard Alk, prod., *The Murder of Fred Hampton* (Chicago: Facets Video, 2007).

7. Charlie Chin, Chris Iijima, and Joanne Nobuko Miyamoto, *A Grain of Sand: Music for the Struggle by Asians in America* (New York: Paredon Records, 1973). This album was produced by Barbara Dane and is the first Asian American album in the Folkways collection at the Smithsonian.

8. C. Bernard Jackson was an African American playwright who founded the Inner City Cultural Center in 1965 in Los Angeles in the wake of the Watts Uprising. It was one of the earliest theaters to promote multiculturalism and nurtured a number of prominent theater artists. From the late 1970s forward, Nobuko was telling Asian American stories through original musical theater and music through a touring band with Benny Yee, Warriors of the Rainbow. She led devised theater work in collaboration with Huong Nguyen and his group, Club o' Noodles. She founded Great Leap in 1978 and grew her solo performance work, multiethnic and intersectional collaborations, workshops, music videos, and festivals, making a home for artists in Los Angeles and beyond.

9. In virtually all states restricting African American intermarriage with Caucasians, Asian intermarriage was also prohibited until 1950.

10. For more on Grace Lee Boggs, see *American Revolutionary: The Evolution of Grace Lee Boggs* (LeeLee Films, 2013), directed by Grace Lee.

1619

Douglas Kearney

Douglas Kearney is a Foundation for Contemporary Arts Cy Twombly awardee and Cave Canem graduate. He has published seven books ranging from poetry to essays to libretti and teaches creative writing at the University of Minnesota, Twin Cities.

1619

(1x6=) 6 (1x9=) 9

GOES UP THE MOUTH OF NO RETURN

69

TO BE AT THE PLACE TO BE*

Come 1619, with entanglement: I think of a route that's a root.

When I think of *entanglement* got me thinking of *entanglement* in the when of 1619, which got me thinking of *berth* and a *birth*.

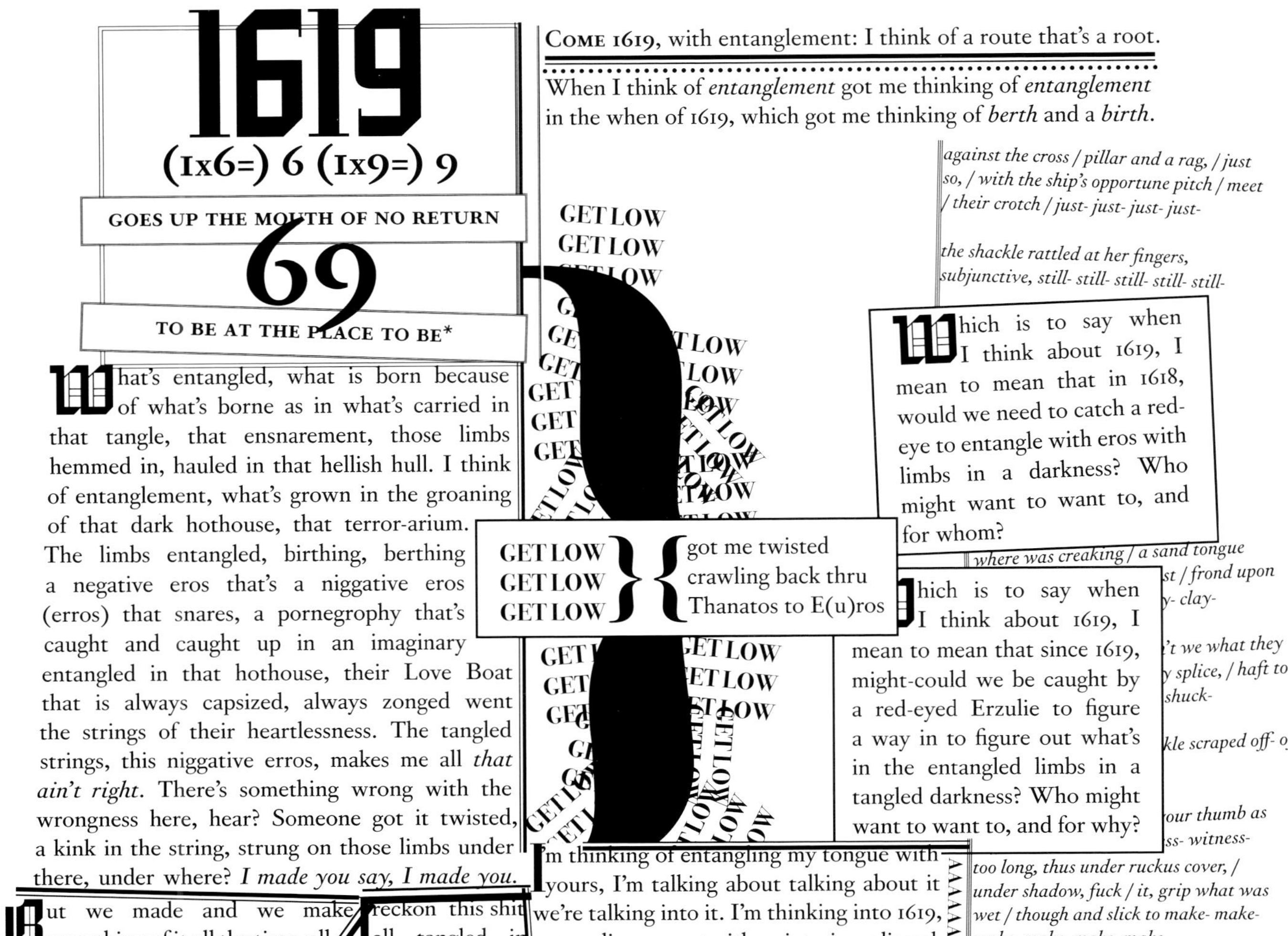

What's entangled, what is born because of what's borne as in what's carried in that tangle, that ensnarement, those limbs hemmed in, hauled in that hellish hull. I think of entanglement, what's grown in the groaning of that dark hothouse, that terror-arium. The limbs entangled, birthing, berthing a negative eros that's a niggative eros (erros) that snares, a pornegrophy that's caught and caught up in an imaginary entangled in that hothouse, their Love Boat that is always capsized, always zonged went the strings of their heartlessness. The tangled strings, this niggative erros, makes me all *that ain't right*. There's something wrong with the wrongness here, hear? Someone got it twisted, a kink in the string, strung on those limbs under there, under where? *I made you say, I made you.*

But we made and we make reckon this shit something of it all the time, all all tangled in

against the cross / pillar and a rag, / just so, / with the ship's opportune pitch / meet / their crotch / just- just- just- just-

the shackle rattled at her fingers, subjunctive, still- still- still- still- still-

Which is to say when I think about 1619, I mean to mean that in 1618, would we need to catch a red-eye to entangle with eros with limbs in a darkness? Who might want to want to, and for whom?

Which is to say when I think about 1619, I mean to mean that since 1619, might-could we be caught by a red-eyed Erzulie to figure a way in to figure out what's in the entangled limbs in a tangled darkness? Who might want to want to, and for why?

I'm thinking of entangling my tongue with yours, I'm talking about talking about it we're talking into it. I'm thinking into 1619, entangling a coast with an interior, a literal

where was creaking / a sand tongue ...st / frond upon ...y- clay- ...'t we what they ...y splice, / haft to ...shuck- ...kle scraped off- off- ...our thumb as ...ss- witness-

too long, thus under ruckus cover, / under shadow, fuck / it, grip what was wet / though and slick to make- make- make- make- make- make-

right? It's 2019, and I'm thinking my own mess—my of 1619 so I'm thinking past own sic—and I don't and thinking past them to wish to make the *error* of think of us now and of essentializing a Nabisco box then and now, then's Blackness (ding), a cracker next, what stay box box-in that got that cheap- passing. Not to ass prize that don't mean jack but give passes, I to jack you up. But entangled here, lack capacity, hurr, I am thinking to this 1619, this as we each one here: the aliveness of here, hurr, this does. here.** Which is an aliveness that's not the snuff flick loop of erros, but red-eyed Erzulie, entangled hurr, what's good, Erzulie? And I don't mean to work two-hands, be two faced, or be too much—but I'm of at least two minds about how Gé Rouge Erzulie could put work in on the trope of entanglement in the berth of a notion. First—what's faithfulness got to do with it? And two: vengeance looks outward, keeping *them* up in the frame. But I'm thinking of 1619, so to the latter, someone's the holes in the 6 and 9.

littoral with a deep dark figure, figuring an entanglement of what a groan grown, laying on my own mess, my own sic, rapt in blood I don't know's my own, I moan, entangled in a spirit in 2019, what I ask to ride me I'm asking to entangle my mind with your mind for to make four heads. A black-ass telepathy, berthed in a birth of niggative capability—the what in *what it do* that is the whut—a theft. A thieving back.

Steal away, steal away, go the song about going till gone. And I think about what comes after 1619. After what was stolen. And I think about entanglement and skin in a darkness and rocking. But it's 1619. I want to think about what's stolen when limbs are entangled in a rocking darkness. But it's 1619...

GET LOW
GET LOW
GET LOW

When I think of 1619, which is to say this 1619, in this place they say Philadelphia, I'm thinking of L. H. Stallings and space and sex war, and I'm thinking of entangling these words with the trace of hers in a room, and so I'm thinking of that space, which was a different space, but now a new space. But then now, I'm thinking of that 1619, so I'm thinking of space and war—so I'm thinking still of //

AAAIIIIIIIIIIIIIIIIIEEEEEEEEEE

in guinea dark, their arms- arms-

the hull held them, rocking in its- its- its- its- its-

skin on what was sore, his leg on what- what- what- what-

it's not bird, though it cries when it's caught- caught- caught-

gone below decks, / skin cooled, perhaps / brine bright perfumed, / gone down where they'd laid, / ere keel come to roll them / in all they left below / there- there- there- there-

their backs against each- each- each-

her hand was- was- was- was-

his hand was- was- was- was-

their hands was- was- was- was-

their hands were- were- were- were-

*If I fix*** to wail till I'm hoarse, due to being entangled in their notting of us, I'm a cheval whose reins is tangled, whose riggings got it twisted. Whose system is rigged? Is a negative eros a rigged system, rigid, too twisted? Fugitive, go rogue. Entanglement of signs, syncretism: Gé Rouge Erzulie, love's got nothing, love's got everything, **** in the berth it's birthed.*

Stallings, but I'm thinking of outer space and it is blue in 1619, and it is deep in 1619, and it is full of fish in 1619, and it is full of salt in 1619, and angler fish troll the bottom of space, their lanterns getting low lighting sea stars getting low in 1619, and the sea floor isn't a corral boneyard of a particular people yet in 1619, though soon come, soon come in 1619, and I'm thinking about space and war and sex in that 1619 so I'm thinking of a ship hold and I'm thinking about warships that are already becoming metaphors that don't know whether they are tenors or vehicles and I am thinking of tangled darknesses and limbs and a hatch coming open and all the light of the black ass sky falling out.

I am thinking of now and on. And on a means of thinking on a tangle. Which is to say: limbs in a darkness, even that darkness, that *1619* darkness, that charnel / carceral darkness, is limbs. And limbs in a darkness, entangled, will find some tangling. Not odd in a loooong darkness; a deeeep darkness. Of such length and depth as to lash tomorrow to a turnt right now. **Erros'** teleology of error, I'm thinking, terror, makes pornegrophy of all limb entanglement in that 1619 darkness—thus we couldn't even touch for us once they touched us. But we give it up, though we don't got to: that 1619 darkness has been knotted / notted / naughted into erros by Euros' eros cum *Prigga Please* overcorrection of the same. Bad faith, not *bad* faith. A cheat. A two-timing done again and again. M: *you gonna believe me or your lying eyes?*

s: *I've never even seen* that *before!*

Gé Rouge Erzulie's sensual ruck cums with a vengeance for the unfaithful. Where there's terror there, the cheval is no mere surface, simple vessel, abject recipient—the cheval a passing passage. For a time, for a time.

Erzulie Freda echo a rocksteady faint some where a whisper when Gé Rouge rides high what some reckon a low road. By whose reckoning? Much is, in English entangled cultures, called *sweet*. Much.

*"…and not to be at the same time." –Andre 3000
**this paper was presented at The Legacy of 1619: The 2019 Callaloo Conference. Dr. Kevin Quashie keynoted on <u>Aliveness</u>, Airea D. Matthews presented a critique of essentialism, and Dr. L. H. Stallings keynoted regarding space and sex wars–all of which pushed this paper–curated by Amber Rose Johnson for the <u>Enacting Entanglements</u> panel–further.
***how to fix to without fixing, that is to lose the fluid that allows you to do what needs doing? that shit gets hard.
****shout-out to Saidiya Hartman

Encircling the Circle

BLOOD MEMORY AND MAKING THE VILLAGE—A CONVERSATION BETWEEN CLEO PARKER ROBINSON AND MALIK ROBINSON

Cleo Parker Robinson and Malik Robinson

Cleo Parker Robinson is founder and artistic director of Cleo Parker Robinson Dance, one of Colorado's premier cultural institutions. Touring her dance ensemble worldwide and creating nationally recognized educational programming, she links extraordinary artists with diverse communities. The recipient of numerous civic and academic awards, she is a renowned choreographer, director, teacher, and activist.

Malik Robinson is executive director of Cleo Parker Robinson Dance. Previously, he developed and directed evidence-based after-school programming, recognized for outstanding impact. Serving as board chair for Dance USA from 2019 to 2021, he continues to serve on the boards of myriad arts organizations, is a member of the Denver Metro Chamber's Leadership Denver Class of 2015, and is a Bonfils Stanton Foundation 2015 Livingston Fellow.

CLEO PARKER ROBINSON: We're often asked about what shaped our mission and work from a cultural and social justice perspective. The answer is clear: the times in which we were living, and where and when we started are the forces that shaped us. Living in Denver, there was a need to connect

Editor's Note: This contribution was edited from a virtual conversation between Cleo Parker Robinson and Malik Robinson on June 15, 2020.

with the rest of the country and the rest of the world. I felt very isolated in the middle of the country. Starting the company out of the very challenging and extraordinary time of the late '60s and into the '70s, coming out of major civil rights awareness and change for our country, affected all kinds of movements. The Black theater movement at that time, which was very connected to the Black dance movement and Black music—melded into a tremendous influence. It was an incredibly dynamic time—everything was changing: people were marching and protesting, having their voices heard about everything, from farmworkers to the Poor Peoples' March, to the Vietnam War, and then the liberation of the hippie movement, it was a blending of all of that. And the arts were intensely vibrant.

I was newly married and had just graduated from Colorado Women's College with no concrete idea of my exact direction. I already had a studio, the Kutsuma Parker School of Dance. I'd been involved in the arts and civil rights through my parents. My father, Jonathan Parker, was African American; my mother, Martha Parker, was white. At Bonfils Theatre, my father was involved in traditional theater, but not as an actor. He'd been grudgingly hired as their first maintenance person of color. But he was also part of the underground theater—really avant-garde work that offered work for artists of color who did not have the opportunity to be in the mainstream. I was very fortunate to grow up in that. My mother was already immersed in the beauty and love of music as an accomplished French horn player. Paul Robeson was my father's greatest influence, but when Mr. Robeson visited Five Points, my parents had to be careful about attending meetings he led, so they'd not be labeled as communists.

Jim Crow laws defined their times. My parents had to travel to five different states to be married, and being a mixed-race couple, they couldn't even enter an apartment together. My mother had to sneak up the back stairs to an apartment above the nightclub of the Rossonian Hotel, where they stayed with a Black dentist and his wife. I often speak about this extraordinary hotel and nightclub, a historic space, now closed for decades, that's just right down the street from our present-day studios in Five Points. In the '40s and '50s, the Rossonian Hotel was like the Harlem of the West with some of the greatest musicians in the world—Duke [Ellington], Bessie Smith, Billie Holiday, Pete Seeger, Freddy Rodriguez Sr.—performing there. It was the only place in Denver where integration took place.

I believe being born in Denver, into this extraordinary, rich music and dance culture that was definitely Black, shaped so much of who I've become. But it was also rich with the culture of whoever came through the community.

MALIK ROBINSON: At that time, being in the Harlem of the West had a heavy influence on the dance company. Other factors that come up for me are connected to your upbringing. I know that the high school you attended, George Washington, was having race riots, and the school was temporarily shut down as a result. I know you were in the middle of attacks that were happening on communities of color at that time, which helped to frame, shape, and inform why we have a dance company.

CPR: I was influenced as well by experiences, from age ten to twelve, living in Dallas, Texas, before returning to Denver in my middle school years. Even though we were very poor, I was involved and entrenched in this extraordinary Black culture. It was very segregated because of Jim Crow laws, so that influenced me probably even more so. Dallas was something totally different from my time in Denver. In Dallas, I went to a segregated all-Black Catholic school where all the priests and nuns were white, and lived in the Black community where families were reliant on one another. We were a community—we knew each other. My grandmother, Mama Cleo, would cook three times on Sunday. We were in the Baptist church every day, and the preacher was at the table with us after Sunday services.

When I came back to Denver, I really didn't even know how to talk about what I'd experienced in Dallas. I just stopped talking because I couldn't figure it all out. Now I was attending an all-white Jewish school and thinking there was no division within the white community. I came to realize there was a deep division between Catholics and Jews, and between those who had more access to resources than others. I became very aware, while young, though I didn't know how to speak about it. I look at pictures of me now, and think, I look like I was Jewish in that high school. I looked like they did, because I was light skinned and my hair was kind of kinky. I felt I could live in both worlds—I even wore a cross and the Star of David at the same time! But I saw myself differently culturally. I felt rhythm differently. I saw the world in different colors.

I had to discover movement. Dance became my way of speaking about what I saw. I tried to give myself a sense of, how do I celebrate that which I know is me? How do I celebrate it with others? How do we heal from some of the stuff that really was painful? For me, dance was healing and universal.

MR: And my childhood home was on the color line of a formerly white neighborhood. White flight was taking place, so we were one of the first in a wave of Black families into the area. I know Denver is starkly different from Dallas, but there are similarities that remind me of my grandfather's stories about raising a family in Denver. He was well aware of those color lines too; even though segregation was supposedly outlawed, it was still very much present.

I think about how those family stories have helped to shape our organization. Our origins are grassroots, and communities looked different then. The first Black attorneys and judges also lived in the neighborhood and were a part of the movement. It was a community, with every economic level represented. Rachel B. Noel was the first Black woman elected to public office in Colorado. She was elected to the Denver school board and was an avid champion for us to have our own building, the historic Shorter African Methodist Episcopal Church. Our building carries the traditions of one of the first Black churches in Colorado. To fund its services, one of the church matriarchs would go down to the gambling shack and make sure all the gamblers pitched in and supported the church services! The church recognized and made sure everyone felt a part of the community. That's a tradition we carry forward.

CPR: *Community* is an interesting word. Oftentimes, it's a coded word when people say *our community* or *my community*. For us, the word *community* has always been huge. There's no way we could have created something that could sustain itself and grow like we have without that support. We've grown slowly but steadily, with magnificent things happening for the company and for young people and elders. Of course, there's been considerable struggle and sacrifice, but you can't get stuck in that.

In terms of our mission, we can't get stuck in the fear of this moment either, whether it's about the coronavirus or the upheaval we're seeing in our cities. Our world faces us in the mirror with a real sense of racism and bias that is just horrendous. It's hard for people to even look at themselves at this moment, in terms of what we've done to one another. But we have to; we can't stagnate or become so frozen from it all that we can't move.

That's what we did in the beginning—we moved. We didn't always know how to move and who to move with, but I've always said, whoever was present, breathing and moving, that's who was with us. For me, that's community, those who align with you. Often in the early days, many of us were just trying to find our own joy, our own voice, and it seemed that nobody else was on that same path. You couldn't even imitate because you didn't see anything to imitate. We had to become pioneers.

So we made our own traditions—in fact we got creative with combining traditions. In our International Summer Dance Institute, culture is quite integrated and diverse. We've built around the idea of "One Spirit, Many Voices." I have a dancer, a kumu from Hawaiʻi, Mauli Ola Cook, come to teach and connect with our children. Then we connect with another teacher, Vusi Makanya, from South Africa, and the two cultures are absolutely coming from the same vibration.

I love the African tradition, because there is no sense of division. Life is a circle, and you want everybody in the circle. You can make many different circles within the main circle, the one circle that everybody is feeling. Right now, I'm really missing that circle—in Zoom meetings we only see one another in squares. Now, I have an even greater appreciation of the concept of having the babies, the little ones, in the middle of the circle; with the youth, the teenagers, surrounding them in a larger circle. You have the adults and the elders on the outermost circle, protecting the inner circles. The children and young people feel protected. Ultimately, everybody joins and becomes one intergenerational circle—a village of creativity and love.

MR: Right now we're in that place of friction and agitation as we try to make this technology work for us. Soon, genius and resiliency will help us innovate and adapt. I'm constantly reminded of ways our ingenuity has kept the circle intact. You can think about our folks going back to the an-

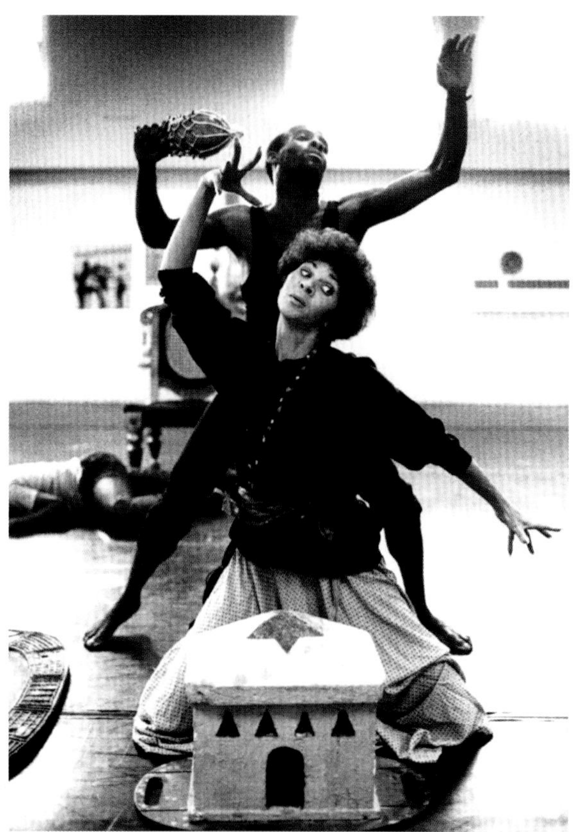

Cleo Parker Robinson as the mambo (the Voodoo priestess) and Cleo Parker Robinson Dance Ensemble member Curtis Frazier in the role of the houngon (the Voodoo priest) in *The Emperor Jones* (directed by Donald McKayle, with Cleo as assistant director) in the Denver Center for the Performing Arts production, 1987. This work later toured under the title of *ve've'*. From the archives of Cleo Parker Robinson Dance.

tebellum days. There were a lot of restrictions on us in terms of how we could move or communicate, and yet we were still able to figure out how to make that work: messages on quilts, rhythms and songs that were sung from plantation to plantation, all forms of communication we adapted. There's nothing that's going to stop that.

CPR: That's what makes us resilient, even during a pandemic, because if we don't have an opportunity, we create one. Oftentimes teaching requires that we share the knowledge that's in the room. When we're dancing or singing, it becomes a collective, an expanded intellectual heightening of what we're capable of experiencing. Sometimes we're surprised. We don't even know what we'll leave with, because we're triggering all those endorphins, we're coming into that spiritual intellectual space. Culturally, I understand that dance—the vibration of it—continues long beyond our lifetime. It has an ancestral spirit to it that comes through the drums. Master Drummer Bataki's father, Alex Cambrelen, played for Katherine Dunham and also for me.

Malik, right after you were born, Alex came to tell me, "I have bad news and good news. Bad news, I will not be able to play drums for you any longer. Good news is, I have taught my son all of the sacred rhythms, and he is now your drummer." Bataki has now been our drummer for the past fifty years. He inspired you, Malik. When you were very young, you and I were at a party with wonderful food and music and drumming. You were the company child. You belonged to everyone. That was hard too, because you had to share me, and I had to share you, but you had a whole village. Anyway, I looked over and Bataki was playing djembe. He took a break for a moment, but the drums never stopped. Someone said, "Cleo, look there." I looked, and Bataki was gone, and there you were, so small, sitting at that drum playing it like you were possessed! You didn't learn to do that. He hadn't taught you.

That's what culture, our blood memories, gives us. Creating a village for us has been so vital. I don't think we've ever had to close our doors. Even though we've sometimes been homeless without a building, we've never stopped. We need to celebrate that, within ourselves and within others. It's the concept of kujichagulia (self-determination) and Sankofa (remembering where we've come from even as we move forward). That's the intersection, that's the connection. And we've been able to do things because we weren't in New York or LA. We were creating from our own authenticity.

MR: I think we in the US put a lot of emphasis on the coasts, but you've talked about this company being born out of the movement. And the movement comes from anywhere we, as a people, are. What we found in Denver has been fertile ground.

Having been exposed to so many different perspectives, so many different walks of life, has largely shaped who I am. I remember having Maya Angelou come in, and watching her work. Listening to Katherine Dunham talk philosophically about transforming society, hearing Kwame Ture talk strategy during social unrest, hearing stories Dick Gregory would tell about the struggle—these were all powerful influences connected to the larger movement. And in Denver, we have this powerful heritage in the Chicano movement led by Corky Gonzales.

Another result of your artistic vision is the fact that we're a repertory company that honors your voice, but not to the exclusion of other voices. You support other artists and other choreographers, but also other leaders in the organization. There's real ownership of the work, but not an idea of sole ownership. It's the idea that we are all caretakers of our mission, and for lifting other voices.

CPR: They're all voices, some that didn't even think that they had a voice. With Project Self-Discovery, we were working with gangs, mostly Bloods, Crips, girl gangs, skinheads, and everyone in between. For them to find another way to self-express, that's more powerful than what they might have inherited, through no fault of their own. If you grow up in a house with a second generation of Bloods, then you're probably gonna be a Blood. You see nothing wrong with that because that gives you some type of identity. You're unable to discover a larger identity that could bring pride to your family and dignity to yourself and give you a more meaningful life. Oftentimes the greatest goal for these young people is to live beyond the age of nineteen without ending up in jail or being killed.

Now we're seeing a lot of violence in our communities. Our young people are trying to understand where we come from, to see where we are, and then where we need to go. There are a lot of things that we may have to revisit in a new way. How do we get back to building communities? We're just a larger world; everything's more complex.

Maybe there's some simplicity, some way we can become addicted to harmony. How do we get addicted to beauty and the things that are truly soulful? I see it in my grandbabies; they speak about beauty all the time. We have to find a way to stay in that mindset, creating villages that aren't just a support for our dancers. How do we bring out the genius in every human being, give and receive this collective cultural wealth, even as the new generation comes forward to inspire us all?

I think about our family who migrated from the South, from Texarkana, Arkansas, from Texas. They were migrating with whatever they were carrying on their backs. My father came that way. He left the South because he didn't want to pick cotton, but he had to prove himself all the time. There's that self-driven place of thinking, "Am I doing it well enough?" But I think part of the culture is actually, "Am I doing it well enough for myself and not just for others?" There's that internal judgment that asks, "What if it's not authentic enough?" Ultimately, it should be: "Am I doing this well enough to help and uplift others?"

Culture and Tradition

A MONUMENT TO OUR RESILIENCE

Ofelia Esparza

Ofelia Esparza is a Chicana printmaker and sixth-generation altarista (altar maker), whose work is informed by a deep spiritual belief in the traditional process. For over forty years, Esparza has shared her cultural knowledge as an educator in the East Los Angeles neighborhood of City Terrace and at the renowned art center Self Help Graphics.

Noche de Ofrenda has become, for me, the highlight of the observances of Día de los Muertos because it draws upon the significance of the altar itself; on the ofrendas, the offerings that we place on it with intention to honor, remember, contemplate, reflect, and to celebrate the lives of our loved ones who have passed on.

Today, when so many lives have been lost to COVID-19, including my own brother Rudolf Estrada (ninety-six) and sister Evangelina Jaquez (eighty-seven), and so many other forms of loss and upheaval have affected our lives, a Noche de Ofrenda gains even more significance to our community. We all need a time for reflection, for gratitude, for healing, and yes, a time for social awareness as a community. As we honor our loved ones, we remember our ancestors who are always with us. We are grateful for their legacy of struggle, survival, and resilience, for their stories, their love of family and culture, and their determination to provide a better life for the next generations.

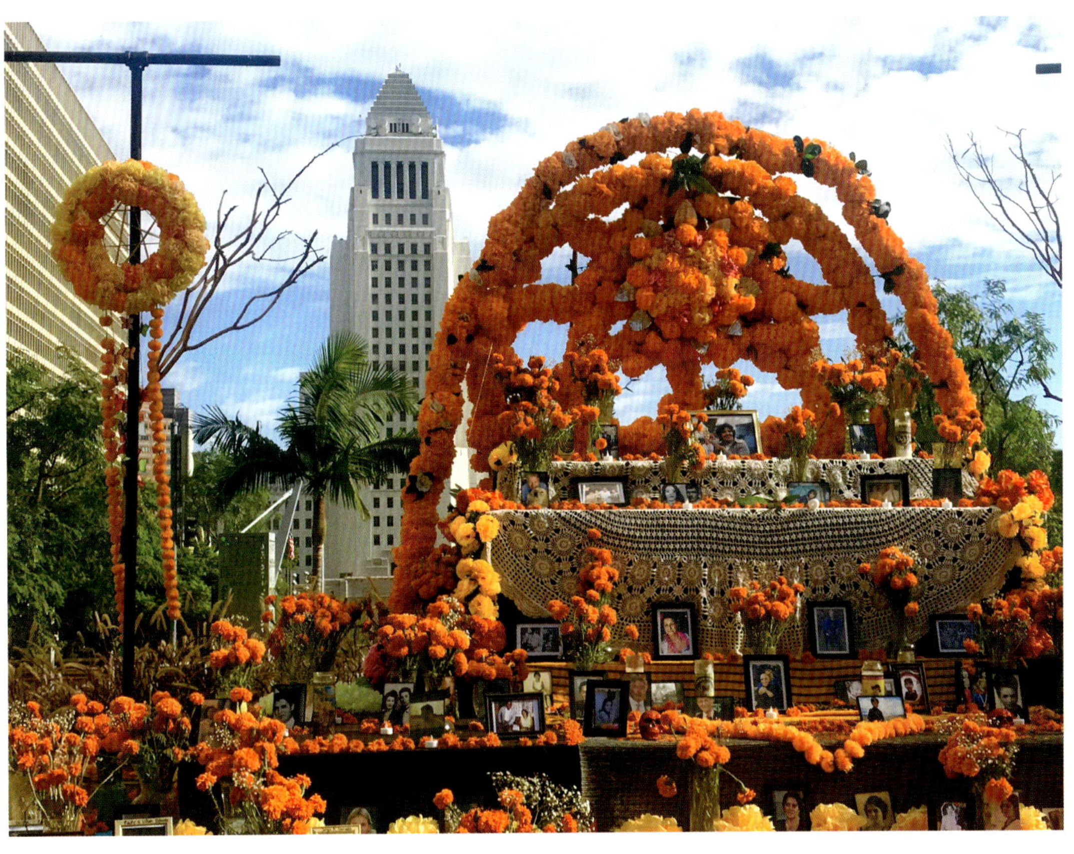

Ofelia Esparza and Rosanna Esparza Ahrens, *Noche de Ofrenda*, 2020. Day of the Dead community altar at Grand Park in downtown Los Angeles. Photo: Carlos Aguilar.

Español

Yanina Chicas

Yanina Chicas, a proud first-generation Salvadoran American, is a DC-based poet who attends the Maret School. She is a member of the 2021 Words Beats & Life poetry slam team. In the future, she wants to become a voice for the Latinx community through poetry or by becoming a lawyer.

Español uno de los idiomas más universal
El idioma que me ayuda comunicar con la gente de 33 países
Pero porque tanto odio hacia el español
Ay todo suena más poderoso con el español
Hasta los regaños de nuestros parientes
"Hija de tu madre, lava los trastes"
Hasta las críticas de las tías
"Y cuando vas adelgazar hija"
Son más dolorosos que mil disparos al corazón

You hear the spice in Spanish
That same spice that took away from my tribe's language
Español uno de los idiomas más universales que mi gente ni siquiera
    quería hablar.
Spaniards, yes you, the colonizers of my lovely country,
You hate me for the way I speak your language,
But stripped me from my native tongue.
I better not try to speak in America because they'll tell me to speak En-
    glish but they forget their colonizers also stripped this country from
    their native tongue.

You see I get thinking how you embarked to a country,
Managed to "discover it" and make up stupid ideologies of our beautiful
    native women,
The ones you seemed to have "adored" for their radiant caramel skin,
Raped them and committed a deadly sin,
Ignored their cries to stop and left them in their own chagrin.

And adding on to that you make us think that we have to fix,
The mix that you created.
You make me so frustrated,
Make my india come out.

Make OUR little curse words come out,
Yes, the ones that hit harder than the chancla my mamita throws,
The ones that have had made my emotional shell harder,
The ones you, Spain, won't accept because
We made YOUR language sound a way better, call it a remix.

Yo te continuó hablando en español,
Even if it damaged our history,
Y aunque, my tribe's language, has vanished.
You did not manage to erase the beauty and built-in strength of my an-
    cestors' skin.
As their kin we ain't just gonna claim the Spanish,
Remember the tribe's heart lives within,
Y va seguir palpitando sin importar lo que nos dicen.

Apsáalooke Feminist #4

Wendy Red Star

I work across disciplines to explore the intersections of Native American ideologies and colonialist structures, both historically and in contemporary society. I was raised on the Apsáalooke (Crow) reservation in Montana; my work is informed by both my cultural heritage and my engagement with many forms of creative expression, including photography, sculpture, video, fiber arts, and performance. An avid researcher of archives and historical narratives, I seek to incorporate and recast my research, offering new and unexpected perspectives in work that is at once inquisitive, witty, and unsettling.

In my series *Apsáalooke Feminist*, I photographed myself and my daughter wearing traditional elk tooth dress, representing my Crow heritage and emphasizing the matrilineality of my tribe. I use the title *Apsáalooke Feminist* to highlight the irony of using the term *feminist* to describe the matrilineal culture of the Crow Nation. Though I regard feminism as an offspring of colonialism, I believe that within the movement there should be room for an Apsáalooke feminism that is historically and culturally specific to Crow women. Intergenerational collaborative work is integral to my practice, along with creating a forum for the expression of Native women's voices in contemporary art. I want Native women to have a place within the art world without being an anomaly or special division, but seen as a part of a current and evolving conversation.

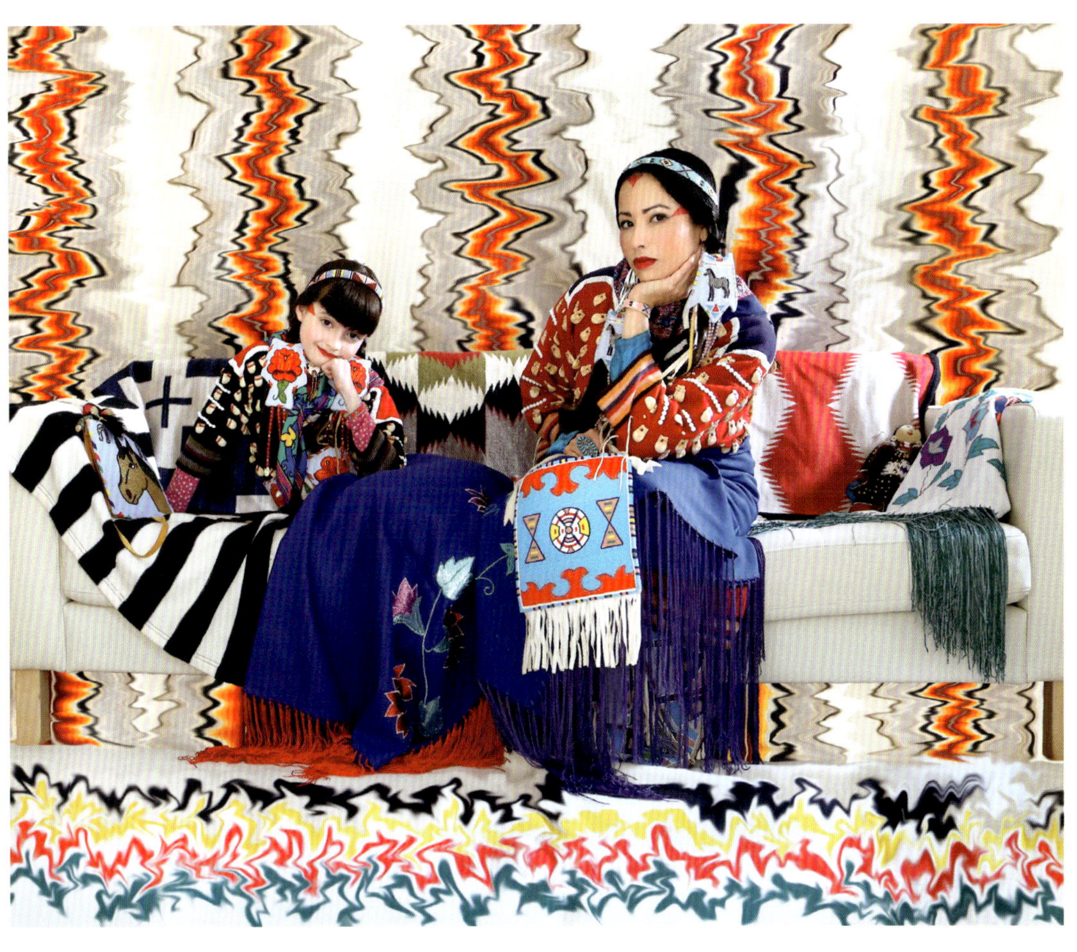

Wendy Red Star, *Apsáalooke Feminist #4*, 2016. Archival pigment print, 35 × 42 in. Photo: Beatrice Red Star Fletcher.

Mother's Words and Grandmother's Thoughts

LIVING THE RIGHT WAY
(A CONVERSATION)

Maribel Alvarez and Ofelia Zepeda

Maribel Alvarez is an anthropologist, folklorist, writer, and curator. She holds the Jim Griffith Chair in Public Folklore at the Southwest Center, University of Arizona. She is the founder of the Southwest Folklife Alliance.

Ofelia Zepeda is a member of the Tohono O'odham Nation. She holds a PhD in linguistics from the University of Arizona and is a recipient of a MacArthur Fellowship for her work in American Indian language education. Her poetry collections include *Ocean Power: Poems from the Desert* (1995) and *Where Clouds Are Formed* (2008).

Applying ancestral knowledge and creativity to cope with the present and to strategize the future can sometimes mean turning upside down the common turns of phrases that we invoke casually to confront a world in trouble. In the following conversation, folklorist and cultural documentarian Dr. Maribel Alvarez speaks with poet and linguist Dr. Ofelia Zepeda (Tohono O'odham) about the zigzag ways of Indigenous wisdom derived from stories, nature, and practical humor before life's challenges, the urge to "fix the earth" hastily, language used as instruction and weapon, and the excruciating learning curve of patience in the face of uncertain outcomes.

Editor's Note: This contribution was edited from a virtual conversation between Maribel Alvarez and Ofelia Zepeda on September 8, 2020.

MARIBEL ALVAREZ: Ofelia, thank you for making space for this exchange. I was introduced recently to the concept of language justice. In public programs, many of us are familiar with an American Sign Language interpreter, or a non-English translator, appearing in the event, in person or online, in a little corner or by the side. But in a framework of justice, that intervention is more than routine. It compels us to ask: What dynamics of power are we privileging when we are listening? What do you make of this notion?

OFELIA ZEPEDA: The use of the word *justice*, in reference to language, is a bit more recent. Of course, we have had the notion of language rights for many years. Indigenous populations have had these terms in their vocabulary for quite some time. Language rights have been important, especially for languages which have been marginalized and impacted negatively by larger dominant languages. The impact in some cases has been dramatic, resulting in language loss. To take a position of language rights, or justice, is also to affirm the belief that all languages must have a place at the table for the benefit of everyone. This means not relegating this responsibility to the edges, as the interest of a few. But this is a very difficult position to hold. Because language is so powerful, especially if you are a large group, it is hard to make room for others.

MA: I have felt myself marked differently in social and professional settings because I speak with an accent. Having grown up with a first language that was not English, occasionally, I may be in a meeting, and when least expected I can sense my language identity markers exposing me in ways I cannot always predict.

OZ: How you sound plays into dynamics of power. Research tells us that even women's voices set them off in power dynamics of group speech different than men. When people hear a woman's voice, they respond differently to the information they are receiving. The same thing happens with people whose first language is not English. It is not that you, as the speaker, lose something, but that others don't understand the value or the context you bring for being bilingual.

MA: You wrote a poem that I feel addresses this strange dynamic of reversal. It is called "Don't Be Like the Enemy."[1] I cite only a few lines:

> This is what she said, "Don't be like the enemy, keep your hair out of
>   your face."
> Tie it back, don't be like a savage.
> Let them see your face, let them know the light in your eyes.

Is this reference to the non-Native person with hair on their face some form of O'odham vernacular knowledge about the other?

OZ: Well, I know that idea comes from my mother's generation. That is a phrase that she used to say to us. We all had thick, long hair, and she was always adamant about making sure that our hair was out of our face. When you went to school, you could not wear the hair hanging down. She would tie it up, braid it, whatever it took to keep it away from your face. And if you messed up your hair, she would say, people might see you as unkempt. Just like what you said about the way that you speak English, that first impression will cause people to read something into it that you are not. So, for her generation, properly cared-for hair was associated with being neat, and neatness was a quality associated with "being civilized."

MA: And "being civilized," of course, was the ultimate colonial put-down—viewing the Indigenous person as less than human.

OZ: Certainly. But the word *enemy* in the poem is more than a simple take on colonizers. For many O'odham, the traditional enemy were the Apache people. I don't know that my mother ever saw Apaches when she was young. I know that she grew up as a young girl hearing the admonition from her father that when she went out in the desert to collect food and things to hide in case she saw somebody she didn't know. Whether it was other raiding tribes or a White settler, she grew up in that era. The O'odham word for enemy can refer to settlers or to other indigenous groups not O'odham. My mother lumped all these people as common threats to O'odham ways of life, as fools who have messy hair in their face because they are always running around. But she also held this idea that a face that is clear does not imply you act with arrogance. Her advice was to never look fully frontal, with your face, even to other O'odham.

MA: This is a complicated telling. It complicates the story of gesture, of Native cultural behavior, in ways I don't think are apparent to the casual reader. It evokes, on one level, heavy words like *enemy* and *savage*. In the context of indigenous history, we recognize in those terms the enterprise of colonialism. But the O'odham point of view you are describing centers the O'odham as a community threatened by many forms of intrusion.

OZ: The poem says, "let them see the light in your eyes, but don't stare." The advice is to cover the face by lowering it slightly, not by using hair. It sounds like a contradiction, but it is not.

MA: In the reference to "lowering the face slightly," you introduce the cultural value of humility. But this is not a humility that implies accepting subjection; it is more about honor and knowing one's correct place in the larger balance of relationships: not too forward, not too shy. The native wisdom you uplift is one that demonstrates a complicated take on humanity.

OZ: Right, it is not simple.

MA: Your poem refuses to allow me, as a listener/reader, the comfort of drawing a one-dimensional portrait of O'odham life.

OZ: And the odd thing is that my mother said those things to us when we were in elementary school. We did not grasp the message in full at that time. We barely scratched the surface of her meaning. As a child, I took things literally. My immediate response was to comb my hair to keep it out of my face, period. It was not until I got much older that I developed a sense of intuition that allowed me to grasp a deeper meaning.

MA: Yes, perhaps even coming to the realization that what she was saying was only partially about hair. I think that was pretty audacious wisdom. There is a poem you wrote, entitled "The Other World," that speaks to this point from the angle of the complications for Native youth between popular culture and a longing to be authentic to their cultural roots.

OZ: Oh, that poem narrates a field trip to the mountains with my granddaughter when she was of elementary school age. Every now and then, we would go way out to some desolate mountain areas, just to camp, or my husband would have a photographic project. She would go with us for a couple of nights. I wanted her to get accustomed to being out in nature, considering she lived in a city.

MA: Here is the first stanza:

> "She said, 'When we get back to
> our world, can we rent a video
> we can all watch?'
> 'What do you mean, our world?
> This place is your world.
> This place of sand, rocks, mesquite,
> rattlesnakes, lizards, and little rain.
> This is yours.'"[2]

And in the next verse we find the nonchalant response from the young woman:

> "Oh, okay, when we get back to the other
> world, can we rent a video...."

You impart a timeless lesson of place and belonging by playing with the possessive pronouns *ours*. But the child does not skip a beat—she redirects the intention of the lesson by invoking, instead, a geography of displacement: "this world" and the "other" world. Cleverly, she accepts Grandma's gift of wisdom. But this claimed world of natural wonder and wisdom has no video stores. It is clear that she wants to be a deft negotiator in both settings!

OZ: Yes, and she was always anticipating getting back "home." She makes it sound like we were gone for a long time. "The first thing I'm going to do when I get back," she says, but the trip was only two nights! She saw the desert as another place, literally a different world. That is the work of poetry, to gently, or fiercely, redirect our interpretations.

MA: In these poems, we connect with your mother's words on one end, and with your granddaughter's thoughts on the other. There is a through line in indigenous knowledge that reckons with the past, posits the fixing of the present, and imagines the future. The summer of 2020, in addition to many other challenges, also brought almost no rain to the desert. What kind of hope can we write into the future when the present reality seems so compromised?

OZ: I know the one big rain we got was in July. It was raining early at night and early in the morning. My mother and her family are from an O'odham village in Sonora, Mexico, where members of the community perform an annual ritual they call "fixing the earth." It is something they do for the benefit of all humanity; it is also done to help bring rain. My mother used to say, "Well, it always rains this time of year (meaning the summer), and that's because we always do the ceremony this time of year." They felt they did their part. But nowadays, it feels that is not enough. To make sense of things, the people say the problem is that the earth has gotten bigger, so the ritual is not able to make the kind of difference it used to. And they say, "But that is okay, because one day it will work again. It may be next summer, or it may not. Maybe two summers from now, it will make a significant enough impact that we will have a good, rainy summer." The community sees that this huge place that we live in is in trouble; such big trouble that the ritual that has always been done, for hundreds or thousands of years, is not enough. But at the same time, they are hopeful. They are not going to stop doing it just because it did not work. They say, "Maybe things will be better."

MA: How do we make sense of that optimism in the face of "big trouble"?

OZ: That is a big question I have been thinking about. It bothers me when the weather report keeps saying how little rain we had. I don't want to be reminded; that's not the point. It's not just the rain. It is all the other things that are interconnected that have gotten us to this point. Some of it, we can control. Some of it, we cannot. But you must do your part. For my parents' generation, that is how you confront a challenge. In a sense, it is hopeful. But it is not hope born out of a shallow wish. The O'odham have always been hopeful and realistic about the environment. Otherwise, they would have never lasted as long as they have in this desert. I find it helpful to think about it this way. I know that is how my parents would think and speak about it.

MA: Perhaps the time horizon of our optimism is too short. When the O'odham reflect that they have been a people in the desert for thousands of years, community wellness is more than the trouble of here and now.

OZ: It can be frustrating. Many people don't have an understanding about how there can be power in waiting.

MA: It can be especially difficult if you are someone who wants to act upon the world to make it better. Artists, poets, are in the business of transformation.

OZ: Maybe "waiting" and "dwelling" are two different things. In some cases, you can be proactive and do certain things. But a lot of times, you just can't. You just wait and see if something will heal itself. I think that demands a different kind of patience. By the way, I'm not very good at waiting.

MA: In the introduction to your book *Ocean Power*, which you entitled "Things That Help Me Begin to Remember," you wrote about cycles, careful observations, and relief. I mean, at some point the desert's heat is unbearable. You write a poem about cooking a tortilla in 115 degrees. But then, the rain breaks the tension. When situations are precarious, every intention counts. You wrote:

> Like the people before them, these women gauged the movement of the summer sun and the amount of work that needed to be done. . . . The women planned their day around the heat and the coolness of the summer day. They knew the climate and felt confident in it.[3]

OZ: There is relief, but then the cycle continues. There will be heat again, unbearable heat.

MA: I suppose I am guilty of overthinking the troubles of the present and the implications for the future. You seem to take a different path to that complicated truth. Your path is not fatalistic or passive in any sense, but you seem to be working with more variables than most of us consider at any single intersection. I am compelled by this beauty you seem determined to uplift.

OZ: Well, I can always try to imagine what my parents would have done if they had lived during the COVID pandemic, for example. They would have listened to the news, be abreast of the issues worldwide. And then again, there is a phrase that many O'odham and other indigenous people use that has to do with "living the right way." That phrase does not refer to the way the pandemic started or suggests that anyone did anything wrong. They would have used it once the pandemic got out of control and people were told how they should behave, how they should live now in order to help stop the spread. I can see my parents taking all those protocols very seriously. Their thoughts would have been, "This is the way we must live now, a new kind of right way to live, until things change again." And I think they would have assessed the severity of the COVID pandemic in light of other big catastrophes they or that the culture lived through. And the lesson they would have derived from it all was that you have to adapt and change to survive and go forward as a culture. And if my parents themselves had not lived through those catastrophes, they would have known the stories through their own parents and their grandparents, and so forth. They had that kind of memory.

MA: But of course, we are very accustomed to seeking immediate resolutions. It has been interesting to hear people describe the longing to go "back to normal." Your view on this layered exercise of grit and savvy was captured in a phrase you used in *Ocean Power*: "Flooding waters were a cautious gift." Thanks for reminding me of the hidden dangers in our binary way of thinking that things are either all good or all bad. I close our time together with your words of wonder:

> To the women, my mother, my grandmother, there was beauty in all these events, the events of a summer rain, the things that preceded the rain and the events afterward. They laughed with joy at all of it.[4]

Notes

1. Ofelia Zepeda, *Ocean Power: Poems from the Desert* (Tucson: University of Arizona Press, 1995), 37.

2. Ofelia Zepeda, *Where Clouds Are Formed* (Tucson: University of Arizona Press, 2008), 27.

3. Zepeda, *Ocean Power*, 1.

4. Zepeda, *Ocean Power*, 3.

The AIM Song

Elisa Harkins

Elisa Harkins is an Indigenous (Cherokee/Muscogee) artist and composer whose work is concerned with translation, language preservation, and Indigenous musicology. Harkins uses the Cherokee and Muscogee languages, music, sculpture, and the body as her tools. Harkins is a Tulsa Artist Fellow and an enrolled member of the Muscogee (Creek) Nation.

The American Indian Movement (AIM) song for me is an anthem, an honor song, and a protest song. It is a way to connect with my deceased grandmother, Lana Turner, whom I never met but I recently learned was an AIM member. My aunt told me that she would drag all of her children (including my father) to AIM meetings. It is also a song of peace that defused a potentially dangerous situation between an Omaha elder and a menacing group of Catholic students. And it was a symbol of unity between Black and Indigenous people at a rally against Trump in downtown Tulsa, Oklahoma, which turned into a Juneteenth celebration. This song's history is like a spiderweb—it is a constellation where I can start to see intergenerational connections.

The American Indian Movement started after the Summer of Love. It was in July of 1968 that Dennis Banks, Russell Means, and Clyde Bellecourt first created this coalition for advocacy and activism for Indigenous people. It is said that before AIM, Indigenous people were completely invisible, then suddenly, someone was willing to give voice to the injustices that were happening to them. It made Indigenous people proud to be Indigenous. And it made it so that Indigenous people could organize and expose the abuse and systemic racism happening to them by the hands of the US government.

I first heard about the AIM song from Louis Gray, an Osage elder. He and his sister, Gina Gray, were at the Institute of American Indian Arts when they heard about the occupation of Wounded Knee in 1973. These

American Indian Movement Song
Sung by Louis Gray (Osage)

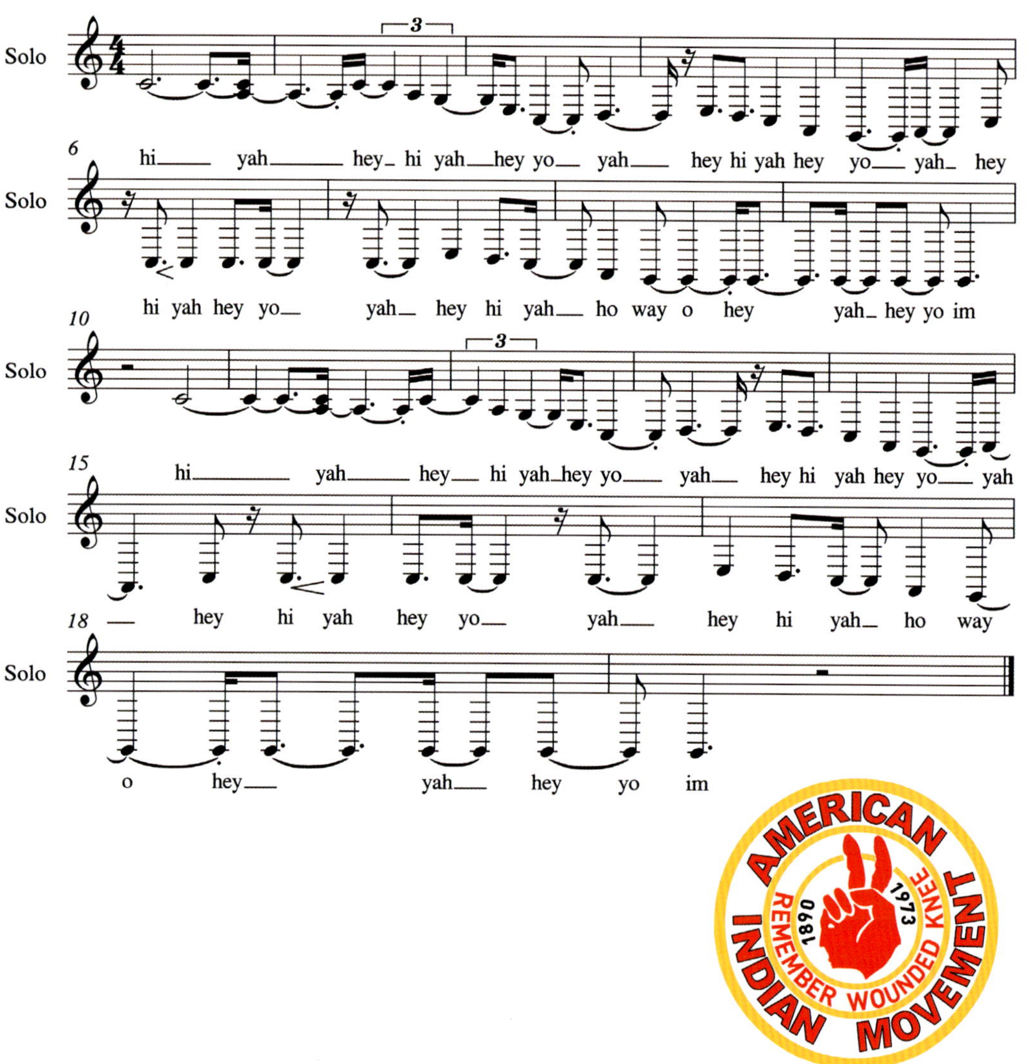

Elisa Harkins, *The AIM Song*, 2020. Signed and numbered
screen print, edition of eight, 27.5 × 19.5 in.

two young college students hitchhiked their way from Santa Fe to the Pine Ridge Indian Reservation in South Dakota to meet up with their older sister Mary Grayce Gray to join the protest. After they arrived, Gina joined Mary and worked in the kitchen preparing meals while Louis was assigned to a bunker. Only nineteen years old at the time, Louis had not come prepared for the cold. He dressed in four layers of clothes, but it was no match for the dead of winter in South Dakota. The blizzards, lack of food, and US marshals shooting at them made conditions tough, but Louis and his sisters continued to support the occupation.

That was where Louis first learned the AIM song. It was a powerful song for those involved in Wounded Knee and the movement. They sang it every time the moment called for it, to get their spirits lifted. They would sing the AIM song if they heard good news; they would sing the AIM song if they heard bad news.

At one point, Louis left his bunker to search for his sisters. He heard that goons were raping women in the movement, and he found them in the nearby town of Porcupine. The press descended upon them, and little to Louis's knowledge, his mother and father saw him on the news, which was broadcast to their home in Denver, Colorado. His father had no idea that his son and two daughters were at Wounded Knee, and after watching Louis on the news, he flew to South Dakota. His father spent two weeks in Porcupine trying to find his children. He slept on benches until the Red Cross was allowed to enter the perimeter of Wounded Knee, and he went along with them.

Earlier that day, a grass fire had started at Wounded Knee, and everyone had tried to stomp it out. There was smoke everywhere. Louis and his sisters were standing in front of the church when they saw, from 200 yards away, a caravan of Red Cross and civil rights activists driving toward them. Even at that distance, Louis could make out William Kunstler, who had defended the Chicago Eight. There were also men in suits, one of which was the Rev. Ralph Abernathy, and the shape of a man who looked familiar. The familiar silhouette emerged from the billowing clouds of smoke and walked toward them on the road. His sister said, "That looks like Dad!" Louis and his sisters stood in disbelief as their father hugged them, telling them he had plane tickets for whoever wanted to go. Gina and Louis decided to fly back to school in Santa Fe while Mary Grayce Gray stayed and became an AIM member, eventually marrying Henry Wahwassuck.

On January 18, 2019, there was an Indigenous Peoples March at the Lincoln Memorial. After the march there was a round dance and a rally. At the rally, a group of three hundred teenage students from Covington Catholic High School (Kentucky) started disrupting the peaceful protest. They were wearing Make America Great Again hats and shirts and yelling an appropriated Māori haka, which they called the "Sumo Chant," along with other jeering and posturing. These taunts were directed toward a group of Black Hebrew Israelites. At this time, Indigenous activist, elder, and pipe holder Nathan Phillips decided to intervene by playing the hand drum and singing the AIM song. During the first few leads of the song, the high school students completely surrounded Phillips and Marcus Frejo, a Pawnee/Seminole singer and activist. As the two were singing, they could hear mocking and laughter, feeling the hatred and bigotry toward Indigenous people. But they kept singing, even with Covington student Nick Sandman standing face to face with Nathan Phillips. Then something interesting happened that no one expected—the Covington students started singing along. Perhaps it was first out of hatred; they were mocking the singing. But then it turned into the students actually learning and singing the AIM song and unwittingly honoring decades of Indigenous struggle. Then one of the students said, "Come on, let's go," and a potentially dangerous situation was dissolved. This song was sung by our ancestors. My grandmother conceived a child at Wounded Knee. She sang this song. It brought her strength and pride. Perhaps the students could feel the history in the song, and perhaps for a moment it took away their hatred.

I currently live in Tulsa, Oklahoma, in the Greenwood District, the historic neighborhood of the 1921 Race Massacre. This was a thriving Black neighborhood full of Black-owned businesses, and it was burned to the ground. The neighborhood was so successful monetarily that it was dubbed Black Wall Street. This metonym was not in reference to stocks and trading, but rather to the wealth and prosperity of the businesses. There were small businesses right next to each other, from lunch counters and barber shops to the Dreamland Theater and the Vernon African Methodist Episcopal Church. In May 1921, a young Black shoe shiner named Dick Rowland was accused of attacking a white female elevator attendant in a building downtown, which resulted in his detainment and threats of lynching. Members of the Greenwood Black community waited outside the jail in fear of these threats coming true. The KKK found this to be an opportunity to challenge the community members, which turned into an armed scuffle, during which shots were fired by those from the Greenwood community. The KKK and mobs of white rioters then decided to storm the Greenwood neighborhood, going from business to business and house to house, murdering people.

On June 20, 2020, the day after Juneteenth, Trump scheduled a campaign rally at the BOK Center in downtown Tulsa. I hadn't planned to go downtown to join the Black Lives Matter march, but my friend Marcus

Frejo (the protester who stood with Nathan Phillips at the Indigenous Peoples March) and his son met me in Greenwood. They were eager to march and asked where the BOK Center was. We drove over to check it out. We saw street medics on the corner and asked where the protest was happening. They told us that the march had left but always returned to that intersection, so Marcus and his son brought out their hand drums and started singing. This started to attract some attention, and some AIM members came over and began to sing the AIM song in solidarity with Black Lives Matter. The three of us joined in, and I started to understand the importance of the song—that we could be in the middle of a protest and not know anyone and start singing this song, and we would find our brothers and sisters. Not only did it attract Indigenous singers, but also Indigenous onlookers, medics, and protesters. You could feel the pride as they offered fists in the air. After a standoff with the police, the protesters decided to march into Greenwood. I followed Marcus and his son as they were drumming and singing, and I joined in, even recognizing a Muscogee (Creek) hymn coming from the pair. As we marched into Greenwood, I saw Marcus and his son hold their drums up high as the protesters joined the Juneteenth gathering, and the street erupted into a joyous celebration. It was a clear victory. We outnumbered the Trump supporters. We had won.

Gullah/Geechee Sea Island Reflections of Futurity

Queen Quet Marquetta L. Goodwine

Queen Quet Marquetta L. Goodwine is a published author, computer scientist, lecturer, mathematician, historian, columnist, preservationist, environmental justice advocate, environmentalist, film consultant, and "The Art-ivist." She is the founder of the premier advocacy organization for the continuation of Gullah/Geechee culture, the Gullah/Geechee Sea Island Coalition.

Sankofa mi yeddi win mi bin da gwine tru de doe. Sankofa hunnuh chillun cum 'gain, but de chillun ain kno. Ef hunnuh ain kno whey hunnuh dey frum, how hunnuh gwine kno whey fa go? Yeah, Sankofa! Like e say een de chuch, "Say so! Say so!"

Within the Gullah/Geechee Nation on the marsh-strewn Sea Islands from Jacksonville, NC, to Jacksonville, FL, proverbs are not just words. They are life! In fact, when one does not understand certain things along your journey, the elders will often simply say, "Just live." However, how do you live in such a way that creates the future you want when you must survive today? This is the question that comes to many an artistic mind along the creative journey. It is one that has to be answered in and from the depth of your soul. This may cause you to take a journey that seems painful, but from it, you will definitely emerge more powerful.

To harness the power of my being, I realized that I couldn't be confined to the titles that many others were comfortable in. I figured this was an outcome of how the stars and moon were aligned when I was conceived, and over time I also realized that much of it needed to be attributed to the ancestral power that enters my being every time I step on Sea Island soil and take in a deep breath of the salt-filled air that surrounds me here in what is often referred to as the Carolina Lowcountry.

When I go out into the fields to harvest foods, I find myself singing the spirituals that were codified in these same fields when my ancestors "worked the plantations." Their indigo-colored souls surround me and syncopate the harmony and the rhythm that sets the pace of my work. Although we grow edible crops now, I am still adorned in cotton, and I give thanks for them and the blood that is still in this soil from their fingers that bled when they touched the cotton bolls to bring in the cash crops that paid masses of people to their exclusion.

Just then in my mind's eye, I picture some of the outstanding artwork bearing Sea Island cotton, indigo, and Carolina gold rice fields and our people within them and that I have in my collection of Gullah art. I think of how once again, we-dem one down ya wha say "WEBE Gullah/Geechee" couldn't be confined by the genres that had been articulated about artistic expressions on canvas so one got created to encompass the ancestral knowledge and imagery that comes out via paint and multimedia in the way ancestral knowledge carved the environment of the southeastern coast into what is considered the Gullah/Geechee cultural landscape.

This Gullah/Geechee landscape is what inspired me and allowed me the zone in which my elders and my ancestors could speak words into my soul that directed what my true name in the presentation arena needed to be. I was awakened in the middle of the night to be donned with the word that fit the description for what I was destined to do.

I am "The Art-ivist." Not "an artist" nor "an activist."[1] I created the terminology decades ago and traveled the world doing activism through the art and have since learned that others have been inspired by hearing the term "The Art-ivist" and would love to do what that is, but to this I find myself responding, "This is not something you teach. This is something that you live."

When I created "art-ivism" and "histo-musical presentations," these things were radical because every other person that knew the stories, songs, and antidotes of native Gullah/Geechees used them amid the Spanish moss–covered oak trees in hush arbors where we were out of earshot of the outsiders—white and non-Gullah/Geechee Black. To speak Gullah/Geechee in public places disrupted those spaces four decades ago when I began, and it still does. The radical ability to code switch between spoken languages, to song, to body movements that bring to life ancestral spirits and speak in the tongues of elders of African Gullah/Geechee wisdom was, and often still is, considered ahead of its time. Yes, it is interestingly seen as futuristic although its base is in that which is ancient.

When one sees the word *futurity* and its relatives, you no doubt think of what is to come. Yet I have elected to be a living Sankofa bird flying forward while my neck is arched back, completing an unbroken circle as a visual arch seen literally and through the spiritual eye. As I dance, I sing, and I speak, I reach backward to the lives of my ancestors that came over during chattel enslavement by no choice of their own and find the drum in their spirit that caused them to march on through these fields and navigate this new landscape in such a way that their very teardrops and drops of blood that hit the soil here left a resounding echo and a pulsation that enters me as my feet connect with the sand in which their footsteps and their very bones are embedded. I am renewed. With this power, the Gullah/Geechee Nation continues to exist. Yes, this is the very definition of futurity to which I have a duty as "The Art-ivist" to continually fly toward while reaching back to get that African mind, that African soul energy, that African power that is sometimes left behind.

Queen Quet leads ancestral tribute libation ceremony at the Gullah/Geechee Nation International Music and Movement Festival, Gasden's Wharf, Charleston, South Carolina. Photo: Kumar L. Goodwine-Kennedy, © Gullah/Geechee Sea Island Coalition. Used with permission from the Gullah/Geechee Sea Island Coalition.

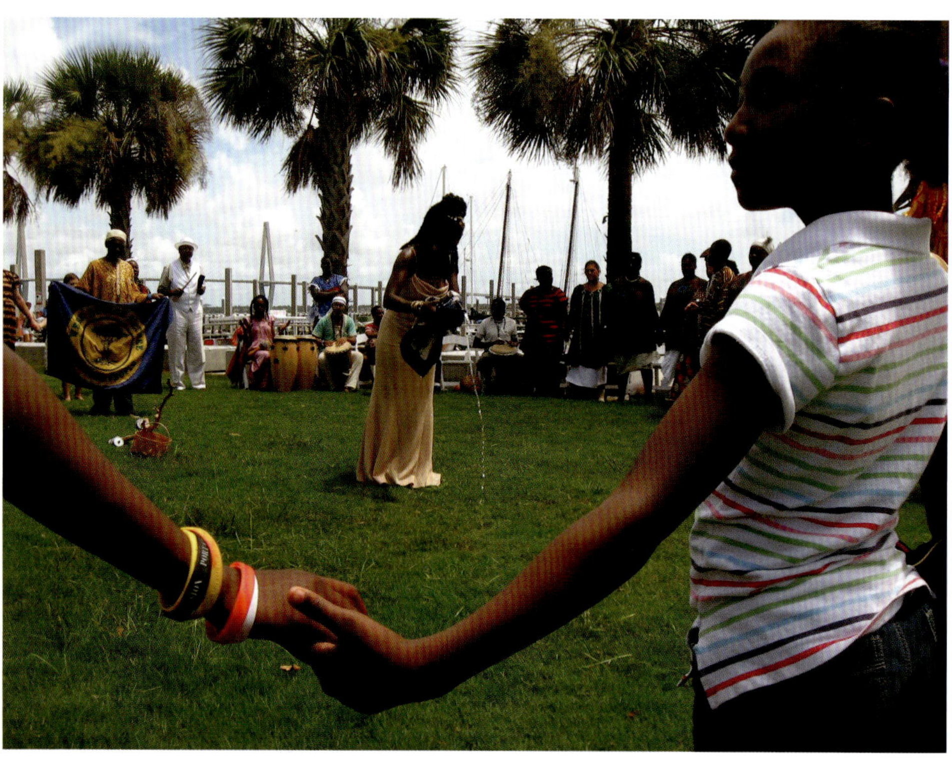

The Gullah/Geechee Nation allows for the space in which to be ever rooted in the soil that my ancestors were initially enslaved on, but were then able to self-emancipate on as well. This is the space that allowed for the Gullah/Geechee people to come together and stand on their right to self-determination on the same spot where over 40 percent of all Africans enslaved in North America were brought through and sold into bondage. This is the place in which the spirituals still live on within our walks syncopated to the polyrhythm that people become familiar with through our Sea Island hand clap that was created when the physical drums were banned—or was it? Maybe the drum actually is the true pace at which our hearts continued to beat in order to keep our blood pumping warm in our veins so that we can continue to create a space in which we not only "just live," but we have a valuable quality of life that we create. If it is up to me, disya wha e da. Disya wha mi da live fa!

So, again, I walk out to the shoreline in rhythm with the waves of the ocean. I stop and give thanks for this ancestral soil that reminds me of a pain-filled past while simultaneously acting as proof of the strength of my ancestors to survive all that they endured while they continued to create. So, I stand to create a new world in which there is equity and equality for all by drawing on the same power that brought about emancipation, self-determination, and "art-ivism," and I continue creating on new platforms digitally and evolving, knowing where I am from and looking forward to where GOD is calling me to go as I hear the ancestral voices in the distance saying, "Yeddi we! Sankofa!"

Note

1. The term *artivist* has also circulated since the 1990s, most notably cited from a "1997 gathering between Chicano artists from East Los Angeles and the Zapatistas in Chiapas, Mexico." "Artivism," Wikipedia, accessed December 8, 2022, https://en.wikipedia.org/wiki/Artivism.

For Paradise

Elizabeth M. Webb

Elizabeth M. Webb, an artist and filmmaker originally from Charlottesville, Virginia, is the senior creative producer for Arts in a Changing America. Her work is invested in issues surrounding race and identity, often using the lens of her own family history of migration and racial passing to explore larger, systemic constructs.

I.

In second grade, I dressed up as a question mark for Halloween. It was a modification of a superhero look, with a fuchsia sequin eye mask, a white apron-cum-cape, and a large cardboard question mark covered in tinfoil pinned to my chest. I wanted to both punctuate and provide an honest answer to the question I was so often asked—"What *are* you?" Question mark.

I like to think this was my first conceptual art piece.

My dark, curly hair and summer tan skin made me stand out in my nearly all-white elementary school in the county that surrounds Charlottesville, Virginia. It might also have explained why I was always cast as Chewbacca in our playground *Star Wars* role-play games, and almost certainly explained why people—classmates and strangers of all ages—felt compelled and entitled to ask me what I was, a question that was often preceded by a "compliment" about my "exotic" appearance.

The truth was: I didn't know much about my family background, at least on my dad's side, and growing up I felt a near responsibility not to ask him about it. It was a subject that I could sense, even from a young age, was painful for him to discuss. So I attempted contentment in my uncertainty, dutifully dodging the "What are you?"s with "What do you mean?"s or the more oblique story I had been told—"My mom's family is from Denmark and Germany. My dad's family has been in America for a long time."

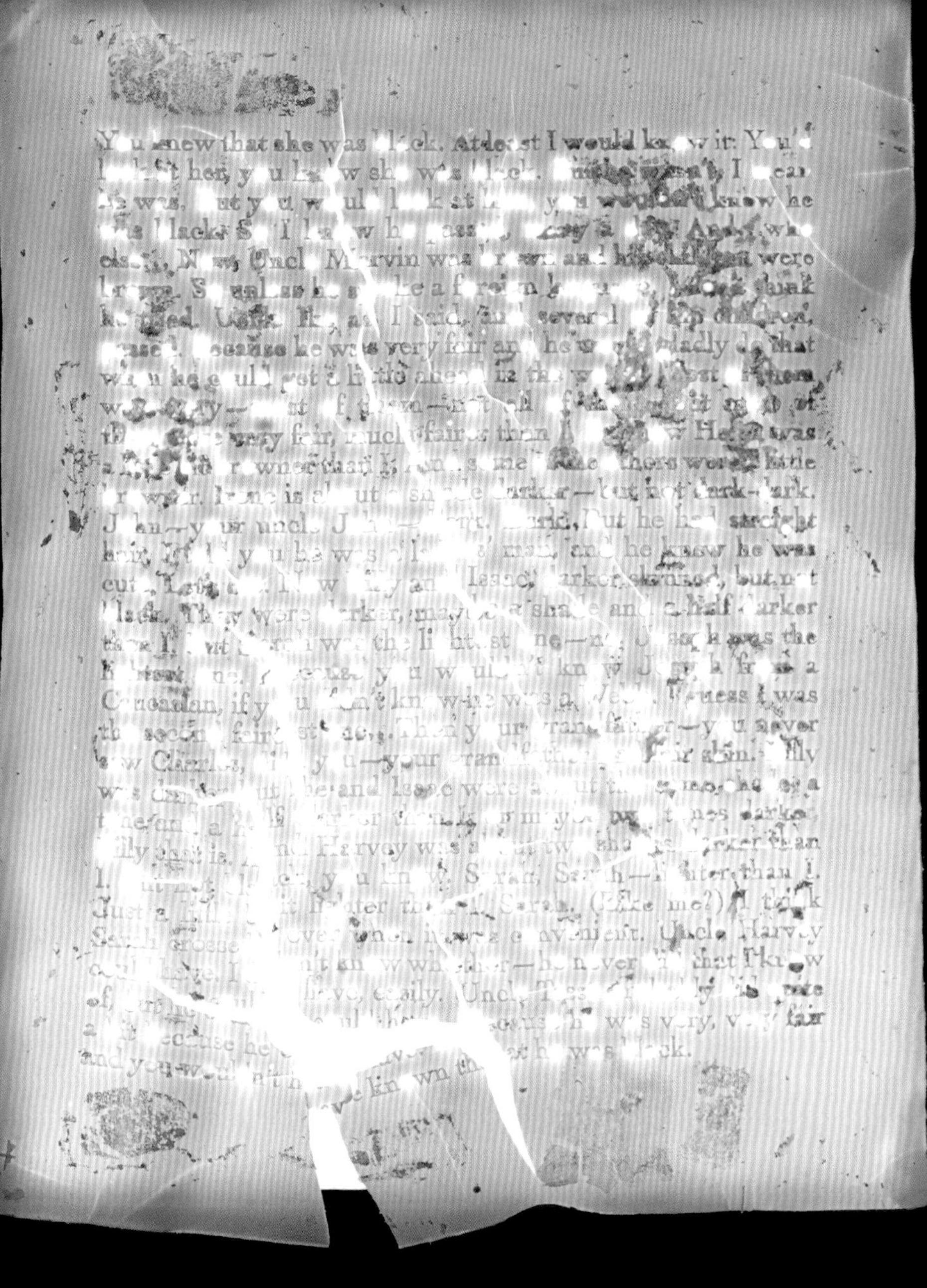

Elizabeth M. Webb, *Cameo Ground (Children of Paradise)*, 2018. Detail view of installation; porcelain, black velvet light box, text, each porcelain panel 8 × 10.5 in.

At eighteen, after many years of reading between the lines, I received from my father a partial answer to the question that so many others had voiced before me. My father's father, a man I'd never met, was Black. He had left my white grandmother and two children in rural Wisconsin just before my dad, their third, was born. My father grew up without a relationship with his own father, but his mixedness, coupled with his family's poverty, did not go unnoticed (or unpunished) in their mostly small, white town. When my father moved to Chicago and discovered that people could not immediately place his identity or point of origin, he eventually grew tired of correcting assumptions and decided to stop "checking the box" altogether. And when he and my mom moved to Charlottesville, Virginia, in the late 1980s and started a family, they chose to raise us in a predominantly white context as part of the majority.

My artistic practice (and equally, my own concept of self) has evolved alongside a process of coming to terms with my family's story as well as understanding the various histories and forms of cultural memory that inform our notions of identity. My discovery was in some ways validating of my experience, but it also gave weight to the deep sense of loss I had carried since childhood. People I could have known. Conversations I could have had. Memories I could have shared. I was drawn to re/build relationships with family members on both sides of the "color line."

I gathered us around the shape of what was lost, hoping to measure it.

II.

When I met my Great-Aunt Jane, she told me a story about her mother, who died in Alabama shortly after giving birth to Jane. She was a Black woman known for her beauty, but there were no recorded images of her. Her name was Paradise. Jane had spent her life determined to find a photograph of her mother. It felt, she told me, like her mother "just didn't exist."

At first, I felt compelled to join Jane in her quest. But when I, too, came up short, I sought refuge in the writings of a lineage of scholars who think through and around absence in the archive—Saidiya Hartman and Krista Thompson, among many others.[1] What would it mean for Paradise to have actively refused the recorded image? To abandon an archival project that was never built to hold her humanity in its fullness? How might her story be transformed from one of loss or lack to one of power and resistance?

Paradise becomes a mythic allegory for femininity and the denial of the gaze that raises larger questions about the nature of beauty, desire, and power. To borrow Kevin Young's terms, Paradise (or her story as substitute) occupies a space of freedom and necessary fiction, hidden in plain sight. She is, all at once, present and absent, the past and the future as imagined present. Her story (and my act of telling it) becomes precisely what her name represents: a freedom just out of reach—one that must be imagined before it can be achieved. In invoking her character, I am what Young would call "storying," or remapping the terms by which my own identity is understood by those around me, as an act of liberation.[2] Her story guides me as I navigate the spaces where power can be found in absence and loss.

No longer looking for an image, I trace her edges in the landscape that witnessed her life. I find pockets of memory, kept between the crisp rows of new-growth pine, along the top edge of her stacked stone chimney, and in the red Alabama clay that clings to your soles.

III.

Jane brought me also to the stories of her twelve siblings, each born in Alabama to Paradise. Many of them moved north to live among uncles who had migrated at different points during the Great Migration, after farming on the tired land handed down to them by their white father had proven unprofitable. When I asked her if any of them passed as white, she listed their shades in relation to her own with ease, as though she had been asked to do so many times before. This interview became the source for *Cameo Ground (Children of Paradise)*, a series of thirteen porcelain panels containing her interview as text. Because we are not given an image of Jane, the scale of skin tone that she outlines in relation to her own becomes relative to an unknown.

The process of making these works includes laser cutting text into paper (so that the text always begins as an absence) and covering the paper in porcelain slip. During the firing process, some words become filled in and others remain holes; fissures and cracks appear and form river-like gaps, and the text moves in and out of legibility. Because of the fickle nature of the process, the vast majority of the pieces are destroyed in the act of making them. The works ask us to read across them to understand the text—an act of reading across difference. I think of these pieces as portraits and cartographies, as maps of absences that also speak to the fragilities of family, perception, identity, and memory.

"When I saw you, I said, 'yep, you're a Webb.' And you can pick your shade, being a Webb."

IV.

In 2020, I moved back to Bedford-Stuyvesant, Brooklyn, just down the block from where my great-great-uncle passed as white to purchase a brownstone in 1939. He then brought the rest of his family up from Alabama, and they became one of the first Black families on the block. My grandfather, too, moved there, after leaving the rural Wisconsin town that proved hostile to a Black man raising a mixed-race family, and started a new life in Brooklyn as a longshoreman on the piers of Red Hook. Though I never met my grandfather, I can imagine that his move to what became known as Little Harlem allowed him to cultivate a greater sense of belonging. Just across the street from my apartment is a new luxury-apartment complex—sprouted from a building that was once the funeral home that prepared my grandfather's body for interment. The neighborhood is changing once again. Retracing his walking paths throughout Bed-Stuy, I think about how we walk/ed upon leaves shed from the same tree, many years apart and from radically different life experiences. Sometimes I run into family members and people who remember him sitting on the corner many years before. My cousin jokes that the family is so big, I probably pass cousins on the street all the time without knowing.

As I work to know these relationships, I notice that vision is fallible but cell memory is felt. The ways we see ourselves in each other go beyond resemblance (though I am comforted by the deep gray eyes and subtle pout many of us seem to share). My family history is a starting point—but my interest in it exists only insofar as it illuminates larger societal structures. Our story is not an uncommon one—it is in many ways quintessentially American, sprouted from a soil tilled by a legacy of white supremacy and erasure. I am invested in creating work that loosens up the ways we are programmed to think, and see, in order to work toward a decolonial visuality— one that defies boundary lines and finds care in the root networks that connect us all.

"You know, you're really white. But you're really Black too.
And I can look at your eyes and tell that."

....

In loving memory of Jane Webb Burrell and Annie Lois Webb Buchanan.

Notes

1. Both Hartman and Thompson have written extensively around themes of archival presence and absence in relation to Blackness. For readers new to their work, good places to start might be Patricia J. Saunders, "Fugitive Dreams of Diaspora: Conversations with Saidiya Hartman," *Anthurium: A Caribbean Studies Journal* 6, no. 1 (2008), https://anthurium.miami.edu/articles/abstract/10.33596/anth.115/; and Krista Thompson, "The Evidence of Things Not Photographed: Slavery and Historical Memory in the British West Indies," *Representations* 113 (winter 2011): 39–71.

2. Kevin Young, "How Not to Be a Slave: On the Black Art of Escape," in *The Grey Album: On the Blackness of Blackness* (Minneapolis, MN: Graywolf Press, 2012). For more on remapping in relation to identities, see Mishuana Goeman, *Mark My Words: Native Women Mapping Our Nations* (Minneapolis: University of Minnesota Press, 2013).

What Is the New Basket That We're Going to Weave?

Lori Lea Pourier

Lori Lea Pourier (Oglala Lakota), a citizen of the Oglala Sioux Tribe, has served as the president of First Peoples Fund since 1999. Lori's early work began at First Nations Development Institute and as the executive director of the international Indigenous Women's Network. She is a 2017 Ford Foundation Art of Change Fellow.

Cecelia Fire Thunder (Oglala Lakota), my huŋka relative, called me yesterday and said, "I almost burned my house down." With her čaŋnúŋpa (ceremonial pipe) in her hands, Cecelia looked up to Unčí Haŋhépi wi, Grandmother Moon, and spoke to her in Lakota. She had admitted to Her how she should not have been hoarding so many things and that from now on she would only start buying things as she needed them. Cecelia mourned deeply for three days but on the fourth day said, "I'm grateful and it is time to move on." She shared with me that at this stage in her life it is important to begin "thinking differently and preparing for what is next." And, "What is it that I really need?" Cecelia will hold the memories of the baskets and the generous gifts she received in her many travels throughout Indian Country. As I reflect on Cecelia's loss and her baskets, I am reminded everything is recycled back to Unčí Maká, Grandmother Earth. My heart is full as she has taught me so much about healing and the gift of life.

Indigenous women weavers say that when babies are born they are gifted with a basket, and when they return to the stars they leave this world with a basket. Inside of that basket is corn for their relatives. Our Ancestors teach us many things while we are here on Earth, and it is up to us to carry on their teachings. If you could take something, what would you take with

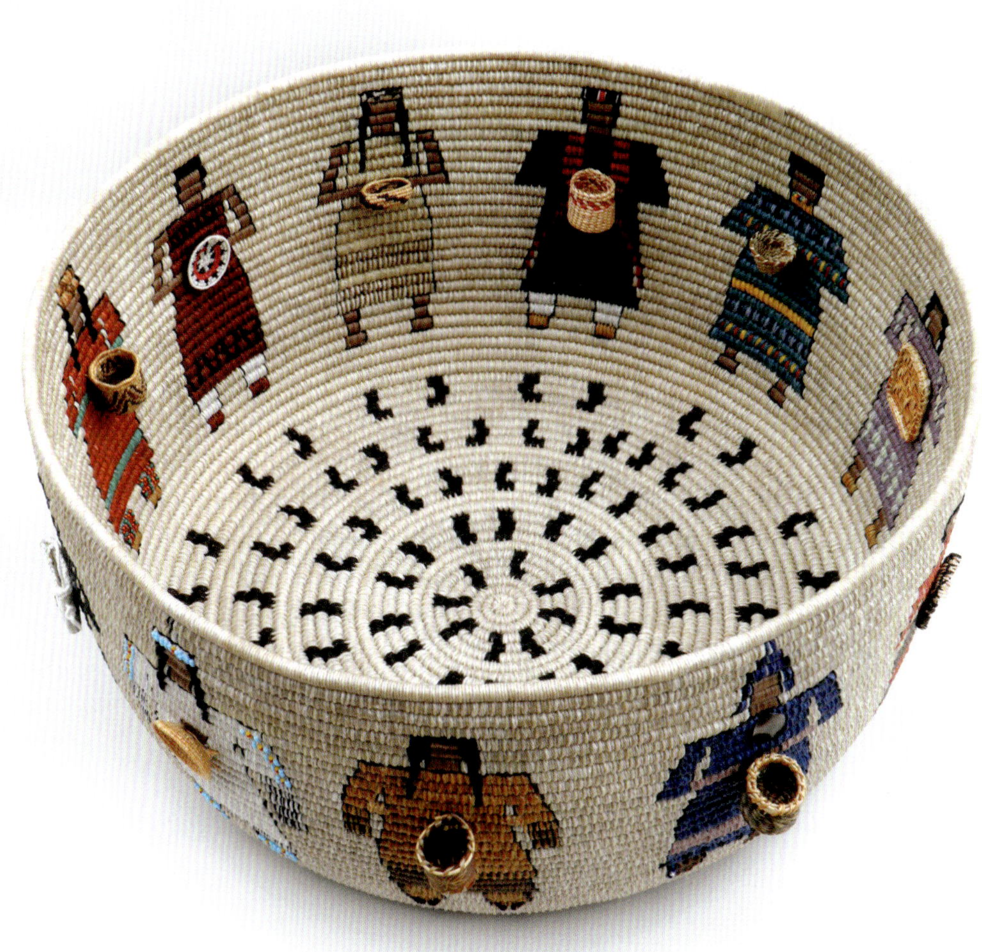

Carol Emarthle-Douglas, *The Gathering of Nations*, 2010.
Mixed media: waxed linen thread, single-rod hemp core,
red and yellow cedar, reed, raffia, sweetgrass, pine needles,
silk thread, cherry bark, artificial sinew, 7 × 11.5 × 11.5 in.
Photo courtesy of the artist. *Note*: Carol Emarthle-Douglas
is a traditional and contemporary basket weaver. Inspired
by her Northern Arapaho and Seminole heritage, she
applies the traditional single stitch coiling method in her
works. For more information, please visit https://www
.cemarthleart.com/.

you? What offering would you place in your basket? And for the future, what is the new basket that we're going to weave?

Our Elders remind us of our teachings and our relationship to star knowledge, Maȟpíya ektá wakán—that which happens in the stars mirrors what happens here on the Earth. I've only begun to learn of the Lakota star knowledge and our creation stories after returning home to Ȟesápa (Black Hills, South Dakota). The Lakota teachings tell us that the Creator placed the Black Hills in the center of Earth for the Oyáte, People, to live. The Lakota Oyáte moved our camps seasonally and by navigating by the stars. Even our tipis were constructed forming inverted shaped cones that mirrored our relationship between the sky and Earth. My huŋka relative Birgil Kills Straight (Oglala Lakota) shared these stories with me when I was young, yet it wasn't until later in my adult years when I began to learn the language and participate in our Lakota ceremonies that I began to understand the importance of these teachings.

In 1996, I returned to Ȟesápa while serving as the executive director of the Indigenous Women's Network (IWN), an international women's movement organization. The work of the IWN was guided by the teachings of the Clan Mothers of the Onondaga and Six Nations. The Sisters of the IWN were directly engaged in political action work and bringing awareness to environmental injustices resulting from federal policies contaminating their natural resources. Many of the Superfund hazardous waste sites identified by the Environmental Protection Agency were directly on or adjacent to American Indian reservations. The IWN women and their members were engaged in self-sufficiency models of community building on their homelands and are actively restoring traditional lifeways.

By 1999, I was pregnant and about to give birth to my daughter when I heard the news that my dear sister Ingrid Washinwatok El-Issa, one of the earliest members and cofounders of IWN, was kidnapped by the FARC in Colombia.[1] She was visiting the U'wa village in northwestern Colombia to share the important work of restoring Indigenous languages and lifeways throughout the United States. Only a few hours after stepping off an international call of American Indian leaders, I went into labor. My daughter was born, and two days later they found Ingrid and two of her traveling companions in Venezuela near the Colombian border.

It was during this time in my life, and the experience of giving birth to my daughter, that I would begin to fully comprehend our ancient star knowledge. Katsi Cook, a Mohawk midwife, helped me during my pregnancy and was also my dear sister Ingrid's midwife some years before. The Lakota star knowledge teaches us that Birth Woman, who lives in the stars near the Wičha Akhiyuhapi, helps women and their unborn children during birth and in easing their pain. Shortly after Ingrid's passing, and as she began her journey back to the stars, I wrote a poem about spirit's passing. It was a time of deep sorrow and the beauty of life, my newborn. It was during this time I came to believe that my daughter, Shahiyela, met her relative as she returned to the stars.

Recently I was reminded once again of our Lakota star knowledge teachings when our spiritual leader Rick Two Dogs (Oglala Lakota) shared a story with those of us wanting to learn more about our cosmologies through our language. He shared with us that Lakota women wore tattoos between our index finger and our thumb so that the wiŋyaŋ, women among the stars, would see the tattoo and know that the woman was traveling from Uŋči Maka, Grandmother Earth, back to the stars. If she had a tattoo, she would continue on her journey through the Milky Way.

My grandmother Alice, and the women one generation before her, are survivors of Indian boarding schools such as the Carlisle Industrial School in Pennsylvania (1838–71). After Carlisle, boarding schools were built on or near Indian reservations. In 1921 at five years old, Grandma Alice attended Cheyenne River Agency Boarding School in South Dakota. At thirteen, she was sent to St. Mary's School for Indian Girls, opened in 1872, also in South Dakota. Although boarding schools were designed to assimilate American Indians, my grandmother and others from her generation were able to retain their language. She went on to teach in the public schools on our reservation until her retirement. My mother, on the other hand, did not learn the language, nor was it taught in the boarding school she attended on the Pine Ridge Indian Reservation where she grew up.

Our knowledge keepers possess the genetic memory that's passed on through the teachings. During the COVID pandemic, Jennie Seminole Parker (Northern Cheyenne), ninety-six years old, joined Lynette Two Bulls (Oglala Lakota), First Peoples Fund 2016 Community Spirit Award recipient, for storytelling on the Yellowbird Facebook page. In 1879, the Northern Cheyennes (Montana) were captured by the US Cavalry and imprisoned in Fort Reno, Oklahoma. A group broke out of the fort during the coldest time of the year. They made it as far as Fort Robinson, Nebraska, trying to return to their homelands. For more than twenty years, the Fort Robinson Outbreak Run has remembered them. It has grown from a handful of youths to one hundred runners who, every January, relay four hundred miles back to Montana to honor their ancestors.[2] Each year in remembrance, Elder Jennie tells the story of her father who survived the breakout, making it back to their homelands in present-day Busby, Montana. Her childhood memories are filled with his stories. She holds the memories today of the generation that survived genocide and whose parents knew what freedom truly meant in this country.

For many, 2020 was a tough year. The hardest thing for us during this pandemic is losing our people to COVID-19. Our way of paying respect is deeply rooted in culture, ceremony, and spiritual practice. As prayerful peoples, we couldn't gather to practice our ceremonies. I can't help but think of all the prayerful people around the world who gather during the Summer Solstice, dancing from sunrise to sunset. As we pray and dance, our feet touch Unčí Maká Mother Earth. We feel her energy and she, ours. It is a time of healing. That didn't occur in 2020.

We are taught that spirit moves through all living things. Culture bearers like Haida weaver Delores Churchill (Tlingit), First Peoples Fund 2002 Community Spirit Award recipient, reminds us that you have to think about where your mind is when practicing traditional art forms such as weaving. They remind us that if we are upset, we should not touch the natural materials because our energy goes into the basket. This way of being is the beauty of our culture bearers.

Growing up, medicine men like Frank Fools Crow and only a handful of families carried the knowledge of the old ways prior to the passing of the American Indian Religious Freedom Act by the US Congress in 1978. Prior to this, our spiritual ceremonies were prohibited by law. My childhood was spent going to Catholic church. It wasn't until my adult years that I began to participate in my own ceremonies on the Pine Ridge Indian Reservation. My daughter, Shahiyela, on the other hand grew up with our traditional ceremonies. It is her generation and those that follow who will carry on the lifeways and teachings of the culture bearers and knowledge keepers.

Our young people are in a stronger place than my generation, my mother's, and my grandmothers'. When we go into ceremonies, we remain connected to our ancestors through our language and our songs. It's in the practice of being in ceremony and in hearing the old songs in Lakota that I know that I am connected to my ancestors.

Listening to Jennie Seminole Parker, one can't help but realize how much was lost. Native peoples, we were at war with this country for a very long time. The generations before us fought for our inherent rights and way of life. They knew what it was like to live free on these lands. When I think of Jennie Seminole Parker, Cecilia Fire Thunder, Delores Churchill, and many others, I carry with me the strength to know that no matter what happens, we are still here, and we are resilient. My spirit is lifted knowing our children will weave and carry with them a new basket of their many stories for generations to come.

Notes

1. Ingrid Washinwatok El-Issa (Menominee Nation, July 31, 1957–c. February 25, 1999) dedicated her life to the rights of Indigenous peoples and was executive director of a fund that endeavored to revitalize Indigenous languages. In 1999, she traveled to Colombia with two colleagues to help the U'wa Tribe set up a school system in the remote highlands. She and her companions were kidnapped and executed by members of a group calling itself the Revolutionary Armed Forces of Colombia.

2. "The Annual Fort Robinson Outbreak Spiritual 400-mile Run is held on January 8–14th, every year, and for the last 25 years. The runners commemorate and replicate the Northern Cheyenne breakout of Fort Robinson, on the actual date and time: January 9th, (1879) 10:30 at night. From the humble beginning of 14 runners; to now 80–100 youth completing the journey from Nebraska to Montana in subzero temperatures. The run originally began as a tribute to the Northern Cheyenne ancestors; now, it has become a forum for healing and wellness; youth leadership and empowerment; cultural & language preservation; environmental justice; and creating social change in our communities." "Fort Robinson Outbreak Spiritual Run," Yellow Bird Life Ways Center, accessed December 8, 2022, https://www.yellowbirdlifeways.org/fortrobinsonrun.

I ka wā ma mua, i ka wā ma hope

'ŌIWI ORIENTATIONS TOWARD A RADICAL FUTURITY

Jamaica Heolimeleikalani Osorio
and Jonathan Kay Kamakawiwoʻole Osorio

Jamaica Heolimeleikalani Osorio is a Kanaka Maoli wahine artist/activist/scholar/educator/storyteller born and raised in Pālolo Valley, Hawaiʻi. She is an assistant professor of Indigenous and Native Hawaiian politics at the University of Hawaiʻi, subject of an award-winning film, *This Is the Way We Rise,* cowriter of the revolutionary VR film *On the Morning You Wake (to the End of the World),* and author of *Remembering Our Intimacies: Moʻolelo, Aloha ʻĀina, and Ea.* She believes that aloha ʻāina can save the world.

Jonathan Kay Kamakawiwoʻole Osorio is a musician, historian, and dean of Hawaiʻinuiākea School of Hawaiian Knowledge. His recent publications include *The Value of Hawaiʻi: Knowing the Past and Shaping the Future,* which he coedited and authored, and *Dismembering Lāhui: A History of the Hawaiian Nation to 1887.*

JAMAICA HEOLIMELEIKALANI OSORIO: When I grew up in a Hawaiian language immersion school, one of the first things they taught us was this idea, "I ka wā ma mua, I ka wā ma hope," which literally means the future is in the past. It's a textbook definition of Indigenous radical futurity—this idea that there are lessons in the past that we need in order to face the challenges of today, and that there's a way of living in the past that will lead us to a different future. There is a rupture that has damaged the relationship between the past and future, that organic flow of energy, of movement and creation. We can call it occupation, we can call it colonialism, we can even call it global warfare. Radical futurity to me is this understanding of us going back to the root to grab something and bring back that knowledge and make it relevant again in the future. ʻŌlelo Hawaiʻi, or Hawaiian language, is what makes this possible for many Hawaiians because it returns you to an ancient timescale, a different way to think about how time moves, how knowledge moves, how language moves, and in all of that, a new reality is possible.

I teach in a political science department, and I teach in the language of English. When we conduct all business and theorizing and work in English, we get caught up in the limits of the English language, and what is limited in our imagination. In the activism that's worked through our family, the activism that's transformed our entire generation, it's hard to find anyone in Hawaiʻi who wouldn't celebrate the revival of the Hawaiian language as being central to everything we've been able to achieve. The stand at Maunakea in 2019 and 2020 would not have happened without a revived Hawaiian language movement.[1] We were prepared for that kind of stand because of what the generation before us started.

JONATHAN KAY KAMAKAWIWOʻOLE OSORIO: I would say "I ka wā ma mua, I ka wā ma hope" is really about orientation. It's about where you face. If one is accustomed to facing the time before—the past, ka wā mua—and treating the thing at your back as the future that you cannot really know, then as you move, you move backwards into your future. More and more things become apparent, things that are happening around you in your peripheral vision.

The political and cultural movement happening in Hawaiʻi didn't necessarily begin with language. It began with an appreciation for our history. At that point, our history was only accessible to us in English. We first had to become really uncomfortable with the English history that was presented to us as young people and how insufficient it is, and how lost it was. I am a historian trained as a Western historian, and one of the things I understand about the Western intellectual tradition is that it adheres to this notion of progress. Through that lens, humans start as little more than animals and live like that for fifty thousand years. And then at some blessed point, we take off and move through the establishment of towns, cities, and agricultural settlements. Then there's technology, there's exploration, there's imperialism. And then over the last five hundred years, a rise to some progressive point in the future that nobody ever identifies, except that we've always been taught that this is better.

As a native person looking at the length of our history—when you see that long period of thousands of years in which people basically lived and took care of one another and had stable societies—we see that as sustainability. We see a departure from this since the 1500s, including exposure to epidemics that destroy countless living beings in the world and contribute to a tremendous unsettling of the work of the world itself.

JAMAICA: We are having a conversation about the ideology of progress, and still we're having this conversation in English. I tell my students early on in our Indigenous politics classes that *progress* is a racist word. It's been used against people across the world to demonstrate a right and wrong way to live. When you talk about orientation, I ka wā ma mua, I ka wā ma hope, as this ancestral orientation to time, and to experience, I think about your relationship to learning the history of Hawai'i through messed-up English sources as a problem of orientation.

Haunani-Kay Trask wrote in *From a Native Daughter* how at some point, it became very clear to her that she was not reading the history of her people. She was reading the colonizer's story of themselves through their telling of her people's history—that they were saying more about themselves than they were saying about Hawaiians.[2] They were obsessed with this idea of linear progress of discovery and exploration. That's an orientational issue.

I think of the taught differences between evolution and progress, the way the Kumulipo teaches us about connectivity, and about genealogy.[3] We don't progress through our movement away from our kūpuna.[4] No, we are empowered through our continuous connection to those kūpuna. And when we're able to use 'Ōlelo Hawai'i to reestablish those connections, it's also giving us back all these pilina, these connections that we had been turned away from by being given a different story.[5] The story of our colonizers is one that is obsessed with looking toward their imaginary future, but the story of our kūpuna is understanding how everything we do is connected to this other point somewhere in pō, the darkness, the obscurity, the realm of the gods where life and chaos is created.

In 2015, at the Critical Ethnic Studies Association Conference in Toronto, a panelist said, "The opposite of violence is not nonviolence; the opposite of violence is creation." Beautiful, right? Violence is not fixed by this idea that we're going to stop violence. Violence is fixed by reestablishing connections, both ancestral and emerging, necessary connections we have to make to each other in our environment that aren't completely possible unless we drastically transform our orientation. To me, that's what radical futurity is about.

JON: There has to be evidence of something changing. And in fact, if you look at the way historians are trained, we are trained to look at change as the thing that matters. The critical focus of the historian is on change itself.

The more we know about our ancestors, we know the stories are not about change. They are about love, about jealousy; they're about things that we understand as human beings. They're about connectedness and relatedness. The notion here is that we exist in a world in which virtually every amazing thing that could ever happen to a person has already happened. What this basically says to any listener is, this is what's possible.

It is a conception of human beings as linked by all these different kinds of relationships to ancestors, to animals, to plants, to places, to trees, and to one another. That is the richness. When you look at the way our ancestors wrote and composed mele for instance, it was always a connection of people, usually romantic, but always in context with some place, with some natural phenomenon, like watching Pele erupt or watching the heavy rains as they rushed down Waiʻaleʻale.[6] All these things are continually putting the listener, the observer of hula, in a place to say, look at the magic of life that we have led collectively as human beings. Why would one imagine a future that was any less magical or beautiful?

JAMAICA: I think there's still a lot to learn from our moʻolelo that have been translated because so many Hawaiians have not yet accessed Hawaiian language.[7]

But it is a completely different experience to come to the language of your ancestors and experience the understanding of why kaona is working, not just as a literary device to make the story more interesting, but to constantly force your discomfort.[8] The nature of our moʻolelo has no singularity. There are multiple mana, different versions of these stories, collapsing into each other. A sentence can mean two wildly different things because we didn't reduce the words with diacriticals, so any single word that could already mean ten different things now could mean fifty different things.[9] We're uncomfortable with that because we have been oriented into a world where we need a straight line from A to B to understand the meaning of what has been put in front of us.

JON: You're right in saying it's unlocked through ʻŌlelo. The first time I began to read mele that was translated into English about places in Hawaiʻi, I really couldn't understand what they were saying, and I couldn't really appreciate the depth of those messages. It's only when you start to read those things in Hawaiian and you start to understand the kaona, the way that words are related to one another so that multiple experiences are connected in one phrase, that you really start to see the amazing richness of our people's life and history.

JAMAICA: This idea of progress—this fixed point and the singularity, this need to meet the demands of progress—implies we need to constantly be consuming. We need to constantly be maximizing our profits that come from consumption, which means that there must be a scarcity of resources and opportunity. We can flip that on its head and say, I've read the stories of my people, sung the songs of my people, and there is no such thing as universal scarcity. There are stories about famine that are meant to teach us something about greed and what happens when we operate as if scarcity is the center of our experience in the world. I want to talk about abundance and alternatives.

JON: We manifested this abundance at Puʻu Huluhulu, which was established during the 2019 attempts to protect Maunakea from further desecration and the building of the Thirty Meter Telescope. Thousands of supporters gathered at this kīpuka, an area that was protected from lava flows and therefore exists as a kind of sanctuary or special area of life among hardened lava fields. Puʻu Huluhulu University was basically a free university—a space for those who gathered there to share our stories that have been told for a thousand years and to learn about contemporary activism.

JAMAICA: This is a perfect example—they tell us, "this land cannot sustain you," and yet there's this kīpuka, which shows you the exact opposite—that life has endured despite this incredible transformation and devastation. The state of Hawaiʻi can't figure out how to care for the health and well-being of our people, the education of our people, the housing needs of our people. But thousands of people move to Puʻu Huluhulu and sustain life without the assistance of the state, the military, or the United States of America. In fact we sustain ourselves in opposition to those ideals—a sort of sovereignty. And there's a few words we use to describe sovereignty in ʻŌlelo Hawaiʻi. I think ea is probably my favorite. It means a breath; it means to rise. It's in everything that's living—it's something that has to be practiced. Ea is decolonial, ea is anticapital, ea is antiracism. It's all these things, and it allows us to think of how else will we live in relation with each other? How else will we build structures and systems of governance that are not rooted in white supremacy and capitalism and the nation-state? It means returning to historical relations with each other, with our lands, understanding our relationship to the sacred, which means understanding positionality in the spaces that we go. It doesn't start with people or even governments or offices. It starts with the land, and how you honor land. And how it is going to honor you back so you can live sustainably.

JON: There was a time when we thought the radical future was just to mention the word *sovereignty*. And there was a time when that radical future meant having the lāhui lay claim to ceded lands, having the state of Hawaiʻi and the Hawaiian Nation coexist.[10] Then the radical future became a return to the kingdom because, after all, the law clearly shows we had a legal right to exist, and the US ended that very legitimate nation-state. But over the years I've come to understand that sovereignty is really just self-control. It's having control over what happens in your life, your family's life, the language you speak, the values, the culture, how you see yourself. Saying "I am not an American" is not even a radical thing. It's just a natural thing to say.

JAMAICA: It's crucial to acknowledge how much our contemporary movement has been informed and supported by Black thought and Black liberation. In the 1970s, in what Haunani-Kay Trask calls "the Birth of the Modern Hawaiian movement," a few organizers, Moanikeʻala Akaka and Kalani ʻOhelo, were sent to a conference in DC where they met with the Black Panthers. They go to Oakland and meet Huey Newton. They bring back this knowledge to their people to talk about direct action and frontline engagement, but also community programs around those frontline engagements. Trask mentioned how Malcolm X's 1964 speech "The Ballot or the Bullet" influenced her 1993 speech at Iolani Palace, "We Are Not American"—one of the most important contemporary speeches in my lifetime.

JON: For Malcolm X and the Black Panthers, it wasn't about achieving equal rights with other Americans. It was about calling into question the ills of American society, whether it was white supremacy or American supremacy— a society essentially living off the productivity and the resources of thousands of other communities and nations around the world.

JAMAICA: Like I said in the beginning, when we talk about how the future is in the past, when we talk about radical futurities, it sounds like something that is quintessentially Hawaiian. But it's also something that is created out of an intimate relationship we've developed and established with people around the globe. ʻAʻole i pau ka ʻike i ka hālau hoʻokahi, not all knowledge is taught in one school. I love what we've learned from Black Afrofuturists—this idea that the apocalypse has already happened before. The transatlantic slave trade, the genocide of Native people across the world, the death of 90 percent of the Hawaiian population due to disease—we have survived the apocalypse. Musicians and artists are articulating this for us in a language we can understand. Public Enemy says Armageddon has been in effect. One of the things we need to take seriously is the fact that we've survived the end of the world, again and again and again, and oftentimes we have survived it through the knowledge of our kūpuna by holding onto our inherited practices like moʻolelo.

As I've grown older, as a teacher, as someone who speaks a lot and tells a lot of stories, it has become very clear to me that when you tell someone a story, share moʻolelo—you're telling them that you love them. When my father sits me down to tell the story of ʻUmi a Līloa, he's telling me, "I love you enough for you to carry one of the most important things that I have, something that my grandmother gave to me and I'm giving to you, and that you will give to someone else." If I say I have ʻike, I have knowledge, I have sight, I have seen something that I want you to see, that's love.

And so, what happens if you tell a people who have been dispossessed for multiple generations, who have been removed from their land, been told that there is only one way to succeed in the world and in the American economy—what if you tell them, earnestly and honestly, that we have been sold a story that does not serve us and there are so many moʻolelo that led our people to abundance for generations before this rupture? And what if we start the work of healing and refer people back to those moʻolelo, so that they might create something radically different, something radically connected to what our kūpuna imagined for us? In a time where so much of that is taken from us, there's nothing more like love than that.

Notes

1. From 2014 to the present, protesters, both Indigenous and non-, halted construction of the Thirty Meter Telescope and brought attention to over fifty years of mismanagement atop Maunakea, a mountain sacred to Kanaka Maoli (https://puuhuluhulu.com/learn).

2. Haunani-Kay Trask, *From a Native Daughter: Colonialism and Sovereignty in Hawaiʻi*, rev. ed. (Honolulu: University of Hawaiʻi Press, 1999).

3. "Kumulipo: origin, genesis, source of life." See Liliʻuokalani, trans., *The Kumulipo: An Hawaiian Creation Myth*, ed. James Kimo Campbell (Kentfield, CA: Pueo Press, 1978). Adapted and translated from *He pule hoolaa alii: He kumulipo no Ka-I-imamao, a ia Alapai Wahine* (Honolulu, 1889); and Lilikalā Kameʻeleihiwa, *Native Land and Foreign Desires: Pehea Lā E Pono Ai?* (Honolulu: Bishop Museum Press, 1992).

4. Kūpuna: grandparents, ancestors.

5. ʻŌlelo Hawaiʻi: Hawaiian language.

6. Mele: song or chant; Pele: lava flow, volcano, named for the volcano goddess Pele.

7. Moʻolelo: story, history.

8. Kaona: hidden meaning, as in Hawaiian poetry.

9. Hawaiian diacritical marks include just two symbols: the glottal stop (ʻokina) and the macron (kahakō). Not only do the ʻokina and kahakō change the sound of a word, they often end up changing its meaning. Lilinoe Andrews, "Hawaiian Diacritical Marks," Historic Hawaiʻi Foundation, December 21, 2018, https://historichawaii.org/2018/12/21/hawaiian-diacritical-marks/.

10. Lāhui: nation, race, tribe, people.

The Art of Peer Pressure

BLACK FIRE UVA!

Kevin Jerome Everson and Claudrena N. Harold

Artist/filmmaker and professor of art at the University of Virginia **Kevin Jerome Everson** has made over 170 films including *Tonsler Park, The Island of St. Matthews, Erie, Ears, Nose and Throat, Sound That, Sugarcoated Arsenic* with Claudrena Harold, and *Park Lanes*. He also has three DVD box sets of his films.

Claudrena N. Harold is a professor at the University of Virginia. She has authored three books, *The Rise and Fall of the Garvey Movement in the Urban South, 1918–1942, New Negro Politics in the Jim Crow South,* and *When Sunday Comes: Gospel Music in the Soul and Hip-Hop Eras.*

> On the basis of some information and a little bit of guesswork you jour-
> ney to a site to see what remains were left behind and to reconstruct the
> world that these remains imply.
> —Toni Morrison, "The Site of Memory," in *The Source of Self-Regard:
> Selected Essays, Speeches, and Meditations* (2019)

On the night of May 4, 1970, at approximately 10:30 p.m., 1,500 students at the University of Virginia (UVA) assembled near the historic Rotunda building to register their outrage at the brutal murder of four coeds at Kent State University in Ohio. Earlier that day, student activists at Kent State had embarked on their fourth round of demonstrations against President Richard Nixon's deployment of US troops to Cambodia. Their protest turned deadly when the Ohio National Guard fired into the large crowd of demonstrators, wounding ten students and killing four others. Anger gripped the nation as more than four hundred colleges and universities erupted in protests over the Kent State murders. If administrators at the University of Virginia expected only an episodic outburst of dissent from their students, they were in for a major surprise. Over the next ten days, students boycotted classes, occupied buildings, and pushed the university's president, Edgar Shannon, into a heated confrontation with state legislators in Richmond. Not content with simply challenging the war in Southeast Asia, student activists addressed larger issues facing the university. On the strike's second day, student leaders composed a list of demands that ranged from ending ROTC to removing all law enforcement officials from the campus to the university publicly "committing itself to accepting 20% as a goal for the enrollment of black students throughout the University." The last demand on the students' list of grievances addressed the labor issue: "We demand that President Shannon express public support for the right of University employees to strike and bargain collectively."[1]

At the center of much of the political upheaval at UVA was James Roebuck. A graduate student in the history department who had recently become the first African American president of the school's student council, Roebuck had the task of mediating the brewing conflict between his peers, the university's president, and a seemingly trigger-happy state all too ready to rely on force to quell dissent. Five days into the strike, Roebuck faced his greatest challenge when local police and the National Guard harassed and arrested dozens of students, invaded several fraternity houses on Rugby Road, and all but turned the university's central grounds into a combat zone.

Roebuck's courageous leadership, along with the students' strident criticisms of militarism, racism, and economic injustice, inspired the second film (*We Demand*) in our Black Fire series. Launched in December 2011, Black Fire currently consists of nine short films: *Sugarcoated Arsenic, U. of Virginia 1976, We Demand, Fastest Man in the State, 70kg, How Can I Ever Be Late, Black Bus Stop, Hampton*, and *Pride*. These films explore the fullness and complexity of Black life at UVA during the post–civil rights era. Though individually distinct in their formal qualities, they reflect our deep interest in the interiority of Black life, particularly those formal and informal spaces where African Americans communed, hobnobbed, prayed, loved, quarreled, reconciled, and moved on. Within these spaces, our gaze fixates on the epic and the quotidian, the sacred and the profane, the individual and the collective.

Instead of standard realism, we favor a strategy that abstracts everyday actions and statements into theatrical gestures, in which archival footage is reedited or restaged, real people perform fictional scenarios based on their own lives, and historical observations intermesh with contemporary narratives. Such an approach requires extensive archival research that extends beyond traditional repositories. Our films tap into historical archives in the basements of Black student organizations and cultural centers, in off-site storage rooms of academic departments, and in oral histories transmitted across generations. In many ways, the decentralized nature of these archives reflects the curatorial practices and ethical commitments of student activists who viewed the documentation and preservation of their organizing efforts as a critical dimension of their activist work. Perhaps no group embraced this commitment more than the Black Student Alliance, which for years refused numerous requests to give their organizational papers to the university's Special Collections Library.

Though thoroughly researched, our films are not interested in providing summative statements on the Black experience. Nor are they interested in providing images of spectacular blackness. In many ways, our art embraces what theorist Nicole Fleetwood calls the "non-iconic." The non-iconic, according to Fleetwood, "is an aesthetic that resists singularity and completeness in narrative; one that exposes the limitations of framing and the temporality and specificity of the moment documented."[2] Toward this goal, we rely on visual archives that privilege those ordinary moments of Black life. One such archive is David Skinner's stunning photographs of African American students, faculty, and workers. Taken largely during the 1970s, these affecting images capture the inner world of Black social and cultural life at the University of Virginia.

Drawing on a rich archive of visual, oral, and written material, we completed our first film, *Sugarcoated Arsenic*, in the fall of 2012. Shot over a three-day period, *Sugarcoated Arsenic* stars Erin Stewart as Vivian Gordon, the director of UVA's African American Studies program from 1974 to 1980. Inspired by Horace Ové's documentary *Baldwin's Nigger*, the opening scene features Gordon delivering a powerful address to an intimate group of Black students. Moving across time and space, Gordon recalls her formative years in segregated Petersburg, reflects on the grace, humility, and brilliance of the historian Luther Porter Jackson, and outlines the particular challenges and opportunities facing African Americans in the post–civil rights era. Her passionate address captures what literary critic Houston Baker calls the poetry of impulse: "black articulateness and lyricism in the very face of violence, catastrophe, rejection and exploitation."[3] Close-ups of both Gordon and the receptive students underscore the beauty and necessity of intergenerational exchange.

At the film's nine-minute mark, the focus dramatically shifts to two stylishly attired students competing in a lively game of foosball. Inspired by a

1974 photograph of two foosball players, the scene underscores the importance of pleasure in building and sustaining community.

Other casual moments captured on film include African Americans playing cards, discussing books, and hobnobbing at a cocktail party. All of these scenes are reenactments of stunning photos of African American students, faculty, and workers during the 1970s.

Even during these moments of leisure, *Sugarcoated Arsenic* never loses its political edge as the stately voice of Vivian Gordon offers political instruction and ancestral wisdom. Drawing from both the visual and the sonic innovations of the Black Power Movement, the film closes with students marching and chanting parts of the Black Panther Party's rallying cry, "Revolution Has Come!"

Filmed during the week of Superstorm Sandy, *Sugarcoated Arsenic* was a labor of love. Not just in terms of the weather conditions but also in terms of the extensive archival research involved in crafting the scenes. During the research process, we unearthed unedited footage of protest marches from 1969 and 1970, reel-to-reel audio of antiwar protests, and videotapes and cassettes of noted Black Studies scholars. And then there were the hundreds of photographs from the 1970s and 1980s, visual evidence of the ingenuity, resourcefulness, and sheer brilliance of UVA's Black community.

Out of this treasure trove of archival material emerged the foundation of our next film, *We Demand*. Shot in the fall of 2014, *We Demand* turns attention to the antiwar movement and focuses on Roebuck, a Philadelphia-born African American who enrolled in UVA's graduate program in 1966. Upon his arrival on campus, he immersed himself in student politics, eventually becoming the president of the school's student council. Several weeks after his election as the council's first Black president, political upheaval engulfed the university as youth activists erupted in protest over the Kent State massacre.

Searching for greater insight into this complex political moment, we journeyed to Philadelphia in the summer of 2014 for a meeting with Roebuck (who since the 1980s had represented the 188th Legislative District, West Philly, in the Pennsylvania House of Representatives). With vivid detail, Roebuck described the tumultuous aftermath of Nixon's invasion of Cambodia and the Kent State murders. His reflections, along with newspaper clippings, antiwar memorabilia and placards, surveillance video, audio, and photos, inspired our next film, *We Demand*.

Released in 2016, *We Demand* features Ricky Goldman as James Roebuck, Richard Warner as Edgar Shannon, and Ryan Leach as student activist Tommy Steele. In the film's opening, we see Roebuck and Steele typing a list of student demands. *We Demand* then segues into President Shannon

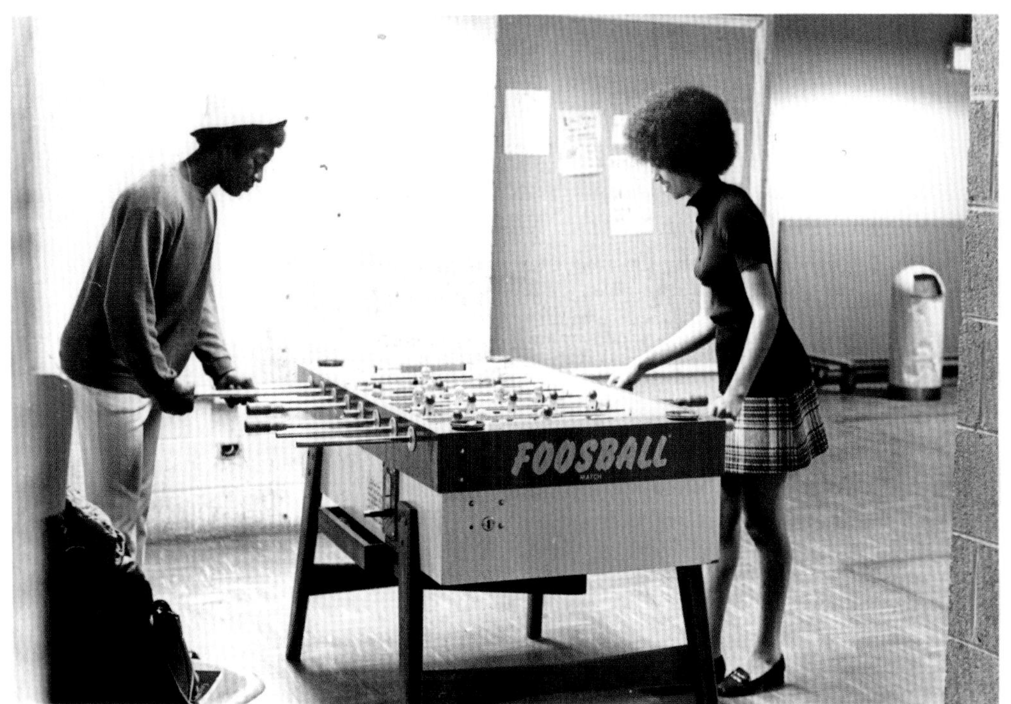

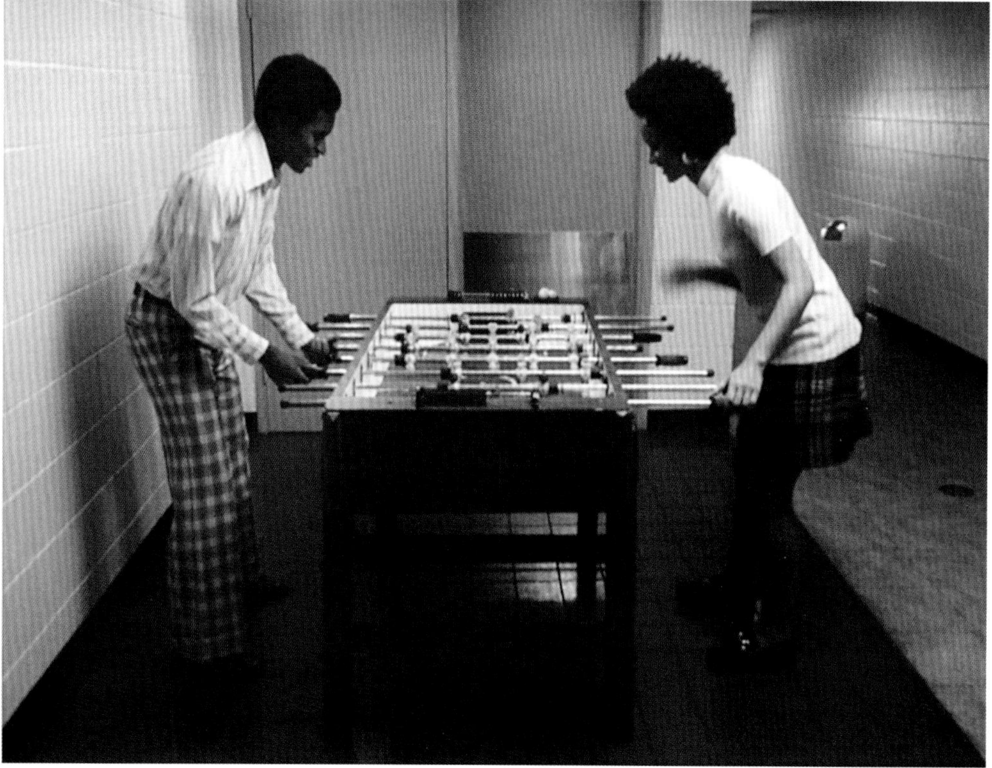

Above: Students playing foosball, 1974. Below:
Sugarcoated Arsenic, directed by Kevin Jerome
Everson and Claudrena N. Harold, 2014. 16 mm
film still. Total running time 20 min.

and James Roebuck preparing for their respective meetings with elected officials in Richmond and Washington, DC. The closing scene finds Steele and Roebuck on the open road, reflecting on the last few days. During the drive back to Charlottesville, Roebuck recounts his journey into activism, reminiscing fondly on the political lessons he received from his mentor, the Reverend Marshall Shepard, his organizing work with the Philadelphia NAACP as an adolescent, and his involvement in the civil rights movement during his undergraduate years at Virginia Union.

Moving from the world of antiwar activism to the sports arena, our next film turned attention to the aesthetics and politics of athletic competition. In *Fastest Man in the State*, Charlottesville native and UVA alumnus Kent Merritt waxes eloquent on his experiences as one of the university's first four Black scholarship athletes. Along with recounting his experiences with racism during the early days of integration, he revisits the particular challenges endured by his teammate and fraternity brother Harrison Davis, who in 1971 took over the quarterback position. If nothing else, Merritt's recollections remind us that the sports arena has never been a politically free zone. His bittersweet memories of the entrenched racism on America's college campuses, along with his reminders of how he and his Black teammates found solace in each other, take on deeper meaning in our current moment, when many athletes have intensified their call for systematic change in this country, particularly around issues related to state-sanctioned violence against African Americans.

Fastest Man in the State benefited immensely from Merritt's generosity and our students' contributions. As had been the case with previous films, we involved students from our courses—Intermediate and Advanced Cinematography, Black Fire, and Introduction to African American and African Studies—in the art-making process. By working as actors and crew members, students are able to envision the university as a site for not just cultural critique but artistic production, a space in which art can be produced, exchanged, debated, and shared across racial, ethnic, and socioeconomic lines. As teachers, we also aim to provide our students (and viewers) with examples of art that decenters the ruling class. Take as a case in point our 2018 film *Black Bus Stop*. That film pays homage to an iconic gathering spot for many African Americans: the Black Bus Stop (BBS). For many African Americans who attended the University of Virginia during the post–civil rights era, the Black Bus Stop was and remains sacred ground. It represents their efforts to affirm their humanity and sense of personhood and built transcendent spaces of communion.

Now the BBS doesn't have an official founding date, but by most accounts it became a popular spot in the late 1970s, the decade when African

Americans built the institutional infrastructure of what some refer to as Black UVA. The Black Bus Stop, located on a central part of campus and not too far from the Business School, was incredibly popular during the 1990s, the peak years of Black enrollment. At the popular hangout, students could be seen talking politics, joking with each other, playing music, setting up dates, and so on. One UVA alumnus called it "the Black Red Carpet."

The seriousness with which Black students regarded the Black Bus Stop became apparent to university administrators in the fall of 1997, when the University Transit Service changed the route and temporarily suspended the stop at the BBS. Over the course of a month, students engaged in protests, sending letters to administrators, holding town hall meetings, and raising questions about the university's commitment to the Black student body. Their efforts proved successful. Within weeks, university administrators resumed the bus system's normal route.

These and other stories about the Black Bus Stop inspired us to make a film that would pay tribute to an iconic space that was not a part of the university's memorial landscape. In the spring of 2018, eight months after a well-organized army of torch-wielding white supremacists marched through the grounds of UVA, we filmed *Black Bus Stop*. For two days, approximately thirty Black fraternity and sorority members from Alpha Phi Alpha, Kappa Alpha Psi, Omega Psi Phi, Delta Sigma Theta, Sigma Gamma Rho, and Phi Beta Sigma assembled near the BBS. Under the glare of the moonlight, the sororities and fraternities danced, strolled, and stomped with dignity and honor. In the aftermath of *Black Bus Stop*'s screening at numerous film festivals, university officials decided to place a historical marker at the iconic gathering place as part of its larger project of reckoning with its racist past. Though appreciative of the university's efforts, our work does not fit neatly into the paradigm of racial repair. Such a paradigm tends to see Black formal and informal institutions as a response to white supremacy or racial exclusion rather than an extension of cultural traditions and forms forged within the institutional matrixes of Black communities.

Our commitment to highlighting these traditions surfaces in the follow-up to *Black Bus Stop*: *Hampton*. Set in the 1970s, *Hampton* follows Black Voices, a gospel choir based at the University of Virginia, as it prepares for a performance in Hampton Roads, embarks on a two-hour bus ride to the concert venue, and then returns to campus after a triumphant performance. With a particular focus on the bus driver (Sandy Williams IV), the film captures the wide range of processes, relationships, emotions, and formal gestures operating in African American gospel music.

The script for *Hampton* draws inspiration from the gospel aesthetic, as well as interviews of two UVA alumni: Chavis Harris, a charter member of Black Voices, and the late Debra Saunders-White, the former president of North Carolina Central, who attended UVA between 1975 and 1979. In their interviews, Harris and Saunders-White detail the centrality of Black Voices in helping them navigate the challenges of the university. In explaining why he and his colleagues selected Black Voices as the choir's name, Harris pointed to the cultural ethos of the Black Power era, as well as the political atmosphere of UVA. He noted, "There were times, like if you were walking on the grounds at night and you were an African American male, and if you were studying and decided to take a break and take a jog like students do all the time, you were probably going to get followed by the university police and stopped." Such encounters intensified Harris's and other Black students' desire for institutional spaces that would not simply challenge white racism but also affirm their humanity. In many ways, Black Voices was a space not just for those in the choir but also for students who appreciated gospel as an art form. This was the case for Saunders-White, who conveyed to us the story of Black Voices' bus trip to Hampton, relating how the university's decision to allow the choir to use one of its buses was the first time she felt as if she actually "belonged" to the university.

With all our film projects, including the latest, *Pride*, we hope to capture how local and national histories are intertwined. We also hope to provide additional opportunities for our students to further develop and express their artistic gifts, see the value of interdisciplinary work, and contribute to the retelling of UVA's rich history. We want them to understand the beauty of collaboration, to appreciate what can be gained from learning together, holding each other accountable, and blending one's talents for the benefit of the collective.

In other words, we want them to know the art and beauty of peer pressure.

Notes

1. Bob Buford, Peter Shea, and Andrew Stickney, *May Days: Crisis in Confrontation* (Charlottesville, VA: Authors, 1970).

2. Nicole Fleetwood, *Troubling Vision: Performance, Visuality, and Blackness* (Chicago: University of Chicago Press, 2011), 64.

3. Houston A. Baker, *I Don't Hate the South: Reflections on Faulkner, Family, and the South* (New York: Oxford University Press, 2007), 76.

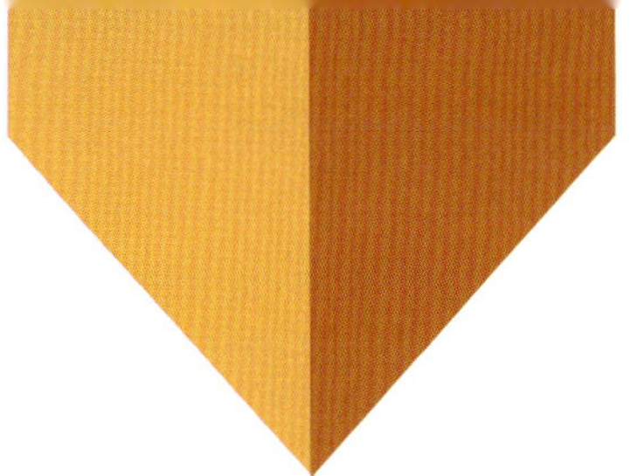

CURRENTS BEYOND

ARTISTS SHIFTING PARADIGMS OF INEQUITY

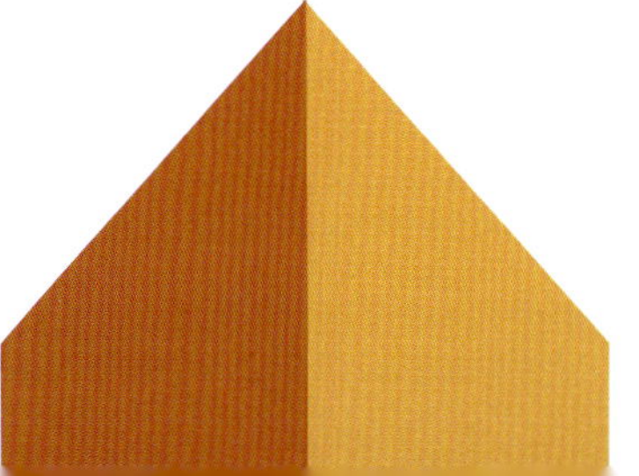

Introduction

Genevieve Fowler

Genevieve Fowler is the former program associate for Arts in a Changing America. She is an LA- and Chicago-based theater director whose practice revolves around the dual tracks of radically inclusive community-based work and postmodernist adaptation of classics for a contemporary audience. Much of Genevieve's theatrical practice has been rooted in lifting up often-unheard voices.

What would a world no longer rooted in white supremacy look like? A world where buried histories of resilience and generational wisdom are celebrated and used as a forward-looking lens to imagine and build a future? In her essay "all organizing is science fiction," **adrienne maree brown** believes that everyone has universes of equity, freedom, and transformation within them. We can create the possibility to, as adrienne maree brown puts it, "bend the future, together, into something we have never experienced: a world where everyone experiences abundance, access, pleasure, human rights, dignity, freedom, transformative justice, peace." The artists and advocates in this section put imagination into action as they work to change the conditions under which we live toward universal good—offering tangible tools, models of creation, and knowledge gathered through the ages to expand our world in creative acts of regeneration and growth. They dream a multiverse into existence in which people and institutions are driven by a diverse set of values, centering and embracing a multiplicity of identities, languages, abilities, and artistic styles.

The Cultural New Deal for Cultural and Racial Justice (CND), authored by a collective of seminal artists and culture bearers committed to transformative action, frames this conversation: "The main question that we all confront now is whether we will emerge from this era choosing to maintain the same systems and beliefs that support the current culture of division and death or if we will instead move forward toward a more just, shared future, guided by worldviews that foster collaboration and mutuality." The authors of the CND put forward a series of concrete actions that create systemic shifts and catalyze personal, institutional, and global transformative thinking. Program director at the Jerome Foundation **Eleanor Savage** joins the CND in offering concrete actions to enact more equitable practices. Savage charges funders and allies to have the courage to move across discomfort in service of racial equity in the arts sector, providing a series of practical actions to implement that evolution.[1] While Savage's work prompts existing institutions to recenter themselves in relation to equity, artists such as **Devin Kenny** use their art to turn exhibition spaces and organizations into centers of action. Kenny's work *What Would Upski Think?* interrogates institutions' willingness to go beyond existing as a platform for visibility and engage in material action by expropriating institutional electricity to mine cryptocurrency for social justice organizations. Their work ultimately asks: will an institution support a cause, even if it's at its own expense?

And still others in this section center the wisdom of their communities to create alternative and nonextractive institutions that embrace artists in their totality. Curator and author **Marlène Ramírez-Cancio** discusses the artist incubator EMERGENYC, which provides an artistic home where individuals can "bring their full selves to bear, existing in all their dimension and intricate code-switches." This home holds space to create from a place of wholeness and weaves a network and lineage of artists working in conversation and community. Dancer and former co-executive director of Allied Media Projects (AMP) **Jeanette Lee** has also helped to build a home for an enormous network of artists by listening to the collective wisdom of forward thinkers who create at the intersection of art and technology. Fueling action through this global web of artists and advocates, AMP takes the tools of the modern world and uses them to drive toward a future of personal, collective, and systemic good. As Lee states, "Because we know that liberation is not a destination at the end of a linear path, but rather a process that's ever unfolding, when we reach the end of one cycle of listening, we begin again."

Dancers **Antoine Hunter** and **Ananya Chatterjea** stress that the power of art exists in its ability to hone our senses to be aware of the unique needs of others. With the Bay Area International Deaf Dance Festival, award-winning Deaf producer, choreographer, dancer, and Deaf advocate Antoine Hunter forged a path centering creativity and dance as a pivot point against ableism. His work challenges audiences and artists to shift their perceptions of the message of dance: "Are you listening? Not just with your ears, but with your heart?" If Hunter asks us to hear fully and completely, then celebrated dancer and founder of Ananya Dance Theatre, Ananya Chatterjea, implores us to use our practice as a vehicle for holding each other's gaze wholly. The context of dance changed vitally for her Twin Cities–based company in the multiple uprisings of 2020; Chatterjea used this moment of turmoil to ground focus in how we practice our art, and how that leads to a new type of sight. **Sky Cubacub** moves beyond asking us to see differently to questioning what we choose to make visible. Through their clothing and accessory line Rebirth Garments, they showcase beauty as grounded in radical visibility and accessibility—a celebratory resistance to what we are so often asked to shun. Their garments are a reclamation of the body in all its various forms, all bountiful with beauty.

This section is further deepened by artists who use ancestral knowledge to shape the future. As conduits of the values and deep wisdom of the past, they connect to the work of the present by shifting policy and practice to sustain all. **Vicky Holt Takamine**, kumu hula, Hawaiian cultural advocate, and founder and executive director of PAʻI Foundation, demonstrates how the historical and cultural innovations of hula practitioners have brought about change in Hawaiʻi's laws and furthered self-determination. Takamine reminds us that ancestral art forms hold power in the present and that, similar to the story of Pele and Hiʻiaka, our current moment is like a volcanic eruption; through destruction comes a time of healing, often initiated by the arts, where "new foliage and life begin to germinate."

Confirming the importance of creating a multigenerational network of experts, gender-nonconforming writer and performance artist **Alok Vaid-Menon** and distinguished LGBT rights activist and writer **Urvashi Vaid** lift up a personal and professional lineage of change. Their work showcases inherited knowledge and intergenerational exchange as a tool for pushing toward a new future, one manifested through the "kernel of possibility" that has been left by those who have come before to create openings for those of younger generations to push through.

Then there are artists working to reveal hidden histories and showcase narratives in all their complexity. Artist and Klamath Tribal Council member **Natalie Ball** holds space between often compartmentalized elements of culture and identity to disrupt historically constructed definitions of *Indian*. Presenting an unearthing and remapping of an intersectional, nuanced experience, Ball's work allows for all to find greater understanding through the casting away of colonialist barriers. Acclaimed artist **Carrie Mae Weems** presents a series of photos from her 2016 series *Scenes & Takes* that celebrates and probes the recent increase in representation of Black and brown bodies on network television shows. Weems notes, "As with much of my work, *Scenes & Takes* grew out of that crack in the cultural armor. I thought it would be important for me to stand in front of, and in, the sets of these shows, to think about what was shifting within the worlds of contemporary expression and popular culture."[2] Physicalizing the presence and power of the Black body in culturally commercial spaces, the series embodies a powerful change in the visual narrative being disseminated through television, showcasing what narratives are important and worth being seen on, in, and around the screen.

Moving outside of traditional materials and institutional spaces, there are artists who are regenerating expansive places for liberatory reflection and re-dreaming. Multimedia artist **Arshia Fatima Haq** creates work that invokes the possibility of transnational solidarity around resistance struggles. In her work *Azadi*, part of a larger skywriting project conceived by Cassils and rafa esparza, Haq moves beyond the gallery space, looking up to the sky. There she exhibits words often prescribed as "other" in a script wrongly associated with terror, reinscribing them as nuanced, multicultural calls to freedom and liberation. Architect and multidisciplinary artist **X** harvests materials from the streets of Chicago to transpose settler colonial architectures with reanimated Indigenous landscapes. His work *SOVEREIGN* creates a deconstructing glitch in colonial time where one can sit in the prosperity of a future without self-constructed or socially created limitations.

So, what would a world no longer rooted in white supremacy look like? It would look like the words and works of the artists, advocates, and culture bearers in this anthology. It would be sculpted by, as adrienne maree brown shares, "people actively working to change the world to tell us stories from the horizons they could see." Horizons not existing peripherally to diversity, inclusion, and equity, but woven together with equity, access, desegregation, community, disruption, and transformation. Horizons reliant on the many tides and currents created by artists dreaming a wave of change into existence, guiding us toward a future ultimately built upon wholeness, humanity, and life.

Notes

1. We are inspired by all who make available their strategies for systemic change and would like to acknowledge Antena Aire for their organizing and resources on language justice. Read their how-to guide, "How to Build Language

Justice," Antena Aire, accessed December 13, 2022, https://antenaantena.org /language-justice/.

2. Carrie Mae Weems, "Carrie Mae Weems: A Crack in the Cultural Armor," *New York Times*, June 1, 2020, https://www.nytimes.com/2020/06/01/opinion /carrie-mae-weems-black-television.html.

Bang Bang

Natalie Ball

Natalie Ball is an artist and Klamath Tribal Council member. She holds an MA in Indigenous contemporary art from Massey University in Aotearoa (New Zealand) and an MFA in painting and printmaking from Yale School of Art. She is the recipient of the Native Arts and Cultures Foundation's 2021 Oregon Native Arts Fellowship, among others.

waqlisaat, my name is Natalie Ball. I locate myself as an Indigenous woman who is Black and Indian. I grew up in Portland's historic Black neighborhood within an active Native community. My dad's parents relocated here from Chiloquin, Oregon, after our tribe, the Klamath Tribes, was terminated by an act of Congress. My mom's family was a part of the Black diaspora that traveled to the Pacific Northwest from rural Arkansas.

I hold space for the intersectionality of Native and Black to exist. This is my attempt to move *Indian* outside of governing discourses to offer a visual genealogy that refuses to line up with the many historically constructed existences of Native Americans. Through autoethnography, I examine internal and external discourses that shape Indigenous identities including blood politics and blood quantum. My studio practice maps personal and historical landscapes, allowing them to hold space for new complex narratives to exist. Humor, form, gesture, and materiality through assemblage are my tools to disrupt mainstream definitions of *Indian*. To have personal, community, and collective histories that reflect the complexity of Native American lives, like my own, is to better understand ourselves, the nation, and necessarily our shared experiences and histories.

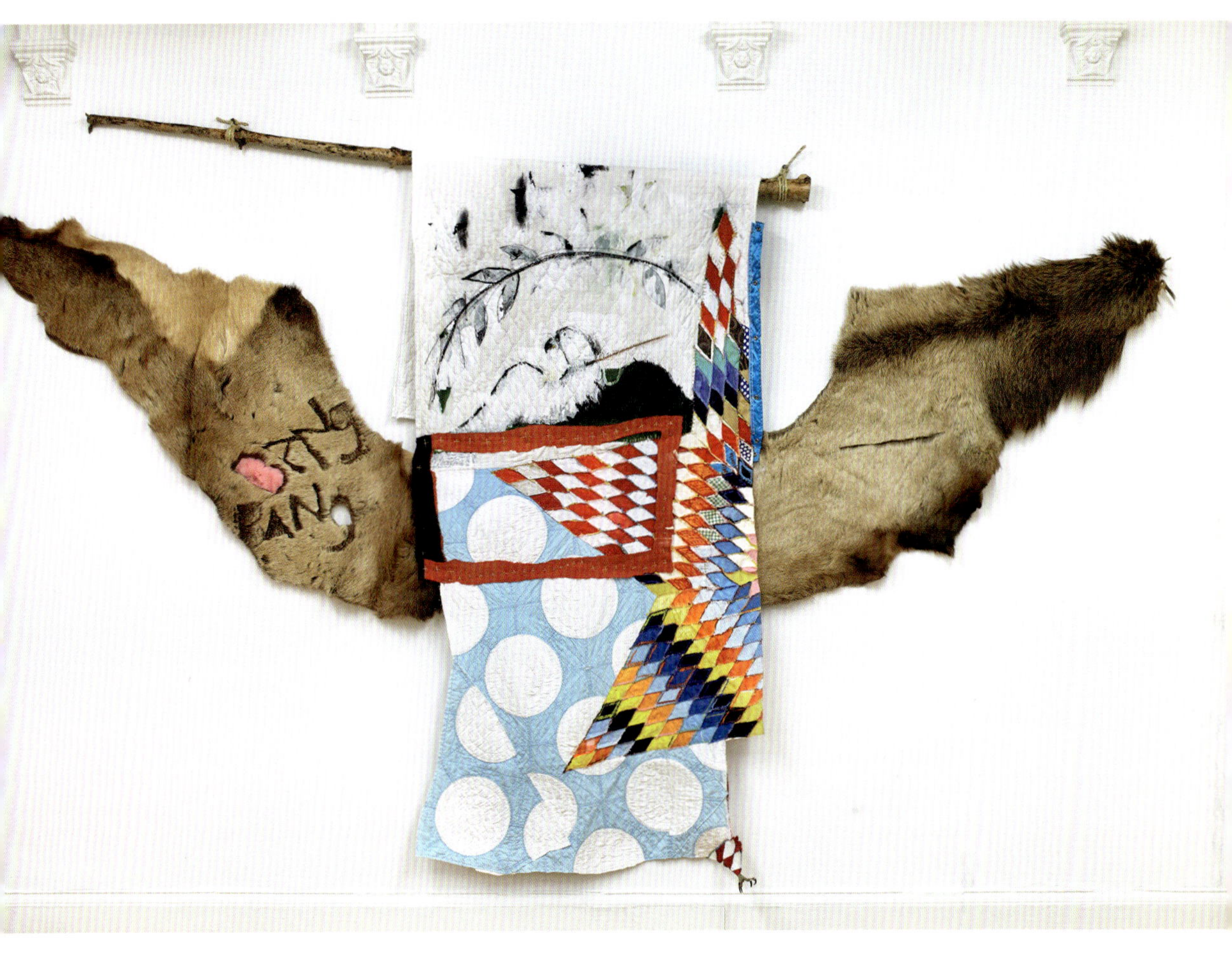

Natalie Ball, *Bang Bang*, 2019. Elk hide, rabbit fur, oil stick, acrylic, charcoal, cotton, pine, and hawk talon, 84 × 124 in. Image courtesy of the artist and Half Gallery, New York.

The Cultural New Deal for Cultural and Racial Justice

This Call was spearheaded by ArtChangeUS, the Center for Cultural Power, First Peoples Fund, the National Association of Latino Arts and Culture, Race Forward, and Sipp Culture. It was written in 2020 by Michele Kumi Baer, Jeff Chang, María López De León, Tara Dorabji, Kassandra L. Khalil, Lori Lea Pourier, Favianna Rodriguez, Nayantara Sen, Carlton Turner, Roberta Uno, and Elizabeth M. Webb, in consultation with Ananya Chatterjea, Ananya Dance Theatre; Sonya Childress, Perspective Fund; Pamela J. Peters; Randy Reinholz, Native Voices; Lula and Erwin Washington and Tamica Washington-Miller, Lula Washington Dance Theatre; Dyani White Hawk; and Carrie Mae Weems. It was translated by Yahaira Carrillo Rosales.

The Cultural New Deal for Cultural and Racial Justice is a call for us to transform our personal, institutional, and global thinking. We believe that culture moves before policy. We believe that culture endures beyond politics. We wrote this Call because our work in culture and arts is inextricably linked to larger social movements for change. We invite you to adopt and adapt this Call to your specific contexts to hold leaders, policy makers, and institutions—and ourselves—responsible, accountable, and transparent in achieving equity and justice.

In these unprecedented times, as justice movements converge, many of us have asked ourselves what the stakes are for the culture we want to advance. We concluded that we needed to change the conditions under which we artists and culture bearers labor and live. The Cultural New Deal for Cultural and Racial Justice points us toward new understandings of how we together can build a culture that is inclusive and sustainable, and leads us toward justice and freedom for all. We urge timetables that are immediate and demonstrate change that is not aspirational, but concrete, measurable, and visible within one to three budget cycles. We offer this Call in the spirit of advancing accountability and collective responsibility and urge you to activate these ideas within your work and our shared future.

A Call for a Cultural New Deal for Cultural and Racial Justice

We are the artists, the culture bearers, the healers of the spirit, the first responders to the community's soul.

In this moment, we face four major threats to our shared existence: a global pandemic; militarized state and vigilante violence, significantly directed at Black people; environmental degradation; and an economic crisis. All of these have been shaped and exacerbated by racism and white supremacy. Black, Indigenous, Native American, Latinx, Chicanx, Arab, MENASA (Middle Eastern, North African, South Asian), Asian, Pacific Islander, and other communities of color, especially those who are Disabled/Deaf and/or LGBTQIA+/Two-Spirit, are dying of these threats—by disease, police/carceral and racial violence, and the health and social inequities that force us into premature death.

The main question that we all confront now is whether we will emerge from this era choosing to maintain the same systems and beliefs that support the current culture of division and death or if we will instead move forward toward a more just, shared future, guided by worldviews that foster collaboration and mutuality.

We come together now to declare that we refuse to return to the white supremacist narratives of segregation, extraction, and domination that deem some of us worthy of sustenance, nurturing, and protection, and others of us surplus, exploitable, and expendable.

In opposition to that worldview, we believe in the power of arts and culture to define and delight, to provoke and persuade, to edify and unite. Our artistic and cultural practices lift up the fullness of our shared humanity, sustain the well-being of all, and lead our social imagination toward transforming our societies and our world.

We recognize that this nation was founded on stolen land and built by stolen labor. Freeing the land means the return of Indigenous lands. We acknowledge that any work we do in the name of justice and healing of this planet must start with respect and support for Indigenous peoples, their knowledge, and their right to self-determination and tribal sovereignty.

We also acknowledge our indebtedness to the movement for Black freedom, and to Black freedom culture, which articulates our dreams of liberation and makes them tangible and imaginable. We will not be free until Black people are free. We stand in defense of Black lives.

The violence of racism has gagged us and hidden our hearts. We know that invisibility, underrepresentation, and misrepresentation exacerbate injustice, dehumanization, and premature death. We who have been silenced for so long must be able to tell our stories. We chant down the monoculture of white supremacy with an expansive diversity of voices.

We assert that place matters, and we root ourselves in community. We are stewards of the places in which we live. We believe in the wisdom of directly impacted communities to be our own storytellers and leaders, to reinscribe history and shape the future.

We ask ourselves the question: arts and culture for what? We work in culture and the arts because we believe that stories weave together the moral fabric of our societies. We aim to build and sustain our communities, those most impacted by racial and cultural inequity. We believe that art and culture are never separate from the undoing of inequities in health, employment, wealth, detention, incarceration, deportation, housing, and the environment.

We know that we work in an arts and culture ecosystem that not only reflects the inequities caused by racism and white supremacy but also reproduces and reinforces those inequities. As leaders and philanthropists talk about recovery for the arts and culture sector, we ask what direction that recovery will take: Will it rebuild systems that maintain racial and cultural injustice? Or will it begin to reverse the legacies of racism and white supremacy in building a new one?

To unmake these systems that oppress all of us, we fight for *cultural equity*, which we define as the condition that all people are fairly resourced in artistic and cultural expression and fairly represented in systems of exhibition, performance, and decision making—which will lead to a redistribution of cultural power.

We fight for *cultural justice*, which we define as the healing of the erasure, suppression, and marginalization of people's artistic and cultural practices. Cultural justice restores and builds for communities of color ways of living, being, and sense making, and allows all of us to express ourselves and be recognized in our full, complex humanity.

Cultural equity and cultural justice are essential for *racial justice*, which we define as the systematic fair treatment of people of all races that results in equitable opportunities and outcomes for everyone. Racial justice moves us all toward a more vibrant, multiracial democracy that advances the self-determination and the sovereignty of all peoples.

We know that the health of our communities depends upon the health of our cultures. Arts and cultural ecosystems keep our communities resilient in hard times. Community health and wellness depend upon strong cultural institutions and strong local cultural economies. We are here to redistribute cultural power from those who believe in domination to those who believe in interdependency, sustainability, and the protection of people and the earth. We work to build communities rooted in openness, belonging, and freedom *for all*.

For these reasons, we call for a Cultural New Deal. It is a call to invest in, support, and sustain the builders of our imagination and the keepers of our cultures. Artists and cultural bearers are never separate from the communities they claim. Their creative ecosystems never exist in isolation. We believe that our work aligns with that of movement-developed platforms, such as that from the Movement for Black Lives, the Poor People's Campaign, Just Recovery, the Women's March, the Green New Deal, Just Transition, the Harriet Tubman Collective, BYP100, the Coalition to Stop Violence against Native Women, and the People's Bailout, whose agendas broadly advance racial and social justice. We add to those our calls to build a healthy, vital, and just culture so that we can anchor, build, and sustain our communities.

In order to end these four existential threats exacerbated by racism and white supremacy, we must pivot from a culture of division and death toward one that values equity, justice, and life. We are not going back to an arts ecosystem that pretended to be neutral but instead preserved deadly whiteness. That culture has failed us. It is time to reset.

We call upon all who agree with us to join with us to meet the urgency of our time.

A Cultural New Deal for Cultural and Racial Justice

We call for an end to racial and cultural inequity and injustice as Black, Indigenous, Native American, Latinx, Chicanx, Arab, MENASA (Middle Eastern, North African, South Asian), Asian, Pacific Islander, and other people of color. Those embodying the intersection of these identities as also Disabled/Deaf and/or LGBTQIA+/Two-Spirit must be centered in this work. We call for:

I.   The support, recognition, and prioritization of the leadership of Black people, Indigenous peoples, and people of color

1. We declare, "No meetings about us, without us." We should not be a minority at the table.
2. We call on institutions, organizations, and culture industry businesses to immediately address inequities in and expand the equitable hiring and promotion of Black, Indigenous, and people of color (BIPOC), especially at the senior leadership level.
3. We call for the redefinition of "recovery ready" funds to be distributed not according to organizational budget size but according to measures of community trust and cultural competency.
4. We call for the building of capacity of BIPOC cultural resource organizations in Black, Indigenous, and communities of color that serve as anchors in our communities.
5. We call upon historically white-led and white-serving organizations to recognize that, in order to transform themselves, they should be learners of cultural equity from leaders of BIPOC communities.

II. The reversal of long-term inequities in funding, hiring, and resources in the arts and culture sector

1. We call for relief funds, stimulus funds, and jobs for artists and arts and cultural organizations for and by Black, Indigenous, and communities of color.
2. We call upon funders, donors, governments, and businesses to redress severe racial and cultural inequity in funding arts organizations for and by Black, Indigenous, and communities of color.
3. We call for investment in BIPOC-led businesses in the arts and culture industries and sectors.
4. We call upon funders, donors, governments, and businesses to divest themselves of investments in companies that do not practice cultural and racial equity and commit to capital investment that uplifts our collective humanity.
5. We call upon large-budget, predominantly white organizations to disclose racial demographics of furloughs, layoffs, and program shrinkage.
6. We call upon all funders, donors, governments, and culture industry businesses to establish and be accountable for equity plans, including furthering diversity of professional full-time staff and boards, providing benefits to all levels of staff, implementing community benefit and antiracism trainings, and

paying artists and community members for labor on advisory
groups, panels, and other services.

7. We call upon funders, donors, governments, and businesses to
collaboratively develop and implement Community Benefits
Agreements that include decision-making participants and
processes, budget transparency, percentage of dollars spent
in the community, percentage for art, and other specific and
ongoing benefits of programs and projects targeting BIPOC
communities.

III. Investment in arts and cultural ecosystems for Black, Indigenous,
and communities of color

1. We call upon all mainstream arts organizations, elected officials,
culture industry leaders, and governments to invest in, protect,
and sustain arts and cultural spaces for Black, Indigenous, and
communities of color.

2. We call upon funders, donors, governments, and businesses to
support and equitably fund culturally rooted BIPOC arts service
organizations with a demonstrated history of trust in their
communities.

3. We call upon funders, donors, governments, and businesses to
support and equitably fund Cultural Community Anchors—arts-
producing organizations that are based in Black, Indigenous, and
communities of color, particularly those leading-edge organizations that have survived despite being underfunded for decades.

4. We call upon historically white-led and white-serving organizations to forge Community Benefits Agreements with BIPOC
communities that center cultural equity and redistribute funds
and power to them.

IV. Investment in building healthy communities through centering
cultural and racial equity

1. We call for the support of cultural institutions and local cultural
economies in order to build healthy communities.

2. We call for support for place-based cultural practices directly tied to the intergenerational education of children, both in
schools and in community cultural spaces—such as escuelitas
or Freedom Schools that elevate a community's history and
culture.

3. We call for the preservation of public spaces as protected spaces
for civic expression, congregation, and experience.

V. Accountability, commitment, and integrity in the pursuit of cultural and racial justice

1. This Call is intended to support work in local, national, and global contexts and should be adapted to specific contexts to hold leaders, policy makers, and institutions—and ourselves—responsible, accountable, and transparent in achieving equity and justice. We call for change processes that include metrics of progress, defined lines of oversight, and timetables. Change must be measurable to be meaningful.

We Begin by Listening

Jeanette Lee

Jeanette Lee (she/her) was a co-executive director of Allied Media Projects (AMP) from 2009 to 2022. She began working with AMP in 2006 as part of the team that led the transition of the Allied Media Conference from Bowling Green, Ohio, to Detroit. Throughout her time at AMP, she led the growth and evolution of the organization through facilitative leadership, innovative program design, resource mobilization, and network cultivation. This essay was written during her time as a co-executive director of AMP.

When I'm orienting a new staff person to work here at Allied Media Projects (AMP), I share the network principles that guide our work and ask the person to reflect on what they mean to them. Inevitably, *We begin by listening* always stands out.

For more than twenty years, AMP has grown a vast and complex network of people aligned around shared principles. We are media makers, artists, educators, healers, visionary organizers, community technologists, abolitionists, archivists, and more. We are confronting the most pressing problems of our day, asking essential questions that get to the heart of things, and designing solutions that are holistic and intersectional. We are overwhelmingly queer and trans, Black and Indigenous, and people of color, who are presuming our power to create the world anew.

We begin by listening is an organizing approach that honors the wisdom and power that people already have. It is a process of seeking out and synthesizing patterns into shared principles that create alignment. The alignment is not around an end goal so much as a way of moving together toward liberation, knowing that the great paradigm shifts we seek must happen internally and interpersonally before they can happen in the world.

And there are so many ways to listen. We listen for different reasons at different moments in the cycles of organizing. These three short stories offer snapshots of how AMP has put the principle *We begin by listening* into practice over the past twenty years.

Listening to Iterate

The AMP network is deeply Detroit rooted but also global. It is held together by a thousand threads of relationship, forged through collaboration over time. The primary space where this network renews itself year after year is the Allied Media Conference (AMC).

The conference is a lot of things—a movement convergence space, a media-based organizing school, a massive party, and a test bed for small experiments in radical community care. It is the fusion of hundreds of people's visions for the world and their dreams of community over twenty years.

The AMC has become what it is through deep listening embedded into its organizing structure, yielding continued iteration with every cycle. No year has ever been perfect, but every single year has been an evolution of the one before it. Listening happens at two levels within the AMC:

Participatory design: Each year there is an open call for the major thematic content areas of the conference, followed by an open call for sessions. This structure allows for someone to say, "I want to convene BIPOC documentary filmmakers" or "I want to do abolitionist dreaming in community with other movement lawyers" or "I want to have a decolonial culinary arts exchange between Indigenous peoples from Turtle Island and Palestine," and then make that thing happen.

The participatory design is not limited to content but extends to the conference experience overall. For example, someone might say, "I want there to be revolutionary childcare space" or "I need access to healing services like reiki and acupuncture to participate fully" or "I want there to be a way of addressing interpersonal conflict that can get us closer to a world without police."

Fusing all these visions together requires great skill and care from AMC staff, who work with dozens of content coordinators over a year to design, curate, and implement their visions.

Essential to all the above is the fact that the conference happens over and over again. Pressure to execute everything perfectly all at once is relieved, because there is always the next year.

Reflection and evaluation: Each year there is an in-depth reflection and evaluation period. Evaluation data generally comes from three sources:

formal survey data, formal and informal debrief conversations with participants and staff, and social media analysis.

Feedback can be hard to receive, especially when it triggers our deep emotional places. So we listen with our whole bodies and pay attention to where we're erecting protective walls around certain kinds of information; what kind of feedback are we latching on to and what kind are we ignoring? We must acknowledge the validity of our emotional responses while still seeking out the gems of learning that are present in every single piece of feedback, positive and negative.

Holding all the complexity helps us learn what worked and didn't work, generating specific ideas for how to do better next time. We look for patterns in the evaluation data and distill a set of lessons from each year, which we publish on our website for transparency. We hope this documentation provides a breadcrumb trail so that we don't have to repeat the same mistakes or forget about the things that worked well. This way, we keep growing toward more ambitious visions and the opportunity to make new mistakes.

Listening to Shift Power

In addition to the Allied Media Conference, AMP supports our network of people and projects making media for liberation through a fiscal sponsorship program and speakers bureau. These two programs grow out of the AMC but also emerge from thirteen years of local organizing here in Detroit. One of our goals through these programs has been to direct the wealth of institutions (primarily philanthropic institutions) to grassroots, BIPOC-led and -serving organizations.

We do this through the administrative services of our programs, but with other Detroit-based social justice organizations, we have also co-led a citywide funder organizing initiative to shift the power dynamics between philanthropy and community organizations. The genesis of this work was a project called the 12 Recommendations for Detroit Funders. The Detroit Peoples' Platform and AMP began this work with the support of the Ford Foundation, shortly after Ford committed to significantly increasing their spending in Detroit, following the city's bankruptcy.

Part 1: Collaborative Vision

We began by listening to Detroit organizers who we saw doing some of the most essential work in the city, the majority of whom did not receive any financial support from Detroit foundations. We conducted twenty audio interviews with people working across issue areas and geographies, asking simple questions about their work and what they needed.

From there, we coded the interviews by theme and worked with a radio producer to edit the interviews into ten short audio collages. We convened all the interviewees, plus members of their organizations and additional partners, for a series of listening sessions. These sessions allowed participants to consider their own ideas and experiences related to others from all over the city. The discussions that followed were incredibly rich and formed the outline for a report from Detroit's grassroots communities to the philanthropic sector, called *Changing the Conversation: Philanthropic Funding and Community Organizing in Detroit*.[1] At the heart of the report were 12 Recommendations to Detroit Funders about how to shift power, invest in BIPOC leadership, and advance systemic change.

Part 2: Presuming Our Power

Once the report was published, we led a series of workshops with local funders and community organizers, coaching philanthropy through the ideas contained and how they might apply them within their institutions. However, changing the practices of specific foundations was not our primary goal. Our goal was to secure funding for an entirely new, community-based social justice fund for Detroit that would embody the 12 Recommendations. We knew that it was important to establish something radically different to which funders could then look as proof of what was possible. But to do that, we had to presume our power to create the thing we needed for ourselves. The Transforming Power Fund was launched in 2018 as Detroit's first social justice fund. To date, it has distributed over $1 million to community organizers and artists who were previously shut out of funding opportunities and are leading the paradigm-shifting work that our city needs.

Listening to Lead

For most of the twenty years of AMP's life, we experienced slow and steady growth. But from 2014 to 2020 we grew exponentially, as our budget nearly doubled each year.

This created incredible growing pains internally, as we struggled to add new staff while orienting them to complex, ever-changing work and a two-decade-long organizational history and culture. In 2018 we celebrated the twentieth anniversary of the Allied Media Conference, producing the largest conference to date, and also purchased a 27,000-square-foot building that was to become our new home. Meanwhile, demand for fiscal sponsorship from AMP and external-facing and internal-facing demands were increasing.

As the executive director of AMP during this period of tremendous growth, I learned that it is nearly impossible to attend to the complexities that accompany such growth externally and internally with equal care. And the moment we stop moving with care, we break. So rather than keep moving for the sake of growth, we had to stop. It was a way of listening with our hearts, and realizing *we can't keep doing things this way anymore.*

Between 2018 and 2021, this listening led to several major revelations for AMP. These are just two:

1. We took a break from producing the Allied Media Conference.

    We called this the Chrysalis Year because we wanted the break to be a period of transformation. We wanted to reemerge as something new. We spent eighteen months in a state of deep reflection and dreaming with our community. We designed new components and said goodbye to ones that no longer served us. We embedded core values into what the conference would become: rooted in care, accountable to Detroit, always iterating. Just when we were preparing to unfurl our new wings, the COVID-19 pandemic threw the chrysalis into chaos. We had to reinvent once again, designing the first-ever all-virtual AMC within a few months. But strangely enough, we were ready. Because we already knew who we wanted to be: rooted in care, accountable to Detroit, always iterating. We just had to find the digital form of that. For so many organizations, the pandemic was a forced chrysalis year. It was a way of grinding some things to a halt against their will and forcing reckonings that were many years in the making. We might have found ourselves there too, if we hadn't listened to our hearts in 2018.

2. We transitioned to a co–executive director leadership model.

    I will always remember this one morning in October 2018. It was the second day of an intense staff retreat in which grievances had been surfacing, emotions were running high, and big decisions had to be made. I was dropping my daughter off at preschool before an early-morning prep meeting with the retreat facilitator. When we reached the preschool, I realized that I had forgotten to bring my daughter's pillow (essential for nap time), and I burst into tears. I sat there sobbing in the parking lot, faced with the impossibility of it all. I think for many executive directors, especially BIPOC and femme executive directors, we live with a feeling that we will give our whole lives to this work, and still it will never be enough. We will make mistakes and we will be eaten alive for them. This logic has a vicious self-fulfilling nature, in which we become terrified of making mistakes and swallow the white supremacist lie of perfectionism. Perfectionism, in turn, makes us harmful to ourselves, our staff, and our communities.

The only solution to this trap I have found is to reject the premise; *we do not have to structure organizations this way*. We can lean into the possibility of other organizational structures if we listen across time and space, to ancestors, movements across the globe, and to the infinite wisdom of the more-than-human world. One of my beloved Detroit elders, Gloria Rivera, continually reminds me that the design solutions we seek can be found in nature, whether the communication networks of mycelium or the distributed leadership of flocking geese.

Shifting to a co–executive director leadership structure is one small step toward something different. At the end of 2020, AMP hired Jenifer Daniels as co–executive director. Our leadership was a Venn diagram of responsibility, with our focus divided by more internal-facing work (Jenifer) and external-facing work (me), and a shared core of organizational visioning and strategy. Even this small shift opened so much. As a leadership team, we had exponentially more bandwidth for listening internally, within our organization, and externally within the wider network that AMP serves. Together, we created a container for leadership in which deep listening was possible, knowing that this capacity is what will shape everything that comes next.

And We Continue...

We begin by listening is a principle that I learned from the media-based organizers who have shaped the Allied Media Projects network over two decades. But long before we crystalized it in the form of a shared principle, it was a practice embedded in pockets of liberatory movement work across space and time: youth sex worker organizers, feminist of color collectives, pirate radio builders, participatory action researchers, electronic music scholars, oral historians, and so many others.

It is a practice that thrives at small, interconnected scales. As AMP continues to grow, we are challenged to hold on to this principle and translate our listening practices to new scales. We are drawing on the wisdom of user experience designers and design justice practitioners in our network to design the tools and systems we need to hold our growth. We are setting strategic priorities that keep us on a path but still nimble, rather than be entrapped inside never-ending strategic planning processes. And because we know that liberation is not a destination at the end of a linear path but rather a process that's ever unfolding, when we reach the end of one cycle of listening, we begin again.

Note

1. Allied Media Projects and Detroit People's Platform, *Changing the Conversation: Philanthropic Funding and Community Organizing in Detroit*, 2017, https://alliedmedia.org/wp-content/uploads/2020/09/Funders_Guidelines_2017.pdf.

EMERGENYC

AN ARTISTIC HOME
FOR EMERGING ARTISTS

Marlène Ramírez-Cancio

Marlène Ramírez-Cancio is a Puerto Rican cultural producer, artist, and educator based in Brooklyn. She is the founding director of EMERGENYC, an incubator and network for emerging artist-activists in New York City and beyond, focused on developing the voice and artistic expression of BIPOC, women, and LGBTQIA+ practitioners.

On a July evening in 2018, queer Afro-Dominican artist Francheska Alcántara rubs the floor of the Brooklyn Museum with bars of jabón de cuaba. Ubiquitous in the Dominican Republic and its diaspora, this soap has a wide variety of household uses, many associated with vainas de mujeres, "women's things," including underwear washing, feminine hygiene, and DIY pregnancy testing—they say if a woman urinates on it, bubbles are a sign of the stork.

The familiar smell of these soap bars, which have the word HISPANO etched in all caps across the front, fills the atrium of the museum. It's a domestic smell: the smell of cleaning house. Alcántara and her collaborators rub soap on tile as they recite "Be Nobody's Darling" by Alice Walker: "Let them look askance at you / And you askance reply," they say, in an unsynced chorus—"but be nobody's darling." It feels like a limpia. A cleansing.

Next, Alcántara invites genderqueer and women-identified audience members to sit in groups of four to play dominoes—a game deeply associated with Dominican masculinity and patriarchal cultural identity. She then unfolds custom-made tabletops across the players' laps so that, collectively, their legs become the legs of the tables. As she hands them large

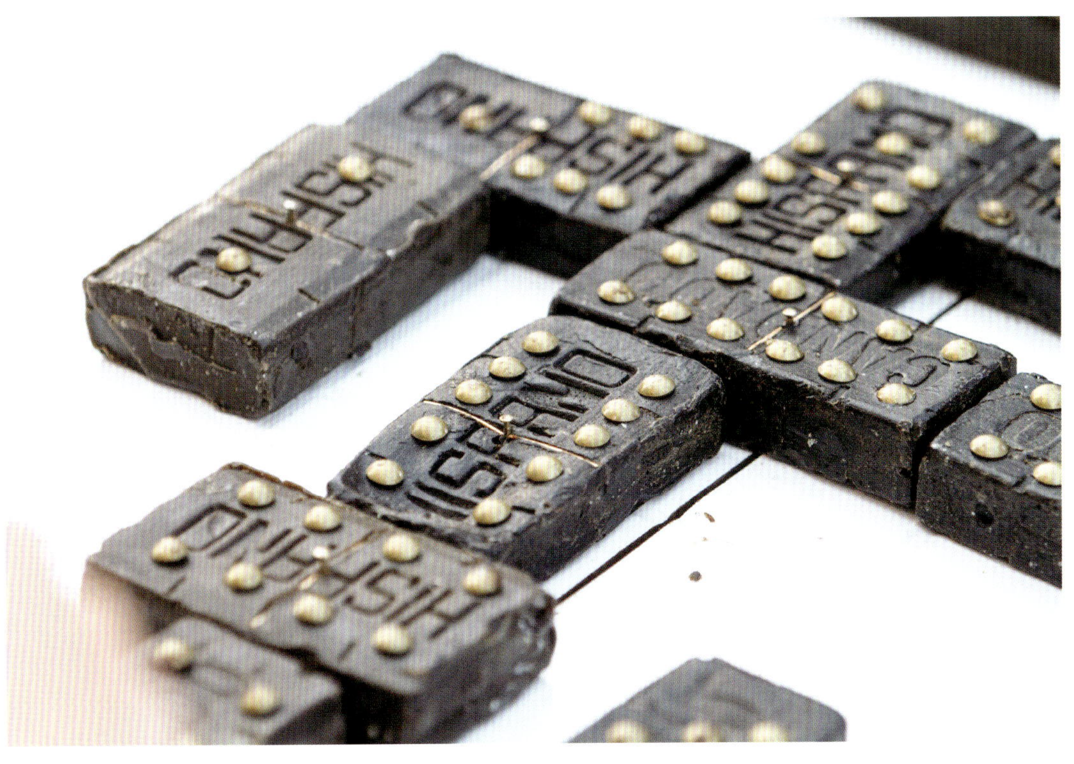

Francheska Alcántara, *A Dominoes Game*, 2018.
Performance. Photo courtesy of the artist.

dominoes fabricated from bars of jabón Hispano, the artist issues a final request: while shuffling and playing, we are urged to discuss the meaning of the word *hispano* in the context of colonial violence. As we connect the dots on the dominoes, we are to connect the dots between Indigenous erasure, antiblackness, misogyny, and neocolonial power structures, while also sharing emergent survival strategies we have engaged in—or wish to invent.

"If they don't give you a seat at the table," Shirley Chisholm once said, "bring a folding chair." In Alcántara's performance, women and nonbinary folks don't just take a seat at the table—they embody the table, replace its materials, and intervene in the rules of engagement, all while engaging in joyful camaraderie.

In *Decolonizing Wealth*, Edgar Villanueva writes that decolonization isn't about setting a place at the table: "the issue is creating a culture of respect, curiosity, acceptance, and love. . . . It's about building ourselves a whole new table—one where we truly belong."[1] In a symbolic move, Alcántara asks us to interrogate dominant paradigms of Hispano identity, to get at the roots (*domino, dominant, domestic*, and Dominican all share the Latin root domus, meaning house) and to redefine our terms, even as we play.

How do emerging queer artists of color like Alcántara find an artistic home, one where they can bring their full selves to bear, existing in all their dimensions and intricate code-switches? What series of encounters, urgencies, dreams, smackdowns, strokes of luck, fits of laughter, wounds, strange coincidences, and acts of mentorship end up leading them to that place? What are the domino effects of each one of those acts?

I first met Alcántara through EMERGENYC (Emerge), the annual artist program I created alongside artist, scholar, and activist george emilio sanchez in 2008 at New York University's (NYU's) Hemispheric Institute of Performance and Politics (Hemi). One of the driving forces of Emerge is to be an artistic home for NYC-based, socially engaged artists like Alcántara. As an incubator, it offers varied entry points into art and activism—prioritizing process, discovery, and reflection, and fostering a brave space for experimentation, interdisciplinary leaps, risk taking, and community building. Over thirteen years, Emerge has activated a strong network of local artivists—most of them people of color, women, immigrants, and LGBTQIA+ folks—who challenge dominant narratives through artistic cultural resistance. They include award-winning playwrights, curators, directors, filmmakers, grant makers, university faculty, arts administrators, healers, and many independent teaching artists.

Alcánatara's performance, *A Dominoes Game*, was presented at the Brooklyn Museum as part of Cuerpxs Radicales: Radical Bodies in Performance, a live art series I curated with Lauren Argentina Zelaya in conjunction with the *Radical Women: Latin American Art, 1960–1984* exhibit. To complement and expand the *Radical Women* show—which itself aimed to shift paradigms by bringing Latin American women into the history of contemporary art— our Cuerpxs Radicales performance series animated the museum space with New York–based, women-identified Latinx artists from countries largely excluded from the original curation. Most of the artists in the series were Emerge alumni or faculty; along with Alcántara, the cohort included QTPOC Emerge alumni Jennif(f)er Tamayo, ray ferreira, STEFA*, and Arantxa Araujo; Emerge faculty Alicia Grullón, Sonia Guiñansaca, and Carmelita Tropicana; and fellow Caribbean artists Joiri Minaya, Awilda Rodríguez Lora, Marsha Parrilla, Linda LaBeija (Linda La), and Ela Troyano.

How Did I Find My Own Home, from Which I Endeavored to Build Other Homes?

The origins of Emerge trace back to July 2000, when I attended the first Hemispheric Institute Encuentro in Rio de Janeiro. Founded by Professor Diana Taylor at NYU, Hemi was born out of the desire to shift the performance studies conversation from the English-only exchanges between the United States and Europe to the multilingual South-North flow of the Americas. Focusing on embodied practices and their impact on culture and politics, Hemi connected artists, scholars, and activists from Argentina to Alaska to forge spaces of creative inquiry and critical practice.

The Encuentro was a convening like I'd never experienced before: part academic conference, part performance festival. It encouraged diverse practitioners across borders, languages, and disciplines to think and create together, outside their silos. As an emerging artist and graduate student at the time, I was thrilled to meet legendary artists like Augusto Boal, Guillermo Gómez-Peña, and Grupo Cultural Yuyachkani; scholars like José Esteban Muñoz, Leda Martins, and Antonio Prieto; activists like HIJOS (children of the disappeared) from Argentina, and Candomblé practitioners from Brazil. At this inaugural two-week-long event, we engaged one another in hands-on workshops, roundtable discussions, keynote lectures, theater performances, and street art actions, all with a hemispheric, decolonial lens. Diana Taylor encapsulated the logic behind Encuentros: "These are ideas that cannot be thought from any *one* place. They have to be thought with other thinkers, with other makers."[2]

And so I found my home in this multidisciplinary, socially engaged transnational community. I participated in the subsequent Encuentros in

Monterrey, Mexico (2001), Lima (2002), and New York City (2003), interviewing artists, performing with my satire collective Fulana, and soaking up as much as I could from workshops, teach-ins, late-night cabarets, and shared meals. In late 2003, I became full-time staff at Hemi in charge of organizing, curating, and documenting the very Encuentros that had been so transformative for me as a participant.

Life Had Shuffled the Dominoes

Over the next four years, we built archives, held an international Indigenous gathering in Belo Horizonte, Brazil, expanded our Americas-wide network, and solidified our presence at NYU. After the Encuentro in Buenos Aires in 2007—at the end of what seemed like an endless Bush administration—we felt an urgency to foster in New York City the same kind of collaborative network of artists, activists, and scholars that we had spent years building throughout the Americas. We wanted to identify emerging artists, hailing from different diasporas, who were working at the intersection of performance and politics, engaged in the long-game project of what José Esteban Muñoz would call worldmaking—those "willful enactments of the self" that, through repetition, across time, make new realities possible.[3] We wanted to grow roots in our home base of New York City, to expand our practice by going hyperlocal—and so we went from crossing borders to crossing boroughs.

We also wanted to create a space that could hold disagreement and anger as well as harmony and love, understanding that not all roads to solidarity are comfortable. In fact, few are. We wanted a program that accepted messy process—as well as full-on, fall-flat-on-your-face failure—as integral to art making, valuing risk taking instead of measurable outcomes of commercial "success." We wanted to activate a local community of artivists that could be themselves, connecting them with others who—as twenty-three-year-old playwright Branden Jacobs-Jenkins wrote in his application in 2008—"would not only be a source of support and inspiration for the duration of the program, but beyond it."

We Named the Program EMERGENYC, Like a Typo for Emergency

Emerge was never an official NYU course—it was not credit bearing and was open to artists regardless of educational background—yet we provided NYU ID cards so they could access university facilities such as libraries, conference rooms, and online archives to advance their research.[4] Participants, faculty, and alumni had credentials to book a meeting room, come in and use free wi-fi, make photocopies, talk with professors, film interviews, and work at our cubicles on their own projects. When we told them, "this is your home," we meant it. It wasn't a transactional relationship. We didn't demand anything in return, other than the benefit of their presence, their perspectives in everyday interactions, their aliveness.

We felt we needed the emerging voices of these artists more than ever; we needed each other in our lives more than ever. The "emergency" of the Bush years came to seem almost quaint in the Trump era. Here was a blatantly racist, misogynistic, homophobic, transphobic, anti-immigrant president targeting the very communities most Emerge participants hailed from. Our Emerge community—which artist-instructor Paloma McGregor once called "POC space inside white space, [where] you can bring your people"—became a vital artistic home for participants and alumni at a time when we all felt under attack.

Life Shuffled the Dominoes Again

On March 11, 2020, we were sent home by NYU for what we thought was "a couple of weeks" due to the novel coronavirus outbreak. We didn't even think to gather our belongings. The thirteenth iteration of Emerge was scheduled to begin on Sunday, April 5, 2020, at Abrons Arts Center. But a few days into the shutdown, an email from Hemi's director said, "With sadness, we need to cancel Emerge for this year."

But how could we cancel? We had already selected a strong cohort of twenty-one artists—we felt an ethical obligation to have them be in community with one another, despite NYU's decision. We scheduled a preliminary meeting with the cohort on March 27 to see how we all felt about going rogue, offering the entire program online, free of charge.

At first, it was difficult to fathom converting a program whose curriculum, designed by george emilio sanchez around Augusto Boal's Theatre of the Oppressed—whose exercises, which he learned directly from Boal, are physical in nature—into a virtual experience. But, in keeping with our commitment to experimentation, we dared to fail. By the end of that meeting, it was clear we had to move ahead with the program because of the pandemic, not despite it.

From April to July 2020, we met online every Sunday morning, as we would have in person. The artistic home provided by the program had now been moved, quite literally, into people's own homes. We could see each other's personal spaces in a way that we wouldn't have before—the stray sock on the bedroom floor, the cat climbing over the headboard, the childhood room that some had to return to—and this created an immediate, profound intimacy. After-class hugs were replaced by emoji-filled texts; instead of gathering at a bar for drinks, participants used our Zoom link off-hours as a sort of clubhouse, rehearsing, celebrating birthdays, sharing space together. We all looked forward to Sundays, our sanctuary of kinship during a time of utter isolation. (Fittingly, the word for Sunday in Spanish, *domingo*, also comes from *domus*, home.)

We went from crossing borders at Hemi Encuentros, to crossing boroughs during twelve years of Emerge, to crossing browsers during the pandemic—which had powerfully opened up borders again, since some folks had to go back home to their countries of origin as the pandemic persisted.

Meanwhile, during the same early days of lockdown, Francheska Alcántara joined the North Bronx Collective, a mutual aid group created in mid-March. Cofounded by fellow Dominican Bronxian artist Alicia Grullón, and run entirely by women of color, the collective distributed food in the Bronx to more than 150 families per week from March to August 2020. Alcántara and Grullón were able to forge this collaboration as activists, in part because of their connections as art makers and cultural organizers. Like Alcántara, Grullón had performed in the Cuerpxs Radicales series at the Brooklyn Museum, and she is part of the Emerge network as an instructor of public performance and street art actions. Together, they stepped up. Like so many community-engaged artists during the pandemic and racial justice uprisings, they showed us artists make natural first responders.

And Then the Dominoes Were Shuffled Again

In August 2020, Hemi's founding director stepped down; in the reshuffling, I set out on my own to run Emerge as an independent initiative. Thanks to george, I was able to form a new core partnership with BAX/Brooklyn Arts Exchange, and for the first time, the call for participants was international. Emerge 2021 brought twenty-four participants together through our screens from NYC (Brooklyn, Manhattan, and the Bronx); Long Island; upstate New York; Los Angeles; the Bay Area; Richmond, Virginia; Philadelphia; Dallas; Austin; Northampton, Massachusetts; San Juan, Puerto Rico; Mexico City; Guadalajara; Guatemala City; Natal, Rio Grande do Norte, Brazil; London; and Berlin. Some had been interested in Emerge for years but had never been able to apply because they were not New

York-based. Finally, they were able to find a community of peers across the globe. And finally, Emerge could grow into what it was always becoming. At NYU, we had exceeded our boundaries—we designed a program, but it quickly became a network. Leveraging connections with established artists and arts institutions, universities, and cultural centers, we are expanding out from an annual program by creating additional workshops, residencies, mentorships, and opportunities with new partner institutions across New York City and beyond. In its expanded form, Emerge harnesses the collective power of these diverse artists, intentionally building a continuity of support for participants and alumni that allows them to take the necessary risks at the core of their practice, develop and present their work, and build power by strengthening their collaborative communities. As Roberta Uno always asks, "What can we do together that we cannot do alone?"

In a 2017 article, Black Lives Matter founder Alicia Garza wrote, "I remember who I was before I gave my life to the movement. Someone was patient with me. Someone saw that I had something to contribute. Someone stuck with me. Someone did the work to increase my commitment. Someone taught me how to be accountable. Someone opened my eyes to the root causes of the problems we face. Someone pushed me to call forward my vision for the future."[5] That is exactly our hope for Emerge—to be one of those forces that can be transformative in an artist's life by fully seeing them, nurturing them over time, connecting them to other someones who will do the same.

And there are many someones out there. These conversations have only just begun—I can hear the sound of the shuffling dominoes. As they click on this reimagined table, I can begin to feel their yet-untold effects.

Notes

1. Edgar Villanueva, *Decolonizing Wealth: Indigenous Wisdom to Heal Divides and Restore Balance* (San Francisco: Berrett-Koehler, 2018).

2. Chris Tabron and Nohemi Contreras, dirs., *Corpolíticas/Body Politics in the Americas: Formations of Race, Class and Gender*, documentary, Encuentro, Hemispheric Institute of Performance and Politics, 2007, https://vimeo.com/2604321.

3. "Disidentification is a point of departure, a process, a building. Although it is a mode of reading and performing, it is ultimately a form of building. This building takes place *in the future and in the present.* . . . Queers of color and other minoritarians have been denied a world. Yet, these citizen subjects are not without resources—they have never been. . . . The minoritarian subject employs disidentification as a crucial practice of contesting social subordination through the project of worldmaking. . . . Our charge as spectators and actors is to continue disidentifying with this world until we achieve new ones." José Esteban Muñoz,

Disidentifications: Queers of Color and the Performance of Politics (Minneapolis: University of Minnesota Press, 1999), 200, original emphasis.

4. Some NYU professors, like Anna Deavere Smith, Diana Taylor, Debra Levine, Tavia Nyong'o, and Karen Finley (among others), led workshops for the program, but the vast majority of instructors, starting with our lead instructor, george emilio sanchez, have been artists with no NYU affiliation, like Peggy Shaw, Avram Finkelstein, Pamela Sneed, Daniel Alexander Jones, Ebony Noelle Golden, and Paloma McGregor.

5. Alicia Garza, "Our Cynicism Will Not Build a Movement. Collaboration Will," MIC, January 26, 2017, https://www.mic.com/articles/166720/blm-co-founder-protesting-isnt-about-who-can-be-the-most-radical-its-about-winning.

Listening through Dance

Antoine Hunter

A Bay Area native, **Purple Fire Crow** (also known as **Mr. Antoine Hunter**) is an award-winning African, Indigenous, Deaf, Disabled, Two-Spirit producer, choreographer, film/theater actor, dancer, dance instructor, model, poet, speaker, mentor, and Deaf advocate. He is the founder and artistic director of Urban Jazz Dance Company and the creator of the Bay Area International Deaf Dance Festival.

Dance saved my life because it was a way to communicate with the world.

Before that, I was extremely depressed. Nobody was taking the time to understand me. And when you can't express yourself, you go crazy.

I come from Oakland, California, home of the Black Panthers. Growing up, I was lucky to have a mom who had crazy love for me; my mother accepts me for who I am. She didn't go, "That's my Deaf son." She went, "That's my son. AND he's Black and he's Deaf." She wanted me to reach my dreams, because in her experience, many people didn't support her dreams. I was involved in as many things as I could get into. Many things involved a lot of communication and difficulty, but running track and field was easy— just run! Yet I couldn't even hear the starting gun go off. Since I couldn't hear, I had to watch. When they went, I just had to go faster. I knew they would be three seconds ahead of me, and I was prepared to work harder. And this experience at a young age—knowing that people would have the privilege to be three seconds ahead of me—translated to my social life. I decided I would be more aware of my surroundings to find a way to get ahead.

I look back to when I went to CalArts [California Institute of the Arts]. I love CalArts. I had never experienced so much art in one place. I was fortunate enough to get involved with costumes, dance, acting, and music. I

Editor's Note: This essay was edited from a conversation between Daniela Alvarez, Antoine Hunter, ASL interpreter Jay Jempson, and Elizabeth M. Webb via Zoom on August 19, 2020.

only slept zero to three hours a day because I didn't want to miss anything. I wanted to soak up everything like a sponge. I was very receptive to learning things there because I think that everyone who goes there feels lost in some way. I felt lost with my identity, but it was a beautiful space for everyone to feel lost and be found. My path/my mission there was clear, but they weren't ready for a Deaf person like me at that time. So I had to get very creative with how I participated. Many people weren't patient with me, but I never let that get to me. I do wish they had understood the need for interpreters. Instead, I had to teach them about it, which took time. I painfully accepted dance class with no interpreter because that was my everyday life. But for the academic portion, I really needed an interpreter. There would be an interpreter for one hour of reading with the class, then three hours of conversation about what we read without an interpreter! What!? It should have been the other way around. I was lost every day. The school system wasn't ready. So it was a teaching moment for all of us. Deaf people who went there after had better access because of my experience. I went back a few years ago, and I'd never seen so many BIPOC people in a dance class there. So I was like [clapping], yes! Good job, CalArts. And there's plenty of space to get better and better.

Urban Jazz Dance Company happened serendipitously. I was not trying to have a dance company at all. I was blessed with the opportunity to travel around the world, see different cultures, and share my knowledge of teaching dance. I often meet people who say to me, "I wish I had the opportunity to do that." And I'd say, "Okay, why not dance with me?" So at a festival, we entered as "Antoine and his dancers," but since I was teaching an urban dance class, they announced our performance as Urban Jazz Dance Company. And that's how we came up with the name. It was a space for people to tell their truth and talk about things that other people didn't want to take the time to listen to or hear. We talked about amazing things—accessibility, slavery, not just dance. It's like jazz music; everyone's all over the place, in harmony, sharing their voices. And every time you come together, it might not be the same. So it's been a beautiful journey for Urban Jazz Dance Company since its launch in 2007. It started with all hearing people, all Black people. But most of my dancers are Deaf now, and we have many races of dancers. Before the dance company, people thought I was the only Deaf dancer. I'm not! We just didn't have a space for Deaf dancers to come together to be visible.

I try to utilize the artistic talents of my company to engage with audiences and communities to empower Deaf and Disabled communities, advocate for human rights and access, and work to end discrimination and prejudice. Hearing people still believe verbal language is superior to signed languages, and Deaf people often feel outcast. This feeling is exponentially increased for Deaf People of Color, as they are oppressed by the white hearing, white Deaf, and the POC hearing communities with a trickle-down domino effect. This affects employment/performance opportunities for Deaf artists of color. Of the 7.75 million Bay Area population (pre-COVID-19 statistics), 2 percent identify as a cultural part of the Deaf community. Deaf People of Color account for 40.8 percent of the Deaf population, whereas Deaf African Americans are 6.7 percent. The Black Deaf population is only 0.7 percent of the total Bay Area population, and 59.4 percent are unemployed.[1] It's important to recognize and acknowledge that both the hearing and white Deaf communities overlook Deaf People of Color and exclude them in employment and visibility opportunities. So I set up the Bay Area International Deaf Dance Festival (BAIDDF) in 2013.

With the festival, we aim to address and expose these dire statistics, break down barriers, and urge our local audiences to take action through arts activism. Something that I didn't notice about the festival that others did was that 92 percent of the dancers were BIPOC people. I was just calling dancers, telling my people to come and dance. Each year the BAIDDF engages fifty artists and approximately 450 attendees from around the world through Deaf-led performances and workshops. I want to add that there are other festivals out there, but oftentimes they are made by hearing for Deaf, and there is always something that doesn't feel like a homecoming but is still fun and very welcoming. I hope the world would allow us Deaf people to create our own space and invite hearing and Deaf, but we need support to allow us to lead and create it ourselves. What if a Deaf person wants to create their own business? Will people truly give funding and support to a leading Deaf business, or must it be introduced/granted permission by a hearing person to be supported? As a Black business, do I need to be supported by a white funder, when most funders are white? We need to wake up and invest with trust in different cultures in America to be more inclusive. When I say wake up to learn Deaf culture, I mean #DeafWoke.

In previous years of the festival, we tended to have about thirty or more different artists coming in from other countries, and maybe about five or six different languages happening at the same time. We have all kinds of Deaf needs, and there are many different Deaf strategies to make it through the world of hearing people. It's an investment in time. But because we understand that in Deaf culture we need more time, we created that space. In 2020 for the virtual edition, we needed even more time. We wanted International Sign Language, American Sign Language, audio description, Colombian Sign Language, Spanish spoken word, Spanish Sign Language, and captions. Virtual platforms like Zoom were not created to have that type of access. So we talked about culture and access. There was no existing platform to provide that access, so we had to create our own. It involved a lot of tears. It involved a lot of sweat. It involved a lot of "Am I on the right path? Who's gonna help me? We don't have enough money." People look at me as a hero, and I'm just trying to survive, that's it. But when we survive and do the work it's all worth the while.

Our festival creates a beautiful space where everyone can be themselves and feel alive. Deaf art is so rich. There's a lot that happens in it. Some people say, "Oh I want to see Deaf dance" and don't really listen to what the artists are sharing. Are you listening? Not just with your ears, but with your heart? I think we've lost the teaching of listening to each other. Because when I look at police abuse, I see no acts of listening. I see the training of attacking. I think they need communication training. You need to learn how to talk to people who are angry, people with mental illness, people with disabilities. People who are Deaf? You need to learn sign language. When I learned deep communication and practiced art, people started understanding how to communicate with me. And there were ripples through that. The big movement I want to share is #IntersectionalityAccessArts—because I've learned so much from blind people, Spanish speakers, from all kinds of people, and I don't want to keep it in. So, please be patient with yourself, be patient with each other, and be willing to change your teaching methods. My teaching changes every minute. I have to be okay with that. You're not changing what you love—you're changing how you get people to receive your love. The last thing I will say is "Zula!" Which means you are brilliant, so don't give up your dreams and hopes.

Note

1. Information that Urban Jazz Dance Company gathered from surveys of the community and several Deaf and hearing leaders.

Scenes & Takes

Carrie Mae Weems

Through image and text, film and performance, and her many convenings with individuals across a multitude of disciplines, **Carrie Mae Weems** has created a complex body of work that centers on her overarching commitment to help us better understand our present moment by examining our collective past.

Images from Carrie Mae Weems, *Scenes & Takes*, 2016.
In order of appearance:

> *Untitled (Director's Cut)*, 2016.
>
> *Untitled (In Suspended Disbelief)*, 2016.
>
> *Untitled (Great Expectations)*, 2016.
>
> *Untitled (To Look Back in Anger)*, 2016.

THE DIRECTOR'S CUT
SCENE 4—TAKE 7
ROLLING...

THE PLOT: SHE'D MADE THE ENDLESS ROUND OF
RELENTLESS AUDITIONS, PRESENTING HERSELF BEFORE
VARIOUS CASTING AGENTS & AWAITS A CALL BACK.

NERVOUSLY, ALLEN SAID, "ARE YOU CRAZY?"
LAUGHINGLY, THE COEN BROTHERS SAID, "FUNNY."
DRYLY, CRONENBERG SAID, "NOT AT THIS TIME."
DISTRACTED, DEMME SAID, "WHAT..."
DISMISSIVELY, SODERBERGH SAID, "WHO?!"
SOFTLY, VON TRIER SAID, "I PREFER SOFT BLONDES."
THOUGHTFULLY, MANN SAID, "HMMM."
FRANKLY, SCORSESE SAID, "FORGET ABOUT IT!"

CUT-PRINT

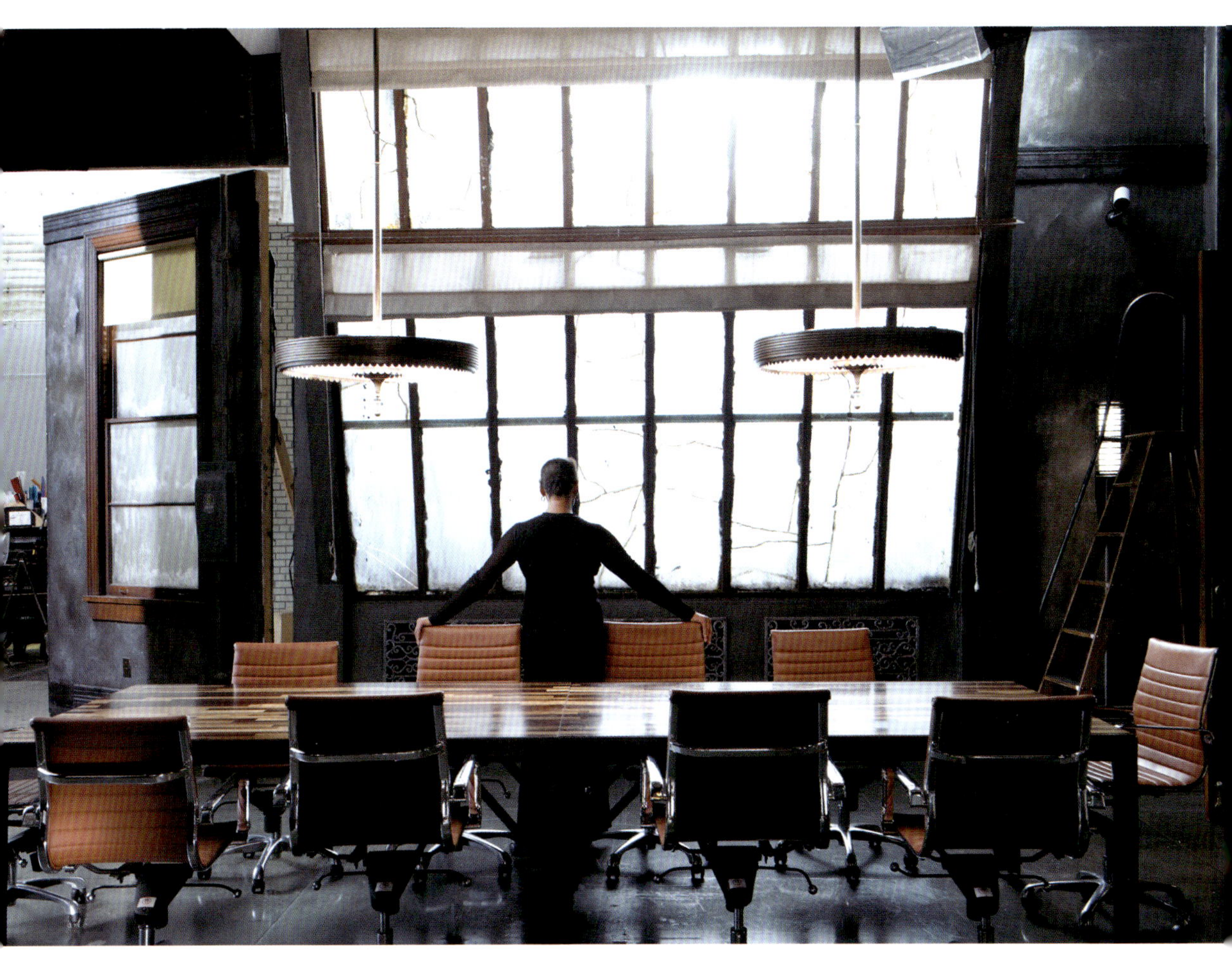

IN SUSPENDED DISBELIEF, SHE FLOATS FROM ROOM TO
ROOM AND SET TO SET, MARKING THE SHIFTS THAT
SEEMED TO RESET THE BAR—HMM, SHOWS EXPLORING THE
OUTER LIMITS OF BLACKNESS AND ITS ABILITY TO HOLD
THE IMAGINATION.

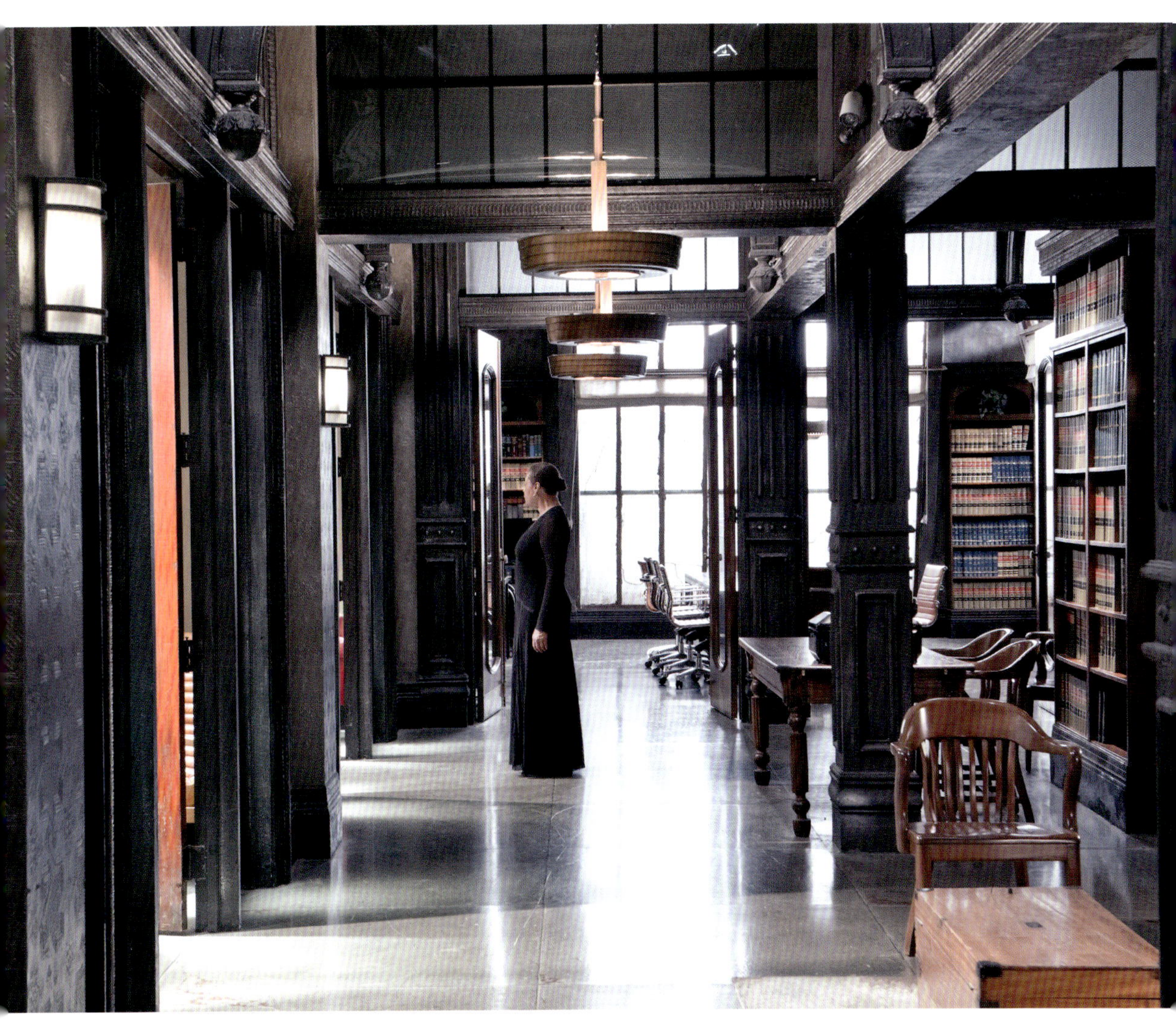

GREAT EXPECTATIONS
VARIOUS DIRECTORS
SCENE 5—TAKE 9
ROLLING...

THE PLOT: A LARGE AUDIENCE GATHERS FOR A MOVIE,
BUT FINDS ITSELF UNSETTLED BY THE APPEARANCE OF AN
UNKNOWN LEADING ACTRESS.

THERE IS COMFORT IN THE FAMILIAR—A MOTHER'S
REASSURING SMILE, THE SOOTHING VOICE OF A PILOT
BEFORE TAKE OFF AND LANDING, THE CONFIDENT VOICE OF
A DOCTOR BEFORE DELIVERING A PAINFUL SHOT OR THE
CODIFIED LOOK OF A LEADING ACTRESS.

THE AUDIENCE TAKES IMMENSE COMFORT IN THE
FAMILIAR. THE UNFAMILIAR HAS LIMITED APPEAL; IT
UNDERMINES EXPECTATIONS. THUS, THE DREAM IS BROKEN,
THE ILLUSION SHATTERED.

CUT-PRINT

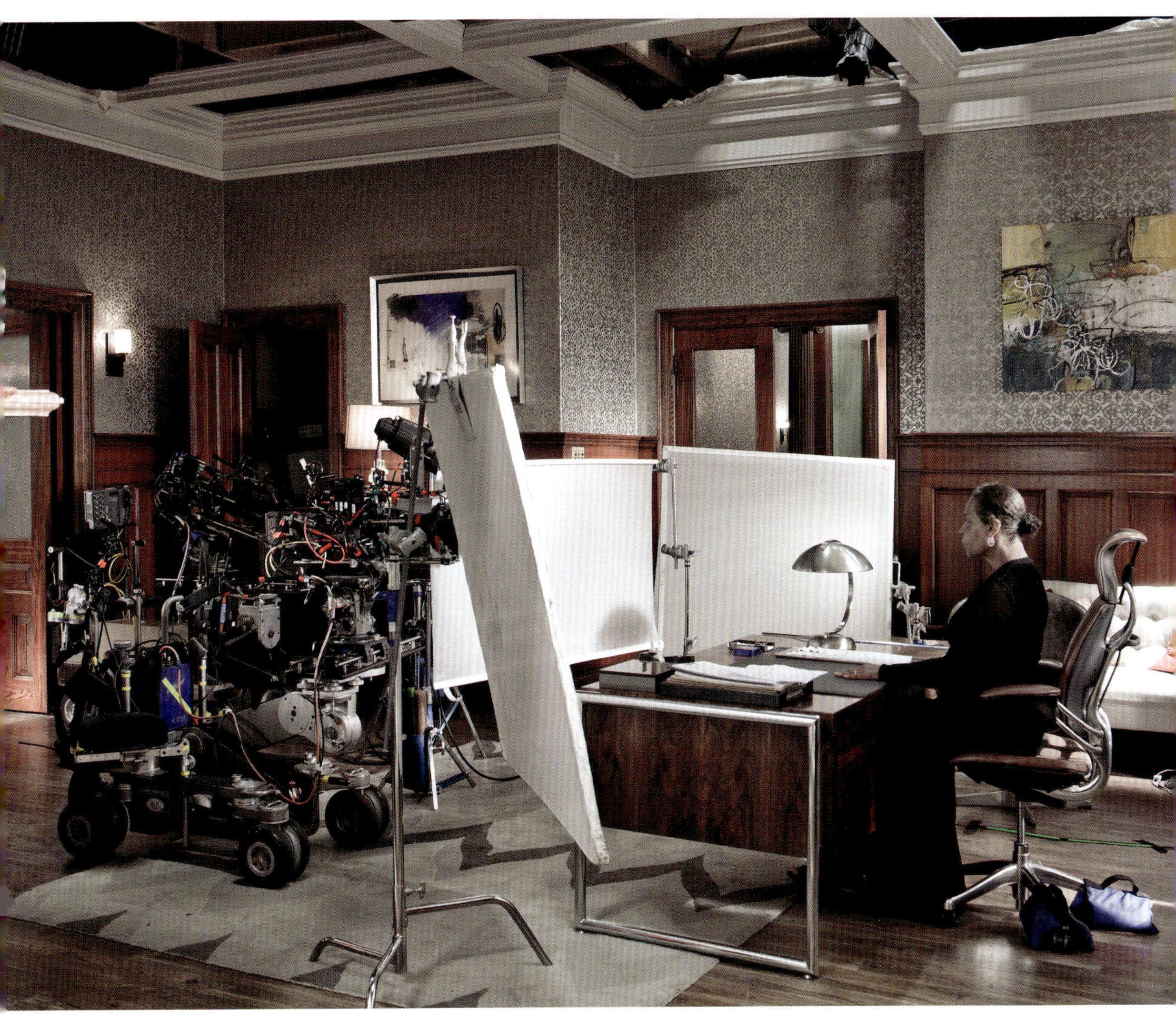

TO LOOK BACK IN ANGER
DIRECTOR: SHONDA RHIMES
SCENE 3—TAKE 5
ROLLING . . .

THE PLOT: TIRED AND EXHAUSTED, A JEALOUS WOMAN
ADOPTS A MURDEROUS WAY TO SEEK REVENGE.

TO LOOK BACK IN ANGER WOULDN'T GET HER FAR, BUT
ENVY HAS A MIND ALL ITS OWN. SHE WAS NO HOLLY
GOLIGHTLY, NO CROSSOVER GIRL, NO KERRY, NO LUPITA,
NO THANDIE. YOUNGER WOMEN WHO HAD EMERGED OUT
OF THE SHADOWS WERE TAKING HER RIGHTFUL PLACE.
AFTER ALL SHE'D BEEN THROUGH, SHE WAS A TAD UPSET
TO SAY THE LEAST.

CUT-PRINT

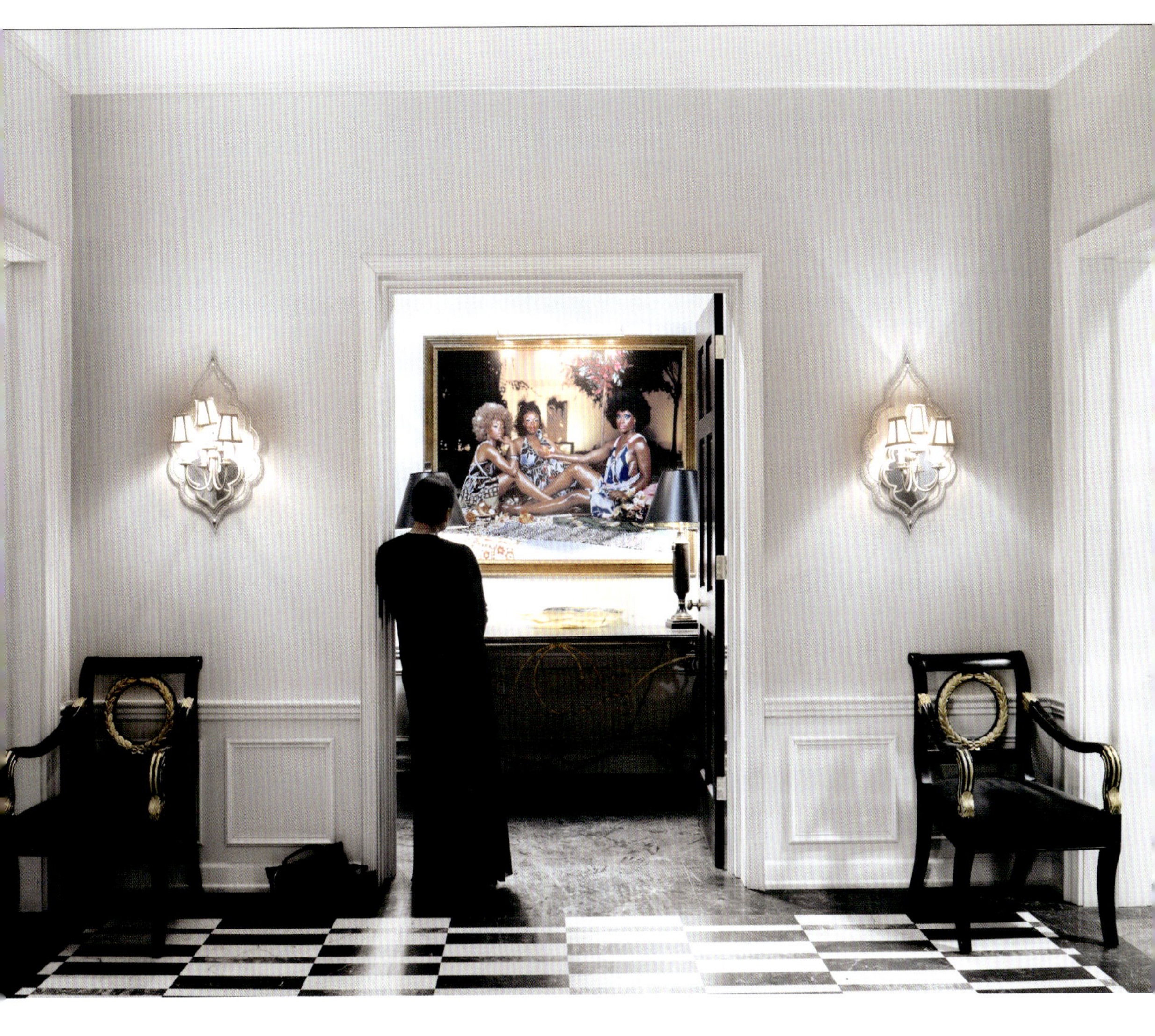

Feminist Coalition and Queer Movements across Time

A CONVERSATION BETWEEN ALOK VAID-MENON AND URVASHI VAID

Alok Vaid-Menon and Urvashi Vaid

....

Alok Vaid-Menon (they/them) is an internationally acclaimed gender-nonconforming writer, performer, and public speaker. As a mixed-media artist, they explore themes of trauma, belonging, and the human condition. They are the author of *Femme in Public* (2017) and *Beyond the Gender Binary* (2020).

....

Urvashi Vaid was a lesbian activist whose work in LGBTQ, feminist, and progressive groups spanned four decades. Through the Vaid Group, Vaid advised nonprofits and donors on strategies that advance racial, gender, and economic justice. Vaid authored several books and original research initiatives, and was cofounder of Donors of Color Network, National LGBTQ Anti-Poverty Action Network, National LGBT/HIV Criminal Justice Working Group, and the Creating Change Conference.

....

Editor's Note: This contribution was edited from a virtual conversation between Alok Vaid-Menon and Urvashi Vaid on September 21, 2020. Urvashi Vaid passed away on May 14, 2022; she is remembered through loved ones and her pioneering activism.

URVASHI VAID: How would you describe the legacy of arts and activism in our family?

ALOK VAID-MENON: We've always been dissident in our own way. And I feel like I was exposed to a kind of counterculture in a way that a lot of my peers weren't. Hearing stories about your childhood, that was the same for you, right?

UV: Yeah, your grandparents, my parents, lived the life of artists. Dad was a college professor, but he was first and foremost a writer. And their circle of friends were all painters and writers and playwrights and poets. And so, what I remember growing up, whether we were in India or in upstate New York, was the community of ideas, and people with ideas, and artists who came through the house. Art was always central.

But I was thinking about activism. I experienced it in a way that might have been different than you did in our family, which was that it was quite bifurcated. You were an artist or you were an activist. My father didn't like political art, although he read a lot and widely. He felt that art that was didactic was really not worth the effort of watching or reading. He did not really get me being an activist till quite late.

AVM: I didn't have that same kind of disconnect, because of you. I think that even though I spent so much time with them, and art was always present, there was always your critique of that art.

And I remember, when your first book, *Virtual Equality*, came out, those foundational debates were so present in my socialization.[1] I read it in my junior year of high school. While I knew that there was a queer world, it was always a sort of urban oasis in New York, and it was so foreign to what I was growing up with in Texas. Reading that book let me know that there was a whole other landscape that I just had never even thought of—which is such a luxury because I, therefore, had some sort of future-oriented vision.

I remember when I was younger, and people would ask me what I wanted to be, I would say, "Oh, I want to be an activist." And people would be like, "What? How is that even an aspiration?" But I think that I was able to have that aspiration because I knew that a political life was possible through you. And I wonder, would I have been able to manifest what I have for myself if I hadn't had that kernel of possibility?

Over a decade after reading it, now I think I have a totally different perception of that book, and your critique at that point. This was in the mid-1990s—you were kind of prescient and anticipating what I think has now really materialized, which was the kind of *simulation* of liberation. Which actually hasn't accomplished any meaningful shift of power. I'd love to hear about what kind of examples were helping you make that argument in the '90s, and is that the same twenty- to thirty-plus years out?

UV: Well, I built that book from the experience of organizing as a grassroots, left, feminist, lesbian—in Boston at *Gay Community News*, and dozens of local groups that I worked on in Boston, then as a nationally focused activist at the National LGBTQ Task Force and in DC and other towns working with local groups. It was a rare experience to plunge into feminist and queer activism when it was emerging, quite radical, outsider politics. It wasn't legitimated.

The insights of *Virtual Equality* came from a few sources. One was very clearly women of color feminism, the Combahee River Collective, which I encountered in 1977. Those ideas were instrumental—that race, class, gender, sexuality, the world of power, and the world of my life are intimately connected; that you can't just work on one piece of it, there's a system to be changed.

The second source for *Virtual Equality* was cultural—poetry and music, protest music and punk rock music. The music was really powerful. The protest folk singers, the folk songs, the labor union songs, the demonstration music—music was always a part of demonstrations, as were the poets. The iconic people for us at that time were writers and artists: Audre Lorde—you'd go anywhere, anytime to hear her speak; Adrienne Rich, same thing; musicians that were in the feminist lesbian space, who were putting out records like Lesbian Concentrate, which was this anti–Anita Bryant anthology of political songs that Olivia Records put out in '77; and then punk rock, which came up in 'the late '70s, which was this antiauthority energy of like, "Oh, yeah, we're going to dislodge you. We're going to do it this way. We can do it ourselves." Patti Smith and that whole movement really affected me.

The third influence was organizing—doing the work of trying to make change, building institutions, volunteering, doing that in the context of a progressive consciousness. I took all that together and reflected on it in the mid-'90s, when I was writing *Virtual Equality*, looking at institutionalization, money, race, insider-outsider strategies, sexism, coalitions, mainstreaming.

AVM: How did you resist the temptation at that moment, when there wasn't that much infrastructure, to say, "Well, acceptance would feel nice"? Because I can make a parallel now to the trans movement, where there's a division between people who are just fighting for trans rights, which is seeking recognition within the preexisting gender structure, and then those of us who are trying to abolish the gender binary altogether, which we understand as a more liberatory project of not just acquiring rights but challenging gender as a system of authority for all people. A lot of the pushback that I receive is people will say, "Well, that's just too utopic. We have to acquire basic recognition right now." How did you resist that kind of temptation when there was such a pull to be included? How were you able to say no to that false promise?

UV: I think because I'm a leftist. When you have a materialist critique of the economic system and of power, you recognize very easily that you can be accommodated or co-opted, and the power system doesn't change. I was able to resist it because I never bought into it. I never wanted to be a corporate lawyer. I never wanted to be in the system. I felt outsider my whole life as a first-generation immigrant.

And then I had a community of comrades. To be in a community of several hundred people who were arguing about gender, sexual liberation, class, power, all the time was very powerful. But I do criticize myself, Alok. Did I really resist? What became of all of those radical dreams? I was in several different lesbian, feminist, radical groups. We had collectives, affinity groups for direct actions, everything. We would talk about things like: We don't want to live in nuclear families. We don't believe in marriage. We want to really make the system change economically so that it works for all people. We implemented very little of that through our movement. The organizations that I helped build are pretty squarely within the nonprofit industrial complex. I'm self-critical about that. I think that what we did do, my generation of leftists, we did create a queer left space.

AVM: One of the things that I have found valuable about hearing you speak about this period is that I think that there's a false tension that's made with my generation of trans and gender-nonconforming consciousness, where we look at that moment of '70s and '80s lesbian feminism and presume it to be trans exclusionary or gender essentialist. But I think that actually words have come to signify different things over time. You describe the kind of lesbianism that you were politically practicing as actually a disidentification with normative womanhood itself. And so it helped me understand that actually, there was a kind of nonbinariness, just by a different name at that time. Can you maybe speak a little bit about what the critique of gender was, in particular from these leftist feminist spaces?

UV: There was a fundamental critique of gender that connects very directly to the critique coming out of your work, and the work of other thinkers and activists who are nonbinary and imagining beyond the gender binary. There was a real rejection of the female gender form, of masculinity and femininity. Monique Wittig's statement "lesbians are not women"—many of us lived by that. I always felt that when we said *dyke*, or *lesbian*, we were declaring a gender identity as well as a sexual orientation. I always said to you, Alok, "Put me in a lineup next to my sisters, and twenty other women, and you'll see that even so-called cisgender has a lot of variance." I think the gender critique at that time was about blowing up the nuclear family, blowing up masculinity and femininity. That never happened. We did very little to change masculinity. Gay men did nothing to change maleness. I mean, one could argue maybe lesbians didn't do enough to change femaleness. I think we did more. We created more space. It is very sad to me that the whole '70s lesbian feminist stuff gets characterized by the antitrans voice, which if you go back and read *Gay Community News*, that wasn't the voice that was being promoted. In fact, it was being criticized by many.

AVM: I think the reason that that division is created is because radical coalitions will always be demonized or criminalized, because those kinds of affinities and connections are so threatening to the power system that they have to disappear or be obliterated. And for me, that sort of continuity is that it's always been gender-nonconforming people who resist the pseudo-embrace of acceptance, because we know that our visible difference disqualifies us from a lot of those rituals of acceptance. And so when I meet people from your generation, there were so many men wearing makeup, quote unquote. So many men wearing skirts. So many butches. And those people have kept that kind of gender-nonconforming spirit and get it.

Because in order to be integrated into that family system, there had to be the kind of subscription to gender roles and gender normativity. And so, a lot of what I write about is that it was a series of political choices that the mainstream movement made to say, "Okay, critiquing the gender system is too much. Straight America is not ready for that." And what a lot of people don't know, and you've written about this too, is that marriage was not even a necessarily organic ask. It was what the right wing was fearing. And then gay people were like, "Oh, wait, maybe we could do that." So it's actually dictated by straight imagination. And then actually the gay political and lesbian political imagination, which was more committed to a critique of patriarchy, got sidelined in order for there to be acceptance.

So I know that you're doing work now around the status of queer women and trans people and the movement. But maybe could you speak to that intimate betrayal of how a movement became more about relationship recognition and marriage, rather than a critique of patriarchy, which it feels like was so central to the kind of imagination you had?

UV: In *Virtual Equality*, my argument was that it was the experience of the AIDS epidemic that made us have to engage more with the mainstream than we ever had before. We needed them to act, we needed them to respond, we needed the institutions to do something to save our lives. We had to find arguments that worked to talk about sex and sexuality. That whole experience in the '80s, with hundreds of thousands of us dying, and the society not caring, just not caring. I'm triggered by COVID, with hundreds of thousands of people dying. I see a similar kind of uncaring. They don't care because it's a lot of poor people and people of color who are dying. If it was hundreds of thousands of white suburbanites dying, forget about it. We wouldn't be sitting here. So in a way, it's similar and different.

That experience scarred my generation. I think it made people want very much to be accepted, to be safe, to be normalized in their families. You don't unlearn gender socialization just by becoming conscious of yourself, and of history, and binariness, and gender nonconformity. We're just structured in these ways, by our upbringing. A lot of women that I know very much wanted to have kids. And the desire came partly from, "I've always wanted to have a family and have kids and raise kids." But the other part of it came from redeeming their rejection from their family of origin. I know dozens and dozens of people who will actually say, "I had a kid or adopted a child and had a reconciliation with my parents through that experience." Participating in family and marriage made us more legible to straight America. Kate Clinton had that great line where she said, "Marriage turned outlaws into in-laws."

But I have some questions for you around your perspective about the disconnect between the movement today around gender and that early feminist work. What do you see as the disconnect, or the sources of that disconnect?

AVM: Well, there's a couple of things. The first thing that I am thinking a lot about is femme phobia. And how there's this initial feminist critique that femininity was manufactured by men, and therefore it is the enemy. And that always felt unambitious to me, because, actually, it's possible to have a point of entry or relationship with femininity that is feminist. And so a lot of what I try to recast transphobia as, is also just femme phobia that's been ongoing. Which is a sort of distrust, or a perception of complicity that's not actually manifest. And that patriarchy more often becomes a critique of femininity and compulsory masculinity than it does become a critique of the gendered system. So femininity is seen as gendered, whereas masculinity is just seen as normative, or default, because of patriarchy. So what I've been trying to trace in my work and in my research is, if you look at early twentieth-century feminist writing, there's a dress reform movement in which a lot of feminists are basically saying, "We will not wear gowns; we will not wear makeup; we will not." And that also fueled the kind of antitrans, antiqueer sentiment as "Look at these foppish ridiculous people." But what I really love about the legacy of people like Sylvia Rivera, and fairies and queens, is that actually there's an embrace of the abject. And I was thinking about that when you were talking about legitimacy, and how queer couples became legitimized through marriage. For me, the crisis of legitimacy is a crisis of unprocessed trauma. If you validate yourself, and if you have a community that validates you, you don't need recognition from the heteronormative power structure. But I think that what I've seen happen in queer movements is a kind of legislative, singular approach as a trauma response. Like, I'm not going to actually process the deep existential pain of being different, so it's easier to be legitimated by these powers that be. And that's why I think, as an artist, I have a different kind of entry to these conversations.

We actually have to heal, and that healing is the work. It's not just secondary or ancillary. There's a relationship, I think, between our political asks and the status of our trauma and our unprocessed grief.

And so I wanted to ask, what do you understand that kind of relationship between organizing and art to be like? Do you have any thoughts on if you wish you had done more of that kind of cultural work? Or is the future perhaps holding that?

UV: I definitely feel cultural political work was an integral part of what I did from the '70s on. I learned how to organize through producing these lesbian, feminist concerts. Roadwork was a great training ground. It was this cultural, political organization, arts organization to put women's culture on the road. I didn't have the talent to be an artist. Or I didn't have the confidence that you have. My art was my ability to organize, to make strategies, to find a way forward, to build a campaign or create a structure to achieve a goal. I can build organizations—it is a skill. I'm not putting it down. Where I expressed my performative side was in speeches. I put a lot of energy into writing and delivering texts. I did a lot of traveling in the '80s and '90s and 2000s.

AVM: Being an artist is the only identity I've ever chosen. And the rest of them feel compulsory. They're about being legible. Whereas being an artist is something that I chose for myself. It's been a rocky road because I had to unlearn what it meant to grow up in the family that we did, which was so invested in a particular knowledge production. Always about the pursuit of academic excellence and a very rational, nonemotional kind of cerebral view of the world. And so I didn't grow up with emotion being stated, it was always implied and in the underbelly.

I did my first solo tour in 2012, which I did as a benefit for Queers for Economic Justice. I had just come back from India, where I was working with the trans movement there. I had some time to kill before school started again, and I had so much fun. Because what I realized is that I could communicate all the ideas that I was learning in a way that was fun, funny, and emotionally gripping. And so I started to develop my performance style, which is a kind of merger of academia, performance arts, protest, sermon. And drawing from so many different, disparate traditions to come up with my aesthetic and way of being.

There's something really miraculous about being on a stage because in so many ways it's what everyone in the world needs. You have an audience to legitimize, to validate some of your most primordial traumas. And you have people that would be like, "You're beautiful," and for a second you believe them. And so I just started to gain so much more confidence by having people actually show up and say, "What you're doing is important. What you're doing is important." Then I began to believe, okay, what I'm doing is important.

But now, I've really shifted, because in the beginning, my priority as an artist was a kind of political checklist of: these are the critiques that I'm wanting to make; here are movement dynamics I want to speak to. I imagine it was very much like those kind of lesbian feminist artists that you were curating in the '70s, very in-community lingo. And then I think I started to change, where I was like, "I'm actually speaking to the human condition." And I hadn't allowed myself to say that. I previously was like, "I'm talking about the intersection of race and transphobia." And then I was like, "No, I'm actually speaking about loneliness." And it's unfair that artists like me get pigeonholed, and I actually want to be able to speak about the world. And I want to be able to comment on the world.

You can change all the policies, you can change all the laws, you can have all the media appearances, etc., but how do we change culture? Because that's the underbelly of what I'm experiencing now as a gender-nonconforming person; I'm the afterlife of the mainstreaming that you write about. When I get attacked, people say, "I'm okay with gay people, but you're too much." And you see that equation has been made, which is, "You're okay, and you're domesticated, respectable, gender-conforming monogamy." But the minute you're wearing a five-inch heel on the subway, you're bringing queerness where it doesn't belong.

And for me art is actually about saying queerness belongs everywhere, and transness and gender nonconformity and emotional expression and creative political expression belong everywhere. But it feels like as an artist who has a political imagination, you have to make the road while walking, because the art world is still so classical and traditional and apolitical. And movement culture is so nonprofitized that I think the only way that I could do what I did was through social media. And that's one thing that I feel like is a huge generational distinction. When I hear about you talking about all these lesbian bands, from the '70s and '80s, that I've never heard of, I always wonder how it would have been different with social media. Because there's no way in hell I could have ever gone from just, like, crashing on people's couches and inviting my friends to selling out the kind of venues I do now, if it wasn't for being able to bypass traditional media. I think your generation often gets disappeared because it wasn't digitized.

UV: It's funny, because you're an artist with a political imagination. I'm a political activist with an artist's imagination. I feel the same kind of frustration that you feel about what gets valued. Imagination doesn't get valued. It's conventional thinking that gets valued. And playing traditionally gets valued by foundations, by those that claim to judge you in different ways. I share your frustration about how devalued art and the creative imagination are. And how central cultural change is to transformation.

To your question about the internet. It's definitely a disadvantage for somebody in my generation. I don't trust it. It's a corporate device. It's a military tool. It's a surveillance strategy. I've never, ever felt comfortable. It's an interesting point that my generation's predigital activism is less known because it is not accessible to people. We used typewriters, and Xerox machines, and press-types to make flyers, for heaven's sake. The history of all that organizing and invention is found in decaying cardboard boxes in storage sheds, not online or in most archives.

But the internet has also been such a powerful tool to find affiliation and build effective communities. You've built these communities. I've admired you so much for that. You've done it twice that I've seen, where you built this community around you of hundreds of thousands of people who are paying attention to a certain set of ideas, sharing them with each other, and telling you things you didn't know. I think of it as an infrastructure to be deployed towards an objective. And if I can facilitate you and other people putting out the idea, that's what I'm interested in. I'm interested in how we create countervailing media channels that do what the right has done so effectively with their media channels. How do I build up other voices that are really producing incredible content, and artists and people? So that's been sort of the role that I'm comfortable in. I like building the infrastructure.

AVM: One of the things that I feel like knowing about your political history has allowed me to do, is to feel a sense of mourning and grief for how the internet has actually been complicit in your critique of *Virtual Equality*. Because queers were given the virtual, and we lost the physical. So it's like, how many lesbian bars are actually left in the US? How many queer community-owned spaces are there actually? A lot of what I'm struggling with in my work is that the internet in one way has made someone like me possible. But also, it has felt like a kind of digital cage. Because it's so much easier to give people internet visibility than it is to give them a real stronghold in culture. The internet is such a great case study of a lot of the ideas that you were putting out in the '90s. Looking at us is not the same thing as regarding us. That visibility is one point of entry, but it's not exhaustive to actually, substantially relating to us. I think what's happened with internet culture now is, it's so easy being exposed to bodies you've never seen before. But you think that exposure is the same thing as what we're asking for. And I think, in a lot of this conversation, a lot of our lives, what we're actually trying to do with imagination, is make people's ambition beyond just meager recognition. Recognition is insufficient to actually address the root causes.

And so, coming to the end of our conversation here, I wanted to maybe ask about the future. We focused on our critiques of the limitations of a kind of political vernacular that's just seeking accommodation. But part of that imaginative work only works if we can actually not articulate but maybe express what could be. So what would you like to see happen in the future with the queer movement?

UV: I used to say that the goal of the queer movement was to disappear, and not be needed. I think differently now. What's happening now is that queer leadership is in the lead or designing the strategies of many social movements. Climate justice, BLM, racial justice, undocumented labor, civil rights, civil liberties, there are strong, brilliant, amazing queer leaders in each of those spaces who are leading the work. The goal of the queer movement should be to run everything! The queer movement will look really different in the future. The queer infrastructure that's single issue is going to shrivel away. What will remain are movements working from a shared worldview to win racial, gender, economic justice. There's an essentialist part of me that does not want queerness to merge into a left or a blended haze—that wonders, what do we bring to the world from our experience being outsiders? What have we learned from being hated? What have we learned from our trauma? And how do we use that knowledge to build a world that cares for people in a different way? I would love for our outsider consciousness to help us build communities of caring, government mechanisms and projects that care for people. The primary structures for caring that we have allowed us to create are family of origin, or churches or faith institutions. Those are the validated structures for caring. Everything else is paid for. I'll pay you to come care for me. I'll pay you to provide this service. I'll pay you to cut my hair. I mean, caring should be paid for, and not unpaid labor—but there's a whole other way that caring needs to be configured as a central organizing principle in the world and not a private afterthought. What do you think?

AVM: I'm trying to abolish the gender binary. So much of what I understand to be the core of the violence that we experience as queer and trans people is rooted in the reduction of billions of complex people into one of two options that are predetermined. Where we take prescribed ideas of what gender should be as what the reality of what gender is. In 2020, one of the biggest fires in the California wildfires was catalyzed by someone doing a gender reveal. And I was like, *this* is the destructive force, the gender binary, not gender-nonconforming people. So all of the energy that people direct to hatred of queer and trans people, if we just took that energy, and we redirected that to the culprit, because the gender binary harms queer and trans people, as well as straight cis people. That's why they harm us— because they only know themselves through repudiation of us because of the gender binary.

The more that I do my research, I'm starting to realize, so much of these ideas of gender were based off of a romanticism of Greek sculpture. And so what I've been trying to actually encapsulate to people is that the joy of being a human is that we are not a statue. That there's something vibrant, and grueling, and difficult, and beautiful, and unruly about being alive that's not about being a statue. We need to learn to see one another for who we are, not what we should be.

Note

1. Urvashi Vaid, *Virtual Equality: The Mainstreaming of Gay and Lesbian Liberation* (New York: Anchor, 1996).

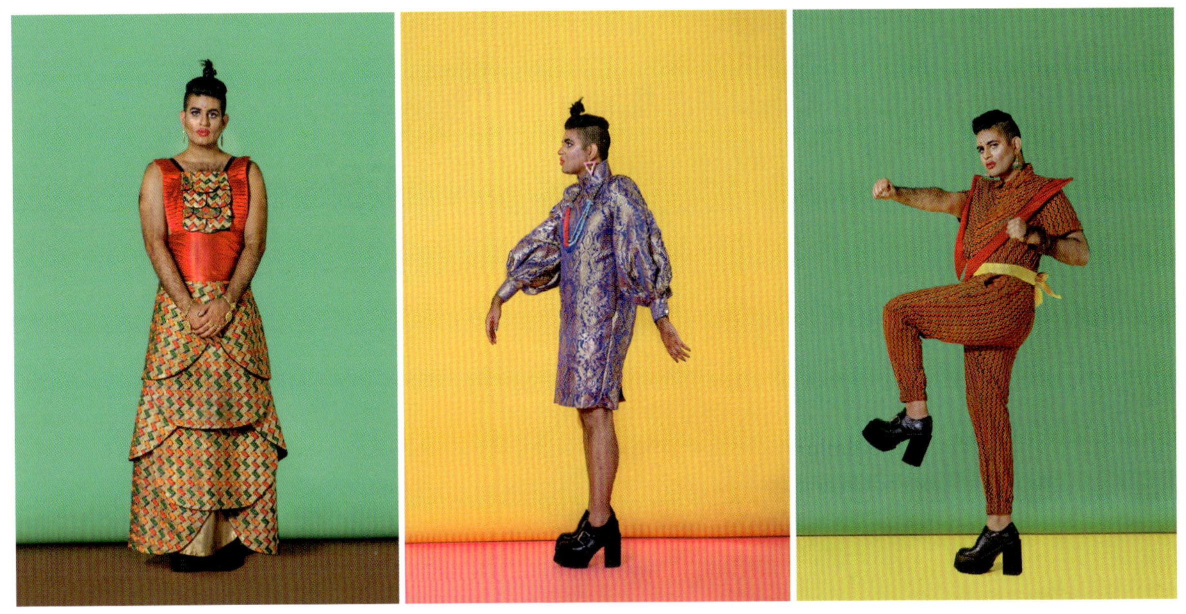

ALOK and Adrianne Keishing, fashion collection,
New Delhi, 2017. Photo: Abhinav Anguria.

What Would Upski Think?

Devin Kenny

Devin Kenny is an artist, writer, musician, and independent curator. Their work centers around products and processes of the African Diaspora in America, with a particular focus on the aesthetics of network culture before and after the advent of the internet. Kenny is a graduate of Cooper Union and received a Master of Fine Arts degree in 2013 from UCLA.

What Would Upski Think? is based on an alternative conception of how arts nonprofits might work to amplify social causes that they otherwise support through exhibitions and visibility. I wondered: Would this support continue if it was in some way at the expense of the institution? What would it look like to go beyond visibility and to rely on material, fiscal action? The piece consists of a 220-volt Antminer that mines cryptocurrency using software called Bail Bloc and distributes the funds to social justice causes.[1] The Antminer produces a lot of noise and requires a great deal of electricity, steeply increasing the electricity bill of the institution. As Grayson Earle described to me, Dark Inquiry developed Bail Bloc as a tongue-in-cheek critique of "slacktivism." Application-specific integrated circuit miners were (and continue to be) largely impractical for the average person mining Bitcoin (BTC), but Bail Bloc distributed the processing burden of mining Monero in a way that was completely benign for the computer user: it doesn't slow down your computer in any noticeable way or hog up memory resources.

For the Artists Space iteration of the project, approximately .33 BTC was mined for Bronx Freedom Fund over the duration of the exhibition (at the time, 1 BTC cost $970).

For the *Rootkits Rootwork* show at MoMA PS1, I was able to secure a group of computers from the MoMA IT department to run the Bail Bloc software 24/7. The software was also installed on the computers of the curatorial

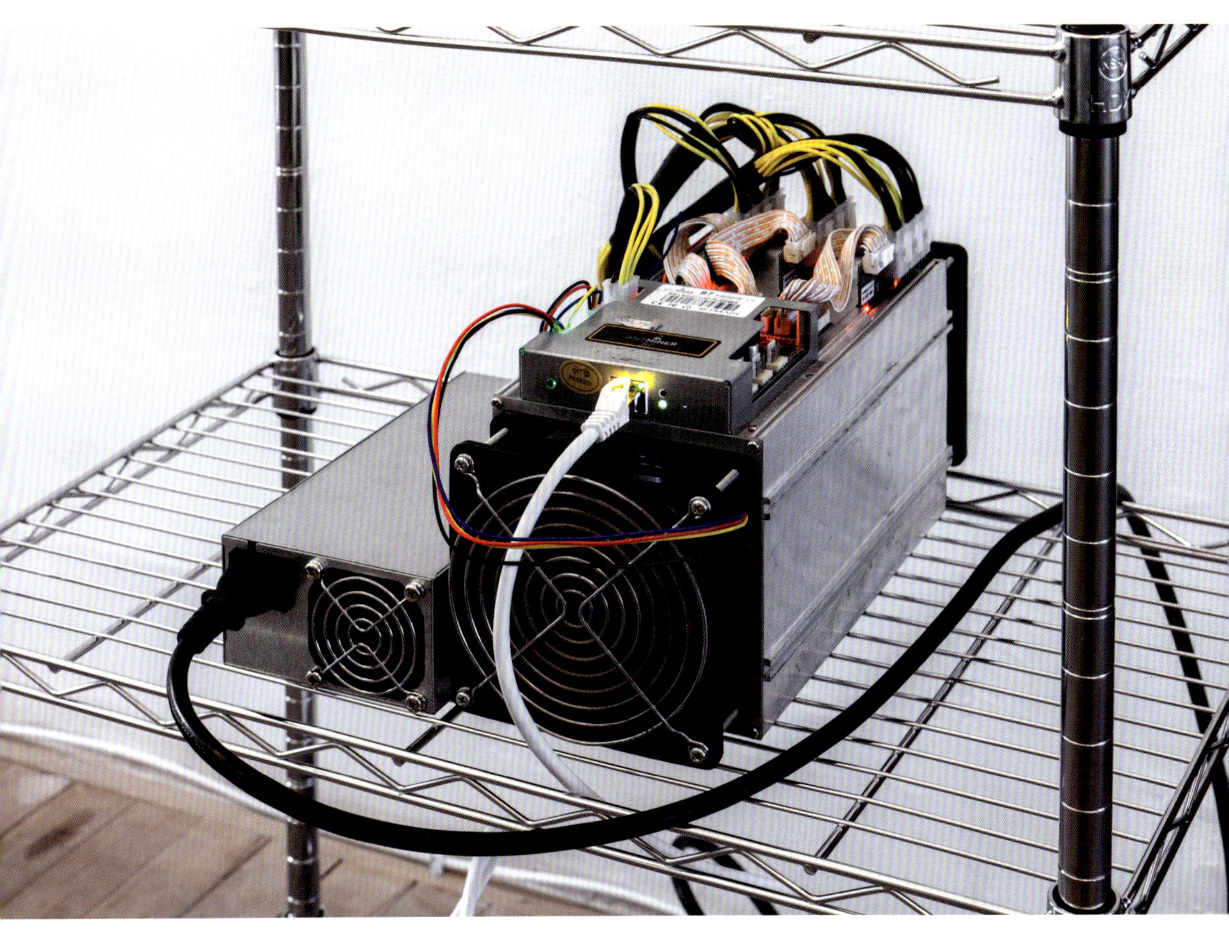

Devin Kenny, *What Would Upski Think?*, 2018.
Bitmain Antminer set to the Bronx Freedom
Fund Bitcoin wallet using institutional electricity,
11.85 × 6.1 × 4.84 in. Artists Space, New York.

staff and mined cryptocurrency for an organization for immigrants facing ICE detention and related legal issues.

Note

1. Antminer is a brand of Bitcoin-mining ASIC (application-specific integrated circuit) hardware created by the company Bitmain.

all organizing is science fiction

adrienne maree brown

adrienne maree brown is the author of *Holding Change: The Way of Emergent Strategy Facilitation and Mediation*, *We Will Not Cancel Us and Other Dreams of Transformative Justice*, *Pleasure Activism: The Politics of Feeling Good*, and *Emergent Strategy: Shaping Change, Changing Worlds*. adrienne is rooted in Detroit.

we are bending the future, together, into something we have never experienced: a world where everyone experiences abundance, access, pleasure, human rights, dignity, freedom, transformative justice, peace.

we long for this, we believe it is possible. but for most of us it is fantasy, dream, a feeling from within, a longing whispered inside the cage of reality, something we have never touched or breathed. science fiction, emphasis on the fiction.

organizers tend to take ourselves so seriously. i was in a self-made closet for a long time as a sci-fi reader. i was sensing strategy and guidance in the pages of fiction, in the words of black sci-fi writers like octavia butler, samuel delany, jewelle gomez, in the anthology *dark matter*. i was reading feminism and decentralization in ursula le guin, network and chaos theory in william gibson. but i was scared that if i admitted how seriously i took the vision and inspiration from those pages, i would be laughed out of the very serious nonfiction rooms where i wanted to be taken seriously as a leader, or at minimum as a reputable follower.

but something i have learned about hiding over time is that what i am hiding is often being hidden by others as well. when i cracked the door open, when i began to share my suspicion that the realm of science and speculative fiction could be a great place to intentionally practice the futures we long for, and that there were writers doing that, that butler was a leader amongst them—there were so many others quietly thinking the same thing! we all just needed a little permission to hoist up our nerd flags and share the depth of our intergalactic black rabbit holes.

one of those thinkers was walidah imarisha. we had crossed each other's paths when she edited an issue of *left turn* magazine dedicated to visionary fiction. i was deeply inspired by that frame and, as language, it synced up precisely with what i had been growing in my heart—the idea is that all of our writing is either advancing or regressing justice. there's not a neutral ground for our art.... what we think of as neutral is often just a mask of normality over the horrific inequalities and injustices that the most privileged few want us to buy into, for their benefit. without an intention of reinforcing systems of harm, we create narratives that perpetuate the tropes we are used to—single white macho man (often matt damon, no shade) magically saves the planet by having all the skills and strength and smarts, while the masses (often brown) await salvation.

in visionary fiction, we center marginalized peoples engaged in bottom-up, collective change. we bring to the center of our stories the characters who have too often been written into the sidelines, the backdrop, or not even mentioned because their role in shaping change is considered irrelevant. we find that the ways our peoples have survived on the margins of economies and histories is actually the most fascinating art of the story—how do we "make a way out of no way"? how do we achieve change with masses of people in absence of millions of dollars or legacy social positioning?

our fiction is also more nuanced than dystopia or utopia. we want to explore that harder, more realistic place in the middle. we have noticed around us that utopia and dystopia generally seem to coexist, the only difference being the perspective, the relative power of the protagonist in a given society or moment. are we the royalty or the servant? are we in the safe community or scrambling for scraps outside the walls? today, right now, there are people living in utopias in which their every need is met and they can ignore the suffering of the world beyond their view. and within a day's travel, sometimes just a few minutes, there are people in squalor, hunger, only seen by the system as threats or burdens. and of course this isn't because we don't have enough. we live in a wildly abundant world, designed to meet our living needs. but we create a growing dystopic field with our choices of how to occupy land, be in relationship, use resources. no, we cannot untangle the mess, we need stories that help us hold the breadth of our own contradictions.

walidah and i created an anthology together, *octavia's brood: science fiction from social justice movements*. to be accurate, it is visionary fiction—twenty stories and two essays. we asked people actively working to change the world to tell us stories from the horizons they could see. we believe that everyone has these universes inside of them, but not everyone feels they have permission to dream, to create the future. so we live most of our lives trapped inside the dreams and imaginings of those who have privilege, who feel empowered to own the future, who imagine mike brown, sandra bland, or elijah mcclain are dangerous, who imagine that walls will make them safe from climate change.

we toured the book, doing workshops to get people writing science fiction together, using sci-fi to imagine creative direct actions. we shared visionary fiction as a transformative process communities can use to flex their collective imagination muscle in addition to visionary fiction. octavia butler's work has inspired emergent strategy, a way to learn and apply emergence science and the complex transformative processes of the natural world to the ways we create change within and through our social justice movements. this work is thriving in Detroit through the Emergent Strategy Ideation Institute, Complex Movements, the Detroit Narrative Agency, and more. it is an exciting time to sit at the intersection of narrative, science, and art. it is an exciting time to be a miraculous and self-aware being, creating.

Rebirth Garments

Sky Cubacub

Sky Cubacub is a nonbinary queer and disabled Filipinx human from Chicago, Illinois. In 2014 they started Rebirth Garments, a clothing and accessory line. They are lead editor of the *Radical Visibility Zine*, a magazine for QueerCrip teens named after their 2015 writing "Radical Visibility: A QueerCrip Dress Reform Movement Manifesto."

A celebratory resistance, Rebirth Garments challenges mainstream beauty standards through centering queer and disabled people of all sizes, ethnicities, and ages, and by using the ideology of Radical Visibility as a guide. Radical Visibility is an unapologetic refusal to assimilate, a claim to our bodies, and a celebratory insistence on highlighting the parts of us that society typically shuns. Rebirth Garments embodies Radical Visibility through the use of bright colors, exuberant fabrics, and innovative designs. My models and clients are asked what would make clothing more accessible to them, what would make clothing more gender affirming, and what they want to highlight. Every garment is handmade, custom designed to the client's measurements, accessibility needs, and aesthetic preferences. Clothing, especially the foundation garment closest to our skin, is our second skin. This foundation has the power to change the way we hold ourselves and gives us the confidence and strength to feel comfortable in our first skin. Rebirth is soft armor. This armor does not necessarily protect against harm, but provides courage and comfort, and allows clients to engage with the world on their terms.

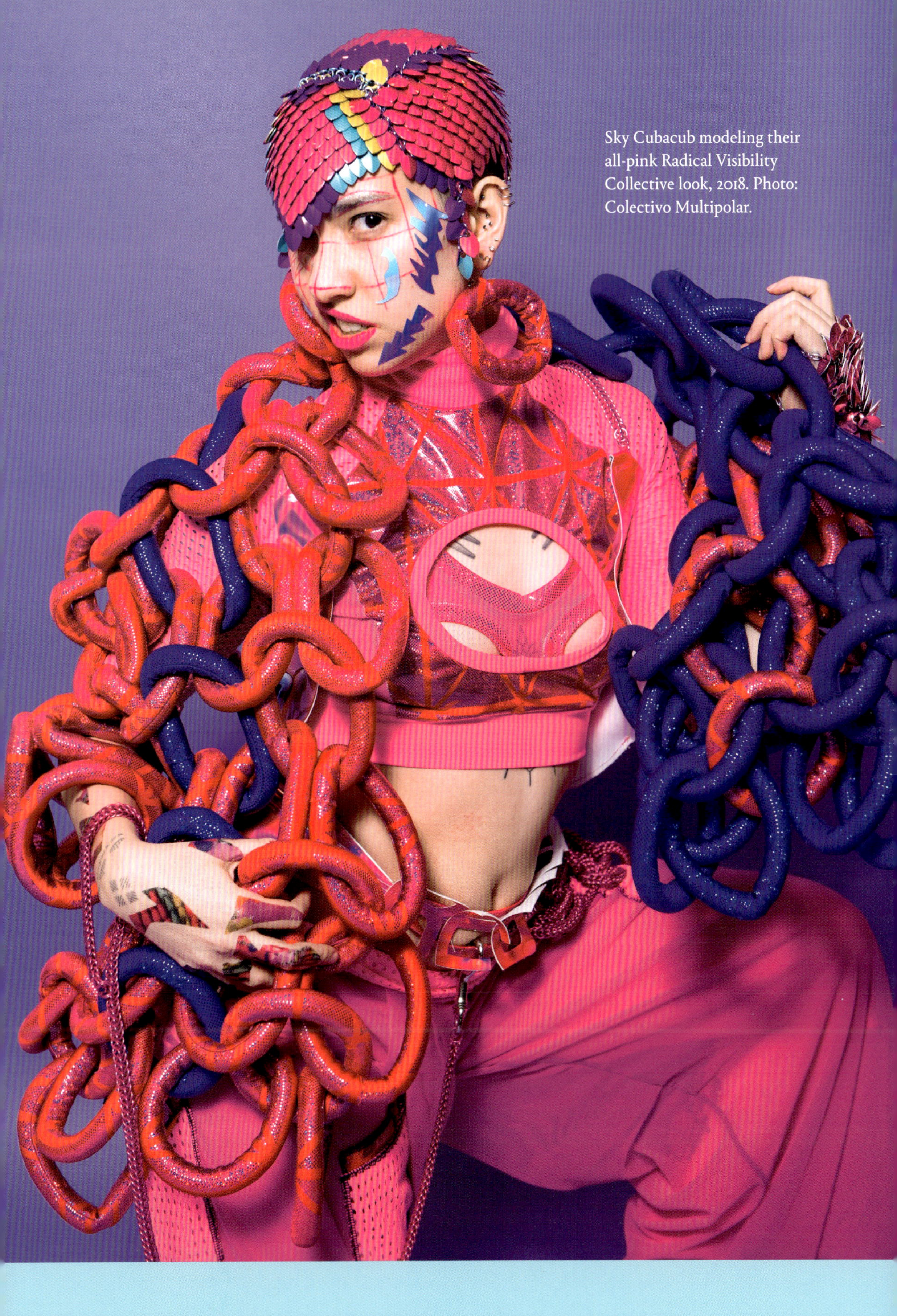

Sky Cubacub modeling their all-pink Radical Visibility Collective look, 2018. Photo: Colectivo Multipolar.

A Call to Action

Eleanor Savage

Eleanor Savage is the president and CEO of the Jerome Foundation and a member of the board of directors for Grantmakers in the Arts. She served as program director of the Jerome Foundation from 2007 to 2023.

In 2015, I was invited to an ArtChangeUS convening of artists, arts leaders, and arts funders to talk about how to shift the paradigm in the philanthropic sphere from diversity, inclusion, and representation to equity, desegregation, and transformation. "A Call to Action" was my admonition that the reigning paradigms in the arts and culture funding world are racism, segregation, and exclusion of people of color and Native American artists—not diversity, and much less equity. I challenged white colleagues in philanthropy to acknowledge and confront racism, and move with urgency to enact racial equity.

As a white butch dyke, serving as the program director at Jerome Foundation, I bring fourteen years of experience in arts philanthropy and fifty-plus years in service to antiracism work as my guiding value and practice. I was born and raised in Macon, Georgia, and currently live in Minneapolis, Minnesota. As I revisit this call to action in 2020, it has been two months since the uprising in Minnesota following George Floyd's murder by police officer Derek Chauvin and three other officers; five months since the dawning of the COVID-19 pandemic and the murder of Ahmaud Arbery by an ex-cop and his son; and four years since Trump's racist regime opened the floodgates for escalating racial violence and white supremacist policies. Rev. Dr. Martin Luther King Jr.'s "fierce urgency of now" is overdue. The need for white people to step up and actively work against racism is beyond urgent—it's imperative. Racism is a national emergency.

Before going any further, I want to share more specifically that racial equity is about developing processes for increasing access and removing

barriers so that artists/organizations of color and Native American artists/
organizations are the owners, planners, and decision makers in the systems
that govern their lives. It is about understanding and dismantling the practices and systems that result in inequity. It is also about acknowledging and
accounting for the historical, generational trauma of inequity.

Since my initial call to action, what progress have foundations made in
addressing racism and moving toward racial equity? There are certainly
field-wide efforts to understand equity, diversity, and inclusion (EDI); some
funders have adopted/publicly posted diversity policies, and many are undergoing EDI and cultural competency trainings with their staff and board
members. A majority of national arts and funder conferences are focused
significantly on EDI-related issues, ranging from funding strategy to breaking down barriers of access, to socially informed investing, to the panel
process and participatory grantmaking.

Yet, what is the impact of this focus on EDI? Are more artists of color
and Native American artists and organizations receiving funding? No. The
level of funding is appallingly disproportionate, with less than 8 percent of
all philanthropic dollars going to communities of color (less than 1 percent
of that to Native communities).

Has there been an increase of artists of color or Native Americans in
staff and leadership positions at funding organizations? No. These numbers
are also appallingly disproportionate, with only 24 percent of foundation
staff and 9 percent of foundation CEOs people of color or Native American.

Has there been a systemic change in the transparency of how funding
decisions are made? No. Individual foundations are making an effort, but
overall there have not been far-reaching changes on this front. Has there
been a field-wide shift to include artists of color and Native American artists and arts leaders in designing programs and making funding decisions?
Again, no significant shifts in the participation in and decision-making
power for BIPOC artists and organizations in grantmaking.

What about the culture of philanthropy? Have EDI trainings and equity
statements impacted the racist assumptions and practices embedded in
grantmaking processes? Yes and no. Hundreds of fierce social justice advocates working in philanthropy are committed to equity and antiracism
with every fiber of their being. Individual funders, national philanthropic
service organizations, and equity initiatives are taking action to operationalize racial equity. There is vital work being done, but organizational efforts
around EDI are slow to move from discussion to action.

No matter the level of organizational commitment to EDI, staff working
in arts philanthropy report ongoing denial and resistance to equity and experiences of blatant racism, both within their organization and from artists

and arts organization constituents. As evidence, I offer some direct comments that I and other program officers have heard in response to efforts to address diversity or equity:

- What am I supposed to tell the white artists who won't get funding because you're imposing a quota requiring that we fund artists of color?
- Our review process is objective and fair (or colorblind). We can't help it if Black artists aren't being funded or if Native artists aren't applying.
- Our priority is artistic excellence, not diversity. We don't believe we should sacrifice quality.
- Dear funder, are you ever going to make grants to white male artists? I looked at the winning proposals; they have nothing to do with fine art. If you are not the right race, you haven't got a prayer in hell of getting a grant.
- If we fund the large organizations, we're supporting opportunities for all. Giving money to small (BIPOC) organizations only supports a specialized niche instead of the whole community.
- How can we trust small organizations with financials that are all over the place? Some have been around for ten years and still have operating budgets under $200,000.
- We don't have enough additional grant dollars to support more grants and we can't just stop funding the (white) people/organizations we've been funding.
- We sent the grant/event/job announcement to all of our mailing lists; if "they" don't apply, how are we supposed to get more people of color?
- I don't have time to give individualized help to applicants who don't know how to prepare applications and can't work with our online grants system/can't "get it together."
- We are open to everyone. There just aren't any qualified (Black, Native American, Latino/a, Asian, or Arab) artists/staff/board members in this community.
- Our board is a fundraising board; there aren't people of color that can give at the appropriate level.
- We don't have a problem with racism. We treat everyone the same.
- We need to make sure we have enough white people on the panel to understand the western European aesthetic and to make sure they're not uncomfortable if they're the only one having to advocate for that.

- Bringing up racial issues is divisive and unnecessary. Telling people their behavior is racist is mean.
- We're an arts organization not an activist organization. We don't have enough time and money to do everything we're already doing. Would it be possible to get an additional grant to support our work on diversity?
- We're a public funder and we have to serve everyone, not just some people wanting special treatment.
- You can't discuss race and diversity in this board meeting because it will upset the directors.
- How do we even know that people of color aren't being supported? Where's the research to prove it? No, we don't collect demographics on our grants because it makes people uncomfortable.
- I am not sure about this white privilege stuff. I think working long hours and being on time is more about Protestant work ethic than whiteness.
- Let's keep talking about these ideas of equity and diversity. We don't want to respond with a knee-jerk reaction. This isn't urgent.
- If we do something around diversity and equity, and we get it wrong, we'll be worse off than if we don't do anything at all.

The messages inherent in these comments expose the tensions that staff and leadership encounter in moving equity from policy to active practice. These are all actual experiences. Rather than dismissing them as rare and ridiculous "Karen or Kevin" moments in arts philanthropy, I encourage us to push through the defensive postures and consider the underlying conflicts with equity:

In order to have diversity or equity, something has to be sacrificed—space for white people: The myth of scarcity serves as justification for avoiding equitable distribution of wealth and is prevalent in philanthropy and the nonprofit arts sector. Resistance to and fear of diversity and equity stem from the fabricated notion that opportunities for white artists and organizations have to be sacrificed to include people of color. What is being sacrificed by the exclusion of BIPOC artists?

Artistic excellence: Grant criteria such as artistic excellence and organizational health are often defined by white norms that are unquestionably accepted as the benchmarks and objective measures for all. Funders who unconsciously use these norms as standards make it difficult, if not impossible, to open the door to other cultural norms and standards.

Organizational focus: Addressing inequity doesn't require becoming a social justice organization, but it does involve an intentional shift in values, actions, and practices. Equity work, like any changes in funding programs and strategies, calls for new skills and competencies and requires resources for learning and implementation. In other words, foundations already do these changes, just not focused on equity.

There's no proof that racism and inequity exist: Many white people are indoctrinated into systemic inequities and racism. They don't believe that racial inequity exists and/or don't understand or acknowledge the long-term impact of these systems. Even when clear data demonstrate the inequities, there are tenacious efforts to justify and hold on to the status quo that favors white artists/organizations. Inequitable systems are set up to perpetuate inequity.

It's hard to find people of color: Many white leaders and staff are not in relationship with BIPOC artists, organizations, and communities. In moving toward racial equity, building relationships and trust between funders and artists and organizations of color is imperative. "Nothing about us, without us, is for us!" is a guiding principle for this work.

The effort to include people of color is a financial burden for white organizations: Many white funders and arts organizations think racial equity simply requires adding a few artists of color to their programs. Some funders support this type of activity instead of directly funding BIPOC organizations. While integration of BIPOC artists in white-led organizations is important, it does not address systemic racism and inequity. Artists of color must participate in planning, decision making, and ownership in order to be moving toward equity. When this work is valued, it is experienced as an asset, not a liability.

Taking in these struggles around fully embracing equity, I want to circle back to the initial question of how we move from racism, segregation, and exclusion of BIPOC artists and organizations to equity, desegregation, and transformation. As a field, philanthropy must first acknowledge racism and inequity and take a stand against it. In the words of Ibram X. Kendi, "The heartbeat of racism is denial." I call on us to learn how to validate the reality of racism and for us to interrupt it, challenge it, be in conversation about it, act against it, and change the systems that perpetuate it.

For white people who self-define as antiracist, I call on us not to position ourselves as separate from covertly and overtly racist people. We have to be accountable for shifting the paradigm of racism within the white community. We have to create space for antiracist learning that is not punitive. This work has to come from a place of love, compassion, and responsibility.

I call on white colleagues in philanthropy to stop acting from places of resistance, denial, fear, passivity, apathy, complacency, and discomfort when confronting racism. These behaviors are as much a part of what keeps racist systems in place as overt violence. Resources abound to learn the history and current reality of racism.

I call on white people to practice antiracism with the same reckless abandon we practice and participate in racism.

The philanthropic arts sector, and philanthropy as a whole, responded immediately to the mass unemployment and closing of organizations due to COVID-19. This demonstrates that we can move quickly and urgently to get money out the door within days. We can convert project funding to general operating support and relax reporting requirements at the speed of an email. We can issue emergency grant funding and raise millions of dollars outside regular grant programs within weeks. I call on the field to honor the heartfelt pledges to not go back to business as usual.

Artists/organizations of color and Native American artists/organizations are organizing in every region and explicitly stating their needs and demands to address inequities. In Minnesota, the Twin Cities Theatres of Color Coalition, formed in 2014, is actively engaging funders to build authentic relationships and make the practices of philanthropy equitable. The MN Artist Coalition, launched in 2020 by artists, is meeting with funders to advocate for radical shifts in philanthropic practice. There is no mystery around what is requested. I call on the field to actively respond to these artists, organizations, and communities, and engage them in decision-making and leadership roles.

How do we operationalize equity? Here are some of the calls to action that I am hearing:

- Shift from transactional to relational engagement with BIPOC arts communities. Build relationships with artists/organizations of color and Native American artists/organizations instead of solely trying to diversify white organizations. If your organization is going to invest time and staff resources around EDI, consider directing those resources to listening and engaging with BIPOC artists in your funding area. Use your resources on relationship and trust building with those most affected by your work.
- Directly fund Black, Native American, and other artists of color and the organizations that serve these communities.
- It's not enough to post "Black Lives Matter" on your website and avow that you value equity. Set explicit goals and develop concrete plans for improving policies and practices. Goals create accountability and communicate transparency around what you seek to accomplish.

- Adopt racial equity as a value to guide your actions. Grantmakers in the Arts (GIA) and many other organizations have strong statements. Look at GIA's Racial Equity Policy and ongoing programming to address racial equity in the arts.
- Hire BIPOC people for staff and leadership roles. Diversify your board of directors. Move to participatory grantmaking processes that directly engage BIPOC artists and arts leaders in decision making and involve them in the program design. There is a direct connection between who decides where the money goes and where the money goes. Contract with BIPOC vendors.
- When working collectively with artists and arts organizations, establishing an equitable power structure involves shared representation in leadership and collective accountability in the decision-making process. Ensure all of the information and processes are accessible to funder representatives, artists, and/or arts organization leadership.
- Join in collaborative action and learning initiatives, working with other funders to share training around dismantling white supremacy and undoing racism, sharing financial resources, and launching funding initiatives. Collective action helps create accountability among funders.
- Shift from project funding to deep investments over time for BIPOC organizations—ten years, twenty years. White nonprofit arts organizations have received consistent funding from the same funders for over fifty years. Think about how to support wealth building versus fundraising.
- Use social and economic position and networks to advocate and expand the voice and power of BIPOC artists and community.
- Artist Favianna Rodriguez from the Center for Cultural Power eloquently expresses the vital role of artists during this time: "Philanthropy must invest in those who shift worldview—the artists, the cultural organizers, and the storytellers who are imagining a new future where we are all freed from the constrictions of white supremacy that destroy our communities and damage our human potential."[1] The case making for the value of arts and culture needs to be centered in racial equity, amplifying the narratives of oppressed communities. Beyond funding, grantmakers can use our nonmonetary resources, including networks and social position, to advocate for the leadership of artists and the resources they need to do their work.

- Envision and imagine what racial equity is. Find funders who are taking action and talk with them about how they are getting to equity and how it works.
- Admit that systemic racism is a reality. The words "systemic racism" are now being said on national news platforms and posted about on corporate websites; Americans are talking about systemic racism![2] Seize the moment to make change!
- Stop perpetuating racism. Racism is a spectrum of practices ranging from unconscious bias to microaggressions to extreme public violence. This system is perpetuated by the unintentional and unexamined ways we go about our day-to-day lives. Develop intervention and disruption protocols to stop racism when it occurs.
- Learn your personal early warning signs of avoidant behavior and zones of discomfort in dealing with racism and practicing antiracism. Develop better muscles for working through these stresses so you are not derailed from taking action. Push past fragility!
- White people need to examine relationships to social and economic power. Stop equating justice and equity for people of color as a loss for white people. This is a fear tactic. Equity benefits everyone. If you as a white person don't understand this, look to antiracist white colleagues for guidance. There are many resources available.
- Be willing to be vulnerable, honest, and open. Be willing to make mistakes and be accountable for them. Be prepared for backlash and resistance to equity and antiracism from white colleagues. It is not comfortable or easy. Hell hath no fury like a white organization getting less funding. It helps to practice your responses to these kinds of conversations with colleagues.
- Acknowledge where the funding dollars come from and be clear about who should be served.
- Create learning opportunities for yourself and colleagues. In Minneapolis, the Racial Equity Funders Collaborative was formed as a learning community, a source of mutual support in and across our organizations, and an organizing body for collective action.[3]
- If you are using panels for your selection process, look at the *RE-Tool: Racial Equity in the Panel Process* as a resource for a wide collection of strategies from arts funders across the United States.[4]
- Resources around every aspect of racial equity work and undoing racism are readily available.

I call on you to use this as a checklist to make transformational change! Engage in radical action and share it with the field.

I leave you with the powerful call from Sarah Bellamy, director, scholar, practitioner of racial healing, and the artistic director of Penumbra Theatre Company in Saint Paul, Minnesota:

White folks, you must dig into your embodied racism, even—especially—if you think it's not there. And this is not just to shift what you say and how you shape your arguments, questions, Facebook posts, tweets. It's not about performing your wokeness. This isn't about what you say—it's about how you act; how your body might be predisposed to rely on a racial inheritance that endangers the lives of others. What's in your guts, in your muscles, in your blood? What are you carrying dormant in your body that springs up when confronted with Black joy, Black power, Black brilliance, Black Blackness in the world? How can you train your bodies to respond differently when you are triggered, when you're in fight-or-flight mode? How can I help you stop yourselves from killing us?[5]

Notes

1. Favianna Rodriguez, *Celestial Navigation: How to Fund Culture Change in the U.S.*, Constellations Convening report, Center for Cultural Power, 2020.

2. "7 Ways We Know Systemic Racism Is Real," Ben and Jerry's, accessed December 13, 2022, https://www.benjerry.com/home/whats-new/2016/systemic-racism-is-real.

3. Maya Beecham, Sharon DeMark, Arleta Little, Sarah Lovan, Glyn Northington, Eleanor Savage, and Erik Takeshita, "Advancing Racial Equity: Racial Equity Funders Collaborative in Minnesota," *GIA Reader*, October 2016, https://www.giarts.org/article/advancing-racial-equity.

4. Eleanor Savage, *RE-Tool: Racial Equity in the Panel Process,* ed. Ama Codjoe, Jerome Foundation, September 2018, https://www.jeromefdn.org/sites/default/files/2018-10/Re-Tool_2018.pdf.

5. Sarah Bellamy, "Performing Whiteness," *Paris Review*, June 8, 2020.

Huliau

Vicky Holt Takamine

Vicky Holt Takamine is the founder and kumu hula (master teacher) of hālau Pua Aliʻi ʻIlima, a school of traditional Hawaiian dance on Oʻahu, Kauaʻi, and New York City. She graduated through the ʻūniki rituals of hula from kumu hula Maiki Aiu Lake. Vicky is also the cofounder and executive director of PAʻI Foundation on Oʻahu.

> *"Hulihia ka mole o ka honua*
> *Hulihia ka ʻale ʻula, ka ʻale lani . . ."*
>> *Overturned the foundation of the earth*
>> *Overturning the red billows, the billowing to the heavens . . .*
> —Paoa, *Pele & Hiʻiaka: A Myth from Hawaiʻi*

The year 2020 will be forever recognized around the world as a time of change, or as Hawaiians would refer to it, Huliau. It is the year when the world was forced to focus on public health issues due to COVID-19, when many of us faced our own racism in the wake of George Floyd's murder, when our economy plunged, and massive unemployment, homelessness, despair, and loss of hope touched many. How we respond to these issues will be the real test of our commitment to our families and communities.

I think about Hawaiʻi's past periods of Huliau. In 1778, Captain Cook arrived from England and opened Hawaiʻi to the rest of the world. Captain Cook's crew brought the first pandemic to Hawaiʻi. The diseases they spread throughout Hawaiʻi decimated our population, estimated to have been around 683,000 in 1778. In his 2015 study, researcher David Swanson, from the University of California, Riverside, estimates that one in every seventeen Native Hawaiians died within two and a half years of exposure to infectious diseases after Captain Cook set foot on the islands. By 1800, the population had declined by 48 percent, and by 1840, 84 percent.[1] In 1810,

Kamehameha I united Hawai'i under one kingdom, and for years after Hawai'i enjoyed sovereignty and economic stability.[2]

Kamehameha I died in 1819, and in 1820 the first Christian missionaries arrived, intent on converting Native Hawaiians to Christianity. One of the first converts was Kamehameha's most influential wife, Ka'ahumanu. And so began another Huliau—the conversion of Native Hawaiians to Christianity, the ban on Hawaiian language in schools and everyday life, hula (Hawaiian dance), and other Native Hawaiian cultural practices and traditions.

Hula practitioners went underground and continued to practice, compose, and create hula, documenting the times and honoring people, places, and historical events. Over the next several decades, hula continued to be taught and performed at private functions, away from the public. However, in 1883 King David Kalākaua declared "Hula is the Language of the Heart. Therefore the heartbeat of the Hawaiian people."[3] Hula and other cultural and artistic practices enjoyed a revival, a new kind of Huliau. It was no longer banned from public performances, and no longer were the creative arts shunned from public display. Christian converts continued to chastise Native Hawaiians for engaging in these "lascivious" celebrations of their cultural practices, and, in their Christian-run schools, Hawaiian language and cultural practices were still banned.

In 1893, with the support of the US Navy, our Hawaiian kingdom was overthrown and our Queen Lili'uokalani was imprisoned in her palace and tried for treason. Then, in 1898, Hawai'i was annexed to the United States, without the permission of Native Hawaiians. I was born in 1947 in the Territory of Hawai'i, and in 1959, Hawai'i became the fiftieth state. I remember the celebration by many. We were let out of school early, but my grandmother wore black; she mourned the loss of our Hawaiian kingdom and the right of self-determination. . . . Huliau.

My sister and I began our study of hula with Maiki Aiu Lake in 1959. I was twelve, my sister, ten. For the next sixteen years, we learned not just hula but Hawaiian language, history, genealogies, ancient mythology, geography, customs, traditions, and much more. My sister and I 'ūniki (graduated through the rituals of hula) in 1975, and I started my school of Hawaiian dance, Pua Ali'i 'Ilima, in 1977. We became part of the Hawaiian Renaissance, the Huliau, to reclaim our Native Hawaiian cultural traditions stolen from our people after colonization. I have been teaching ever since.

Just before my kumu, Maiki Aiu Lake, passed away, we chatted on the phone. I was in my mid-thirties, and she asked me how old I was. She said I was still young, but that when I turned fifty, I would be doing the most important work of my life. I didn't think about that conversation until years later.

In February 1997, the year I was to turn fifty, the Hawai'i State Legislature introduced legislation that would restrict Native Hawaiian gathering rights. Yet under the Hawai'i state constitution, Native Hawaiians are guaranteed the right to gather the natural and cultural resources that are vital to our cultural practices. After submitting my testimony against the bill and watching it move quickly through State Senate and House committees, I gathered the most influential master teachers of hula together as the 'Īlio'ulaokalani (The red dogs of the heavens) Coalition. We rallied at the state capitol, drumming and chanting for twenty-four hours to kill the bills. It was the most powerful demonstration of the power of hula in modern times. Since then, the hula community has gathered to effectively make a difference on environmental, political, and social justice issues. . . . Huliau.

Hula practitioners continue to lead the public through peaceful cultural demonstrations and marches to protect our Native rights, educational institutions, and the natural and cultural resources vital to our cultural practices and sacred sites. Today, hula people conduct daily rituals at Mauna Kea, objecting to the desecration of our most sacred mountain, the home of the Hawaiian god Wākea, Sky Father, and the goddesses Lilinoe, Waiau, Kuahu'ula, and Poli'ahu. We joined the Black Lives Matter demonstrations and marches through Waikīkī, sharing our cultural traditions of oli (Hawaiian chant) and hula (Hawaiian dance) and have joined the Native Americans at Standing Rock. We remain vigilant at the legislature to ensure that the rights of our people are protected.

I think of our Hawaiian kingdom in this one hundredth year of the women's suffrage movement and the right to vote. Under the Hawaiian kingdom, Queen Ka'ahumanu, the wife of King Kamehameha the Great, had immense power and influence. She was the Kuhina Nui, equal to the rank of a prime minister. Queen Lili'uokalani was the last queen of Hawai'i—extremely intelligent and talented, a powerful figure and beloved ruler of Hawai'i. Women in the Hawaiian kingdom enjoyed the right to vote, but they lost that right when Hawai'i became a territory of the United States. And while we now have the right to vote once more, the United States has still not elected a woman as president to lead its nation.

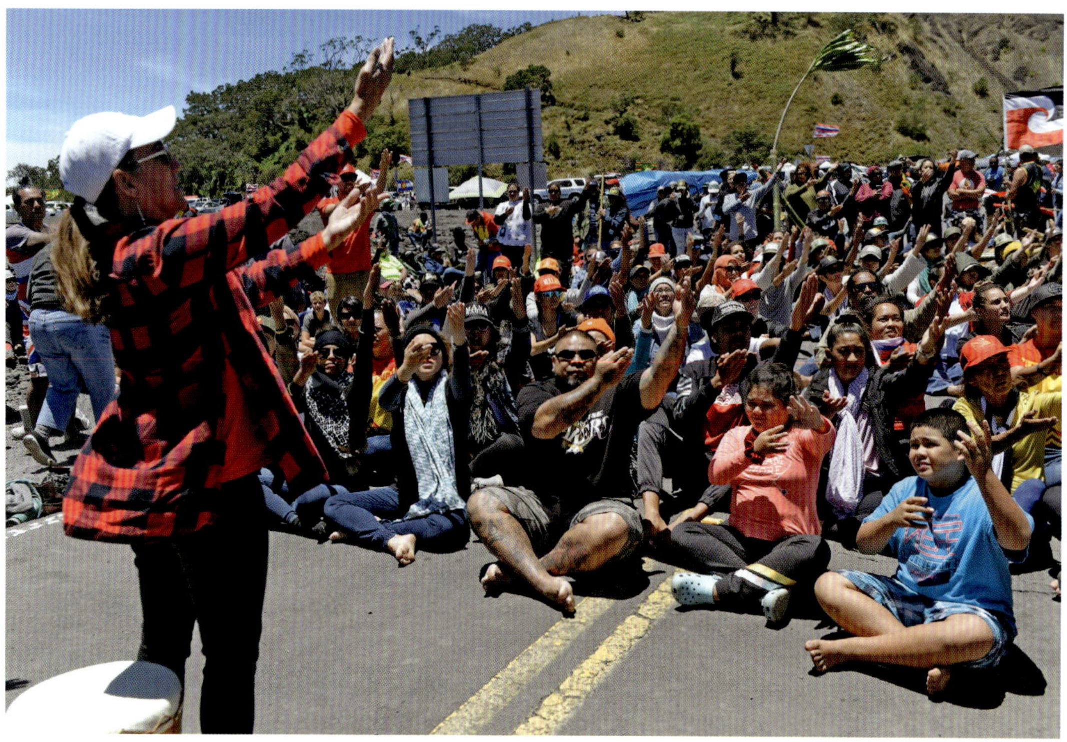

Vicky Holt Takamine teaches hula movements to groups gathered to protect Mauna Kea, 2019. Photo: Bruce Asato for the *Honolulu Star-Advertiser*.

I think of the pandemic like a volcanic eruption, similar to the story of Pele and Hiʻiaka. The goddess of fire and volcano, Pele, arrives in Hawaiʻi, searching for a new home. She starts in the north, at Mokupāpapa, or Kure Atoll, and works her way down the island chain, clearing the lands, creating new features, craters, and extending the islands' borders. Following the destruction of the lands, Hiʻiaka, the youngest sister of Pele, is sent back across these islands in search of Pele's lover, and as she travels, she helps to heal the islands. New foliage and life begin to germinate.

As we navigate the next few years, I wonder what lies ahead. What kind of society will we be? Who will survive? Will we be more compassionate, loving, caring to one another? Will there be justice for all?

The year 2020 will be forever recognized around the world as a time of change, of Huliau. We approach this time of change with hope and optimism that we can make changes in our communities to build a better society—one that is more just, compassionate, and loving. The creative arts sector has always been at the forefront of effecting change in our society, giving the movement voice, power, and beauty.

We have an opportunity as hula poʻe (people), artists, and cultural practitioners to lead our communities, build a better world, model a more just and inclusive society, and create better systems to meet the needs of our community.

Notes

1. David Swanson, "A New Estimate of the Hawaiian Population for 1778, the Year of First European Contact," *Hūlili* 11, no. 2 (2019): 203–22.

2. For further study responding to this period, please see the works of Native Hawaiian scholars like Haunani K. Trask, Noenoe Silva, Jon Kamakawiwoʻole Osorio, Jamaica Heoli Osorio, Kāwika Tengan, J. Kehaulani Kauanui, Emalani Case, Noelani Goodyear-Kaʻōpua, and Keanu Sai.

3. The 60th Annual Merrie Monarch Festival, April 9–15, 2023, https://www.merriemonarch.com/.

SOVEREIGN

X

X, M.Arch, MFA (Koasati/Chamoru), is a multidisciplinary artist and architect specializing in land, architectural, and new media installation. His work illuminates the liminal space between the ancestral plane and our accelerating posthuman world. His work is exhibited and collected internationally, including the Chicago Architecture Biennial, Museum of Contemporary Native Art, and Ars Electronica.

SOVEREIGN was created with invasive phragmites harvested from the city streets of Chicago, wrapped around steel rebar and set within the urban grid of present-day Zhegagoynak. The work functions as a glitch in colonial time, acting to invert the settler colonial architecture of the city to carve out a moment of respite and return. The silhouette of a hut, which is traditionally wrapped in respective materials like birch bark, or palmetto thatching, depending on woodland region, is articulated here, only using materials harvested from the settler colonial landscape as it currently exists. *SOVEREIGN* is a material departure but ancestral return to the principles of resourcefulness for survival, augmenting and reanimating the Indigenous landscape to interrupt the accelerating colonial world.

The trajectory of my practice is an exploration of the human interface between our built environment, technology, history, futurity, our own self-relevance, and how we navigate this relationship to construct our notions of order. My work directly engages the notions of a posthuman world but actualizes to activate the possibility of our own prosperity, by painting our self-constructed limitations and deconstructing them. I believe that art can transcend representation and become something sacred that embodies life itself. I believe that through a multiplicity of creation and being, our knowledge can be embedded into the landscape, providing access for future generations of prosperity.

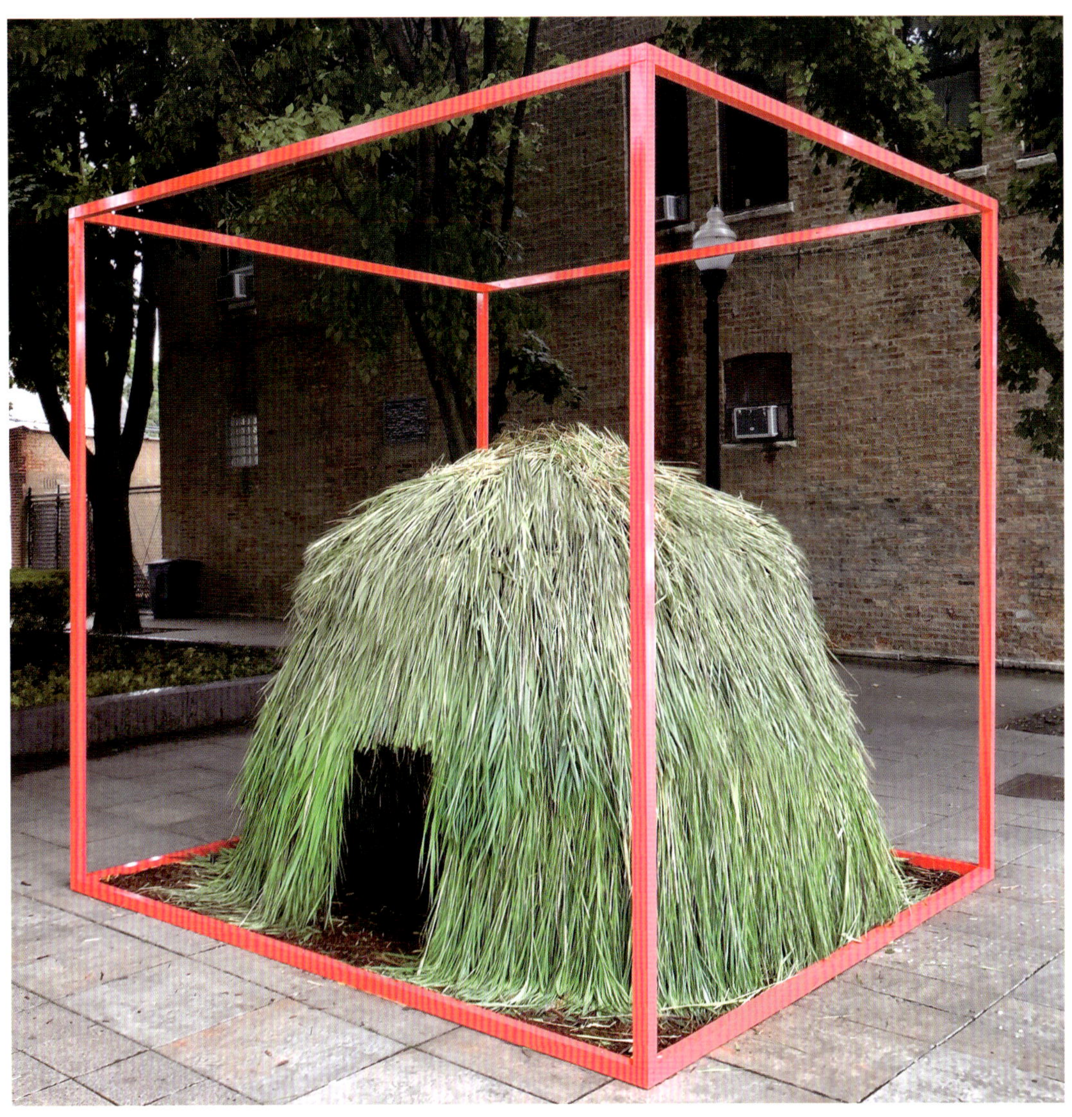

X, *SOVEREIGN*, 2019. Steel, rebar, invasive phragmites grass harvested by the artist, 10 × 10 × 10 ft. For Nomadicube, curated by M. Bernstein. Photo: X.

Flexing Hope Is a Practice

Ananya Chatterjea

Ananya Chatterjea's work as choreographer, dancer, and thinker brings together contemporary dance and social justice choreography. She is artistic director of Ananya Dance Theatre, a dance company of BIPOC women and femmes, and cofounder of the Shawngrām Institute for Performance and Social Justice. Her second book, *Heat and Alterity in Contemporary Dance: South-South Choreographies*, was published in 2020.

I live and work in Mni Sota Makoce, the unceded homelands of the Dakota peoples, and I begin by lifting up the principle that has been taught to me, Mitakuye Oyasin: We are all related.[1] This inevitable relatedness has indeed been 2020's lesson as we have struggled through multiple pandemics. It is also the principle that will support us in imagining different ways to inhabit our ecosystem as we begin to realize the Cultural New Deal.[2]

In the spring and summer of 2020, as we in the Twin Cities were scrambling to work in compliance with the governor's shelter-in-place orders, George Floyd was brutally murdered in our city. I participated in the grief-laden protest and witnessed how it turned violent at the Third Precinct police station, when tear gas and rubber pellets shot through the air while a community responded from generational trauma, even as it was infiltrated by white supremacists from outside. The Uprising followed, scorching many of the buildings along the main arteries of the Twin Cities. And then, the affordable housing crisis became even worse, and hundreds of unhoused peoples, forced out of the temporary shelters they had built, sought some respite by converging in encampments in the city's public parks.

I had been creating a piece about home, borders, boundaries, loss, and belonging, with the artists in my company. When we reconvened at a park after the Uprising, we had to grapple with a vitally changed context for dance. This park, about ten blocks from the now burned-down Third Precinct station, soon became home to the Sanctuary, an encampment of primarily Black, Indigenous, and Latinx women and femmes. We learned to navigate our solidarity with the unhoused community by supporting mutual aid organizing, inviting them to our training sessions if they were interested, but also trying to protect their privacy. As the encampment grew, we moved out from under the shade of the trees where we had begun rehearsing. We found ourselves building capacity to dance for hours in the hot sun with masks, dodge multiple flying balls from the various group sports with whom we shared the field, and deal both with the slippery gravel of the baseball diamond, which blew up clouds of dust with every footwork, and the unyielding asphalt of the tennis court, which amplified the heat of the sun beating down on us.

Sometimes it felt like the very aesthetic core we had worked so hard to define for so many years was impossible to maintain. The heaviness of shoes on our feet and the uneven ground on which we danced often prevented us from articulating the clear and sharp rhythmic footwork that is the hallmark of our work. So we honed in on our principle of remaining "grounded and nimble" and built in long traveling phrases instead to conjure energy from the ground. And even as we had to give up the femme intimacy and touch at the root of our feminist movement's vocabulary, we practiced sharpening our gazes over the line of our masks and articulating emotionality and connection through the reachings of our spine. And in this practice of flexing to adapt to present circumstances, prioritizing the stories on the ground on which we danced, and of collectively reciting our bols, syllabic accompaniments, over the sirens of police cars speeding by us, dancing deepened into a practice of listening, healing, and transformation more than ever, and of building solidarity. Reflecting on the process, I am reminded of adrienne maree brown's powerful notion of "emergent strategy" as a mode of emphasizing "critical connections over critical mass, building authentic relationships, listening with all the senses of the body and the mind . . . how we intentionally change the ways that grow our capacity to embody the just and liberated worlds we long for."[3] I am inspired by the call of many Black and brown feminists to align ourselves with natural ecosystems, observe and learn from plant and animal life, so we can upend the pervasive capitalist violence of our societies and investigate how to be with each other differently.

The Cultural New Deal reminds us that the struggle for cultural justice is urgent because creative work can unlock our imaginations of a different world, where racial, economic, sexual justice are possible. It also reminds us that transformation will have to be a long-term goal, approached strategically, dismantling systemic hierarchies and redesigning the field from equitable perspectives. This work is complex because of the multiple and interlocking flows of violence that undergird the cultural sector, enabling both top-down and lateral harm. In other words, we have to both make space for decolonizing crucial notions of beauty, excellence, and what makes for artistic value (so we can stand confidently in our own creative practices) and battle the philosophy of scarcity and necessary competition against each other that decimates the possibility of solidarity (so we can create supportive communities).

Yet, because we are racialized in specific ways, Indigenous, Black, and brown artists are often positioned along a pecking order in the hierarchy of preference and desirability among decision makers. Positioned in contestation to each other in this ladder of apparent meritocracy, we are systemically pushed to ignore the specific histories that locate us on uneven ground, even when we stand adjacent, or close to, one another. This promotes identity-on-steroids races, based on a nonviable assumption of the same starting line, and limits our capacity to revitalize solidarity through the power of our differences.

In rejecting the blinkered histories we have been taught and that obscure lineages of connectivity among Black and brown communities, I have been investigating possibilities of meetings across different geographies and time frames, historic, futuristic, generational, individual, for reasons other than the wars summoned by capitalism. For one, I have been fascinated with precolonial Indian Ocean sea routes that connected traders and others from across Asia and Africa and created shared practices such as indigo dyeing. In 2018, I made a piece, *Shātrangā, Women Weaving Worlds*, exploring real and imagined relationships painstakingly woven by Black and brown women and femmes, and the labor of repairing connections when disrupted by capitalism. The research and choreographic process taught me about different kinds of transnational meetings and mostly undocumented histories we have to conjure from the waterways of story, myth, and imagination. Dancing this ensemble piece, navigating complex pathways and uneven-beat cumulative rhythm cycles, reiterated the importance of holding each other's gaze, really seeing each other while moving through the complex choreography.

Seeing each other, recognizing our implication in violent systems, and pushing toward transformation is foundational to the work outlined in the Cultural New Deal. For me, it has been vital to hold up again and again that it is not sufficient to critique white supremacy but to acknowledge how it has multiplied itself in global fascisms, all the more dangerous for co-opting the language of decolonizing and masquerading as movements for equality. Thanks to the teachings of powerful Dalit leaders, we know that even though race and caste are different, Black Lives Matter is shining light on the parallel movement for Dalit Lives Matter, and we are being called to recognize how the workings of fascist governments, racism, casteism, sexism, homophobia, ableism lodge themselves in our brains. So what is the work we have to do to refuse co-optation by capitalism's mandate of competitive individualism, resist the proliferation of global systems of hate, and keep alive lineages and traces of relationships that have existed among us as we forge new solidarities? How can we make self-reflexivity an instinctive practice, so we are always vigilant about our implication in systemic privilege, and remain connected to Dr. Cornel West's notion of "Radical Love"—seeing the world from the lens of the most oppressed communities of the world?

While dancing has been vital to me at this time as a practice that always reminds me of being present, mindful of dancing fully without running into others, fulfilling my rhythm while attentive to the counterpoint others are articulating, I want to remind us that the crucial focus is on how we practice, not what. After all, the liberatory power of dance has been harnessed by supercapitalist televised competition-based shows and spectacularized routines, among other co-optations. The Uprising has taught me to value even more deeply a practice of dancing that can prepare our somatic beings for sharing vibration and light, conjure connection and spirit, find a commons of justice and affirmation, and come to know embodied difference. Going, in a moment, from fast rhythmic footwork, sweeping arm gestures, to slow, extended flow sequences has reinforced the learning necessary to move nimbly, from forcefully pushing back against state and systemic violences to listening carefully within communities experiencing layers of harm. So that we can break the chain of violence begetting violence begetting violence and learn to regulate our breathing so we are able to integrate our nervous systems inside community contexts that need oxygen, instead of responding from perpetually heightened states of alert or dissociation.

And in this process of playing the long game, I have come to imbue my dancing with a practice of hope. I have been reminded that hope is not something external but is a muscle that has to be worked every day, with nuance, so it is realistic even as it is audacious, perhaps open-ended but always leveraging justice. Asking myself, "What does the choreography of courageous hope look like?" has infused my improvisations with all kinds of joy and surprise, and has welded the notion of innovation with just world making. To inspire this work that so many of us are charged with at this time, I invoke two brilliant poets. One, June Jordan, whose 1978 "Poem for South African Women" reminded us to stand with each other:

> And who will join this standing up
> and the ones who stood without sweet company
> will sing and sing
> back into the mountains and
> if necessary
> even under the sea
>
> *we are the ones we have been waiting for.*[4]

And next, Faiz Ahmad Faiz, beloved poet of South Asia, who exhorted us to refuse silence:

> Bol, ke lab azad hei tere
> Bol zabaan ab tak teri hei
> Teri sutwan jism hei tera
> Bol ke jaan ab tak teri hei.
>
> Speak, for your lips are free!
> Speak, your tongue is still yours!
> Your upright body is still yours!
> Speak, for your life is still yours![5]

May we continue to align our dancing with justice.

Notes

1. I thank my Dakota sister, healer, and community leader Janice Bad Moccasin for this teaching.
2. See "The Cultural New Deal for Cultural and Racial Justice" at the beginning of this section.
3. adrienne maree brown, *Emergent Strategy: Shaping Change, Changing Worlds* (Chico, CA: AK Press, 2017), 7.
4. June Jordan's poem was presented at the UN on August 9, 1978, to commemorate the protest of forty thousand women and children on August 9, 1956, against the dompas laws of the apartheid government in South Africa. It was later published in her anthology of poems, June Jordan, *Passion: New Poems 1977–1980* (Boston: Beacon, 1980).

5. Faiz Ahmed Faiz's 1941 poem was published variously. It is part of *Poems by Faiz*, translated from the Urdu and with an introduction and notes by V. G. Kiernan (London: Allen and Unwin, 1971). The translation here is my own. Widely associated with the Progressive Movement of his time, the poem continues to be relevant and has been sung and recited widely across South Asia.

Azadi

Arshia Fatima Haq

Arshia Fatima Haq works across multiple media—film, installation, sound, performance—in feminist modes outside of the Western model. She is the founder of Discostan, a collaborative decolonial project and record label. Her work has been presented nationally and internationally in museums, galleries, nightclubs, and the streets.

For my contribution to *In Plain Sight*, I chose to invoke the concept of *azadi*. The simplest translation of this word is *freedom*, and it is used in Urdu, Farsi, Hindi, Kurdish, Pashto, Azeri, Balochi, Armenian, Kurdish, Punjabi, Bengali, and Kashmiri, among others. The word has more nuanced connotations of liberation, autonomy, and independence; in many regions, it also evokes and embodies political layers of resistance struggles. Using this word imagines the possibility of a transnational solidarity around these struggles. As well, I was thinking about how the complexity and infinite resonances of a particular script, Arabic, have been reduced to signify terror or "the other" within the American context, and also how all related scripts—Farsi, Urdu, and so on—are conflated within this reduction. In using the Urdu script in addition to the Roman letters of English in writing *azadi*, I invoke the subtle subversion of writing freedom in a "foreign" and often-feared script across the sky.

Arshia Fatima Haq, *Azadi*, performed in July 2020. Documentation by Labkhand Olfatmanesh. *In Plain Sight*, conceived by Cassils and rafa esparza, is a coalition of eighty artists fighting migrant detention and the culture of incarceration.

AFTERWORD

Daniela Alvarez and Elizabeth M. Webb

Daniela Alvarez is the REFRAME and research manager for ArtChangeUS and the public programs coordinator at the Getty Museum in Los Angeles. Her work as a cultural organizer and programmer centers on promoting community benefits and in creating spaces of belonging.

Elizabeth M. Webb, an artist and filmmaker originally from Charlottesville, Virginia, is the senior creative producer for ArtChangeUS. Her work is invested in issues surrounding race and identity, often using the lens of her own family history of migration and racial passing to explore larger, systemic constructs.

> stay metaphysical. stay knowing vision is a process
> and seeing is not always believing.
> stay questioning the frame—including this one here.

—**taisha paggett,** "vestibular mantra
(or radical virtuosities for a brave new dance)"

> divorce greed
> from the concept of *more*, for here the *more*
> is a radiant hope. more eyes looking
> at others, building rooms from stale
> air, set on finding the root of pain
> and giving it a much-deserved burn.

—**Sarah Yanni,** "emergence"

Throughout our organizing work with ArtChangeUS, we made certain to ground our exchanges in artistic practice, forefronting art as the foundation of experience and celebration of our collective journey. And so it is fitting to end here, with the life-giving poetry of Sarah Yanni.

Jeff Chang once noted that culture moves before policy; Roberta Uno added that culture *endures and thrives beyond politics.* We believe that culture is the expansive force that lets us know that *enduring and thriving is possible.* The voices in this volume, along with the many more outside its pages, are part of a groundswell of cultural practice and organizing that visions and creates a thriving future of endurance. We give gratitude to all who have joined us along this journey—every artist who questioned the frame and made it stronger, every organizer who chose a circle instead of a straight line, every participant who activated these spaces with their presence, and the many partners who have become our accomplices and family.

In 2015, our founder and former director, Roberta Uno, made an intentional choice to build a leadership pipeline to lift the next generation of artists and cultural workers. As ArtChangeUS transitions from having a storied field leader at the helm to a model led by next-generation sagacious cultural practitioners, we look to those who came before us as well as those who will come after us. We carry our collective experiences as we continue this work, in service of picking locks rather than keeping gates, in acknowledgment of place as a holder of deep knowledge and memory, and in trust and stewardship of relationships, both ongoing and new—"for here the *more* is a radiant hope."

We are honored to continue this work with ardor.

emergence

(after adrienne maree brown)

Sarah Sophia Yanni

Sarah Sophia Yanni is a Mexican Egyptian writer, educator, and editor. She is the author of the chapbook *ternura / tenderness* (Bottlecap Press) and was a finalist for *BOMB Magazine*'s 2020 Poetry Contest, Poetry Online's 2021 Launch Prize, and the *Hayden's Ferry Review* Inaugural Poetry Contest. She is managing editor of *TQR* and holds an MFA from CalArts.

and when the storm comes
swirling up, bringing hordes
of ancient stuff that once
resided on the ocean floor, what
will we do with our hands?

the challenge—to recall the working mode
before the collapse began.

it will happen, undoubtedly.

we must prepare ourselves
with minimal objects: journals carried
during brief times of clarity, something
passed down maternally,
for luck. a mind yanked from the dark, filtering years and years
of story to arrive from babble
to glistening wisdom.

and remember to be adaptive, in
the imperfect forms that all ideals take. with tools like
the breath, jaws become more
than gaps for the exhale. they calm, bodies
reaching the final hum of a once
crescendoed chorus, and in
that stilling state, intention starts to spin.

both the self and critical mass. a small
thing punched through walls, spilling
from the hole, lifted out and touched
by a tired population. divorce greed
from the concept of *more*, for here the *more*
is a radiant hope. more eyes looking
at others, building rooms from stale
air, set on finding the root of pain
and giving it a much-deserved burn.

becoming less heavy
or reliant on the term *impossible*, focused less
on the tangible present, and more on
the dust that settles onto futures, next week, next
year, a time when we're
no longer present but the modes
and their feelings are anything
but insignificant.

that is how it will happen. and that is what we'll do.
palms with a thin coat of sweat, open
and warm, reaching to grab a softer version
of tomorrow.

ACKNOWLEDGMENTS

We would also like to thank our beloved Core Partners: Maribel Alvarez, Marc Bamuthi Joseph, P. Carl, Halima Afi Cassells, Jeff Chang, Teddy Cruz, Jane Golden, Vicky Holt Takamine, James Kass, Robert van Leer, Wendy Levy, María López De León, Rick Noguchi, Anne Pasternak, Lori Lea Pourier, Favianna Rodriguez, Garth Ross, Annette Evans Smith, Diana Taylor, John Kuo Wei Tchen, Carlton Turner, Clyde Valentín, Jose Antonio Vargas, Detroit Consortium (Devon Akmon, Cézanne Charles, Juanita Moore, ill Weaver), Minneapolis/St. Paul Consortium (Ananya Chatterjea, Dipankar Mukherjee, Meena Natarajan), Los Angeles Consortium (Alison De La Cruz, Ben Johnson, Amy Kitchener, Natalie Marrero, Debra Padilla, Randy Reinholz, Jean Bruce Scott, Tamica Washington-Miller); our institutional and administrative homes: Steven Lavine and California Institute of the Arts (2015–20), Citizen Engagement Laboratory (2015–17), NEO Philanthropy (2017–ongoing), Hemispheric Institute of Performance and Politics at New York University (2015–22); and all the people and organizations that generously opened their homes to us throughout our programming.

Our dedicated former staff members: Kristen Adele Calhoun, Genevieve Fowler, Nadine Friedman-Roberts, Kassandra L. Khalil, and Namiko Uno; and current Cultural New Deal program manager Michele Kumi Baer.

Our fellows for constantly reminding us of the brilliance of coming generations: Daniel Alcazar, Ratri Anindyajati, Rosa Boshier, Morgan Camper, Genevieve Fowler, Juan Carlos Herrera, Sarah Ibrahim, Derek Jackson, Vinhay Keo, Toran X. Moore, Silvi Naçi, Eloy Neira, Aydinaneth Ortiz, Maia Paroginog, Frederick Douglass Ramsey Jr., Abigail Salling, T. J. Tario, Jazmín Urrea, Sarah Sophia Yanni, and Evelyn Hang Yin.

Our funders for believing in our vision and praxis: Andrew W. Mellon Foundation, Annenberg Foundation, Art for Justice Fund, Bush Foundation, Doris Duke Charitable Foundation, Ford Foundation, Hewlett Foundation, HRK Foundation, Institute for International Education,

Jerome Foundation, Kresge Foundation, LA County Arts Commission, Los Angeles Department of Cultural Affairs, McKnight Foundation, Nathan Cummings Foundation, Rasmuson Foundation, Silicon Valley Community Foundation, Surdna Foundation, and Unbound Philanthropy. Special gratitude to Maurine Knighton, Darren Walker, Margaret Morton, Lane Harwell, Rocío Aranda-Alvarado, Emiko Ono, John McGuirk, Inés Familiar Miller, Regina R. Smith, Elizabeth Alexander, Don Chen, F. Javier Torres-Campos, and Sinéad López for making this book possible.

Our incomparable editorial team: Elizabeth Ault, Aimee Harrison, Benjamin Kossak, and Ihsan Taylor at Duke University Press; copy editor Karen Fisher; assistant editors Kapena Alapaʻi, Genevieve Fowler, Kassandra L. Khalil, and Sarah Sophia Yanni; and our anonymous peer reviewers.

And our families, friends, and loved ones in this realm and others, whose generous spirits guide us toward a brighter future.